P9-DOB-412

REGISTRATION CODE

REGISTRATION CODE

IMPORTANT

HERE IS YOUR REGISTRATION CODE TO ACCESS MCGRAW-HILL
PREMIUM CONTENT AND MCGRAW-HILL ONLINE RESOURCES

For key premium online resources you need THIS CODE to
gain access. Once the code is entered, you will be able to
use the web resources for the length of your course.

Access is provided only if you have purchased a new book.

If the registration code is missing from this book, please visit the registration
screen on our website of within your WebCT or Blackboard course instructions
are also available on how to obtain your new code. Your registration code can
be used only once to establish access. It is not transferable.

To gain access to these online resources

1. USE your web browser to go to: **www.mhhe.com/pricearch1**

2. CLICK on "First Time User"

3. ENTER the Registration Code printed on the tear-off bookmark on the right

4. After you have entered your registration code, click on "Register"

5. FOLLOW the instructions to setup your personal UserID and Password

6. WRITE your UserID and Password down for future reference. Keep it in a safe place.

If your course is using WebCT or Blackboard, you'll be able to use this code to
access the McGraw-Hill content within your instructor's online course.

To gain access to the McGraw-Hill content in your instructor's WebCT or
Blackboard course simply log into the course with the user ID and Password provided by your instructor. Enter the registration code exactly as it appears to the
right when prompted by the system. You will only need to use this code the first
time you click on McGraw-Hill content.

These instructions are specifically for student access. Instructors are not required
to register via the above instructions.

Thank you, and welcome to your
McGraw-Hill Online Resources.
ISBN-13: 978-0-07-326925-1
ISBN-10: 0-07-326925-5
T/A Price: Principles of Archaeology, 1e

9 780073 269252

PRINCIPLES OF ARCHAEOLOGY

PRINCIPLES OF
ARCHAEOLOGY

T. Douglas Price   *University of Wisconsin-Madison*

Boston   Burr Ridge, IL   Dubuque, IA   Madison, WI   New York   San Francisco   St. Louis
Bangkok   Bogotá   Caracas   Kuala Lumpur   Lisbon   London   Madrid   Mexico City
Milan   Montreal   New Delhi   Santiago   Seoul   Singapore   Sydney   Taipei   Toronto

This book is for Annalise Price

Mc Graw Hill **Higher Education**

Published by McGraw-Hill, an imprint of The McGraw-Hill Companies, Inc., 1221 Avenue of the Americas, New York, NY 10020. Copyright © 2007. All rights reserved. No part of this publication may be reproduced or distributed in any form or by any means, or stored in a database or retrieval system, without the prior written consent of The McGraw-Hill Companies, Inc., including, but not limited to, in any network or other electronic storage or transmission, or broadcast for distance learning.

This book is printed on acid-free paper.

1 2 3 4 5 6 7 8 9 0 WCK/WCK 0 9 8 7 6

ISBN-13: 978-0-07-296148-5
ISBN-10: 0-07-296148-1

Vice President and Editor in Chief: *Emily Barrosse*
Publisher: *Phil Butcher*
Editorial Coordinator: *Teresa Treacy*
Marketing Manager: *Dan Loch*
Developmental Editor: *Pam Gordon*
Project Manager: *Christina Gimlin*
Manuscript Editor: *Patricia Ohlenroth*
Text and Cover Designer: *Jeanne Schreiber*
Art Editor: *Robin Mouat*

Illustrators: *John and Judy Waller, Dartmouth Publishing, Rennie Evans*
Manager, Photo Research: *Brian J. Pecko*
Permissions Editor: *Marty Granahan*
Media Producer: *Michele Borrelli*
Production Supervisor: *Richard DeVitto*
Composition: *9.5/12 Palatino by Thompson Type*
Printing: *45# Publisher's Matte, Quebecor World*

About the cover: A series of scenes from archaeology are depicted on the front and back covers. Front cover (top) and spine: A gold funeral mask from the Bronze Age Greek site of Mycenae, originally said to be the mask of Agamemnon. © Nimatallah/Art Resource, NY. Front cover (three small photos, left-right): Chinese archaeologists cleaning the remains of chariots and horses at a newly-discovered Bronze Age tomb near Anyang, China. © Reuters/Landov; Zahi Hawass, chief of Egypt's Supreme Council of Antiquities, examines a brilliantly colored mummy dating back more than 2,300 years. © AP/Wide World Photos; Kelly Knudson at work in the Laboratory for Archaeological Chemistry preparing enamel samples for isotopic analysis. © Courtesy Jason Knudsen. Front cover (large photo): Castlerigg Stone Circle from the Neolithic period in Cumbria, England. © Digital Vision. Back cover (top): A rollout view of a ceramic vase from the Classic Maya period. © Justin Kerr/Kerr Associates. Back cover (bottom): Archaeologists examine a carved stone monument from Turkey ca. 900 BC. © Mehmet Gulbiz/Images&Stories.

Credits: The credits section for this book begins on page C-1 and is considered an extension of the copyright page.

Library of Congress Cataloging-in-Publication Data
Price, T. Douglas (Theron Douglas)
   Principles of archaeology / T. Douglas Price.
      p. cm.
   Includes bibliographical references and index.
   ISBN-13 978-0-07-296148-5; ISBN-10 0-07-296148-1(alk. paper)
      1. Archaeology.   2. Archaeology—Methodology.   I. Title.
   CC165.P69 2006
930.1—dc22   2006044933

The Internet addresses listed in the text were accurate at the time of publication. The inclusion of a Web site does not indicate an endorsement by the authors or McGraw-Hill, and McGraw-Hill does not guarantee the accuracy of the information presented at these sites.

www.mhhe.com

Brief Contents

v

Contents

CHAPTER 13 Archaeobotany 349

CHAPTER 14 Bioarchaeology 377

Preface

SOME BACKGROUND

When I was nine years old, I was lucky enough to visit the remains of a massive Roman tomb along a roadside in northern Spain. Standing there, I was completely in awe of the crumbling walls of that ancient stone mausoleum; I wondered who made it, why it was built, and how old it was. My parents told me about the Romans and how archaeologists studied such ruins. I decided then and there that I wanted to be an archaeologist. That happened and I have been one now for many years. I love what I do. It is a wonderful job, filled with travel, fieldwork, discovery, ideas and intellectual challenges, interesting friends and quirky colleagues, demanding and delightful students, and endless ways to learn more about the past.

I would like to share this fascinating field with you. This book is written primarily to introduce college students to the ideas and methods of today's archaeology, where research in the field and laboratory combine to uncover our past. It's intended to tell you about this intriguing subject that combines so many disciplines and skills in the study of earlier human behavior. I hope that this book may encourage some of you to consider archaeology as a career and to enter this exciting field of study. If nothing else, I hope it will help you to better understand the world around you and to appreciate the inherent allure of the past.

There are generally two sorts of introductory courses in archaeology at our universities. One kind offers an overview of what archaeologists have learned about the past. These are world prehistory classes. There are several good textbooks for these overview courses. Gary Feinman and I have written one such introduction to world prehistory called *Images of the Past*. That book provides a survey of the human past from our earliest ancestors and the first use of stone tools through the development of art and more complex societies in the Upper Paleolithic, the origins and spread of agriculture, and the rise of early states in the Old and New Worlds. It's about facts and knowledge.

A second kind of course offers a consideration of the methods and ideas, or principles, of archaeology—about how archaeologists look at the past and how they obtain the information they use to make sense of the past. *Principles of Archaeology* is written for this kind of course about theories and techniques.

There are also several other textbooks available on this aspect of archaeology, but I think most of them are too complicated. It's not easy to write a straightforward book about the theories and techniques of archaeology because of the great diversity and breadth of the subject. Archaeologists do all kinds of things, including research, teaching, public outreach, excavations, rescue work and cultural resource management, museum exhibitions, caring for monuments and parks, writing grant proposals—they even write books.

Archaeologists go in all sorts of directions to learn more about the past. The tools of modern archaeology are numerous and the areas of interest are myriad. That's one of the reasons it's so fascinating in the first place. However, there is so much involved in modern archaeology that one book simply cannot cover its entirety.

I have opted for a direct approach, focusing on fundamentals. I have included what I think is more important and more appealing, and I have incorporated the information that I think a first course in archaeology ought to cover. I have also described interesting sites and situations from both the New World and the Old that I feel serve as intriguing examples of methods and theories. At the same time, I have included some of the cutting-edge, breakthrough areas where science and technology are telling us new and exciting things about the past.

This is not a reference book. I have tried not to overload the text by covering all of archaeology, or hundreds of sites, or the full range of different methods or ideas that have appeared. For information on other aspects of archaeology, outside the scope of this text, I will point you toward suggested readings and websites. By having a text that covers the fundamentals, my hope is that you will be able to focus on what is essential. I will also try to point out why it's important to know certain things in the book. It's much easier to learn something if there is a reason for it!

THE TEXT THEMES

There are several recurrent themes in *Principles of Archaeology*. The first concerns how archaeologists think and learn about the past. While it is important to master the methods and theories of archaeology, I believe that it is equally important for you to get a sense of how archaeologists think. This first theme is therefore intended to encourage you to reflect on the process of how archaeologists come to know the past. While this text presents a number of important methods and theories, my hope is that this book will allow you to go beyond a basic reading to being able to think for yourself. As part of this "thinking" theme, a number of the chapters include a final section where you can work on some fairly typical projects in archaeology, using method, data, and theory.

A second theme of the text, one I also feel strongly about, concerns the preservation of the past. I am not a tree hugger; I don't want to restore our local park to the ice sheet, tundra, or oak forest that existed there at various times in the past. But I do know that archaeological sites are being destroyed at a rate much faster than they can be studied or saved as modern civilizations expand across the earth. Looting, careless development, and the wanton destruction of archaeological resources can eliminate any future opportunity to learn from our past. If we are to have archaeology in the coming decades, it is essential that fundamental information be recorded or protected before there is nothing left to be studied. For this reason, ways and means to save and protect archaeological sites are the second theme of this book. My goal is to encourage you to understand and help with the effort.

A third theme concerns the important role of science in archaeology. Scientific approaches to understanding the past are growing rapidly and are very important. Major discoveries in the future will come from the laboratory as much as from the ground. For this reason, students of archaeology need to learn about the possibilities and potential of the various laboratory and instrumental techniques that are employed in the study of the past. To this end, there is a separate chapter in this book on archaeometry, also known as "instrumental" archaeology. In addition, in a number of the other chapters, studies involving chemical and physical means of analysis are emphasized in the examples that are used.

THE ORGANIZATION OF THE TEXT

Archaeology is not rocket science; it's mostly common sense. Archaeologists collect information about the past, they study it, and they try to make sense of it. Archaeological materials are discovered and provide evidence of past human activities. This body of evidence must be analyzed in order to define basic facts such as age, use, location, and movement. Archaeologists have a powerful set of tools for investigating the evidence they discover. Evidence and the results of analysis provide a body of information about the past, but these are facts and estimates that must be interpreted to have meaning. Theories, hypotheses, ideas, and assumptions are bridging concepts that archaeologists use to interpret—to attach meaning—to evidence and analytical results.

Three stages—discovery, analysis, and interpretation—make up the heart of doing archaeology. This book is organized following these same basic steps to take you, the reader, along a path to learn more about the human past. On the way, I will try to keep things simple, straightforward, and interesting. I think that makes them easier to learn.

This book has four parts. I have included an opening essay at the start of each part, which explains the subject and contents and which will help you get a sense of what is to come.

Part 1 is an introduction in three chapters. These initial chapters are important because they provide background for the other sections, and they introduce significant themes that recur throughout the book.

Chapter 1 is an introduction to archaeology, about what it is and what it is not. It includes some discussion of the role of evolution and the scientific method, about why we should study archaeology, along with some information on careers so that you can see how many interesting opportunities there are in the field as you begin your study.

Chapter 2, "Doing Archaeology," provides a lengthy description of the recovery and investigation of the royal graves at Sipán, Peru, some of the richest tombs ever found in the Americas. Through the story of Sipán, this chapter inaugurates the organization and themes of the book; with information on doing archaeological research (discovery, analysis, and interpretation), archaeological thinking, preserving the past, and science in archaeology.

Chapter 3 offers a brief history of archaeological research as a basis for understanding the discipline and its distinctive perspectives. This history provides a background for understanding how archaeology has developed over time and how archaeologists think about the past. This chapter could also be read in conjunction with Chapter 16 as an introduction to theory, ideas, and interpretation in archaeology.

The principles of archaeology comprise the next three parts of the book and the three stages of archaeological research. **Part 2** describes the *discovery* of archaeological information, including the questions that are asked (what archaeologists want to know) in Chapter 4, the archaeological record (the nature of the evidence) in Chapter 5, and the methods of fieldwork in Chapter 6.

Part 3 concerns the various kinds of *analyses* that are done, assembled in a series of chapters dealing with the classification of the materials and statistics (Chapter 7), the dating of evidence (Chapter 8), geology and archaeology (Chapter 9), stone tools (Chapter 10), pottery (Chapter 11), animal bones (Chapter 12), plant remains (Chapter 13), graves and human skeletal remains (Chapter 14), and the physical and chemical composition of archaeological materials (Chapter 15).

Part 4 deals with *interpretation* and responsibility. Chapter 16 involves the theoretical ways in which archaeologists look at the past, where questions and ideas come from. The concluding Chapter 17 deals with the ethics and responsibilities of archaeology in today's world and offers more details on what can and is being done to protect the past and involve the public interest.

THE FEATURES OF THE BOOK

The features in the text are designed to help you master the material and to highlight the themes. Learning is largely about recognizing what is important to remember, and I have incorporated both organizational and structural means for emphasizing what's of the essence in archaeology.

I have also taken a consistent approach to the format of the chapters in the book, beginning with a running narrative in each. This running text includes both the ideas and methods that comprise the basics of how archaeology is done. It is the heart of the book. Along with the running text, I have included three distinct sections called introductions, examples, and conclusions.

The *Introduction* provides an overview of the subject matter, themes, and organization of the chapter. In order to gain attention and draw you into the content of the chapter, the *Introduction* begins by focusing on a distinctive image that I hope conveys some of the fascination of the field. *Examples* are intermingled through each chapter. *Examples* are case studies from important archaeological investigations throughout the world to illustrate some of the concepts and methods that are described and to show how archaeologists think and work. I am a strong believer in learning by example, so there are numerous case studies, sometimes several to a chapter. The *Conclusions* synthesize the contents of the chapter and place that information in a larger context.

There are also three types of boxes sprinkled through the chapters that are intended to highlight the three themes. In the first kind of box, called *Archaeological Thinking*, I highlight situations where reason and ideas have resulted in new insight into past human behavior—where innovative thoughts have had important consequences. In the second box type, called *Protecting the Past*, I focus on what is or is not being done to protect some of the sites and places discussed in the text. This will give you some idea of the various problems and the solutions involved in preserving our common cultural heritage. The third kind of box, *Science in Archaeology*, will emphasize studies in which instrumental and analytical techniques provide new information about the past.

Several other features support the first theme of encouraging you to think like an archaeologist. To this end, this book is problem-oriented; it is about the problems that archaeologists encounter and how they resolve them. Marginal quotes and several personal statements from archaeologists themselves allow you to hear the voices of the field and to learn how archaeologists themselves have thought about problems they have faced. So that you can get a personal sense of this process, I have also inserted a project section at the end of a number of the chapters with archaeological data or directions to involve you with a number of thought-provoking questions. These projects will be self-contained on perforated pages so that they can be removed. You can also find a digital version of these projects at the Student's Online Learning Center (www.mhhe.com/pricearch1), which is discussed in detail later in this preface.

A few final features serve to help you learn more. Each chapter opens with an outline giving you a preview of what is to come. Technical terms and important concepts in archaeology are indicated in bold type in the text with definitions in the margins; all these words are also assembled in a glossary at the back of the book. Following foreign or unusual terms and names, I have included a pronunciation guide in parentheses. There is also an index at the back of the book to help you find names or topics quickly among the pages.

I have placed a few study questions at the end of each chapter to help you review the contents. A suggested list of general readings appears at the end of each chapter as well, while a more complete list of references sits at the back of the book. Specific citations within the written text were avoided in favor of a more readable prose, but references on specific topics can be found at the back of the book under the name of the individual associated with the work. You can also search this bibliography at the Online Learning Center by keyword.

Also at the back, you will find a brief summary of our human past in an appendix. In order to have some sense of the periods and places that you will encounter in this book, this section provides a whirlwind tour of prehistory with some timelines, major periods, general trends, and important sites. You may want to refer to this section for more information on some of the sites or time periods you encounter in the text.

In addition to these features, I have tried to provide a sense of the size of areas and structures from archaeological sites in the text by referring to modern features, such as city blocks, football fields, and the like. An appendix in the back of the book offers some English–metric measure conversions and equivalents to help make sizes more comprehensible.

Because archaeology is a very visual subject, I have included lots of illustrations—some 500 photographs and drawings. Emphasis in the selection of these illustrations has been on quality and clarity. It is essential to see and study the maps, plans, artifacts, and places that comprise the archaeological record. Maps are shown with a small inset globe to provide better geographic orientation. Illustrations highlight the important features of a subject. Multistep drawings and photographs explain more complex issues, such as making pottery. Cartoons are intended to provide a lighter look at the subject of archaeology. I have also included what are commonly called artist's reconstructions in a number of places through the book. These reconstructions are an attempt to depict what archaeological places may have looked like at the time they were in use. While these reconstructions are often inspiring, it is important to remember that they are highly speculative, based in part on archaeological knowledge and part on the artist's imagination.

An important note on dates: The age of archaeological materials is given in several ways in this book. Dates greater than 10,000 years ago are described in years before the present (bp) or in millions of years ago (m.y.a.). Dates younger than 10,000 years ago are given in calendar years before Christ, BC, or *anno Domini* ("in the year of the Lord"), AD. (Most archaeologists don't use the terms B.C.E. [Before the Common Era] or C.E.—the Common Era.) These dates for the last 10,000 years have been corrected, or calibrated to actual calendar years, because of a minor error in radiocarbon dating. Another term used for more recent periods of time is millennium, 1000 years. The millennia before Christ run in reverse—for example, the first millennium goes from 1 BC to 1000 BC.

Supplements

As a full-service publisher of quality educational products, McGraw-Hill does much more than just sell textbooks. They create and publish an extensive array of print, video, and digital supplements for students and instructors. *Principles of Archaeology* boasts a comprehensive supplements package. Orders of new (versus used) textbooks help defray the cost of developing such supplements, which is substantial. Please consult your local McGraw-Hill representative for more information on any of the supplements.

For the Student

The Student's Online Learning Center (by Adam Wetsman, Rio Hondo College). This free, Web-based, partially password-protected, student supplement features a large number of interactive exercises and activities, helpful study tools, links and useful information at www.mhhe.com/pricearch1. To access the password-protected areas of the site, students must purchase a new copy of the text. The website is designed specifically to complement the individual chapters of the book. In-text icons guide students to information on a particular topic that is available on the website.

Exciting Interactivity

- Internet exercises—offer chapter-related links to World Wide Web sites and activities for students to complete based on the sites.

Useful Study Tools

- Chapter objectives, outlines, and summaries—are designed to give students signposts for understanding and recognizing key chapter content.

- Multiple choice and true/false questions—give students the opportunity to quiz themselves on chapter content and visuals.

- Essay questions—allow students to explore key chapter concepts through their own writing.

- Chapter key terms and glossary—define key terms.

- Audio glossary—helps students with words that are difficult to pronounce through audio pronunciation assistance.

- Bibliography—gives students the opportunity to search and explore topics of interest through additional readings on chapter-related topics.

Helpful Links

- General Web links—offer chapter-by-chapter links for further research.

- Links to *New York Times* articles—give students immediate access to articles on chapter-related content.

Useful Information

- FAQ's about Archaeology Careers in the United States—gives students answers to questions on available jobs, necessary education and training, picking a college or university, basic texts on the field, going on a dig, and getting more information.
- Career opportunities—offer students related links to useful information on careers in anthropology.

For the Instructor

The Instructor's Resource CD-ROM (by Adam Wetsman). This indispensable, easy-to-use instructor disk provides a variety of features:

- Image Library—offers professors the opportunity to create custom-made, professional-looking presentations and handouts by providing electronic versions of many of the maps, tables, line art, and photos from the text. All images are ready to be used in any applicable teaching tools.
- PowerPoint lecture slides—give professors ready-made, chapter-by-chapter presentation notes, including art from the text.
- Instructor's Manual—offers chapter outlines, chapter summaries, learning objectives, lecture-launcher ideas, and suggested films and videos.
- Computerized test bank—offers numerous multiple choice, short answer, and essay questions in an easy-to-use program that is available for both Windows and Macintosh computers.

The Instructor's Online Learning Center (by Adam Wetsman). This password-protected site offers:

- Access to all of the student online materials.
- Access to many of the instructor support materials found on The Instructor's Resource CD-ROM, including the Image Library, the PowerPoint lecture slides, and the Instructor's Manual.
- Links to professional resources—for anthropological sites on the World Wide Web.

PageOut: The Course Website Development Center. All online content for the text is supported by WebCT, Blackboard, eCollege.com, and other course management systems. Additionally, McGraw-Hill's PageOut service is available to get professors and their courses up and running online in a matter of hours, at no cost. PageOut was designed for instructors just beginning to explore web options. Even a novice computer user can create a course website with a template provided by McGraw-Hill (no programming knowledge necessary). To learn more about PageOut, visit www.mhhe.com/pageout.

Videotapes. A wide variety of full-length videotapes from the Films for the Humanities and Sciences series are available to adopters of the text.

ACKNOWLEDGMENTS

Any book is a major undertaking—it's probably a good thing that authors don't remember that fact when they begin. A book also requires the efforts of numerous individuals in addition to the author. There are many people to thank, who have graciously provided their time, comments, information, and/or illustrations. Their help is both essential and greatly appreciated. This group includes Mark Aldenderfer, Søren Andersen, Eleni Asouti, Joe Ball, Ernie Boszhardt, Göran Burenhult, Elizabeth Burson, Jim Burton, Tom Christensen, Christiane Clados, Meg Conkey, Lawrence Conyers, Bernd Cromer, Erwin Cziesla, Marie Danforth, Andrew Elkerton, Gary Feinman, Dave Frederick, Paul Goldberg, Bill Green, Paul Green, Peter Vemming Hansen, Sönke Hartz, Brian Hayden, Barbara Heath, Clara Helfferich, Ian Hodder, Kasper Johansen, Greg Johnson, Annie Katzenberg, John Kelly, Lucretia Kelly, Doug Kennett, Mark Kenoyer, Jason Krantz, Kelly Knudson, Dan Lieberman, Linda Manzanilla, Joyce Marcus, Mark Michel, William Middleton, George Milner, Paul Mullins, Wes Niewoehner, Christopher O'Brien, Inger Österholm, Duane Peter, Nicole Pigeot, Kathleen Pigg, Tom Pleger, Jennifer Price, Karen Rehm, John Rick, Larry Ross, Matt Sanger, Sissel Schroeder, Tom Server, Payson Sheets, Bruce Smith, James Stoltman, David Hurst Thomas, Ruth Tringham, Clive Waddington, Christian Wells, Robert Whallon, Barbara Winter, Henry Wright, and Jason Yaeger. Special thanks to Joe Ball, Rhonda Foster, Paul Green, Maureen Kavanagh, Larry Ross, Tina Thurston, and Anne Underhill for their personal sections. Dale Croes made an important contribution to the "Responsibilities" chapter, as he does to the field as a whole. Also loads of thanks to Adam Wetsman, who has done so much fine work on the teaching supplements for the book.

I would also like to express my appreciation to the people who acted as reviewers of the volume. There were several stages in the review process and the thoughtfulness, comments, and ideas of these readers have helped greatly to make this book better. Thanks to:

Joseph Walter Ball, San Diego State University

Brian D. Bates, Longwood University

Mary C. Beaudry, Boston University

Donald Blakeslee, Wichita State University

Mary Theresa Bonhage-Freund, Alma College

Christina Brewer, Saddleback Community College

Clarence R. Geier, James Madison University

Paul R. Green, Old Dominion University

Julie Hanson, Boston University

Curtiss Hoffman, Bridgewater State University

Andrea Hunter, Northern Arizona University

Lawrence H. Keeley, University of Illinois at Chicago

Barry Lewis, University of Illinois

Patricia Carol Martz, California State University, Los Angeles

Randall McGuire, Binghamton University

Sean Rafferty, University at Albany, SUNY

Dean Snow, Pennsylvania State University

There are also a few organizations and institutions I must acknowledge. The University of Wisconsin-Madison provided the year of leave during which much of this book was written. Our wonderful UW libraries and their electronic wizardry supplied a constant stream of articles and reference material to a distant land. The ability to receive an email with a scan or digital version of any article I could name made this book possible. The World Wide Web and Google have made my life much easier as a ready source of information and reference. Finally, the staff at McGraw-Hill Higher Education—a great bunch to work with, most competent and helpful, friendly, brave, clean, and irreverent. That group includes Christina Gimlin, project manager; Brian Pecko, photo researcher; Robin Mouat, art editor; Marty Granahan, literary permissions editor; Rich DeVitto, production supervisor; Dan Loch, mar-

keting manager; Michele Borrelli, media producer; and Teresa Treacy, editorial coordinator. I would like to particularly single out Jeanne Schreiber, who did the design work; Patricia Ohlenroth, my copy editor who made innumerable and significant improvements in the manuscript; Kevin Witt, the former anthropology editor who was the calm in the storm; and Pam Gordon, my development editor who is responsible for keeping everything together and in motion and who has a remarkable ability to know and communicate what's important in a manuscript.

Finally, I would like to thank all of the students over the years who have allowed me the privilege of teaching them about archaeology—a profound pleasure. This one's for you.

CONCLUSION

I have written this book for a variety of reasons. Archaeology is an inherently intriguing subject to many people. I find it fascinating. I believe that archaeology provides an important part of human knowledge. It helps us understand ourselves, where we have come from, what we have experienced, how we have survived, and even where we may be going. Enrollment in archaeology courses in colleges and universities continues to grow. Media coverage of new discoveries and interpretations appears almost daily. In order to understand this subject better and to put it into the context of our lives today, it is important to know about how archaeology works and how archaeologists think about the past.

It is my hope that this book, *Principles of Archaeology*, will help you understand what it is that archaeologists do. Perhaps it will help you decide to become an archaeologist or to be a better one. I hope that the path here through discovery, analysis, and interpretation will be smooth, and that you will enjoy the journey. If you have any suggestions about how to improve this book, I would be happy to hear from you.

—T. Douglas Price
Madison
December 2005

About the Author

Doug Price is Weinstein Professor of European Archaeology and Director of the Laboratory for Archaeological Chemistry at the University of Wisconsin-Madison, where he has been on the faculty for more than 30 years. His current research involves fieldwork dealing with the beginnings of agriculture in Denmark and lab studies using strontium isotopes in human tooth enamel to look at questions of prehistoric migration. His is the author of a number of books and articles on archaeology and has been involved in fieldwork in Ireland, Wisconsin, Michigan, the Netherlands, Peru, Israel, Guatemala, Mexico, and New Mexico. He likes archaeology, children, cooking, football, and the family dog. He doesn't like long, self-promoting descriptions of a book's author.

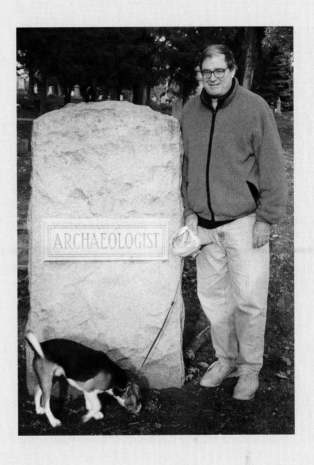

Also Available from McGraw-Hill

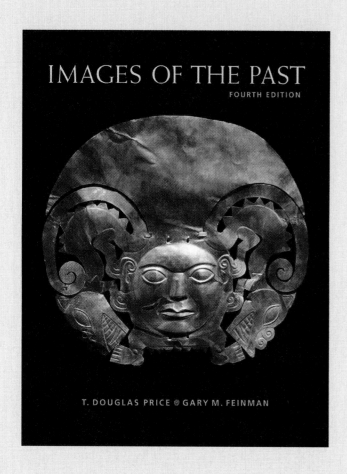

IMAGES OF THE PAST
FOURTH EDITION

T. DOUGLAS PRICE • GARY M. FEINMAN

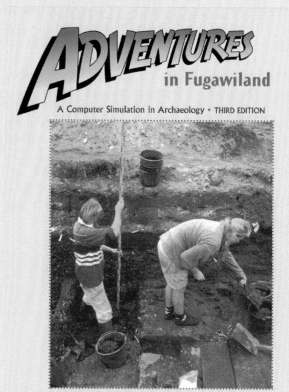

ADVENTURES in Fugawiland

A Computer Simulation in Archaeology • THIRD EDITION

T. Douglas Price • Anne Birgitte Gebauer

Walkthrough

Offering a Unique Approach to Introducing Students to Archaeology

AN IMPORTANT EMPHASIS ON HAVING STUDENTS THINK FOR THEMSELVES

The first major theme of the text concerns how archaeologists think and learn about the past and offers students multiple examples and opportunities to explore archaeology using method, data, and theory on their own.

AN ESSENTIAL FOCUS ON PRESERVING THE PAST AND ETHICS

A second major theme of the text concerns the ways and means to save and protect archaeological sites and encourages students to help with the effort.

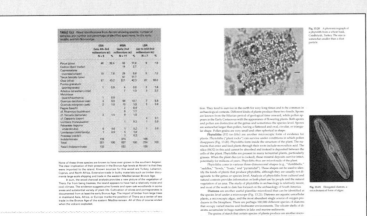

AN ENTICING VIEW OF THE ROLE OF SCIENCE IN ARCHAEOLOGY

The third and last major theme of the text illustrates the importance of the laboratory and instrumental techniques in archaeology and conveys the changing nature of the discipline.

Featuring Understandable and Unique Coverage of Complex Content

A FUNDAMENTAL TEXT

Students are introduced to all of the important theories and techniques in archaeology that are essential to a first-year course and are not overloaded with encyclopedic coverage of the entire discipline.

A STRAIGHTFOWARD ORGANIZATION

The text's organization follows the three basic steps of the archaeological process of discovery, analysis, and interpretation, giving students a logical progression through the course content.

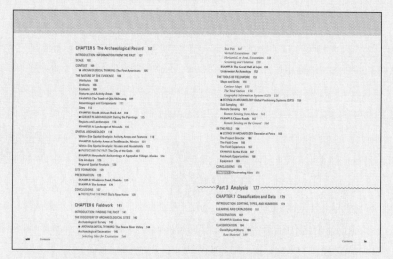

UNIQUE AND ESSENTIAL CONTENT

Chapter 2 offers students an overall look at the process of doing archaeology before they move on to the detail of the later chapters by describing the recovery and study of the royal grave at Sipán, Peru. Chapter 7 includes a substantial section on basic statistics in archaeology and Chapter 15 focuses on archaeometry.

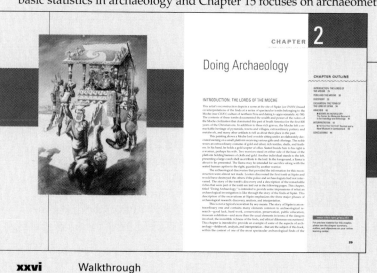

Engaging Readers with an Exciting Narrative, Fascinating Case Studies, and a Spectacular Visual Presentation

ENTICING CHAPTER OPENERS

Chapter introductions draw students into the topic at hand by focusing on a distinctive image or group of images that conveys the fascination of the field.

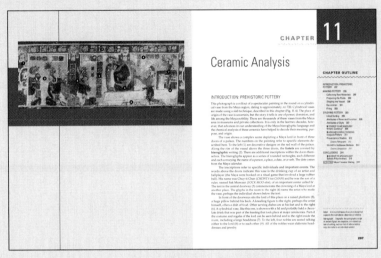

FASCINATING CASE STUDIES

Examples of important archaeological investigations from throughout the world illustrate concepts and methods and show archaeology in action.

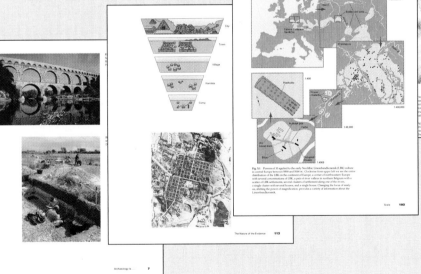

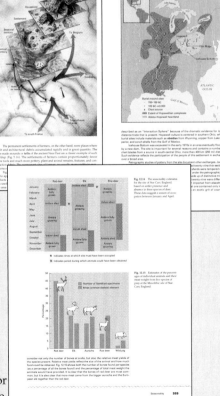

AN EXTREMELY VISUAL TEXT

Five hundred illustrations—including photos, line art, maps (many with orientation globes), plans, and cartoons—allow for presentation with great clarity, and a stunning depiction of the diversity and splendor of archaeology.

Helping Students Succeed with a Unique,
Extensive Learning System

UNIQUE PROJECTS THAT ALLOW STUDENTS TO DO ARCHAEOLOGY THEMSELVES

Students are allowed to try out the concepts introduced in the chapters through hands-on projects, which involve students with archaeological data and questions.

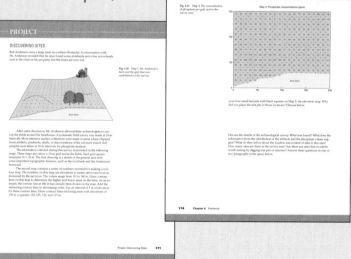

FEATURES THAT PROMOTE THE MAIN THEMES OF THE TEXT

Three kinds of boxes (Archaeological Thinking, Protecting the Past, and Science in Archaeology) appear throughout the text and encourage students to consider the overall themes of the text and how they relate to specific chapter content.

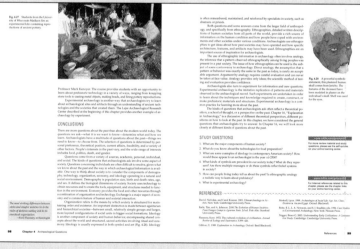

SUPPORT THAT ASSISTS WITH CONTENT, ENCOURAGES CRITICAL THINKING AND FURTHER STUDY, AND HELPS STUDENTS UNDERSTAND WHAT IS IMPORTANT

Part openers, chapter outlines, marginal glossary terms and quotes, chapter conclusions, study questions, and references, help students master course content and allow students to understand the big picture.

Providing Comprehensive Supplemental Support
for Students and Professors

A DYNAMIC STUDENT SUPPLEMENT

An Online Learning Center available at
www.mhhe.com/pricearch1 is chock full of
study tools, activities, links, and useful
information, and is linked to the text through
in-text icons.

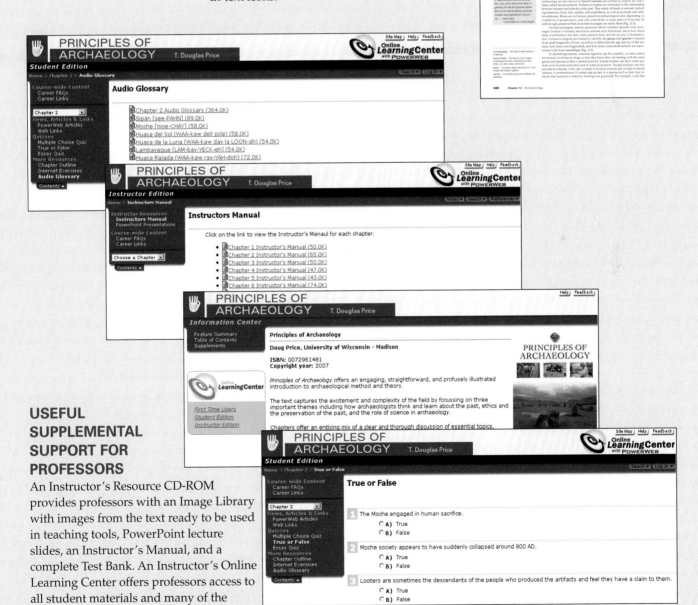

USEFUL SUPPLEMENTAL SUPPORT FOR PROFESSORS

An Instructor's Resource CD-ROM
provides professors with an Image Library
with images from the text ready to be used
in teaching tools, PowerPoint lecture
slides, an Instructor's Manual, and a
complete Test Bank. An Instructor's Online
Learning Center offers professors access to
all student materials and many of the
instructor support materials found on the
Instructor's Resource CD-ROM along with
links to professional resources.

INTRODUCTION

Principles of Archaeology is presented in four major sections: Part 1, Introduction; Part 2, Discovery; Part 3, Analysis; and Part 4, Interpretation. These sections are intended to follow the major stages of archaeological research and to provide some information on how and what archaeologists do. This first part is in three chapters, and it provides background for the other sections and introduces the important themes that recur throughout the book.

Chapter 1 is an introduction to archaeology, about what it is and what it is not, and about why we should study archaeology. It also has some information on careers in archaeology so you can get an idea of how many interesting opportunities there are in the field as you begin your study. This chapter contains descriptions of three kinds of jobs in archaeology by offering a look at a day in the life of a university professor, a state archaeologist, and a museum curator.

Chapter 2, "Doing Archaeology," provides a lengthy description of the recovery and study of a royal grave at Sipán, Peru, one of the richest tombs ever found in the Americas. This is not a typical archaeological excavation by any means, but it makes for a good starting point in an investigation of archaeology because it provides a look at a spectacular grave and the remarkable archaeological effort that rescued the contents of the grave and information about the tomb for the people of Peru. This chapter inaugurates the organization and themes of the book: doing archaeological research (discovery, analysis, and interpretation), thinking about archaeology, protecting the past, and science in archaeology.

Chapter 3 offers a brief history of archaeology from its beginnings as a pastime of the rich and famous to a serious scientific discipline. The history of archaeology and the development of thought and important ideas in the field are closely related. Knowledge is a construction that requires many minds over many years. Understanding the history of archaeology allows us to better understand current perspectives.

Not in Part 1, but also a kind of introduction to the past, is the appendix— "A Brief History of the Human Past." This section in the back of the book provides a condensed overview of world archaeology from the first humans through the rise of Greece and Rome, along with some information on the archaeology of more recent times. It is intended to give you some background for the ideas and information in Principles of Archaeology. If you need to know more about a place or time period in archaeology, you might begin your search there.

An Introduction to Archaeology

INTRODUCTION: WHAT IS ARCHAEOLOGY?

Every summer outside of Lynchburg, Virginia, a group of professional archaeologists, students, and other interested folks move the earth and sift the soil at the place known as Poplar Forest, the second home and a plantation of Thomas Jefferson from 1809 until his death in 1826. Jefferson was a wealthy landowner, scholar, inventor, architect, and politician, and the third president of the United States. He also undertook some of the earliest archaeological excavations in North America (which are described in Chapter 3). Jefferson referred to the large octagonal house he built at Poplar Forest as his most valuable possession, and he had many possessions, including a number of slaves. More than ninety slaves lived at Poplar Forest during Jefferson's time. These individuals worked the fields, tended the stock, and built roads and buildings. They were the masons, blacksmiths, carpenters, spinners, weavers, and servants that kept the plantation running and profitable.

Despite the significant role these people played at Poplar Forest, little was written about them. History does not have a particularly good memory when it comes to the less fortunate. Letters and other documents provide some information about life at Poplar Forest. Jefferson and his overseers left written records about work schedules, births, deaths, and the expenses of a large plantation, but these accounts contain little about the everyday lives of the slaves. Archaeology can recover some of this missing information and has played a major role in increasing our understanding of the conditions of slavery in the United States. For example, archaeological research tells us about the size and construction of the slave homes, people's possessions, diet, and daily activities. The uncovered artifacts also reveal aspects of private enterprise and private lives.

The photos at the beginning of this chapter are from the archaeological project at Poplar Forest. They show (clockwise from upper left) the octagonal mansion that Jefferson built, surveying and testing in the field, excavations, a reconstruction of slave homes at the Quarter Site, screening the soil for artifacts, and drawing pits and discolorations on the ground.

Archaeologists have found two areas of slave residence, the Quarter Site and the North Hill site, at Poplar Forest. At both places, the slaves built houses at the edges of the fields. Four of these buildings have been excavated, including single-family log cabins and a duplex for an extended family. Archaeologists believe that these cabins were probably crowded and dark, so many daily activities must have taken place outdoors, often in a yard that was largely out of the overseer's sight.

www.mhhe.com/pricearch1

For preview material for this chapter, please see the chapter summary, outline, and objectives on your online learning center.

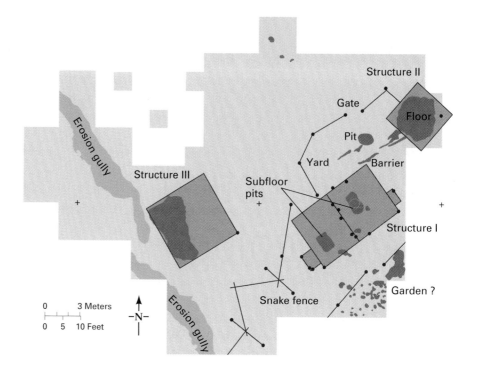

Fig. 1.1 Plan of the structures and features at the Quarter Site excavations at Poplar Forest. Three structures, two single-family cabins and a duplex structure, can be seen, each with a large pit or root cellar in the center. Indications of fencing, a garden, and a yard can also be seen.

A single house, which predated Jefferson's residence at Poplar Forest, was uncovered at the North Hill site. This house, like the three at the Quarter Site, was a log cabin and probably had a wooden chimney. Pieces of the clay lining used in such chimneys were found at both sites. The house at North Hill also had a large pit in the floor. Artifacts found in the storage cellar and around the house included burned seeds and animal bones, woodworking and farming tools, several silver Spanish coins, and items of clothing and adornment, such as buttons, shoe buckles, and beads.

The three cabins at the Quarter Site were probably occupied by four families between 1790 and 1812, the time of Jefferson's residence (Fig. 1.1). The largest building (5 × 8 m [15 × 25 ft]) was a "duplex" of two large rooms that probably housed separate families. Each room had a deep root cellar like the house at North Hill. The remaining two structures were considerably smaller and probably also served as residences. The archaeological evidence documents a variety of activities at this site, including sewing, cooking, handicrafts, and keeping animals. The remains of a garden were also observed next to one of the cabins.

The plantation provisioned the enslaved with food (pork, corn, wheat flour, and salt) and cloth for clothing, bedding, and blankets. Women who married at the plantation were given a cook pot and a bed as a reward. The plant and animal remains found at the site reflect an ethnic diet. Some thirty-three different species of domestic and wild plants were found at the North Hill site, including fruits, grains, nuts, vegetables, medicinal herbs, and spices. These plants include both those cultivated at the plantation and other species collected in the wild or grown in gardens. Jefferson bought garden produce, ducks, chickens, and eggs from the slave quarters. Interestingly, sorghum was found at the North Hill site, though this cereal was unfamiliar to Jefferson at the time. This plant, originally African, may have been grown in the slave gardens without the knowledge of the overseer because it does not appear in Jefferson's records.

Only a small number of animal bones were found at the two sites, mostly from pigs, the staple meat in the diet. Cow and chicken bones were few in number. The most common bones were from the feet and skull of the pig, suggesting

Fig. 1.2 Buttons, buckles, and beads used for personal adornment, excavated at the Poplar Forest sites.

that the best cuts of meat may have gone to the plantation owners. In addition to the domestic animals, the remains of deer, squirrels, possums, a raccoon, and fish were also found. Lead shot and gunflints for a rifle were found in the excavations, suggesting that the slaves had some firearms. Bones were heavily fragmented, perhaps as a consequence of meal preparation. African dishes were often one-pot meals, in which a variety of meats and vegetables were chopped or broken up and added to a stew or soup.

More than 120 beads, buttons, and buckles were found in the houses and yard at the Quarter Site (Fig. 1.2). These are items of personal adornment, worn by the slaves at Poplar Forest. These objects were not provided by the owners and must have been acquired independently by the slaves. These finds suggest that people expressed individual tastes and differences by purchasing or acquiring fancy buttons, ribbons, and buckles.

At Poplar Forest, archaeology provides some of the details of everyday life that are missing in historical accounts. These details indicate that there was a home life that included individual pursuits and personal activities. One can only hope that the horror of slavery and the arduous existence of the slaves was perhaps muted to some extent by this home life. "Home," to the slaves, meant their living quarters, which they often had to build and furnish themselves. They also supplemented the food provided by the plantation by gardening, gathering, and hunting, which in turn helped promote traditional dietary and medicinal practices. Among their personal activities was the generation of income from the sale of produce from their gardens, chicken coops, and other private endeavors. They also purchased and wore items of personal adornment, perhaps as a means of identifying one's self amid the anonymity of slavery.

The archaeology of Poplar Forest provides a glimpse of America's past. Archaeology is a kind of time machine for visiting the millennia that have gone before. There are many things we will never know, but what can be learned is often surprising and intriguing. The principles of archaeology provide a means for looking into the past. This chapter is intended to introduce you to what it means to be an archaeologist. The first two sections of the chapter consider what archaeology is and what it is not. Archaeology has value both as a repository of information on the human past and as one of the best ways to determine what actually happened (as opposed to what people wish had happened or what didn't happen).

There are certain guiding principles that provide a foundation for the natural sciences and for archaeology in particular. The scientific method and the theory of evolution are baselines of archaeological research. While not all archaeologists will agree with this statement, almost all would accept the importance of both the scientific method and the theory of evolution to the discipline.

The scientific method is a technique for eliminating incorrect answers in our search for an understanding of the past. It is a means for evaluating our ideas and ensuring that explanations are accurate. The scientific method leads, not to truth, but to a clearer understanding of the phenomenon under investigation. The use of the scientific method is critical in science, medicine, and engineering, where many issues are a matter of life or death. Most people would not want an important drug developed using only the guesswork of one researcher, and the scientific method helps prevent this. It helps ensure that bad ideas are eliminated through experimentation and testing. In archaeology—not a life-or-death discipline—the scientific method helps to focus our understanding of the past.

Evolution is the fundamental theory in the biological sciences. It explains the rise and current state of life on earth. Evolution involves mutation and natural selection, along with other mechanisms, in changing the genetic code of plant and animal species to enable them to adapt to a changing environment. It explains how humans evolved from the apes and helps us to understand the emergence of the modern *Homo sapiens.* A controversy exists between the proponents of evolution and those of creationism and intelligent design. Along with evolution, this controversy is considered in this chapter in an attempt to situate archaeology in the debate.

A third section in this chapter addresses the question of why we should bother to study the past. A final section considers archaeology as a career. This last part provides some basic information about the profession of archaeology and three short stories of archaeologists in different kinds of jobs.

ARCHAEOLOGY IS . . .

What is archaeology? A subject can be defined by both what it is and what it is not. Archaeology is many things to many people. In some ways, the tagline on the cover of *Archaeology* magazine says it all—adventure, discovery, culture, history, and travel.

Archaeology is the source of information about our human past. It is both a popular pastime and an academic discipline, and it involves both amateur and professional practitioners. Archaeology can be found on popular television shows and in obscure scientific journals. It is everywhere. The artifacts and architecture of the past dot the landscape (Fig. 1.3). A few hours spent in a plowed field almost anywhere will reveal something from antiquity.

Archaeology, then, is the study of our human past, combining the themes of time and change, using the material remains that have survived. Archaeology focuses on past human behavior and change in society over time. Archaeologists study past human culture across an enormous amount of time and space, essentially the last several million years and all of the continents except Antarctica. In one sense, archaeology is the investigation of the choices that our ancestors have made as they evolved from the first humans to the historical present.

Archaeology is also a detective story, a mystery far more complex and harder to solve than most crimes because the clues to past human behavior are enigmatic—broken, decomposed, and often missing. Piecing together these bits of information to make sense of the activities of our ancestors is a challenge. This challenge—and the ingenuity, technology, and hard work necessary to solve it—provides both the excitement and the frustration of archaeology.

Archaeology is a fascinating field, in part because the subject matter is highly diverse and highly human. There are so many times and places involved,

Archaeology is the search for FACTS, not truth. If it's truth you're looking for, Prof. Tyree's Philosophy course is right down the hall. . . . Forget any ideas about lost cities, exotic travel and digging up the world . . . we do not follow maps to buried treasure and "X" never ever marks the spot. . . . Seventy percent of all archaeology is done in the library.
—Indiana Jones, fictional archaeologist

Archaeology is a science that must be lived, must be seasoned with humanity.
—Mortimer Wheeler, archaeologist

archaeology The study of our human past, combining the themes of time and change, using the material remains that have survived.

Fig. 1.3 Archaeology is often hauntingly beautiful. This is the Roman aqueduct still standing at Pont du Gard near Nîmes, France.

Fig. 1.4 Excavations of a large trench at a Stone Age site in Denmark.

so many questions to be asked. Archaeology accommodates an extraordinarily wide range of interests: chemistry, zoology, human biology, ceramics, classics, computers, experiments, geology, history, stone tools, museums, human fossils, theory, genetics, scuba diving, and much, much more. Many of these subjects are discussed in the following chapters.

Another way to regard the nature of archaeology is to consider how it fits among academic fields of study. Archaeology is usually situated as a social science or among the humanities in a university setting. In much of the world, autonomous institutes or departments of archaeology are the norm. Among the largest of these are the Institute of Archaeology in London, with nearly 500 students and over 70 academic teaching staff; the six-story Maison de l'Archéologie et de l'Ethnologie in Paris, with offices for 260 archaeologists; and the Institute of Archaeology, Chinese Academy of Social Sciences, in Beijing, with several hundred archaeologists.

In the United States, for historical reasons, archaeology is usually part of a department of anthropology, which combines archaeology with **biological anthropology** and **cultural (social) anthropology**, all focused on humans and culture. Biological anthropology is the study of the biological nature of our nearest relatives and ourselves. Biological anthropologists study bones, blood, genetics, growth, demography, and other aspects of both living humans and primates, like the monkeys and apes, and their fossilized remains. Cultural, or social, anthropologists study living peoples and focus on the shared aspects of the human experience, describing both the differences and the common characteristics that exist. **Linguistics**—the study of human languages—is sometimes included in anthropology but often found in another academic department.

In fact, archaeology extends across a number of disciplines—the natural sciences for the collection and analysis of the material remains of past human activity, the social sciences for questions about human behavior and the major themes of technology, demography, diet and subsistence, economy, and behavior, and the humanities for the study of human creativity, art, and design.

In anthropology departments, archaeology is sometimes called **anthropological archaeology**, or **prehistory**. Anthropological archaeology refers specifically to archaeological investigations that seek to answer the larger, fundamental questions about humans and human behavior that are part of anthropological enquiry. Prehistory refers to the time of humans before the written record placed us in history. Many archaeologists do study prehistory, but many also study literate societies such as the Maya and Aztec and the urban civilizations of ancient Mesopotamia and China, where writing began. The term *prehistory* is often misused and applied to these early literate civilizations as well.

Historical archaeology—archaeology in combination with the written record—borders on the field of history and usually refers specifically to the archaeology of civilizations of the Renaissance and Industrial Era (Fig. 1.5). The historical record is limited and archaeology can complement the written record and provide more insight on our own recent past. It is difficult, in fact, to understand how our great grandparents lived. What was life like 50, or 100, or 200 years ago? One example of how historical archaeology can tell us about our own past was described at the beginning of this chapter in the section on Poplar Forest. Another example of how archaeology can tell us about history comes from the Little Big Horn. Custer's Last Stand in AD 1876 is an enduring part of American history, taught in almost every school in the country. Yet there are few written accounts of the battle between the Seventh Calvary and the Sioux and Cheyenne in existence. Little was known of the details and progress of the battle until archaeologists investigated the site at Little Big Horn in Montana in the mid-1980s. The archaeological detective work across the battlefield revealed spent cartridges, fired bullets, personal items, and human remains that told much of the progress and

Archaeology is one of those special fields where the public appeal and interest of the subject is combined with the intellectual pursuits of science. . . . Archaeology is surely a major example of that linkage, along with astronomy and cosmology, so close to the old existential questions of all thinking humans.
—Philip Morrison, physicist

biological anthropology   The study of the biological nature of our nearest relatives and ourselves.

cultural (social) anthropology   The study of living peoples with a focus on the shared aspects of the human experience.

linguistics   The study of human languages.

anthropological archaeology   Archaeological investigations that seek to answer the larger, fundamental questions about humans and human behavior taught in departments of anthropology.

prehistory   The time in the past before written history, often synonymous with *archaeology*.

historical archaeology   Refers primarily to the *archaeology* of the civilizations of the recent industrial era, since 1700 or so.

Fig. 1.5 Representation of Jamestown, one of the earliest English colonies in North America, founded in AD 1607, at Jamestown settlement, a living-history museum of seventeenth-century Virginia.

nature of the conflict. A much clearer picture of a scattered and lengthy running engagement has now emerged.

Archaeology can also be taught in a department of classics or art history or religious studies. **Classical archaeology** is concerned with the literate Mediterranean civilizations of Greece and Rome. Departments of classics teach the literature, architecture, language, and archaeology of the classic civilizations. Biblical archaeology, focused on past places and things in the Holy Land, can be found in departments of religion. Archaeologists interested in geology and landscape formation are sometimes housed in departments of geology or geography.

Another important distinction in archaeology is made between academic archaeology and **cultural resource management (CRM)**. Two important laws passed in the 1960s largely established this field: the National Historic Preservation Act of 1966 and the National Environmental Policy Act of 1969.

These laws require a consideration of whether a proposed action, e.g., construction, will affect archaeological or historical sites. The U.S. Environmental Protection Agency requires an environmental impact study to determine whether important sites are in danger of destruction prior to the start of federally funded construction. Both federal agencies and private corporations must provide information on the effect their construction projects may have on the history and prehistory of the area. This legislation has led to the substantial growth of archaeology in both government and private sectors with the creation of state and federal agencies and private companies to conduct and evaluate these impact studies. Various kinds of construction—reservoirs, highways, sewage systems, and power lines, to name just a few—require such archaeological surveys and environmental impact statements, and businesses, governments, and private citizens must pay to have such impact studies made. This kind of work, known as cultural resource management, is an important part of archaeology and it is done by people at universities, museums, government agencies, and private companies.

Archaeology is a profession and a vocation, an academic pursuit and a popular pastime, combining demanding science and romantic perspectives. Practicing archaeologists are trained in universities and take jobs doing research, teaching, and protecting the past. Professionals and amateurs are serious about learning and about demanding proof about what happened in the past. Yet because the past is both obscure and fascinating, archaeology is a subject that attracts wild speculation, alternative views, and charlatans—and that is what archaeology and true archaeologists are not.

classical archaeology   A branch of *archaeology* primarily concerned with the literate Mediterranean civilizations of Greece and Rome.

cultural resource management (CRM)   Historical preservation in the United States involves *survey* and *excavation* to determine that historical and cultural resources are not being destroyed by development and construction.

ARCHAEOLOGY IS NOT . . .

OK, now a pop quiz. Please answer true or false to the following questions.

1. The first humans appeared almost 50 million years ago.
2. All archaeological sites are protected under the law.
3. Archaeology is the study of ancient humans and dinosaurs.
4. New York and London are at approximately the same latitude.
5. The earliest human remains come from Southeast Asia.
6. The first ten million years of our existence on earth were spent in Africa.
7. Evolution cannot explain how humans came to be on earth.
8. The earliest human ancestors appeared around 60,000 years ago.
9. The sun revolves around the earth.
10. Stonehenge was built by the Druids.

All of the answers are false. There are many misconceptions about the past and about archaeology, due in part to an absence of knowledge and in part to the presence of charlatans and the popularity of **pseudoscience**.

This section of Chapter 1 deals with what archaeology is not, what has been called the fraud, myth, and mystery of the past. It is important to be alert to this aspect of archaeology and to emphasize the importance of questioning, criticism, and proof in discussions of the past. There are hundreds of fraudulent examples in archaeology, fake finds from the past. People search for Atlantis; members of mother earth cults eat the soil at important archaeological sites; the Shroud of Turin (Chapter 8) draws thousands of devoted pilgrims. In almost every country, fake artifacts have been promoted as genuine for financial or political reasons. The mysteries of the past continue to mesmerize and seduce. Sometimes professional archaeologists are fooled as well.

A well-known forgery, the Piltdown Man, provides an example here. In addition, the pseudoscience of Erich von Däniken offers a case study of the potency of archaeological mystery. Finally, some thoughts on the evaluation of claims about the past, scientific or otherwise, are expressed.

 EXAMPLE ~~~~~~~~~~~~~~~~~~~~~~~~~~~~~~~~

THE PILTDOWN MAN

Late in the year AD 1912, a lawyer, Charles Dawson, and a respected geologist, Arthur Smith Woodward, presented their new discoveries of fossil remains to the Geological Society in London (Fig. 1.6). Their finds included part of a thick human skull, a fragment of an apelike lower jaw, some animal remains, and even early stone tools. They estimated that these fossils found close together near a place called Piltdown in southern England were 500,000 years old.

Piltdown was a forgery, but for 40 years the remains were accepted as an important part of our evolutionary development. Piltdown was proclaimed genuine and was called the "missing link" between apes and humans by several of the most important British scientists of the day.

Piltdown was finally debunked many years later by chemical tests that showed that the skull and jaw were neither the same age nor very old. (This study is described in Chapter 15, on archaeometry.) It was a fake. The bones had been heavily stained and chemically treated to make them appear ancient. Diagnostic anatomical features were broken off or filed down to change the appearance of the jaw. Today, the word *Piltdown* is a term of ridicule, used to label fraudulent research. The identity of the

pseudoscience False or misleading claims about the nature of the world or the past, masquerading as science.

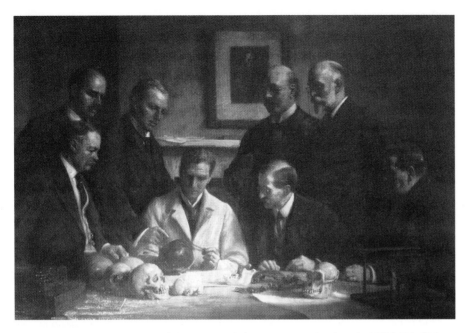

Fig. 1.6 A painting of some of the principal characters involved in the Piltdown discovery and examination. Dawson and Woodward are in the back row to the right.

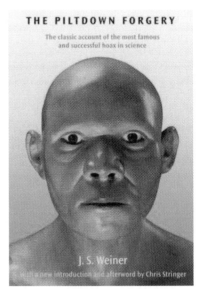

Fig. 1.7 A revised edition of the 1955 book by J. S. Weiner that indicted Charles Dawson as the culprit in the Piltdown forgery.

perpetrator(s) of the forgery is still debated but Charles Dawson is often implicated (Fig. 1.7).

Why did this fraud fool the experts? There are of course a number of reasons. For the most part, the forgery was well done and not seriously questioned. The scientists wanted to believe the find because it fit preconceived notions. Moreover, Germany and France already had important human fossils, discovered decades before Piltdown. Perhaps national pride blinded the researchers to the scratch marks made by the filing of the jaw and teeth.

 EXAMPLE

ERICH VON DÄNIKEN

Since the initial publication of *Chariots of the Gods* in 1970 (now in its 44th edition), Erich von Däniken has been at the forefront of alien archaeology. Von Däniken, a Swiss entrepreneur, argues that many prehistoric monuments were actually built by aliens who visited earth in the past. He says, for example, that alien landing and launching pads are recognizable at several archaeological sites. He suggests that the famous Nasca lines in the desert of southern Peru were signposts for space travelers. He also once told the *National Enquirer* that he could leave his body at will and transcend space and time. Von Däniken has even claimed that God was an ancient astronaut.

A TV special called "In Search of Ancient Astronauts" ensured von Däniken's fame in the United States. His books have been translated into thirty-two languages, and more than 60 million copies have been sold. Most recently, von Däniken and his colleagues have opened a new family attraction near Interlaken, Switzerland, appropriately called Mystery Park (Fig. 1.8). Examples of the alien presence in the past have become amusement park rides and displays at the attraction.

> *People should learn the meaning of astonishment.*
> —Erich von Däniken, author

Fig. 1.8 The Mystery Park amusement area in Interlaken, Switzerland.

Although his claims are demonstrably fraudulent, von Däniken's words continue to enthrall many readers and viewers. For example, von Däniken mistakenly described the soft, carvable volcanic tuff used for the giant heads on Easter Island as one of the hardest rocks on earth. He also said that archaeologists did not know how the Egyptians moved the massive construction stones for the pyramids, when in fact we do. The list is long. Many of the statements of pseudoscience are false or unverifiable.

EVALUATING SCIENCE AND PSEUDOSCIENCE

Why do people believe such myths, hoaxes, or lies? Because there is so much in the world around us that is uncertain or unknown, answers, right or wrong, are usually welcome. Too often, however, such answers are uncritically accepted as truth.

An essential distinction must be made in archaeology, and other fields, between science and pseudoscience. Science is a method for evaluating the correctness of explanations. Pseudoscience is a technique for creating "truth."

Pseudoscience is the name given to the myriad of stories and explanations proposed by charlatans, swindlers, and true believers. It is false science, based on either deceit or belief, founded in perception, not observation, and it often involves the paranormal, bizarre statements, and allegations that are often said to be beyond the reach of science and scientists. Pseudoscience avoids or disavows the scientific method and makes unsubstantiated claims to truth. Some may ask what the harm of a few fantastic stories might be. The answer is that misconceptions and false facts can create many problems, in medicine, in diet, and in archaeology. It is important to be accurate in our understanding of the world around us, and accurate information requires reason, evaluation, and testing.

If you have reason to doubt the validity of a claim or explanation about the past (or anything else for that matter), you should ask questions. What is the evidence for the claim? What are the credentials of the claimant? Is this a reasonable argument? Have other experts or professionals substantiated the argument? Does the claim involve intangible or unknown forces or individuals? In most cases, it is better to be dubious than naïve or gullible.

Perhaps the best criterion to use in evaluating the claims of pseudoscience, or science, is the principle of Occam's razor. Occam was a fourteenth-century English theologian who espoused a philosophy of simplicity: the simplest solution

I maintain there is much more wonder in science than in pseudoscience. And in addition, to whatever measure this term has any meaning, science has the additional virtue, and it is not an inconsiderable one, of being true.
—Carl Sagan, astronomer

is often the correct one. This principle that also applies in the case of claims about the past.

The Scientific Method

Science, in fact, has developed in order to separate fact from fiction. Science is a method for seeking the real nature of the universe through observation and experimentation. Science seeks to falsify or disprove hypotheses, rather than prove them. Scientists are skeptics, with good reason.

The scientific method is one of critique; all ideas are assumed to be wrong until proven otherwise. This practice is perhaps best understood in the context of medicine. If all drugs were automatically assumed to work before they were given to patients, there would be many casualties and people would be afraid of doctors. Drugs are assumed to be dangerous before their benefits and safety can be repeatedly demonstrated. The same is true of scientific ideas in archaeology and other fields, although the consequences are usually not as dramatic.

Science is careful evaluation. The scientific method usually begins with an observation—water turns solid. An idea or a guess, a hypothesis, about how or why that happens is put forth—maybe cold makes water hard. The hypothesis is evaluated or tested—put water in freezer, water turns hard. If the hypothesis passes the test, it can become a theory, not a truth—cold freezes water to ice. This theory is not truth because there may be other factors or forces that we don't know about that turn water to a solid. A **theory** is just a generally accepted explanation.

Science in archaeology is really an argument by an accumulation of evidence, rather than by experimentation. What makes archaeology a science is the testing or evaluation of the answers until we are confident they are not wrong. The science of archaeology lies in bridging the gap between the information we recover and the questions we seek to answer. Finding ways to evaluate ideas and claims is called operationalizing a study, defining abstract ideas in terms of measurable outcomes in the search for knowledge.

One example of such a bridge between information and ideas comes from a study of ancient coins from Europe and Asia that were minted before AD 1500 and found in North America. Among these coins is a Viking coin from Maine that may well predate Columbus and Chinese coins that were found at Indian sites on the Northwest Coast of North America. There are also a number of less reliable reports of Greek, Roman, and Hebrew coins found in North America. These coins have given rise to claims for contact between the New World and the Mediterranean prior to the arrival of Columbus.

Jeremiah Epstein, an archaeologist at the University of Texas, carefully examined forty of these claims to determine if they had any validity. Epstein compiled a detailed list of the coins with their original date, the year and place of discovery, and circumstances of the find. His work indicated that most of the coins were found in the twentieth century and the majority of those since World War II, when Americans began to visit Europe in large numbers as soldiers and tourists. Moreover, the original dates on the coins are scattered over a long period of time, most of Greek and Roman history, without any clear clusters. The location of the find was also revealing. Most of the coins were found in the eastern and especially the southern states. Intriguingly, the majority of the coins were found in interior areas of the country and not on the coasts. Voyages from the Mediterranean, whether intentional or accidental, would likely have come ashore in the southeastern United States and it seems unlikely that those early sailors would have moved deep into the interior of the continent. Furthermore, almost all the coins were found in modern settings, which also raises questions about their authenticity. Only four of the coins come from an archaeological context at Indian sites in North America, and none of these examples could be verified as reliable or authentic.

> All of our science, when measured against reality, is primitive and childlike—and yet it is the most precious thing we have.
> —Albert Einstein, physicist

> There are dozens of ways to do good archaeology. To define the range of acceptable archaeological methods, we will at times emphasize the extremes. One extreme is largely scientific, the other is largely humanistic. One extreme is pretty objective, the other is quite subjective. One extreme values ecology, the other prizes the role of ideas. Sometimes these approaches co-exist, sometimes they clash.
> —David Hurst Thomas, real archaeologist

theory   A generally accepted explanation of observed events or relationships.

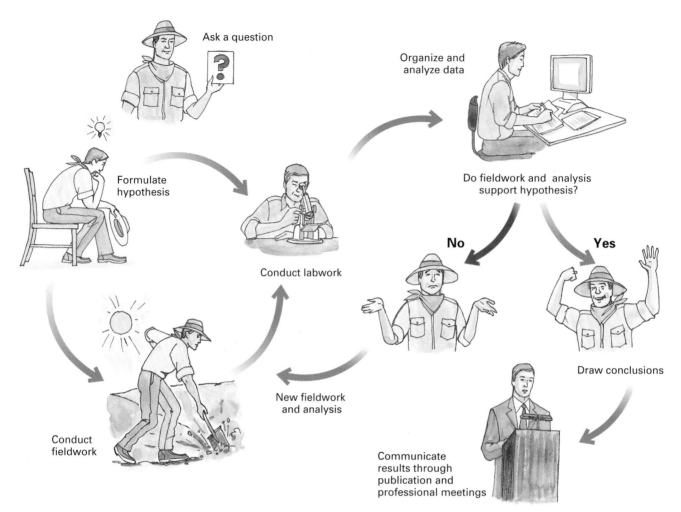

Ask a question

Formulate hypothesis

Conduct labwork

Conduct fieldwork

New fieldwork and analysis

Organize and analyze data

Do fieldwork and analysis support hypothesis?

No   **Yes**

Draw conclusions

Communicate results through publication and professional meetings

Fig. 1.9 The scientific method in archaeology is a way of evaluating ideas to eliminate wrong ones by testing and retesting. Once a research question is selected, possible answers are evaluated through field and lab investigations. If the results don't support the answer, the process begins again. If the results do support the answer, conclusions are published.

Science is a way of thinking much more than it is a body of knowledge.
—Carl Sagan, astronomer

The real purpose of the scientific method is to make sure Nature hasn't misled you into thinking you know something you don't actually know.
—Robert Pirsig, author

Epstein's careful compilation of information on the coins and their context and the questions he asked to determine if they were authentic in origin and place of discovery are a classic example of the scientific method in action. Epstein used science to evaluate the claims for early contact. First, he operationalized his study by developing criteria for verifying the hypothesis of early contact. He then refuted the claims based on the evidence he accumulated. When Epstein looked for patterns in the information that would support or contradict the presence of the coins in North America before Columbus, he found in every case that the evidence would not support an argument for early contact between the Mediterranean and North America. The simplest and most plausible explanations for the cases he examined were that either the coins had been lost in more recent times or they were frauds.

Most archaeologists accept that it is not truth they are seeking, but rather a better understanding of the past and its human inhabitants. Thus, archaeological research adds to the body of knowledge; it rarely provides final answers. Answers in the social sciences are difficult to come by because human behavior and decision making are involved and we do not yet adequately understand these phenomena.

Fig. 1.9 schematically depicts the scientific method in archaeology. It is a research strategy that begins with the formulation of the problem or question. For example, is layer A older than layer B? Was this stone tool used for cutting meat? How many people lived in this house? Once a question is asked, it is necessary to come up with ideas or possible answers to the question. Evaluating those hypothetical answers is the crux of the scientific method. Archaeologists conduct fieldwork and undertake a variety of analyses to evaluate the hypothetical answers.

Their fieldwork and analysis then generate new questions and answers. The process continues to spiral, with wrong answers being eliminated and new questions constantly being generated. Answers that appear to be correct are then made public to a wide audience. Negative evidence is also published so that other scientists will not take the same path again.

Evolution

www.mhhe.com/pricearch1

For a Web-based activity on Charles Darwin, please see the Internet exercises on your online learning center.

Evolution is a fundamental concept in natural and biological science. It is a scientific theory that best explains the existence of life on earth. Change, modification, variation, these themes describe the course of evolution from the first self-replicating molecules to the fully modern humans of today. Most of the evolution of life on earth is marked by biological evolution from one species to another to adapt to new conditions. Evolution allows life to change.

The theory of natural selection, formulated by Charles Darwin and Alfred Russel Wallace in the middle of the nineteenth century, explains this process of change. Darwin coined the term *natural selection* to account for the increase in offspring of those individuals who survived from one generation to the next. He introduced the concept in his 1859 publication *On the Origin of Species by Means of Natural Selection.* Darwin pointed out that all organisms produce more offspring than can survive and that the individuals that survive do so because of certain advantageous characteristics they possess.

In other words, the surviving organisms are better adapted to the world that confronts them. For example, offspring with better hearing or eyesight can more effectively avoid predators or find more food. Nature's choice of better-adapted individuals—the "survival of the fittest," according to Darwin—leads to continual change in the species, as their more advantageous characteristics are passed genetically from one generation to the next. This basic process gave rise to the myriad creatures that occupy the world today. Evolutionary change is often described as differential reproductive success, and natural selection is the principal, though not the exclusive, mechanism responsible for it. Of course, as environmental conditions change, those physical characteristics that enhance survival and successful parenting also may vary.

As humans, we have another and unique means of adaptation that involves learned behavior. Culture is a means for human adaptation based on experience, learning, and the use of tools. Cultural and biological responses to cold conditions provide an example. Body hair increased on animals like the woolly mammoth, which was a biological response. Humans, on the other hand, built fires to stay warm—a cultural response. Within limits, culture enables us to modify and enhance our behavior without a corresponding change in our genetic makeup. As a consequence, biological evolution and natural selection alone cannot explain the culturally acquired traits of the human species.

The prehistoric record of our ancestors is characterized by both biological evolution and cultural development. Biological, rather than cultural, changes dominated our first several million years of existence. The evolution of our earliest forebears is highlighted by key changes in movement, body size, teeth, and the size and organization of the brain. The last hundred thousand years or so of our presence on the planet are marked primarily by cultural changes rather than by biological ones. The transmission of cultural traits through learning occurs much more rapidly than Darwinian evolution.

Views on evolution evolve over time as well. New mechanisms for evolution have been proposed in recent years, and there is ongoing discussion about the level in populations at which selection operates, whether on groups or individuals. There is also debate about the pace of change—whether major evolutionary modifications occurred gradually, as Darwin emphasized, or rather abruptly and suddenly. Stephen Jay Gould and Niles Eldredge of Harvard University describe the uneven pace of evolution as **punctuated equilibrium**. It now seems that some biological shifts occur gradually, as Darwin described, whereas others may occur in relatively rapid spurts following long periods of stasis, or little change. This view of evolution is a modification to the theory, but the basic tenets of evolution have withstood many tests and offer the best way to understand the emergence of life and early humans.

Evolution and Creationism

Evolution is both fact and theory. The theory of evolution describes the mechanisms that cause changes in the plants and animals of the earth over time. Biological evolution involves changes in genetic characteristics over time. That is a fact. The evidence for evolution—fossil, anatomical, genetic—is so strong that it is also fact. Exactly how evolution operated in the past is not always clear. Thus, the mechanisms of evolution involve theory. But that doesn't change the facts. Remember that gravity is also a theory. Almost all archaeologists and other scientists affirm the validity of an evolutionary perspective.

Creationists, on the other hand, believe that the earth and its creatures were created by God, as recorded in Genesis in the Bible. In fact, the biblical creation is an origin myth, one of many different stories that cultures around the world use to explain their beginnings. Most of the world's religions have their own creation stories. Many creationists in the United States believe that God made the earth and all the animals as they exist today in a period of seven days. The term *intelligent design* is sometimes used today to avoid religious overtones. But proponents of intelligent design believe that the complexity of organisms and life on earth is evidence for the existence of a cosmic architect. Creationists do not believe that one form of life changes into another and they cite several arguments against evolution: there is no evidence in recorded history of one species turning into another, the fossil record does not show gradual change, scientific dating methods are flawed, and genetic data do not consistently provide evidence for evolution.

In spite of the preponderance of evidence for evolution, the concept contradicts the religious beliefs of many and has led to a continuing controversy in the United States. Debates rage about whether evolution should be taught in schools. In fact, the Supreme Court ruled in 1987 that creationism was religious and therefore could not be promoted in public schools. Most major religious groups have accepted the fact that evolution is not at odds with their view of creation and human origins. In 2006, the Roman Catholic church restated its support for evolution, praising a U.S. court decision that rejected intelligent design as non-scientific. But the push for teaching creationism in the schools has continued.

WHY STUDY ARCHAEOLOGY?

A very reasonable question concerns the relevance of archaeology. Why should we study archaeology? Why is it important to know what happened in prehistory? Why do we need to know about the past?

One basic reason to learn about archaeology is simply a curiosity about the past. Public opinion in the United States is very positive with regard to archaeology. A recent poll revealed that 76% of those questioned expressed a strong interest in archaeology and 90% thought archaeology should be taught in high school. Reasons for this interest were varied: learning about how people lived in the past, connecting the past to the present, and the thrill of discovery were mentioned. Archaeology is clearly of inherent interest to the general public. Stories appear almost daily in our newspapers and on television. The Internet is crowded with pages about archaeology and our human past. The giant heads of Easter Island (Fig. 1.10) are just one of many fascinating stories that have been reported in the media.

www.mhhe.com/pricearch1

For a Web-based activity on Evolution and Creationism, please see the Internet exercises on your online learning center.

punctuated equilibrium   Abrupt and sudden changes in the pace of evolution.

Fig. 1.10 Mysterious heads from Easter Island in the Pacific are among the fascinating remains of the extraordinary things that our ancestors made.

But this fascination with archaeology stems from the inherent significance of the subject. There is, of course, an exciting mystery involved in uncovering treasures in the earth, but more than that, archaeology tells us about ourselves and how we got to be the way we are. Ultimately, it is the lessons about our past that archaeology provides that convey its significance. The human condition is one that has changed and will change over time. To know our place and to have confidence about where we are going are essential ingredients for the success of our species.

For most of our human career, we have lived as gatherers and/or hunters. The roots of human behavior are to be found in that past. The changes that took place in that time were both biological and cultural—primarily biological at the beginning, almost exclusively cultural toward the end. Our earliest ancestors appeared more than 6 million years ago in Africa. The first groups of farmers have been found in western Asia around 11,000 years ago. During the intervening period our activities shifted from a peripatetic quest for food by small groups of a generic apelike ancestor to an elaborate pattern of intensive food collecting and storing by large groups of fully modern humans living in permanent communities.

www.mhhe.com/pricearch1

For a Web-based activity on Careers in Archaeology, please see the Internet exercises on your online learning center.

In fact, hunter-gatherers have continued to exist at the margins of modern society until very recently. To unravel the beginnings of humanness, the origins of fully modern behavior, and our background as foragers through archaeology is essential to understanding ourselves and our place in nature. In a sense, our life in mega–urban societies with intricately structured hierarchical organizations, highly advanced technologies, and extraordinary communication and exchange is too new to be understood without knowledge of the baseline behaviors from which it derived.

The role of archaeology ultimately is to describe the course of human development, to tell us about our origins. That knowledge can provide both pride and confidence in our species, along with a much greater awareness of our oneness. Of course, this may not seem so important in an age when recent polls indicate that the majority of Americans do not know that the earth travels around the sun every 365 days and continue to believe that humans and dinosaurs did battle in the past. But then again, maybe that is why it is so important. Archaeology has the opportunity to greatly extend the fundamental contributions that have been made to human knowledge and society.

CAREERS IN ARCHAEOLOGY

There are many different ways to participate in archaeology: watch a TV program, read a book, visit a museum, or tour an archaeological site. For those with a more serious interest and a desire to pursue a career in archaeology, an advanced degree is normally required, either a Master of Arts (MA) or Science (MS) or a Doctorate of Philosophy (PhD).

Degrees in archaeology are offered by academic departments in colleges and universities. Undergraduate students interested in archaeology usually take courses in anthropology, geography, geology, zoology, botany, soils, and the like to learn basic information about the discipline and related fields. Participation in fieldwork is an important activity at all levels in one's education in archaeology. Problems and questions of field research are complex, and gaining experience in a variety of situations and time periods is a great way to learn about the past. To gain field experience, students often enroll in field schools, summer training programs in archaeological survey and excavation that are offered as credit courses by many universities. Fieldwork is often the crucible where students learn if archaeology is really the career they want to follow.

Interested undergraduate students apply to graduate school during their senior year or soon after graduation. There are also returning students who have decided to pursue their interest in archaeology. Application to graduate schools usually requires an undergraduate transcript, letters of recommendation, scores from the Graduate Record Examination (GRE), and a statement of interest, along with a processing fee.

Calvin and Hobbs © 1988 Watterson. Dist. by Universal Press Syndicate. Reprinted with permission. All rights reserved.

Most graduate students start their studies with some specific interest in a time or place or subject matter. Most have an undergraduate background in archaeology and often some field experience. Advanced degrees require a major commitment in time, energy, and money.

A master's degree involves 1 to 3 years of coursework on average and may require a written thesis as well. Many programs include a comprehensive examination at the end of the master's curriculum. The goal of a master's program normally is to instill a broad general knowledge, both practical and theoretical, about the field of archaeology that will allow the student to perform well in the discipline. There are also more focused MA and MS programs in which specific skills are taught, such as cultural resource management, human osteology, and geographic information systems.

The Doctor of Philosophy degree takes an average of 7.5 years, including the time required to obtain the master's, and is intended to provide specialized knowledge of particular areas of archaeology and to demonstrate exceptional research skills. Coursework is usually part of the curriculum, but the major part of PhD studies involves research. A PhD dissertation, the culmination of this degree program, is essentially a book describing the questions, methods, and results of a substantial research project.

With a master's or doctorate in hand, there are many directions to explore, although not a large number of jobs. Archaeologists work in several kinds of jobs: as professors teaching and doing research in universities and colleges, as curators cataloging and investigating artifacts in museums, as professional archaeologists in commercial firms doing fieldwork and writing reports on the impact of development on cultural resources, and in such government positions as rangers, researchers, and managers of archaeological and historic resources on federally owned lands. A variety of other fields of study are involved in assisting archaeology to learn about the past, including botany, chemistry, classics, genetics, geography, geology, physics, zoology, and many others. In this sense, archaeology combines many interests and directions in a single discipline.

If you are serious about a career in archaeology and want to learn more, get in touch with your local college or university, contact the Society for American Archaeology or the Archaeological Institute of America for information, or search the Web. There are thousands of websites that offer information on this fascinating field. A very useful document called Frequently Asked Questions about a Career in Archaeology by David Carlson can be found at the Society for American Archaeology website on teaching.

Survey Says . . .

To understand archaeology, it is essential to know what archaeologists do and how they do it. The preceding section provided some information on the education needed to become an archaeologist. But what are archaeologists like as people, what do they do, what kinds of jobs do they have, and how much money do they make?

A great deal of information about American archaeologists was compiled in 1994 by the Society for American Archaeology, the national organization for archaeologists. The Society surveyed its 5000 members to find out who they were and what they were like. Nearly one-third replied and their answers were published in 1997 in a book called *The American Archaeologist: A Profile,* by Melinda Zeder. Although this information is now somewhat out of date, it is the most recent summary available.

In the 1994 survey, approximately 36.5% of the respondents were female. Today that number would be closer to 40%. In 1994, and still true today, American archaeology is a profession with few minorities. Of the 1644 replies to the questionnaire, 1470 (89%) reported that they were of European ancestry, only

If anyone were to ask me why I have spent my life studying prehistory, I would only say that I have remained under the spell of a subject which seeks to discover how we became human beings endowed with minds and souls before we had learned to write.

—Grahame Clark, archaeologist

I am an archaeologist and devote my time to trying to gather information about the behavior of men long since dead. I like doing this and my society pays me quite well for doing it. Yet neither I nor society can see any practical application for the information I gather; we are indeed quite sure it will not increase the production of bombs or butter.

—V. Gordon Childe, archaeologist

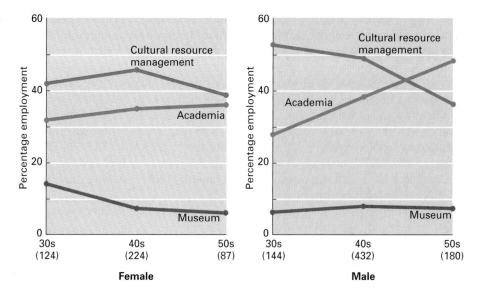

Fig. 1.11 Female and male employment in archaeology by age and career. Ages are grouped into 30s, 40s, and 50s. The numbers beneath the age groups indicate how many individuals responded to the questionnaire. For example, for women in their 40s, 8% are employed in museums, 35% in academia, and 47% in CRM work.

I became an archaeologist because I wanted to drive around in a big Land Rover, smoking, cursing, and finding treasure.

—Carmel Schrire, archaeologist

2 people were African American, 4 were Asian, 15 were Hispanic, and 10 were Native Americans. A total of 142 (9%) listed themselves as "Other"—persons who likely objected to being classified. Eliminating this "other" category, 98% claimed a Euro–American heritage.

Another important question asked archaeologists where they worked. Four categories of employment were used: academic, museum, private, and government. The private and government sectors are generally related and similar in terms of the job and are involved with the management of cultural resources. Among the respondents to the survey, about 38 percent were employed in colleges and universities, about 10% in museums, 18% in government agencies, and another 24% in private firms, leaving about 10% as students or unemployed. Archaeologists in government agencies and private firms are primarily involved with cultural resource management (CRM). A major distinction in archaeology can be made between academic and CRM employment. In the 1994 survey, these two areas were roughly equal in size (academic = 38%, CRM = 42%). But CRM continues to grow; today more than 50% of active archaeologists are involved in this field.

The survey also provided information on the gender of those employed in archaeology. Fig. 1.11 shows the number of individuals who responded to the survey by sex, age, and position. It shows that academic jobs were most common for males and females and older archaeologists, but less frequent than government and private (CRM) jobs combined. The higher proportion of younger people in the government and private sector points to growth in these areas compared to the academic arena. Museum jobs were the least common among the respondents.

The survey of archaeologists also asked about job satisfaction. Although most students would prefer employment in an academic position, people working in the private sector report a higher job satisfaction level than those in universities. Salaries are good in the private sector; nearly 40% of the individuals who started in the 1970s were making more than $60,000 a year in 1994 and nearly half of those were making more than $80,000.

Museums are a desirable work setting. The survey showed that museum archaeologists are the worst paid, but the most satisfied. Women in particular prefer museum work to other work settings and they find it satisfying, but they are poorly paid. Government archaeology is considered the least attractive of all, but the work is well paid and 80% of government archaeologists describe themselves as satisfied.

How much money do archaeologists actually make? Table 1.1 provides some estimates of current salaries. Three levels of employment can be compared

TABLE 1.1 Career paths in archaeology, job description, education, opportunities, and salary range.

Career	General duties	Degree	Opportunities	Salary
Teacher/Professor	Teaching, research, and service	PhD	Relatively few jobs	$30,000–$100,000 + benefits
Museum Curator	Collections management, research, exhibitions	BA to PhD	Relatively few jobs	$30,000–$100,000 + benefits
CRM Archaeologist	Project planning and supervision, report writing	BA to PhD	Some higher-level jobs, many lower-level positions	$30,000–$80,000 + benefits
CRM Manager	Compliance, management, contract writing	BA to MA	Many jobs with national or state government agencies	$40,000–$70,000 + benefits
General Labor (field and lab)	Survey, excavation, cataloging	Some college and experience	Many short-term jobs with private companies	$6 to $15/hour

Source: Sutton and Yohe: 75.

in the survey depending on time of service and achievement. Assistant professors in academia and field directors in the CRM sector have similar pay scales, generally between $40,000 and $60,000 and up to $80,000. In the next level, associate professor or project manager, the majority of respondents earn more than $60,000. The best-paid positions are full professors and presidents of private CRM firms. Of these individuals who make more than $80,000 a year, the CRM presidents generally do better. Approximately 27% of the heads of private firms and 7% of full professors in the sample made over $100,000 a year. Promotion rates are also better in the private sector. In academia, it normally requires 6 years for an assistant professor to become an associate professor and another 6 years for an associate to become a full professor. Promotion in the private sector is not as structured and moving up the corporate ladder may take substantially less time.

More specific salary data are available from a 2004 survey of membership by the Society for American Archaeology and the Society for Historic Archaeology. There were 2143 respondents to the survey. The average salary based on *education*, for those whose primary position was listed as archaeologist, ranged from $40,098 for a BS or a BA compared to $61,365 for respondents with a PhD. The highest-paying positions included full professor (average salary $84,483), owner of a CRM company ($83,280), museum director ($67,114), and park archaeologist ($59,136).

A Day in the Life . . .

Many people think that being an archaeologist would be a great job, but few know what it is that archaeologists actually do. As we have mentioned, most archaeologists work in universities and colleges, in private or government positions involved with cultural resource management, or at museums, where they are responsible for collections of archaeological materials and provide exhibits and educational opportunities for the public.

Much of the work that archaeologists do involves a lot of organizational and administrative tasks. University faculty spend a good bit of time teaching and interacting with students. CRM specialists often work with government forms and paperwork, mainly in project review; museum personnel spend time managing collections and exhibits and dealing with the public. Aside from these

Fig. 1.12 Tina Thurston and students examine finds from Denmark.

tasks, many archaeologists also continue their research projects, though research and writing often can only take place in the few hours that one can manage outside of the normal requirements of a day's work.

In order to give you a sense of what archaeologists actually do at work, in the following pages three individuals describe a typical day or provide an overview of their job in academia, government, and a museum. The days presented here are composites, representative of the different activities that are involved in doing these jobs.

University Professor: Tina Thurston

Tina Thurston is Assistant Professor in the Department of Anthropology at the State University of New York at Buffalo. She received her PhD in anthropology from the University of Wisconsin-Madison in 1996. Her interest in Scandinavia began at an early age as she traveled with her actor-parents, who spent part of each year onstage in Sweden and Denmark. Her studies spurred her interest in the role of settlement pattern in the development of political society. She followed this interest to investigate the nature and timing of the rise of the state in the late Iron Age in southern Sweden. Tina teaches a number of courses and seminars at the university, including world civilizations and landscape archaeology. Her fieldwork takes place in northern Denmark, where she is investigating an Iron Age settlement (Fig. 1.12).

A Day in the Life of a University Professor   As an archaeologist who teaches at a large university, the State University of New York, University at Buffalo, I have a number of roles. One, of course, is the role of professor, a person who not only teaches and advises undergraduate and graduate students but also is responsible for organizing and carrying out the business of the university and my department within it. Another role is that of author. I spend huge amounts of time writing various types of material, from reviews of my colleagues' grants to articles on my fieldwork. Finally, I must plan and conduct research and fieldwork—with an emphasis on planning, which occurs almost all year long—in preparation for the excavations that people generally associate with being an archaeologist. My work is funded by grants, and every few years I must write and submit a new proposal if I'm to keep doing my research. Luckily, this is year 2 of a 3-year grant, so I only have to submit a short report on how the prior year's work turned out.

6:00 am—Like many people, as well as the new mother of a baby girl, I want everyone's day to get off to a good start, so I get up early. Our family has breakfast together, and today my husband keeps our daughter at home with him—he is an artist and works in his studio on our property in the countryside a half hour's drive from my university. Two other days a week, when I'm not teaching, I'll take our little girl to school with me and keep her in my office.

7:45 am—I get an email message from the director of the museum with whom I work collaboratively in Denmark. He tells me about the two sites we wanted to excavate this summer; one farmer has given his permission, while the other has not. The second farmer is doing an experiment with fertilizer in the field where we want to work. He says we can dig it up anytime after he harvests his crops, but that will be in late August, which is too late for us. This is bad news; I will have to find a substitute site. My grant from the National Science Foundation only lasts for 3 years, so if things have to be put off, other things must replace them or we won't meet our goals or deadlines.

8 am—In the museum, I meet a student who is working on our ceramics for her master's thesis. We pull out several trays of sherds from the long rows of storage racks before deciding which sites have the best-preserved evidence for settlement during the Viking to Medieval transition. We will have to take these into the field with us to compare with material from the upcoming dig—if we get permission from the new farmer, that is.

9 am—I get to the lecture hall a few minutes early to open the technology cabinet and get the computer going. I spend a lot of time making Web pages with text and pictures for students to see in class and use for study. The class, on the conquest of the Aztecs, lasts 50 minutes.

10 am—I return to my office after discussions with my teaching assistants and some students after class, and email a map and the names of landowners to the museum director in Denmark so he can ask some other farmers about digging on their land this summer. After that, I continue with my writing projects, occasionally stopping to answer emails as they come in. I also send out an email reminder to my crew for this summer, a combination of experienced graduate students and undergraduates that will attend a field school with us. This summer, we will have a group of over twenty people on the project, and there is a lot of organizing to do.

12:30 pm—I am on the Faculty Senate that helps govern the university and have a meeting across campus today at 1:30. I leave early to stop by the bank. I recently had my grant funds transferred to me by the university—now I must wire them to the Danish bank we use during the field season. As I'm about to leave, a senior colleague in the department stops by to tell me we have gotten permission from the dean to hire a new archaeologist. That's great news!

1:30 pm—The Faculty Senate meeting lasts a couple of hours, but I leave early because I have a graduate seminar from 3:30 to 6 pm and I have to get back to my office.

3 pm—I stop by the Anthropology Department office before class to check my mail. There, I find a number of folders containing student petitions. I am also the director of Undergraduate Studies, so I have to approve and sign off on several types of forms.

3:30–6 pm—Today, I teach a graduate seminar. I absolutely love teaching both undergraduates and graduate students, although it requires a lot of preparation. Even though I've read the articles the students have read for this week many times, I have to review all of them each time I teach the course so that they are fresh in my mind as we discuss them in detail for two and a half hours, so I need to prepare for several days prior to the seminar.

7 pm—Tonight, one of my graduate students is giving a talk on her dissertation fieldwork at the Buffalo Museum of Science, where the local chapter of the

New York State Archaeological Society meets. I want to be there to show my support for her. There will be many undergraduate and graduate archaeology students attending too, so I look forward to seeing them outside of class.

10 pm—I get home late tonight so my husband has made dinner. We spend some time together with our daughter before going to bed. Tomorrow, I don't teach, so I hope to get a lot of writing in, as well as more organizing for the summer's fieldwork.

State Archaeologist: Maureen Kavanagh

Fig. 1.13 Maureen Kavanagh in Maryland.

Maureen Kavanagh is Chief of the Office of Archaeology for the Maryland Historical Trust (Fig. 1.13). She did her undergraduate studies at Tufts University and earned a master's degree in anthropology at the University of Wisconsin-Madison in 1979. The Maryland Historical Trust was formed in 1961 to assist the people of Maryland in identifying, studying, evaluating, preserving, protecting, and interpreting the state's significant prehistoric and historic districts, sites, structures, cultural landscapes, heritage areas, cultural objects, and artifacts, as well as less tangible human and community traditions. The Trust currently has seventy-eight staff members, an active underwater archaeology program, and facilities that include an archaeological curation and conservation lab.

A Day in the Life of a State Archaeologist   8:30 am—Meet briefly to discuss plans for the day. Two staff members are headed out for a field visit to a stratified Archaic site being excavated by an archaeological consulting firm as part of a highway mitigation project. On the way back, they will stop at a seventeenth-century site in a park on the Chesapeake Bay to evaluate erosion caused by a recent storm. I will call ahead to the park manager to let him know they are visiting today. Finish catching up on phone requests and email.

9:00–10:30 am—Log new archaeological site inventory forms into computer system. Contact several consultants who filled out forms for clarification on some information, and notify all by email of site numbers assigned. Transfer forms to staff, who will map site locations into GIS and file them in the library.

10:30–11:30 am—Finish preparing Powerpoint presentation on a Late Woodland village in Frederick County excavated by the state amateur society and archaeology office. Presentation will be given in the evening; one goal is to promote public support for a county-level archaeology program.

11:30 am–12:00 pm—Lunch.

12:00–1:30 pm—Meet with archaeologists from consulting firm to develop a scope of work for a survey being recommended by our office for a research park in Cecil County.

1:30–1:40 pm—Receive call from concerned citizen about a housing development being built on the site of a former farmstead and cemetery. Explain the role of the office in reviewing projects that have state or federal funding or permitting, and check the project log database to see if the office has received that project for review.

1:40–3:00 pm—Review twenty development projects for impact to archaeological resources. Check project maps using GIS to determine if surveys have been done in the impact areas and whether or not sites have been recorded. Determine that three of the projects fall into areas of high probability for archaeological resources, and recommend that Phase I archaeological survey be done.

3:00–3:15 pm—Contact amateur archaeologist who has expressed interest in donating large personal artifact collection to the state. Arrange for visit to assess condition of collection to determine its research value.

3:15–3:45 pm—Finish reviewing a draft Phase I archaeological survey report. Write letter to consultant with comments to address in final report.

3:45–4:15 pm—Receive phone call from police in Wicomico County. They have been notified of human bones encountered at a construction site and have determined that the bones are not recent. Contact archaeology professor at a university near the site to go out to evaluate.

4:15–4:45 pm—Review a bill introduced in the state legislature on treatment of unmarked cemeteries. Write comments on the legislation, suggesting some changes, and send them to the legislative liaison that coordinates agency reviews.

4:45–5:00 pm—Finish answering email and phone calls. Burn Powerpoint CD; leave for evening lecture.

Museum Curator: Anne P. Underhill

Anne Underhill is Associate Curator of Asian Anthropology at the Field Museum of Natural History in Chicago. She received her PhD in anthropology from the University of British Columbia in 1990. For her dissertation and recently published book, she analyzed burials from published Chinese archaeological reports and pottery stored in Chinese museums. She has also done an ethnoarchaeological study of potters in western China who use traditional techniques. Her research interests involve the development of complex societies in northern China, craft specialization, mortuary ritual, and regional settlement organization. In the early 1990s, new laws permitted Anne to organize one of the first international archaeological projects in China in many years. Since 1995, her team has conducted ten seasons of systematic regional survey and three seasons of excavation at a late-prehistoric site dating to ca. 2600–1900 BC (Fig. 1.14).

A Day in the Life of a Museum Curator   Working at the Field Museum of Natural History in Chicago as a curator in the Department of Anthropology during the past five years has involved a greater variety of activities than I ever expected. It is rewarding because I have the opportunity to be involved in public education, college-level education, caring for our vast collections of artifacts, and archaeological field research. With respect to public education, I act as a content specialist for new exhibits at the museum—for permanent halls as well as temporary exhibits. During the course of a year, I also give several public lectures about my archaeological research in China for adults and students of all ages, such as high school students who have studied archaeology or who are learning Chinese.

I am also Adjunct Associate Professor at two local universities, University of Illinois-Chicago and Northwestern, where I teach archaeology and anthropology classes. I enjoy the opportunity to help PhD students in archaeology who work in different parts of Asia and who focus on topics such as the development of complex societies and craft specialization. Another component of my job is to

Fig. 1.14   Anne Underhill with her Chinese colleagues at the excavations at Liangchengzhen.

FUTURE ARCHAEOLOGY

OUR BEST GUESS IS THAT IT WAS SOME SORT OF LATE 20TH CENTURY PRISON...

WILEY

answer inquiries by the public about their own collections. We are glad to tell people what we can about technology or cultural context, but as a matter of policy we do not make estimates about monetary value. My department helps a large number of students and scholars, both local and international, do research on our archaeological and ethnographic collections.

As you can imagine, I devote a great deal of time to my archaeological field research in China and to writing. The fieldwork itself takes about one month (if we are surveying) or three months (if we are excavating) each year. There is a lot of work to do before and after as well, such as planning the research, buying equipment, making travel plans for the team, and writing reports (about the finances as well as the results). Analyzing the results takes several months. Like archaeologists everywhere I must spend a great deal of time writing grant applications to fund the research and articles presenting the results. I also have enjoyed the opportunity to write more articles about the late-prehistoric and early-historic periods of China. My job is always challenging and never dull!

CONCLUSIONS

Archaeology is the study of the human past. Archaeologists use the material remains and residues that have survived the passage of time to learn about the lives and activities of our ancestors. Archaeology is not easy; the pieces of the past are the broken fragments and discarded trash of the former inhabitants of our earth. Archaeologists use a wide range of techniques and perspectives to explore that information and learn about the past.

Archaeology is also the science of the past, using observation and evaluation to test ideas and theories about what happened in antiquity. It provides a fascinating and frequently beautiful window on the ancient world. It does not involve speculation or myths about our ancestors and their ways, and it is not pseudoscience or fiction. Instead, archaeologists rigorously try to make accurate statements about the past.

We have all been taught that opinions count, and they do. At the same time, the old saying that you cannot believe everything you hear rings true when it comes to archaeology. Not all opinions are correct and we constantly evaluate the accuracy of the opinions and information we receive. The scientific method is basically a way of carefully evaluating opinions to separate fact from opinion. Opinions in archaeology are the answers, ideas, explanations, and hypotheses that are offered to explain something. Evaluation is the testing part of the scientific method that is essential to weed out wrong or inaccurate opinions and ideas.

Archaeology can be exciting, exotic, and fun; it can also be boring and tedious. Archaeology is usually a rewarding career. There are not a lot of archaeologists, perhaps 10,000 in the United States today. Most spend only a few weeks a year doing fieldwork, while the rest of their time is spent in the office, laboratory, or classroom. According to surveys, most archaeologists are white, and somewhat more than half are males. Some archaeologists work in universities and museums teaching, curating, and studying the past, but more work in the government and the private sector protecting and preserving the past. Most archaeologists enjoy their work.

STUDY QUESTIONS

1. What does archaeology mean? How would you define the term?

2. What is pseudoscience? Can you think of some examples of pseudoscience you have encountered?

3. Is archaeology relevant for today? Why study archaeology?

4. What kinds of jobs are available for archaeologists?

5. What kinds of things do archaeologists do? Would you like to be an archaeologist?

www.mhhe.com/pricearch1

For more review material and study questions, please see the self-quizzes on your online learning center.

REFERENCES

Alcock, Susan E., and Robin G. Osborne, eds. n.d. *Classical Archaeology.* Oxford: Blackwell Publishing.

Feder, K. 2005. *Frauds, Myths, and Mysteries: Science and Pseudoscience in Archaeology.* 5th ed. New York: McGraw-Hill.

Hall, Martin, and Stephen Silliman, eds. 2006. *Historical Archaeology.* Oxford: Blackwell Publishing.

Heath, Barbara. 1999. *Hidden Lives: The Archaeology of Slave Life at Thomas Jefferson's Poplar Forest.* Charlottesville: University of Virginia Press.

Neumann, Thomas N., and Robert M. Sanford. 2001. *Cultural Resources Archaeology.* London: Rowman & Littlefield.

Shermer, Michael. 1997. *Why People Believe Weird Things: Pseudoscience, Superstition, and Other Confusions of Our Time.* New York: W.H. Freeman and Company.

Tyler, Norman. 1999. *Historic Preservation: An Introduction to Its History, Principles, and Practice.* New York: W.H. Norton.

www.mhhe.com/pricearch1

For Internet references related to this chapter, please see the chapter links on your online learning center.

CHAPTER 2

Doing Archaeology

INTRODUCTION: THE LORDS OF THE MOCHE

This artist's reconstruction depicts a scene at the site of Sipán (*see-PAHN*) based on interpretations of the finds at a series of spectacular tombs belonging to the Moche (*moe-CHAY*) culture of northern Peru and dating to approximately AD 300. The contents of these tombs documented the wealth and power of the rulers of the Moche civilization that dominated this part of South America for the first 800 years of the Christian era. In addition to these rich graves, the Moche left a remarkable heritage of pyramids, towns and villages, extraordinary pottery and metalwork, and many other artifacts to tell us about their place in the past.

This painting shows a Moche lord or noble sitting under an elaborately decorated awning on a small platform receiving various gifts and offerings. The noble wears an extraordinary costume of gold and silver, rich textiles, shells, and feathers. In his hand, he holds a gold scepter of office. Seated beside him to his right is a woman, perhaps his wife. Two warriors stand on either side of the base of the platform holding banners of cloth and gold. Another individual stands to the left, presenting a large conch shell as a tribute to the lord. In the foreground, a llama is about to be presented. The llama may be intended for sacrifice along with the seated human captive to the right, guarded by another warrior.

The archaeological discoveries that provided the information for this reconstruction were almost not made. Looters discovered the first tomb at Sipán and would have destroyed the others if the police and archaeologists had not intervened. The story of the tomb's discovery and a description of the remarkable riches that were part of the tomb are laid out in the following pages. This chapter, titled "Doing Archaeology," is intended to provide some impressions of what an archaeological investigation is like through the story of the finds at Sipán. This description of the excavations at Sipán emphasizes the three major phases of archaeological research: discovery, analysis, and interpretation.

This is not a typical excavation by any means. The story of Sipán is an extraordinary one and contains many elements common to archaeological research—good luck, hard work, conservation, preservation, public education, museum exhibition—and more than the usual elements in terms of the dangers involved, the incredible richness of the finds, and ethical dilemmas encountered. This chapter is intended to provide an example of some of the aspects of archaeology—fieldwork, analysis, and interpretation—that are the subject of this book, within the context of one of the most spectacular archaeological finds of the

www.mhhe.com/pricearch1

For preview material for this chapter, please see the chapter summary, outline, and objectives on your online learning center.

Fig. 2.1 The coast of Peru is one of the driest places on earth because of an unusual combination of hydrological and topographic factors.

twentieth century. We begin with a brief introduction to the environment of coastal Peru and to the Moche culture.

PERU AND THE MOCHE

Many years ago, I spent 4 months along the coast of Peru, surveying and excavating archaeological sites. Much of the area was arid desert. While surveying, we would walk past the bodies of birds that had died months earlier but simply had not decomposed in this desiccated environment. Excavations at a 1000-year-old site uncovered llama dung, fingernail clippings, and plant fibers, among other finds. Almost everything was preserved in the extremely dry conditions.

The combination of the cold Pacific waters and the massive Andes Mountains creates one of the driest places on earth (Fig. 2.1). The coastal region of western South America is a ribbon of land only a few tens of kilometers wide between the sea and the Andes Mountains. The Atlantic trade winds come from the east, and when they hit the Andes, they push high into the atmosphere. The moisture in these warm winds then falls on the jungles on the eastern slopes of the Andes. The low pressure caused by the uplift of the Atlantic winds quickly draws in the cold Pacific air that carries little water. As a result, there is little rainfall on the west coast. Less than 5 cm (2 in) of rain falls each year.

Stretching from southern Ecuador through Peru and along much of the coast to Chile, this wasteland is broken only by a series of east-west rivers flowing out of the Andes, crossing the desert to the sea, and creating oases for life in this arid region. These river valleys were the focus of a series of prehistoric societies before the Spanish arrived in AD 1533 and conquered the indigenous populations.

Beginning around the time of Christ, a major civilization emerged in the Moche River valley on the north coast of Peru and rose to dominate the region over the next 800 years. The center of this civilization was at the site of Moche itself, with a population of perhaps 10,000 people. Two major pyramids—the

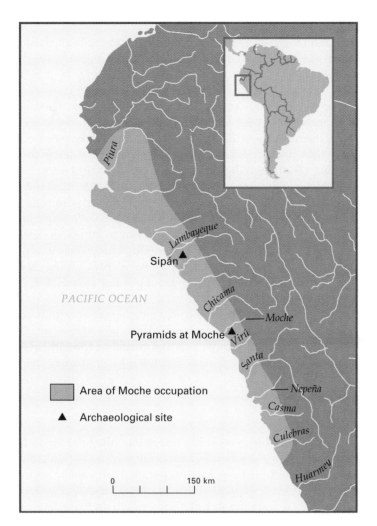

Fig. 2.2 The north coast of Peru, showing the extent of the Moche civilization and the location of the sites mentioned in the text. The lighter colored area shows the extent of the Moche culture.

Map labels: Piura, Lambayeque, Sipán ▲, PACIFIC OCEAN, Chicama, Moche, Pyramids at Moche ▲, Virú, Santa, Nepeña, Casma, Culebras, Huarmey

■ Area of Moche occupation
▲ Archaeological site

0   150 km

Huaca del Sol (*WAA-kaw dell sole*) and the Huaca de la Luna (*WAA-kaw day la LOON-ah*)—dominate the horizon at Moche. The two structures are separated by a 500-m (1650-ft) wide plaza. The Huaca del Sol rises 40 m (130 ft), like a fifteen-story building, above the river valley and covers more than a soccer field at its base—the largest structure ever built in prehistoric South America. The pyramid is made up of more than 140 million sun-dried bricks. The Huaca de la Luna is only slightly smaller, 30 m (100 ft) high, and includes a complex of platforms, walls, and courtyards.

The Moche civilization encompassed a series of coastal valleys over a distance of 550 km (341 mi) from the north to the south (Fig. 2.2). Trade relations extended even farther. For example, the Moche obtained the gemstone lapis lazuli from mines in Chile, spondylus shell and mother-of-pearl from the coast of Ecuador, and a variety of animals, such as boa constrictors, parrots, toucans, and monkeys, from the jungles to the north and east. The presence of these animals is known from scenes on Moche pottery.

There were large Moche centers with major construction in six of the river valleys. The Moche used large adobe bricks to build pyramids, temples, palaces, and fortresses. In addition to the several large centers, the Moche people lived in farmsteads and villages. They dug irrigation canals up to 100 km (62 mi) long to bring water from the Andes to their fields. In these fields, they cultivated corn, beans, guava, avocados, squash, chili peppers, melons, cotton, and peanuts. The cold ocean waters are particularly rich in this region, and the sea and its

Fig. 2.3 Stirrup-spout portrait vessel of a haughty Moche noble with elaborate helmet and ear ornaments.

estuaries also provided the Moche with an abundance of fish, shrimp, crabs, crayfish, and mollusks. Domesticated animals added to the larder and included the llama, guinea pig, and ducks. Wild plants and animals were collected and hunted as well.

The Moche left a marvelous archive of their activities, environment, and ideology in a variety of arts and crafts made of many different materials. They were technically very adept but left no written records. Everything we know about them comes from archaeology. The arid conditions of the Peruvian coast mean that many perishables, such as basketry, leather, plants, and even human remains, are preserved, creating a rich archaeological record of the region.

Much of the art appears to be associated with ritual and ceremony and with the upper crust of this society. Precious metals, for example, were the exclusive property of the elite. Textiles of cotton and wool were spectacular, as evidenced by the twill weaves and metal plaques woven into cloth designs. Moche pottery is also among the most spectacular produced anywhere at any time and included portrait heads, animals, landscapes, vegetables, and scenes of everyday (and night) life. The so-called stirrup-spout portrait vessels (Fig. 2.3) are particularly fine examples of Moche art and craft.

Moche society appears to have collapsed suddenly around AD 800. The cause of their demise is unknown but is thought to have involved either conquest by outsiders or some kind of environmental or climatic catastrophe. Later civilizations, including the Chimu and the Inka, controlled this region prior to the Spanish conquest.

DISCOVERY

An important Moche center lies near the village of Sipán in the Lambayeque (*LAM-bay-YECK-eh*) Valley, in a remote area some 200 km (125 mi) north of Moche itself. Here there are three massive pyramids and adobe structures known collectively as the Huaca Rajada (*WAA-kaw ray-YAH-dah*) (Fig. 2.4). The largest structure covers an area the size of a soccer field and rises almost 60 m (200 ft), the height of a twenty-story building. A second pyramid, directly adjacent to the first, is smaller at the base but about the same height and also has a flat top. The third structure is rather nondescript, a little smaller than a football field and 10 m (30 ft) high. This last structure was the burial place of the lords of Sipán. But their initial discovery, as is often the case, did not involve an archaeologist.

The looting of archaeological treasures has probably been going on in Peru at least since the time of the Inka. People from the farming village at Sipán have been robbing archaeological sites in the area for generations. Poverty and unemployment are powerful incentives to get cash by a variety of means. Although the Peruvian government outlawed looting and trafficking in pre-Hispanic artifacts almost 50 years ago, the practice continues. Given the amount of tomb robbing that has taken place, it is surprising that anything is left for archaeologists to find. The looters dig deep holes with picks and shovels and often find ceramic vessels or stone and shell or metal beads, which they sell. Occasionally, they find something more.

In November 1986, local looters started tunneling into the third and smallest pyramid at Sipán. Working at night for several months, the looters dug 7 m (22 ft) into the structure and beneath the royal tomb of a Moche ruler. The ceiling of their tunnel collapsed, depositing the contents of the tomb in the looters' hands. The looters then removed at least ten large sacks full of extraordinary gold, silver, and gilded copper objects. In the process, the robbers also destroyed a huge quantity of pottery, bone, feathers, cloth, and other materials that were of no interest to them.

An angry dispute among the looters over the division of the treasure led to a fight and the murder of one of the participants. Another unhappy looter got

Moche artistic expression is amazingly varied. Animals, plants, anthropomorphized demons or deities, and a wide range of life scenes are shown, including the hunting of animals, fishing, combat, the punishment of prisoners and criminals, sexual acts, and the pomp of rulers seated on thrones or carried in litters. Architectural details—temples, pyramids, and houses—are all depicted in Moche art, as are features of clothing and adornment. The degree of realism with which Moche art is expressed and the wide spectrum of subject matter make it one of the most appealing of all pre-Columbian art styles.

—Christopher Donnan,
archaeologist

Fig. 2.4 Huaca Rajada in the Lambayeque Valley on the north coast of Peru. The small mound in the left foreground was the place of the tombs of Sipán.

away from the group and went to the police, who then arrested two of the thieves and seized one bag of the treasure.

By this time the director of the Museo Nacional Bruning in Lambayeque, Walter Alva, had been called in by the police to help identify the stolen materials and the looters themselves. When Alva and the police visited the site, most of the local community had descended on the pyramids and were digging and sifting frantically to try to find more gold. It took the police some time to chase these people away and restore order.

Eventually, the police seized the ringleader of the looters and another sack with a few artifacts. This man had been shot by the police and later died; another individual was wounded in the raid. Local people were greatly angered by these events and began to threaten the authorities, the archaeologists, and the site itself.

Because of the extent of destruction by the original looters and the very real danger that the pyramid would be completely destroyed by continued looting due to the enormous riches that had been found, Walter Alva decided to immediately organize an archaeological project to learn as much as possible about the tomb and the pyramid (Fig. 2.5). The excavators could not have imagined at that moment that they would uncover the richest burial ever found in the Americas.

The site was soon put under long-term police guard to discourage further looting. The pyramid was encircled with barbwire, and a fortified guard post for the police was erected on top to keep the looters at bay. Unfortunately, most of the items looted from the tomb were sold into the antiquities market and will never be recovered. An American art dealer was responsible for the export and sale of

Fig. 2.5 Archaeologist Walter Alva and an assistant holding a scepter missed by the looters in the despoiled tomb at Sipán. The tunnel into the pyramid can be seen in the background.

Fig. 2.6 Artist's reconstruction of the three adobe structures at Sipán. The lake in the background fills the quarry for some of the mud bricks in the pyramids. The royal tombs were found in the smallest structure, in the left foreground.

much of the treasure from the looted tomb. Buyers from the United States, Europe, and Japan paid huge prices for pieces of the treasure. In 1987, the smugglers tried to sell one of the ornaments for $1.6 million.

At the start of excavations, the angry looters and villagers surrounded the pyramid, throwing stones and bottles and continuously threatening the archaeologists. Gunshots were exchanged between the police and a few of the looters, and tear gas was used to disperse the crowds. Walter Alva and the field crew slept in the tunnels and niches of the pyramid, reluctant to leave the protection of the police. Alva even carried a loaded pistol to protect himself.

After a few months, the crowd had grown to several hundred individuals and the situation was extremely tense. Finally, in a dramatic gesture, Alva cut through the barbwire and brought the angry mob in to see the open coffin of the Lord of Sipán. He explained that this was their ancestor, their heritage, a lord who when he died was dressed in gold. Alva's courageous act captured the hearts of the protestors. Eventually, the villagers helped to protect the site from further damage. The people began to see the tomb not as a gold mine to be plundered but as the almost magical shrine of an esteemed ancestor. Alva and his crew showed the tomb to more than 6000 visitors over the course of the excavations.

[Looters] tend to be people who live on the land. They are the descendants of the people who produced the artifacts and feel they have a claim to them . . . [they] feel the archaeologists are looting themselves.
—Dan Sandweiss, author

EXCAVATION: THE TOMB OF THE LORD OF SIPÁN

The excavations led by Walter Alva continued from 1987 through 1990. Over many months of careful work, the archaeologists uncovered three fabulous tombs in the small adobe pyramid. In each case, the central figure was elaborately costumed in exquisitely crafted gold and silver ornaments, elaborate woven clothing, and worked shell, gemstones, and gold and silver regalia of all kinds. The

Fig. 2.7 Excavations at Tomb 1 in the top of the coffin of the Lord of Sipán.

tombs were named after the presumed role of the individual in the central burial. The first tomb excavated, described below, belonged to the Lord of Sipán (Fig. 2.7). Tomb 2 contained the High Priest of Sipán and Tomb 3 belonged to the Old Lord of Sipán. The discussion below relates the finds only at Tomb 1, beginning with the discovery of the grave and the excavation of the central coffin and its contents. Other individuals and objects from the tomb are then described. Subsequent sections discuss some of the analysis and interpretation of the tomb and its contents, and the consequences of the project.

Alva began by excavating a series of meter-square units on top of the pyramid and soon found an area filled with sand and small stones, distinct from the adobe bricks of the pyramid itself. This area measured 5 m (15 ft) on a side and was excavated to a depth of 4 m (12 ft) before the discoveries began to appear. First came the skeleton of a 20-year-old man wrapped in a cotton cloth. He was lying on his back wearing a copper helmet and holding a round copper shield. The man was probably a warrior intended as a guardian for the treasures below. Interestingly, his feet had been removed before he was buried above the tomb.

At 4.5 m (14 ft) below the surface, and half a meter below the footless guardian, were seventeen wooden roof beams from the tomb chamber itself. The presence of the intact beams indicated that the chamber below had not been disturbed. Immediately beneath the roof beams the excavations uncovered the remains of large wooden planks and copper straps holding them together. These planks were the lid of a coffin that lay in the very center of the burial chamber. Both wood and metal were valued commodities in the arid desert of Peru, and these materials alone presaged a rich grave.

The excavations continued slowly and carefully, because Alva knew that haste would result in errors. The details of each object and level encountered were mapped and photographed. Excavations were carried out from scaffolding erected on top of the coffin and other finds to prevent the destruction of the materials below the feet of the excavators. A group of about twenty-five individuals worked at the site, including professional archaeologists, students, and hired laborers. Beneath the coffin lid were the decomposed remains of a red cloth shroud and under it another cloth, this one with gilded copper circles sewn into the cloth. Underneath

Fig. 2.8 The tomb of the Lord of Sipán exposed during excavation with a mass of grave goods, clothing, and jewelry.

that second cloth was another with square copper platelets attached. The three shrouds were wrapped completely around the contents of the coffin (Fig. 2.8).

After the upper pieces of the shrouds were removed, the remaining contents of the coffin began to appear, including several spear points and a headdress with feather ornaments (Fig. 2.9). On top of the headdress was an **ingot** of pure gold about the size of a child's hand. Beneath the headdress and ingot were several so-called banners. These are heavy cotton cloth rectangles, about 60 cm (2 ft) on a side, covered with sewn-on metal plates and human figures of gilded copper. Banners had never been excavated before but had been seen depicted in scenes painted on Moche pottery, which showed high-status males holding up banners in display.

Beneath the banners was a large, headless figure of gilded copper with arms and legs with a small male figure—similar to those on the banners—in the center. The function of this copper object is unknown. Next came a wide cloth belt with legs and feet with metal claws woven into the fabric, perhaps part of another headdress.

The next layer contained a series of **pectorals**—wide, biblike necklaces—made from tens of thousands of shell and copper beads (Fig. 2.10). Three complete pectorals were eventually removed in a painstaking excavation process designed to keep the bead designs from each pectoral apart. The shirt of the interred individual came next. Like the banners, it was cloth covered with metal platelets of gilded copper. It would have looked like a shirt of mirrors glimmering in the sun when it was worn. Four more beaded pectorals were found underneath the shirt.

Fragments of the skeleton began to emerge as these pectorals were removed and it was possible to see that the body had been placed on its back. Next to the skeleton the amount and quality of the jewelry increased. There were four large nose ornaments. Two were crescent-shaped pieces of gold and silver about 10 cm high and 15 cm wide (4 in × 6 in) that would have been attached to the nasal septum by a narrow hole. These nose ornaments would have covered the lower half of the face. The other two nose ornaments were circles of silver and gold. Together, the ornaments range in size from a jar lid to half a dinner plate and may have been intended to represent phases of the moon and to be worn at different times of the month. It appears that the entire ceremonial wardrobe of the warrior-priest was buried with him.

Three pairs of ear ornaments were found beside the skull. These masterpieces of metal and lapidary work display such detailed craftwork that a magnifying glass is needed to appreciate all the detail. One set of these ornaments shows a warrior, another a deer, and the third ducks. They are made from gold, turquoise, and shell. The warrior ornaments are especially exceptional. On these

ingot A casting of pure metal intended for transport and reuse, usually oblong or disk shaped.

pectorals Wide, biblike necklaces or plates worn over the chest area, part of costume or armor.

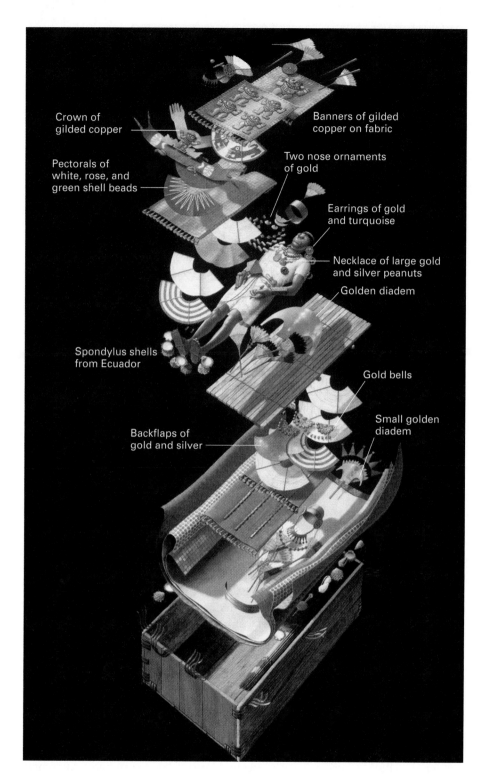

Crown of gilded copper

Pectorals of white, rose, and green shell beads

Spondylus shells from Ecuador

Backflaps of gold and silver

Banners of gilded copper on fabric

Two nose ornaments of gold

Earrings of gold and turquoise

Necklace of large gold and silver peanuts

Golden diadem

Gold bells

Small golden diadem

Fig. 2.9 An exploded view of the finds in the coffin of the Lord of Sipán. Many of these items are described in more detail in the text.

ornaments, a warrior figure about the size of a thumb stands with a golden war club in one hand and a small shield in the other (Fig. 2.11). The warrior is dressed in a costume similar to those found in the tombs, with a necklace of large gold beads, an elaborate gold and turquoise headdress, a gold nose ornament, and large gold and turquoise ear spools. On either side of the central figure on the ear ornament are two smaller helmeted warriors shown in profile with an elaborate gold headdress. These ear ornaments are considered among the finest examples of ancient jewelry ever made.

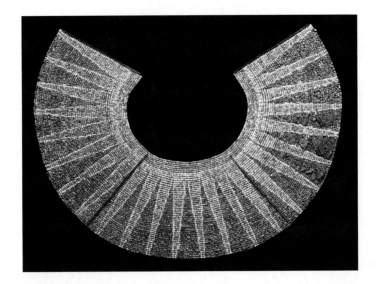

Fig. 2.10 One of the beaded pectorals found with the Lord of Sipán.

Fig. 2.11 One of the warrior ear ornaments, found near the skull of the Lord of Sipán.

www.mhhe.com/pricearch1

For a Web-based activity on Moche art and other aspects of this culture, please see the Internet exercises on your online learning center.

Beneath this set of jewelry excavators found even more remarkable artifacts around the face of the deceased ruler. The lower face was covered with a gold sheet shaped into a life-size replica of the upper neck, chin, mouth, and cheeks. Beneath this piece were a nose cover, a set of teeth, and two eyes made of sheet gold placed in position on the face of the corpse.

Three necklaces of large, hollow beads were found around the neck, one of simple gold balls, one of silver human heads 4 cm (1.5 in) in diameter, and one of gold and silver peanuts up to 9 cm (4 in) in length, about three times actual size. A fourth necklace of sixteen round gold disks, 4.5 cm (1.5 in) in diameter, was found next to the other three.

Two sacrificial axes, one gold and one silver, were placed on the chest of the man. He wore beaded bracelets on both arms containing hundreds of gold, shell, and turquoise beads with copper beads used for spacers. Gold and silver ingots were found next to his hands, and silver sandals were attached to the feet. A remarkably well-made scepter of gold and silver was found held in each hand. One of these scepters had a large golden box on top decorated with similar low-relief scenes of a warrior killing a nude sacrificial victim. The second scepter had two figures on its top, showing a richly dressed individual standing in front of a roped and nude captive, another dramatic scene of dominance and power.

Once the skeleton was removed, more of the artifacts were exposed. An enormous crescent-shaped gold headdress ornament, more than 60 cm (2 ft) in width, appeared along with copper rods with badly decomposed feathers. Some of the feathers were identified as coming from a flamingo and would have been coral red in color.

Beneath the body and huge headdress, the inventory of artifacts continued. Among the pieces of jewelry were gold and silver backflaps—large, metal fins about 45 cm (18 in) in length that hung from the back of the costume. The gold backflap weighed almost a kilogram, today valued at something like $12,000 in metal alone. Both backflaps depict a fanged human figure holding a sacrificial knife in one hand and a human head in the other. This individual is known as the decapitator and has appeared in painted scenes on pottery depicting events in the lives of the nobles of Sipán (Fig. 2.12). A semicircle of eight small, circular bells or rattles surrounds this figure on each flap. A set of two elaborate gilded copper rattles would also have been attached at the back of the costume.

It became clear with the recovery of the backflaps that the Moche had been very meticulous in the costuming and display of the corpse. Gold ornaments and equipment were on the right side of the individual, and silver was worn on the left. On the back of the costume, this pattern was reversed. There is a sense from

Fig. 2.12 Moche pottery depiction of the funeral and burial of a noble individual. The two individuals atop the right platform use ropes or belts to lower a coffin into a tomb. Ceremony and sacrifice take place in the scene to the left.

the coffin and its contents that every item, every color, every material, and every position of an item was fraught with meaning.

More pectorals, banners, and feathers, cloth, and metal parts of headdresses were found beneath the layer with the backflaps. There was also a necklace of large, hollow beads in the form of human heads (Fig. 2.14). The same kinds of objects were found at the top of the coffin, suggesting that the contents were placed in such a way that the body lay between the same sequence of objects. There was near the bottom a smaller, crescent-shaped, gold headdress ornament as well, and a broad copper belt that may have been part of a crown. All of these items were inside the three cloth shrouds originally encountered under the lid of the coffin.

In the bottom of the casket were two types of brightly colored seashells of species that are only found to the north in the warmer waters off the coast of Ecuador. Also on the floor of the coffin were a series of copper war clubs, spear points, and shields.

The other finds in the tomb, surrounding the coffin, were also remarkable (Fig. 2.13). The tomb itself was a large chamber cut into the pyramid, approximately 12 × 10 m (36 ft × 30 ft) in area and about 6 m (20 ft) high, the size of a modern two-car garage. A low **adobe** bench had been built around the central burial in the tomb. Hundreds of pottery vessels, probably containing offerings of food, were placed in niches in the bench. Eight other individuals were also buried in the tomb. Of these eight, five were in cane coffins surrounding the plank casket of the Lord of Sipán. Three contained women: two adolescents at his head and one adult female at his feet. The other two were males buried on each side of the lord, one with a dog and the other wearing the uniform and equipment of a warrior. A llama had also been placed under each male coffin. Another individual was a 9- or 10-year-old child placed in a sitting position near the head of the lord. Finally, in a niche in the wall of the tomb, a woman had been placed in a cross-legged sitting position.

Human sacrifice was a sad but ubiquitous practice in many prehistoric societies. Yet it appears in this case that not all the individuals in the tomb had been sacrificed at the time of the burial. The three female skeletons around the plank coffin were somewhat decomposed and jumbled, suggesting that they may have been dead for some time before reburial in the tomb.

The excavations of this tomb took a total of 12 months of 6-day weeks to complete, initially under duress because of the protesting villagers. Later in the course of work, the meager funds for excavation were almost exhausted. A local pasta maker donated a truckload of noodles that were used for a time to help pay

adobe   A brick made of earth and straw and dried by the sun.

Fig. 2.13 Artist's reconstruction of the tomb of the Lord of Sipán, showing the various offerings and burials surrounding the central coffin.

Fig. 2.14 A necklace with large gold and silver beads inlaid with shell in the form of feline human heads.

the workers at the site. In addition, an archaeologist from UCLA, Christopher Donnan, helped with equipment and funds to keep the project going. Eventually, Donnan and Alva were able to obtain funding from the National Geographic Society to conduct the full excavations of the several tombs at the site. German donations also helped to pay the enormous costs of conserving the finds.

ANALYSIS

Much of the conservation of the materials from the tombs at Sipán will continue for years, and the results are gradually being reported. Conservation efforts have been spearheaded by the Römisch-Germanisches Zentralmuseum (Roman-German Central Museum) in Mainz, Germany, and by the Bruning Museum in

The Center for Materials Research in Archaeology and Ethnology

Heather Lechtman, an archaeologist at MIT and an expert on ancient metallurgy, analyzed these plated artifacts and was able to determine how they were made. Apparently, the Moche metalworkers dissolved gold in a solution of water and corrosive minerals, such as salt and potassium nitrate, and then added bicarbonate of soda. Boiling this solution created an electromagnetic coating process that attached the gold to a copper item placed in the bath. Subsequent heating of the object in a kiln sealed the gold to the copper and smoothed its surface.

Lechtman is one of the founders and the director of the Center for Materials Research in Archaeology and Ethnology. Established in 1977, CMRAE is a consortium of eight Massachusetts educational and cultural institutions that promote the use of science and engineering in the pursuit of archaeology and ethnography. The consortium members are Boston University, Brandeis University, Har-

vard University, Massachusetts Institute of Technology, the University of Massachusetts-Amherst, the University of Massachusetts-Boston, the Boston Museum of Fine Arts, Tufts University, and Wellesley College.

Each of the consortium members provides faculty, staff, and laboratory facilities for research and education in the technological study of cultural materials. Plant and animal food remains, human skeletal material, and metal, ceramic, stone, bone, and fiber artifacts are the objects of study, along with the environments within which these materials were produced and used. Using advanced analytical techniques in biological, chemical, geological, physical, and materials science, the goal of this educational group is to increase our knowledge of past and present societies by making the natural and engineering sciences an important tool in archaeology and ethnography.

Lambayeque. Both conservation and analysis of the materials have involved various specialists.

John Verano of Tulane University was responsible for studying the human remains from the Sipán investigations. His analysis of several hundred Moche burials from this area provided a picture of population demography. From his analysis, Verano found that most individuals who survived infancy and childhood eventually died between the ages of 35 and 40. Females had a slightly longer life expectancy than males. Verano also noted that the average height for Moche males was 158 cm (5 ft 3 in) and for females 147 cm (4 ft 11 in). In fact, the Moche were about 1 cm (.4 in) taller than the present inhabitants of the north coast of Peru.

Verano's examination of the skeleton in the plank coffin indicated it was a male, approximately 35–45 years of age and 1.65 m (5 ft 5 in) tall, substantially larger than average for the Moche. The good condition of his teeth indicated that he had an adequate diet or well-prepared food so that the normal wear and decay, seen in other individuals from this time, were absent. The skeleton was badly preserved but the excavators were able to coat the bones with resin before removal to harden and hold them together. His bones showed no signs of injury; there was little indication of hard labor in the muscle attachments. The back of the head was flat, likely from the use of a cradleboard in infancy. This trait, called **occipital flattening**, was found in 60% of Moche males and females. The male in the coffin also showed no evidence of the cause of death, but then most diseases do not leave traces in bone. In fact, there was no evidence of the cause of death of any of the individuals buried in Tomb 1. However, unlike the three females and the lord himself, the other individuals were likely killed as sacrifices at the time of the burial ceremony.

Analysis of the metal objects in the tomb has been another significant area of study for archaeologists. Hundreds of metal objects have been found in the lord's tomb. The gold, silver, and copper objects found are both spectacular and technologically quite sophisticated. The Moche were clearly extraordinary metalworkers. Scenes depicted in Moche pottery show the use of blowpipes with a furnace that they must have used to produce the sorts of high temperatures necessary

occipital flattening   A flattening of the back of the head caused by hard crib boards in infancy. Noted among the Moche and many other Native American groups in the New World.

Fig. 2.15 A reconstruction of the costume of the Lord of Sipán, showing the full costume of headdress, helmet, mask, pectorals, and textiles.

to melt certain metals (on the order of 1300°C). The Moche used combinations of alloys of gold, silver, and copper and had such sophisticated technologies as **lost wax casting** and **annealing**. They even made some **bronze**. While some of the objects were pure gold or silver, many were gilded copper, made using a technique apparently known only to the Moche at the time. The sophistication of the gilding technique soon led archaeologists to investigate its methodology. See science in archaeology on the previous page.

INTERPRETATION

The riches in the central plank coffin of the Lord of Sipán are simply astonishing; words alone cannot convey the quality of workmanship and rare materials. Although many items in the grave did not survive, especially fine cloth and wooden objects, the contents that were recovered are extraordinary and present a tangible record of the wealth and power of the lords of Sipán.

The contents of the tomb and the coffin itself, both corporeal and material, are evidence of the indisputably high status and power of rulers who controlled the lives of their subjects. The grave contents of the Lord of Sipán suggest he was a warrior and priest. This individual was often depicted in paintings on Moche ceramics as the overseer of sacrificial ceremonies in a costume with paired backflaps, a crescent-shaped headdress, large circular ear decorations, a crescent nose ornament, and a pair of bells hanging from his belt (Fig. 2.15). This person is also shown in military situations, accompanied by a dog and often with a lamp-shaped scepter.

All of these elements were found in and around the tombs. A series of small rooms on the south side of the pyramid with the tombs contained hundreds of ceramic vessels, quantities of wood ash and organic residues, llama and human bones, and a number of miniature copper objects. These materials suggest the remains of feasting. Amputated hands and feet were also uncovered near the tombs at Sipán. These sacrificial offerings would seem to indicate not only that key participants in the sacrifice ceremony were buried in the pyramid but also that the event itself probably took place on or near the pyramid.

Some information on the nature of Moche society can be garnered from the burials in these tombs and the more typical burials found in cemeteries and villages from this period. The important burials from the tombs appear to reflect four different categories of individuals—ruling lords, priests, military leaders, and the retainers and assistants to these individuals. Walter Alva noted that persons associated with political or military power were interred in the northern sec-

lost wax casting A technique for creating detailed metal castings using wax as the mold. The molten metal replaces the wax and replicates the mold.

annealing A process of repeated heating and cooling to make metal tougher and less brittle.

bronze A mixture of tin (or arsenic) and copper that produced a harder metal. Produced in both the Old and New Worlds.

Tourism and a New Museum in Lambayeque

The results and consequences of the discovery and excavations at Sipán are still rumbling through the archaeology of the Americas and Peru. The nation of Peru has benefited greatly from the discoveries in both material and ideological ways. In August 2003, a spectacular new facility called the Royal Tombs of Sipán Museum was inaugurated in Lambayeque (Fig. 2.16). The museum provides access to the most important archaeological finds from the site in an exceptional exhibition that combines scientific accuracy, maximum security, and modern display. The Lambayeque region is now on the tourist route and Sipán is a major attraction, helping the economy of the region. And one of the original looters—the leader of the mob of protestors in 1987—is now the head tour guide for visitors to the site.

Fig. 2.16 The new Museo de Tumbas Reales de Sipán in Lambayeque, Peru, houses the finds from a number of royal tombs.

tion of the funerary platform, and religious individuals were placed in the southern part. In addition to the important personages, there were a series of sacrificial victims in the tombs that may have been slaves, prisoners, or volunteers. Apart from the tombs, the most numerous burials in Moche society are of common people, interred in simple graves with some pottery and very little metal in the burial grounds and settlements.

The contents of the royal tombs at Sipán are very similar to what is known from important looted tombs at two sites in other valleys of the Moche civilization. The close relationship in material and ideology between the elite in these distant areas suggests that the major valleys may have had their own nobility and that these elite families and individuals were closely connected with each other.

Knowledge of the ideology of the Moche comes from the finds at the tomb excavations and other sources. For example, several different **ethnographically** known groups in South America, including the Inka, associate color and metals with concepts of the cosmos and afterlife. Yellow is often associated with the sun and with gold; silver is pale and white and connected to the moon. The combination of gold and silver in costume and display among the Moche no doubt invokes this relationship. Alva and Donnan have discussed the duality of silver and gold and their complementary cosmological meaning. Gold and the sun were associated with life, silver and the moon more closely related to death. The combination of gold and silver found with the elite conveys their power and control of the lives and deaths of the Moche people. Only high-status individuals were buried with precious metals. What little metal there was in common graves was found only in objects made of copper.

Aside from increasing our knowledge of Moche ideology, the Sipán excavations also provide a clearer understanding of Moche social and economic organization. Moche society was marked by greater differences in wealth and status than previously believed. Although there are depictions of powerful individuals surrounded by rays or bolts of lightning in scenes on pottery vessels, there was little evidence for royal burials or a special elite class until these tombs were found. The elaborate costumes buried with these nobles would have demanded

ethnographic *Ethnography* is the study and description of human societies. Ethnographers are anthropologists who study societies in a variety of places around the world.

many highly skilled artisans to create and replenish the great number of objects of wealth that were buried.

The royal tombs have also yielded significant clues about Moche art and religion. It is now clear that at least some of the art documents actual events enacted by real people. The treasures of the Sipán tombs are priceless, but of even greater value is the information we have gained on prehistoric South America and the Moche—a fascinating ancient civilization.

CONCLUSIONS

The Sipán project reflects multiple aspects of archaeology, and like other such endeavors, it was difficult and expensive. In many ways, it is remarkable that archaeology gets done at all. There are so many demands to be met—energy, time, money, permission, and motivation. Yet in spite of it all, there are many archaeology success stories and exciting results often appear. That is certainly true in the case of Sipán.

The discovery of the site by nonprofessionals is typical. Fortunately, looting is not so common in most places, but then, of course, the contents of a site are rarely so extraordinary. Excavations at Sipán were painstaking and difficult, but the efforts, beliefs, and will of Walter Alva ensured that Sipán could be scientifically studied and that the results would provide valued information about the prehistory of the Moche and Peru. In addition, the interest and funding that were generated by discoveries at Sipán provided the incentive for scientific excavation of other tombs in the area that may help researchers answer specific questions about the nature of Moche political power and ceremony.

The conservation of the excavated materials from Sipán was an enormous undertaking as well. The German conservators who began the process also trained their Peruvian counterparts in modern methods of conservation. Those skills are now employed and taught to others by the Peruvians, exemplifying yet another benefit to the people of the region in addition to the finds at Sipán.

The ethical aspects of Sipán discoveries are also a lesson, involving several different groups of people. The local looters and villagers at the start of the project were angry that the police and archaeologists were preventing them from taking treasure that they believed was rightfully theirs. The dramatic act by Walter Alva, opening the excavations to the looters and telling them of their heritage, changed that situation. Alva has emphasized that the excavation was carried out exclusively by Peruvians and that the discoveries belonged to the Peruvian nation—and not to grave robbers. Looting is still an enormous problem in South America, but attitudes are gradually changing. Disparities in wealth today mean that looting and other crimes will continue until social ills are corrected. That is true in many places.

Another group entangled with the Sipán discoveries, one without ethical concerns, includes the smugglers and buyers of Moche art in the United States and Europe. At the end of March 1988, a colleague of the illicit art dealer turned informant and provided U.S. Customs' agents with enough information to allow them to raid the homes of a number of the new owners of the Sipán loot. These people were some of the more influential members of society in Southern California. More than sixty agents were involved in the largest seizure of stolen pre-Columbian art in U.S. history. Among the places where this art was found was the Santa Barbara Museum of Art.

Although the legal action that followed the seizure of these materials was limited at best, some of the treasure was, in fact, returned to Peru. One of the leading dealers was sentenced to prison for a short time, a first in U.S. history, for dealing in pre-Columbian antiquities. In 1990, a presidential decree banned the importation of antiquities from Sipán. After that law expired, a memorandum of understanding was signed in 1997, prohibiting U.S. trade in Peruvian artifacts.

A lot of this has nothing to do with the niceties of North American ethics. In Peru, everyone who has a shovel and is poor digs. To sit up here in our comfortable air-conditioned places and say those people shouldn't loot . . . is a nicety that we can afford and they cannot.
—Julie Jones, museum curator

The archaeologists are a third group involved in ethical issues surrounding the discoveries at Sipán. Both Alva and Donnan were the subject of various accusations and attacks. While some of the artifacts were smuggled out of Peru shortly after their discovery, others remained in the hands of a private collector in Lima. Donnan visited this man and photographed some of the finds, as he had done with other collectors. Some of Donnan's photographs appeared in the first *National Geographic* article on the site. This issue is discussed again in Chapter 17, "Responsibilities."

Donnan's activities have been strongly condemned by some archaeologists, who argue that professionals should have no contact whatsoever with looters and smugglers, that to do so validates their activities and gives them some legitimacy that they do not deserve. The president of the Society for American Archaeology at the time criticized Donnan for his relationship with the collectors, saying, "I take a fairly hard line [with looted objects]. If knowledge is lost, that's too bad."

Donnan has responded that he decries the looting, but these objects and artifacts would be lost to science unless he tracked them down and photographed and recorded them for posterity. It's a dicey argument without clear-cut answers. Walter Alva has supported Donnan, and other archaeologists realize that some archive should be made of these materials before they disappear. At the same time, trafficking in antiquities is illegal and individuals involved should be reported to the authorities, something Donnan did not do.

Many people have benefited from the Sipán project. Information from the research has been made available to the public and the profession of archaeology. A number of publications on the excavations, the tombs, and the contents have appeared in popular magazines such as *National Geographic, Archaeology,* and *Natural History,* as well as in scientific journals and several books. As the analysis of the finds continues, more information will appear that reveals the extraordinary nature of the Moche civilization.

The wealth of Andes civilizations is breathtaking. The Spanish conquest of the Inka and the rest of South America revealed vast riches—it was that fabled El Dorado. The Spanish stripped the walls of the Inka capital of sheet gold, took the golden animals from the emperor's golden garden, and looted ancient tombs from the mountains to the sea. So vast were these riches that it is said that the European Renaissance was financed by the gold the Spanish took from Peru in the conquest. It is difficult to imagine that although this looting has been going on for centuries, there are still tombs, like the one of the Lord of Sipán, unopened.

STUDY QUESTIONS

1. Why is looting often pandemic in places with a rich archaeological heritage?
2. What do grave goods tell us about the life of an individual?
3. Are warfare and human sacrifice typical for many prehistoric human societies?
4. How do rulers become so powerful in these societies? What enforces their status and authority?
5. What do the finds at Sipán tell us about Moche beliefs in an afterlife?

There's no way of course that the discovery will solve the economic crisis, but we have managed to get the Lambayeque region on the tourist circuit. Local people are getting their self-respect back and now feel proud of being descendants of the Moche culture, which has generated such admiration around the world. National Geographic has devoted reports to the site and foreign television stations from Japan, Australia, the United States, and Chile have filmed it. There are now colleges, universities, restaurants, and shops named after the Lord of Sipán. The name has entered the language and enhanced the region's identity. People have been able to see for themselves the very positive effects of the discovery and the archaeological project to save it.
—Walter Alva, archaeologist

www.mhhe.com/pricearch1

For a Web-based activity on Christopher Donnan, please see the Internet exercises on your online learning center.

www.mhhe.com/pricearch1

For more review material and study questions, please see the self-quizzes on your online learning center.

www.mhhe.com/pricearch1

For Internet references related to this chapter, please see the chapter links on your online learning center.

REFERENCES

Alva, Walter, and Christopher B. Donnan. 1993. *Royal Tombs of Sipán.* Los Angeles: UCLA Fowler Museum of Cultural History.

Donnan, Christopher B. 1978. *Moche Art of Peru.* Los Angeles: UCLA Museum of Culture History.

———. 1991. Archaeology and looting: Preserving the record. *Science* 251:498.

Lechtman, Heather, A. Erly, and E. J. Barry, Jr. 1982. New perspectives on Moche metallurgy: Techniques of gilding copper at Loma Negra, Northern Peru. *American Antiquity* 47:3–30.

A Brief History of Archaeology

INTRODUCTION: THE HISTORY OF PREHISTORY

This drawing of the site of Chichen Itza (*CHEECH-in EAT-zah*) in the Yucatan of Mexico is one of many made by two explorers during the first half of the nineteenth century. A London artist, Frederick Catherwood, and a New York lawyer, John Lloyd Stephens, visited the region twice between 1839 and 1841 and recorded their findings in words and drawings. They discovered more than a hundred Maya sites and fifteen lost cities. Catherwood used an optical device known as a *camera lucida* to make vivid, accurate, and captivating drawings of the ruins and sculptures. Stephens was so fascinated by the site of Copan that he purchased the ruins from their owner for $50. The site today is the property of the Honduran government. Stephens and Catherwood's two illustrated books on their adventures, titled *Incidents of Travel,* were national bestsellers in 1841 and 1843 and revealed the spectacular Maya civilization to England and North America for the first time. These books, now over 160 years old, remain among the more compelling accounts of ancient Maya ruins and provide an early and important record in the history of archaeology.

Like most academic disciplines today, archaeology did not really exist as a separate branch of study until the second half of the nineteenth century. The history of the discipline of archaeology follows closely the path that each of us takes to learn almost any subject—from awareness to interest to questioning to investigation and, eventually, to understanding. Archaeology is also a product of the times in the sense that current issues and concerns influence the development of the discipline. For example, the period of exploration that accompanied the European colonization of large parts of the world was one of discovery—many new archaeological regions and sites were recognized and new questions were asked. The period after World War II was generally one of optimism and a sense that everything could be known using modern technology and ideas. A growing awareness that too many people threatened the environment led to greater concern with population and environment in archaeological thinking. Today in archaeology, there is growing concern with globalization, ethical issues, and responsible behavior.

In the following pages, the history of the field is examined in three major time periods: pre-1900, 1900–1950, and 1950–2000. Descriptions of three investigations offer some sense of how archaeology was done in these different eras: Thomas Jefferson's mound excavation in Virginia in the late eighteenth century, a major British project in Iraq in the 1920s (Woolley at Ur), and a cultural resource

www.mhhe.com/pricearch1

For preview material for this chapter, please see the chapter summary, outline, and objectives on your online learning center.

Fig. 3.1 One of the etchings from the *Description de l'Égypte* volumes shows a fanciful head of the sphinx being measured by French engineers from Napoleon's army.

management project in Illinois in the late 1970s and 1980s (FAI–270). Some comments about the status of archaeology today conclude the chapter.

www.mhhe.com/pricearch1

For a Web-based activity on the history of archaeology, please see the Internet exercises on your online learning center.

It is impossible to describe the interest with which I explored these ruins. The ground was entirely new; there were no guide-books or guides; the whole was virgin soil. We could not see ten yards before us, and never knew what we should stumble upon next. At one time we stopped to cut away branches and vines which concealed the face of a monument, and then to dig around and bring to light a fragment, a sculptured corner of which protruded from the earth.

—John Lloyd Stephens, explorer

BEFORE 1900

Several stages mark archaeology's birth and childhood. Prior to AD 1800, only a few points of light mark an early fascination with the human past during what has been called the romantic phase of archaeology. These include the celebrated examples of William Stukeley's (1687–1765) work at Stonehenge, Avebury, and elsewhere in Britain, published in 1740 and 1743, and Thomas Jefferson's (1743–1826) excavation of a mound in Virginia in 1784. Such studies represent notable exceptions to the prevailing theological views that defined the origin, chronology, and course of human life from biblical orthodoxy.

An emergent phase of archaeology began after 1800. This era was marked by the creation of museums of antiquity, the appointment of the first university chairs in archaeology, and the initiation of more systematic fieldwork in various parts of Europe and the New World. By the beginning of the nineteenth century, the museums of Europe were filling with artifacts from the collections of exotic memorabilia assembled from colonies and ports of call around the world by ship captains and wealthy dilettantes. Napoleon was conquering large parts of Europe and ventured into Egypt at the turn of the nineteenth century. His engineers and scientists recorded the achievements of the pharaohs in a series of volumes titled *Description de l'Égypte* that captivated the European public (Fig. 3.1).

In Denmark, Christian Jörgensen Thomsen was appointed first director of the new National Museum in 1819 and established the chronological foundation for Old World archaeology with his three-age system of stone, bronze, and iron (Fig. 3.2). In the 1840s, Thomsen's successor, J. J. A. Worsaae, conducted extensive fieldwork and documented Thomsen's theories.

Elsewhere, excavations were being conducted in a variety of places. In the Netherlands, C J. C. Reuvens was appointed to the first chair in archaeology at the University of Leiden in 1818 and began fieldwork in various parts of the country.

Jacques Boucher de Perthes, excavating in his native France in the 1830s–1850s, uncovered the bones of extinct animals in association with handaxes and argued that humanity was clearly older than the orthodox 6000-year date. Kalina and Krolmus published *Pagan Sacrificial Places, Graves and Antiquities in Bohemia* in 1836, based on fieldwork and the study of museum collections. In

Fig. 3.2 Christian Thomsen, first director of the National Museum of Denmark.

Middle America, Stephens and Catherwood were exploring and illustrating the Maya ruins, as described at the opening of this chapter. In North America, Squire and Davis recorded and reported on the extraordinary *Ancient Monuments of the Mississippi Valley* in 1848 (Fig. 3.3).

The second half of the nineteenth century marked a formative stage in the professionalization of archaeology. Darwin's 1859 publication *On the Origin of the Species* crystallized the intellectual foment of the time and led eventually to acceptance of the antiquity of earth, humans, and the process of evolution. Darwin's work was an intellectual turning point in our understanding of the past. This period also saw the emergence of antiquarian studies—distinguished from history and natural science. Museums of natural history were the primary base for archaeological researchers, but academic positions were increasing in number. The first dissertation in the United States in any field was written in 1861. The first PhD in archaeology in the United States was granted at Harvard University in 1894, little more than a century ago. Interest during this time was largely in the classical, the exotic, in treasure and inscriptions, but eventually shifted toward ancient technologies and more commonplace artifacts. Few archaeological journals existed and only a handful of general texts were available. Several basic tenets of scientific archaeology emerged during this period: the principles of stratigraphic excavation, the significance of common artifacts, the documentation of fieldwork with notes, maps, drawings, and photography, and the publication of results.

Around the globe, intrepid individuals were investigating local prehistory. F. Keller described the discovery of Swiss lake dwellings during a period of extremely low water levels in the winter of 1853–1854. The Italian archaeologist Giuseppe Fiorelli directed excavations at Pompeii in the 1860s, excavating entire room blocks and recording stratigraphic layers. Two noted British prehistorians developed methods of excavation and analysis. Working in England, Augustus

Fig. 3.3 A plan from Squire and Davis, 1848, *Ancient Monuments of the Mississippi Valley,* showing the Hopeton Work in Ohio, with a series of major earthworks, mounds, and a causeway.

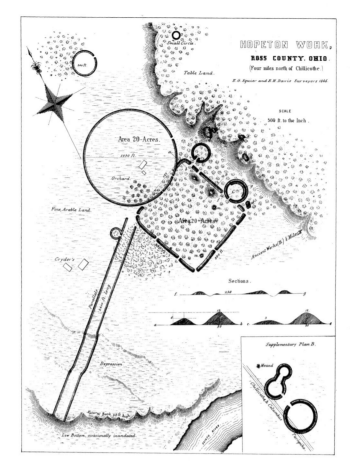

Fig. 3.4 Flinders Petrie in Egypt.

Henry Lane-Fox Pitt-Rivers—"the father of scientific excavation"—stressed the significance of simple artifacts for understanding the past. William Matthew Flinders Petrie demonstrated the importance of stratigraphic excavation and comparative artifact analysis in the study of the chronology of early Egypt (Fig. 3.4). In the 1870s, Heinrich Schliemann popularized his finds at Troy and Mycenae with dramatic newspaper accounts that captivated the public. Henry Austen Layard opened the mound of Babylon and exposed the Assyrians. Sir Arthur Evans uncovered and reconstructed the home of the Minoan civilization at Knossos. John L. Stephens and Frederick Catherwood wandered the jungles of Central America and reported the mystery of the Maya to fascinated newspaper audiences.

 **EXAMPLE** 〰〰〰〰〰〰〰〰〰〰〰〰〰〰〰〰〰〰〰〰〰〰

JEFFERSON AT RIVANNA RIVER

Thomas Jefferson (1743–1826), one of the founding fathers of the United States, was many things—scholar, politician, architect, musician, inventor, horticulturalist, president, and slave owner. Jefferson was also interested in the past. As a practical man, he believed that the way to learn about that past was to excavate the remains of earlier societies. Jefferson grew up on the frontier of Virginia and encountered Native Americans regularly in his early years. That interaction must have instilled a lifelong interest in the past of Virginia and in its native peoples. In fact, Jefferson devoted part of the only book he ever wrote, *Notes on the State of Virginia,* published in 1787, to the history of the original inhabitants of the state (Fig. 3.5).

The Spanish conquistadores, who explored parts of North America during the first half of the sixteenth century, saw large earthen mounds constructed and used by the Native American populations in the southeastern United States. Remarkably, 200 years later their observations had been forgotten, supplanted by a new explanation for the mounds that involved a people known as the Moundbuilders. This myth of the Moundbuilders, as it has come to be known, arose among the early European settlers. When these settlers arrived, they met Native American populations decimated by disease and conflict. The small numbers of these individuals who remained were greatly weakened. Europeans refused to believe that these groups could have been responsible for the numerous large mounds and spectacular artifacts. To account for these constructions, the settlers adopted a story of another race of people, the Moundbuilders, who were responsible for the fine artifacts and earthworks, but who had since disappeared and been replaced by Native Americans. This perspective, of course, helped to justify the land grab that was taking place since the Indians could not be the original owners of the land.

For Jefferson, the origins of the Virginia Indians were less clear and he set out to learn more about the mounds, who built them, and why. In 1784, Jefferson carefully excavated a large burial mound near the Rivanna (*riv-VAHN-ah*) River on his own property. His excavations are remarkable for the methods he used and the careful observations he made. His notes contain details on the size of the mound, the growth of trees on the mound, the various layers encountered in the excavations, and the human remains and artifacts that he found. Some of the materials from his excavations he kept in his home at Monticello, but the largest portion of the collection was sent to the American Philosophical Society in Philadelphia for safekeeping and future study.

Jefferson estimated that perhaps 1000 individuals had been buried in the mound. His reasoned, stratigraphic analysis showed that the construction of the mound was done in several discrete episodes of enlargement and interment. Each new group of burials was covered and groups were separated by a layer of stones and earth. The absence of wounds on the bodies and the presence of children among the dead suggested to Jefferson that the burials were not related to warfare or militarism, as others had surmised. He correctly concluded that the mound was constructed by the ancestors of the Native Americans who were living in Virginia during his childhood. Jefferson argued on the basis of the skeletal remains, and linguistic research that he conducted, that the ancestors of these people had come from Asia. His results were generally ignored in the United States and, in part because of this lack of interest, Jefferson's book sold better in France than it did in his native Virginia.

Jefferson's archaeology, although he did not use the term, was remarkable in several aspects. He was one of the very first individuals in the Americas to conduct any kind of excavation. Empirical studies were not yet in fashion. Not only did he excavate; he did it carefully and recorded stratigraphic observations that helped him to understand the construction and function of the mound. Finally, Jefferson's research was problem oriented; he was trying to answer questions about the origins of the Virginia Indians.

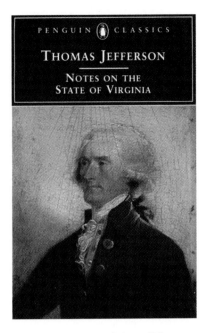

Fig. 3.5 A recent edition of Thomas Jefferson's *Notes on the State of Virginia,* originally published in 1787.

I proceeded then to make a perpendicular cut through the body of the barrow, that I might examine its internal structure. This passed about three feet from its center, was opened to the former surface of the earth, and was wide enough for a man to walk through and examine its sides. At the bottom, that is, on the level of the circumjacent plain, I found bones; above these a few stones . . . then a large interval of earth, then a stratum of bones, and so on. . . .

—Thomas Jefferson, president

1900–1950

The years from 1900 to World War II were a classic stage of exploration and the investigation of culture history. Culture history focused on the questions of when and where major changes and innovations happened and on the source of those changes. Primary sources for change were thought to be innovation and diffusion. New artifacts and ideas were either local inventions or borrowed, or carried, from elsewhere.

A century ago archaeology was unknown to most. But during the first decades of the twentieth century, spectacular new sites were made public as

Fig. 3.6 Hiram Bingham's discovery of Machu Picchu at the edges of the Inka empire ignited the American public's interest in archaeology in 1910.

Fig. 3.7 Dorothy Garrod, the first female professor of archaeology at Cambridge University.

archaeologists visited distant lands in search of the origins of civilization. Howard Carter at Tutankhamen's tomb in Egypt, Leonard Woolley at the Royal Cemetery of Ur (*UHR*) in Iraq, and Hiram Bingham's discovery of Machu Picchu (*MACH-eew PEACH-eew*) in Peru (Fig. 3.6) are some of the hallmarks of that period of wonder. In Mesoamerica, the Carnegie projects integrated hieroglyphic inscriptions and massive excavations to derive new understandings of the ancient Maya civilization. V. Gordon Childe defined the concept of an "archaeological culture" and synthesized much of European prehistory. These years also were a time of large-scale public works projects in Europe and North America; enormous excavations produced mountains of artifacts and information, revealing the richness of the archaeological record, often even in the less remote regions of the world.

It was during these times of discovery that archaeology became a staple in academic settings. Autonomous departments of archaeology were created in many parts of the world. In the United States archaeology was combined with cultural and physical anthropology (and sometimes linguistics) into a single departmental unit. The subdisciplines of anthropology often were joined with sociology, and sometimes other disciplines as well. The faculties of such departments usually had less than ten members and a small number of students, and specializations were geographic and occasionally chronological. The first female to earn a PhD in archaeology in the United States was Frederica de Laguna in 1933; Dorothy Garrod was made Disney Professor of Archaeology (and the first female professor) at Cambridge University in 1939 (Fig. 3.7). By 1940, archaeology had become an attempt to ascertain the time and space parameters of material remains from the past. In this same interval, *archaeology* became a household word.

Yet fifty years ago, our knowledge of the past and development of archaeology as a science were still relatively limited. There was no widely useful method for absolute dating, the origins of humanity were thought to have been less than 500,000 years ago, and the first farmers were said to have emerged in Egypt around 4000 BC. In 1946, there were 661 members in the Society for American Archaeology, with a roughly comparable number of archaeologists in all of Europe. Ethnoarchaeology had barely been imagined. Historical and underwater archaeology were in their infancy. The standard use of quantitative techniques and the explicit elaboration of the theoretical frameworks that underpin field studies were still nascent endeavors.

EXAMPLE

WOOLLEY AT UR

Charles Leonard Woolley (1880–1960) made one of the great archaeological discoveries of the twentieth century, comparable to Howard Carter's find of the tomb of King Tut in Egypt just a few years earlier. Woolley was born in London, son of a clergyman, and attended Oxford University. He began his career at the Ashmolean Museum in Oxford as an assistant keeper in 1905 and became interested in the ancient Near East. He worked with T. E. Lawrence (of Arabia fame) in Egypt, Syria, and Iraq during the decade between 1910 and 1920 (Fig. 3.8).

From 1922 until 1934, he directed the project that would bring his fame, the joint Oxford University–University of Pennsylvania effort at the site of Ur of the Chaldees, the fabled home of biblical Abraham and capital of an ancient civilization in the modern country of Iraq. Iraq had been part of the Ottoman Empire from the sixteenth century on and was invaded and occupied by Britain during World War I. In 1920, the League of Nations established the British Mandate over Iraq and the archaeologists began to arrive.

The site of Ur is located in southern Mesopotamia, the land between the Euphrates and Tigris rivers, close to the Persian Gulf (Fig. 3.9). Ur was one of the earliest urban city-states, inhabited by perhaps 200,000 people during its peak around 2500 BC, a period known as the Early Dynastic. At this time, bureaucratic organization, social stratification, trade, crafts, and writing were all highly developed.

The site is enormous, and today it is largely a moonscape of sand and mudbrick. The mounded remains in the center of the site cover an oval area approximately 1200 m by 800 m (2500 ft) (the size of a small airport). The ruins stand up to 20 m (65 ft) above the featureless, flat, surrounding plain. The **ziggurat** (*ZIG-uhr-aht*), or temple pyramid, on the northwest end of the site woud have been substantially higher, perhaps 80–100 m (300 ft). A long, broken line of smaller mounds—the remains of buildings—extends more than 1.5 km (1 mi) to the north.

Mesopotamia, the cradle of the first states and cities, is a huge basin filled with fine sediments deposited for millennia by the Tigris and Euphrates. Rainfall is limited and the area is essentially a desert between the two rivers. This region was largely unoccupied until the discovery of irrigation; canals carried water from the rivers and created very fertile agricultural lands. The irrigated farmland is a great natural resource but there is little else for hundreds of kilometers—no stone, no wood, no metals. Virtually all of these raw materials had to be imported. The only readily available resource was the soil itself, made into bricks of mud sun-dried to harden. The lack of

Fig. 3.8 Leonard Woolley (right) with his foreman, Hamoudi Ibn Shaikh Ibrahim, at Ur.

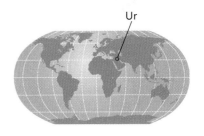

Ur

Fig. 3.9 Aerial photo of the site of Ur in southwestern Iraq. The large structure near the center of the photo is the ziggurat. Surrounding this structure can be seen the foundations of many other large buildings.

ziggurat A large, solid, mudbrick stepped tower. Stairways lead to a small temple on top.

Fig. 3.10 Woolley's excavations of the "death pit" at Ur, an enormous excavation done by hand by hundreds of local workers.

www.mhhe.com/pricearch1

For a Web-based activity on the site of Ur, please see the Internet exercises on your online learning center.

rain meant this material would last for years. Today, it has largely turned back to dust and blows around the cores of the mounds and architectural remnants that still stand.

Woolley's workers first exposed an enormous pyramid or ziggurat at the site along with the remains of smaller temples and residences. The most spectacular finds at Ur, however, were the royal tombs containing the remains of nearly 2000 people. The royal tombs were vaulted brick or stone chambers at the bottom of a shaft dug deeply into the earth. Access was provided by ramps leading down to the chamber, filled in when the tomb was closed. The body of the ruler was placed in the center of the chamber with great quantities of grave furnishings, equipment, and sacrifices. Several of the tombs included wheeled wagons or sleds and horses or oxen to carry some of the grave goods. Servants and attendants were found both in the chamber with the deceased king or queen and in the adjacent area that Woolley called the "death pit" (Fig. 3.10).

The rich grave goods provide graphic evidence of the opulent wealth of the kings and queens, the superb craftsmanship, and the pronounced social stratification of this early Mesopotamian civilization (Fig. 3.11). Perhaps the best-known vault is thought to contain the body of a queen. Woolley sent a telegram to the University Museum in 1928, written in Latin to conceal the news: "I found the intact tomb, stone built and vaulted with bricks, of Queen Puabi adorned with a dress in which gems, flower crown, and animal figures are woven. Tomb magnificent with jewels and golden cups."

Queen Puabi was lying on her back on a bed, accompanied by female attendants. Two wagons drawn by oxen and attended by male servants had been backed down the entry ramp, where fifty-nine bodies, mostly female, were on the ground near the tomb chambers. All retainers were lavishly bedecked with ornaments crafted

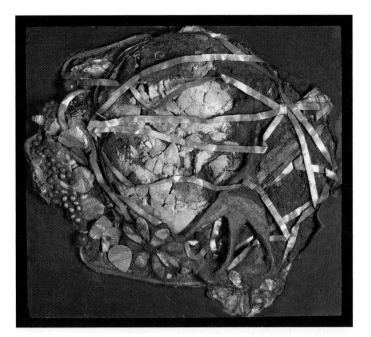

Fig. 3.11 The crushed skull, headdress, and jewelry of Queen Puabi's burial at Ur.

of gold, silver, carnelian, lapis lazuli, and turquoise. Woolley believed that all the people and animals buried with the queen entered the vault alive. After the queen and her possessions were placed in the pit, the animals were dispatched by their keepers, who then consumed the poison that had been waiting for them in the tomb. No violence is evident in the arrangement of the corpses.

Woolley attempted to work out the relative chronology of the tombs, sorting them from earlier to later. The cemetery area was small and crowded with tombs and burials from different periods. Graves were superimposed one over another and earlier graves had frequently been disturbed by later ones. Woolley knew that the depth of the chamber was unimportant because the graves had been dug down from an irregular surface. Woolley developed a system of dating the tombs by association through a series of changes in pottery, stone, and metal artifacts that could be used to establish the chronological order of the tombs.

Woolley was knighted by the English king in 1935. He wrote twenty-five books about his research, including *Spadework: Adventures in Archaeology,* published in 1953, and *Excavations at Ur: A Record of 12 Years' Work* in 1954. His career is a classic example of archaeology in the first part of the twentieth century, a period of exploration and discovery, when theory was almost unknown, scientific techniques were just emerging, and archaeologists were often adventurers.

1950–2000

The second half of the twentieth century was a stage of growth and confidence, followed by doubt and reassessment, a "postclassic" period of development involving a quest for both data and theory and an explosion of new scientific methods. Brian Fagan of the University of California at Santa Barbara described these changes as the result of developments in three areas: (1) computers and new scientific methods, (2) theoretical advances, and (3) the increasing number of archaeologists. Prior to 1950 in North America, fewer than 100 PhDs had been granted in archaeology, compared to the thousands held by those working today. In the

When the archaeologist progresses beyond the single specimen, he is studying the phenomena of culture. I join a number of contemporaries in believing that archaeology is moving in the direction of its establishment as a more important segment of the developing science of culture than it has been in the past.

—James A. Ford, archaeologist

The Ancient City of Ur

The ancient city of Ur—known today as Tell el-Muqayyar, the Mound of Tar—was once a heavily populated green island in the center of the Euphrates River in southern Iraq, amid rich, irrigated agricultural fields on both sides of the river. Today, this isolated area lies between Baghdad and the Persian Gulf in a wasteland of blowing sand. Two events brought about the end of ancient Ur. The river changed its course and moved away, and the cultivated lands developed a crust of salt, rendering them unusable due to continuous farming and the evaporation of irrigation waters. After Woolley's excavations and the restoration of the ziggurat and some of the building walls at Ur, the site became a minor tourist attraction as the biblical home of Abraham and one of the world's first cities.

In normal times in Iraq, everything below the plow zone belongs to the state, following the Napoleonic and later Ottoman code of law. All major sites are owned by the state and protected by guards from what is called the state's Antiquities Department. The first director general of antiquities in Iraq, Gertrude Bell, pushed through strong legislation, specifically about the protection of monuments, sites, and Ur itself.

In recent years, the site has suffered as part of the U.S. invasions of Iraq (Fig. 3.12). Part of the site was bombed in the 1991 invasion in the hostilities that affected a number of archaeological sites. Rocket or shell-fire damaged the brickwork of the ziggurat. The Saddam regime built a large air base called "Talil" just south of Ur. When the United States took over the base in April

Fig. 3.12 U.S. troops and humvees at the base of the ziggurat at Ur in 2003.

2001, they expanded the base perimeter to include the site. American forces stationed in the area vandalized the site, spray-painting graffiti and slogans on the monuments and stealing ancient bricks with cuneiform inscriptions, before it was put off-limits by the U.S. military. Some of the treasures of the site and the tombs, stored or on display in the National Museum in Baghdad, were stolen by looters at the start of the war in 2003. The U.S. Congress passed an Emergency Protection for Iraqi Cultural Antiquities act in late 2004 to try to preserve these archaeological materials. The future of Iraq and Ur is uncertain at the present time.

year 2000, there were more than 6500 members in the National Society for American Archaeology and perhaps 10,000 practicing archaeologists in the United States.

The immediate postwar years were an extraordinary time. Questions turned to the antecedents of civilization as interest grew in human ancestors, in hunters and gatherers, and in early farmers. Archaeologists began to think about the goals and meaning of archaeology, beyond the simple issues of shovel and trowel. Emphasis switched from culture history to culture process, the study of how societies operate and change. An exemplary, multidisciplinary approach was introduced in projects such as Grahame Clark's excavations at Star Carr in England, the Braidwoods' investigations in Iraqi Kurdistan, and Richard MacNeish's studies in the Tehuacán (*tay-wah-CAHN*) Valley of Mexico. Other projects of this type included Gordon Willey's search for regional settlement patterns in the Virú Valley of Peru and the Leakey family's extraordinary quest at Olduvai Gorge (Fig. 3.13), leading to the discovery of the earliest hominids in Africa.

The next generation of giants in the discipline made their names during the decades that followed World War II. François Bordes (1919–1981) excavated and prescribed a basic order for much of the European Paleolithic. Lewis Binford defined archaeology as a science and explicitly called for the investigation of culture process (Fig. 3.14). David Clarke (1937–1976) argued for an analytical archaeology to investigate the past. Glynn Isaac (1937–1985) foraged into the obscure behavior

Fig. 3.13 Louis and Mary Leakey at work on Olduvai Gorge, ca. 1963.

of early hominids. Kent Flannery of the University of Michigan kept things honest with a humorous, practical sense of how to study the past.

In the context of the optimism and expansionism of the immediate postwar decades, the discipline of archaeology diversified. Culture history gave way to culture process in the 1960s and 1970s as archaeology became a mix of science and anthropology. The "new archaeology," midwifed by Lewis Binford, David Clarke, and their students, emphasized deductive reasoning, quantitative methods, and a search for general laws and process. The focus on process led to the term *processual archaeology* for this perspective.

During the 1980s, a self-proclaimed "post-processual" group of archaeologists, led by Ian Hodder of Stanford University, questioned many of the basic premises of the discipline and pointed to new directions and goals in the pursuit of the past. Emphasis was placed on interpretation and the importance of symbol, ideology, and cognition in the operation of society (Fig. 3.15). Explanation became text, biased by the internal goals and agenda of each individual author. Archaeology was to be pluralistic, with many points of view, all equally valid; a version of political correctness arrived in archaeology.

At the same time that post-processualism was being defined, several evolutionary and environmental approaches regained a foothold in North America under a variety of titles: optimal foraging theory, evolutionary ecology, evolutionary archaeology, and neo-Darwinism. New ideas melded with old as archaeologists passed through theoretical minefields and emerged on the other side with more sense of how the social and ideological—along with technology and the environment—were significant factors in shaping our past. These issues are considered in more detail in Chapter 16, "Explanation in Archaeology."

In that same period, the archaeology of heritage grew enormously in importance around the globe. The archaeology of heritage involves the protection of the past through legislation and the creation of organizations to preserve our common cultural inheritance. Institutions such as the National Register of Historic Places, the National Park Service Archaeology and Ethnography Program, the State Historic Preservation Offices, English Heritage, and others in countries around the world were founded at this time. The legislated requirements for impact

Fig. 3.14 Lewis R. Binford, Southern Methodist University.

Fig. 3.15 *Reading the Past,* by Ian Hodder, 1986.

assessments prior to construction and the mitigation of the destruction of cultural resources led to a new industry of archaeology in the private and government sectors. Historical preservation became a business, and archaeology became a job.

Many factors contributed to an increasing emphasis on the preservation of archaeological sites and resources, including the green movement, a greater awareness of the rapid tempo of site destruction, a concern for the rights of native peoples, the commercial importance of archaeology as a magnet for tourism, and the rebirth of interest in archaeology for nationalistic and political motives. A large cadre of professional archaeologists, a majority of the discipline by the end of the twentieth century, are no longer found in the halls of universities or museums; rather, these individuals operate in government agencies and private businesses for the purpose of rescuing, preserving, and managing our heritage. The amount of funding expended in heritage preservation is estimated to be on the order of twenty to fifty times that available for academic research. This trend has resulted in more diversified interests and goals in archaeology and has generated an enormous body of new information about the past.

 **EXAMPLE** ~~~~~~~~~~~~~~~~~~~~~~~~~~~~~~~~

THE FAI–270 PROJECT

The Archaeological Resources Protection Act of 1979 provided for the protection of archaeological resources located on public lands and Indian lands; defined archaeological resources to be any material remains of past human life or activities that are of archaeological interest and are at least 100 years old; encouraged cooperation between groups and individuals in possession of archaeological resources from public or Indian lands with special permit and disposition rules for the protection of archaeological resources on Indian lands in light of the American Indian Religious Freedom Act; provided that information regarding the nature and location of archaeological resources may remain confidential; and established civil and criminal penalties, including forfeiture of vehicles, fines of up to $100,000, and imprisonment of up to 5 years for second violations for the unauthorized appropriation, alteration, exchange, or other handling of archaeological resources with rewards for furnishing infor-mation about such unauthorized acts. (U.S. Congress, Office of Technology Assessment, 1986)

As mentioned, prior to the start of any federally funded construction, the U.S. Environmental Protection Agency requires an impact study to determine whether important archaeological or historical sites are in danger of destruction. Both federal agencies and private corporations must provide information on the effect their projects may have on the history and prehistory of an area. Various kinds of construction— reservoirs, highways, sewage systems, power lines, to name just a few—require archaeological surveys and impact statements. This kind of archaeology, known as cultural resource management (CRM), has become very important in the past 25 years. More than half of the archaeologists in the United States today are in CRM-related fields for private businesses, government agencies, and some universities.

These CRM projects usually involve three stages. An initial archive and field survey is made to see if archaeological or historical artifacts are present. If such materials are found, a second stage of more detailed testing and evaluation is undertaken. If these results are positive, a third stage may involve a full program of excavation and recovery or mitigation. Mitigation may involve moving the place of construction, rerouting right of ways, or more complete excavation.

CRM projects vary greatly in size and scope. Many of these evaluations are relatively small scale and require only a few days or weeks for the determination of the impact of construction. Major building projects (for example, dams, pipelines, and highways), on the other hand, may require years of fieldwork, analysis, and report writing to complete an evaluation.

The FAI–270 project in eastern Illinois was one of the largest CRM projects in U.S. history. The designation FAI–270 refers to Federal Aid Interstate 270 (later renumbered 255), a six-lane expressway to be constructed as part of a long-term expansion of the highway system around St. Louis, Missouri. The 270 segment, begun in 1975, was planned to run north-south along the Illinois side of the Mississippi River, carrying traffic around St. Louis. This area is known as the "American Bottom" and lies just south of the confluence of the Illinois, Missouri, and Mississippi rivers (Fig. 3.16). The American Bottom is extremely fertile land with a variety of environmental zones, including swamps, ponds, forests, and wet prairie grasslands.

The planned route of the highway ran along one side of the Cahokia Mounds State Historic Site. Cahokia (*kah-HOKE-ee-ah*) is one of only twenty World Heritage sites in the United States (discussed in Chapter 17) and the location of the largest man-made earthen mound in North America (Fig. 3.17). At its peak between AD 1050 and 1250, Cahokia was the most extensive site north of Mexico and may have had a population as high as 30,000 people. The site includes more than 100 earthen mounds, residential areas, plazas, and many other features in an area of 16 km² (6 sq mi). The enormous Monk's Mound has a base of almost 300 × 250 m (1000 × 750 ft), approximately 7 hectares (18 acres), and rises in four terraces to a height of 30 m (100 ft).

The original FAI–270 highway plan involved approximately 1000 acres of land to be impacted by construction. The combination of the major prehistoric center at Cahokia and the very rich environment of the American Bottom meant that a large number of archaeological sites from many periods lay in the right-of-way for the six-lane interstate.

The primary contractor for the highway, the Illinois Department of Transportation (IDOT), asked the University of Illinois at Champagne-Urbana (UICU) to undertake the CRM work on the project. The directors of this project hired archaeologists from all over the country in 1977. Several other universities and museums were involved as well as the project grew in size.

The FAI–270 investigations were planned from the start to learn more about the natural environment of the American Bottom and its very rich archaeological record

www.mhhe.com/pricearch1

For a Web-based activity on Cultural Resource Management, please see the Internet exercises on your online learning center.

American Bottom

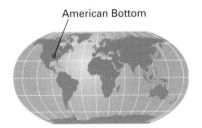

Fig. 3.16 The FAI–270 project study area of the American Bottom, east of St. Louis, Missouri, on the floodplain of the Mississippi River in western Illinois. Note the many former lakes in existence in this region. Major mound groups in this area are shown in red.

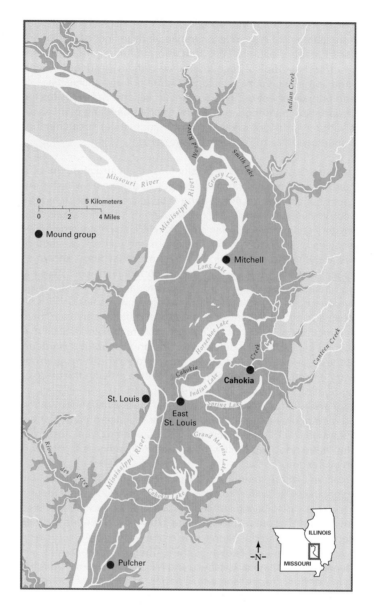

Fig. 3.17 Monk's Mound at Cahokia, this pyramid is the largest prehistoric earthwork in the United States and Canada. Note the cars along the highway for a sense of size.

Fig. 3.18 Aerial view of excavations at the Range Site, showing houses from the Mississippian period. People shown on the right-hand side of the photo give a sense of the scale of the excavations.

along the corridor of the planned highway. The design of the project included three major questions that would direct research. (1) What was the nature of the transition from the Late Archaic to Early Woodland period? (2) What kinds of settlements and community plans characterized the Late Woodland and Mississippian periods? What can this information tell us about the rise of more complex societies? (3) What is the evidence for the rise and fall of the site of Cahokia outside the boundaries of the site itself?

Initial surveys of the right-of-way identified 59 new sites. Testing and evaluation of these sites continued until 1982. At the same time, the preparations for the highway generated new development in the area and required more archaeological survey. After this stage of the project, a total of 102 archaeological sites had been identified. Excavations were undertaken at the 20 most promising sites that had been located in the survey (Fig. 3.18). The research questions of the project meant that excavations were undertaken for large-scale recovery of community plans at the archaeological sites. Earthmoving equipment was used to expose the subsurface of many of these locations to help reveal the larger site plan. This was new information for many of the time periods encountered and provided important new data.

Answers to those initial questions were not easily discovered. The Late Archaic was a time of hunter-gatherers in this region, prior to the introduction of ceramics. This period also witnessed the adoption of squash, probably domesticated in Mexico, and several native North American domesticates such as sunflower, marsh elder, and gourds. Subsistence was based on a range of activities including hunting, fishing, fowling, and gardening, along with nut, seed, and shellfish collection. Settlements from this period were large and rich in artifacts and features, and some appeared to be sedentary.

The transition to the Woodland period took place ca. 600 BC with the introduction of pottery and a number of new types of artifacts. The Early Woodland appears to represent the arrival of new groups of people in the American Bottom. Sites were small, short-term occupations with limited deposits of artifacts. The Woodland Period continued until approximately AD 800 and the beginning of the Mississippian period and the rise of the center of Cahokia. Several spectacular artifacts dating from the Mississippian period were discovered by the project (Fig. 3.19).

The FAI–270 project involved more than 1000 archaeologists, fieldwork lasted from 1978 until 1985, and the reports still continue to appear. At least thirty books and numerous scientific articles have been published on various aspects of the project and the finds. The funding for the archaeological portion of the project was more

Fig. 3.19 One of the discoveries of the FAI–270 project, the Birger Figurine, carved from pipestone, a depiction of a woman hoeing or hitting a cat-faced snake that wraps around her.

than $4,000,000, a tiny portion of the entire highway construction budget of hundreds of millions of dollars.

In the end, the FAI–270 project managed to rescue a huge amount of information before the road construction disturbed the area. The results of this project were summarized by the noted American archaeologist James Griffin (1905–1997) in 1984: "Seldom if ever has so much been added to archaeological knowledge, by so many participants, supported by so much money. Together these participants comprised a non-institutionalized, unfortunately short-lived, archaeological institute of high quality."

TODAY: THE FUTURE OF THE PAST

It is clear that the field of archaeology is growing rapidly and changing substantially. The numbers of academic programs, private businesses, books, journals, reports, society members, students, and archaeologists in general have increased several times over in the past 25 years. New questions, new technologies, new directions, and new needs are rapidly emerging. Specialization is also on the rise—there are many kinds of archaeologies and archaeologists, each with their own scientific journals and societies.

In some ways, archaeology today resembles the field of geology 25 years ago. Geology has existed longer in academia as one of the first of the natural sciences. In the past 25 years, the scientific and instrumental aspects of geology have become much more important as departments have emphasized chemical

House Size and Population

The rise of corn agriculture and a remarkable expansion in population and cultural complexity mark the Mississippian period in the American Bottom. Settlements were large and permanent. Based on information collected during the FAI–270 project, an intriguing pattern is seen in which house size and the number of structures increased (Fig. 3.20) while site size decreased. This pattern suggests growing population in the context of a need for more farmland. A number of sites with earthen mounds are known from the beginning of the Mississippian period, distributed roughly every 20 km (12 mi) across the American Bottom. Clearly differences in status and power were emerging at that time, culminating in the town-and-mound pattern of stratified sociopolitical organization that characterized this period. Four levels of a settlement hierarchy could be identified: small settlements without mounds, sites with a single mound, sites with a number of mounds, and the center at Cahokia itself. Native American occupation of the American Bottom declined after AD 1300 and ended with the westward expansion of European-American settlement in the eighteenth century.

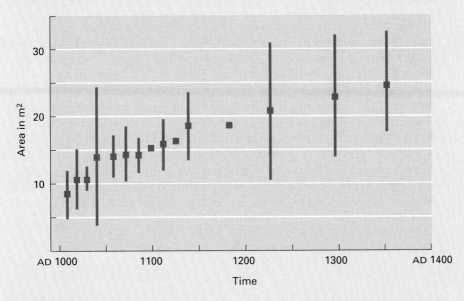

Fig. 3.20 A plot of house size at Mississippian sites in the American Bottom through time, between AD 1000 and 1400. The square marks the average house size at a site, and the vertical bar shows the range of size. A single square symbol indicates a single house was found. The dates for the individual sites are approximate. This information was obtained by the FAI–270 project.

and physical methods of laboratory analysis and a quantitative curriculum. Many departments of geology have been renamed geological science or geophysics. Archaeology, a younger discipline and one that must examine human behavior as a measurable variable, lies just at the beginning of a substantial laboratory phase. The first department of archaeological science was formed in Britain a few years ago.

It seems clear that the scientific orientation of archaeology will continue to expand along with more subjective perspectives. Professor Philip Morrison of MIT pointed to the increasing importance of science and archaeology in the world at a conference in 1992. "Basic research in the natural sciences will need to become more prized and better understood by students, parents, press, and Congress. I expect that one of the best ways will be to engage more non-science students in the sciences; links between humanities and natural science will be more and more sought, studied, and examined. Archeology is surely a major example of that linkage, along with astronomy and cosmology, so close to the old existential questions of all thinking humans."

There are problems and pitfalls. Along with inevitable specialization in the field, efforts must be made to retain an emphasis on synthesis and integration so that questions and answers are matched. The financing of archaeological research is a continuing problem. Fieldwork and laboratory analysis become more expensive, while available funding remains stable or declines. The illicit trade in antiquities and the rapid growth in world population and development are quickly removing large numbers of artifacts and sites from the public domain and archaeological access. Greater public awareness of these problems and further national and international action is needed if our human past is going to survive.

CONCLUSIONS

As British archaeologist Glyn Daniel (1914–1986) remarked some years ago, "The present state of archaeology cannot be divorced from its past state." The foundation of what we know today was laid down in the twentieth century. We are currently constructing the first floors of an edifice of knowledge the final height of which is yet unknown. We have to accept the fact that 50 or 100 years from now future archaeologists will look back on this time today with the same nostalgic disdain that we often hear expressed for the archaeology of the early and middle twentieth century. We need to appreciate that each archaeologist will add only a few bits and pieces to the great tower of knowledge that is the construction of the human past. Maybe one of the most important lessons of archaeology is that we can build only on what has been laid down before, like the ziggurats and pyramids we excavate. That's why the construction process itself is such an important undertaking.

www.mhhe.com/pricearch1

For more review material and study questions, please see the self-quizzes on your online learning center.

STUDY QUESTIONS

1. What were the first beginnings of archaeology?
2. How did archaeology become more scientific and less of a hobby?
3. Who were the major figures in archaeology in the twentieth century?
4. What are the current directions and trends in archaeology?
5. What does the history of archaeology tell us about the future of the discipline?

REFERENCES

Bahn, P. G., ed. 1996. *The Cambridge Illustrated History of Archaeology.* Cambridge: Cambridge University Press.

———., ed. 1996. *The Story of Archaeology: The 100 Great Discoveries.* London: Weidenfeld & Nicolson.

Feinman, G. M., and T. D. Price. 2001. *Archaeology at the Millennium.* New York: Kluwer.

Hodder, I. 1992. *Theory and Practice in Archaeology.* London: Routledge.

Meltzer, D. J., D. D. Fowler, and J. A. Sabloff, eds. 1986. *American Archaeology: Past and Future.* Washington, D.C.: Smithsonian Institution Press.

Trigger, Bruce. 1989. *A History of Archaeological Thought.* Cambridge: Cambridge University Press.

Willey, G. R., and J. A. Sabloff. 1993. *A History of American Archaeology,* 3rd ed. New York: W.H. Freeman and Company.

www.mhhe.com/pricearch1

For Internet references related to this chapter, please see the chapter links on your online learning center.

DISCOVERY

Fieldwork is the best-known part of archaeology. Pith helmets, mummies, and golden treasure usually form the popular vision of archaeology. But fieldwork is rarely done without a purpose. That purpose involves discovery—learning what kinds of materials are present or seeking the answers to questions. Archaeology is a discipline, a science, a field of study concerned with finding answers to questions about the human past. It is the questions that archaeologists seek to answer and the problems to be resolved that drive fieldwork and the process of discovery. As the archaeologist David Thomas once said, the importance of archaeology is "not what you find, it's what you find out."

The daily life of ancient people is a continuing source of fascination. There are endless questions about them at a variety of different levels. Questions range from the raw material and function of artifacts to the operation of societies and the nature of human cognition. They concern events and process, stability and change, invention and the commonplace. Larger questions relate to the major changes in human behavior and society in the past.

The three chapters in this second part of *Principles of Archaeology* deal with the issues of questions and discovery. Chapter 4, "Archaeological Questions," concerns what archaeologists want to know. Chapter 5, "The Archaeological Record," investigates where archaeological information comes from. Chapter 6, "Fieldwork," delves into how archaeologists get this information.

4

Archaeological Questions

INTRODUCTION: THE SUBJECT MATTER OF ARCHAEOLOGY

This is a photograph of an Iron Age settlement at Lejre (*LIE-ruh*) in Denmark. A village like this one should date to around AD 100. There is a conundrum here, of course: Photography was not invented until the nineteenth century AD. Lejre is a present-day archaeological research center in the Danish countryside. Archaeologists and other folks try to reconstruct the past by building houses and tombs, cultivating fields and herding animals, and making the tools, pottery, and clothing needed for everyday life. Lejre welcomes more than 20,000 visitors a year and is one of the more popular tourist destinations in Denmark.

Lejre sits in a lovely rolling landscape of forest, lakes, bogs, and fields. Walking through the center, you pass a group of wild boar, then a small lake with children paddling dugout wooden canoes and chopping wood with ancient-looking iron axes. The smell of wood smoke wafts everywhere. Beyond the thatch-roofed administrative building, you enter an open grass meadow with scattered sheep, mounds and large, stone tombs, a small pond, and—in the distance—the Lejre hallmark, a living Iron Age village.

The center runs as a private, nonprofit foundation and is supported by grants, gifts, and admission fees. It is open to the public and professional archaeologists alike. While tourists wander through the landscape and villages, archaeologists and friends build houses, plow fields, make stone tools, hammer red-hot iron, and weave wools. The goal is to gain new knowledge about people in the past, their living conditions, technology, methods of cultivation, and the like through practical experiments—learning by doing. At the same time, engaging the public fascination in archaeology is a very positive aspect of the center's activities, encouraging the support of archaeology as a discipline.

Lejre is a large-scale example of experimental archaeology, attempting to reproduce the tools, architecture, and landscapes of antiquity. **Experimental archaeology** is one of the ways that archaeologists try to answer questions about the past. How was an artifact made? How was a pit used? How was a tomb built? What happened when a house burned? At the same time, experiments raise new questions and expand the scope of what it is that archaeologists want to know. Questions are the subject of this chapter: What do archaeologists want to know?

In all walks of life, the questions we ask and the answers we receive determine what we know. For that reason, archaeological questions are the most important part of gaining knowledge about the past. It is essential to define the questions to be answered before beginning any research. The package of questions,

www.mhhe.com/pricearch1

For preview material for this chapter, please see the chapter summary, outline, and objectives on your online learning center.

experimental archaeology Modern experiments to reproduce *artifacts, architecture,* and/or techniques from the past.

intended methods, research area, and planned analysis is called the **research design**—the overall strategy for answering a question about the past.

So, what do archaeologists want to know? Archaeologists study humans in the past. But what about humans is of interest?

Imagine a time machine that can take an archaeologist to any place and time in the past for two hours. The time and place selected reveal the interests of the archaeologist who turns the dial. The things that he or she records during that two-hour visit tell us what that person wants to know, the questions they have about the past. Some questions are basic: What did people eat? How did they get their food? What kind of house did they live in? How was society organized? Other questions are more esoteric: How did people bury their dead? How did they calculate time? How did they view the universe? What did they think about? There are as many questions as archaeologists and, in fact, many more.

Given this multitude of potential questions, what do archaeologists want to know? There are the fundamental questions about the past that are appropriate anywhere, anytime: Who? What? When? Where? and Why? Much of what archaeologists do is intended to answer these questions. What is the archaeological evidence and where is it found? How old is it and who made it? How was it used? Why was it made? Many of these derive from existential issues about ourselves. Where did we come from? Why are we here? Where are we going?

In addition to such fundamental issues, there are larger questions about human origins. These questions focus on major changes in the human condition along the path through prehistory to the present. Where and when did the human lineage diverge from its apelike relatives? When, where, and why did fully modern humans appear? Why did hunter-gatherers begin to tame animals and plants in the world around them and begin farming? What is responsible for the beginnings of social inequality and where does this change in social organization first appear? What do we know about the rise of the first states and empires?

This chapter is intended to introduce some of the important questions that archaeologists try to answer and some of the background to these questions. Most of these questions deal with various aspects of human society and its environment, including demography, technology, economy, organization, and ideology. Sources of questions are also varied and include common sense, ethnography, experimental archaeology, and ethnoarchaeology. Ethnography, the study of the culture and life of living peoples, provides a rich body of information about how humans have adapted and survived in various places around the globe. Archaeologists use this information to look for similarities between people of today and prehistoric remains, a practice known as ethnographic analogy. **Ethnoarchaeology** is the study of living peoples by archaeologists intent on gaining useful information for learning about the past. These topics are covered in the following pages of the chapter.

WHAT DO ARCHAEOLOGISTS WANT TO KNOW?

The questions that archaeologists seek to answer about the past involve a larger concept about the way of life of prehistoric peoples, how human societies coped with their physical and social environments, and how our predecessors viewed their world. That basic concept—and the primary unit of analysis in archaeology—is **culture**.

Culture is a complement to our biology. Most of the evolution of life on earth is marked by biological evolution from one species to another in order to adapt to changing environments. As humans, however, we have a second, unique system for adaptation that involves learned behavior. Culture is a nonbiological means of human adaptation based on intelligence, experience, learning, and the use of tools. Culture is our advantage for survival. It is learned behavior passed on from generation to generation, through language and education. It is the set of choices

The problem of creativity, of the source of fruitful theories and the questions they generate is not solved by scientific methods. Despite the high hopes of some fierce sciencemongers, there are no clear and certain methods of producing good ideas; scientific method is concerned with the process to follow once the question has been asked.
—Albert Spaulding, archaeologist

research design The overall strategy of intended methods, research area, and planned analysis for answering a question or questions about the past.

ethnoarchaeology Archaeological study of living societies for information to help better understand the past.

culture A means of human adaptation based on intelligence, experience, learning, and the use of *tools;* the general set of behaviors and knowledge that humans use to survive and adapt.

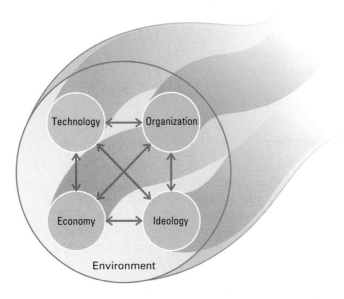

Fig. 4.1 A simple, schematic view of the major components of human society in the environment, and the interaction among them. It is important to remember that the environment includes other human societies as well as climate, vegetation, fauna, and geology.

we have for dealing with needs, changes, and stress. Culture operates to help us survive, to obtain the basic necessities of life—food, water, shelter, and safety—as well as to fulfill the needs of our psyche. This is the focus of archaeology—the search for evidence of our cultural development through time.

Archaeologists use the term *culture* in two ways. *Culture* in the singular can refer to the generic set of behaviors and knowledge that humans share as a hallmark of our species. Humans have culture. *Culture* also is used in the plural to describe **archaeological cultures**, specific human groups and societies in the past.

There are many ways to look at past cultures. One schematic view sees cultures composed of components—a combination of technology, economy, organization, and ideology set in a natural and social environment. Fig. 4.1 is a simple diagram of these components in the environment and the general interaction among them. The components are closely related and they all interact with each other and the environment. Social organization affects economy and vice versa. Ideology is related to environment. Technology and economy affect the environment.

Human societies have a size dimension as well that involves both population—the biological group of individuals that constitutes a society—and geographic space. **Demography**—the study of population—is an important concern in archaeology, and paleodemography is the study of past populations.

The questions that archaeologists ask about past societies then focus on several aspects. **Environment** refers to the natural and social milieu in which human societies operate, the source of food and materials for subsisting and surviving, as well as a source of change and stress. **Technology** includes the material, equipment, techniques, and knowledge that allow people to convert natural resources into tools, food, clothing, shelter, and other products they need or want. **Economy** refers to the methods that society uses to obtain food, water, and resources for maintenance and growth. **Organization** focuses on how relationships in society—among individuals, groups, and other societies—are arranged and how interaction takes place. **Ideology** is that realm of culture that involves the unknown and the satisfaction of distinctly human psychological needs. Ideology provides an explanation of human, natural, and supernatural relationships. These aspects of human culture and society are discussed in more detail in the following pages.

The components of human society—technology, economy, organization, and ideology—are also closely interrelated in prehistoric materials. The same artifact

archaeological culture A group of related materials from a region that indicate a common or shared way of doing things.

demography The study of human populations with a focus on size, age and sex distribution, birth and death rates, and migration. Prehistoric demography is also known as paleodemography.

environment The natural and social milieu in which human societies operate.

technology The material, equipment, techniques, and knowledge that allow humans to convert natural resources into *tools*, food, clothing, shelter, and other products they need or want.

economy The means and methods that society uses to obtain food, water, and resources for maintenance and growth.

organization Structure and interaction in human society, including relationships among individuals, groups, and other societies.

ideology The explanation of human, natural, and supernatural relationships through belief, *ritual*, and ceremony.

or object may involve aspects of each. A type of knife found exclusively in women's graves may hold information on the manufacture of tools, about the environmental resources that it was used on, on the nature of women's work, on the relationship between sexes in the society, and on ideas about death. Environment, technology, economy, organization, and ideology thus are different, but related, dimensions of past cultures and of human life, and they are an important focus of archaeological investigations.

Environment

Our environment sets the basic conditions for human life. It provides the essentials for our existence in the form of food, water, and raw materials. Human life is directly conditioned by its environment; thus human groups cannot be understood outside the natural and social environment in which they operate. The environment in which human society operates includes natural resources in the form of water, plants, animals, and minerals, as well as climate, catastrophe, and other human societies. One of the jobs of archaeologists is to describe and define the environment of past societies.

Environment operates for human benefit and detriment. In addition to providing essential resources for life, the environment also is the source of storms, floods, earthquakes, volcanic eruptions, tsunamis, and other major disasters, all of which can have a significant impact on the world (see Chapter 9, "Geoarchaeology"). Climate change and catastrophic events also shape human culture and society. Climate in particular is major factor in human life. Much of our evolutionary history as a species took place during the Pleistocene geological epoch, for example, a period of extreme cold, continental ice sheets, and substantially lower sea levels, between 10,000 and 2,000,000 years ago.

Fig. 4.2 depicts a simple example of the relationship between society and environment, in this case an early farming culture in Neolithic Europe and a land-

Fig. 4.2 The use of forest resources during the early Neolithic in Central Europe. The diagram shows the natural forest and cultivated fields at the top and the kinds of resources of timber, branches, and nuts that are available for construction, tool manufacture, firewood, and human and animal food.

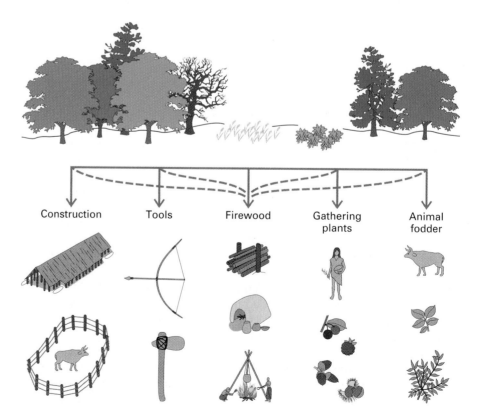

TABLE 4.1 Representative population densities for various human groups. There is a dramatic increase in human population in more complex societies.

Name of group	Location	Type	Density/km^2
Naskapi	Canada	Hunter-gatherers	0.005
Copper Eskimo	Canada	Hunter-gatherers	0.012
Shoshone	Nevada	Hunter-gatherers	0.012
Aranda	Australia	Hunter-gatherers	0.031
Paiute	Nevada	Hunter-gatherers	0.035
Kung	Botswana	Hunter-gatherers	0.097
Shoshone	California	Hunter-gatherers	0.23
Nootka	NWCoast US	Hunter-gatherers	0.66
Tsimshian	NWCoast US	Hunter-gatherers	0.82
Yoruk	Oregon US	Hunter-gatherers	1.81
Canada	Canada	Nation	3
Maring	New Guinea	Farmers	15
United States	United States	Nation	31
Gurumba	New Guinea	Farmers	44
World	Earth	Globe	45
Muyeng	Cameroon	Farmers	60
France	France	Nation	109
Hide of Tur	Cameroon	Farmers	120
Dugam Dani	New Guinea	Farmers	160
United Kingdom	United Kingdom	Nation	243
Japan	Japan	Nation	338
Bangladesh	Bangladesh	Nation	1019
Madison	Wisconsin US	City	1160
New York City	United States	City	4434
Bombay	India	City	49,202

scape of forest and fields. The environment provided timber for construction, wood for tools, firewood, and plants for food and animal fodder. Without these resources, early farming societies—villages and people—could not have existed.

Demography

Prehistoric demography (or paleodemography) is the study of human populations in the past. The important characteristics of a population from the perspective of demography include size (the number of individuals), vital statistics (sex and age distribution, birth and death rates, and migration), and geographic extent. A living **population** is all of the people living at a place or in a region. In this sense, population could refer to the people in a house, a school, a town, an area, a country, or the earth. An archaeological population generally refers to the people related through membership in the same group. An archaeological population can mean a house, a site, or a region and can range in size from a few to many tens of thousands. A **burial** (or death) **population** is the set of human remains found interred in a site or cemetery.

Human populations occupy geographic space. Another aspect of demography is **population density**, the number of people per square kilometer (Table 4.1). The population density of human populations has increased over time and is

population   (1) All of the people living at a place or in a *region*. An archaeological population generally refers to the people related through membership in the same group. (2) All of the items or units of interest in statistical sampling.

burial population   The set of human remains found interred in a *site* or cemetery.

population density   The number of people per unit of area, e.g., square kilometer.

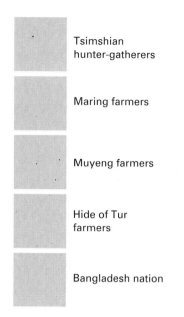

Tsimshian
hunter-gatherers

Maring farmers

Muyeng farmers

Hide of Tur
farmers

Bangladesh nation

Fig. 4.3 A schematic depiction of population density in selected human societies, showing a range from 0.82 to more than 1000 persons per square kilometer.

sometimes argued to be one of the major forces of social change. A schematic representation of these differences in population density is shown in Fig. 4.3.

Geographic space can be defined as home range, territory, country, or empire, depending on the nature of the society present. **Home range** generally refers to the area used by mobile hunter-gatherers. The term is borrowed from zoology, where it refers to the specific geographic area an animal uses for feeding and other activities. **Territory** implies a recognized and defended area utilized by a group or society, often associated with agricultural societies. A **country** is a sovereign region, marked by boundaries and defended by military power. An **empire** is an even larger sovereign space, expanded by military conquest and encompassing several countries and/or territories.

Archaeologists and biological anthropologists attempt the difficult task of estimating past human population sizes. Archaeologists make estimates based on site size, number of houses, number of graves, total area of house floor at a site, or assumed amount of food available or consumed (see the section "Ethnography and Archaeology" later in this chapter). The problems with archaeological estimates include the fact that complete sites are rarely excavated, so that the total number of structures is usually unknown. Also, the sites of hunter-gatherers in the past often do not reveal living structures at all. In addition, it is often impossible to know how many structures were occupied at the same moment in time. The number of individuals per structure is highly variable and using an average value per household may seriously over- or underestimate the total for the settlement. Thus, although archaeologists often make estimates of site populations, it is understood that these are only approximations.

Biological anthropologists and bioarchaeologists use biological information from human skeletal remains in graves and cemeteries to describe the major characteristics of a population. For example, the human skeleton can provide important information on both the sex and the age of the person at the time of death (see Chapter 14, "Bioarchaeology"). Estimates of population size, however, are difficult using burial evidence because burial populations are not directly representative of the living population. Burial populations contain more individuals from younger and older age groups, who are more susceptible to death. The bioarchaeologists must project from the death population to the living population using what are called model life tables. Again, such projections are only approximations.

Some years ago, archaeologist Bruce Trigger of McGill University made an estimate of human population for the region of Lower Nubia (southern Egypt and northern Sudan) along the Nile River between 3500 BC and AD 1500, a period of almost 5000 years. Trigger focused on the cemeteries in this region. He assumed that each village had one burial ground and that everyone from the village was buried there. The number of graves in many of these cemeteries was known. Trigger noted that the smaller cemeteries with just a few tens of burials did not change in size over time. There was a clear increase in the larger cemeteries over time, however, with the earlier larger cemeteries containing 100–200 graves and the later larger cemeteries having several thousand burials. Trigger developed a formula to predict living population from the size of the cemetery and the number of modern inhabitants. He then calculated the population for thirteen time periods between 3500 BC and AD 1500. Trigger's estimates show the population growing from ca. 2000 to almost 60,000 people during the Late Nubian period.

Trigger's study is summarized graphically in Fig. 4.4. The chronology and major archaeological cultures are indicated at the top of the diagram. Population estimates for these periods are shown, along with the height of the Nile flood, agricultural productivity, and episodes of conflict. There is an apparent break in the occupation of Lower Nubia during the Napatan period, indicated by an absence of archaeological evidence.

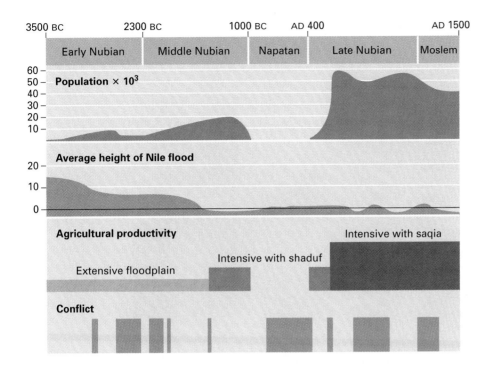

Fig. 4.4 Trigger's estimates for population, height of the Nile, agricultural productivity, and conflict in Lower Nubia between 3500 BC and AD 1500.

While the graph is a composite of estimates, there are some clear patterns revealed. Population grows rather steadily before the Napatan period to approximately 20,000 people and then explodes following the Napatan to its maximum before today of almost 60,000. Flood heights of the Nile tend to stabilize after 1500 BC, so that agriculture becomes more predictable. At the same time, intensive methods of agriculture are introduced, involving first the **shaduf** (a manual water hoist) and later the **saqia** (oxen-powered water wheel). Agricultural productivity increases dramatically with each innovation. The incidence and intensity of conflict is also a factor in population in Lower Nubia. It is clear from the graph that long-term warfare and unstable political situations result in a reduction in human population.

Estimates of such vital statistics as birth and death rates of past populations are also made from burial populations. Birth and death rates (fertility and mortality) in a population are determined from the numbers of individuals in different age classes in the burial population. An example from the 5500-year-old Black Earth site in southern Illinois is described below to illustrate these concepts.

 EXAMPLE ~~~~~~

THE BLACK EARTH SITE

The expansion of open-pit coal mining in southern Illinois in the 1970s led to archaeological survey and excavation and the rescue of an important early site dating from 4500 to 3000 BC (Fig. 4.5). The name for the site, Black Earth, comes from the distinct black sediments—accumulations of trash, waste materials, and charcoal and ash from thousands of campfires—that stand out against the natural yellow-brown soils of the area. It is an enormous site, more than a city block in size, and the archaeological materials are found up to 1.5 m (5 ft) beneath the ground.

The Black Earth site sits along a low ridge, next to a series of shallow lakes and swamps and close to a range of hills. The occupants used the river, lakes, and swamps

Black Earth

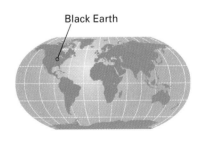

~~~~~~

shaduf A manual water hoist used for irrigation in ancient Egypt.

saqia An oxen-powered water wheel used for irrigation in ancient Egypt.

Fig. 4.5 Excavations at the Black Earth site in the 1970s, exposing pits and graves.

for aquatic resources and exploited the uplands behind the settlement as well. Preserved plant and animal remains document the diet of the inhabitants.

The primary food resources included turtles and fish, deer, turkey, and nuts, especially from the hickory tree. These nuts were available in autumn and could easily be stored and used throughout the winter for food. Seeds from hackberry, wild grape, persimmon, bedstraw, and wild bean were also common. The rich resources of the area and the availability of food throughout the year permitted permanent settlement at the Black Earth site.

In addition to the settlement remains, there was a substantial cemetery at the Black Earth site (Fig. 4.6). The contents of the graves provided important evidence of tools, as well as ornamental and ceremonial items (Table 4.2). Materials placed in the graves were likely the property of the deceased or were placed with the dead as a kind of offering. These objects were found intact at the burial sites, unlike most everyday objects, which were generally discarded when they were broken or no longer useful.

Only about 25% of the individuals were buried with objects in their graves. The distribution of grave goods at the site is of interest to archaeologists because it provides clues to status and activities (Table 4.3). Male graves contained the majority of the grave goods of all types and most of the ornamental and ceremonial items. Women received more utilitarian items than anything else. Subadults (juvenile individuals less than 18 years of age) received the fewest grave goods of any type.

Males were generally buried with equipment to obtain food or other resources, while females were buried with tools to process or prepare these raw materials.

Fig. 4.6 Burial 102 at the Black Earth site with a group of grave goods at the right shoulder.

Women were buried with scraping tools, bone awls, and needles. Only males were buried with ornamental objects, such as bone pins and decorated bones, along with spear heads, worked stone drills and axes, and small animal bones. A "medicine bundle" was placed near the head of a 43-year-old male. This cluster contained forty-five objects, including eagle talons, part of a bear paw, a miniature axe, pieces of slate, red ochre, and a dog's tooth. One perforated disk of marine shell, probably from the Atlantic Ocean or the Gulf of Mexico, was found around the neck of a buried infant. Copper from the Great Lakes area was found with an adult male at the Black Earth site. A copper wedge had been placed at the top of the neck of the skeleton, perhaps as a substitute for the missing skull of this particular individual.

The evidence from the burial population provided substantial information on the demography of the site occupants. At least 154 burials were found. The investigators estimate that originally there may have been more than 500 graves in total from both excavated and unexcavated areas.

Of the 154 burials from the Black Earth site, age could be determined for only 124 individuals and sex for 87 skeletons. The reasons for this are that the sex of juvenile individuals is difficult to determine, and that some of the skeletal material was so fragmentary that information about the individual's age was lost. The number and percentage of individuals in age and sex categories are shown in Table 4.4 and 4.5. Age categories of infant (0–3 years of age), child (3–12), adolescent (12–18), young adult (18–35), middle-age adult (35–50), and old adult (50+ years of age) are those that can be distinguished using human skeletal remains. Infants accounted for 23% of the burials.

Males had a shorter lifespan than females. They also account for 57% of all the identified burials, slightly outnumbering females in the cemetery by 50 to 37, a ratio of 1.4 to 1. This ratio suggests that males were more likely to be buried than females since there were likely almost equal numbers of both sexes. Height of sexes was also determined. Adult males averaged 1.7 m (5 ft 6 in) in height, while females were 1.6 m (5 ft 2 in) tall. The graphic distribution of burials in the population by age and sex is shown in Fig. 4.7. The percent of males and females in each age group from 15 to 60 provides

TABLE 4.2 Grave goods buried with individuals at the Black Earth site.

Function	Adult male	Adult female	Child
Utilitarian	Mussel shell	Mussel shell	Mussel shell
	Bone awl	Bone awl	Utilized flake
	Worked antler	Worked antler	Ground stone
	Unworked deer bone	Unworked deer bone	
	Projectile point	Bone needle	
	Chert core	Hafted scraper	
	Drill	Chert biface	
	Scraper		
	Utilized flake		
	Axe fragment		
Ornamental	Shell pendant	Shell pendant	Shell pendant
	Bone pin		Shell bead
	Anculosa-shell bead		Mussel-shell bead
	Antler bead		Circular shell disk
	Plummet		Crinoid-stem bead
	Bar gorget		
Ceremonial	Decorated bone	Worked turtle shell	Turtle shell cup
	Animal bone (not deer)	Animal bone (bird)	Red ochre
	Elk antler cup	Red ochre	Water-worn pebble
	Red ochre		Fluorspar crystal
	Fossil		
	Fluorspar crystal		
	Worked shale		
	Worked stone		
	Hematite		
	Water-worn pebble		
	Banded slate		
	Miniature grooved axe		

TABLE 4.3 The number and percentage of types of grave goods in utilitarian, ornamental, and ceremonial categories by sex and age from the Black Earth site. Males and females are adults.

Sex/age	Utilitarian		Ornamental		Ceremonial		Total grave goods	
	No.	%	No.	%	No.	%	No.	%
Male	13	26	6	12	9	18	17	34
Female	10	27	2	5	1	3	10	27
Juvenile	2	6	3	12	3	10	7	23

a picture of the age and sex distribution in the population. The information shows that females clearly live longer than males. The two oldest members of the burial population were female.

Mortality is an indicator of how human groups interact with their environment. A graph of the life expectancy of the population from the Black Earth site indicates

TABLE 4.4 Number and percentage of human burials by age class from the Black Earth site.		
Age	Number	Percent
Infant (0–3 years)	26	23
Child (3–12 years)	3	2
Adolescent (12–18 years)	9	7
Young Adult (18–35 years)	36	29
Middle-Age Adult (35–50 years)	4	36
Old Adult (50+ years)	3	2
Adult?	3	2
TOTAL	124	99

TABLE 4.5 Number and percentage of human burials by sex from the Black Earth site.		
Sex	Number	Percent
Male	50	57
Female	37	43
TOTAL	87	100

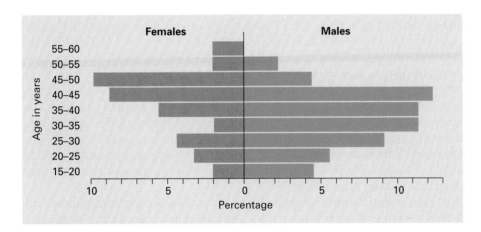

Fig. 4.7 The demographic distribution of burials in the population by age and sex from the Black Earth site, Illinois.

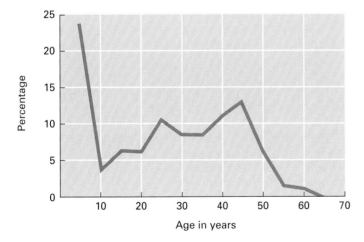

Fig. 4.8 Survivor curve for the burial population from the Black Earth site.

that infant mortality was very high (Fig. 4.8). Of all the individuals who died before age 18, two-thirds died in the first year of life. Almost 25% of the burial population died before the age of 5. Overall life expectancy from birth was 23.9 years. Male life expectancy after childhood was only 32 years; for females, 38 years. The oldest individual in the group was almost 60 years of age. Male deaths increase slightly with age and peak between 40–45 years of age. Female deaths show two peaks, one at 20–25 and another at 40–50. The younger peak may be related in part to deaths during childbirth.

Technology

Technology is an interface between human society and the environment. It is the means by which people interact directly with their natural environment. Technology includes the tools, facilities, and knowledge used to obtain or create resources for human existence. It is also the aspect of past culture that is most readily observed in archaeological data. The fragments of the tools and architecture that people used in the past, made of durable materials such as stone, ceramic, and metal, are the most common archaeological remains.

Changes in technology over time provide clear indicators of the development of material culture as well as diagnostic information about the age of various materials. For example, it is possible to trace dramatic changes in the flint points for spears and arrows in the Stone Age of southern Scandinavia from approximately 12,500 to 3500 BC from larger-stemmed and pointed forms to smaller, geometric shapes with wider leading edges. Experiments involving firing these points into animal corpses document the increasing effectiveness of the points over time. Smaller, more symmetric points result in smoother and more accurate arrow flights. Wider leading edges do more internal damage to the animal than the sharp points that tend to pass directly through the body. Fig. 4.9 shows the evolution of the hammer from the early stone forms to more recent metal tools in a 1922 depiction. The last step in the sequence is a huge steam-driven hammer designed by James Naisymth in 1842.

New materials and technologies can appear in a region through invention, diffusion, or migration. **Invention** is the creation or development of new ideas or techniques for solving problems. **Diffusion**, on the other hand, involves borrowing from other areas and results in the spread of new ideas or techniques from one group to another. **Migration** is a specific kind of diffusion that involves for-

Fig. 4.9 The evolutionary history of the hammer from simple pounding stones to James Naismyth's 1842 steam hammer.

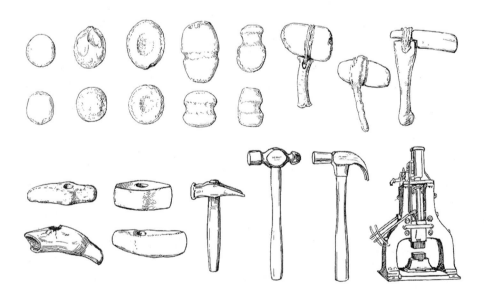

invention   The creation or development of new ideas or techniques for solving problems.

diffusion   The spread of new ideas or materials from one group to another.

migration   Movement of new people into an area.

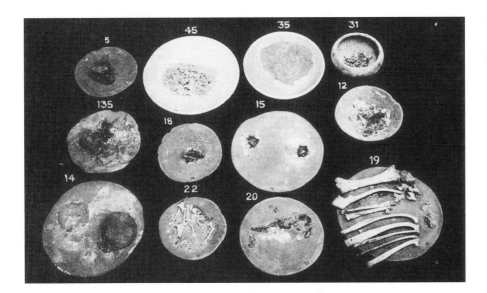

Fig. 4.10 The food offerings in the tomb of an Egyptian noblewoman from ca. 2700 BC. The plates contain bread, berries, kidneys, ribs of beef, quail, pigeon, fish, fruit, and cakes.

eign people bringing new ideas and/or materials to an area. One of the challenges of archaeology is to determine which of these factors was responsible for the appearance of new things.

Economy

Economy concerns how people obtain foods, material, and goods to sustain their lives. One major aspect of prehistoric economy is subsistence. **Subsistence** refers to the activities and materials that people use to feed themselves. Archaeologists use the term *subsistence pattern* to describe the plants and animals that prehistoric people ate, the activities required to obtain those foods, and the procurement and preparation techniques and implements used to turn those plants and animals into food.

The term *hunting and gathering* describes one such pattern in which wild animals are hunted and wild plants are gathered for subsistence. The terms *hunter-gatherer* and *forager* are used to designate the people who practice this pattern. An example of a hunting and gathering society comes from the Jomon culture of Japan, described in the example below. Such societies were generally smaller, less sedentary, and more egalitarian than farming groups. These issues are discussed in more detail in a subsequent section on organization.

Agriculture is another major form of subsistence pattern, which involves the herding of domesticated animals and/or the cultivation of domesticated plants. As opposed to the forager, who collects food from the wild, the farmer produces food from domesticated species and cultivated land. The initial domestication of plants and animals took place in several different areas of the world between 10,000 and 4000 years ago. The basic distinction between wild and domestic foods provides one of the major divisions in human prehistory, between the hunter-gatherers of the Paleolithic and the farmers of the Neolithic. Fig. 4.10 shows the preserved remains of a meal buried with an Egyptian noblewoman from the second dynasty, about 2700 BC. The plates contain servings of a variety of meats and vegetables that were probably part of the diet of elite individuals in ancient Egypt. The menu contains both wild and domestic foods, indicating that wild foods remained an important part of the human diet well after the development of agriculture.

"We tried hunting and we tried gathering, but now we usually eat out."

subsistence   The activities and materials that people use to obtain food.

hunter-gatherers   People who obtain their food from wild plants and animals, not domesticated species.

foragers   Nonfarmers; groups who subsist by hunting, collecting, fishing, and the like without domesticated plants or animals.

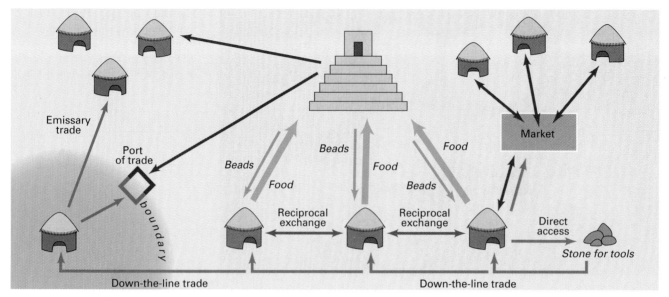

Fig. 4.11 A schematic depiction of different types of exchange and trade within society. The diagram shows several households and a palace. Distinctions between reciprocity and redistribution are indicated by the width of lines showing exchange. Down-the-line trade is a process that moves specific goods farther from their source in a sequence of trades. Redistribution involves the movement of food or goods to a central place from which these materials are rationed or provided to part of the population. The green houses represent another society. Trade involves the movement of goods in exchange for value. Societies trade with one another directly, through ports of trade (a common ground) or emissary trade (traveling merchants or foreign residence). A market is a place where trade and exchange take place involving barter or a common currency.

exchange   Transfer of material or information among individuals or groups.

reciprocity   The *exchange* of items of roughly equal value.

redistribution   The movement of goods to a central place from which they are rationed or portioned out to members of society.

trade   Economic transactions between individuals or groups involving bartering, buying, or selling.

Exchange is another important aspect of economy. One way to study interaction within and between societies is to look at the distribution of items of exchange. Individuals and groups exchange materials and ideas. When artifacts such as stone axes, obsidian knives, metal spear points, or certain kinds of food pass from person to person, or group to group, archaeologists speak of "exchange."

Three kinds of exchange can be distinguished: reciprocity, redistribution, and trade (Fig. 4.11). **Reciprocity** involves the exchange of items of roughly equal value. Barter is a form of reciprocal exchange. Reciprocity or reciprocal exchange sometimes takes the form of gift giving, where objects of value are given to build alliances and friendship or to create debts. **Redistribution** involves the movement of goods to a central place from where they are rationed or portioned out to select members of society. Such a system of redistribution might be used to support relatives, an army, or priests, or craftsmen or the pyramid builders of ancient Egypt, for example. The social security system in the United States is an example of redistribution in the economy today.

Economic transactions known as **trade** involve bartering, buying, or selling goods. Trade usually takes place in some sort of market economy, perhaps using a monetary standard. A market is a place where trade and exchange take place using barter or a common currency. Trade is common in our own economic system today when objects are bought and sold for the purpose of making a profit. This level of exchange often involves a complex society with professional artisans, regular supplies of raw material, extensive transportation systems, protection of markets and traders against pirates, and enough customers to make the business worthwhile.

Archaeologists frequently examine exchange and trade through the study of "exotic materials." The presence of objects and materials that are not available or locally produced in an area provides immediate evidence of connections and interaction. Of great use in such investigations are artifacts or materials that come from a known location. There are many cases of such movement in exotic materials, often in the form of rare stones or minerals. There were no natural sources of turquoise in ancient Mexico, for example, but this beautiful blue-green stone was imported from Arizona and used in the costumes and jewelry of the elite in Aztec Mexico.

The economic activities of prehistoric peoples were organized in different ways. A fundamental mechanism for the efficient organization of tasks is a **division of labor**. Separate groups or segments of society perform different activities as part of an efficient organization of the economic process. A basic example is seen in many groups of hunter-gatherers, where the division of labor is often by sex and production is at the level of the individual. Males are primarily hunters, and females are primarily gatherers. Both groups contribute food to the subsistence of the society. In agricultural societies, households are an important unit of production for food and other essential materials. Economies become increasingly specialized through time, with larger groups or entire communities involved in the production of specific items. The emergence of specialist groups of producers such as potters, metalsmiths, and bead makers marks advanced agricultural societies. The organization of production can assume even more formal structures, such as guilds or unions, in more complex civilizations.

 EXAKMPLE ⟿⟿⟿⟿⟿⟿⟿⟿⟿⟿⟿⟿⟿⟿⟿⟿

JOMON JAPAN

The Jomon (*JOE-moan*) period in Japan, dating from 10,000 to 300 BC, is a fascinating time, known for elaborate and well-developed technology. Almost 50,000 sites have been discovered from this period. Among the artifacts found at the sites were clay vessels. Pottery containers were invented very early in Japan, probably before 10,000 years ago. These fired clay vessels occur often at Jomon sites, and their forms became increasingly elaborate over time. The word *jomon* means **cord-marking**, referring to the kind of decoration applied to the pottery before firing: cord-wrapped sticks pressed into the wet clay to create a design.

Jomon villages varied greatly in size and often were occupied for a long time—several hundred years or more, in some cases. The inland settlements generally contained 4–8 pithouses, although more than 50 structures from a single site have been identified. **Pithouses** were substantial circular or rectangular structures built of large support posts, containing elaborate, stone-lined hearths. Villages were often arranged in a horseshoe shape and may have been divided into two groups of residential units, one on either side of the horseshoe. Communal structures for various purposes were built around the periphery of the village, and burials occurred individually near houses or in the communal structures.

Subsistence was based primarily on wild resources, although some cultivated plants may have been included in the diet. More than 180 species of plant foods have been identified from Jomon settlements, including fleshy fruits such as grapes, blackberries, and elderberries, aquatic plants with edible seeds, and tubers. Nuts apparently played a major role in subsistence because the shells of walnuts, chestnuts, acorns, and buckeyes occur at many sites. In the later Jomon, root crops, such as taro, yams, and arrowroot, may have been under cultivation in western Japan, along with some cereals, such as buckwheat and barley. Chipped stone hoes were common at sites from this time. Rice, however, was apparently not cultivated in significant quantities until toward the end of the Jomon period.

The importance of hunting is indicated by the abundance of arrowheads at many Jomon sites. Inland hunting focused largely on deer and boars, but bears, antelopes, monkeys, hares, martens, and other small mammals were also taken. Marine foods and coastal settlements predominated in eastern Japan, particularly after 4000 BC. Fishing was important at sites on the rivers, estuaries, and the ocean. Salmon and other freshwater fish were caught in the rivers. Bones from such deepwater species as tuna and shark were also found in the deposits. Fishing equipment included net floats of bark and pumice, net weights, fishhooks, harpoons, and dugout canoes. Over thirty different species of shellfish have been reported.

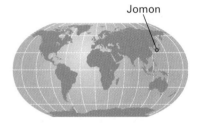

www.mhhe.com/pricearch1

For a Web-based activity on ancient Japan, please see the Internet exercises on your online learning center.

division of labor   Organization of tasks involving different groups doing different activities for the sake of efficiency.

cord-marking   A distinctive decoration on *pottery* produced by pressing a cord-wrapped stick into the soft *clay* of a pot before firing.

pithouse   A dwelling constructed over a hole in the ground, semisubterranean structure; a structure built on a semisubterranean foundation.

Fig. 4.12 A schematic depiction of human subsistence activities in the Jomon culture of Japan at ca. 3000 BC. The diagram shows the kinds and quantities of foods that were used during the course of the year by coastal Jomon hunter-gatherers. The width of the area for different food-stuffs inside the circles indicates their contribution. Winter is shown at the top of the circle and the seasons move counterclockwise to spring, summer, and autumn. The diagram shows large-game hunting as a primary subsistence activity in the winter, with sea mammal hunting and fishing providing a major part of the diet in the summer. Plants contributed substantially to the diet in the fall and spring.

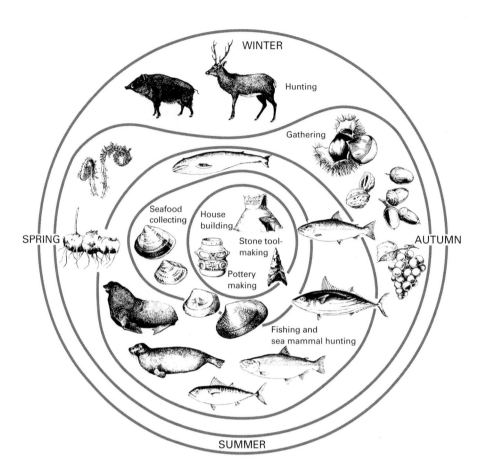

kinship Relationships between individual members in society based on family ties.

lineages Genealogies, lines of descent that are used to extend relationships and determine membership in a group; the relationship between individual members in society on the basis of their family ties.

moieties Organizational division of some societies into two large, kin-related groups; moieties are composed of clans.

sodalities Groups or clubs within society whose members come from different *lineages* and share common interests or goals.

Organization

Organization refers to the roles and relationships in society and concerns inter-action between women and men and among different segments of society, such as families, age classes, labor units, or ethnic groups. Organization structures many aspects of society, including social interaction, marriage, economic activity, and political relationships. Kinship and marriage systems, lineage, sodality, rank, and class are important aspects of social organization and means for structuring social relationships.

Kinship defines the relationship between individual members in society based on family ties. *Grandmother, brother, uncle,* and *niece* are some terms that re-late us to other people through kinship. Marriage systems tie unrelated individu-als together through sanctified kinship, and rules for these relationships are carefully delineated by society. Families and households are the fundamental units of human society. **Lineages** are genealogies, lines of descent that extend re-lationships and determine membership in a group. A lineage is composed of liv-ing and ancestral generations of related families. Lineages provide a means for calculating one's relationships through lines of ancestry from one generation to the next. Members of the same lineage often work together as a corporate group. Several lineages together make up a clan, a larger descent group. In some cases, clans are divided among two branches, or **moieties**—dual-descent organizations (Fig. 4.13).

A lineage is a descent group whose members trace their heritage from a common, often mythical, founder ancestor (Fig. 4.14). **Sodalities** are groups or clubs within society whose members share common interests or goals. Member-

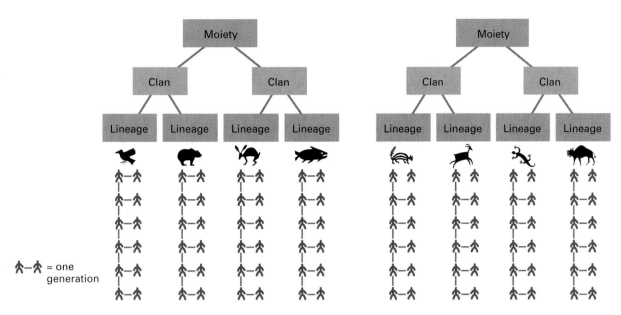

Fig. 4.13 A schematic representation of lineages, clans, and moieties in the organization of a human society. Lineages are lines of descent calculated through generations, often from a common mythical ancestor. Four lineages of descent from mythical figures are suggested in this schematic view. Each stick figure represents a generation.

Fig. 4.14 The hierarchical structure of Maya society, with the ruler at the top, nobles, priests, and warriors in positions of high status, and farmers and slaves at the base of the pyramid.

ship is usually determined by sex and/or age. These groups, such as dance organizations, warrior societies, or guilds, often include members from different lineages. Lineages—lines of descent—integrate societies vertically across generations; sodalities integrate societies horizontally, crosscutting generations.

Many societies of hunter-gatherers are described as egalitarian, with more or less equal relations between the members of the group. Agricultural societies are usually larger and often distinguish separate groups within society defined by inherited status differences based on rank or class. **Rank** refers to inherited positions in descent groups; everyone is ranked in terms of status relative to all other people. The firstborn of the highest ranked group is the highest position in such a

rank Inherited positions in societies based on birth order and ancestry.

society. In ranked societies, each individual has a unique place in the order of relationships. **Class** societies, on the other hand, are hierarchically structured by distinctions between groups, or classes, of people that define levels, or strata, in society. The term *stratified* is also used to describe such organization. Class is inherited and encompasses large groups of individuals. Class can determine one's job, location of residence, marriage opportunities, and financial status. The caste system of India was an example of a rigidly stratified class system. In modern capitalist societies, upper, middle, and lower classes describe the structure.

One of the most significant changes in human organization was the shift from egalitarian to hierarchical structures following the origins of agriculture. Hierarchical organizations have one or more levels of control above the majority of the people in the society. Higher status characterizes these elite and privileged groups that control much of the wealth, power, and decision making in society. It is often reflected archaeologically in more elaborate and valued material possessions. In such a hierarchy, detailed information and requests flow from the base of the hierarchy upward, and responses and commands flow from the top down.

Government operates in a hierarchical manner as well, from local representatives to municipal government, state government, and federal government. The geographic sphere of control and decision making varies with the level in the hierarchy. So, for example, the municipal government repairs local roads, and the federal government builds an interstate system. In a general sense, political organization is a reflection of the increasing complexity that is witnessed in human society through time. As societies became larger, organizational changes took place that resulted in hierarchical levels, closer integration, and more linear decision making.

One of the more common trends in the organization of past societies is an increase in complexity over time. **Complexity** refers to increasing numbers of units in society and more integration between those units. More units are a result of growth and social, economic, and ideological specialization. Such differentiation may be reflected in the distinctions between villages, towns, and cities that began to appear with chiefdoms and states. More integration is a result of hierarchical organization and the emergence of ranked or stratified groups within society, where power and decision making are in the hands of a few.

There are several ways to describe or characterize such hierarchies in human society. One of the most common uses the terms *bands, tribes, chiefdoms,* and *states* to distinguish four different levels of political organization. **Bands** and tribes describe relatively small-scale societies of hunter-gatherers or farmers where relationships are generally egalitarian and decision making is consensual. Power and property are distributed among all the members of the population. Status is earned through achievements and is ephemeral, held only by the individual who gained it and not passed to offspring. **Tribes** are larger and more sedentary than bands in general and are usually involved in subsistence agriculture.

Chiefdoms and **states** are larger, often territorial societies where relationships are defined by inequality. Organization in these societies is hierarchical, with a permanent political structure. Agriculture is usually intensive, and relations with other societies often conflictual. Status is hereditary and assigned by birth order (rank) in chiefdoms or by class affiliation (stratification) in states, as in the stratified society of the ancient Maya (Fig. 4.14). Chiefdoms and states are also normally associated with monumental architecture in the form of massive earthworks and constructions like pyramids, ziggurats, platforms, and palaces. Towns and cities are often found in chiefdoms and states, respectively. States are also territorial and can be distinguished from chiefdoms by greater population, size, complexity, and a permanent bureaucracy. Robert Carneiro of the American Museum of Natural History defined a state as an autonomous political unit with various communities within its territory, having a centralized government with the power to collect taxes, draft men for work or war, and decree and enforce laws.

class Distinctions between groups of people that define levels, or strata, in society.

complexity Organization of society involving more units in society and more integration between those units.

bands Small-scale societies of *hunter-gatherers* where relationships are generally egalitarian and decision making is consensual.

tribes Small-scale societies of farmers where relationships are generally egalitarian and decision making is consensual.

chiefdom A large, kinship-based political unit of several communities where status is hereditary and assigned by birth order *(rank)*.

state A large-scale, autonomous, and territorial political unit and class society having a centralized government with the power to collect taxes, draft men for work or war, and decree and enforce laws.

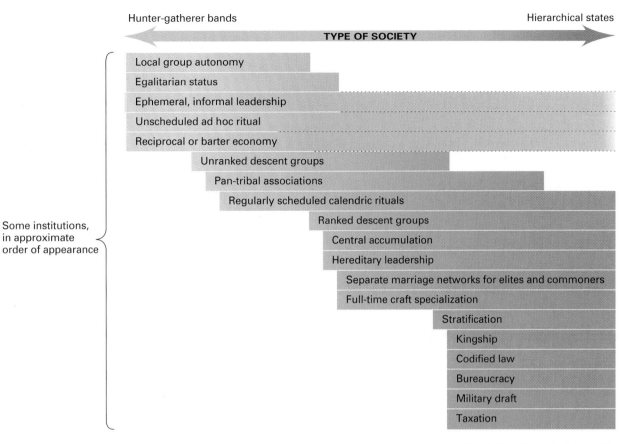

Hunter-gatherer bands   Hierarchical states

TYPE OF SOCIETY

Some institutions, in approximate order of appearance:

- Local group autonomy
- Egalitarian status
- Ephemeral, informal leadership
- Unscheduled ad hoc ritual
- Reciprocal or barter economy
- Unranked descent groups
- Pan-tribal associations
- Regularly scheduled calendric rituals
- Ranked descent groups
- Central accumulation
- Hereditary leadership
- Separate marriage networks for elites and commoners
- Full-time craft specialization
- Stratification
- Kingship
- Codified law
- Bureaucracy
- Military draft
- Taxation

Fig. 4.15 Characteristics of human societies in the evolution from hunter-gatherers to states.

Not all archaeologists find the band-tribe-chiefdom-state model to be useful, but most would recognize the substantial changes that take place as societies become larger and more complex. Some of the changes in social, economic, and political organization from hunter-gatherers to states are summarized in Fig. 4.15. The organization of society moves from egalitarian relationships and ephemeral leadership to ranked, then stratified, hierarchies and hereditary rulers. Reciprocal economies are transformed into elaborate trade systems with craft specialization and markets. Administrative, military, and ritual activities are formalized into permanent segments of society.

Ideology

Ideology is the means by which people structure their ideas about the universe, their own place in that universe, and their relationships with one another and with other things and beings around them. Ideology is the way that a people view and understand their world, and it affects much of what people do. Ideology is reflected in the clothes we wear, the food we eat, and the places in which we live. It encompasses the norms, values, and beliefs held by a society.

The ideology of a society is often expressed in ceremony and pageant surrounding important rites of passage through life: birth, adulthood, weddings, and death. It is usually embodied in specialists who maintain ritual knowledge and direct the ceremonies and activities that keep such ideology active and pertinent. In egalitarian societies, such individuals are often known as **shamans**—specialists in ritual and healing, and seers of the future. In hierarchical societies, such specialists are seen in powerful groups, such as cults, sects, priesthoods, or formalized **religions**.

shamans Specialists in ritual and healing, seers of the future in *hunter-gatherer* and *subsistence* farming societies.

religion Formalized *ritual*, a belief system that promotes *cosmology*, *ideology*, morals, and values in human society.

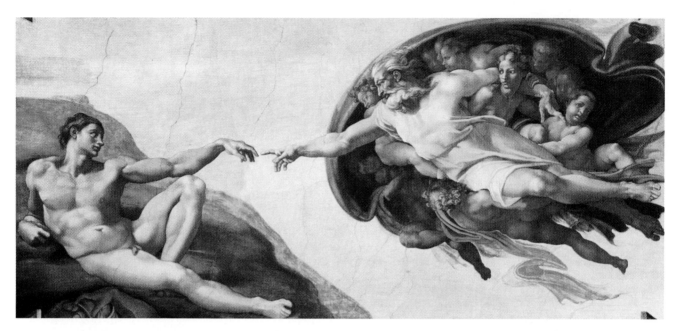

Fig. 4.16 The ceiling of the Sistine Chapel in the Vatican, painted by Michelangelo, depicts some major elements of the Christian origin myth. Adam, the first man, on the left, is given life by the touch of God.

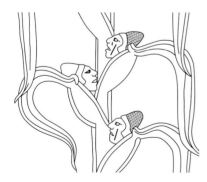

Fig. 4.17 A depiction of ears of corn with human heads in a mural from highland Mexico ca. AD 600, emphasizing the belief that maize (corn) was the source and staple of humanity. This symbolism expresses an integrated view of environment, subsistence, and belief.

The chief aspects of ideology include cosmology, iconography, ritual, and religion. Ideology is a reflection of **cosmology**—explanations of the origins of the universe, of life, and of society. Most societies have distinctive cosmologies—origin myths—that account for their beginnings. Roman cosmology, for example, invoked the twins Romulus and Remus, legendary beings raised by a she-wolf, as the founders of Rome. Genesis and the story of Adam provide the origin myth for the Christian religion (Fig. 4.16). Most origin myths have common features—creation, floods, doomsdays, and important protagonists.

Iconography concerns the pictorial representations of beliefs, ideas, and concepts. Belief systems have powerful symbols to reiterate their meaning, and ritual sanctifies and validates that message. Iconography involves symbols, depictions, and designs that are expressions of ideology. Christian crosses, Jewish stars, and Islamic crescents are powerful icons of ideological concepts. These symbols convey enormous meaning and incite powerful responses in both believers and nonbelievers. School mascots, corporate logos, flags, and certain faces incorporate a wide range of themes and ideas related to specific social or political units and their ideological position. Symbols in the prehistoric world took many forms as well, including the decoration of place, artifact, and person.

Symbols are often expressed in artwork that is created for various reasons, including aesthetic, political, and ritual. The art in archaeology occurs in a variety of media—cave walls, bark, bone, antler, stone, ceramic, feathers, cloth, and many other materials. Human and animal forms dominate the motifs of most Stone Age depictions, while more schematic and abstract designs are found in later, complex societies. Fig. 4.17 depicts aspects of the origin myth of the peoples of highland Mexico 1400 years ago.

Though much of prehistoric art had psychological and ideological roots, ideology is particularly obvious in the art of later civilizations, often in the guise of propaganda. Distinctive motifs, like modern corporate icons, can be found everywhere the power of a particular political entity extends. This pattern can be seen in the double crown of the Egyptian pharaoh, the were-jaguar motif of the Olmec of Mexico, and many other contexts.

Ritual is a ubiquitous practice in human society and a manifestation of ideology. It usually involves symbolic, prescribed, and structured behaviors that are often repetitive in nature. Aspects of ritual behavior include animism, dance, div-

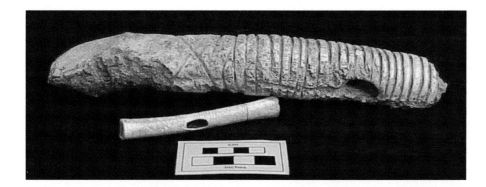

Fig. 4.18 A bone rasp and whistle, music instruments from the Upper Mississippi Valley used in dance, ceremony, and ritual.

Fig. 4.19 The colossal heads of the Olmec culture of Mexico are icons of gods or rulers dating from approximately 900 BC.

ination, magic, music, mythology, rites of passage, sorcery and witchcraft, shamans and priests, and taboos and totems. The practice of ritual and ceremony produces both information and artifacts (Figs. 4.18 and 4.19). Artifacts associated with various aspects of ritual behavior sometimes show up in the archaeological record, and the term *ritual* is sometimes used to describe material remains that are not readily understood in terms of technology, organization, or economy.

Ritual is often contrasted with the secular and practical. This distinction may well be a recent, not a prehistoric, reality. The separation of church and state is a phenomenon of the Age of Enlightenment that began in Europe in the eighteenth century. Ritual is a way of dealing with the unknown, but the consequences

cosmology   Explanations of the origins of the universe, of life, and of society.

iconography   The pictorial representations of beliefs, ideas, symbols, and concepts.

symbol   Depiction or design which expresses larger concept, often ideological.

rituals   Symbolic, prescribed, and structured behaviors that are often repetitive in nature and related to belief systems.

Ritual in Ancient Oaxaca

Ideology can be difficult to grasp in archaeology. It is hard to determine whether certain places or artifacts were important for practical or ideological reasons, whether used for daily life or ritual. It is also the case that such distinctions may not have been made in the prehistoric world. In some special circumstances, however, it is possible to investigate ritual behavior. An intriguing study comes from ancient **Mesoamerica**, an anthropological term for the area of Mexico, Guatemala, Belize, and parts of Honduras and Salvador where several early civilizations, including the Aztec and Maya, emerged.

Sedentary village life began around 1800 BC in Mesoamerica. Society changed very rapidly after that as long-distance exchange, status differentiation, and monumental construction began to appear in the Olmec (*ol-MECK*) culture on the Gulf Coast of Mexico. Kent Flannery and Joyce Marcus of the University of Michigan conducted extensive investigations of this time period in the Valley of Oaxaca (*wah-HOCK-uh*) in the southern highlands of Mexico. By 1300 BC, there were at least a dozen small villages of 8–10 nuclear families living in small, thatched-roof houses in the valley. Each house was separated from its neighbors by 30–40 m (100–125 ft) and had its own yard, work areas, storage pits, and garbage dumps. The largest of these was San Jose Mogoté (*SAN hoe-ZAY moe-go-TAY*), with 20–30 households and the only one with a distinctive public building, located in the center of the village.

Flannery and Marcus found a number of unusual artifacts at San Jose Mogoté. They used information on the distribution of these items within the village to interpret the organization of ritual at the individual, household, and community levels (Fig. 4.20). Trumpets made of conch shell from the seacoast at least 200 km (120 mi) distant were found in the public building. Fragments of conch shell—waste material from making the trumpets—showed up in one of the houses in the village where a craftsman must have lived. A variety of musical instruments, including deer scapula rasps, antler drumsticks, and turtle shell drums, have been found both at the public building and in the storage pits of the houses. The turtle shell is from the coast, and the deer bone and antler are local.

Other items were also imported, perhaps as part of costumes for ritual dances and ceremony. Figurines of masked dancers support this suggestion. Crocodile jaws and macaw feathers from jungle areas in the coastal lowlands were used as personal decoration. Local items apparently used in costumes included armadillo shell and clay masks.

Ceremonial activities at San Jose Mogoté may have included self-mutilation and sacrifice. The region is a dry one and rainfall for the crops is unreliable. Even today the inhabitants of the area worry a great deal about the weather and hold ceremonies to invite the rain. The Spanish conquistadores in the sixteenth century reported that the native inhabitants of this area prayed to the gods, asking for more rain. They sacrificed drops of their own blood—drawn from tongues, ears, or sex organs—with a pointed object. Sharp spines from marine stingrays and fish have been found in the houses and public areas of San Jose Mogoté, probably for similar bloodletting ceremonies. People sometimes also sacrificed animals and other humans. Flannery and Marcus' investigations at San Jose Mogoté have provided extraordinary insight on the nature and organization of ceremonial activities in ancient Mexico.

Ritual: All-purpose explanation used where nothing else comes to mind.
—Paul Bahn, archaeologist

Mesoamerica Anthropological term for the area of Mexico, Guatemala, Belize, and parts of Honduras and El Salvador where several early civilizations, including the Aztec and Maya, emerged.

are sometimes more tangible. The beginnings of written language in China, for example, were associated with a ritual practice for predicting the future, known as scapulamancy. Different symbols were drawn on the thin shoulder blade bone (scapula) from a deer, sheep, or ox. The scapula was then placed over a fire and heated slowly until it charred and cracked. The patterns of charring and cracks on the symbols were then read as an omen or message about the future. This practice, in fact, gave rise to writing, a practical and powerful means of communication.

As used in archaeology, the term *ritual* encompasses various aspects of past behavior, including religion, ceremony, and belief. Religion is a formalized framework of belief and behavior that helps humans cope with the unknown—that is, deal with the uncertainties and fears of life on earth. Anthropologist Roy Rappaport described religion as having three components: sacred propositions, ritual, and religious experience. The first of these, sacred propositions, are society's most powerful beliefs, and they are held by the faithful. These propositions provide the basis for ritual practices. Rituals can then create religious experiences, which in turn reiterate belief in sacred propositions.

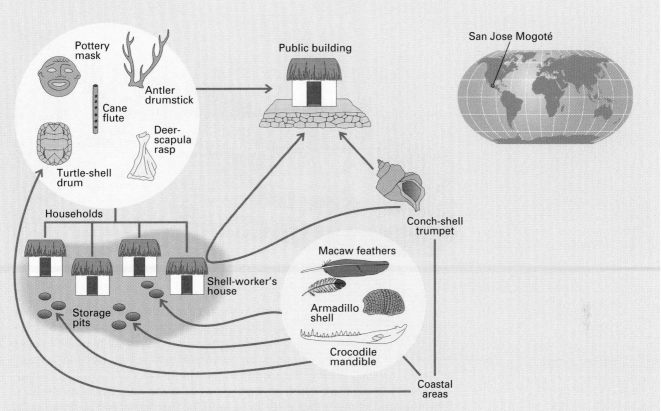

Fig. 4.20 Evidence of trade, craft activities, and ceremony from the artifacts found at San Jose Mogoté. All of the artifacts are used for music and costume in communal dance and ceremony at the large public building. Local materials included antler, cane, deer bone, and pottery. Materials imported from coastal areas at least 200 km (120 mi) to the south included conch shell, macaw feathers, armadillo and turtle shells, and crocodile mandibles. The conch shell was fashioned into a trumpet at the house of a specialist in shell working.

Religion is an organized belief system that promotes cosmology, morals, and values in human society. It takes many forms, from the highly prescribed versions we know today—with elaborate ceremony, explicit rules, and centers of wealth and administrative hierarchy—to the more informal practices of egalitarian societies. Religion is manifested in ritual and ceremony and observed archaeologically in religious artifacts and architecture.

ETHNOGRAPHY AND ARCHAEOLOGY

When anthropology departments were formed in U.S. universities in the late nineteenth century, the native peoples of North America were the primary focus of their attention. This focus was developed in part because travel and communication to other parts of the world were limited, while Native Americans were both visible and accessible to anthropologists in the United States. Anthropology departments were constituted to study Native Americans and other aboriginal peoples from a "four-field" point of view: biological, archaeological, ethnographic, and linguistic. Archaeology and ethnography were thus housed together.

Fig. 4.21 A village of long, plank houses on the Northwest Coast of North America.

Ethnography is the study of living human cultures, traditionally non-Western, through the practice of participant observation and detailed descriptions of observed practices, activities, behaviors, and beliefs. Ethnographies have provided a rich body of information on varieties of human behavior and the myriad ways in which people live around the world. In North America, ethnographers study living Native American peoples, and archaeologists study the past. Here, the connections between the living and the past have been obvious, and a cozy relationship has existed between these two academic fields. Archaeologists have been able to use the observations of ethnographers to help interpret the prehistoric remains that they have found. Today, a special branch of ethnography combines sources from history, archaeology, and oral traditions in the search for answers about past peoples, a method called **ethnohistory**.

Ethnographic reports are a major source of information for ideas and models of past human behavior. Archaeologists often look for comparisons between ethnographies and archaeology to explain things, a practice known as **ethnographic analogy**. For example, ethnographic reports in the early twentieth century that the Northwest Coast Indians in North America lived in longhouses (Fig. 4.21) provide models for archaeologists studying excavated residential structures built hundreds of years earlier in that region. Comparing the known present to the unknown past by analogy is an important way that archaeologists construct knowledge. Analogies can provide some understanding of an unknown phenomenon by suggesting that it is similar to something that is known today. Analogy involves argument by inference, assuming that similar relationships existed between similar materials in the past. Analogy provides a means for explaining artifacts, features, and other material aspects of past human behavior.

There is a continuing debate, however, in archaeology about how to use analogy and whether it is appropriate for understanding past human cultures. Alison Wylie and Ian Hodder have distinguished formal and relational analogy. Formal analogies simply point out similarities in two situations and suggest that other relationships are present. Relational analogies refer to the use of analogy where direct relationships can be observed, such as historical or ethnohistorical situations. Thus, one can be relatively confident in arguing that a crescent-shaped stone artifact from Alaska was a knife when Inuit groups in the Arctic today still use an almost identical steel model (Fig. 4.22). On the other hand, a strange

ethnography   The detailed investigation of a group of people, traditionally non-Western, through participant observation and descriptions of practices, activities, behaviors, and beliefs.

ethnohistory   Branch of ethnography that combines sources from history, *archaeology,* and oral traditions in the search for answers about past peoples.

ethnographic analogy   Comparison between *ethnography* and *archaeology* to explain similar things.

Fig. 4.22   Past and present versions of the ulu, the preferred knife of many Arctic peoples. Photograph of an Inuit woman using an ulu for skinning seals in the 1920s with a modern retail version of the knife on the left of the photo. Prehistoric versions of this knife were made of stone.

25,000-year-old bone artifact from the French Paleolithic has no ethnographic equivalent and its intended use remains unknown.

The issues of continuity, similarity, and scale are key to the successful use of analogy. Historical continuity increases the chances that items and behaviors are comparable from the present to the past. The more similar ethnographic and archaeological objects or remains are, the more likely they were used in a similar manner. Finally, the scale of the inquiry is important. Simple artifacts are more likely to yield useful analogies than comparison of complex settlement systems or cosmologies. An example of the use of ethnographic information to estimate house and site population is provided below.

> *Existing peoples can only be used as sources for reconstructing the lives of prehistoric peoples with extreme caution and within well-defined limits, since one is otherwise in danger of assuming what one is after all trying to discover.*
> —Grahame Clark, archaeologist

 EXAMPLE ∿∿∿∿∿∿∿∿∿∿∿∿∿∿∿∿∿∿∿∿∿∿∿∿∿∿∿∿∿

FLOOR AREA AND SETTLEMENT POPULATION

One of the questions that an archaeologist usually asks is how many people lived at a site. Population size is an important characteristic of a community and helpful in understanding the nature of the settlement. At the same time, determining the number of inhabitants at a site is not easy. Just calculating the size of a site is difficult because in many cases not all of a site can be excavated. Moreover, huts and houses are rare at the archaeological sites before the advent of farming. The rise of agricultural villages resulted in more substantial house construction, and in some cases archaeologists can get a reasonable idea of the number of structures present.

Many assumptions have to be made in estimating site population. For example, it is necessary either to assume that houses were all occupied at the same time or to make an additional assumption about the proportion that were in use. Even if the number of houses is known, how many people lived in each one? This is a difficult question to answer because this information is simply not available from the past.

To overcome such obstacles, archaeologists sometimes turn to ethnographic data to learn more about the relationship between material culture and human behavior. Some years ago, Raoul Naroll investigated this relationship to learn more about settlement population. Naroll collected cross-cultural information from descriptions

TABLE 4.6 Ethnographic data for floor area and settlement population.

Society	Largest settlement	Estimated population	Estimated floor area (m²)
Vanua Levu	Nakaroka	75	413
Eyak	Algonik	120	836
Kapauku	Borekubo	181	362
Wintun	Anonymous	200	900
Klallam	Port Angeles	200	2420
Hupa	Tsewenalding	200	2490
Ifaluk	Ifaluk	252	3024
Ramkokamekra	Ponto	298	6075
Bella Coola	Bella Coola	400	16,320
Kiwai	Oromsapua	400	1432
Tikopia	Tikopia	1260	8570
Cuna	Ustupu	1800	5460
Iroquois	Anonymous	3000	13,370
Kazak	Anonymous	3000	63,000
Ila	Kasenga	3000	47,000
Tonga	Nukualofa	5000	111,500
Zulu	Anonymous	15,000	65,612
Inka	Cuzco	200,000	167,220

Source: Naroll 1962.

Fig. 4.23 A graph of the relationship between settlement size and site area. Note that the two axes of the graph are logarithmic. Settlement population ranges between 75 and 200,000 people; floor area ranges from 400 to 167,000 m². There is a strong positive relationship between these two variables.

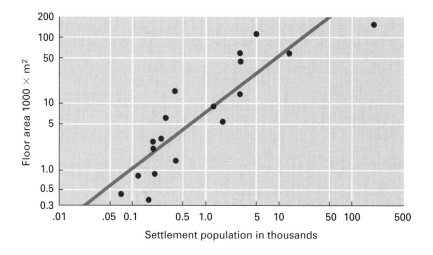

of ethnographically reported societies. He was able to find eighteen societies where data on both population and site size were available (Table 4.6). Site size was often not directly measured, however, because it was difficult to define. Instead, Naroll measured "dwelling area" at the settlement as indicated by the total area under roof for all dwellings. This variable translates as house floor area at archaeological sites since the roofs are gone.

Naroll took the information he had assembled and graphed it together in a cross-plot, settlement population versus floor area (Fig. 4.23). Because the numbers go from a few hundred to hundreds of thousands, he used a logarithmic scale on both axes of the graph. The nature of the graph is not so important. What is important is the linear relationship between population and floor area: Population and floor area increase together at the eighteen ethnographic settlements. If the total floor area is high, population is high. That means there is a predictable relationship between these two measures, that one of the measures can be used to estimate the other. Thus, Naroll provided archaeologists with a means for estimating population from house floor area based on ethnographic data. The study predicts that site population is approximately one person for each 10 m^2 of floor area. While Naroll's original formulation has been critiqued and revised over the years, it offers a useful perspective on this important archaeological question.

ETHNOARCHAEOLOGY

Ethnographic information has certain limitations since past human behavior is much more diverse than what has been recorded in the ethnographic literature on living peoples. There are, for example, no ethnographies of Neanderthals. In addition, it is often the case that ethnographers were not interested in or did not record the kinds of information important to archaeologists, such as diet and subsistence, burial practices, technology, and much more.

In recent years, archaeologists themselves have begun studying living societies around the globe to obtain more information on human behavior and activities that would produce an archaeological record. Ethnoarchaeology is the study of living peoples by archaeologists to gain useful information for learning about the past. Archaeologists live with hunter-gatherers to learn about how people spend their time, hunting practices, and how bones accumulate at a living site (Fig. 4.24). They may, for example, study villages in the Middle East to learn about house construction and the use of space in hot, dry climates. They may also study the ritual activities of modern Maya peoples in order to learn more about Mesoamerican belief systems and religious practices.

The example of ethnoarchaeology described below comes from South Asia and concerns the manufacture and use of beads in ancient and modern Pakistan.

The past is a foreign country; they do things differently there.
—L. P. Hartley, historian

Fig. 4.24 A !Kung San camp in Botswana. Living hunter-gatherers in this area have been the subject of numerous ethnoarchaeological studies.

HARAPPAN BEADS

www.mhhe.com/pricearch1

For a Web-based activity on Indus Valley civilization, please see the Internet exercises on your online learning center.

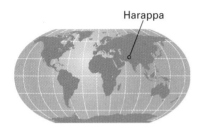

Harappa

One of the world's early state-level societies emerged in the valley and tributaries of the Indus River in eastern Pakistan. The Bronze Age Harappan (*har-RAAP-ahn*) civilization flourished between 2800 and 1900 BC and encompassed more than 1500 cities, towns, and villages in an area the size of western Europe. Major hallmarks of the Harappan state included an as-yet-undeciphered written script, systems of weights and measures, planned cities with elite and common living areas, and distinctive symbols and motifs. A considerable degree of occupational specialization also characterized Indus society. Some smaller sites concentrated on a specific industry, craft, or trade, including bead making, shell working, ceramic production, and copper working. Metallurgy was well developed, and copper and bronze were used for a variety of tools and weapons. A striking feature of Harappan society is the extent of the standardization of weights. Precisely shaped pieces of stone were used everywhere as counterweights in balances. Construction bricks also had standard dimensions. In fact, ceramic forms and even ornamentation were remarkably similar at sites throughout the Indus region.

One of the major centers of this society was at the site of Harappa itself, a large walled city of more than 150 ha (ca. 375 acres), about half the size of Central Park in New York City and roughly 5 km (3 mi) in circumference. The population of the ancient city is estimated to have been between 40,000 and 80,000 people. Indus cities generally were not as large as those in Mesopotamia, but they appear to have been more systematically planned, with streets and centralized drainage networks for individual houses. As part of this systematic planning, there were also designated living and working quarters for bead makers, coppersmiths, weavers, and other craftspeople. One's profession was probably an important factor in social differentiation.

Excavations at Harappa led by Mark Kenoyer and Richard Meadow since 1986 have exposed the prehistory of the city and revealed many aspects of its economy and subsistence. During the course of the excavations, tens of thousands of beads, drills, and pieces of bead-making debris have been recovered. It is clear that the ancient Harappans wore a good bit of jewelry to identify themselves and probably to display their social position (Fig. 4.25). The artisans of the Indus civilization used complex grinding, drilling, and decorating methods to make many kinds of beads from minerals imported often over long distances. Common raw materials used to make beads included steatite, terracotta, and faience; more valuable, exotic stones such as agate, jasper, carnelian, lapis lazuli, garnet, serpentine, and amazonite were also imported for making beads. Precious metals such as copper, bronze, gold, and silver were used on occasion as well. Some types of beads were heated to bring out the color in the mineral; others were painted or glazed.

Kenoyer has investigated bead production in Harappan society thoroughly and conducted ethnoarchaeological studies of bead makers in Pakistan today to learn more about the past. Ethnoarchaeology allows archaeologists to observe the cycles of production, use, and deposition of the materials that make up the archaeological record within the context of living human societies. In the case of bead making, Kenoyer's research questions concerned the technique and control of production as a means of understanding political organization at Harappa. He wanted to know how the production of beads was organized and who controlled it.

Kenoyer's questions led him to the city of Cambay in Pakistan to study the manufacture of carnelian beads, as well as levels of organization and the control of production. Cambay has been a center of bead production for at least 3000 years and traditional production methods continue there. Today, raw materials for the beads are transported to the city in unworked form to discourage theft. Kenoyer recorded the stages of production in the modern workshops as follows (Fig. 4.26): Nodules of agate are dried and heated to produce more color and enhance their fracture qualities. The first breaking of the nodule results in large flakes, which are then shaped into coarse blanks, or roughouts. A second stage of heating intensifies the color and leads to the second stage of flaking, which shapes the roughout into a biconical bead shape. The intensive labor of grinding, polishing, and careful drilling is followed by a final heating stage that produces the finished bead.

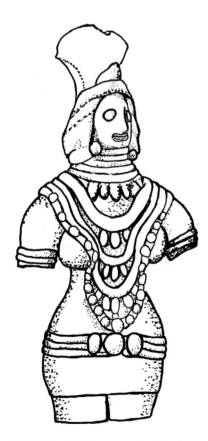

Fig. 4.25 A Harappan clay figurine depicts the important role of beads in costume and decoration.

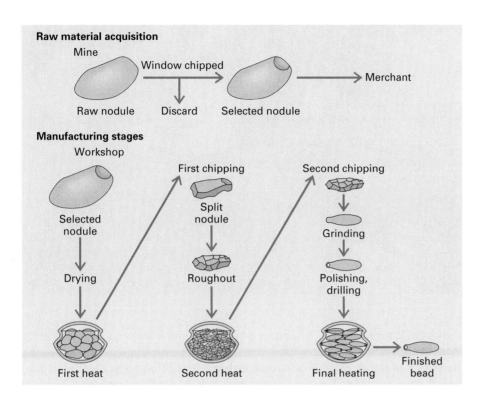

Raw material acquisition

Fig. 4.26 A schematic diagram of the production of elongated agate beads in the Indus Valley civilization, ca. 2500 BC.

Kenoyer learned a great deal from the ethnoarchaeological study. For example, he observed differences in beads produced by large group workshops and those made by individual craftsmen. The large workshops produced more standardized forms of beads and individuals created more irregular beads. Kenoyer's study led to new strategies for excavation at the site of Harappa to ensure that relevant information on bead making was found. In general, ethnoarchaeological studies at Harappa have provided valuable information about the Harappan culture, including the determination of trade routes, the extent of trade and exchange, the organization of production, and the nature and context of status differentiation, as well as changing patterns of social interaction across the site.

EXPERIMENTAL ARCHAEOLOGY

www.mhhe.com/pricearch1

For a Web-based activity on experimental archaeology, please see the Internet exercises on your online learning center.

One of the ways that archaeologists try to answer old questions and find new ones to ask is by experiment. Experimental archaeology is the "hands-on" investigation of past human activity and behavior, a do-it-yourself way to test theories about how artifacts and architecture were made and used. Virtually every archaeologist has tried to understand archaeological remains through the replication of ancient technologies. Experimental archaeology is done in many ways and at many different scales through the reconstruction and recreation of environmental conditions and ancient technologies, buildings, transport, tools, and equipment. Examples of experimental archaeology include making flint tools, butchering an animal, making a bone fish hook, constructing an adobe house, cutting trees with stone axes, and building a copy of a prehistoric boat and sailing it.

Fig. 4.27 shows students at the University of Wisconsin-Madison lighting an experimental kiln they built for firing reproductions of ceramic vessels from the Harappan culture. These students are participants in a course on experimental archaeology that meets almost every summer on the university campus, taught by

Fig. 4.27 Students from the University of Wisconsin-Madison fire an experimental kiln containing reproductions of ancient pottery.

Professor Mark Kenoyer. The course provides students with an opportunity to learn about prehistoric technology in a variety of ways, ranging from knapping stone tools to casting metal objects, making beads, and firing pottery reproductions.

Experimental archaeology is another way that archaeologists try to learn about archaeological sites and artifacts through an understanding of ancient technologies and the societies that created them. The Lejre Archaeological Research Center described at the beginning of this chapter provides another example of archaeology by experiment.

CONCLUSIONS

There are more questions about the past than about the modern world today. The questions we ask—what it is we want to know—determine what and how we learn. Archaeologists have a multitude of questions about the past—things we need to know—to choose from. The selection of questions is determined by personal preference, theoretical position, current affairs, feasibility, and a variety of other factors. People's interests in the past vary, and the wide range of interests includes food, politics, death, and gender.

Questions come from a variety of sources, academic, personal, individual, and social. The kinds of questions that archaeologists ask involve some aspect of society. Questions concerning individuals are often difficult to resolve, given what we know about the past and the way in which archaeological information is available. One way to think about society is to consider the components of demography, technology, organization, economy, and ideology operating in a natural and social environment. Demography is population size, birth and death rates, age, and sex. It defines the biological dimensions of society. Society uses technology to obtain resources and to create the tools, equipment, and structures needed to function in the environment. Economy provides the food and other resources through a combination of organization and technology. Exchange is a major aspect of economy and a common feature of human and societal interaction.

Organization refers to the means by which society is structured for maintaining order and existence. An important distinction is made between egalitarian and hierarchical societies—between small, relatively simple groups and larger, more layered configurations of social units in bigger social formations. Ideology is another component of society and human behavior, encompassing shared concepts about the world and structured, sacred activities involving ritual and ceremony. Ideology is usually expressed in both symbol and art (Fig. 4.28). Ideology

The most striking differences between states and simpler societies lie in the realm of decision making and its hierarchical organization.
—Kent Flannery, archaeologist

is often remembered, maintained, and reinforced by specialists in society, such as shamans or priests.

Both questions and some answers come from the larger field of anthropology, and specifically from ethnography. Ethnographies, detailed written descriptions of human societies from all parts of the world, provide a rich source of information on the human condition and how people have coped with environments and other societies under various conditions. Archaeologists use ethnographies to get ideas about how past societies may have operated and how specific architecture, features, and artifacts may have been used. Ethnographies are an important source of inspiration for archaeologists.

The use of ethnographic information in archaeology often involves analogy, the inference that a pattern observed ethnographically among living peoples was present in a past society. The issue of how ethnographies can be used is the subject of some controversy in archaeology. Direct analogy, the assumption that a pattern or behavior was exactly the same in the past as today, is rarely an acceptable argument. Argument by analogy requires careful evaluation and can never be taken at face value. Analogy provides only ideas; the scientific method of testing and evaluation provides confidence.

Archaeologists also turn to experiment for information and new questions. Experimental archaeology is the imitative replication of patterns and materials observed in the archaeological record. Such experiments are undertaken in order to learn about the techniques and knowledge required to create, construct, or make prehistoric materials and structures. Experimental archaeology is a common practice for learning more about the past.

The kinds of questions that archaeologists ask often reflect a theoretical position, a school of thought, or a perspective on the past. Chapter 16, "Explanation in Archaeology," is a discussion of different theoretical perspectives, different positions on how to look at the past. In this chapter, we have considered the general questions that archaeologists try to answer. In Chapter 16, we will look more closely at different kinds of questions about the past.

Fig. 4.28 A powerful symbolic statement, this plastered human skull comes from Jericho. The features of the deceased have been modeled in plaster on the individual's skull. Shell was used for the eyes.

STUDY QUESTIONS

1. What are the major components of human society?

2. What do you know about the technologies for food preparation?

3. What are some examples of ideology in contemporary American society? How would these appear to an archaeologist in the year AD 2500?

4. What kinds of symbols are prevalent in our society today? What do they represent? Are there multiple messages or do these symbols reflect belief systems in society?

5. How can people living today tell us about the past? Is ethnographic analogy a realistic way to learn about prehistory?

6. What is experimental archaeology?

www.mhhe.com/pricearch1

For more review material and study questions, please see the self-quizzes on your online learning center.

www.mhhe.com/pricearch1

For Internet references related to this chapter, please see the chapter links on your online learning center.

REFERENCES

David, Nicholas, and Carol Kramer. 2001. *Ethnoarchaeology in Action.* New York: Cambridge University Press.

Earle, Tim, and A. Johnson. 2000. *The Evolution of Human Societies: From Forager Group to Agrarian State.* 2d ed. Palo Alto: Stanford University Press.

Flannery, Kent. 1972. The cultural evolution of civilization. *Annual Review of Ecology and Systematics* 3:399–426.

Gibbon, G. 1989. *Explanation in Archaeology.* Oxford: Basil Blackwell.

Meskell, Lynn. 1999. *Archaeologies of Social Life: Age, Sex, Class, Etcetera in Ancient Egypt.* Oxford: Blackwell.

Reitz, E. J., L. A. Newsom, and S. J. Scudder, eds. 1996. *Case Studies in Environmental Archaeology.* New York: Plenum Press.

Trigger, Bruce G. 2003. *Understanding Early Civilizations: A Comparative Study.* Cambridge: Cambridge University Press.

Coppergate Site
1. Modern (1750–present)
2. Post-Medieval (1550–1750)
3. Medieval (1200–1550)
4. Norman (1067–1200)
5. Viking III (975–1067)
6. Viking II (925–975)
7. Viking I (850–925)
8. Anglian (400–850)
9. Roman (AD 71–400)

CHAPTER 5

The Archaeological Record

INTRODUCTION: INFORMATION FROM THE PAST

The drawing on the opposite page captures one major aspect of archaeology. The place depicted is York in northern England. This modern city has been the site of continuous habitation since Roman times in the first century AD. The drawing shows nine different levels of occupation and earth that have accumulated in the city center. Also shown, as active inhabitants, are the Anglians around AD 650, the Vikings around AD 950, the medieval population around AD 1400, and visitors to the Jorvik Viking center in modern York. Jorvik (*YORE-vick*) was the Viking name for York. The Center provides a museum, learning activities, and re-creations of the Viking settlement and is one of the most popular attractions in the region. The center sits directly over the excavations of the old Viking town and visitors are able to see the places that archaeologists uncovered and to examine the evidence for the Viking presence.

The layers and materials beneath modern York are the archaeological record—the traces of the past surviving to the present. This record is composed of many different kinds of materials and information, including the artifacts, the sediments, and the structures left behind. Archaeologists investigate this record to learn about human activity and behavior in the past. How the archaeological record forms and the nature of its contents—both material and contextual—are the subjects of this chapter.

Every field of endeavor—plumbing, chemistry, bee keeping, bar tending, archaeology—has its own vocabulary. In archaeology, the objects that survive from the past are sometimes referred to as **material culture**—the tangible, preserved evidence of past human activities. This body of evidence that archaeologists work with is part of the **archaeological record**, the information about the past that has survived to the present. This record includes both past materials and the context in which they are found. Context is the association and relationships between objects that are together in the same place. This chapter examines the important properties of scale and context in the study of archaeological evidence.

Archaeological evidence takes various forms at different scales. Most of the information that archaeologists use to learn about the past comes from artifacts, sites, and regions. **Artifacts** are the objects and materials that people have made and used. **Sites** are accumulations of such artifacts and features, representing the places where people lived or carried out certain activities. **Regions** are large areas, often containing a number of sites that have been physically or conceptually modified. In addition to artifacts, sites, and regions, archaeologists also study attributes, features, ecofacts, assemblages, and landscapes, among other things. The meanings of these terms and others are discussed in detail in this chapter.

Archaeological sites are a basic unit of study. Sites form and change over time, and a few are eventually investigated by archaeologists. It is essential to consider the processes involved in the formation and transformation of archaeological materials. Archaeologists study the static, silent, erratic, and fragmentary record of archaeology to understand the dynamic, intact, vibrant pattern of human life in the past. We need to know as much as possible about how one becomes the other—for example, how living behavior becomes static material culture. Site formation is the term used to describe this process. Preservation is one aspect of site formation and this topic is also considered in some detail in this chapter.

SCALE

Two keys for archaeological thinking (and many other things) are scale and context. Thinking about archaeology usually involves scale and context. It is important to keep these factors in mind when considering how things fit together and when looking for patterns. **Scale** has to do with size and is a major consideration in the analysis of archaeological materials. Scale in archaeology involves different levels of discovery, analysis, and interpretation. Important levels of archaeological scale include **attributes** (characteristics of archaeological materials and information), individual objects (artifacts and ecofacts), culturally related sets of objects (assemblages and components), spatially related groups of objects (sites), and places in geographic space (landscapes and regions). At each level, larger units in scale and number are involved. Changing the scale of our enquiry also changes the way we look at the evidence. (See Chapter 6 for more on the term *scale* and its use in the description of map and illustration size.)

A powerful way to visualize scale was documented in a short film called *Powers of 10*. The phrase refers to the mathematical shorthand known as scientific notation that allows large or small numbers to be written in an abbreviated fashion. A long number like 1,222,000,000.00 could be written in shorthand as 1.222×10^9. The power of ten refers to the number of positive or negative decimal places in the number.

Powers of 10 provided a graphic picture of the world that began with a wide view and increased the magnification by a power of 10 step-by-step, zooming from the span of the universe to a picnic along the shore of Lake Michigan, into the hand of one of the participants, through the cells inside, into the DNA and the subatomic particles of atoms. It was an extraordinary, and powerful, depiction of scale, and it portrayed how the world around us exists on myriad levels.

A similar perspective helps the archaeologist understand the past. An example of scale in archaeology can be seen in Fig. 5.1. In this case, focus is on the Linearbandkeramik (LBK) (*LYNN-ee-er-BAND-kehr-am-ick*) farmers of central Europe around 5250 BC. The scale increases in powers of ten as we move from a view of the European continent to a single farmhouse belonging to the LBK period. Each step in the sequence, each increase in magnification by a power of 10, provides new information about these early European farmers. In the broader view, we see where the LBK occurs in Europe; at larger scales the locations of settlements are visible as well as the relationships among settlements and houses. At the highest magnification, we see the construction techniques of individual houses. We could, of course, zoom even further into a house to look at features and artifacts, attributes of the artifacts, or even the chemistry of pottery or the ancient DNA in the bone of the buried inhabitants.

This concept of scale applies to time as well as geographic space. We can talk about time in the past at large scale or small scale, in days, weeks, months, years, decades, centuries, millennia, tens of thousands, hundreds of thousands, or millions of years. The resolution of most of archaeology is in tens to hundreds of

material culture Tangible, surviving evidence of human activities.

archaeological record The body of information about the past that has survived to the present.

artifacts The objects and materials that people have made and used.

sites Accumulations of artifacts and features, representing the places where people lived or carried out certain activities.

regions Large geographic areas, containing a number of archaeological sites, that have been physically or conceptually modified.

scale (1) Different levels of discovery, analysis, and interpretation in *archaeology;* or (2) the size of a map relative to the area it portrays.

attributes Detailed characteristics of archaeological materials and information.

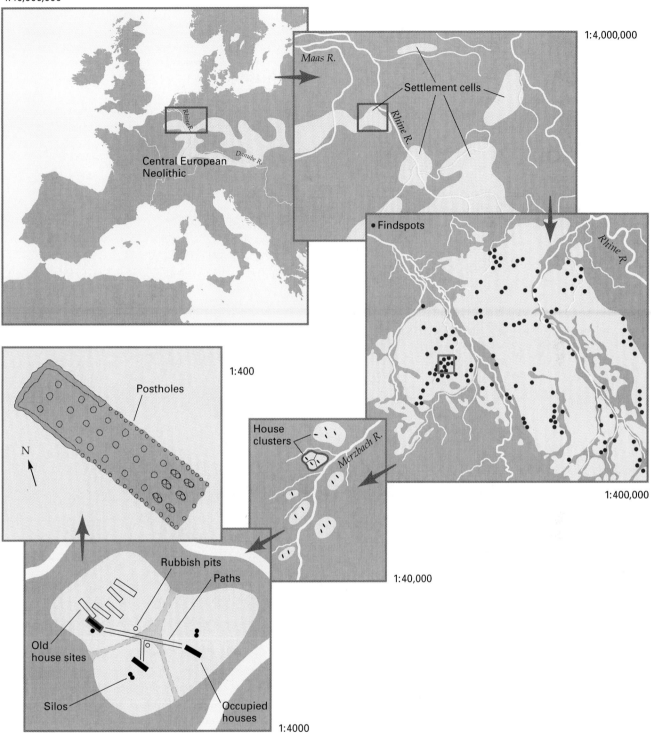

1:40,000,000

1:4,000,000

Maas R.

Settlement cells

Rhine R.

• Findspots

Rhine R.

1:400,000

House
clusters

Merzbach R.

1:40,000

1:400

Postholes

N

Rubbish pits

Paths

Old
house sites

Silos

Occupied
houses

1:4000

Fig. 5.1 Powers of 10 applied to the early Neolithic Linearbandkeramik (LBK) culture
in central Europe between 5500 and 5000 BC. Clockwise from upper left we see the entire
distribution of the LBK on the continent of Europe, a corner of northwestern Europe
with several concentrations of LBK, a pair of river valleys in northern Belgium with a
scatter of LBK settlements, several clusters of settlement along one of the rivers,
a single cluster with several houses, and a single house. Changing the focus of analysis, shifting the power of magnification, provides a variety of information about the
Linearbandkeramik.

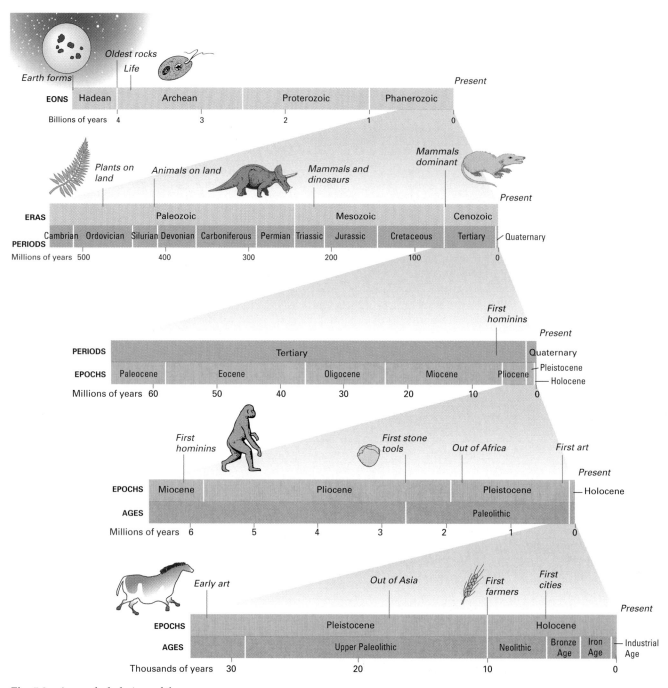

Fig. 5.2 An exploded view of the scale of time. The chronology of the earth's history with finer divisions of millions and thousands of years. From the formation of the earth until the present in geological and archaeological time. Archaeological time is shown in blue.

years at best but in some instances we can discuss shorter- or longer-term phenomena: for example, the volcanic destruction of Pompeii took place in a matter of hours; the evolution of stone tools happened over more than 2 million years.

One way to visualize the scale of time is depicted in Fig. 5.2. Changing the scale brings finer resolution and more detail to the chronological period of interest. In this example, the top of the time scale shows the history of the earth from 4.6 billion years ago to the present, highlighted by the appearance of rocks and life. The second step shows 550 million years of geological eras, dominated by the arrival of plants and animals on land and the dominance of the dinosaurs. The third stage in our timescale shows the past 65 million years or so of the Cenozoic era, when mammals became dominant and the first human ancestors appeared. The fourth scale covers the past 6.5 million years, from the Miocene to the Holocene epoch, and from the first **hominins** to the appearance of *Homo sapiens*. In the

The First Americans

A classic example of context comes from the discovery of early humans in North America. The age of the first people in the Americas is still debated, but 100 years ago most scholars thought that American Indians had arrived only a few hundred years before Europeans in the New World. In 1927, however, stone spear points were discovered among the bones of extinct bison at a place near Folsom, New Mexico (Fig. 5.3). Stone points of this type had been known for some time and the bones of an extinct form of the bison are not uncommon in the southwestern United States. It was the context of the extinct animals and the human artifacts, found together in time and space, that convinced a skeptical audience of professional archaeologists and the general public that humans had been present in the area for thousands of years. Since the original discovery, radiocarbon dates from this site have established the age at 8500 BC.

Fig. 5.3 Archaeological context. This photograph shows the discovery in the early twentieth century of a stone spear point (a Folsom Paleoindian point) in association with the ribs of an extinct form of bison. This evidence was used to confirm the antiquity of humans in the New World.

Folsom

final scale, of the past 35,000 years or so, we see the beginnings of art, the emergence of the first farmers, and the appearance of the first cities. We could, of course, keep expanding our timescale to show more detail and more recent history.

What is important to remember is that archaeologists work at different scales of geographic and chronological information to learn about the past. It's essential to keep the scale of the analysis in mind when considering the questions that need to be answered.

CONTEXT

Context is another essential aspect of archaeological information. Context has to do with place and association among archaeological items and the situation in which they occur. Are objects found in distinctive locations? Are objects found together with other items? Are sites found in specific places? Are regions characterized by specific landmarks or monuments?

Context has two meanings in archaeology—(1) the location of artifacts in association with other items and materials, and (2) the matrix in which artifacts are found. At a basic level, context concerns relationships among artifacts. Items that are found together in the same pit, in the same layer, or in the same sediment, for example, are assumed to be related in terms of time and activity. That is to say, objects in the same context are thought to have been in use together in time and geographic space, roughly contemporary, and involved in the same activities or resulting from similar behaviors.

In a broader sense, context is the physical setting, location, and association of artifacts and features. Context is of major importance in archaeology and provides much of the essential information for the determination of authenticity and

hominin   Early human ancestor, fossil form (replaces the term *hominid*).

context   Place and association among the archaeological materials and the situation in which they occur.

significance. Context is essential for learning about age, use, and meaning. The more that is known about the context of archaeological remains, the more that can be learned about the past, both of the artifacts themselves and of the people who made them.

A distinction is made between primary and secondary context. An object in its original position of discard or deposition, in the place where it was left, is said to be in **primary context** or **in situ** (Latin: "in place"). Objects that have been moved from their original place of deposition are in secondary context and less useful for learning about the past. When artifacts are removed from their original location, without proper excavation and documentation, contextual information is lost forever. Looters are unconcerned with the context of archaeological materials. Peter Cannon-Brookes described looted artifacts as "cultural orphans, which, torn from their contexts, remain forever dumb and virtually useless for scholarly purposes."

An important term in the realm of context is **provenience**, or place of origin. The synonymous term *provenance* is used in art history and classical archaeology to describe the history of an object's ownership. The provenience of an artifact is the place where it was found, a very important piece of information. Artifacts and other archaeological objects with an unknown provenience provide very little information for learning about the past. Provenience implies context, meaning that there is additional information available about the object of interest.

THE NATURE OF THE EVIDENCE

The archaeological record, then, is found in a variety of contexts at different scales. Archaeological information takes many forms. We will focus on attributes, artifacts, ecofacts, features, assemblages, sites, and regions or landscapes in the following pages. This discussion will begin with smaller, more detailed and specific, and move to larger and more general views of the archaeological record. Later sections in this chapter deal with how the record is formed and preserved.

Attributes

An attribute is a characteristic or trait. All things have attributes. Even a black hole has many attributes, including location, size, intensity, and age. In archaeology, attributes are the characteristics of artifacts, features, sites, assemblages, or landscapes—the details of archaeological information that we use to describe these remains. Attributes are the traits, measurements, and properties of archaeological materials. Most of this information is recorded in the laboratory after artifacts have been cleaned and cataloged.

Four primary attributes are used to classify archaeological artifacts: (1) age—how old is it? (2) form—the size and basic shape of an object; (3) technology—the characteristics of raw materials and manufacturing technique; and (4) style—the color, texture, and decoration of an object. Attributes can be visible (e.g., color, length, shape), microscopic (e.g., edge wear, pollen species), or invisible (e.g., weight, chemistry, density).

Attributes are variable from one object to the next. They can be metric (measured, described in numbers) or nonmetric (described in words). Fig. 5.4 shows some of the attributes that could be recorded on an arrowhead.

The number of potential attributes for almost any object is virtually unlimited. Table 5.1 lists some of the attributes of the pottery at an 800-year-old site in south-central Indiana. This list includes attributes of the form, technology, and style of the pottery. For example, temper is a technological attribute. It is a material added to clay to make pottery. Several different materials were used for temper at this site, including grit, shell, limestone, and a combination of grit and shell. Rim profile is an aspect of form. Stylistic attributes record the locations and kinds of decoration (e.g., smoothed, cord-marked, fabric-marked), design motifs (e.g., plain,

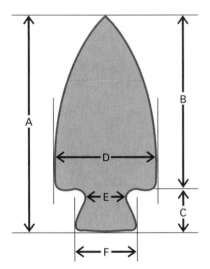

Fig. 5.4 Some of the metric attributes of an arrowhead: A. maximum length; B. blade length; C. stem length; D. maximum width; E. neck width; F. stem width.

primary context The original position of an object in its place of discard or deposition; in place (Latin: *in situ*).

in situ The original position of an object in its place of discard or deposition; in place; primary context.

provenience The place of discovery or origin. Where an item is from (a.k.a. provenance in *classical archaeology*).

TABLE 5.1 Some nonmetric attributes of prehistoric pottery from the Clampitt site in south-central Indiana, dating to ca. AD 1200.

Temper

1. grit
2. shell
3. limestone
4. grit and shell
5. sand

Surface Treatment Rim

1. smoothed
2. cord-marked
3. smoothed cord-marked
4. fabric-marked

Surface Treatment Neck/Shoulder

1. smoothed
2. cord-marked
3. smoothed cord-marked
4. fabric-marked

Surface Treatment Body

1. smoothed
2. cord-marked
3. smoothed cord-marked
4. fabric-marked

Surface Treatment Lip

1. smoothed
2. cord-marked
3. smoothed cord-marked
4. fabric-marked

Rim Form

1. thickened
2. unthickened
3. rolled

Rim Profile

1. straight
2. cambered (recurved)
3. excurvate (flared)
4. incurvate (constricted orifice)

Lip Form

1. flat
2. round

3. round and narrow
4. beveled

Lip Motif

1. plain
2. oblique
3. transverse
4. chevron (alt. obliques)
5. horizontal (channeled)

Lip Technique

1. none
2. cord-wrapped dowel impressed
3. tool-impressed
4. plain dowel impressed
5. punctate (ovoid)
6. punctate (circular)

Rim Motif

1. plain
2. obliques
3. chevrons (alt. obliques)
4. parallel (alt. obliques)
5. verticals
6. circles (punctates)
7. horizontal lines

Rim Technique

1. none
2. cord-wrapped dowel impressed
3. incised (<2.0 mm wide)
4. punctates

Neck Motif

1. plain
2. curvilinear guilloche
3. rectilinear guilloche
4. indeterminate guilloche
5. obliques

Neck Technique

1. none
2. cord-wrapped dowel impressed
3. incised (<2.0 mm wide)
4. trailed (>2.0 mm wide)

oblique, transverse, chevron, horizontal), and the shapes of lips and rims. More information on ceramic attributes can be found in Chapter 11, on ceramic analysis.

Archaeologists must select the attributes that contain information of interest for the questions they seek to answer. For example, questions about technology would focus on aspects of manufacture; questions about change over time might focus on attributes of style. Attributes are discussed in more detail in several chapters, including "Classification and Data" (Chapter 7), "Lithic Analysis" (Chapter 10), and "Ceramic Analysis" (Chapter 11).

Artifacts

Artifacts are portable objects shaped, modified, or created by people. They are combinations of attributes, having a variety of characteristics. Artifacts are tools, instruments, toys, clothing, furniture, jewelry, weapons, and the many other items that we make and use to survive and often to improve our lives.

Stone, pottery, and plant and animal remains are some of the more common categories of archaeological materials. Each of these classes of material culture is the subject of another chapter, which examines the nature of and variation in these objects. Chapter 10 focuses on stone tools and considers the ways that lithic materials are obtained, how they are shaped into tools, and how archaeologists use information from the artifacts. Chapter 11 deals with ceramics, how they are made, and the kinds of information they provide for archaeologists. Many other kinds of artifacts, made from metal, bone, glass, wood, shell, and so on are the subject of specialist studies. References to such studies are provided in the bibliography at the back of the book.

Ecofacts

Ecofacts are unmodified, natural items found in archaeological contexts, usually brought to a site by its occupants and useful for the study of past human activity. Ecofacts, such as animal bones and plant remains, are used to reconstruct the environment of a site and the range of resources that people ate and used. Ecofacts can be classified as organic (plant and animal) or inorganic (sediment and stone). Plant and animal remains are also referred to as **flora** and **fauna**, respectively; these terms are used almost interchangeably. Ecofacts are usually studied by archaeologists or specialists with training in zoology, botany, or geology. Bones are an extremely important category of evidence. Animal bones are the objects of study for archaeozoology, discussed in Chapter 12. Plant remains tell archaeobotanists about the environment, climate, local vegetation, and diet of prehistoric groups and are considered in Chapter 13. Human bones fall in the special realm of bioarchaeologists, described in Chapter 14.

The most important inorganic ecofacts are the various sediments uncovered by excavation. Deposits of soils and sediments result from both human and natural processes. These sediments and deposits are studied by geoarchaeologists. The types of sediments present at a site may indicate the source of the material that was deposited. Examples might include water-lain silts from a flood, volcanic ash, or frost-cracked rocks from the ceiling of a cave. Geoarchaeology and the study of such sediments are the subject of Chapter 9.

Features and Activity Areas

Feature is the term for nonportable facilities and structures that humans dig or build. Features are modifications of the earth—constructions used for shelter, movement, and various other activities, such as cooking, storage, religious rites, water control, and the like. They may be structures like houses or pits, or fences or field systems defining an area used for special purposes. Features also include

ecofacts   Unmodified, natural items found in archaeological contexts, often plant or animal material.

flora   Generic term for the archaeological remains of plants; the general class of plants.

fauna   Generic term for the archaeological remains of animals; the general class of animals.

features   The permanent facilities and structures that people construct in or on the earth.

midden   Any substantial accumulation of garbage or waste at a locus of human activity; archaeological deposits of trash and/or shells that accumulate in heaps and mounds. A shell midden is a specific type of midden composed largely of mollusk shells.

inhumation   Burial of all or part of a corpse; contrast with *cremation.*

cremation   The incinerated remains of a human body.

cenotaph   An empty grave, without a body.

activity area   Location of specific tasks or behaviors within a site.

canals, bridges, paths or roads for moving water or people, and constructions like fireplaces, drying racks, and traps. Burials are a specific kind of feature discussed below. Features are usually studied in the field since they are fixed in place, but occasionally burials, hoards, or other special remains may be removed as a block (French: "*en bloc*") and taken to the lab for further excavation and analysis.

Features are important for understanding the distribution and organization of human activities at a site. For example, the size, elaboration, and location of houses or graves may suggest differences in wealth and status. Fireplaces are usually a focus on human activity. Pits are common on archaeological sites and were likely used for a variety of purposes, including storage, burial, refuse, hearths, and more. Postholes and postmolds are other common features on archaeological sites and provide important clues as to the size, shape, and location of structures. Such features are discussed in more detail in Chapter 6, "Fieldwork."

Some features result from the accumulation of garbage and debris, rather than intentional construction. A **midden** is any substantial accumulation of garbage or waste at a place of human activity. Examples include heaps of waste material at workshops and quarries. A midden may be part of the cultural layer at a site, or, found alone, a midden itself would be a site. Studies of such features may provide information on strategies for obtaining food or raw material, how the raw material was used and distributed, and whether it was scarce or abundant.

Burials, constructed for the interment of the dead, are usually in the form of graves or tombs; graves are dug into the ground, while tombs may be constructed either above or below ground. Burials can be either inhumations or cremations. **Inhumation** refers to burial of the corpse, while **cremations** are the burned or incinerated remains of a human body. Burials can be single or multiple, with more than one individual. An example of an extraordinary tomb in central China is described below. There are graves known as **cenotaphs** that do not contain a body; an individual died at sea or in a foreign place and the body was not recovered for burial. More information on the study of human remains can be found in Chapter 14, "Bioarchaeology."

Activity areas are locations of specific tasks or behaviors focused on a single or limited purpose at a site. Activity areas may be a combination of artifacts and features utilized in the performance of a specialized task. Examples would be stone tool production, hide working, ceramic firing, food preparation, tool repair, and ceremony. Activity areas provide evidence for the function of a location and the use of a site. They are present at most kinds of archaeological sites where humans performed tasks, ate food, or did other things.

 EXAMPLE ~~~~~~~~~~~~~~~~~~~~~~~~~~~~~~

THE TOMB OF QIN SHIHUANG

Graves and tombs are a special part of the archaeological record for a number of reasons. Graves usually contain human remains and are often considered sacred ground. They also contain largely complete objects that were intentionally placed in the grave. In addition, graves are usually the product of a process of ritual and ceremony intended to make a place sacred or hallowed.

Graves and tombs take a variety of forms, from simple shallow pits with a single individual interred, to mass burials of jumbled bodies, to the elaborate tombs of sovereigns and the elite. Examples of these elaborate tombs are among the most famous finds in archaeology—the tombs of Tutankhamen, the Lord of Sipán (Chapter 2), and others. But the largest and most elaborate of elite tombs are found in China.

Chinese civilization began some 2000 years before Christ. By the time of Rome, China had been joined into an enormous empire, stretching over 1.3 million km² (515,000 mi), an area slightly larger than the modern country of South Africa. The

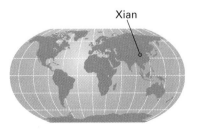
Xian

Fig. 5.5 A plan of the tomb of Qin Shihuang outside the city of Xian, China. The known features around the burial mound are indicated but most of the enormous area, including the primary tomb under Mount Li, has not been excavated. The scale in the upper right corner is 1 km.

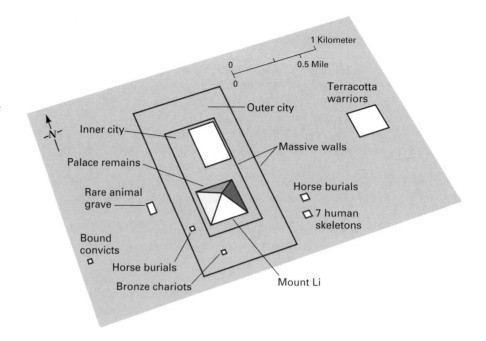

man responsible for this was Qin Shihuang, also known as Shi Huang Ti. He inherited the throne of the Qin (*CHIN*) kingdom at the age of 13 in 246 BC. The name of China probably comes from this word. During the first 25 years of his reign, he frequently engaged in battle, eventually conquering six other major kingdoms and creating the empire.

As soon as Shi Huang Ti became king, he began building his tomb. According to written documents from the time, 700,000 laborers from all parts of the country worked for 36 years on the project, building a subterranean palace for the emperor to inhabit for the rest of eternity. Archaeologists estimate the size of the subterranean palace, built at the bottom of a 32-m-deep pit (100 ft, like a ten-story underground parking garage), to be about 160 × 180 m (400 × 525 ft), the equivalent of three large soccer fields (Fig. 5.5).

The architects of the tomb conceived of it as a universe in miniature. All the country's major waterways were reproduced in mercury within the tomb. The emperor's outer coffin was made of copper, and fine vessels, precious stones, and other rarities were buried with him. Heavenly constellations were painted on the ceiling, with pearls for stars. The designers of the tomb's security system, a series of mechanized crossbows, were sealed inside the tomb to die so that none of the tomb's secrets could be divulged. This underground palace has not yet been excavated.

The palace tomb was buried under an enormous mound of earth, called Mount Li, originally 46 m (150 ft) tall, the height of a fifteen-story building. Outside the mound was an outer city enclosed by a high rectangular stone wall 7 m (23 ft) thick at the base. The total complex covered 200 ha (500 acres). Today, most of the walls and temples have been removed. Various offerings and accompanying materials were buried in a huge area surrounding the palace tomb. The total area of the tomb, buried offerings, and grounds is more than 55 km² (20 mi²; about the size of Manhattan). Most of this area has never been excavated.

About 1370 m (4500 ft) east of Mount Li, excavations have revealed an astonishing spectacle. Guarding the east gate to the emperor's tomb is a brick-floored, 1.2-ha (3-acre) chamber filled with terracotta soldiers and horses. Collapsed pillars indicate that a roof once covered the buried paradeground. Some 6000 terracotta figures have been exposed, along with wooden chariots. The terracotta warriors are slightly larger than life-size and are arranged in battle formations, are dressed in uniforms of various rank, and carry real weapons—swords, spears, and crossbows (Fig. 5.6). Traces of pigment indicate that the uniforms were brightly colored. Of the excavated figures, none look exactly alike; their facial expressions vary, suggesting that they were realistic portraits of different individuals in the emperor's honor guard. Even the horses

Fig. 5.6 One of the buried chambers filled with terracotta warriors at the east gate of the tomb of Qin Shihuang. This 1.2-hectare (3-acre; 1.5 soccer fields) area is filled with an army of almost 6000 distinctive figures and their weapons.

were very finely crafted, appearing alert and tense, as they would be in battle. This find of the warriors alone is often described as the eighth wonder of the ancient world.

Since the original discovery of the terracotta warriors, many more buried chambers have been found in the area of the tomb. There are almost 100 pits with warriors, archers, chariots, and horses in a large zone surrounding the tomb. In the area between the inner and outer cities, archaeologists have found a buried chamber for stables, thirty-one chambers for birds and rare animals, forty-eight tombs for imperial concubines who were buried alive with the emperor, and three sites of homes of officials in charge of gardens and temples. Some twenty unexcavated tombs probably hold the remains of his councilors and retainers.

Most of the tomb area and its many chambers have not been excavated. The complex is a project that will require generations of Chinese archaeologists to uncover. And, in fact, it is only one of many tombs in a region that was the capital of China through several important imperial dynasties.

Assemblages and Components

An **assemblage** is a related set of different things. Archaeological assemblages occur at different scales and in different contexts. *Assemblage* is a generic term that can be used at the level of a region, a site, a structure, or an activity. All of the artifacts from a site or layer are often referred to as an assemblage. Sometimes a more specific term is used, such as the *lithic assemblage* or the *ceramic assemblage,* to refer to the stone tools or pottery from that site or layer. Assemblages contain a substantial amount of information because they are combinations of artifacts in context. Assemblages of artifacts can reveal the age, function, and cultural affiliation of a site.

On a larger scale, the term *assemblage* is sometimes used to describe all the artifacts and features that define an archaeological culture. For example, the assemblage of Acheulean artifacts from the Lower Paleolithic in Europe includes handaxes, cleavers, and various flake tools. The term *industry* is used to characterize one product or type that appears in a number of assemblages. The handaxe industry associated with the Acheulean would be an example.

The term *component* is often applied to an assemblage from a single layer, living floor, or occupation level. Component implies a set of materials in contemporary use by the same group of people. A **multicomponent** site contains different episodes or time periods of activity. Surface sites are sometimes multicomponent. A **single-component** layer or site would be the remains of a single episode of human activities.

assemblage   A related set of different things.

industry   One object or *artifact* type that appears in a number of *assemblages*.

component   An *assemblage* from a single layer, *living floor,* or *occupation horizon;* a set of materials in contemporary use by the same group of people.

multicomponent   A mixture of different episodes or periods of activity.

single component   The remains of a single episode of human activities.

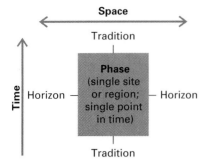

Space

Tradition

Horizon — **Phase** (single site or region; single point in time) — Horizon

Tradition

Time

Fig. 5.7 The significance of tradition, horizon, and phase in time and space.

occupation horizon   The layer or stratum that accumulates during an episode of human habitation and activity.

living floor   The actual places where people lived and carried out their activities.

tradition   The continuity of similar *artifacts* and design through time.

horizon   Layer or *assemblage* associated with geological strata or archaeological contents—usage includes a soil horizon, a cultural horizon; the geographic extent of similar artifacts and design in space.

phase   A particular period in time and space where an *assemblage* occurs.

open-air sites   Sites on land and uncovered, in contrast to *sites* in caves or *rockshelters*.

rockshelter   A shallow cave or overhang, defined by having a width greater than its depth.

surface sites   Sites visible on the surface of the ground.

nonsite (off-site)   The areas between archaeological *sites* where there are occasional traces of human activity in the form of isolated *artifacts*, *features*, or other evidence.

residential sites   Places of habitation where people live and carry out the everyday activities that sustain life.

camp   A short-term, temporary settlement, usually associated with *hunter-gatherers* or nomads.

hamlet   A small village with just a handful of houses and a small number of inhabitants.

village   A small residential unit of permanent houses with a population of less than a few hundred.

town   Larger than a village with internal differentiation in size and location of structures and usually containing one or more public buildings.

city   An urban agglomeration with a population of 10,000 or more, internal differentiation, and distinct civic or ceremonial areas within its boundaries.

extractive sites   Nonresidential localities where some members of the society obtain food or other resources.

Related terms include *occupation, living floor, tradition, horizon,* and *phase.* An **occupation horizon** is the layer or strata that accumulated during an episode of human habitation and activity. A **living floor** refers to the actual places where people lived and carried out their activities. A living floor might be found inside a house structure, around a hearth, or in huts at a campsite. Both terms assume the same group in residence for a continuous period of time.

In the New World, the terms *tradition* and *horizon* are sometimes used to describe large-scale archaeological patterns in time and geographic space (Fig. 5.7). **Tradition** refers to the continuity of similar artifacts and design through time. **Horizon** defines the geographic extent of similar artifacts and design in space. A **phase**, then, is the term for a particular point in time and space where these materials occur—a set of sites or assemblages in a certain region within a specific period of time.

Sites

Archaeological sites are places of human behavior, concentrations of the material remains of past activities. Sites are accumulations of artifacts and features. Any place that people changed by digging, building, or leaving artifacts in the past is an archaeological site. Sites take many different forms and are found in a variety of places on the landscape. Important attributes of sites include location, function, and age. Sites can be on land or underwater. Shipwrecks, for example, are a special kind of underwater archaeological site. **Open-air sites** on land are distinguished from sites in caves or rockshelters. A **rockshelter** is a shallow cave or overhang, defined by having a width greater than its depth.

Sites are also distinguished as surface or buried. **Surface sites** are visible on the surface of the ground and can be recorded in archaeological surveys. They often have a buried component but may also be found only on the top of the ground. The visibility of surface sites is a function of vegetation, soil conditions, and several other factors. Archaeological survey for surface sites is best under conditions of limited vegetation and loose, dry soils. **Nonsite**, or off-site, describes the areas between archaeological sites where there are occasional traces of human activity in the form of isolated artifacts, features, or other evidence.

A distinction can be made between residential and nonresidential sites. **Residential sites** are places of habitation where people live and carry out the everyday activities that sustain life. The term *settlement* is sometimes used for places of residence. Residential sites can be distinguished as mobile or sedentary settlements. Hunter-gatherers and pastoral nomads are often mobile and change their place of residence throughout the year. Some hunter-gatherers and most farmers are sedentary, remaining in residence at the same locale year-round.

Camps, hamlets, villages, towns, and cities provide a useful fivefold division of residential sites (Fig. 5.8). **Camps**, or campsites, are short-term, temporary settlements usually associated with hunter-gatherers or nomads. The number of inhabitants in a camp is usually a few tens of people. A **hamlet** is a small village with just a handful of houses and a small number of inhabitants. **Villages** are small residential units of permanent houses with populations numbering a hundred or so. **Towns** are larger than villages and exhibit some internal differentiation in the size and location of structures. Towns usually contain one or more public buildings. The population of a town numbers in the hundreds to a thousand or so. **Cities** are very large, with populations of several thousand or more inhabitants (Fig. 5.9). Cities have substantial internal differentiation and distinct civic or ceremonial areas within their boundaries. Cities may be defined by boundaries of walls or fortifications. Towns and especially cities usually contain some form of monumental architecture—pyramids, palaces, walls, fortifications, and the like.

Extractive sites are nonresidential localities where some members of society obtain food or other resources. Activity in these areas is limited and specialized.

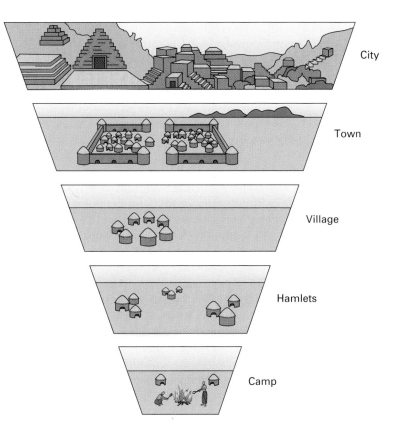

City

Town

Village

Hamlets

Camp

Fig. 5.8 The types of residential sites that are found in the archaeological record include camps, hamlets and villages, towns, and cities.

Fig. 5.9 An aerial photo of the ancient Roman city of Timgad in Algeria. The city was built from scratch in AD 100 according to Roman plan and contains baths, markets, arches, temples, libraries, a forum, theaters, and homes for more than 15,000 inhabitants.

Examples include kill sites, where animals are killed and butchered, quarries and mines, where mineral resources are obtained, fields and gardens, where food is grown, and isolated trading sites, where exchange and economic activities are focused.

A **shell midden** is a specialized kind of extractive site—a dumping ground for the food remains of shell from mussels, oysters, or other species—found along seacoasts and riverbanks in various parts of the world. Shell middens were sometimes the result of extractive activities and sometimes associated with residential settlement.

Some kinds of nonresidential, nonextractive sites are features of the landscape, including fortifications, such as walls and earthworks, ditches and canals, and roads and trails. Ritual places and monuments are other kinds of nonresidential, nonextractive sites. This category includes isolated monuments, such as mounds and pyramids, standing stones, shrines and altars, isolated graves or cemeteries, and rock art.

Rock art is one kind of evidence—part of the archaeological record—that is found on all the inhabited continents. Rock art is known from virtually all the states in the United States. The first rock art appeared toward the end of the Paleolithic, after 30,000 years ago, in Europe, Africa, and Australia. Humans decorated the world around them and rocks are one of the places where that art has sometimes been preserved. The cave and rock art of prehistory are of two major types. **Pictographs** were made by the application of pigment to rock surfaces (e.g., cave paintings); **petroglyphs** were made by removing the outer surface of a rock by carving or hammering. An example of rock art from the later prehistory of southern Africa, one of the richest regions in the world for pictographs, is discussed below.

 EXAMPLE ~~~~~~~~~~~~~~~~~~~~~~~~~~~~

SOUTH AFRICAN ROCK ART

Rock art sites are scattered across the landscape of southern Africa. The panel shown in Fig. 5.10 depicts both eland (large antelopes) and humans. Rock painting in this region is thought to be at least 25,000 years old and paintings are normally found

Fig. 5.10 Rock painting from southern Africa depicting eland and humans.

around shelters or overhangs and were made using fingers, animal fur brushes, sticks, and feathers. The pigments came from various materials: iron oxides were used for the red and yellow, charcoal or burnt bone for the black, and fine clay for the white.

Ancient art is studied by a variety of scholars—archaeologists, anthropologists, and art historians—to better understand the paintings and their significance. The eland is thought to be a powerful animal among the San people who probably produced this art. Such artworks were often created during times of ritual and ceremony. The outstretched legs of the two individuals in the center of the panel may reflect one of the symptoms of trance associated with ceremony. Clearly, this art would have been an important part of the landscape for these people.

www.mhhe.com/pricearch1

For a Web-based activity on cave art, please see the Internet exercises on your online learning center.

SCIENCE IN ARCHAEOLOGY

Dating the Paintings

Until recently, the antiquity of rock art was a contentious issue. The methods and techniques for dating rock are very limited because of the nature of the medium. Most of the art is on vertical faces of rock, not deposited in stratigraphic layers that can be dated. The materials used for painting and engraving are not readily amenable to dating techniques. The black, white, red, and orange pigments used in South Africa, and elsewhere, are largely inorganic and contain very little or no carbon. In addition, very little actual material is used for the painting and left on the rock, making standard dating methods difficult. In a few cases, the tools used to produce the art or drops of pigment have been found deposited in stratigraphic position associated with materials that have been dated.

Because of these problems, only a few absolute dates (see Chapter 8, "Dating") have been available from rock art sites. The antiquity of the art in many places has not been known. Now, however, archaeological scientists using new techniques are dating the rock surface just beneath the painting, rather than the actual pigments. This method results in dates that may be a little older than the actual paintings, but presumably not by much.

To date the rock, researchers carefully collect samples of mineral salts known as oxalates just behind missing flakes of pigment in the rock art. Oxalates form on the rock surfaces in dark, damp caves and build up over time like layers of dust. To get a radiocarbon date from the oxalates, the carbon in the mineral salts must be converted to carbon dioxide either chemically or with a laser. An accelerator mass spectrometer (AMS) is then used for radiocarbon dating (see Chapter 8, "Dating").

Southern Africa now is known to have one of the oldest rock art traditions in the world. This new dating technique revealed the rock art to be thousands of years older than previously thought. Evidence from painted stones in a cave deposit in Namibia shows that an artistic tradition, with the ritual and symbolism that is associated with it, extends back at least 25,000 years.

Just recently, the antiquity of art and decoration in South Africa has been pushed back much deeper into the past. Excavations at Blombos (*BLAHM-bos*) Cave have recovered evidence of rock engraving dating to approximately 77,000 bp. Two engraved slabs of ochre with geometric patterns at the cave are more than 35,000 years older than the oldest art anywhere else in the world (Fig. 5.11). These specimens are beyond the range of radiocarbon measurement and have been dated by a technique known as thermoluminescence (see Chapter 8, "Dating").

Fig. 5.11 One of the two engraved pieces of red ochre stone from Blombos Cave in South Africa, dated to 77,000 bp.

Regions and Landscapes

Two different terms are often used to describe larger geographic areas. Regions are physical areas of space; **landscapes** are conceptual, perceived areas. These terms are often used interchangeably in archaeology. Questions about regions and landscapes focus on how material culture is distributed in space, whether clustered or not, and how the distribution is related to both geomorphological and cultural processes. These studies involve large areas ranging in size from a few acres to areas the size of a county or state or even larger, depending on the subject of interest. For example, discussions of certain types of projectile points from the Paleoindian region encompass much of North America (see Fig. 7.19).

Regional archaeology tends to focus on the distribution of artifacts or sites across an area, especially on large-scale patterns in human behavior and how humans use the environment. Regional studies often involve the analysis of settlement patterns or the study of specific features of the environment. Questions in this area have concerned resource availability, carrying capacity (how many people could be supported by the available resources), or the spacing of sites, features, or objects, for example.

Landscape archaeology has a different focus. There are two kinds of landscapes—natural landscapes and cultural landscapes. Natural landscapes involve geology, bodies of water, vegetation, animals, climate, and the like. Cultural landscapes are the type of landscape often described in archaeology. They involve human changes in the natural landscape and include both physical changes, such as construction, cultivation, and overgrazing, and human perception of the landscape—that is, how the area is understood and incorporated in human understanding: as sacred or profane, as rich or poor, as wet or dry, as theirs or ours, or in a variety of other ways. Landscape archaeology tends to emphasize the spaces between the sites or artifacts and often focuses on the cultural or built environment of paths, fields, water-control constructions, monuments, and sacred sites. Such studies often attempt to understand the reasons behind the modification of the landscape in terms of economy, politics, or social or religious goals. These approaches assume that landscapes were dynamic and have undergone long-term changes and development.

Monuments are an important category of archaeological remains, found either within sites or across the landscape. Various kinds of monuments, either singly or in groups, are found in most parts of the world. They take a variety of forms, including earthworks such as **mounds** (aka barrows, tumuli), enclosures or fortifications, and stone structures, such as standing stones, stelae, tombs, shrines, temples, and more. **Stelae** are stone monuments, carved and/or painted with designs and/or inscriptions. The Maya of Central America carved spectacular stelae commemorating major events in the lives of their rulers. In the midwestern United States, Native American groups built large earthen mounds in the shapes of animals, as described in the next section.

> *We are the children of our landscape; it dictates behavior and even thought in the measure to which we are responsive to it.*
> —Lawrence Durrell, author

shell midden   A specialized kind of extractive site, a mound made up of large dumps of shell from mussels, oysters, or other species.

rock art   Decoration of rock surface by painting, pecking, or engraving.

pictographs   *Rock art* made by the application of pigment to rock surfaces.

petroglyphs   *Rock art* made by removing the outer surface of a rock by carving or hammering.

landscape   A humanly modified or perceived area.

mound (a.k.a. *barrows*, tumuli)   A built pile or heap of earth or stones, resembling a very small hill, usually a burial monument.

stela   A stone monument, carved and/or painted with designs and/or inscriptions, common in the Maya region (plural: *stelae*).

 EXAMPLE ~~~~~~~~~~~~~~~~~~~~~~~~~~~~~~~~~~

A LANDSCAPE OF MOUNDS

Native American groups built earthen mounds and structures across parts of North America in the past. Thousands of distintinctively shaped earthen mounds dot the landscape of southern Wisconsin and the bordering regions of Illinois, Iowa, and Minnesota (Fig. 5.12). The mounds occur individually and in groups, often on high

Fig. 5.12 A procession of eleven bear mounds along a ridge top at Effigy Mounds National Monument, along the Mississippi River in northeastern Iowa. The mounds are outlined in white to make them more visible in the photograph.

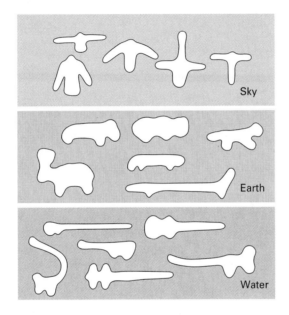

Sky

Earth

Water

Fig. 5.13 Effigy mound shapes include birds, mammals, turtles, and a few human forms. Various forms are thought to be related to the sky, earth, and water spirits.

points near water. They were built between AD 700 and 1200 and vary in size from 5 to more than 200 m (15–600 ft) in length and 1–3 m (3–10 ft in height). These mounds are effigies—built in the shapes of mammals (bear, panther, deer, wolf), reptiles (turtle), and birds (goose, eagle, hawk). The animals are shown in profile or plan (bird's-eye) view (Fig. 5.13). There are also a few examples of human figures known. Human burials, either as bundles or cremations, have sometimes been found in these mounds. Burials were usually placed in the central part of the animal, near the head or heart.

Some of the animals are found throughout the entire area of the Effigy Mound Culture, but others have a more restricted distribution. In recent years, it has become clear from information in the legends of Native American groups in Wisconsin that specific animals represent ideological symbols of different parts of the perceived environment. Birds, for example, signify the air; bears denote the land; panthers are a water spirit. With that information in hand, the different distributions of the mounds can be better understood. It is likely that different groups of people associated themselves with particular motifs. As can be seen in Fig. 5.14, the bears and birds predominate in western Wisconsin, while the panthers are much more common in southeastern Wisconsin. South-central Wisconsin has a combination of all three motifs, often in the same mound group. Clearly, these mounds were an important part of the ideological landscape that prehistoric peoples in southern Wisconsin created around themselves.

Fig. 5.14 The distribution of effigy mound shapes in the state of Wisconsin. This map emphasizes the different distributions of the bear and panther forms. Both overlap with birds in the south-central part of the state.

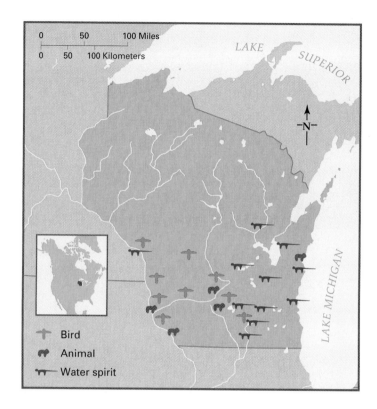

SPATIAL ARCHAEOLOGY

Spatial archaeology is the study of how and why prehistoric remains are distributed across geographic space. Investigations range from the analysis of the location of individual activities within a site to the distribution of sites or monuments in a region. Four levels of spatial information are of interest to archaeologists: (1) small activity areas or features within a site; (2) house floors within a site; (3) sites; and (4) sets of sites within a larger region (Fig. 5.15). Each level provides different kinds of information on the activities and behavior patterns of people in the past. These levels of analysis are discussed below.

Within-Site Spatial Analysis: Activity Areas and Features

Within-site spatial patterning in archaeology is usually seen in the form of activity areas, individual features, architectural units, or houses. Houses and households are discussed in the next section. A small area of artifacts and/or features within a site contains important information in its spatial patterns and relationships. Such patterns may represent activity areas, single deposits, or individual rooms, plazas, courtyards, or other architectural elements. Activity areas can be identified at short-term camps and within urban areas.

There are major differences in the archaeological evidence from the camps of hunter-gatherers and that from the villages, towns, and cities of farming populations. Hunter-gatherers were often mobile groups who moved regularly during the year. Their camps were usually short-term occupations and debris accumulations are minor. Such foragers built fireplaces and occasionally structures, but the number of features at such sites is also often limited. Because pottery was a late invention, largely associated with farming populations, the camps of hunter-gatherers normally contain more stone tools and animal bones than anything else if preservation is good.

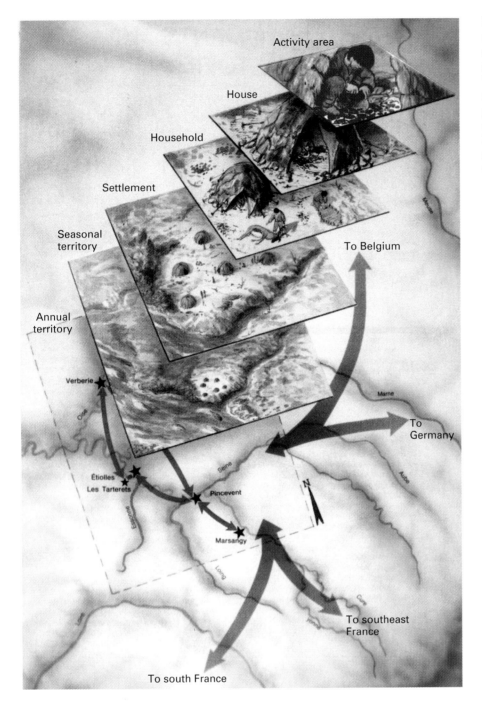

Fig. 5.15 Some of the spatial units of the archaeological record: activity area, house, household, settlement, seasonal territory, annual territory. These units increase in size, number of artifacts and features, and geographic scale. The units are nested—activity areas are found in houses or households, households make up settlements, and settlements mark the seasonal and annual territory.

The permanent settlements of farmers, on the other hand, were places where trash and architectural debris accumulated rapidly and in great quantity. The man-made mounds or **tells** of the ancient Near East are a classic example of such buildup (Fig. 5.16). The settlements of farmers contain proportionately fewer stone tools and much more pottery, plant and animal remains, features, and construction debris. The permanent sites of farmers are usually more visible in excavations or on the landscape itself.

Fig. 5.17 shows a plan of a Mesolithic campsite on a small Danish island dating to approximately 5000 BC. Excavations at the site revealed the distribution of artifacts and features from a hunter-gatherer occupation, and this information was used to reconstruct distinct areas of activity and refuse deposition at the site. The area of primary occupation was identified by the presence of several hearths

tell An accumulated mound of occupation debris; man-made settlement mounds of earth and trash that accumulate from the decomposition of mud-brick, common in Southwest Asia and Southeast Europe.

Fig. 5.16 The ancient city and fortress of Bam in southeastern Iran dates back more than 2000 years and sits on a tell that is even older. Parts of the site were destroyed by an earthquake in 2003.

Fig. 5.17 A Mesolithic site in Denmark, with identified activity areas on this small island. The primary activities appear to have been hide working and flint tool manufacture. Various areas of refuse and waste deposit are found at the edges of the island. The dark line at 1.5-m (5-ft) elevation marks the water level at the time of the occupation of the island. The area of primary occupation was identified by the presence of several hearths and a mix of artifacts. The shading shows the trenches and horizontal excavations at the site.

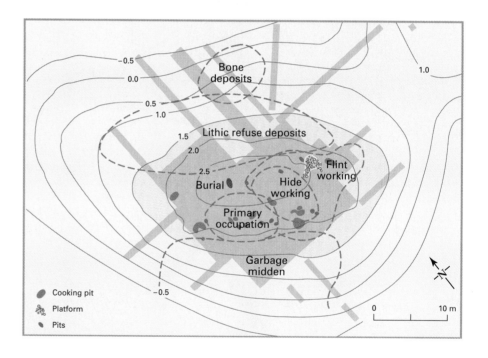

and a mix of artifacts. Artifacts indicated two major activities: hide working and flint tool manufacture. The various areas of refuse and waste deposit were found at the edges of the island.

In reality, the reconstruction of activity areas is often difficult for a variety of reasons. Among these reasons is that actual living floors with in situ artifacts are rare at both temporary and permanent settlements. At both kinds of sites, the inhabitants often cleaned areas of frequent use. Sweeping an area results in the removal of many of the larger pieces of debris. At seasonal hunter-gatherer sites, like the one in Fig. 5.17, larger artifacts and ecofacts were frequently tossed in the water, leaving only the smaller fragments and artifacts on the actual living area. Another factor masking activity areas comes from what Robert Ascher called the smearing or blending of patterns due to movement and the changing locations of activity during a stay. In addition, it is often the case that temporary locations of habitation are frequently reoccupied because of the good qualities of the setting. Reoccupation will also result in new uses of the living area, and more smearing of previous patterns will take place.

The discovery of activity areas within sedentary settlements is also difficult. Artifacts and debris are usually cleaned from the packed-earth or plaster floors of houses in such communities. Permanent fixtures in such houses, however, such as fireplaces, storage areas, platforms, and the like may provide an indication of how the house was used. The example below documents ritual activity areas both inside and outside the houses at residential units in the ancient city of Teotihuacán.

EXAMPLE

ACTIVITY AREAS AT TEOTIHUACÁN, MEXICO

The site of Teotihuacán (*TAY-oh-tee-wah-KAHN*) was one of the largest cities in the ancient world around AD 100. Located outside modern Mexico City in the highlands of Mexico, the ancient city housed 150,000 people in a series of large apartment compounds covering an area of some 25 km² (10 mi²). Much of Teotihuacán has been surveyed and mapped by archaeologists, providing fine resolution on the use of this large, urban area (Fig. 5.18). More than 5000 compounds, structures, and activity areas were recorded in the survey.

Several residential compounds have been excavated. The compound of Oztoyahualco (*ose-TOY-yah-WHELK-co*) in the northeast quarter of the city has been the focus of detailed study of internal activity areas. One aspect of the study involved the identification of areas for ritual and ceremonial activities. The compound itself likely housed three extended families in a series of rooms; the location of each family unit is indicated in Fig. 5.19. Each family unit was the locus of daily life, and a variety of activities took place within each domestic area. Each unit consisted of a number of rooms, courtyards, and passageways. It also had specific areas for food preparation and consumption, animal butchering, refuse deposition, sleeping, and other activities.

Courtyards were a focus of many activities, including various ceremonies and rituals. Small altars dedicated to household deities were built in these open spaces.

Teotihuacán

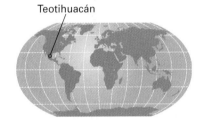

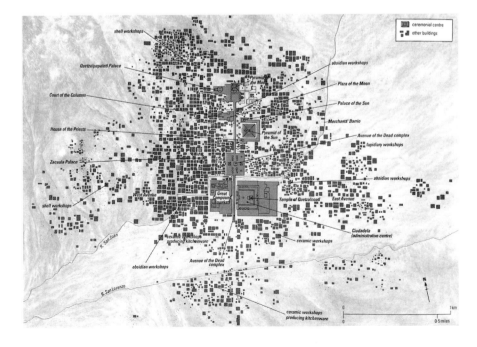

Fig. 5.18 A map of the ancient city of Teotihuacán in the central highlands of Mexico. The central north–south axis marks the major civic and ceremonial buildings at the site. The residential compound of Oztoyahualco lies in the northeast quadrant of the city, which covered more than 25 km² (10 mi²) at its height.

Spatial Archaeology **121**

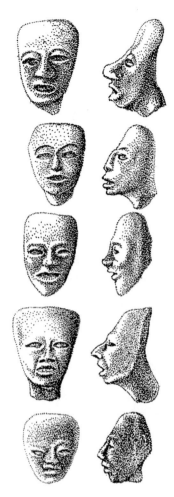

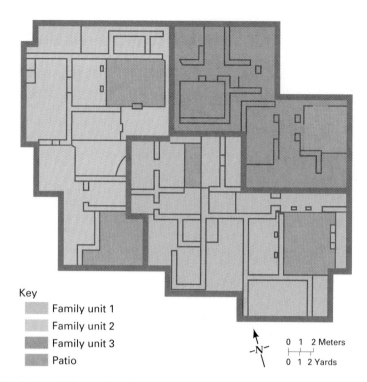

Key

Family unit 1
Family unit 2
Family unit 3
Patio

0 1 2 Meters
0 1 2 Yards

Fig. 5.19 A plan of the residential compound of Oztoyahualco in the ancient city of Teotihuacán in the central highlands of Mexico. The compound is approximately 25 m (75 ft) in width and contains three separate family residence areas, marked by the thick internal walls.

Fig. 5.20 Portrait ceramic figurines from the residential compound of Oztoyahualco, probably depicting some of the inhabitants of the site.

Courtyards were also a place of burial; eighteen graves were unearthed within the compound. A number of artifacts document the importance of the courtyards as ritual activity centers, including fragments of pottery vessels for burning incense and a variety of objects associated with a particular god. In addition, there were many clay figurines found, including portrait heads (Fig. 5.20) that may depict important residents of the compound.

Within-Site Spatial Analysis: Houses and Households

Houses are residential structures delimited by walls or other boundaries and enclosing artifacts and features used in domestic activities. The archaeology of households has become a subject of great interest in recent years. Houses are a locus of residential activity for an individual or group (the household) during the occupation of a site. Households are the basic building block of many human groups. These units organize and carry out the primary functions of reproduction and child rearing, subsistence, production and maintenance, and decision making that keep societies existing and vibrant.

An example of the spatial analysis of house floors is shown in Fig. 5.22. There are two views of the same house at the site of Uncas (*OONK-cuz*) in northern Oklahoma, ca. AD 1000. The plan on the left shows the outline of the house and the location of a variety of artifact types, bone, and antler. The plan on the right indicates the probable areas of activity within the house based on the distribution of different artifacts and the hearth. For example, scrapers were concentrated in the northwest quadrant of the house and are assumed to have been used for preparing animal hides for use as clothing. Areas of food preparation and

The City of the Gods

Teotihuacán—the spectacular "city of the gods"—was named to the UNESCO list of World Heritage Sites in 1987 and is protected in Mexico by presidential decree. The original city was approximately 25 km^2 (10 mi^2) in area, but the center of the protected archaeological zone today covers only 1.6 km^2 (1 mi^2). The protected area includes more than 5000 structures, ranging from the Temple of the Sun (Fig. 5.21) to residential compounds and craft workshops, and includes two canalized rivers, a major avenue, and ceremonial caves.

There are three concentric zones of the site that are protected: (A) a highly protected central portion where the Pyramids of the Sun and Moon, the Avenue of the Dead and the most important structures of the ancient city are located; (B) the modern towns of San Martin de Las Piramides and San Juan Teotihuacán; and (C) the periphery of the ancient city, where construction is permitted under certain conditions.

The site has been threatened several times over the course of the past century. Originally, a new airport for Mexico City was planned for the area. Today, the explosive growth of Mexico City has filled most of the surrounding valleys with the barrios of some of the 22,000,000 inhabitants of the city, and the expansion continues.

The most recent threat came from Wal-Mart and drew an emotional response from the people of the area. A number of groups protested the construction of a superstore less than 4 km (2.5 mi) from the center of the site. They argued against the scenic pollution and the additional development that the store would generate. The government, however, noted that Wal-Mart had used the proper channels to seek authorization and that the store would be built in Zone C, where construction is permitted. Many local people were happy to see the Wal-Mart arrive as a source of employment and cheaper goods and supplies.

Teotihuacán will always remain. It is an enormous center of temples and massive pyramids, an important part of the heritage of the nation of Mexico, and one of the most visited tourist attractions in the New World. At the same time, the wear and tear of tourism and the elements of nature slowly erode the surfaces of the buildings and mar paintings and other building details.

Fig 5.21 Teotihuacán, looking south along the Avenue of the Dead, from the Pyramid of the Moon. Note the Pyramid of the Sun 65 m (200 ft) high in the left center of the photo.

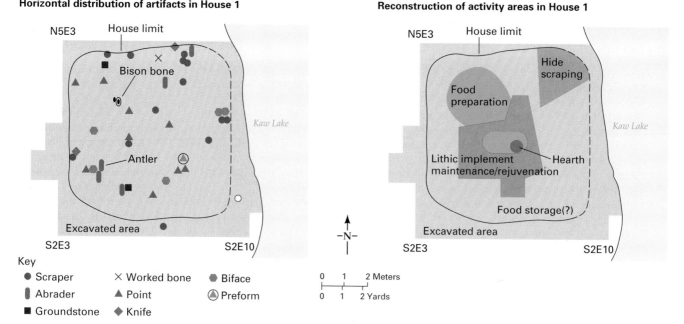

Horizontal distribution of artifacts in House 1

N5E3   House limit

Bison bone

Antler

Excavated area

S2E3   S2E10

Reconstruction of activity areas in House 1

N5E3   House limit

Hide scraping

Food preparation

Kaw Lake

Lithic implement maintenance/rejuvenation — Hearth

Food storage(?)

Excavated area

S2E3   S2E10

Key

● Scraper   × Worked bone   ● Biface
▮ Abrader   ▲ Point   ⊛ Preform
■ Groundstone ◆ Knife

–N–

0   1   2 Meters
0   1   2 Yards

Fig. 5.22 Activity areas within House 1 at the Uncas site in north-central Oklahoma. Left, horizontal distribution of artifacts; right, reconstruction of activity areas within the house.

storage, hide scraping, and stone tool repair have been identified in this hypothetical reconstruction.

A variety of information is available from the study and analysis of archaeological households, providing substantial insight on the organization and operation of these basic units of society. The spatial organization of the living surface or the floor of a structure may define areas for activities such as cooking, tool manufacturing, craft production, and weaving, or for certain facilities, such as sleeping or storage areas. These differences may indicate a division of male and female space and activities, how many people lived in a household, and the structure of the family—nuclear, extended, or polygynous, for example. An example of a household study from the period of European contact in Alaska is discussed below. Another example, the slave quarters at Poplar Forest, Virginia, can be found at the beginning of Chapter 1.

◉ **EXAMPLE** 〜〜〜〜〜〜〜〜〜〜〜〜〜〜〜

HOUSEHOLD ARCHAEOLOGY AT AGAYADAN VILLAGE, ALASKA

The Aleutian Islands of Alaska are home to some of the more interesting hunter-gatherers in North America. Although the area lies near the Arctic Circle, it is one of rich resources and large communities of hunter-gatherers. In the period between AD 1400 and 1800, these groups were characterized by an economy based on rich maritime and riverine resources, substantial villages organized by ranking, and large dwellings occupied by several nuclear families and their slaves. British and Russian explorers and traders in ivory and fur came to the area and spoke of visiting similar houses in the eighteenth century.

A total of twenty houses were visible on the surface as large depressions in the ground at the site of Agayadan (*OGG-aye-ya-dahn*) Village. These multifamily houses often have a number of side chambers or rooms and are described as nucleus-satellite structures (Fig. 5.23). Excavations of three houses of varying size at the site by Brian Hoffman of Hamline University have provided fascinating information on household organization and status differences. The largest house was 15 × 7 m (50 × 22 ft) in size; a medium-sized and a smaller house were also examined. The population of the site at its maximum is estimated to have been between 200 and 425 individuals.

Agayadan Village

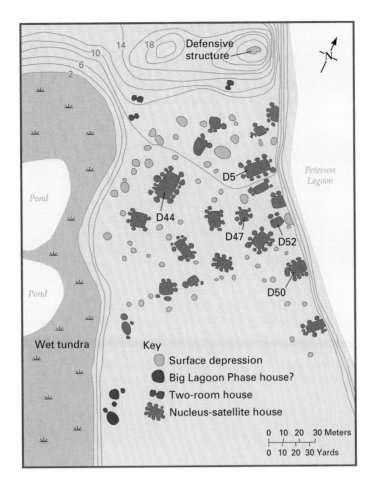

Fig. 5.23 The nucleus-satellite houses and other surface depressions at Agayadan Village. In addition to these houses, a number of other pits and smaller houses can be seen. There is a defensive earthwork located on a high point just to the north of the site. The three excavated houses were D-5, D-47, and D-50.

Fig. 5.24 Drawing of the interior of an Unalaska house by John Webber, a member of Captain Cook's expedition in 1778.

Careful removal of the living floor of these houses and analysis of the minutiae of debris have revealed information on occupation and abandonment. The timber houses had a central, open area; the areas closer to the walls were separated into smaller family spaces by a small trough. The contents of the three houses included more than 1500 artifacts of bone, stone, wood, and other materials, along with thousands of pieces of waste stone, bone, iron, and ochre.

A huge set of animal bones and shells were identified. The diet was based on food from the sea and rivers, including seals, sea lions, salmon, flatfish, ducks, gulls, and other shorebirds. Land mammals were not common among the animal bones. The season of death of the various mammals and fish suggests that the site was largely abandoned during the summer but occupied for the remainder of the year. The coast where the site is located was likely very wet during the summer when the frozen ground thawed and rainwater accumulated in low-lying areas.

Distinct communal and private areas were recognized in these multifamily dwellings. Features in the houses included hearths, roasting pits, and storage pits. Hearths for heat and cooking and roasting pits were located in central, communal areas of the houses; storage pits and workshop activities were associated with individual family compartments in the houses.

Most of the differences between the houses are related to the number and status of the occupants. Amber beads were found in all three houses, but 90% of the other artifacts for personal adornment (beads, pendants, lip plugs, and buckles of jet, ivory, and calcite) were found in the largest of the three houses. The inhabitants of the largest house also seem to have worked harder or had more slaves; they stored more foods, harvested more salmon, and spent more time making items for trade, including delicately carved trinkets of ivory and limestone and finely sewn clothing.

The end of the village likely came from violent encounters with Russian whalers as a consequence of the Russian War in 1764. Historical Russian documents record an attack on a village, probably Agayadan, describing the murder of a number of the inhabitants. Artifacts found in the medium-sized house support this interpretation. The contents of the house had been intentionally smashed or burned, and several musket balls of a common Russian caliber were found embedded in the floor.

Site Analysis

A site or living surface might include a habitation area with one or more shelters and fireplaces, different activity areas for food preparation, curing of animal skins and hides, and the manufacture of various artifacts, perhaps storage equipment, and a midden or trash area. A site is often a composite of artifacts, features, activity areas, structures, and midden (Fig. 5.25). The day-to-day activities of the occupants may be reflected in the various structures and activity areas found throughout the settlement. Structures at a site may be solid and substantial in the case of permanently settled communities in a village or townlike setting. Short-term or seasonal settlements, however, may leave little trace of construction.

Spatial patterning within a site can provide information about the number of houses and people at the settlement and on their relationships with one another, as well as the kinds of activities that went on at the site. The site of Meer in Belgium, described in Chapter 10, provides an example of the spatial analysis of a camp of hunter-gatherers from the Late Paleolithic.

Regional Spatial Analysis

Regional studies are growing in importance in archaeology. Approaches that relate variables of interaction among human groups are of particular interest. These variables include (1) the size and nature of groups involved; (2) the nature of the interaction, and (3) the physical space across which interaction occurs. Settlement pattern analysis is the regional study of settlements and focuses on the type of sites present. The camps of hunter-gatherers, for example, present very different patterns than the cities, towns, and villages of settled farmers. Important questions about the sites of hunter-gatherers concern the season and length of occupation, the kinds of foods and resources consumed, and the number of inhabitants. In the following text, we discuss the forager-collector model for hunter-gatherers and provide an example of the regional analysis of state-level settlement patterns.

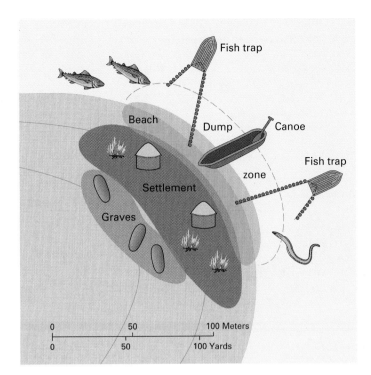

Fig. 5.25 A hypothetical plan of a hunter-gatherer camp along the seacoast of Denmark some 7000 years ago. Sites are located at good fishing places directly at the water's edge. Fixed fishing equipment is set in the water off the site. Garbage and debris from the site is often thrown in the water nearest the site, creating a dump zone. There is a landing area at the beach. The living floor is situated next to the coastline and contains residential and activity areas marked by scatters of artifacts and concentrations of hearths. Behind the settlement on slightly higher ground are places for burial of the dead. These sites are linear deposits 20–30 m (60–100 ft) in length and 10–20 m (30–60 ft) in width along the coast.

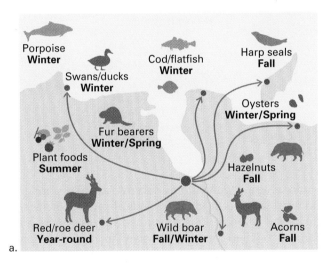

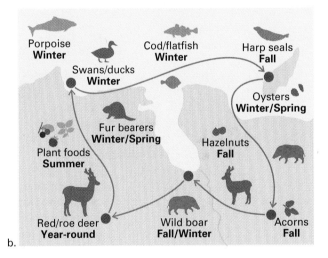

Fig. 5.26 A schematic representation of foraging and collecting patterns of subsistence and settlement among hunter-gatherers. (a) Collectors occupy a fixed base camp. A number of smaller, temporary, specialized hunting and gathering sites are used to extract resources from the environment and return them to the base. (b) Foragers move residential camps regularly during the year to take advantage of seasonally abundant food resources.

Some years ago Lewis Binford suggested a useful model for the study of hunter-gatherer settlement. Binford distinguished foraging and collecting patterns based on residential mobility (Fig. 5.26). Foragers move people to food, while collectors have more permanent residences and bring foods back to their base. Foragers follow what is known as an **annual round or cycle**, moving regularly from place to place and from year to year across the landscape. In essence, this is a distinction between more and less mobile strategies for survival. Binford intended this distinction to represent two ends of a continuum, in which prehistoric hunter-gatherers might find a strategy at either end or somewhere in the middle between foraging and collecting.

Among village farmers, differences in the size and architectural elaboration of houses may be evidence of status differentiation, a situation where some people have more wealth, power, and control over goods and labor than others. The arrangement of houses in a town or city also may reflect social organization

Fig. 5.27 The nature of social, political, economic, and religious relationships among settlements in a region. Relationships vary depending on the context.

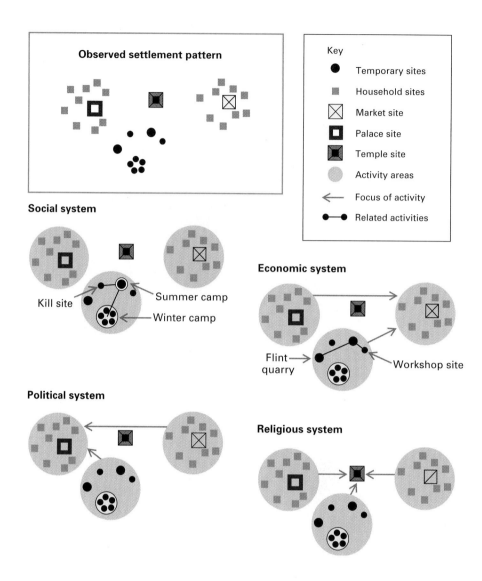

in the separation of poor and wealthy households. Concerns for privacy and protection in the form of fences, palisades, or ditches may indicate private ownership or conditions of competition or warfare. Settlement studies also may reveal areas of economic specialization, with skilled craftsmen involved in the production of certain materials, while other items are made in individual households.

Regional settlement patterns can provide a variety of information on the prehistoric use of the landscape. Several different kinds of sites are often found in an area. Residential settlements of various sizes and durations are typical targets for investigation. Such sites can vary from camps to villages, towns, or ancient cities. Fig. 5.27 depicts several groups of settlements in a region—temporary sites, households, markets, palaces, and temples. The relationships among these sites, and the groups of people who occupied them, vary depending on social, political, economic, or religious context. For example, social relationships—marriage and kinship—define three distinct socially related units. Everyone participates in ceremonies at the isolated temple site, but political allegiances connect the different groups to the palace. Economically, food, raw materials, and finished products are traded at the market site.

The study of ancient civilizations has frequently involved the investigation of settlement location and distribution. One important approach in such studies employs the so-called **gravity model**, borrowed from cultural geography. This model predicts that the expected interaction between two populations is equal to

gravity model A concept from geography whereby interaction among settlements is based on size, similar to interaction among planets based on gravity. Bigger communities have more interaction and influence on smaller communities.

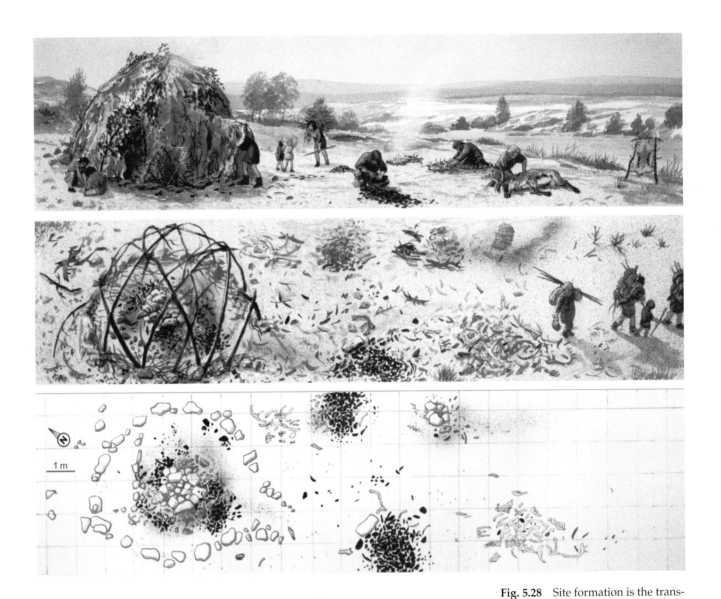

Fig. 5.28 Site formation is the transformation of past human behavior into the archaeological record. A Stone Age campsite with hut and activity areas becomes a scatter of stones, bones, charcoal, postholes, and discolorations.

the product of the size of the two groups divided by the square of the distance between them. You can think about such a model in terms of stars, planets, and moons, and the effects of gravity. Heavier celestial bodies have more gravity and more effect on other bodies, depending on how far apart they are. Bigger towns and cities have more influence than smaller communities.

SITE FORMATION

Archaeology is the study of past human behavior. But archaeologists cannot directly observe the behavior we are trying to understand. Instead, we observe the archaeological record that preserves only material culture and context. Dynamic behavior has been coded into static and decomposed evidence. It's a bit like crime scene investigation, only much more difficult. Archaeologists need to solve a mystery but have only a few bits and pieces of clues. Time and decomposition have removed much of the evidence that was originally present. In order to understand the past, it is essential to find connections between human behavior in the past and the artifacts that survive to the present. An important aspect of these connections is how archaeological sites are created, a process known as **site formation**.

Fig. 5.28 depicts the transformation of the camp of a small group of hunter-gatherers into an archaeological site. The living place—with huts, fireplaces,

site formation The processes involved in the creation of archaeological sites.

TABLE 5.2 Some natural and cultural formation and transformation processes affecting archaeological sites.

Process	Formation		Transformation	
	Natural	**Cultural**	**Natural**	**Cultural**
Erosion and deposition	X		X	
Catastrophe	X		X	
Past human activity		X		X
Bioturbation			X	X
Modern human activity				X
Looting				X

Source: Mark Q. Sutton and Robert M. Yohe. 2003. *Archaeology: The Science of the Human Past.* Boston: Allyn & Bacon.

drying rack, and several activity areas—disintegrates over time into scatters of stone tools and waste, construction stone, and concentrations of bone, ochre, and charcoal.

Some years ago, Michael Schiffer of the University of Arizona wrote about this issue in a book called *Behavioral Archaeology.* Schiffer distinguished **systemic context** (the actual use of artifacts and features in the past or present) from the **archaeological context** in which they are found. In his book, Schiffer focused on the factors that affect artifacts and features during the change from systemic to archaeological context. He noted that one set of activities creates or forms the archaeological record (formation processes) and another set of activities and processes transforms the buried record over time (transformation processes). Schiffer distinguished these processes as cultural or natural transformations of the archaeological record (Table 5.2). **Cultural transformation** of the archaeological record is the result of human activity; **natural transformation** is the result of geological, hydrological, and chemical activity while artifacts are lying on or buried in the ground.

One way to think about the formation of the archaeological record is to consider the life history of an artifact. Fig. 5.29 schematically charts the life of an artifact from the acquisition of raw material to the manufacture of the artifact. The debris from manufacture is waste material deposited in the archaeological record. The artifact itself can be lost, used, or stored and enter the archaeological record. Lost artifacts can be scavenged and reused. Broken or exhausted artifacts are discarded or recycled until finally discarded. Artifacts can also be cached (stored) in the ground or elsewhere for later retrieval or buried for ritual reasons. These cached objects can be retrieved or forgotten. Scavenging is another activity that often returns lost or discarded artifacts into the use cycle. In some cases, scavenging and reuse may take place thousands of years later.

Artifacts and features either remain on the surface of the ground or are covered by sediments over time through a natural or cultural process. Flooding, airborne dust, earthworm activity, **slopewash**, continued human presence, and many other activities can result in the accumulation of sediments and the eventual burial of archaeological remains. Some further aspects of site burial are discussed in Chapter 9, "Geoarchaeology."

Taphonomy is the term used in paleontology and archaeology for the study of what happens to a plant or animal between its death and the time it is found as a fossil or archaeological remain. This interim includes decomposition, postmortem transport, burial, and other chemical, biological, and geological activities that affect the remains of the organism. Discovery of the taphonomic processes that

systemic context   The actual use of *artifacts* and *features* in the past or present.

archaeological context   The buried or surface context in which archaeological remains are found; what survives to the present.

cultural transformation   Modification of the *archaeological record* caused by human activity.

natural transformation   Modification of the archaeological record by geological, hydrological, or chemical activity.

slopewash   Gradual movement of sediments from higher to lower ground as a natural process of erosion and deposition.

taphonomy   The study of what happens to a plant or animal between its death and the time it is found as a fossil or archaeological remain.

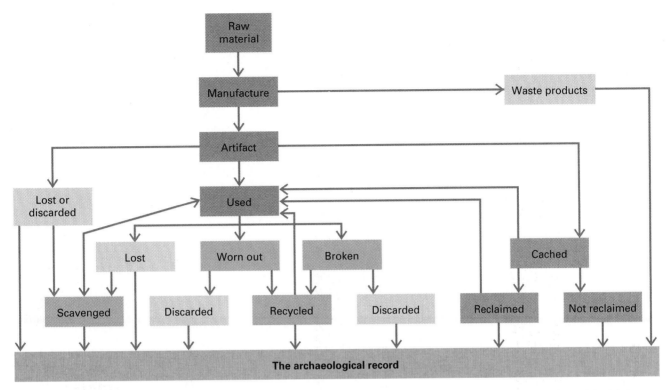

Fig. 5.29 Diagram of the life history of an artifact from raw material to the archaeological record.

occurred provides a better understanding of the environment and life history of the organism. The importance of taphonomy in the study of animal bones in archaeology is discussed in Chapter 12.

The study of the natural and cultural transformation of past human activity into an archaeological site is essentially the taphonomy of behavior. Following burial, a number of disturbances can affect the location, context, and preservation of the archaeological materials in the ground (Fig. 5.30). Cultural transformations include digging, burning, building, and the like. Looting results in the intentional destruction of archaeological materials.

Natural transformation of archaeological remains can take place through subsequent erosion by waves or water currents, wind, or ice, or through catastrophic transformations due to flood, earthquake, or other events. Natural transformations also result from plant and animal activities such as root growth or animal digging—a phenomenon known as **bioturbation**. Burrowing animals like rabbits, moles, and many others dig tunnels and nests deep into the ground and destroy features and change the positions of archaeological materials. For example, porcupines digging tunnels and dens in certain rockshelters and caves of the Near East have completely scrambled archaeological deposits from the Paleolithic. The roots of trees and other plants can also displace artifacts in the ground and alter the conditions of preservation. When large trees fall or are blown over, the root system is levered out of the ground and brings with it a huge ball of soil and sediments. Such tree falls were a common event in the past, as today, and often disturbed archaeological sites.

Fig. 5.31 illustrates how formation and transformation processes might operate on a 2-million-year-old Stone Age site from East Africa. The scenario begins with a simple site created by a group of early humans carrying animal parts and stone tools to the shade of a large tree. While there, they make tools, butcher the animal parts, break some of the bones for marrow, and eat and sleep. When they leave, the humans might remove some of the tools or food, thus erasing some evidence of their activities. Several things then happen in this scenario. Other animals bring their kills to the shade of the tree. Scavengers remove bones and other

[Archaeology is] the discipline with the theory and practice for the recovery of unobservable hominid behavior patterns from indirect traces in bad samples.
—David Clarke, archaeologist

*The day we die, then the wind comes,
To wipe out the traces of our feet,
The wind creates dust which covers
The traces that were where we walked.*
—San chant, quoted by Colin Turnbull, anthropologist

bioturbation Disturbance of the *archaeological record* from plant and animal activities such as root growth or animal digging.

Site Formation **131**

Fig. 5.30 Cultural and natural formation and transformation of an archaeological site. A sequence of occupation episodes interrupted by natural events of flooding, decomposition, and modern construction.

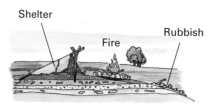

2000 years ago: Hunting camp (acquisition, manufacture, use, and deposition behavior).

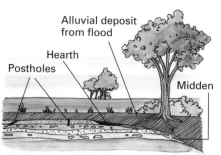

1800 years ago: Flood covers remains of camp with silt (transformational process).

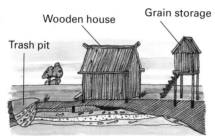

1500 years ago: Farming village built on silt (new cycle of acquisition, manufacture, use, and deposition behavior).

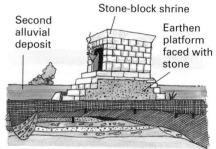

1000 years ago: New flood destroys farming village (transformational process); stone shrine built on new ground surface (new cycles of acquisition, manufacture, use, and deposition behavior).

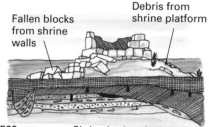

500 years ago: Shrine is abandoned and begins to disintegrate, forming mound (depositional and natural transformational processes).

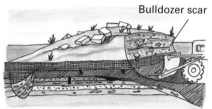

Today: Mound is quarried for fill to be used in highway construction (cultural transformational process).

Fig. 5.31 A schematic view of some of the events and processes that create and modify Stone Age archaeological sites, in this case, a hypothetical site ca. 2 million years old. In addition to the disturbances shown, roots and animal burrows can move artifacts and destroy or modify features.

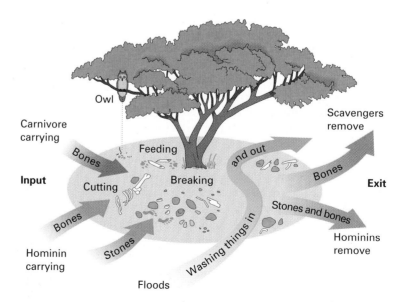

animal parts. Flash floods cross the base of the tree, removing some artifacts and features and leaving others behind. Predator birds land in the tree and leave their droppings. Eventually, the place is buried in sediment or volcanic ash and becomes an archaeological site. As this scenario shows, time and the elements can differentially remove much of the evidence of past human behavior.

PRESERVATION

One of the primary processes affecting the formation of an archaeological site is preservation. Once objects and features are buried in the ground, the forces of nature initiate a process of decay and decomposition. The effects of this process depend on a number of conditions, including temperature, moisture, acidity, and setting. In most situations, many of the materials originally present at a site disappear over time, leaving only the most durable artifacts. Archaeologists thus normally find only a tiny proportion of the total material culture that was present in the past. Fig. 5.32 shows before and after (past and present) views of the material culture of some hypothetical hunter-gatherers, following the decomposition

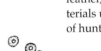

Fig. 5.32 The effects of decay are depicted in this figure. (a) What remains of the artifact assemblage after time and decomposition have removed the organic portion. Only the stone fishing weights, the stone axe, and small stone projectile points remain. Archaeologists usually find only a tiny remainder of the materials used in the past. (b) The range of bone, antler, wood, horn, plant, feather, sinew, stone, and shell materials used by a hypothetical group of hunter-gatherers.

a.

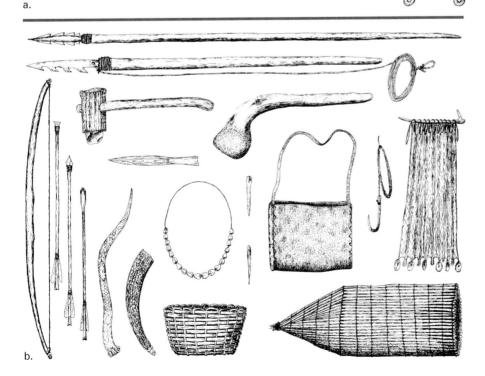

b.

Fig. 5.33 One of the natural processes affecting archaeological sites is differential preservation. Comparison of wet and dry conditions is shown in the graph for various kinds of materials. Inorganic items fare better than soft organic materials under poor conditions for preservation. Extremely arid conditions are also conducive to good preservation.

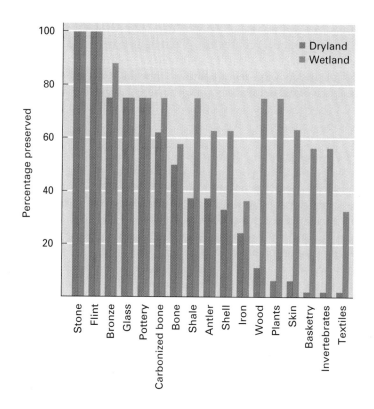

TABLE 5.3 Conditions of preservation and survival for various classes of archaeological remains.

Material	Normal survival time	Conditions for preservation	Conditions for decomposition
Stone	Millions of years	Most	Exposure in erosional environments
Copper/bronze	Millions of years	Most	Moisture, oxygen
Gold	Millions of years	Most	Few
Glass	Millions of years	Most	Plowing, acidic soils
Ceramics	Thousands of years	Most	Freeze-thaw, plowing, acidic soils
Iron	Hundreds of years	Few, no oxygen	Moisture, oxygen
Bone	Months to years	Rapid burial, wet, burning, alkaline soils, fossilization	Surface exposure, wet-dry conditions, acidic soils
Plants	Weeks to years	Dry, cold, wet	Moisture, warm temperatures, acidic soils
Flesh	Days to weeks	Dry, cold, wet	Moisture, warm temperatures, acidic soils

Source: Based on Sutton and Yohe 2003, 103.

of the organic component of the materials. Only objects of stone remain after the passage of time in this case.

One of the most important conditions affecting preservation is moisture. Very dry or very wet conditions will foster preservation, but damp conditions or a situation of a shifting wet and dry environment promotes decomposition. Fig. 5.33 depicts the approximate levels of preservation at dryland and wetland sites. At such sites, inorganic materials usually are preserved, and organic materials usually disappear.

Table 5.3 offers a summary of materials and conditions of preservation for a variety of archaeological finds. In essence, inorganic materials—stone, metal, glass, ceramics—can survive for very long periods under varying conditions of preservation. Organic materials—bone, wood, plant materials, meat—often the most common trash, generally disappear at archaeological sites except under rare conditions of aridity or wetness.

Two examples of remarkable preservation are documented below: the Windover materials from Archaic Florida and the Iceman from the Italian Alps.

 EXAMPLE ～～～～～～～～～～～～～～～～～～～

WINDOVER POND, FLORIDA

Near the spaceport of Cape Canaveral, Florida, lies one of the more remarkable archaeological finds from North America. The Windover site is a pond cemetery used by the people who lived and died along Florida's Atlantic coast between 8000 and 7000 years ago (Fig. 5.34). Archaic hunter-gatherers buried their dead in the small pond there. The waterlogged conditions and unusually low acidity of the pond have preserved the people and the gifts with which they were buried to a remarkable degree.

At least 168 deceased individuals were staked down underwater on the soft mud floor of the pond. Most were placed on their side with their face to the north. One female was buried facedown and the remains of her last meal were found in the stomach area. The contents included fish scales and bone, nut fragments, and seeds

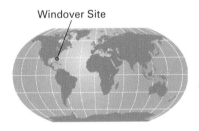

Windover Site

Fig. 5.34 Excavations at the Windover site in Florida. The pond has been drained to permit excavations to take place.

Fig. 5.35 Preserved skull containing brain tissue from the Windover excavations. The brain case was opened in a search for preserved tissue.

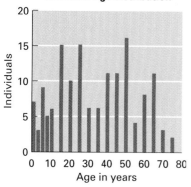

Fig. 5.36 The age distribution of individuals buried at the Windover site. A high number of children are present and a few individuals lived to be more than 60 years of age.

from grasses and berries. Ancient DNA and bits of brain tissue were preserved in more than ninety of the individuals (Fig. 5.35).

The large number of burials provided important information about this population of hunter-gatherers. The age of the buried individuals is shown in Fig. 5.36. Age at death ranged from infant to around 60 years, although a few individuals lived to be even older. A high mortality rate for the young is seen from the equal proportions of children and adults in the cemetery. Intriguing signs of both compassion and conflict were found in the skeletal material. Several of the individuals in the population had debilitating diseases or injuries—yet they survived for a number of years, clearly cared for by others. In addition, there were a number of traumatic injuries that resulted from blows to the head and limbs and wounds from pointed weapons in the skeletal remains as well. These injuries were observed in both adults and children.

Large numbers of artifacts have also been preserved. There were more than eighty-five examples of weaving, basketry, woodworking, and clothing. The textiles—bits of cloth and bags—are the oldest woven materials found in North America. The fabric was made with fibers from local plants, probably palm, with weaving techniques requiring a loom. Other artifacts included a small bird bone decorated with fine, geometric lines, a hollow bone perhaps used as a whistle, bone hammers with wooden handles, shark teeth, and stone points. The grave of a 45-year-old male contained the fabric from grave wrappings, several pointed bone awls, a number of bone needles, a large tooth from a puma, a drilled shark tooth, and a finely made stone projectile point.

Many of these artifacts were completely unknown prior to the discovery of Windover. The pieces of fabric have pushed back our knowledge of weaving technology by thousands of years. The human remains provide an extraordinary glimpse of the ancient inhabitants of Florida. The skeletal remains tell us about the demography and aspects of life of the population. The brain tissue and DNA tell us about the biology of the people and their relationships with each other and with other Native American groups in North America. Remarkable conditions of preservation are responsible for this unique opportunity.

Today, the site is once again a quiet, dark pond in the Windover neighborhood. After the last season of excavation, the dark peat was pushed back into the pond and the place restored to its previous condition.

⊙ EXAMPLE

THE ICEMAN

One of the most extraordinary archaeological finds of the last century was made in 1991 in the high Alps, on the border between Italy and Austria. Hikers noticed a human body, half-frozen, facedown, in the snow and ice along the trail (Fig. 5.37). The hikers contacted the authorities, who assumed it was the body of an unfortunate mountaineer; a number of people die in the Alps every year. The remains were somewhat carelessly removed from the ice and taken to a morgue. After inspection of the body, and particularly the items found with the corpse, it became clear that this was not the result of a recent climbing accident—it was the frozen mummy of a man from the Stone Age.

The Iceman is the highest archaeological find in Europe, at 3200 m (10,500 ft). Sometime fairly soon after his death, snow buried his body; there are no traces of scavenging by birds or other animals. He is mummified, dried by the sun, wind, and ice of the mountaintops. Over time, a small glacier on the mountaintop expanded to cover the depression in which the Iceman lay. Amazingly, this thick, heavy layer of ice did not crush the body, but sealed it into a small depression for 6000 years, as if in a huge freezer. That glacier retreated during the warm summer of 1991 and exposed the corpse.

The body was taken to the University of Innsbruck for study. More than 150 specialists have been examining all aspects of Ötzi (*UT-zee*), as he has come to be known, named after the nearby Ötz valley. The extent of preservation is remarkable; most of

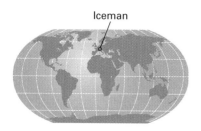

Iceman

Fig. 5.37 The Iceman as he was discovered in the high Alps along the border between Italy and Austria; his body emerged from the melting ice of a mountain glacier.

the internal organs, as well as the eyeballs, are intact. Although the body was hairless from the effects of freezing and thawing, hair was found around the body. Tattoos were clearly visible on his back and right leg. X-rays revealed several broken ribs and indicate that the Iceman suffered from arthritis in his neck, lower back, and right hip. An absence of stomach contents and the presence of material in the large intestine indicate that he had not eaten for 8 hours. His last meal included unleavened bread, some greens, and meat. DNA analysis identified the meat as coming from red deer (European elk). Analysis of pollen in the stomach contents indicates he died between March and June. The Iceman was approximately 50 years old at the time of his death. Radiocarbon dates from the body and the equipment the Iceman carried indicate an age of around 4300 BC, clearly in the Neolithic period.

The Iceman was carrying a substantial amount of gear with him, consisting of seven articles of clothing and a number of pieces of equipment. His clothing included a large belt with a pouch, which held up a leather loincloth and skin leggings, a coat of deerskin, a cape of woven grass, a conical leather cap with fur on the inside and a chin strap, and shoes of calfskin stuffed with grass.

The equipment included a bow and quiver of arrows, bow strings, bone points, a bone needle, a hafted copper axe, a wooden rucksack frame, two birchbark containers, a hafted knife of flint and its sheath, several flint tools (including a scraper, an awl, a flake, and a tool for pressure flaking flint), a net (perhaps for catching birds), a piece of ibex horn, a marble pendant, and birch fungus (possibly used as medicine). Most of the arrows were unfinished; he carried several items that were incomplete or in need of repair. No food was found among his possessions. One of the more interesting finds is the axe; it is almost pure copper. This new metal documents the widespread use of copper during the latter half of the Neolithic period. Copper was being mined and smelted in several areas of eastern Europe by this time and traded as far as Scandinavia.

The difficult questions about the Iceman include where he came from, how he died, and what he was doing so high in the Alps. He probably came from valleys to the south in Italy, less than a day's walk away. He carried a small ember of charcoal, for use in starting fires, from the wood of trees that grow south of the Alps. Pollen found in his intestines came from the hornbeam tree, which also grew only to the south of the Alps. The grains of wheat attached to his clothing and in his last meal indicate connections with farming villages. His lungs are black with the hearth smoke that filled early Neolithic houses. Recent studies have revealed several wounds. Deep cuts to his hand and wrist suggest he was in an armed struggle and an arrowhead lodged in his back may well have been the cause of death. It now seems that the Iceman died as a result of violent conflict. Why he died high in the peaks of the Alps remains a mystery.

CONCLUSIONS

Sometimes a picture is worth thousands of words. The diagram in Fig. 5.38 has a lot of parts, but it is a wonderful illustration of how archaeologists think about past human societies, how the things we study—people, artifacts, assemblages,

Fig. 5.38 This diagram shows the relationships between some of the major units of archaeological analysis and their social equivalents. These relationships show that attributes are the product of individuals; artifacts reflect group activities; components are produced by groups of people; and regional assemblages are the material remains of archaeological cultures. These relationships are not written in stone but often are appropriate to the material evidence that archaeologists study. These assumptions also tend to ignore the effects of change over time, which are always an important aspect of this evidence. The diagram depicts an abstract situation in the prehistory of the southwestern United States but is applicable in most places.

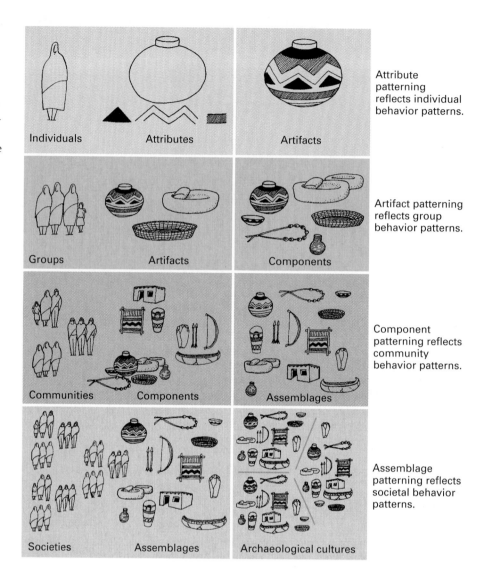

Attribute patterning reflects individual behavior patterns.

Artifact patterning reflects group behavior patterns.

Component patterning reflects community behavior patterns.

Assemblage patterning reflects societal behavior patterns.

and cultures—are related. The diagram shows the social correlates of archaeological evidence—how we go from static material to the dynamics of human organization. It is worth spending some time considering what is depicted here. This illustration, designed by James Deetz, is an enormous simplification, of course, but the basic relationships that are depicted are extremely useful for thinking about how we classify the archaeological record.

There are several levels of evidence that are used—attributes, artifacts, components, and assemblages. Individual or idiosyncratic behavior is reflected in the attributes that appear on artifacts and features. Designs on pottery reflect both social norms and personal choice. Individuals, households, groups, communities, and entire societies may be reflected in the different levels of artifact and feature patterning. The spatial implications of such patterning are also important—individuals are found at points on the landscape at any one moment in time, activities take place in a relatively small area, communities cover small to large areas depending on their size, and cultures cover regions. Spatial archaeology is the investigation of the location and geographic aspects of sites and the human use of the landscape.

This chapter has considered the nature of the archaeological record and the importance of context and scale in thinking about the past. The archaeological record is composed of both material and context. Context refers to the relationships between the materials of the archaeological record. Materials include a variety of objects—attributes, artifacts, ecofacts, features, sites, assemblages, and

Ötzi's New Home

The Iceman is one of those rare finds in archaeology that attract enormous public attention because of the unusual conditions of preservation. The mysteries of the Iceman—how the body was preserved for so long, and how and why he died—add to the aura of intrigue surrounding the discovery. Equally important, however, is how much we are learning from the Iceman about the artifacts, clothing, and equipment of the Neolithic—and especially how those people were not very different from ourselves.

The Iceman has now returned to the cold. His body today is displayed through a small window in a large freezer in a $1.9 million exhibit in the South Tyrol Archaeological Museum in Bolzano, Italy. Ötzi now lies on a glass tabletop, surrounded by walls of ice blocks and a small viewing window. The new ice cell has a constant temperature of –21°F (–30°C) and a humidity of 99%, conditions that will keep the corpse of the Iceman preserved.

The museum also contains the artifacts that accompanied the Iceman on his long journey through time. Today, the Iceman and the museum are bringing thousands of visitors to this rather out-of-the-way region of northern Italy.

landscapes. These materials and the information of context, scale, and place provide the basic evidence for archaeological research.

In order to better understand the context, scale, and place of the evidence, archaeologists investigate the processes that formed the archaeological record. Formation processes are part of the creation of archaeological sites and their transformation after formation. Natural formation involves nonhuman processes of erosion, deposition, and disturbance. Plant and animal disturbances are referred to as bioturbation. Other natural changes to a site involve wind and water erosion and deposition, freeze and thaw conditions, and the chemistry of soils and sediment. Catastrophic events also result in natural changes to the archaeological record. Cultural changes to the archaeological record involve human activities, such as digging, building, and looting, which often disturb or destroy remains from the past.

Conditions for preservation are a critical aspect of the archaeological record and determine what kinds of evidence remain for study. Conditions for preservation vary with temperature, moisture, and acidity. Very wet and very dry conditions generally favor the survival of more fragile remains from the past, while intermediate conditions usually mean the disappearance of organic materials at archaeological sites.

STUDY QUESTIONS

1. What is the archaeological record?
2. What are the major types of archaeological evidence?
3. Why is it important to understand the processes that form the archaeological record?
4. What kinds of natural changes can take place at archaeological sites?
5. Can you list ten different kinds of archaeological sites?

www.mhhe.com/pricearch1

For more review material and study questions, please see the self-quizzes on your online learning center.

www.mhhe.com/pricearch1

For Internet references related to this chapter, please see the chapter links on your online learning center.

REFERENCES

Allison, Penelope, ed. 1999. *The Archaeology of Household Activities.* New York: Routledge.

Deetz, James. 1967. *Invitation to Archaeology.* Garden City, N.Y.: Natural History Press.

Dincauze, D. F. 2000. *Environmental Archaeology.* Cambridge: Cambridge University Press.

Peebles, Christopher, and Susan Kus. 1977. Some archaeological correlates of ranked societies. *American Antiquity* 42:421–448.

Schiffer, M. B. 1987. *Formation Processes of the Archaeological Record.* Albuquerque: University of New Mexico Press.

Trigger, Bruce. 1968. The determinants of settlement patterns. In *Settlement Archaeology,* edited by K. C. Chang, 53–78. Palo Alto: National Press.

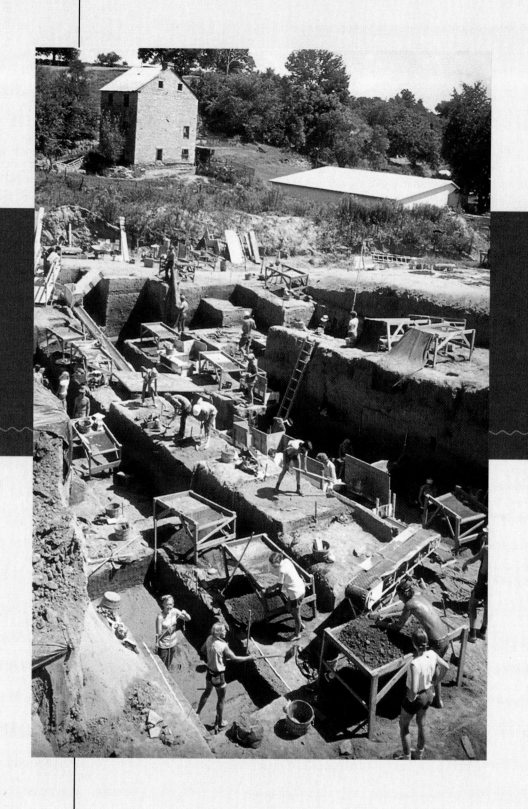

Fieldwork

INTRODUCTION: FINDING THE PAST

The photograph on the opposite page shows one of the better-known projects in the history of American archaeology. The excavations at the Koster (*KAH-stir*) site in Illinois in the 1970s opened an enormous area and exposed a deep series of cultural layers. The Koster site was the location of settlement for a series of human groups over a period of 10,000 years of occupation. There are at least twenty-six separate **living horizons** present, and major villages were present around 3300, 5000, and 6600 BC. The finds from the site include many thousands of artifacts, the earliest house structures in North America, one of the earliest domesticated dog burials in the New World (5000 BC), and objects brought to the site from as far away as the Great Lakes and the Gulf of Mexico.

The research at Koster was one of the activities of the Center for American Archaeology (CAA), which was established in the area in 1953 and has become a major focal point for education, training, and research. The CAA is located in the small town of Kampsville, Illinois, and over the years has purchased a number of buildings in the town to incorporate into the archaeological facilities. For example, a former general store is now the CAA Museum and Visitor Center with artifacts, exhibits, and media displays.

A nonprofit enterprise, the Center for American Archaeology today continues a program of archaeological research in east-central Illinois. The CAA's mission is to discover and disseminate the unwritten story of earlier Americans' lifeways, accomplishments, and changing natural environment. Several generations of students, schoolteachers, and interested vocational archaeologists have benefited from participation in the fieldwork of the center.

It is almost impossible to overstate the importance of fieldwork in archaeology. It is the essential means for obtaining the basic information that archaeologists use to understand the past. It is often difficult, tedious, and monotonous. It frequently takes place under less than ideal circumstances and it is usually inadequately funded. Assembling the time, energy, money, permission, equipment, and crew necessary for a field project is a major undertaking. At the same time, fieldwork is a memorable experience—physically, socially, and intellectually.

This chapter is an introduction to the methods of fieldwork that provide the primary evidence for archaeology. I have been doing fieldwork for more than forty years, and I still enjoy the challenges. It is the most inspiring activity possible for an archaeologist. In the field, I constantly find myself asking new questions, recognizing old errors, and gaining insight more than in any other context.

living horizon (*occupation horizon, living floor*)
The actual surface of occupation at an archaeological site, sometimes preserved under unusual conditions of deposition.

I insist that students participate in fieldwork. Without an involvement in the recovery of archaeological data, it is very difficult to appreciate all of the factors that shape and modify the information we have to use. Archaeological remains are usually fragmentary, disturbed, and in complex depositional environments. An appreciation of the many limitations of archaeological evidence is essential for a realistic perspective on what we can learn about the past.

Archaeologists study past human behavior, from the time of our early ancestors to the historical present. Most of the information about the past comes from artifacts, sites, and regions. Artifacts are the objects and materials that people made and used in the past. Sites are accumulations of such artifacts, representing the places where people resided or carried out various activities. Regions are areas with a number of sites where groups of people lived and interacted with others and the environment. Learning about the past involves the discovery, analysis, and interpretation of artifacts, sites, regions, and other archaeological information.

This chapter is about the discovery process, the search for and recovery of archaeological information. Much of the information gathering for archaeological studies involves **fieldwork** that is intended to locate artifacts and sites. Artifacts and sites are found either on the surface or beneath the ground. **Survey** is used to discover artifacts on the ground; **excavations** are used to expose buried materials. Survey and excavation can be combined in a project intended to learn about a particular area, or they take place independently, depending on the goals of the project. Fieldwork and discovery are part of research designed to answer questions about the past. Survey and excavation are used in both basic research about the past and in cultural resource management, protecting the past from modern development.

Survey and excavation are the primary discovery techniques of field archaeology. Following a discussion of these fieldwork methods, some of the tools for fieldwork are described, including maps and grids, soil sampling, and various kinds of remote sensing designed to look onto or through the ground for archaeological remains. People and equipment are also important parts of fieldwork, and the last segment of this chapter considers the project director, the field crew, the field experience, and some of the tools and equipment that are needed for a successful archaeological project.

THE DISCOVERY OF ARCHAEOLOGICAL SITES

To understand the past, and before survey or excavation can even begin, archaeologists must locate the places where people lived and left the remains of residence and other activities. Finding sites requires a combination of methods that includes research in libraries and archives, communication with **amateur archaeologists** and local people, and fieldwork.

Archaeological materials are most commonly discovered by accident. Digging and construction activities often uncover prehistoric objects; farmers and individuals in the outdoors come upon artifacts. Amateur archaeologists often know a great deal about the prehistory of their local area and frequently find sites while walking fields and looking for artifacts. It is essential that these finds be reported to a local historical society, museum, or university. The past is too important not to share.

The discovery of archaeological sites depends in part on what is already known about an area in terms of its landscape, environment, and history. Prior to beginning fieldwork, archaeologists check the relevant written material on the time period and place of interest. This research will reveal the present state of knowledge, indicate what is not known, as well as what is, and help establish directions for further research. Such library research is also essential to ensure that investigations similar to the ones that are planned have not already been carried out.

fieldwork   Collectively known as fieldwork, an important part of archaeological research involves *survey* for and *excavation* of archaeological materials, practices normally done outdoors (in the field).

survey   (1) A systematic *reconnaissance* of the landscape for *artifacts* and *sites* on the ground through aerial photography, field walking, soil analysis, or geophysical prospecting; (2) mapping of sites and areas using surveying instruments such as a *total station* or *GPS*.

excavation   The exposure, recording, and recovery of buried materials from the past.

amateur archaeologist   In contrast to professional archaeologists, who are educated in the discipline, amateur or vocational archaeologists collect *artifacts*, study *archaeology*, and participate in professionally run excavations. Amateur archaeologists are an important part of the field and have made substantial contributions to our knowledge of the past.

Fig. 6.1 Field survey in Denmark; the small red flags mark the location of finds on the surface of the plowed field. This site was from the Neolithic period.

The next step is a visit to the local historical society or other archaeological institutions, such as museums or university departments, where records for the area are maintained. Such places generally keep an archive of information on the location and contents of known archaeological and historical sites. Study of these records will indicate what types of sites are already present, and perhaps their size and general content of artifacts. This information can provide an initial list of findspots and their locations on maps.

Archaeological Survey

The next step in discovering the past involves fieldwork. There are two kinds of surveying that archaeologists do that need to be distinguished. Archaeologists do surveying by field walking or **reconnaissance** to look for artifacts and sites on the landscape. An archaeological survey is a systematic search of the landscape for artifacts and sites. Archaeologists also do **instrumental surveying** to make maps and plans of the places and areas of interest. Reconnaissance produces a list of sites and their contents; instrumental surveying produces a map. Both of these types of surveying are discussed in the following pages, starting with the search for sites.

As a start, all landowners in the selected area should be contacted to learn what they have found previously on their lands, to examine any collections of artifacts they may have, and to obtain permission to survey their property.

Archaeological reconnaissance, or field survey, involves systematic field walking. This means walking up and down cultivated fields and exposed surfaces at regular intervals (Fig. 6.1) determined by the size of the sites that may be in the area. If the smallest sites are likely to be 20 m (60 ft) in diameter, there is a good chance of finding them by walking at intervals of 10–15 m (30–50 ft) between surveyors. It may also be necessary to walk over an area several times during the year, or over several years, to collect enough artifacts to determine the contents and approximate age of a site.

When an artifact is found, the object is counted and sometimes put in a bag, and the location of the find is recorded. The surrounding area should be searched carefully by walking back and forth at close intervals. It is important to determine whether the artifact is a single isolated find or whether there are more artifacts, architecture, or unusual discolorations on the surface that might indicate features like fireplaces or pits. If there is a site, it is important to establish the area covered by artifacts to determine the size of the site and to obtain an estimate of the density of artifacts.

> *The simplest way to find sites is to ask somebody who knows where they are. . . . Be aware that the most important sites are not found by archaeologists at all—instead they are found accidentally by farmers, quarrymen, construction workers, or aerial photographers.*
> —Paul Bahn, archaeologist

> *The way to do fieldwork is never to come up for air until it is all over.*
> —Margaret Mead, anthropologist

reconnaissance The search for *artifacts* and *sites* by *survey* or field walking.

instrumental surveying Making maps and plans of places and areas of archaeological interest using *survey* instruments such as a *total station* or global positioning satellite systems.

The Reese River Valley

One of the more intriguing projects in American archaeology during the second half of the twentieth century was the result of student research. David Hurst Thomas, then a graduate student at the University of California-Davis, conducted this study for his PhD degree. Thomas wanted to evaluate the important ethnographic work of Julian Steward, one of the doyens of American anthropology. Steward had written extensively about the Native American hunter-gatherers, collectively known as the Shoshoneans (*show-SHOW-knee-ins*), who lived in the Great Basin of western North America.

The Great Basin is a harsh expanse of dry desert and high mountains between the Rockies and the Sierra Nevada, a huge area that includes most of Nevada, western Utah, southeastern Oregon, California east of the Sierra, and a small, dusty part of northern Mexico. It is an enormous region of low-lying flatlands (basins) and mountains (ranges) with relatively arid climate. The limited rainfall in this area accumulates in the basins as lakes and **playas**. The landscape is varied and rather sparse (Fig. 6.2). The lower and higher regions are covered with sagebrush and other scrub. Cottonwood, aspen, and willow grow along the waterways. A woodland of piñon and juniper trees spreads along the mountainsides. Piñon trees produce an abundant, nutritious, and tasty crop of pine nuts.

The Shoshoneans lived in this difficult region. These people moved regularly from place to place, exploiting specific foods that were available at different times of the year, following a **seasonal round**. Rich crops of piñon nuts were harvested in the fall and provided stored food for the winter. Indian rice-grass growing in the low-lying wetlands produced nutritious seeds that were collected in the summer. Antelope, rabbit, deer, and mountain sheep were hunted and trapped. Fish, wildfowl, and other resources in the lakes and wetlands were added to the larder.

This way of life was largely destroyed by the European settlement of the West, beginning in the 1850s. Julian Steward interviewed surviving descendants of the original peoples of this area in the 1930s and reconstructed their aboriginal way of life. Dave Thomas wanted to evaluate whether Steward's reconstruction of the remembered patterns of subsistence and settlement was accurate. For example, Steward suggested that larger groups of people were cooperating in the collection of the piñon nuts during fall and smaller groups were harvesting more widely distributed resources elsewhere at other times of the year in a regular annual cycle of subsistence and settlement. Steward defined an important concept, **ecological constraint**—the limitations of the natural environment—which he argued determined and limited the population, settlement pattern, and economy of the Shoshonean peoples.

To evaluate Steward's model, Thomas began an archaeological study in the Reese River Valley of Nevada, in the western part of the Great Basin. Thomas reasoned that the distribution of prehistoric artifacts should mimic the utilization of the landscape. For example, if Steward was correct, artifacts should be more abundant and clustered in environmental zones with rich resources. To investigate such questions, Thomas needed to know how artifacts were found on the landscape. He planned a survey of the area to record the distribution of artifacts. Because the valley was large and he could not survey the entire area, he decided to look at only part of it. He selected a 22 × 30 km (15 × 20 mi) cross section of the valley as his **study area** (Fig. 6.3). Thomas divided this segment of the valley into four "life zones": (1) the lower-lying stream and margins; (2) lower sagebrush-grass on the valley floor, around 1675 m (5500 ft) in elevation; (3) piñon-juniper, 1800–2400 m (6000–8000 ft) in elevation; and (4) upper sagebrush-grass, above 2400 m (8000 ft).

Because the entire 660-km² (250-mi²) study area was still too large to survey, Thomas could investigate only a **sample**, a small part of the whole. To be sure that the places he looked at covered the entire area, Thomas used a statistical procedure known as random sampling. To do this, he placed a grid of squares, 500 m (1600 ft, about 1/3 of a mile) on a side, on a map of the study area. Each square was numbered. A total of 1400 grid squares were needed to cover the roughly 300 square miles of the study area.

Thomas then used the life zones to "stratify" his sample; that is to say, he took a random sample of 10% of the squares in each life zone. Stratified random sampling ensured that the 140 squares selected were scattered across the landscape and that the different areas had adequate coverage. Fig. 6.3 shows the locations of

Fig. 6.2 The Reese River Valley today with the lower sagebrush-grass on the valley floor and the beginnings of the piñon-juniper along the lower slopes of the mountains.

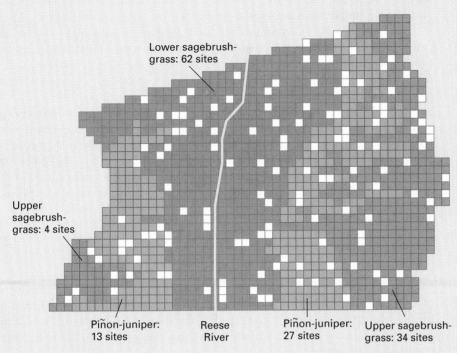

Lower sagebrush-grass: 62 sites

Upper sagebrush-grass: 4 sites

Piñon-juniper: 13 sites

Reese River

Piñon-juniper: 27 sites

Upper sagebrush-grass: 34 sites

Reese River Valley

Fig. 6.3 The Reese River Valley survey region marked with grid squares 500 m (1600 ft) on a side. The different environmental zones are shown, along with the number of sites found in each zone. The open squares are the ones sampled in the project. The course of the Reese River is shown running from top to bottom through the center of the map.

the sample squares within the different life zones. This procedure assumes that the locations of these life zones have not changed over time and that most archaeological materials still lie on the surface of the ground, unburied and visible.

The fieldwork then involved locating on the ground in the Reese River Valley, each of the 140 grid squares to be sampled marking its boundaries, and collecting all of the artifacts within those boundaries. Several crews of six people each surveyed the grid squares, walking between one and two squares each day. The entire survey took four months and recorded about 80,000 stone artifacts, of which 2500 were intentionally shaped tools. These tools were then classified as to purpose; for example, as hunting equipment (e.g., arrowheads, butchering tools) or domestic equipment (e.g., flakes from making tools, grinding stones for preparing food, seed knives for harvesting seeds).

The geographic distribution of different kinds of tools is of essence. Two general areas of base camp settlement were distinguished within the study region. "Shoreline" settlement was concentrated in a series of large sites along the Reese River in the middle of the lower sagebrush-grass zone. The artifacts in this zone indicate that subsistence was focused on abundant wild grass and root crops that ripen in the late spring and early summer. This diet was probably supplemented with the rabbits and rodents that lived there.

The second major zone of habitation was the piñon-juniper woodlands on the lower mountain slopes. Arti-

facts in this area were concentrated on flat-topped ridges that were optimal places to stay. Settlement was placed here to be able to harvest the fall nut crop in preparation for the winter. Artifacts at these sites document activities such as hide working and clothing manufacture. Deer and mountain sheep likely also supplemented the diet.

From this information, Thomas was able to define a **dual-residence** settlement pattern. Special-purpose locations were found. Butchering tools were found in several spots on the valley floor where rabbits and antelopes may have been hunted. Knives and grinding stones were found in other isolated concentrations in the sagebrush-grass zone, resulting from women's seed-gathering activities. Male hunting camps with points and flakes from sharpening stone tools were found in the piñon-juniper belts. This interpretation assumes that gendered activities were the same in prehistory as reported in the ethnographic record compiled by Julian Steward.

In fact, the results from the archaeological survey very much confirmed the pattern that Steward had reconstructed from interviews with the descendants of these prehistoric groups. The information from the survey also answered important archaeological questions, showing that excavation is not the only way to learn about the past. In this instance, the combination of archaeological survey, hard work, ethnographic interviews, and bright minds documented the life of the prehistoric inhabitants of the Great Basin. It seems that these hunter-gatherers had a very successful relationship with nature in what appears to us a rather difficult environment.

Fig. 6.4 Excavations in progress in a Wisconsin cornfield. In this photo, the corn crop has been removed and the excavators are shoveling the topsoil into a wheelbarrow to be screened.

playa A dry lake bed, common *geomorphological* feature in the western United States.

seasonal round (a.k.a. annual cycle) The pattern of subsistence and settlement found among *hunter-gatherers* who change residence regularly during the course of a year.

ecological constraint Limitations on human activity imposed by the *environment*. For example, arid conditions are an ecological constraint on agriculture.

study area A generic term for the *region* of focus of a research project.

sample A portion of a whole (n); to take a part of a deposit, site, feature, or artifact for analysis (v). The term *sampling* describes the process of taking a sample. This can be a one-time event, a series of actions, or a statistical process. Statistical sampling is a specific method for taking *samples* that allows probability estimates to be made about the *population* that is being sampled. Archaeologists almost always take *samples*, but only rarely is this done in a statistical fashion.

dual-residence A subsistence and settlement pattern observed among some groups of *hunter-gatherers* who live in two places at different seasons during the course of a year.

field notes The records of a field project of *survey* or *excavation* with description of activities, finds, records of samples, drawings, photographs, and the like. An important document of the research project.

Information must be recorded about each findspot. These **field notes** should include (1) the location, site number, map number; (2) what was found, types and number of artifacts, fire-cracked stones, charcoal, etc.; and (3) observations about the site, discoloration in the soil, the presence of mounds, nearby streams or water, and other pertinent environmental information.

A description of the conditions for making observations might also be useful information for later comparison of what was found at different places. A plowed field where stones and potsherds have been exposed by a recent rain offers the optimal conditions for surveying. Dusty conditions, vegetation, stony ground, and dim light make observation much more difficult.

It is not always possible to make a complete reconnaissance of the entire area under investigation. Roads and construction and forests, crops, and other vegetation often cover substantial parts of the landscape and make it impossible to see the ground. It may be possible to survey only a portion of the entire area thoroughly, but that portion should be representative of the larger region of the investigation. The larger the proportion of the research area that can be surveyed, the better.

Archaeological Excavation

Excavation is the technique that archaeologists use to uncover buried remains from the past (Fig. 6.4). Buried materials usually are more abundant and better preserved than those found on the surface. In excavations, accurate information can be observed in the arrangement and relationships of structures, artifacts, plant and animal remains, and other materials. Thus, excavation often is essential to obtain more information.

Excavations are conducted to answer specific questions that the archaeologist would like to resolve. Questions may include who lived at a site, what did they eat, what did they do, where did they get raw materials for making tools and equipment, what kinds of relations did they have with their neighbors, and how was their society organized and structured? Learning the answers to such questions is one of the reasons that most archaeologists got interested in the subject in the first place.

Selecting Sites for Excavation

The choice of a site for excavation is determined by several factors, including the potential threat to the archaeological remains. Sites are often chosen for excavation because they appear to be well preserved or to contain new information that will help to better understand the prehistory of a particular region. The choice of a site for excavation is sometimes based on the results of a survey. An initial survey of an area, including coring and testing of promising sites, might indicate that one or several sites would be worth excavating. Careful surface collection and testing must be carried out at the site selected for excavation in order to make sure the site can provide the kinds of information that are needed and to assist in planning the excavation. Archaeological sites are being ruined at a rapid rate by the growth and development of modern civilization and there is a serious and real concern about the loss of undisturbed sites for future research. Sites threatened by modern construction are also good candidates for excavation in order to save the information and objects that would otherwise be lost.

In cultural resource management projects, the strategy for evaluating the presence and importance of historical and archaeological remains is well defined. Initial reconnaissance during Phase I involves field walking and small-scale shovel testing where the surface of the ground is covered by vegetation or debris. Sites of interest found during Phase I are tested more carefully using small excavations and other methods to assess the level of preservation and significance of the materials and to explore questions such as the age, function, size, and place-

ment of the site during this second investigation (Phase II). Places that are identified as having significant importance may be subject to Phase III activities of full-scale excavation and exposure to learn more about the site.

It is important to know as much as possible about a site prior to full-scale excavation in order to choose the best strategy for the project. At every excavation, an archaeologist is faced with a series of decisions about how to acquire the best-documented information under the circumstances. Accurate notes and records of the layers, structures, and artifacts at a site are essential, not only for the investigator, but also to create a permanent archive of information about the site that is available to others. In ideal circumstances, a site could be fully excavated and everything recorded in the finest detail. In the real world, however, constraints on time and funding and a need to leave a portion of the site for future archaeologists make it standard procedure not to excavate entire sites. This ethical practice recognizes that future archaeological techniques may make it possible to learn more about the site and its contents than can be done today.

Test Pits

Preliminary examination of a site usually involves making a few small excavations to preview the site. These test excavations can be small, vertical pits, perhaps 1 × 1 m (ca. 3 × 3 ft) in size, or a series of one or more trenches across the site. The test squares to be excavated might also be placed in rows (Fig. 6.5) or a chessboardlike pattern across the site, or their location might be chosen by random sampling. Another technique, used commonly in American archaeology today, is called shovel testing. This method involves regularly spaced small holes about the width of a shovel dug below the plow zone to see if there are any

> *Every archaeological site is itself a document. It can be read by a skilled excavator, but it is destroyed by the very process which enables us to read it. Unlike the study of an ancient document, the study of a site by excavation is an unrepeatable experiment.*
> —Philip Barker, archaeologist

artifacts or other archaeological indicators buried in the ground. Shovel testing is often used where the surface of the ground is hidden or obscured by vegetation such as meadow, pasture, or forested areas.

The size and number of test pits to be excavated depend on the kind of information being sought. In some cases, it is difficult to visualize the stratigraphy, or set of layers, observed in the small test pits. One or two long trenches across the site may provide a better view of the sequence of deposits.

Vertical Excavations

Excavations can be vertical or horizontal. The photograph of the Koster site at the opening of this chapter shows excavations that are deep in the ground (vertical) and expose a broad (horizontal) area. Vertical excavation takes the form of squares or rectangles carefully positioned across a site to expose stratigraphy and artifact contents. By studying the vertical walls (**sections**) of these excavations, archaeologists can observe buried layers in the earth.

The stratigraphy, or layers of natural sediments and human deposits, reveals how the site was formed and accumulated. The relationships between deposits in the stratigraphic sequence indicate the chronological arrangement of the layers. The bottom layer is deposited first as the oldest layer in the sequence. The subsequent layers are progressively younger. The stratigraphic sequence provides a relative chronology, whereby layers and the artifacts they contain can be determined to be "younger than" or "older than" other layers and artifacts in the same sequence.

The thickness of a layer is determined not so much by the length of time that it took to accumulate as by the natural and human activities involved in the deposition of the materials. For example, heaps of shells may accumulate very rapidly into high shell middens; the collapse of houses with earth or sod walls can result in very thick layers; and stone tool manufacture can produce large quantities of debris. On the other hand, the place where an animal was killed and butchered—a kill site—may leave almost no archaeological trace.

Assessment of the context and relative position of layers allows an archaeologist to interpret the depositional history from the stratigraphic sequence. An approximate date of the layers may be derived from artifacts with a known age found in a particular layer. For example, a hubcap from a 1935 Ford would indicate that the layer could be no older than 1935. The ages of many types of ancient pottery and stone tools are also known and can be used to suggest an approximate date for archaeological levels. Layers sometimes may also be dated by means of absolute techniques like radiocarbon dating, discussed in Chapter 8, "Dating." Stratigraphy, the study of layers of sediments at archaeological sites, is discussed in more detail in Chapter 9, "Geoarchaeology."

Horizontal, or Area, Excavations

Horizontal, or area, excavations expose large open areas of ground, one layer at a time. Area excavations are intended to recover information on site arrangement and structures (Fig. 6.6). Such excavations may expose actual prehistoric living areas where a group of people carried out everyday activities.

Human activities in the past—digging, construction, burning, burial, and the like—left visible changes in the ground. These archaeological features include postholes, fireplaces, storage pits, walls, graves, and many others. For example, holes were often dug in the ground to insert wooden posts as part of a construction. Such **postholes** provide a great deal of information on the size and shape of structures and site arrangement. A complex network of postholes or walls may appear within an excavated area, revealing the outline of houses, fences, or other structures. A series of postholes filled with one kind of soil to the same depth can be connected to indicate a single stage of construction. If postholes filled with one type of soil were dug into postholes with another kind of soil, the former is likely the result of a different phase or period of construction. One example of

section (a.k.a. profile) The walls of trenches and squares in excavations that show a cross section of the deposits and reveal the sequence and methods of formation.

posthole The hole or depression left when a post is removed from the ground, an indication of construction posts.

Fig. 6.6 Horizontal excavations at a Mesolithic site in Denmark. Artifacts are being left in situ in order to map their exact location for the analysis of spatial patterning.

Fig. 6.7 Archaeologist drawing a plan view in the field, using a string grid as a guide.

postholes in archaeology is described below in the section on the Great Hall at Lejre, Denmark.

Several different kinds of burials can be found. Simple **inhumation** is the burial of the whole body. Such graves usually contain an articulated skeleton with all the bones in their correct anatomical positions. Secondary burials are the result of burial of some of the skeleton, after the flesh and soft tissue has disappeared. Usually the skull and larger bones are present, often in a small pile or bundle. **Cremations** are burials of the ash and small, carbonized bones from bodies that have been burned prior to burial.

When the site stratigraphy is relatively simple—with only one or two stages of occupation and thin layers of artifacts and other materials—it is sometimes possible to separate the remains from each stage of occupation. In such cases, it is advantageous to expose large surfaces of the same layer to get an overview of the distribution of features and artifacts at the settlement. Following removal of the topsoil, the surface is scraped with trowels or shovels, loose soil is removed, and features and artifacts are uncovered. The uncovered surface is then carefully recorded, usually in drawings and photographs (Fig. 6.7). Important artifacts and

inhumation   Burial of all or part of a corpse; contrast with *cremation.*

cremation   A funereal practice involving immolation of the corpse. Cremation burials usually consist of ash and a few fragments of bone and teeth and are often found in urns and small pits. Also, the incinerated remains of a human body. Contrast with *inhumation.*

Fig. 6.8 Dry screening sediments to find smaller artifacts.

features are numbered individually. A separate catalog can then be made of all the artifacts, with their inventory number, type of material, kind of artifact, location, and layer. The recorded objects are removed one at a time and put in bags with labels showing their number.

A variety of samples are taken from different layers in the walls of the excavation and from the occupation floor. Soil samples are taken to help define and characterize the deposits at the site. Pollen samples are sometimes taken to assist in defining the vegetation in and around the site. Samples of charcoal and bone are taken for radiocarbon dating at many sites.

The surface of the sediments beneath the occupation layer is uncovered and cleaned. Unusual colors in the soil may reveal features such as pits and postholes, which are recorded in photos and drawings. Features are normally dissected by excavating one-quarter or one-half of the pit or posthole at a time in order to remove the contents and determine the function of the feature. This produces a vertical section through the middle of the feature and allows a view of how it was formed.

At the end of the dig, the excavation has to be filled up and undisturbed portions of the site protected in the best possible manner. Records, artifacts, and samples must be moved back to the home laboratory to be cataloged and prepared for analysis. After the fieldwork come more detailed analyses of the recovered materials, the writing of excavation reports, and the preparation of publications, all of which require much more work and time than the excavation itself. One estimate has suggested about 5 weeks of analysis and writing from each week of excavation. Final results of the investigations are then made available to the public and to professional archaeologists through articles in scientific journals and published reports.

Screening and Flotation

The excavated soils are usually sifted through screens and/or washed with water to find small objects, fragments of bone, and plant remains (Fig. 6.8). The terms *screening*, *sieving*, and *sifting* are generally synonymous in archaeological jargon. Dry sieving works reasonably well in loose, dry soils but water screening is recommended in most situations to ensure more complete recovery of small items. Water screening involves the use of water to wash the sediment away from the excavated material. In most cases, this means that archaeologists move excavated soil to an area where screens and hoses are available. Water is sprayed on the soil in the screens to remove the sediment and leave the artifacts. The water removes the dirt from the objects and makes everything easier to see and identify.

screening Sifting or sieving of *sediments* through fine screens to separate them from *artifacts* and *ecofacts*.

Mesolithic sites in Denmark were excavated with occasional dry screening for years. The general picture from these excavations was that fish and plants were not very important in the human diet of the time. The introduction of wet screening, however, resulted in the discovery of enormous amounts of fishbone and nutshell in the sieves, changing the picture of subsistence substantially. Mesh size of the screen is variable from place to place and from archaeologist to archaeologist. Mesh size is always a compromise between the time it takes to process samples and the goals of the project. Mesh sizes between 2 and 4 mm (0.08–0.16 in) are commonly used in archaeology. A nested set of screens with decreasing mesh size toward the bottom is sometimes used to improve efficiency.

Flotation has become a standard technique at sites where carbonized plant remains are preserved. Normal water sieving tends to destroy fragile materials such as plant remains. Flotation involves the use of tubs of water for separating sediment and artifacts from the plant remains. The basic principle is simple: Carbonized plant remains are lighter than water and will float to the top and can be skimmed from the surface of the water. Basic flotation can be done with buckets, but more elaborate machines are available for large-scale flotation. Because this technique is time-consuming, samples of the archaeological sediments are used rather than all of the materials from the site. Samples are usually taken from hearths, storage areas, and other places where plant remains are likely to have been carbonized. This technique is discussed in more detail in Chapter 13, "Archaeobotany."

 EXAMPLE ~~~~~~~~~~~~~~~~~~~~~~~~~~~~~~~~~~~

THE GREAT HALL AT LEJRE

Ancient Scandinavia is perhaps best known because of the Vikings who pillaged and settled much of the North Atlantic around AD 1000. Denmark has a long list of kings and queens, starting with Gorm around AD 935. Gorm was king of "all Denmark" and the Vikings are assumed to have established the first significant political state in Scandinavia. There were earlier kings, described in various historical sources, going back another century or so, but these individuals likely ruled lesser regions than all of Denmark and are sometimes considered more mythical than real.

But legends have weight. These stories name the place called Gammel Lejre (*GAHM-ul LIE-ruh*) as a once-powerful center. The legends describe a ship sailing there with gold, weapons, and a young boy, a gift to the people from the gods. The boy child became King Skjold. For several generations, he and his descendants ruled a kingdom from Gammel Lejre (Old Lejre). The royal seat was a great "Hjort-hallen" (red deer hall) where many important events are said to have taken place. Eventually, however, rivals for power killed the king and his warriors, and their magnificent hall was razed to the ground, ending the reign at Gammel Lejre.

Horizontal excavations in 1986 by the Roskilde Museum near the town of Gammel Lejre, outside of Copenhagen, revealed dramatic evidence for substantial wealth and power in the past. These excavations uncovered the postholes and features of an enormous wooden structure from an earlier time (Fig. 6.9). The excavations revealed traces of a hall 48 m in length and 11 m wide (150 × 35 ft)—a total area of 500 m^2 (5400 ft^2). The evidence came in the form of enormous wooden posts and postholes in the ground marking the major vertical timbers in the building. The building had convex walls with sloping timber braces on the outside. This huge hall was probably the largest building in northern Europe at the time. The most powerful person in the land probably lived there.

A plan of the postholes that were excavated (Fig. 6.10) reveals a ninth-century Viking Age hall (in gray in the figure), built over a less-well-preserved, earlier timber building (in black). The wall posts and the rows of postholes from both interior and exterior supporting posts are visible on the plan. The two halls, although separated

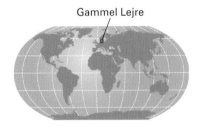

Gammel Lejre

Fig. 6.9 Aerial photo of the great hall at Lejre, Denmark. Shaving cream has been used to mark the outlines of the massive posts that supported the roof and walls of this structure.

Fig. 6.10 Plan of the Two Great Halls at Gammel Lejre. The two structures can be seen in the earlier building (black) and the later construction (gray). Because of their similarity, the second structure is clearly seen as a rebuilding of the former one.

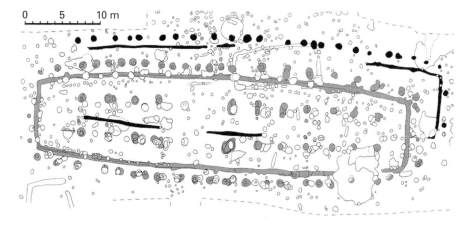

by three centuries in time, are of similar construction. The Viking hall used some of the supporting postholes from the previous construction. The archaeology presents a picture of continuous habitation between the two major episodes of construction. The buildings were repaired in the intervening period and some posts were replaced four or five times. Animal bones found in postholes from the oldest hall are radiocarbon-dated to around the year AD 660, documenting the existence of those legendary early rulers long before the Vikings.

Underwater Archaeology

Most archaeology takes place on dry land, but an increasingly important part of archaeology is being done under the sea. Underwater archaeology became famous with the recovery of Bronze Age shipwrecks in the Mediterranean several decades ago, focusing largely on shipwrecks from around the world. The excavation of the *Mary Rose* in England, described in Chapter 14, "Bioarchaeology," provides another example.

But more and more, underwater survey and excavation are being done to find archaeological sites that were submerged by rising lake or sea levels (Fig. 6.11). The painted Paleolithic cave of Cosquer (*KOS-care*) off the Mediterranean coast of France is one example. Many submerged Neolithic settlements have been discovered and excavated in Switzerland and France. In the small country of Denmark, underwater reconnaissance by amateur divers and professional archaeologists has archived more than 2000 sites from the Stone Age alone. The finds include settlements, wooden fishing weirs, dugout canoes and a variety of artifacts.

Although survey and excavation conditions are more difficult underwater, the logistics complex, and the costs substantially greater, the exceptional preservation of organic materials often makes the effort worthwhile. Excavation underwater usually proceeds in very much the same way as on land. The exception has to do with equipment for vacuuming or washing away sediments from the archaeological remains. Otherwise, excavations are done in grid units, recording artifacts and stratigraphy, in order to document the location and context of the finds.

THE TOOLS OF FIELDWORK

Archaeological projects in the field require tools and information to operate effectively. These tools include maps and positioning information to locate sites and artifacts exactly in geographic space. Locational information is essential for

www.mhhe.com/pricearch1

For a Web-based activity on underwater archaeology, please see the Internet exercises on your online learning center.

Fig. 6.12 Excavations at an Upper Paleolithic site in France. The site grid is marked here by a series of hanging wires at 1-m (ca. 3-ft) intervals that can be raised or lowered to mark the grid units on the floor of the cave.

understanding and reconstructing context. Maps are one of the most important tools of fieldwork. Topographic maps (showing the topography, or shape, of the land surface with elevation lines) are available for most areas. In the United States, the U.S. Geological Survey compiles and distributes these maps. Such maps contain a great deal of information about longitude and latitude, elevation, slope, and the location of water, roads, towns, and other features.

Archaeologists also make their own maps and plans. The technologies of satellite location, laser measurement, and computer mapping have greatly enhanced this capability. Discussed in this chapter are the technologies of the total station, global positioning satellites, and geographic information systems.

Other technologies aid the archaeologist in further determining the location of a site. Digging in the ground is hard work, expensive, and time-consuming. Therefore, archaeologists today try to peer into earth for archaeological remains before they dig using a variety of techniques and technologies that are usually listed under the rubric of remote sensing. These include methods such as soil chemistry and various electrical and electromagnetic techniques involving magnetism, radar, and resistivity, which are described in this chapter. Examples of such methods in use include soil chemistry at a Maya site in Guatemala, satellite imagery of ancient roads in Arizona, and georadar on the ground in the Near East.

Maps and Grids

Accurate mapping of layers and artifacts is the key to the proper recording of information on an archaeological project. Maps and plans are made by instrumental surveying, a technique used by land surveyors and cartographers. A grid is

Fig. 6.13 A drawing grid in action. One member of the field crew measures the location of points to be drawn while the other compiles the plan. This excavation is at the Basilica di Torcello on Torcello Island, Venice, Italy.

marked out across the surface of an area prior to reconnaissance or excavation to be used for all horizontal measurements. A site grid represents a coordinate system, usually with lines running north–south and east–west at regular intervals. Intervals along the two axes of the grid are designated with a system of letters or numbers or both. The grid lines and measurements within each grid square are measured as distances in meters and centimeters north and east of the baselines at the edge of the excavations.

The site grid might also be oriented according to local topography or archaeological features such as mounds or middens. In a narrow cave, for example, the grid is often aligned to the long axis of the chamber (Fig. 6.12). At coastal sites, trenches are sometimes excavated perpendicular to the coastline in order to study stratigraphy and site formation in relation to the coast.

Location of the site and the site grid in relation to global latitude, longitude, and elevation above sea level must be determined. A control point, or site **datum**, must be located in the neighborhood of the excavation as a point of origin for vertical measurements. A pre-existing datum point like a surveyor's benchmark may be used if available. Otherwise, a permanent feature like a rock outcrop or building foundation might be marked and used as the datum point.

Vertical location in the excavation is best determined using a surveying instrument, set at a known elevation, and sighting on a vertical measuring rod. Measurements at the site should be converted to meters above sea level, or the elevation of the datum line may simply be recorded. The Geological Survey has established fixed points of known elevation at many points on the landscape in many countries so that surveyors and others can establish their position. These fixed points for survey are rapidly being replaced by systems employing the Global Positioning System (GPS), described below.

Grids are also used for more precise drawings of features and artifacts. A **drawing grid** (a.k.a. a planning frame), usually a 1-m^2 (ca. 3-ft^2) wooden frame with a grid of string or thin rods at 20-cm (8-in) intervals, is placed on the ground or on the section to enable the draftsperson to more quickly and accurately map the finds (Fig. 6.13).

Contour Maps

Information from the field survey can be plotted on a map to provide a better record of the location and distribution of the finds. A **contour map** of an area shows the topography, the three-dimensional surface of the place. One way to

datum A point with known locational coordinates and elevation; a fixed point for *surveying*.

drawing grid (a.k.a. planning frame) Normally a 1-m^2 (10-ft^2) frame of wood or aluminum fitted with a grid of string or wire at 20-cm (ca. 8-in) intervals. It is used for drawing detailed plans of vertical sections or horizontal floors in archaeological *excavations*.

contour map A schematic map of topography, the three-dimensional surface of the earth or other features. Contours are conventionally shown as a series of curved, concentric lines reflecting elevation or relief of a surface.

Fig. 6.14 A volcanic island with lines marking elevation at 500-m intervals; (below) the same lines seen from above appear as contours of the landscape.

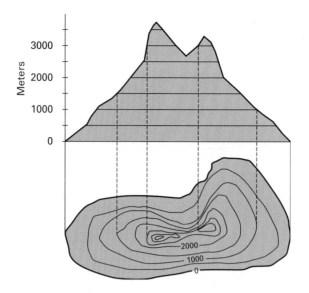

visualize a contour map is to consider a high volcanic island (Fig. 6.14). In this case, the island has two peaks with a saddle, or low area, in between. Elevations of the island between sea level (0) and 3700 m are marked by horizontal lines at 500-m (1500-ft) intervals. If the lines were marked on the white volcanic ash with dark soil and viewed from directly above, the island would look like a contour map. Lines that are close together indicate a steep slope; widely spaced contour lines indicate a flat area or gentle slope. The contour lines on this 3-D depiction reveal the shape of the mountain. The view of this mountain from directly above would appear as a two-dimensional contour map. The lines are like steps on a staircase. If you flattened the staircase with a steamroller, you would still see the individual steps from above.

The elevation of the ground is measured in feet or meters above sea level or a known fixed point, or datum. The United States Geological Survey (USGS) has placed these fixed points all over the country so that surveyors can measure from them and establish the elevation, latitude, and longitude of a place. Surveyors formerly used an optical instrument, a kind of telescope, known as a level or transit to determine the elevation from the fixed point to the new area. Today, surveying is done with electronic instruments called total stations and satellite locator devices known as Global Positioning System (GPS). These instruments are discussed below.

Fig. 6.15 shows how to measure from a fixed datum to a new point and determine the elevation there using the traditional method. The measurement begins at a datum placed by the USGS at an elevation of 50 meters above sea level (asl). The level is first set up at Station 1 some distance away and aimed at the USGS datum. A measuring stick (**stadia rod**) is placed on the datum and the height of the level instrument above the datum is measured. In this case, the instrument is 10.4 m above the datum. The stadia rod is then moved inland some distance to a higher elevation and the level turned to read the elevation of this new location. Now the level, which has not moved, reads 1.2 m. That means that the ground where the stadia rod stands is 9.2 m (10.4 − 1.2) higher than the USGS datum, or 59.2 m asl. This new point is called a benchmark. This process is repeated until the point of interest is reached—in this case an archaeological site—with an elevation of 80.2 m.

At this point, it is possible to measure the elevation of the topography in terms of meters above sea level in order to produce a contour map. A contour map is a series of concentric contour lines at different elevations in the area. To create this map, a grid is laid out and measurements of the elevation of the ground are

stadia rod   Essentially, a very long ruler that is held vertically and read by an optical surveying instrument to determine distance above the ground.

scale   A ratio representing the size of an illustration, map, or reproduction in a publication.

alidade   An optical surveying instrument used for making contour maps.

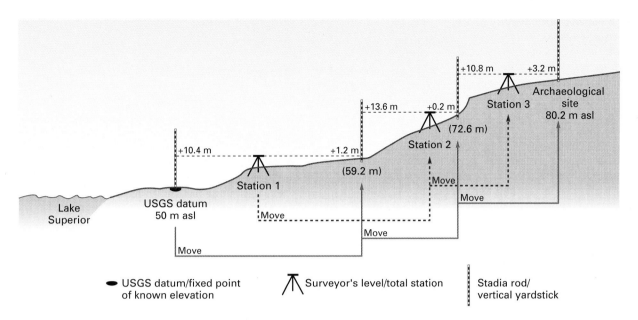

+10.8 m +3.2 m

+13.6 m +0.2 m

Station 3

Archaeological
site
80.2 m asl

(72.6 m)

Station 2

+10.4 m +1.2 m

Move

Station 1

(59.2 m)

Move

USGS datum
50 m asl

Move

Lake
Superior

Move

Move

● USGS datum/fixed point
of known elevation

⋀ Surveyor's level/total station

Stadia rod/
vertical yardstick

Fig. 6.15 The use of a level or transit to find the elevation of an archaeological site upslope from a small lake. The USGS datum is a point of known elevation placed by the government.

taken at regular intervals across the grid. Elevation is measured using an optical or electronic instrument. Elevation, or contour, lines are then drawn on the map connecting points of equal elevation. Concentric contour lines are normally drawn at a regular interval, for example at 1 meter or 500 feet. In Fig. 6.16, the interval is 10 meters.

It is necessary to interpolate values between measured points when drawing lines in order to plot the specific contour. This can be done by actually measuring on the map or simply estimating the value between the two points. For example, in Fig. 6.17, values between 99 and 103 m and between 95 and 103 m are shown as measured to determine where the 100 m contour line crosses between the measured grid points.

Contour maps or maps of any kind require display of the **scale** of the map to provide the viewer with information on the size of the area on the map and a sense of distance. A map can be depicted at a number of different sizes depending on the page or paper limits. Scale can be given as a ratio representing the size of an illustration or map in relation to the actual size of the object it represents. Examples of such ratios would be 1:10, 1:50, and 1:250,000. Scales are usually shown in metric or English systems of measurement or both. A north arrow is normally provided on a map for orientation.

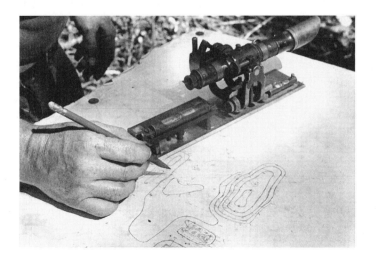

Fig. 6.16 Survey and mapping with an **alidade**. This old-fashioned, simple optical instrument was used by archaeologists for many years. Here, the archaeologist is shown drawing contour lines on the site map. Elevations are read using the instrument and a stadia rod. Today, surveying is normally done with electronic instruments.

Fig. 6.17 Interpolating elevation from known grid points.

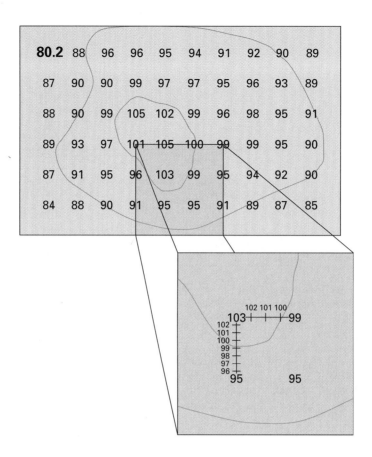

Mapping projects are greatly simplified today with the use of satellites, computers, and lasers. A total station can measure distance and elevation from a fixed point in a matter of seconds. Global positioning satellites (GPS) can determine the latitude, longitude, and elevation of a fixed point within minutes. Geographic information systems (GIS) can combine this data with the archaeological materials to produce useful maps and databases in a few hours.

The Total Station

Today traditional optical survey instruments have been replaced by electronic equipment that measures both horizontal and vertical directions simultaneously. This instrument is called a **total station**. There are two components: the instrument mounted on a tripod at a fixed point or base station, and a target or prism that is moved and used to return a signal to the instrument (Fig. 6.18). Total stations use an infrared or laser signal to calculate distance and three-dimensional angles to determine the precise location of the target in terms of grid coordinates and elevation. Built-in computers do the calculations and record measurements and other information during the process. The total station can be used to produce contour maps and to locate artifacts and architecture precisely in three dimensions (latitude, longitude, and elevation).

Geographic Information Systems (GIS)

Geographic Information Systems (GIS) are a potent means for recording, analyzing, and presenting geographic or spatial information in archaeology. GIS resulted from the marriage of computers and cartography (mapmaking) and has become an essential part of archaeology's tool kit. A GIS representation of an archaeological project would include a set of maps or plans of the area of interest

total station A modern *surveying* instrument using an infrared laser and computer to calculate distance and three-dimensional angles to determine the precise location of a target in terms of grid coordinates and elevation. Replaces levels, *alidades*, transits, and theolodites.

Geographic Information Systems (GIS) A computer program(s) for the storage, display, and analysis of geographic and spatial data. The basic concept involves the use of overlaid maps of an area in combination with locational information and spatial analytical capabilities.

Global Positioning System (GPS) A locational and navigational system for determining precise three-dimensional coordinates (longitude, latitude, and elevation) of any place on the earth's surface. Satellites broadcast locational information used by GPS equipment to determine the exact position. Replaces traditional, manual land-survey methods.

Fig. 6.18 A total station in use mapping an archaeological site in the highlands of Peru. Two members of the field crew work at the total station and two others are locating and marking map points with the reflecting target for the total station. The total station uses a laser beam to measure the distance and angle between the instrument and the target and then calculates the exact position of the target.

www.mhhe.com/pricearch1

For a Web-based activity on GIS, please see the Internet exercises on your online learning center.

 SCIENCE IN ARCHAEOLOGY

Global Positioning System (GPS)

One of the major achievements of the twentieth century was the deployment of a series of satellites broadcasting information for determining exact locations on the earth's surface. Familiar now as handheld locator systems and driving guides, **GPS** was originally created for the Department of Defense (DOD) and the targeting of intercontinental ballistic weapons. In essence, approximately fifty satellites provide fixed points in space from which a computer can determine the specific latitude, longitude, and elevation of any place on earth (Fig. 6.19). The end of the Cold War made this system available to the public, and eventually the DOD removed the restrictions on its accuracy. Today, it is possible to use portable GPS equipment to determine precise locations within a few centimeters.

The use of GPS is now standard in archaeology as a basic means for locating sites and other features on the landscape and for mapping larger areas. The next stage in the use of GPS will take advantage of enhanced resolution, allowing GPS to replace traditional methods of surveying and mapping and to be used at excavations

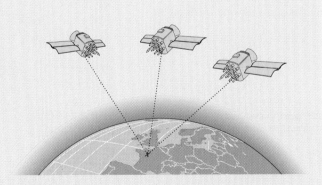

Fig. 6.19 Artist's depiction of three GPS satellites in orbit beaming location signals to the ground.

for recording the precise location of artifacts, architecture, and other features. The combination of GPS for determining location and Geographic Information Systems for recording and mapping information provides a powerful set of tools for archaeology.

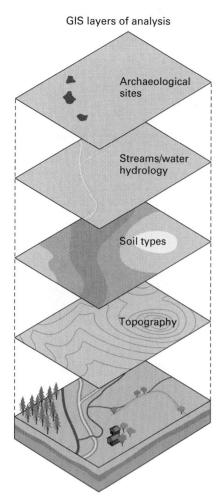

GIS layers of analysis

Archaeological sites

Streams/water hydrology

Soil types

Topography

Fig. 6.20 A GIS display of the state of New York with various layers shown, including relief on the bottom, county boundaries in the middle, and watersheds on top.

and a series of locations in that area (Fig. 6.20). The size and scale of the area of interest are flexible; the maps may include areas as large as continents or as small as individual structures or features on an excavation. Information on each location (e.g., region, site, or artifact) can be stored in a linked database and recalled immediately. The data can also be analyzed statistically and the results presented in cartographic form. The power of GIS lies in its ability to show various kinds of information from a geographic perspective.

A good example of GIS lies in its use as a database for national or state-level site files. GIS allows one to find sites from a specific time period, for example, and to display the locations of those sites on the map. Different kinds of maps (e.g., elevation, water, soils, vegetation, modern construction, rainfall) can then be examined alongside the distribution of sites to see if patterns emerge. Such site files also are used in planning and development. The database is checked when new construction projects are proposed to determine if any known archaeological or historical places will be impacted.

One interesting feature of GIS is its ability to generate "visibility" models—that is, to determine what can be seen from a particular spot on the basis of height of land and position on the landscape. Two perspectives can be used: line of sight to determine if one point can be seen from another, and viewshed to determine visible areas of the landscape from a particular point. These models are often useful in understanding the locations of monuments and tombs. Fig. 6.21 shows the landscape around the monument of Stonehenge in southern England. The lines and small dots depict all the prehistoric sites in the area. The colored dots show

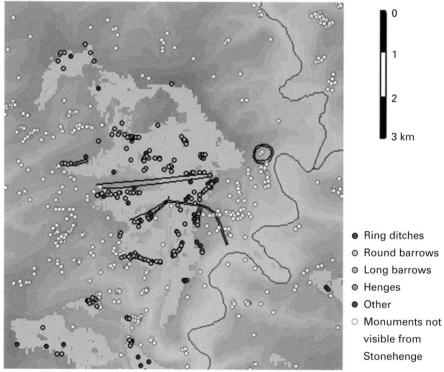

0
1
2
3 km

● Ring ditches
◎ Round barrows
◉ Long barrows
⊕ Henges
● Other
○ Monuments not visible from Stonehenge

Fig. 6.21 A GIS viewshed analysis of the portions of the landscape in southern England that are visible from the ground (shown in gray) at the sight of Stonehenge. The computer is used to determine what is visible in the lines of sight from the monument. The computer cannot account for trees and vegetation in such a reconstruction. Notice that many of the other monuments in the area can be seen from Stonehenge (shown in color). The linear features are called avenues or **cursus monuments**.

cursus monument Paired linear earthworks that mark an avenue or long, rectangular area in Neolithic Europe.

those mounds and places that can be seen from Stonehenge itself. The light area is that part of the landscape visible from the site of Stonehenge.

GIS is also being used to project where archaeological remains might be expected. This use is popular with planners because it is cheaper than fieldwork. The technique is called "predictive modeling." Associations between known archaeological sites and environmental features such as soil type, distance to water, exposure, and the like can be determined. If sites tend to occur primarily on a particular kind of soil and within a certain distance of water, GIS can be used to identify those areas on a map. For example, good agricultural soils and a high water table are often correlated with the locations of farming villages in early Neolithic Europe.

Soil Sampling

Archaeological remains are frequently buried in the ground beneath the sediments that have accumulated since their deposition. Objects found on the surface often have been brought up from deeper layers by digging or plowing and may indicate a buried site. Materials found on the surface usually provide only a partial indication of the information that can be obtained from a buried site.

Once buried sites have been located by survey and recorded, other kinds of fieldwork can begin to uncover more about them. Drilling or boring into the ground with an **auger** or corer produces a column of soil showing the sequence of layers and samples of sediments at the site (Fig. 6.22). Small test pits, perhaps 1×1 m (3×3 ft) in size, dug into the ground can provide similar information and might be necessary to determine if a buried site is present. A number of corings and/or test pits often are made, following a regular pattern over the surface of the site. Soil samples should be collected from all parts of the site and at different depths.

Physical and chemical analysis of soil samples may provide information about the origins of the deposits, the water content and fertility of the soil, the amount of organic material, and the basic chemistry of the soil. For example, phosphate analysis of the sediments from a site may reveal traces of human activities. Phosphate is found in bone, feces, urine, and other organic matters that accumulate in and around human habitation. It appears as a strong blue color in the soil sample when hydrochloric and ascorbic acids are added. Areas with higher concentrations of phosphate will show up as stronger blue colors in such analyses.

Phosphate testing may supplement surface surveys in areas where vegetation prevents observations of the surface or where cultural layers are deeply buried under the topsoil. Within a known habitation area, these tests may be used to determine the extent of the site and detect special areas such as house floors. Other chemical elements in archaeological soils are also very informative with regard to past human activity. More information on elemental analyses and archaeological sediments can be found in Chapter 15, "Archaeometry."

Other objects in the soil are also informative. Materials found in soil samples often include pieces of wood and plants, seeds, fragments of insects, mollusk shells, hair, or chips of bone or stone. Such items provide information on the formation of the layers, the local environment, and the nature of past human activities. For example, small chips that result from the manufacture of arrowheads and other stone tools can come up in borings and test pits, indicating that other buried artifacts may be present.

Remote Sensing

Remote sensing involves instrumental techniques for peering onto or into the ground without digging. These prospecting techniques detect differences in the vegetation or subsoil and the presence of prehistoric features and disturbances. Such methods include metal detectors and magnetometers (measuring magnetic

Fig. 6.22 A geologist examines the sediments in a core taken from deposits at a Mesolithic site in Denmark.

auger (a.k.a. corer, borer)   A tool for drilling holes, used in *archaeology* for coring into soil and taking samples.

remote sensing   A variety of techniques used for obtaining information about surface or buried objects. Aboveground techniques normally involve aircraft or satellites using photography, radar, and other methods to locate and map *features* on or near the surface. Belowground techniques use radar, resistivity, magnetic properties, or chemistry to search for buried features.

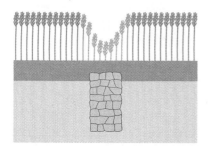

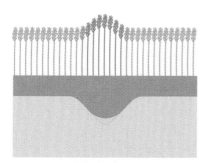

Fig. 6.23 Differences in vegetation due to buried archaeological remains visible from the air. The diagram shows a wall (top) and a ditch (bottom) in a cultivated field. During dry years and when the crop is ripe, these differences can be seen. Buried walls result in less moisture and shorter, drier vegetation. Buried ditches contain more moisture and produce green, rich vegetation compared to the rest of the field.

variations in the ground), resistivity (measuring the electrical conductivity of the soil), and the use of ground penetrating radar. In each case, the instrument or its sensors are moved over the ground in a systematic way, usually following a site grid, and the locations of anomalies are recorded. Anomalies are values that are different from the general background readings at the site.

Remote Sensing from Above

Air photographs also can provide information on the locations of archaeological sites. Old foundations or prehistoric agricultural fields, overgrown with vegetation and almost hidden on the surface, may appear in air photographs. When prehistoric structures were originally abandoned, the depressions often filled with rich topsoil. This means better growth conditions for vegetation. In fields of wheat, for example, such different soil conditions might result in a distinctive pattern showing the outlines of houses or whole villages (Fig. 6.23).

Satellite photography and other technology are also being used increasingly in archaeology to look at regional patterns of land use and to locate specific features on the landscape. A variety of instruments can scan the electromagnetic spectrum emitted from the earth's surface. The **Thermal Infrared Multispectral Scanner (TIMS)**, for example, uses a six-channel scanner to measure the thermal radiation on the ground with an accuracy of 0.1°C. Different sediments and soils have distinctive temperatures, invisible to the human eye, which the TIMS can record. Differences in soil texture and moisture have revealed prehistoric fields and roadways in the Maya region of Mesoamerica.

Radar instruments bounce energy beams off the ground and read the returning signal. Radar can penetrate darkness, cloud cover, thick jungle canopies, and even the ground. Microwave radar is beamed into the ground and the echo often reflects buried features. **Synthetic Aperture Radar (SAR)** beams energy waves to the ground surface and the reflected energy is recorded. SAR is particularly sensitive to linear and geometric features on the earth. Satellite instruments can be programmed to seek certain "signatures" that are known beforehand to identify certain kinds of features on the ground, such as canals, causeways, or rectilinear features.

Chaco Canyon

Thermal Infrared Multispectral Scanner (TIMS) A satellite instrument that records multiple wavelengths of light reflected from the earth's surface.

Synthetic Aperture Radar (SAR) An instrument that beams energy waves to the ground surface and records the reflected energy.

 EXAMPLE 〜〜〜〜〜〜〜〜〜〜

CHACO ROADS

In AD 1050, Chaco Canyon, Arizona, had a population of some 5500 people living in large, multiroom apartment complexes known as pueblos. Towns and villages were connected to each other and the outside world by more than 600 km (400 mi) of roads. These roads are not simple paths. Chaco roads are remarkably broad—usually 8–10 m (25–35 ft) in width—comparable to modern two-lane highways. Most of these roads are marked by lines of rock or dug lightly into the ground. This extraordinary system extends in some cases more than 50 km (30 mi) to distant areas. Rock-cut stairways in the canyon cliffs provide for vertical movement along the roads. The roads were initially observed on the ground but the extent and pattern of the system were not imagined until satellite photography of the area became available (Fig. 6.24).

These roads are mysterious. They appear to be much wider and more substantial than needed for the foot traffic in the region. They are also discontinuous, often composed of a number of short segments. Many of the roads have no destination, simply ending out in the countryside (Fig. 6.25). Various explanations for their use based on economic, connective, or religious reasons have been suggested. Present-day Pueblo people, descendants of the Chaco and other groups of this part of Arizona, place great spiritual importance on directions and connections with nature. Perhaps the road system enhanced Chaco Canyon's position in both the physical and spiritual worlds.

Fig. 6.24 False-co[lor] satellite photogra[phy of the] road system. Th[e...] the linear featu[res...] the lower right-hand co[rner...] low lines are current-day roads which follow topography and the path of least resistance in construction. In contrast, the prehistoric roads are strikingly linear.

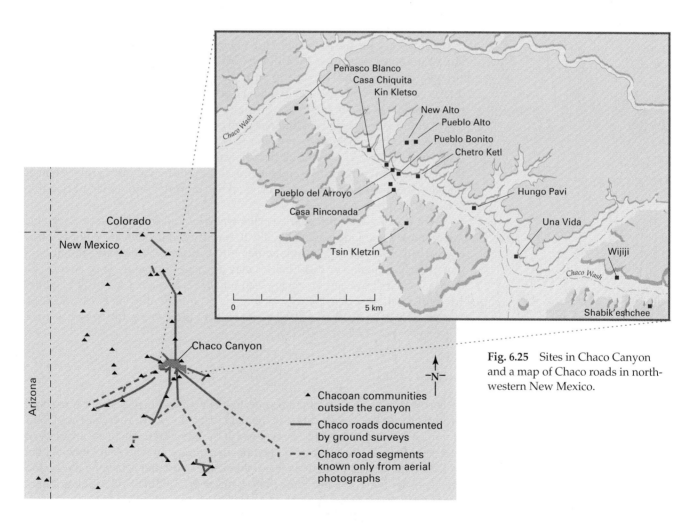

Peñasco Blanco
Casa Chiquita
Kin Kletso
New Alto
Pueblo Alto
Pueblo Bonito
Chetro Ketl
Pueblo del Arroyo
Casa Rinconada
Hungo Pavi
Tsin Kletzin
Una Vida
Wijiji
Chaco Wash
Shabik'eshchee

0   5 km

Colorado
New Mexico
Arizona
Chaco Canyon
—N—

▲ Chacoan communities outside the canyon
— Chaco roads documented by ground surveys
--- Chaco road segments known only from aerial photographs

Fig. 6.25 Sites in Chaco Canyon and a map of Chaco roads in northwestern New Mexico.

Remote Sensing on the Ground

Several different kinds of detectors can be used at archaeological sites to look for buried artifacts and features, including metal detectors, magnetometers, resistivity meters, and georadar.

Metal detectors register the presence of metal objects on the surface or buried in the soil. Metal detectors emit an electromagnetic field that is disrupted by the presence of metal objects in the ground. Metal detectors are of limited value at many sites since nonmetallic objects are not detected and since most archaeological sites in North America do not contain metals. Metal detectors are very useful at historic sites where iron tools and other metal objects are common.

Magnetometers are a more sophisticated form of detector and record variations in magnetic fields. A magnetometer, or gradiometer as it is also known, measures the earth's magnetic field at an archaeological site. The instrument is usually carried across the site following a regular grid pattern. Certain features at a site create minor disturbances in the earth's magnetic field that can be measured by the magnetometer. For example, rocks, metals, or changes in the density or composition of deposits from the presence of foreign materials, including imported rocks and metal, can create magnetic anomalies at a site, as can changes in deposits or local materials that have been altered magnetically by firing (hearths, kilns, burned houses, and the like). The information from the magnetometer on variation in the magnetic field at the site is processed in a computer and a map of the anomalies and altered deposits can be generated.

Resistivity refers to the ability of material to conduct electricity. In archaeology, a **resistivity meter** is used to measure soil conductivity and map differences in soils that may be due to the presence of buried disturbances such as fireplaces, burials, or other structures. Resistivity works best when the buried features are strongly differentiated, especially with disturbances such as stone walls and ditches. Different materials have different resistances, which are linked to moisture content, and therefore porosity. Variation in the composition and water content of different soils results in differences in electrical conductivity. The technique involves attaching the resistivity meter to two or more metal probes that are inserted into the soil. A low-voltage electrical current is passed between the probes, the measurement is recorded, and the process is repeated along a grid system at the site. The measured data are processed by computer and a plan of possible buried structures is produced.

Ground penetrating radar (also known as georadar) sends electromagnetic waves into the ground—something like the sonar used in submarine hunts. Low-energy radar waves register anomalies in the subsoil, which are shown on a graph. Such anomalies or disturbances may be caused by nature or by human activities. As with any remote sensing technique, it is necessary to "ground truth" the results with test pits or excavation to verify and identify such disturbances. The example below from the famous site of Petra (*PET-tra*) in the Near East may help explain how GPR works.

IN THE FIELD

Archaeological projects are about people, too. The following pages offer some brief information on the project director, the field crew, the field experience, and field equipment in order to provide some sense of the adventure. There are a variety of roles to be filled on a survey or excavation, depending on where and how big the project is. The project director oversees the whole effort and is usually the person who plans the work, organizes the project, raises the funding, and makes arrangements for permission, equipment, and crew. Large projects may have one or more specialists present as well, ranging from photographers to cooks, artists, surveyors, and archaeological experts in plant, animal, and human remains.

metal detectors   Instruments that emit an electromagnetic field, which is disrupted by the presence of metal objects in the ground, used for finding buried metal objects.

magnetometer (a.k.a. gradiometer)   Measures the earth's magnetic field at an archaeological *site* to locate buried walls and pits.

resistivity meter   Used to measure electrical conductivity in soils, which may be due to the presence of buried disturbances such as fireplaces, burials, or other structures.

Ground Penetrating Radar (GPR) (a.k.a. georadar)   An instrument that sends radar waves through the ground to reveal buried features.

Georadar at Petra

Petra is a fascinating ancient city in Jordan, located in the desert, hidden by steep sandstone cliffs and hills among a series of wadis (canyons). The entrance to the city, known as the Siq, is through a narrow defile between high cliffs. Petra was founded some 600 years before Christ. Its defensive and hidden situation protected the city until the Romans finally conquered it around AD 100. The city was abandoned sometime after AD 500. A number of the major buildings at Petra are still visible, with their facades carved on the cliffs and their interiors cut into the soft rock. Among the buildings and ruins are a number of open, empty spaces on the floor of the canyon.

Petra

a.

These canyon floors have been buried in sediment from episodic rainstorms and flash floods. No one was quite sure what was under the sands. For that reason, Lawrence Conyers of the University of Denver undertook a georadar survey of some of these open, flat areas in the wadis. The radar instrument was moved back and forth in a systematic grid and the echoes recorded (Fig. 6.26a,b). The data from the instrument were then computer-processed to provide a plan view of a large structure buried under the sediments. Based on information from the survey, Conyers made test excavations, which uncovered the walls of a rectangular stone building (Fig. 6.26c).

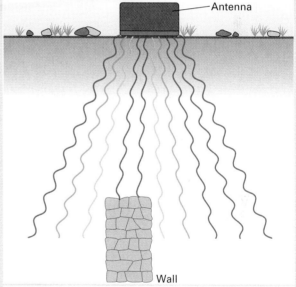
Antenna
Wall
b.

Fig. 6.26 Georadar in action. (a) Lawrence Conyers and assistant pull the ground penetrating radar (GPR) across an open area at Petra. (b) Schematic drawing of the instrument in use, emitting microwaves and measuring the response with an antenna. (c) A computer-generated display of the results of the magnetometer survey showing the outline of a structure buried in the middle of the open area. Test pits at this location revealed that stone walls were being recorded by the GPR.

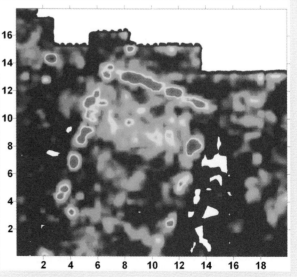
c.

The field crew consists of the students, volunteers, and laborers that together provide the work force for survey or excavation. The composition and interaction of the field crew are largely responsible for the success of the field season. Fieldwork is usually a valuable and exceptional experience for all involved. In fact, the social and intellectual context of an archaeological project is a major reason that most archaeologists like to dig.

Field equipment involves a wide range of tools, instruments, and utensils, again depending on the location, isolation, and funding of the project. Projects in the rain forest of Guatemala, for example, need generators, portable kitchens, tents, and a wide range of camping equipment in addition to archaeological items. Other projects may require construction trailers, fencing, backhoes, power augers, and a variety of other materials. The basics of archaeological equipment, both project and personal, are listed at the end of this section.

The Project Director

Directing a field survey or excavation requires a variety of skills and knowledge for planning a field season, raising money to pay for the work, supervising and training a crew of volunteers or students, recording information from a site with notes, drawings, and photographs, and measuring and mapping the locations of all finds, samples, and features. Excavations require reams of notes, drawings, and other paperwork. The director must keep an excavation log or diary, recording the course of the excavations, the work schedule, the number of people working, accounts of expenses, dimensions and positioning of excavation areas, layout of the measuring system, and all the finds. There must be recording systems for all measurements, for observations and interpretations, and for all drawings, photos, and samples.

The project director must monitor progress in the field laboratory as well, where finds are washed, sorted, cataloged, and bagged for storage. Some knowledge of preservation techniques is necessary on the part of the director to conserve fragile objects. The director also needs to be able to deal with people and manage social relationships under demanding conditions in often isolated field camps. The director needs to be a jack-of-all-trades to be successful.

The Field Crew

Excavation is a labor-intensive undertaking, and the field crew is the most important part of the project. This crew is the group of people involved in the actual digging process, unearthing the sites and artifacts. Members of the field crew on a CRM project are hourly employees of a private company or paid employees of a museum or government agency. Field crews on academic research projects are often composed of a variety of individuals, young and old, ranging from professional archaeologists with advanced degrees to undergraduate and graduate students, and sometimes just people interested in the subject. In addition to student and volunteer help on an academic project, there are sometimes paid day laborers employed as well. Particularly in developing countries, where labor is cheaper, archaeologists may hire local individuals to do necessary construction, earth moving, and some detailed excavation.

The U.S. Department of Labor has an official listing for field crew members in the department's Directory of Occupations. The listing is "29020 Archeological Technician" and the description of the position is as follows:

> Provides technical support to professional archeologist, utilizing a basic understanding of anthropological and archaeological field techniques in connection with locating, testing and evaluating cultural resource sites. Conducts pre-field office research, field surveys and site testing, using a variety of reference materials, interviews with source individuals, aerial photographs and

technical instruments. Searches areas of proposed projects for evidence of historic and prehistoric remains. Determines exact location of sites and marks them on maps and aerial photographs. Records information on site survey form and prepares an archaeological reconnaissance report needed for evaluation and management of the project. Insures that work assignments are carried out in safe and timely manner according to established standards and procedures. Reviews work in progress and reports to superiors relative to the completion date and other standards set in report. Cleans and catalogs artifacts recovered from inventories and excavations.

There is also a union for field crew, the United Archaeological Field Technicians. Their website is at http://members.aol.com/UAFT/home.htm.

An essential position on larger field projects is the crew chief, basically the foreman of the project, usually in charge of day-to-day operations and the ongoing practicalities of the fieldwork. Crew chiefs are experienced archaeologists, sometimes graduate students working on their dissertations as part of the project.

The Field Experience

Archaeology is the science of the past, but it is also a social experience in the present. Fieldwork can require a few days, weeks, or months, walking miles each day with your head down in survey of the ground, or moving tons of earth to expose buried levels. Excavations are hard work, often in uncomfortable conditions—hot sun, chilling rain, freezing temperatures, sticky mud, biting insects. Excavations are sometimes carried out in remote and difficult places, requiring patience and endurance. Archaeology is also good dirty fun. The experience of working, and relaxing, with others who enjoy the same things can be unforgettable. The discovery process is captivating, and sharing that excitement with colleagues and comrades enhances the entire experience.

Fieldwork is finally an extraordinary learning experience. One realizes the difficulties involved in recovering information from the past and comes to appreciate how much has been learned. In addition, a constant stream of questions about the past and the significance of place, artifact, and context come to mind while in the field. All in all, archaeological fieldwork can be a most stimulating activity.

Most people enjoy the process of fieldwork more than just about anything else. It's the perfect combination of physical activity and mental work—problem solving. Not to mention the great company. How many other fields let you engage emotionally, intellectually, and physically with their subject matter on so many levels? . . . Ostensibly, we're out there to find things and record things so we can come to conclusions. But is that what archaeologists enjoy most about their job? Is that what keeps bringing them back? I don't believe it. . . . Field archaeology is just too much fun.

—Adrian Praetzellis, archaeologist

 **EXAMPLE** ～～～～～～～～～～～～～～～

IN THE FIELD

But what is working in the field really like? Paul Green, now a senior cultural resources manager for the federal government (Fig. 6.27), has worked on sites in both the United States and Europe, with crew sizes ranging from one to about seventeen people. Here are some of his impressions.

My second major field season was as a crew member working in the Burgundy region of eastern France with Carole Crumley, an Iron Age specialist, at the University of North Carolina. In late July, during an unusually hot summer, we were winding up the long field season excavating the remains of a Celtic hill fort. This was a fortified site of the Gaelic-speaking peoples conquered by Julius Caesar in the first century BC. Most of the season we had been carefully digging 5-cm (2-in) levels in an area near the ramparts, constructed of rough, jagged boulders. One day, a local mayor speculated that the long-sought water source, or cistern, used by the inhabitants of the site would be found under a large thornbush in a depression near the summit of the mountain.

As the main dig area was winding down, the site director, Alan Downer, asked me to put in a 1 × 2 m (3 × 6 ft) test unit where the mayor had indicated. The pesky thornbush required about an hour and several puncture wounds to remove. Afterward, it took only a few minutes to discover that the area was full of large cobbles,

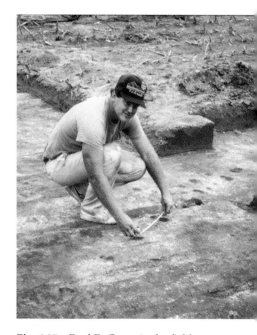

Fig. 6.27 Paul R. Green in the field, measuring the posts of a proto-historic Algonkian longhouse in coastal North Carolina.

small boulders, and a yellowish soil quite unlike what was found near the fortress walls. It was impossible to excavate with a trowel. I removed the boulders one by one and put the yellow soil through the sifting screen, with no resulting finds. Down went the unit through large chunks of yellow soil and boulders: 1 meter, 2 meters. It was starting to look uncomfortably like a grave.

Sometime in the next day or so, I was standing on the bottom of the unit and placed a shovel into the soil. Instead of the monotonous rocks and yellow soil, dark chocolate brown sediment appeared, loaded with large fragments of bright orange roofing tile and big chunks of charcoal. Al and I talked about the new layer and what it might mean, since nothing like it had been seen before on the site. He asked me to enlarge the unit to a 2 × 2 m size so we could better evaluate the new finds.

Several days later, and now definitely near the "site-closing" date, we sat in the bottom of the unit, staring at and trying to understand the "grid east" wall in front of us. A few centimeters of gravel on top, meters of boulders and yellow fill below, then the new find. How did it fit with a Celtic hill fort? Al reached out and casually brushed the unit wall with a small whisk. Some soil crumbs fell away and the smooth, dressed face of a stone block stared back at us. We were dumbstruck. He brushed again and block after block became visible. The unit wall had almost perfectly coincided with the stone wall of some unknown structure. We had found part of a completely forgotten church from the medieval period.

The find completely changed the direction of the dig. Over the last few days of that season and over several more years, excavations revealed the wall to be part of a larger complex. Its collapsed walls had produced the stone rubble and limey fill I had first dug through. Beneath the church were the remnants of a small Roman-period temple, or *fanum,* to which the roof tiles and burnt embers belonged. Finds included a figurine, coins, and pottery. And further down, we found artifacts and deposits of the Celts. These included pottery and silvered bronze coins, which still gleamed in the soil.

I've never forgotten the strange twists of that first season, the excitement of the new finds, and unraveling some of the mystery on that French mountain. Or the first time that you see, truly see, prehistoric features in the ground and, while excavating them, understand how they came to be. Most vividly, for a lifetime you remember the people, those who worked with you, who housed and perhaps fed you, and the "locals" with their questions and long, wondering gazes.

Yes, fieldwork is physically tough and the days are long, but the "fringe benefits" are fantastic. You travel to new, sometimes exotic, places and work with smart, creative, and energetic people with interests much like yours. Some memories fade with time, like blisters, thorns, bug bites, tree roots, and stifling heat. Others stay with you, like discovering a medieval church where none was suspected, below that a Roman temple, and below that remains of Caesar's Celtic foes, including coins shining brightly against the chocolate-colored dirt.

www.mhhe.com/pricearch1

For a Web-based activity on fieldwork opportunities, please see the Internet exercises on your online learning center.

Fieldwork Opportunities

Every archaeologist should participate in fieldwork. Though not everyone enjoys the field experience and not every branch of archaeology involves regular fieldwork, the experience is essential to being a competent and professional member of the discipline. Students in archaeology are urged to take part in fieldwork as part of their education. Many graduate students are involved in fieldwork over the summers of their studies.

CRM archaeological projects often hire students on a seasonal basis to do fieldwork. Academic projects usually take students into the field to participate in the research. Both CRM and academic employers usually look for students with some experience in fieldwork. This situation makes for a bit of a conundrum—you need experience to get a job, so where do you get the experience? Probably

TABLE 6.1	Individual excavation kit.
2-m folding ruler	nails
3-m measuring tape	notebook
4-in trowel	nylon string
artifact bags	pen and pencil
dental picks	permanent marker
disposable scalpel	plumb bob
dustpan	small paintbrush
kneeling mat	small palette knife
labels	whisk broom
line level	

TABLE 6.2	Some excavation equipment.
Digging	shovels, spades, picks, backhoe, rake, hammers, wheelbarrows, ladder, kneeling pads, auger, dustpans, buckets, tubs, brushes, brooms, water sprayer, artifact bags, labels and tags
Drawing	drawing table/boards, planning frame, drawing paper/film, graph paper, pencils/lead/erasers
Photography	cameras, photo sign board, north arrow and scale, small bellows
Sieving	screens, water pump and hoses, artifact bags, sorting boxes, permanent markers
Survey/mapping	surveying instruments, plumb bob, stadia rods, ranging rods, chaining pins, measuring tapes, large nails, string, wooden stakes, survey flags
Survival	tables, chairs, water coolers, parasols, insect repellent, sun screen, rain gear, rubber boots, beer

the best place to begin in archaeology, unless you are fortunate enough to be invited on a project, is to participate in a field school. Universities around the United States, Canada, and Britain conduct student training projects known as field schools.

Field schools are conducted as part of larger projects or specifically for the training of students. Students pay a fee, ranging from a few hundred to a few thousand dollars, for the opportunity to take part in a field project. Course credit is often given for participation so that the field school counts as coursework in a degree program. Field schools expose students to a variety of tools, methods, and techniques and usually provide an important first exposure to outdoor archaeology. Field school certification is a documentation of experience in archaeology and usually provides an opportunity for further fieldwork and employment.

Opportunities for field school participation are often posted in the anthropology departments at universities. In addition, there are several online sites for fieldwork opportunities that include field schools:

1. www.archaeological.org/webinfo.php?page=10016
   The Archaeological Institute of America. Probably the largest and most comprehensive listing of fieldwork opportunities on the Web.

2. www.archaeologyfieldwork.com
   Jennifer Palmer runs a website with employment, volunteer, field school, and internship openings with a variety of information.

3. www.bajr.org/index.html
   British Archaeological Jobs Resources. A list of jobs and fieldwork opportunities in the United Kingdom, along with other information for and about archaeology.

Equipment

Most excavations are organized so that each excavator has a small kit of tools in addition to the common excavation equipment. Table 6.1 lists some contents of an individual kit, and Table 6.2 lists the basic equipment for the project. These lists will vary from individual to individual and site to site depending on conditions, personal preferences, and location.

CONCLUSIONS

Prehistoric sites are often found through a combination of accident, archival research, and fieldwork. Archival research provides information on what is already known about an area. Fieldwork often results in the discovery of the unknown. When new sites are found, surface survey, testing, boring, and several geophysical methods are available to determine the size and possible contents of the prehistoric deposit. A number of recent technological developments have greatly improved efficiency and accuracy in archaeological fieldwork in areas of surveying (total station, GIS, GPS) and remote sensing (georadar, magnetometry, resistivity, soil chemistry). However, once a site is discovered and defined from the surface, excavations are often necessary to expose what lies beneath.

Archaeological excavation is a technique for recovering objects and information about the past from the ground. Excavation strategies vary greatly depending on the type of site, the period of time, the nature of the deposits, and the research questions under consideration. Two general types of excavations are horizontal and vertical, focusing respectively on specific horizons of human activity and on the stratigraphy and chronological nature of the deposits. Excavations are demanding but essential for providing the basic material for analysis and interpretation. Underwater archaeology is another aspect of fieldwork, conducted by archaeologists trained as divers. Although the conditions of work are more demanding because of the logistics and demands of being underwater, the methods and results of this research do not differ greatly from those of archaeology on land.

DISCOVERING SITES

Bob Anderson owns a large farm in northern Kentucky. A conversation with Mr. Anderson revealed that he once found some potsherds and a few arrowheads next to the river on his property, but the items are now lost.

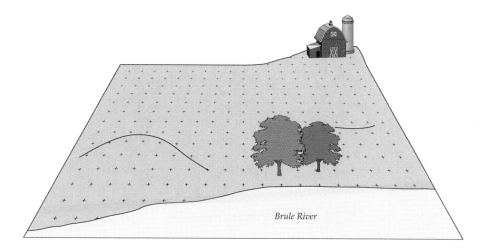

Fig. 6.28 Map 1: Mr. Anderson's farm and the grid that was established for the survey.

Brule River

After some discussion, Mr. Anderson allowed three archaeologists to survey the fields around his farmhouse. A systematic field survey was made at 10-m intervals. More intensive surface collections were made in areas where chipped stone artifacts, potsherds, shells, or discolorations of the soil were found. Soil samples were taken at 10-m intervals for phosphate analysis.

The information collected during this survey is provided on the following maps. These maps also show a 10-m grid across the fields. Each grid square measures 10 × 10 m. The first drawing is a sketch of the general area with some important topographic features, such as the riverbank and the Andersons' farmyard.

The second map contains a series of numbers recorded for making a contour map. The numbers on this map are elevations in meters above sea level as measured by the surveyor. The values range from 111 to 140 m. Draw contour lines on this map to determine the higher and lower areas on the farm. As an example, the contour line at 140 m has already been drawn on the map. Add the remaining contour lines in decreasing order. Use an interval of 5 m of elevation for these contour lines. Draw contour lines enclosing areas with elevations of 135 m or greater, 130, 125, 120, and 115 m.

Fig. 6.29 Map 2: Elevation of each grid unit from the mapping work.

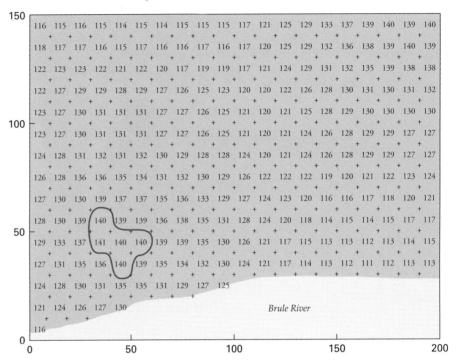

Map 1: Elevation in meters above sea level

Where are the higher areas on the farm?

_____

_____

_____

_____

_____

Map 3 shows the number of chipped stone pieces, potsherds, and other artifacts that were collected in each 10-m grid unit during the survey. The values range from 0 per grid unit to a maximum of 60 artifacts per grid unit. In order to better visualize what these numbers mean, it is useful to draw contour lines around the areas of high artifact density. Draw contour lines of artifact density on the map. Use a contour interval of 10 artifacts per grid unit. Draw lines enclosing areas of more than 10, 20, 30, 40, 50, and 60 artifacts per grid unit. What is the relationship between elevation and artifact density?

_____

_____

_____

_____

_____

Map 2: Number of artifacts per grid unit

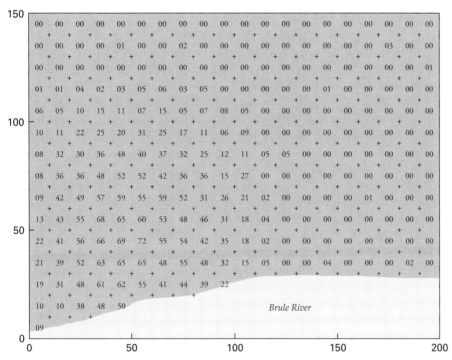

Fig. 6.30 Map 3: The number of artifacts collected per grid unit in the survey.

Map 4 shows levels of phosphate in the area in parts per million (ppm) in the soil samples. Values range from 50 ppm to 120 ppm across the survey area. Higher levels are indicative of more human, or animal, activity. There is some residual phosphate almost everywhere here due to artificial fertilizers. Draw contour lines on Map 4 to represent the concentrations of phosphate as an indicator of human activity. Use an interval of 20 ppm to draw contour lines on Map 4. Draw contour lines enclosing grid units containing more than 60, 80, and 100 ppm of phosphate in the soil.

What does the phosphate say about the location of human activity in relation to elevation and artifact density?

_____

_____

_____

_____

_____

You have time and permission to excavate four small 1 × 1 m test pits in the field of Farmer Anderson. Where would you place these test pits given what you have learned from the distribution of artifacts and phosphate? Mark the location of

Fig. 6.31 Map 4: The concentration of phosphate per grid unit in the survey area.

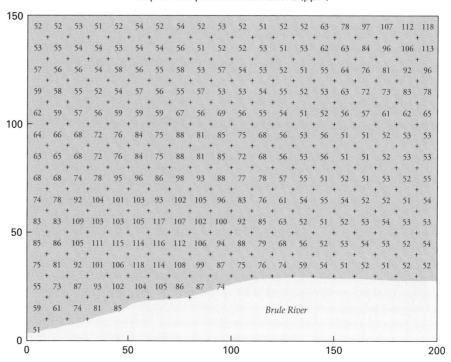

Map 3: Phosphate concentrations (ppm)

your four small test pits with black squares on Map 2, the elevation map. Why did you place the test pits in those locations? Discuss below.

_____

_____

_____

_____

Discuss the results of the archaeological survey. What was found? What does the information from the distribution of the artifacts and the phosphate values suggest? What do they tell us about the location and content of sites in this area? How many sites are there in the survey area? Are there any sites that would be worth testing by digging test pits or trenches? Answer these questions in one or two paragraphs in the space below.

_____

_____

_____

_____

_____

_____

_____

_____

STUDY QUESTIONS

1. What are the major techniques for the discovery of archaeological remains?

2. How are maps made and why are they important?

3. Excavations are expensive and time-consuming. Why are they necessary?

4. What techniques are available for remote sensing—that is, for looking into the ground without digging?

5. What are the differences between archaeology underwater and on land?

www.mhhe.com/pricearch1

For more review material and study questions, please see the self-quizzes on your online learning center.

REFERENCES

Caple, Chris. 2000. *Conservation Skills: Judgement, Method and Decision Making.* London: Routledge.

Collis, John. 2001. *Digging Up the Past: An Introduction to Archaeological Excavation.* Stroud: Sutton Publishing.

Gaffney, V., and J. Gater. 2003. *Revealing the Buried Past: Geophysics for Archaeologists.* Stroud: Tempus.

Greene, Kevin. 2002. *Archaeology: An Introduction.* 4th ed. London: Routledge.

Peregrine, Peter N. 2001. *Archaeological Research: A Brief Introduction.* Upper Saddle River, NJ: Prentice Hall.

Roskams, Steve. 2001. *Excavation.* Cambridge Manuals in Archaeology. Cambridge: Cambridge University Press.

Sutton, Mark Q., and Brooke S. Arkush. 2002. *Archaeological Laboratory Methods: An Introduction.* 3rd ed. Dubuque: Kendall/Hunt Publishing.

Zimmerman, L. J., and William Green. 2003. *The Archaeologist's Toolkit.* Walnut Creek, Calif.: AltaMira Press.

www.mhhe.com/pricearch1

For Internet references related to this chapter, please see the chapter links on your online learning center.

ANALYSIS

After the fieldwork, the materials collected in survey and excavation must be cleaned, conserved, sorted, classified, and counted. Then come the specialist studies, the detailed analyses, the compilation of data, the writing of excavation reports and scientific articles, all of which require much more work and time than the actual fieldwork. As mentioned, one estimate suggests there are about 5 weeks of analysis and writing for each week of excavation—and that estimate is probably low!

The chapters in Part 3 of *Principles of Archaeology* focus on some of the different analyses that characterize archaeological research. Chapter 7 considers classification and data: how archaeologists divide things into groups, record information, and look at the numbers—the first steps in analysis. Chapter 8 is a discussion of the major dating methods that are used to determine the age of the things that are found.

Specialists are needed to examine and interpret the wide range of materials and information found at archaeological sites. Geoarchaeology, the study of the geological setting and the details of the sediments encasing archaeological remains, is described in Chapter 9. Lithic analysis of the stone tools that are a common material on many archaeological sites is the subject of Chapter 10. Ceramic analysis concerns the study of ancient pottery, a major aspect of archaeological research at many sites, and it is covered in Chapter 11. Chapter 12 discusses archaeozoology, the investigation of the animal bones that represent the remains of meals and manufacturing activities, and Chapter 13 introduces archaeobotany, the study of plant remains, both visible and microscopic, that are found at a site. The next chapter, 14, looks at bioarchaeology, the investigation of human skeletal remains from archaeological contexts. Finally, Chapter 15 discusses archaeometry, the application of chemical and physical sciences to archaeological materials. There are of course other kinds of materials and artifacts found at archaeological sites—wood, metal, ground stone, textiles, glass, and more. References to studies of such materials are found in the bibliography at the end of the book, or you can search online for the kind of material in which you are interested.

Classification and Data

INTRODUCTION: SORTING, TYPES, AND NUMBERS

In this photograph, a hunter from Botswana in southern Africa carefully applies the poison juice from a beetle larva to the front of his arrow. He belongs to a larger group of hunter-gatherers in the region known as the San. The bows and arrows that the San used were lightly constructed and the arrow would not bring down a prey animal without the poison.

Polly Wiessner, an archaeologist at the University of Utah, has conducted ethnoarchaeological studies in several different parts of the world. Her experiences in Africa, New Guinea, Vietnam, and Australia have provided a rich body of information on the variety of human behavior. She spent a large part of the 1970s among the San in the Kalahari Desert of southern Africa, a rather desolate place during the dry season, and a region of little interest to farmers. She published a report on some of her work in 1983 entitled *Style and Social Information in Kalahari San Projectile Points*.

Wiessner began her article with an anecdote from the American West—a circle of covered wagons and a horde of Indian riders. An arrow slams into the wagon next to a cavalry scout, who calmly studies the weapon and reports that they are under attack by Apaches. This cliché highlights Wiessner's focus on variation in artifacts and particularly on style, an attempt to determine if archaeologists can distinguish groups of people in the past using stylistic variation in artifacts. As Wiessner noted, the differences seen in a group of artifacts can be due to time, function, or style. Part of the archaeologist's task is to distinguish these different sources of variation, and it's a hard job.

In southern Africa among the San, Wiessner made detailed notes on the objects the people made and used. She was particularly interested in arrows and beaded decoration such as on bags, headbands, belts, and the like. These objects showed significant differences, reflecting variation in material culture.

The arrows that the San men made had a metal point and a poisoned shaft. The shaft was a length of yellow reed with a notch at one end to fit the bowstring. Both ends of the shaft were lashed with sinew to strengthen the reed. The business end of the reed held a thin piece of bone. The bone acted as a **foreshaft** for the arrow, designed to detach after impacting the animal and leave the poison in the animal. Finally, the point was attached. The metal points were hammered and filed into shape from a piece of fence wire. The highly toxic poison was put on the front of the arrow just behind the point.

foreshaft   Part of an arrow, designed to detach with the point after impacting the animal in order to preserve the longer shaft of the arrow, which falls away.

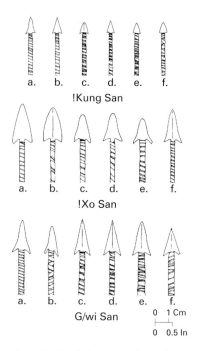

Fig. 7.1 Typical arrows from three groups of San hunters in southern Africa. The points are made from identical materials by related groups of people, and there are clear differences among the groups that match distinctive language dialects.

www.mhhe.com/pricearch1

For preview material for this chapter, please see the chapter summary, outline, and objectives on your online learning center.

Most of the hunters could identify their own arrows and those of their close colleagues. These arrows were traded widely among the men and were given distinctive characteristics by their makers. It was also the case that the hunter who killed an animal got a larger share of the meat, making the recognition of one's arrows advantageous. Wiessner asked the men how they identified arrows and compiled their answers. The most important characteristics were the shape of the barbs and the body and the size of the point. Wiessner then studied the arrow points of the different groups to see if they showed real differences. She determined that there were clear distinctions between the groups, but that very little difference could be seen among individuals within a group (Fig. 7.1). The distribution of a group's projectile points coincided with the location of the people in that group who spoke a certain dialect. On the basis of her studies, Wiessner distinguished between what she called an "assertive" kind of style that portrays individual or personal identity, and an "emblematic" style that displays group identity.

This chapter is about the differences in the archaeological record and about how archaeologists cope with that variation. Just as we try to break time and space into smaller units, we need to put the information from past societies into smaller, more manageable bits of information. Classification is the primary means for categorizing large bodies of data. To deal with large amounts of information and numbers, archaeologists also use statistics and graphs to summarize and display the data they compile. These subjects are discussed in more detail in this chapter.

This chapter is also about categories and classification, information and data—how archaeologists organize, measure, and describe the materials they collect during fieldwork and after they have cleaned, cataloged, and conserved them. Archaeological fieldwork produces many kinds of materials and information. These objects, drawings, measurements, photos, and the like comprise an enormous body of data. The survey of the valley around the ancient Mexican city of Teotihuacán (Chapter 5) recorded more than 5000 structures in the region. Excavations at ancient cities, with their accumulations of architecture and refuse, process hundreds of thousands of pieces of pottery in a single season. My own excavations at the Stone Age site of Smakkerup Huse in Denmark recovered a total of 225 kg (560 lbs.) of flint and other worked stone, 150 kg (330 lb) of bone and antler, wood, nutshell, and other plant remains, and many other interesting artifacts. The numbers far exceed the quantities implied by the weight. There were tens of thousands of pieces of flint, hazelnut shell, and fishbone, and thousands of bone and antler fragments. As these quantities illustrate, the amount of material that is excavated and processed in an excavation can be overwhelming.

A major part of archaeology consists of analysis—searching through this huge body of material and information for more facts. Much of the search involves studying the artifacts that are recovered. Archaeologists spend a great deal of time studying artifacts (and other information) and creating new data to describe the finds and their characteristics. Analysis is the search for pattern in the body of information that results from excavation and classification.

In this chapter, the preparation and analysis of archaeological materials is first considered in terms of the initial cleaning, cataloging, and conservation of finds. The next major step is the classification of materials into useful and meaningful categories for further analysis. Classification focuses on the raw material, technology, function, and style of artifacts. The classification and counting of archaeological materials and the measurement and description of their characteristics produce even more data and information. Presentation and comparison of such data is best accomplished with the use of statistics to summarize and display the information of relevance. Statistics provide descriptive measures of average and range in a set of data to condense many numbers into few. Statistics are also useful for making decisions about similarities and differences in numbers using probability. The visual display of data is another way to condense information

Fig. 7.2 Numbering and cataloging the finds from the excavation is a demanding job because of the size and number of the pieces.

and make it more understandable. Such displays include various plots and graphs that summarize large quantities of information into a bar, line, or dot. Cleaning, cataloging, conservation, and classification are essential before the more detailed analyses of specific kinds of finds—described in later chapters—can begin.

CLEANING AND CATALOGING

When the finds come in from the field, they have to be processed (Fig. 7.2). That process involves a number of steps that are intended to turn dirty and broken pieces of the past into relatively clean, stable, and archived information. It is usually necessary to clean the objects so that the evidence of the kind of material, the type of artifact, and so forth can be seen. It is also essential to clean these objects so that mold and fungus don't grow on them during storage. Cleaning is usually done with water and brush. Certain kinds of artifacts are not washed at all because they may be too fragile or might contain information that could be removed or damaged by cleaning.

Most finds are also cleaned so that they can be numbered and cataloged. Artifacts and ecofacts are numbered so that they can be removed from the labeled bags from the excavation and then studied with similar objects from other parts of the excavation. Numbers are usually applied in permanent ink, or sometimes with bar codes, depending on the size and nature of the materials.

The finds from an archaeological project represent a huge investment of time, money, and energy. Archaeological materials are nonrenewable resources, so they must be treated as valuable objects and stored for future study and comparison. Archaeological finds are stored in university departments, in museums, in government facilities, and other places as an archive and record of the work that was done and the information that was found.

In order to be able to find these materials in the future and to know what is present, it is essential to archive the finds according to a logical system. Essentially that means that the finds are entered into a catalog of permanent records. The catalog entry for each object includes a description of the kind of artifact, the type of raw material, the color, the overall shape and measurements, techniques of manufacturing, presumed function, decoration, and provenience information.

Fig. 7.3 A page from a field catalog with an unusual flint artifact.

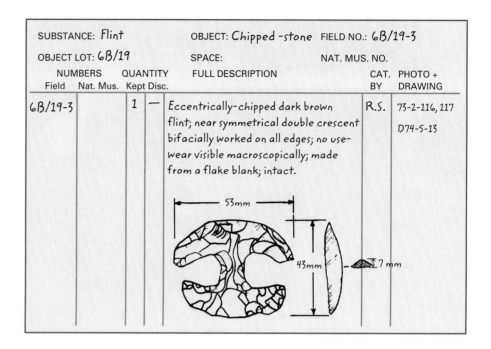

SUBSTANCE: Flint				OBJECT: Chipped-stone	FIELD NO.: 6B/19-3		
OBJECT LOT: 6B/19				SPACE:	NAT. MUS. NO.		
NUMBERS		QUANTITY		FULL DESCRIPTION		CAT.	PHOTO +
Field	Nat. Mus.	Kept	Disc.			BY	DRAWING
6B/19-3		1	—	Eccentrically-chipped dark brown flint; near symmetrical double crescent bifacially worked on all edges; no use-wear visible macroscopically; made from a flake blank; intact.		R.S.	73-2-116, 117 D74-5-13

This catalog could be supplemented with an accurate drawing and a photograph of the find. A sample field catalog sheet is shown in Fig. 7.3. An inventory of the materials from the excavation then can be made by counting and recording the number of finds in each category of material, such as chipped stone, ground stone, or pottery.

Once the artifacts and other finds have been cataloged and the analysis is done, they are stored in a museum or other appropriate facility. Museums and storage facilities maintain a master catalog and assign an accession number to each curated collection. This number supplements, but does not replace, catalog numbers used by the submitter of the materials.

CONSERVATION

The **conservation** of archaeological materials is critically important, yet often neglected. Less durable artifacts decompose when removed from their original burial conditions, and conservation is essential to preserve these items. Unfortunately, there are few trained conservators or facilities for this kind of archaeology in the United States. Conservators are usually employed at museums and some government organizations to curate and maintain a wide range of prehistoric and historic materials.

Conservation involves two primary activities: preservation and restoration. Preservation involves stabilizing the condition of the finds through the use of mechanical and chemical means. The state of excavated materials varies widely. Stone and ceramic artifacts usually fare well in the ground, but metals behave very differently. Iron oxidizes and rusts; silver tarnishes and disintegrates; bronze and copper turn green and corrode; and gold only dulls in luster. Damage to organic materials such as wood, metal, bone, and fabric is even greater under a variety of burial environments. Conservation treatments that may be both extensive and expensive are required (Fig. 7.4).

Restoration involves altering the material and/or structure of the artifact or ecofact to return it to a more original condition in order to make it more understandable, usually for display or educational reasons. But conservators prefer to preserve items, rather than restore them, in most instances because their goal is "nontoxic, minimal intervention artifact stabilization."

www.mhhe.com/pricearch1

For a Web-based activity on preservation projects, please see the Internet exercises on your online learning center.

conservation Preservation and restoration of archaeological materials in the laboratory and museum.

restoration Altering the material and/or structure of an artifact or structure to return it to a more original condition.

Fig. 7.4 Wood treatment tank at the Conservation Department, York Archaeological Trust. This tank is for timbers and other large pieces of wood.

Conservation treatments for artifacts can be active or passive. Active preservation is similar to treating ill or injured patients with chemicals, plaster casts, prosthetics, and other means to repair damage and improve their health. In this way, conservators are like doctors for artifacts. Passive treatments seek to improve the conditions under which the find is kept in order to prevent further deterioration. Passive conservation is more cost effective since a large number of finds can be stored under similar conditions of preservation. Documentation of treatment is an essential part of conservation as many techniques of preservation can alter the physical and chemical characteristics of the find. Some conservation techniques can dramatically affect the results of analytical methods such as radiocarbon dating or chemical analysis. Careful records are kept of the preservatives and materials that are used, along with observations of any changes in the original objects.

The example below describes the treatment of the Lindow Man, a 2000-year-old body from the bogs of northwest England.

 EXAMPLE ~~~~~~~~~~~~~~~~~~~~~~~~~~~~

LINDOW MAN

Archaeologists rarely find flesh on the bones of the past. Much of what we know about our ancestors and their lives comes from the detective work of piecing together information from fragments of pots and tools, discarded bones and buried skeletons—the broken, forgotten, and hidden remnants of what human society once created. Unusual situations, especially in the case of human bodies preserved from the past, immediately capture our attention. These discoveries emphasize the fragile nature of the human condition.

Among the most remarkable prehistoric bodies are the "bog people" from northern Europe. Hundreds of individuals have been found in the peat bogs, dating to the centuries around the birth of Christ. These bogs have marvelous preservative powers. The accumulation of peat and organic detritus that fills these swamps and mires contains tannic acid from the needles of coniferous trees. Tannic acid, used for

www.mhhe.com/pricearch1

For a Web-based activity on Lindow Man, please see the Internet exercises on your online learning center.

Lindow Man

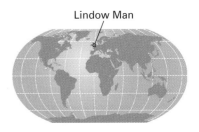

Conservation **183**

Fig. 7.5 The head and torso of Lindow Man, a well-preserved bog body found in England. The man had been bludgeoned with an axe, strangled, and stabbed in the throat.

The sense of wonder they [bog bodies] conjure up is combined with the feeling that they have in some way cheated death, to live again. The forces behind the violent and often complex deaths they suffered are beyond mere scientific enquiry to convey.

—R. Turner, author

tanning hides, is one essential factor in the preservation of the skin of the bog bodies. The second factor is the waterlogged condition of the bogs, which creates an environment where bacteria cannot break down soft tissues.

Lindow Man is one of the famous bog bodies of northern Europe (Fig. 7.5), found in a marsh near the city of Manchester, England, in 1984. The finds included the head, torso, and right foot of a male in his twenties. Radiocarbon dates from the body indicate a date of death between the birth of Christ and AD 120. The deaths of the people found in the bogs are usually not the result of accidental drowning or disappearance. Humans were intentionally sacrificed to the sacred bogs. Lindow Man, for example, was bludgeoned with an axe and strangled and his throat was cut before he was placed in the waters of the bog. There is some indication that his body was painted with a blue-green paint or dye, perhaps a tribal war paint described by Julius Caesar in his encounters with the Celts.

Lindow Man provides an extraordinary example of the innovative techniques of archaeological conservation. Excavated in 1984, the remains were taken to the British Museum in London for analysis and conservation. Fifty specialists were called in to examine Lindow Man. They dated him, X-rayed him, analyzed his stomach contents, determined his blood type, checked his teeth, and reconstructed his face. After the analyses, the standard sequence of conservation treatments—cleaning, mounting, consolidation, and reconstruction—began.

As a first step, as soon as one side of the body had been cleaned, a cast was made using materials similar to those used on broken limbs. This cast of both sides of the remains became a mount that could be used to turn the body without damage. Once removed from the bog, without care, the body would have dried up and shrunken quickly, eventually disintegrating to dust. Throughout the scientific examination and conservation, the body was kept moist by spraying it with distilled water and covering exposed parts with a household plastic wrap. The body was also stored in a cooler at 4°C after 2 hours of treatment.

Within a few months of his discovery, however, the Lindow Man began to deteriorate. The conservation issues were complex with Lindow Man and had not been tried before at the British Museum. The members of the conservation department consulted with experts in other countries and finally decided to use a new approach involving freeze-drying. After the remains were carefully cleaned again, the body was submerged in a tank of a **hydrophilic** lubricant called polyethylene glycol for 4 weeks. Hydrophilic compounds have an affinity for water and helped to remove this substance from the corpse.

Then the body was placed in a special freezer. When the temperature had reached –20°C (–7°F), a vacuum was applied so that the water in the cells of the tissue would sublime (evaporate). As the water disappeared, the waxy, water-soluble polyethylene glycol took its place as a solid residue. This solid strengthens the cell walls and reduces the major problems of drying, shrinking, and hardening with waterlogged materials. The body was then slowly unthawed, weighed, and measured to see if the conservation had caused significant changes. The procedure worked very well; the skin remained supple and shrinkage was less than 5%. In addition, the museum staff determined how the preserved tissue would react to light and humidity in order to determine the best conditions for storage and display.

Today, Lindow Man is one of the biggest attractions at the British Museum, enclosed in a small glass showcase tucked away in a cranny of the museum, around the corner from the Egyptian mummy room. The relative humidity and temperature in the display case is strictly controlled. Flash photography is prohibited and light levels around the case are subdued so that no harmful ultraviolet radiation touches the only surviving human face from British prehistory.

CLASSIFICATION

Following the initial cleaning, recording, and conservation of materials, finds are classified into more specific categories and types. Classification is a way of creating order in a mass of archaeological materials by grouping items into similar cat-

hydrophilic   Chemical compounds with an affinity for water which are used to remove water from artifacts during conservation.

egories for analysis. Classification is the process of putting objects into groups on the basis of shared characteristics.

Understanding the world around us is a complicated process. One of the first things that we learn to do as children is to classify and identify what we encounter—people, places, things, animals, minerals, vegetables, and so on. Identification is the process of recognizing the category an object belongs in. Classifying is the process of creating those categories. We constantly classify and identify. It is the way that we make sense of the world; how we order the chaos around us into categories, classes, or groups of items so we don't have to deal with everything at once.

Classification provides order—we sort different kinds of mp3 players, insects, clothing, seashells, people, and everything else into groups. Think about music. There are thousands of songs you have heard and it's impossible to remember everything. But when you classify your favorite music, cataloging songs in your mind by artist and genre perhaps, they are much easier to remember. If you want to tell someone else about your musical tastes, you talk about types or genres of music—alternative, bluegrass, country, folk, funk, jazz, hip hop, and so on. You are classifying the world around you.

The illustration below provides a case for classification (Fig. 7.6). There are thirty-three houses shown. Are they the same or different? If they are different, how many kinds of houses are there? These questions involve classification and identification. Deciding on the different kinds of houses is classification; deciding to which group a house belongs is identification.

Another lesson from this example is that different people will group these houses in different ways (e.g., all the same, black vs. white roofs, houses on ground vs. stilts, door east vs. door west, etc.). Archaeologists usually fall into one of two groups—splitters and lumpers. Splitters are people who tend to create lots of categories; lumpers tend to see only a few. Classification is not an objective process and classifications are not rigid or necessarily right. Classifications are tools, not solutions. They are developed to solve a problem and to answer specific questions.

Our classifications of the world around us depend on what we want to know. An example of how classification works can be seen in Fig. 7.7. In the upper photo, a number of objects from a modern household are classified by raw material: metal, wood, rubber, and plastic. In the lower photo, the same items are grouped by function—food preparation, hygiene, repair/maintenance, and leisure. These items could be grouped in a variety of other ways—e.g., by color, room in house, date of manufacture, owner, hardness, sharpness, and so on—depending on what we want to know.

Most scientific disciplines classify the things they study—biologists use the Linnaean system to identify species of plants and animals, chemists read the periodic table of the elements, astronomers see different types of stars, geologists have named many types of rocks. All group similar kinds of things together in categories on the basis of shared characteristics. Much of what archaeologists do involves classifying the evidence from the past—artifacts, features, architecture, sites, landscapes, etc.—into groups of related items.

Archaeologists sort through the objects and information that have survived from the past to create order. This process makes cataloging, describing, analyzing, and reporting the finds more manageable. Classification proceeds through steps, creating hierarchies of categories. Some objects readily fall into categories and can be easily classified. Most materials from the past, however, are highly variable and difficult to classify. Classification can be done in several ways, but most systems are either intuitive or objective. Intuitive classification involves visual sorting of items based on prior knowledge. Objective classification involves measurement of some characteristics of the objects (length, weight, color, hardness) and sorting them into groups based on the measurements.

There are, in fact, several important concepts involved in classification—groups, types, guides, and keys. **Grouping** is the process of sorting things into

We need more rather than fewer classifications, different classifications, always new classifications, to meet new needs.

—J. O. Brew, archaeologist

Fig. 7.6 Hypothetical village of different house types.

classification The process of putting objects into groups on the basis of shared characteristics.

grouping The process of sorting things into piles, or groups, of similar items without predetermined categories.

Fig. 7.7 Everyday household objects can be classified in many different ways, including by cost, owner, location, raw material, or function. In this example, the same objects are sorted by raw material (a), and by function (b).

a.

b.

piles, or groups, of similar items without predetermined categories. Grouping is an initial step toward classification. Classification is the general process of sorting items into known categories—placing items in labeled boxes. A classification is any described set of groups. A **typology** is a formal system of classification for assigning time and space meaning to archaeological materials. The units of a typology are called types—types of projectile points, types of pottery, or types of sites, for example. Guides and keys are aides for identifying items. A **guide**, like a guide to the birds of North America, is a listing of the different types, or species, that are present and the important characteristics of each. A guide is intended to help identify the types. **Keys** are condensed guides, listing the characteristics of important types. This may sound a bit confusing, but in essence archaeologists classify the material and information that they study, often using typologies to create standardized categories.

A published typology is a guide to classifying one group or type of archaeological material. The diagram in Fig. 7.8 shows a series of projectile point types from the Northwestern Plains of the United States along with their approximate age. Over time, types appear and disappear, replaced by new forms. General trends in the case of these point types include smaller size and a notched base.

Classifications of archaeological material are usually hierarchical, ordered from more general to more specific. A *hierarchical classification* starts with an object. Repeated decisions are made about the category in which the object belongs, based on different attributes. Hierarchical classification creates a kind of family tree of artifact types.

Classifications are considered today as arbitrary frameworks for categorizing materials to bring order to a chaotic jumble of artifacts and information. This has not always been the case, and a short history of archaeological thinking about classification and typology provides an example of how methods for ordering the past have developed.

One of the early approaches to typology utilized the concept of the *fossile directeur*, or diagnostic artifact. This French term is borrowed from geology and paleontology and refers to the "indicator fossil." In paleontology, a single fossil species has often been used as a marker of a time horizon. The presence of even one bone of that species indicates the time period in which that animal existed. A *fossile directeur* can provide a date for the entire deposit or layer of fossils. This approach was used in archaeology in the nineteenth and early twentieth centuries to characterize archaeological assemblages. The discovery of a single diagnostic artifact was used to provide the age and cultural affiliation for an entire layer or assemblage of artifacts. Of course, artifacts don't behave like biological species. There are real limitations to this approach in archaeology, largely because so much information is ignored. As dating methods have improved using other materials, archaeologists have moved away from the *fossile directeur* approach and toward more detailed analyses of artifact assemblages.

In the 1950s, an important debate developed among archaeologists about the meaning of types. Do the types that archaeologists define have significance in the past or only in the present? The two major players in this argument were Jim Ford (1911–1968) and Al Spaulding (1914–1990). Ford argued that types were artificial classifications of materials from the past, created by archaeologists. Ford believed that types were used to solve a problem and, for Ford, that problem was chronology. Ford used types to learn about the temporal dimension of variation in artifacts.

Spaulding, on the other hand, believed that archaeologists discovered "natural" types that were real and also recognized by the people who had made them. These natural types were thought of as a kind of "mental template," a concept shared by members of the same group and used as a guide for making artifacts and architecture. Spaulding argued that types could be discovered using statistical techniques that revealed clusters or associations of attributes.

David Clarke elaborated on this idea, describing archaeological types as packages of various attributes (Fig. 7.9). For example, a projectile point could be summarized by a series of measurements of size and shape.

Today, classification is widely regarded as an artificial construct, designed for solving specific problems. It is unlikely that we can reproduce how our ancestors visualized their world.

Classification is important in archaeology for several reasons. Sorting provides some order to the mass of materials that are recovered in archaeological fieldwork. Description of archaeological materials is less dense and tedious when reference is made to a known category or type. Classification greatly facilitates comparison of assemblages or sites by reducing a huge quantity of information to a more manageable and understandable summary. The next section of this

typology A formal system of classification for assigning time and space meaning to archaeological materials.

guide A listing of the different types, or species, that are present, and the distinguishing characteristics of each.

keys Condensed guides, listing the characteristics of important types.

fossile directeur (French: *indicator fossil*) A single fossil species as a marker of a time horizon.

3 A typology of projectile from the Northwestern Plains of the United States.

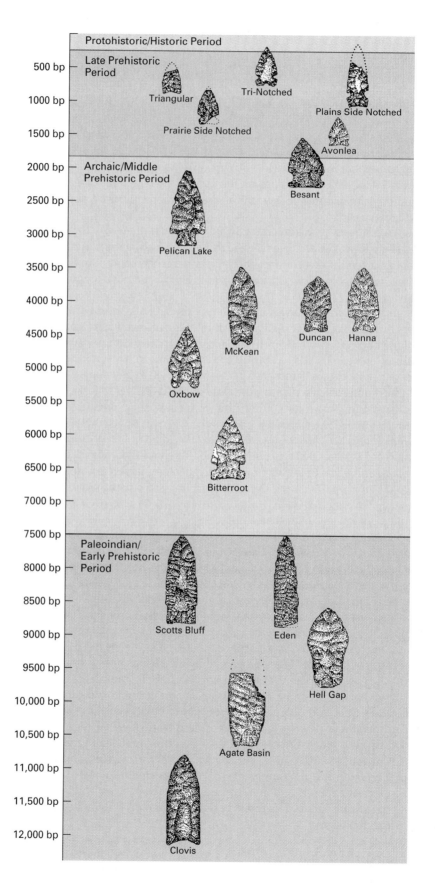

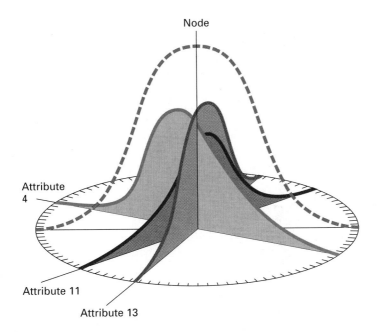

Node

Attribute 4

Attribute 11

Attribute 13

Fig. 7.9 David Clarke's concept of an archaeological type as the node of a number of attributes. While each attribute varied, a type was defined by the most typical state of a series of attributes.

chapter provides some details on the classification of artifacts, the attributes that are important, and how types vary in time and geographic space. This follows an example on the classification of Iroquois pottery.

Classifying Artifacts

Objects made by human hands have a number of characteristics that are helpful in understanding past human behavior. These characteristics provide the basis for sorting and classification, and they are related to the differences among objects. The major differences among prehistoric objects are normally due to variation in raw material, technique of manufacture, function, and style. Raw material involves the basic properties of the material and where it came from. Artifacts are shaped from a raw material using a certain technique for an intended purpose. Use of an artifact may leave distinctive traces of wear, damage, or residue. In addition, some characteristics of an object may be due to errors in manufacture. Beyond raw material, technique of manufacture, and function, these items may have other distinctive features related to style—design, fashion, symbol, or tradition. Artifacts can carry substantial symbolic meaning for the original owners. We can describe these important attributes that differentiate humanmade objects as raw material, technology, function, and style.

One of the major problems in classifying objects is that it is often difficult to distinguish these major attributes because an artifact frequently combines several of them. Think about a simple wooden yellow pencil. The raw material is mostly natural wood, graphite, and rubber with a little circle of metal and some paint. The shape is long and thin with a hexagonal cross-section. These characteristics are largely related to function, so the pencil can be held comfortably in the hand. The graphite core is the focus of function, of course, to put visible marks on paper. What about the yellow color? Why is the pencil yellow? Are there printed messages on the pencil—the name of the manufacturer, a business, a person, a logo, or an institution? These messages are advertisements with a commercial or ideological purpose. The pencil, in this case, functions both as a writing implement and as a vehicle for advertising.

Raw Materials

The variety of materials in use in the world today is remarkable, as synthetics (e.g., plastics, metal alloys, silicon, and "space-age materials") have become such

> *Most intellectual problems are, ultimately, problems of classification and nomenclature.*
> —S. I. Hayakawa, semanticist and senator

Iroquois Pottery

The example in Fig. 7.10 illustrates a decision tree for classifying an artifact. An initial sorting of materials during excavation separates natural objects and human artifacts. Finds in the field are often sorted by raw material. A standard distinction of animal, mineral, or vegetable is used early in the sorting process to distinguish clay artifacts from stone, bone, metal, and other materials. Fired clay ceramics are then separated from other clay artifacts.

Within the group of ceramics, in this case, the pottery known as Owasco is separated and a classification of this material (Fig. 7.10) provides a more detailed description of the differences that are present. Specific attributes of the pottery are used to define smaller classification groups. The presence or absence of collars on the vessels provides an initial separation in the decision tree. Among the collared vessels, the presence or absence of decoration distinguishes the next level. The absence of an out-folded notched lip marks the next group that can be sorted on the basis of a beaded design on the exterior surface and distinguished from vessels with an incised design on the neck. In this classification, specific types are named and the two types of decorated pots lacking collars are called Castle Creek Beaded and Castle Creek Incised Neck.

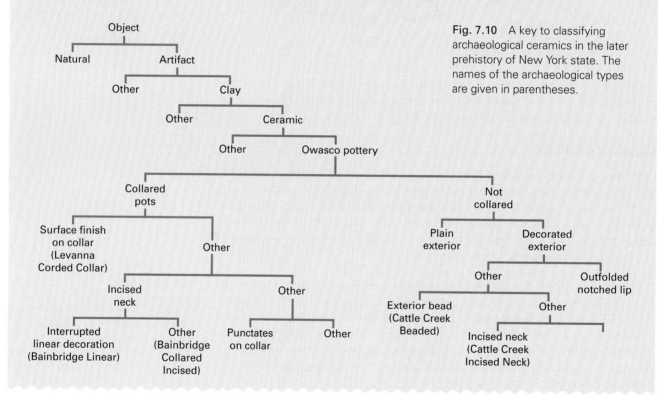

Fig. 7.10 A key to classifying archaeological ceramics in the later prehistory of New York state. The names of the archaeological types are given in parentheses.

an important part of our material culture. In the past, however, the available raw material was largely limited to what nature provided. The list of useful materials grew as human knowledge and technology advanced. Stone, bone, and wood dominated technology in the Paleolithic. With the Neolithic came advances in ceramics, plasters, and eventually metals.

Raw material is a fundamental criterion for separating categories of artifacts in archaeology, and usually one of the more obvious characteristics of an artifact. Animal, mineral, and vegetal materials are some readily recognizable categories into which artifacts made of stone, bone, clay, antler, and wood can be sorted. In the past as in the present, materials have been selected based on how appropriate they are for the intended use of an object. Hard stone is necessary to make sharp-edged flakes. Pliable branches are needed to build a hut. Bone or antler can be shaped into a fishhook. Clay, straw, and water are mixed and baked to make bricks. Given the link between an object's function and the substance out of which

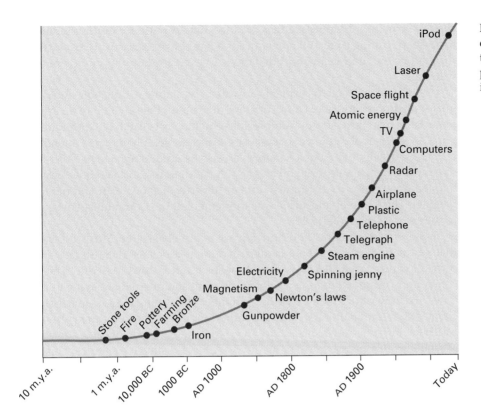

Fig. 7.11 A schematic view of the evolution of technology. Note that the time scale is logarithmic. The pace of invention has greatly increased over time.

it is made, raw material selection is clearly an essential aspect of early human behavior. Raw material selection is also influenced by other factors, including the availability of material. One of the reasons suggested for the low number of stone tools in the Paleolithic of East Asia is the use of bamboo or other hard woods as a substitute for cutting edges.

Technology

Technology is a combination of technique, or method, and knowledge, or skill. Production technology is an important feature of any artifact. Prehistoric peoples used a variety of means to make artifacts. Stone was broken, flaked, ground, pecked, and polished to achieve different shapes and effects. Early stone axes were made by flaking; later stone axes were produced by polishing. Even later axes were produced by casting molten stone (metal).

The evolution of technology in human history takes place at an ever-increasing rate. Fig. 7.11 is a plot of technological developments against time.

It is useful to distinguish two general categories of technologies for making tools and equipment. Manufacturing techniques can be either additive or subtractive. **Additive techniques**, like making ceramics or building a house, involve incremental steps and the addition of material to the object or structure. A bigger object is made from smaller pieces. Problems encountered or errors made can usually be corrected by undoing the last action. **Subtractive techniques**, on the other hand, involve the continuous removal of material from a larger original piece. Techniques such as knapping stone or carving wood are subtractive methods. Errors are not easily removed or hidden in subtractive technologies. More flaws and irregularities are observed in the products of subtractive technologies, resulting in more variability and greater difficulty in classification.

Function and Style

Function refers to the purpose of an artifact—the action or activity for which it was used or intended. Different actions require tools or facilities of different

additive techniques   Ways of making things like ceramics or building a house that involve incremental steps and the addition of material to the object or structure. A bigger object is made from smaller pieces. Compare *subtractive techniques*.

subtractive techniques   Ways of making things like stone *tools* or wood carvings that involve the continuous removal of material from a larger original piece. Compare *additive techniques*.

function   The use of an *artifact;* the action or activity for which it was made.

Fig. 7.12 The hammer and sickle, a powerful political symbol.

shapes, structure, hardness, edges, and the like. A knife for cutting requires a hard, sharp cutting edge. A hammer needs a hard broad surface on a heavy object that can be moved over a short distance. A vessel for holding liquids must be watertight.

Archaeologists often "explain" an artifact by stating its function, and distinguish function from style. Unfortunately, describing the function of an artifact, feature, or structure is rarely simple since such objects can have different purposes. A single tool can have several uses, for example. A hammer is intended to hit things, usually nails, but a hammer can also be used to remove nails, to knock down walls, crack nuts, or to break glass. A hammer is also a symbol. A carpenter's hammer helps to distinguish him or her from a shoemaker and her or his hammer. The hammer and sickle was the symbol of the Communist Party in the former Soviet Union (Fig. 7.12).

Material, technique, and function are relatively straightforward concepts that we can understand in both modern and prehistoric materials. **Style** is a more difficult concept; we all know what it means but it is hard to define. The term comes from a Latin word for a writing implement and referred originally to differences in handwriting. Today, style has a number of meanings. A person has style, a city has style, and hair is "styled." An important difference in meaning exists between having style and being a style. Style is a distinctive way of being something. Most things that people make or modify have style-distinctive features. This style is a way of doing things, it is an expected norm, and it is a learned behavior.

A useful distinction is made in archaeology between the things that people do of their own free will vs. the things that people have to do. This is basically the difference between style and function. Functional is practical and necessary; stylistic is creative and optional. Archaeologists regard style as an important aspect of the artifacts and features that they find. Style is what makes these objects distinctive and different. For example, a tool for hammering nails is a hammer. That is its function, its use. To hammer a nail, it needs a handle to hold onto and a hard, heavy end to strike the nail.

If hammers were purely functional, they would all look alike. But they do not. Carpenter's hammers from different times and places are distinctively different. This aspect of how hammers appear is in part a result of style, a result of tradition, of variation, or the different ways that people do things. The style of iron axes in colonial America also differed visibly depending on their origin, but they were all intended for cutting trees (Fig. 7.13).

Style can be individual, idiosyncratic, a result of personal behavior. Style can also be shared among a group of people as a learned way of doing things. It can be a recognized emblem of group membership, such as a flag or shield or other design on objects identifying the group. Nations use such symbols intentionally. Prehistoric groups may have used group style intentionally in some cases, but often style was not a deliberate addition.

Fig. 7.13 Stylistic or traditional differences among iron axes made and used in colonial America. These axes, of British, German, and English styles, were intended for the same purposes.

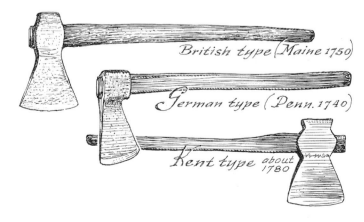

British type (Maine 1750)

German type (Penn. 1740)

Kent type about 1780

style A distinctive way of being or doing.

seriation An archaeological method for ordering.

Styles of Gravestones

Some years ago, archaeologist James Deetz (1930–2000) studied the designs on gravestones in New England to understand changes in style over time (Fig. 7.14). Gravestones are great for such a study because the year they were made is marked on the stone. Thus the date of the stone is known precisely and time is controlled in the study.

Deetz recorded the type of design and year from a large number of graves. He distinguished three major motifs—the death's head, the cherub, and the urn and willow (Fig. 7.15)—and plotted the percentage of each motif for ten-year intervals between 1720 and 1820. Deetz was able to show that these designs were styles that appeared and were very popular, and that they then disappeared over time. According to his findings, the death's head was the only style present during the first 40 years and it disappeared in the 1780s. The cherub appeared in the 1760s, peaked in the 1780s, and disappeared in the 1800s. The urn and willow design made a brief appearance in the 1770s but did not catch on until the 1790s. Deetz' study demonstrated that styles clearly change over time as fashions. This principle is the basis for an archaeological dating technique known as **seriation**.

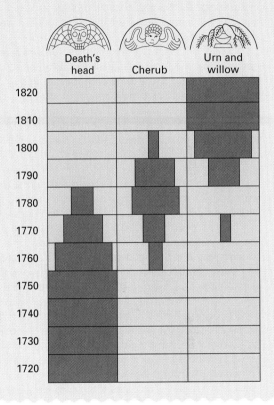

Fig. 7.14 The death's head motif found in New England cemeteries in the eighteenth century.

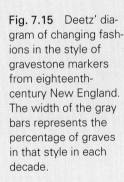

Fig. 7.15 Deetz' diagram of changing fashions in the style of gravestone markers from eighteenth-century New England. The width of the gray bars represents the percentage of graves in that style in each decade.

Archaeologists have tried to define style with varying degrees of success. It's one of those concepts that tend to defy definition. In one sense, style is the distinctive way that something is done. By looking at how people dress, how they wear their hair, how pants are worn, and the kinds of shoes they wear, we know what style means to these people. The same is true when archaeologists look at projectile points or types of pottery or house construction or many other items. These things have a purpose, a function, but beyond function they have distinctive styles, different ways they were made. Style is assumed to be something that is learned from parents, peers, tradition, and society.

There is an individual or idiosyncratic form of style; it is how we as individuals do things. At the same time, there are larger spheres of stylistic behavior that reflect how members of the same family, or same town, or same state, or same society do things. These are not individual but, rather, cultural forms of stylistic behavior.

Seriation

Before the advent of absolute dating methods like radio-carbon dating, it was difficult for archaeologists to determine the age of their finds except in very general terms. At the beginning of the twentieth century, the earliest human ancestors were thought to be perhaps 100,000 years old. Younger materials could sometimes be dated if some association with established chronologies could be found. For example, the dynasties of pharaohs in Egypt had been dated accurately using the Egyptian calendar. Artifacts from known time periods in Egypt found in Europe or the Near East could provide an approximate age. But the instances where this was possible were few and far between.

One of the responses to this situation was the invention of a new method to establish the chronological order of archaeological finds to be used for dating by association. The concept of stratigraphy and superpositioning made it clear that layers succeeding one another went from oldest to youngest from bottom to top. But what about finds that did not come from stratigraphic layers? How could these materials be ordered?

The British archaeologist Flinders Petrie (see Chapter 3, "A Brief History of Archaeology") laid the groundwork for this method in Egypt when he ordered sets of ceramics from Egyptian tombs (Fig. 7.16). Flinders Petrie used the criteria that at least one type should be present in the next assemblage in the order. This is a simple way of seriating, or ordering, a sequence of finds in archaeology based on the presence or absence of types in each assemblage and arranging them in chronological order.

A more common situation is one in which an archaeologist orders, or seriates, a series of artifact assemblages based on the relative abundance, or frequency, of types in each assemblage. This is usually done with ceramic assemblages, and one of the first applications involved large assemblages of pottery sherds from sites in the Maya region. The dates of the sites were not known but the percentage—frequency—of the pottery types in each assemblage could be calculated. This method is known as frequency seriation.

Frequency seriation is based on the archaeological principle involving change in the popularity of style over time. Assuming that types of pottery represent styles, like other fashions their popularity should increase after they appear, reach a peak, decline, and eventually disappear. This phenomenon is graphed in Fig. 7.17. Archae-

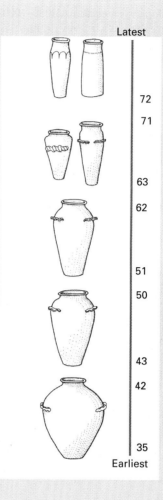

Fig. 7.16 Flinders Petrie's time-ordering of ceramics from Egypt. Petrie seriated sets of ceramic grave offerings based on the presence of the same type in the adjacent set. The sequence goes oldest to youngest from bottom to top.

ologists employ this principle to order ceramic assemblages chronologically using frequency seriation. One minor change is to shift the graph to a vertical orientation and to indicate the popularity (frequency) on both sides of the axis of the graph. This is known as a battleship curve because it resembles the outline of a battleship seen from above. Again, if time goes from bottom to top, a type of pottery appears, grows in popularity, declines, and disappears.

The key to frequency seriation is to look at a number of different types over time and to arrange the battleship

Variation in Time

Groups of similar items defined by criteria of raw material, technique, function, and/or style, vary in time and geographic space. Raw materials change; techniques of manufacture improve and become more efficient; innovation creates improvements in technology; and style, like fashion, changes over time. Style and time are intimately related in archaeological typologies. It is usually style that

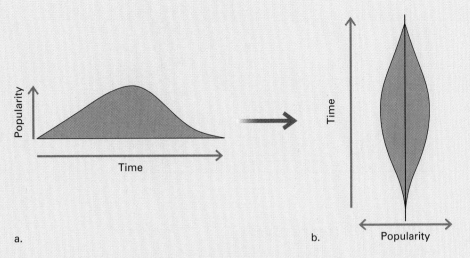

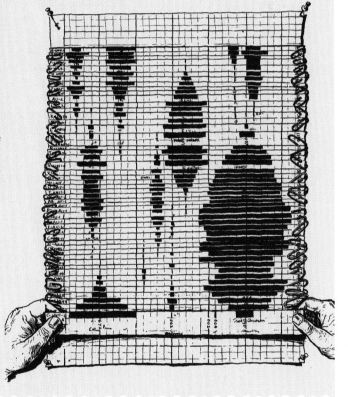

Fig. 7.17 A graph of the popularity of a fashion or style over time (a). The popularity of the item (e.g., number of people wearing this item) increases from its initial appearance and peaks, declines, and disappears. (b) The same graph turned vertically and relative popularity is centered on the vertical axis. This is known as a battleship curve.

curves for each type so that they best fit together showing the sequence over time. Some types will increase in relative popularity while others decrease. This method can be seen in Fig. 7.18, which shows the original frequency seriation conducted by James Ford with the pottery from the Maya area sites. Ford's diagram was done by hand using strips of paper with the frequency of each type indicated. Each strip represented one site. The strips were then rearranged until the best set of battleship curves could be found, and that was assumed to be the best chronological order. Today, there are a variety of computer algorithms that can calculate seriations much more easily. Absolute dating methods are often available to help order assemblages as well.

Fig. 7.18 The original James Ford diagram showing the hand-ordered technique of using paper strips. Each strip represents the ceramics from one Maya area site, and each bar on the strip is the percentage of a certain pottery type in the larger set. The strips are arranged and re-arranged until the best pattern of battleship curves is achieved. That order should represent the chronological order of the assemblages as calculated using frequency seriation. In this example, there are fifty paper strips for assemblages and eleven types of pottery represented.

provides the most information on change over time and variation over space in archaeology. Function changes more slowly. For example, arrowheads are sharpened pieces of stone intended to sit on the end of an arrow shaft and, when fired, to pierce and kill an animal. The function is specific. However, the shape of arrowheads in various times and places varies enormously due to the traditions and choices of the maker. That is style.

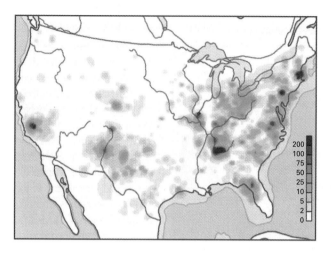

Fig. 7.19 Geographic distribution of all Paleoindian projectile points in the lower forty-eight United States (number of points = 12,791), using county level information.

Variation in Geographic Space

Types also vary in geographic space. Mapping the distribution of specific artifact types has been a favorite pastime in archaeology for more than a century. The geographic extent of particular types provides information on the distribution of the human groups that made and used that type and helps to identify exotic or unusual finds. This spatial information is an important aspect of archaeological knowledge.

Fig. 7.19 plots the geographic distribution of Paleoindian projectile points in the United States. The map shows the density of these distinctive spearheads as the number of finds per 1000 square miles. The map was made by counting the numbers of the projectile points listed by county in the archaeological archives of the states and plotting them as the number per 1000 square miles to get a regular pattern. Contour lines were then drawn to show the areas with high and low densities. The range in density is from 0 to 200 points and the contours are shown in the legend on the right side of the map. The map emphasizes the higher density of finds east of the Mississippi River, along the Rio Grande River in Texas and New Mexico, and in California. This pattern may reflect the density of Paleoindian peoples in the continental United States some 10,000 years ago. In addition, more points are found where there are more collectors; that may account for part of the distribution, particularly east of the Mississippi. The high density on the Wyoming-Colorado border is due to long-term archaeological investigations in this region.

DATA

Objects themselves are not data. Animal bones, potsherds, stone tools, or fireplaces are not data. **Data** are the **observations**, counts, and measurements of these material items. Data are information, usually in the form of numbers, which are created and collected in archaeological research, and elsewhere of course. The word *data* is plural (singular: *datum*) and there are lots of data in archaeology. The counts of different types or classes of artifacts are data, as are the classes and types themselves. The thickness of pottery, the size of Roman towns, the color of Middle Paleolithic flint, the types of Viking ships, the count of radiocarbon isotopes in a sample, the population of Maya sites, the kinds of Mesolithic artifacts, the count of pollen grains on a microscope slide, the number of samples of tooth enamel—these and more are data.

Data are created when we observe, count, or measure. They are often recorded as numbers, although other kinds of information (words and images)

data Information; the observations and measurements of archaeological materials.

observations The values recorded in a data set.

can also be data. For example, the count of artifacts per square meter in an excavation is a number, but the color of a stone tool is a word or phrase and a photograph or drawing of a stratigraphic section is an image. Numbers, however, are the most familiar kind of data and the focus of this discussion.

Numbers

First off, why numbers? Many people don't like numbers, but in fact numbers usually make life easier. Numbers are a kind of code, a way of simplifying the world around us. Rather than saying sheep, sheep, sheep, sheep, sheep, sheep, sheep, we say seven sheep. If we had a lot of different animals, we might want to code them as well. For example, if dog = 1, cat = 2, cow = 3, horse = 4, chicken = 5, pig = 6, sheep = 7, and goat = 8, then our seven sheep would be 7, 7. There are various reasons for such coding. One is to save time and space in writing, or to condense information; another is to be able to use numerical information in calculations, especially in computing.

Numbers can be presented in different ways: counts, proportions, or measurements. Counts are the simplest kind of number; tallies of objects, types, features, bones, pollen, and so on are simple, sequential whole numbers that express how many. We use counts of things constantly in our lives.

Proportions and percentages are also important and useful kinds of numbers. They tell us the ratio of the number of a specific item or category to the number of a larger body of items or categories. It is, for example, useful to know what percentage of your monthly income you spend on rent or mortgage. Too high a percentage is risky. Percentages are expressed in a range from 0 to 100%. Proportions are expressed as a ratio between 0 and 1. Both express fractions and are calculated by dividing the number of specific items by the number of total items. For example, if we had 100 animal bones and 22 of the bones were from cows, 22 divided by 100 is 0.22. That is a proportion. To get percentage, we multiply by 100; cow bones are 22% of the total animal bones.

Percentages are especially useful for comparing amounts of specific items from different contexts or places. For example, site 1 has 2000 animal bones with 50 cow bones; site 2 has 200 bones with 25 cow bones. Site 1 has more cow bones (50 compared to 25), but a lower percentage of cow bones compared to site 2 (2.5% vs. 12.5%). Thus, cows were more important in the diet at site 2.

Measured numbers (also known as ratio data; see scales of measurement below) are the most precise. Length, volume, density, concentration, diameter, and chemical composition can be measured with tools and instruments to provide precise, real numbers using decimal places. These numbers are powerful because all kinds of mathematical operations are possible with them.

There are other kinds of numbers as well, and some discussion of these may provide a better understanding of data. Numbers and data come from observation and measurement. The three common **scales of measurement** used for recording data are nominal, ordinal, and ratio (Table 7.1). There is also a fourth scale called interval between ordinal and ratio measurement. Interval data, like Fahrenheit degrees, are rare in archaeology and often treated as ratio scale measurements.

Nominal scales record basic information as unordered observations. Nominal scale data are usually described with lists of names or other words. The observations in the scale have no numerical meaning and are simply categorical. Answers to questions like "What is your major?" or "Do you own an iPod?" are nominal because they yield data such as "anthropology" or "no." Archaeological examples would be categories of colors, sex, types, classes, species, or building designations at an ancient city. There is no numerical relationship among the categories. Even if we assign numbers to code types of animals (e.g., cow = 2, chicken = 4), we cannot say that a chicken is twice as much as a cow. It makes no sense. The presence or absence of a characteristic is a simple case of nominal scale

Nominal	Ordinal	Ratio
Gender	Movie ratings (1–4 stars)	Degrees Celsius
Marital status	USDA Beef Grades (select, choice, prime)	Percentage
Names		Length or size measurements
A list of words	Size of sites or artifacts (small, medium, large)	Weight
	Relative dates (older, younger, youngest)	

TABLE 7.1 Examples of scales of measurement data.

data. We can only count the number of objects in each category of nominal data. Nominal scale information is most common in archaeology.

Ordinal scale data is ranked information. Rank is established by the criteria of "greater than," "equal to," or "less than." The interval or distance between adjacent numbers in the scale is unknown. Ordinal data has an ordered relationship between numbers, so that one is, for example, bigger, or longer, or rounder, or darker than another in a series. Examples include sediment classes (sand, silt, clay, ranked from coarse to fine), site size (from small to large), artifact size (small, medium, large), estimates of quantities (few, average, many), and the like.

Ratio scale measurements are values with a true zero point. Answers to questions like "How tall are you?" or "What is your G.P.A.?" are numerical. Ratios are equivalent at this scale of measurement, for example, the ratio of 2 to 1 is the same as the ratio of 8 to 4. These are real numbers measured in centimeters, square meters, grams, cubic centimeters, parts per millions, and the like. These numbers are mathematically useful and can be multiplied and divided as well as added and subtracted. We could talk about the weight of a chicken and a cow and note that the cow weighed 100 times as much as the chicken.

A distinction between qualitative and quantitative numbers is also useful. Qualitative data (a.k.a. discrete or nonparametric data) are determined subjectively or judgmentally and include nominal and ordinal scales of measurement. You have to make a decision about which category on the scale an object belongs to. Quantitative numbers (a.k.a. continuous or parametric data) are measured by comparison to a fixed or known scale (e.g., inches, square meters, meters above sea level, and degrees Centigrade) using tools or instruments such as rulers, balances, spectrometers, and the like.

Some researchers distinguish between categories and variables when recording data. Categories are differences that are described in qualitative scales of measurement, while variables are measured differences in variation that are recorded in a ratio scale. Other scientists tend to use the word *variable* for all kinds of recorded observations.

These scales of measurement are important when considering how to use the numbers or what statistics should be applied. There are different kinds of statistics for different scales of measurements. For example, parametric and nonparametric statistical tests require quantitative and qualitative data, respectively. Some basic statistics are described below.

Basic Statistics

ordinal scale of measurement Ranked information with an ordered relationship between numbers.

ratio scale of measurement Measurements with a true zero point made using an instrument.

A large batch of data—tens or hundreds of numbers, for example—can be daunting and hard to comprehend. Fortunately, there are some simple techniques to control, condense, and visualize numerical information. The term *statistics* is often used loosely to describe a technique for summarizing and manipulating data. But,

TABLE 7.2 Length and width measurements on San projectile points in Fig. 7.1 from three different groups of people (!Kung, !Xo, and G/wi), and basic descriptive statistics.

Group	!Kung		!Xo		G/wi	
Point	Length (cm)	Width (cm)	Length (cm)	Width (cm)	Length (cm)	Width (cm)
A	1.2	0.8	2.8	1.5	2.1	1.3
B	1.2	0.7	2.4	1.4	1.7	1.0
C	0.8	0.6	1.7	1.2	2.4	1.2
D	0.9	0.5	2.0	1.4	2.2	1.3
E	0.8	0.5	1.6	1.4	2.3	1.4
F	0.7	0.6	2.3	1.3	1.7	1.2
Sum	5.6	3.7	12.8	8.2	12.4	7.4
Mean	0.93	0.62	2.13	1.37	2.07	1.23
Variance	0.05	0.01	0.21	0.01	0.09	0.02
s.d.	0.22	0.12	0.45	0.10	0.30	0.14

in fact, the end goal is what is important: to make sense of numerical information. Much of the analysis of numbers is more common "sensical" than statistical.

Statistics can be either descriptive or inferential. **Descriptive statistics** are useful for condensing information and for the comparison of numbers in different sets of data. **Inferential statistics** are used for making decisions about data and relationships among variables. We will concentrate on descriptive statistics and just take a glance at inferential methods in this chapter. Descriptive statistics such as the median and the mean are measures of the central tendency of a set of numbers. Descriptive statistics like the standard deviation are measures of the **range**, or dispersion, of the data.

Mean, Median, and Mode

Mean, median, and mode are different ways to express the concept of average in data using a single number. Average means middle or normal but does not have a mathematical value. The scale of measurement is important in deciding how to describe the average value.

The **mean** (designated as X-bar, $\bar{x}$) is the average measure for ratio scale data. The mean is calculated from numerical values by totaling the sum of the values and dividing by the number of observations. Means are usually given with a decimal point and are ratios.

To demonstrate the calculation of the mean, we can use the arrow points from southern Africa discussed at the beginning of the chapter (Fig. 7.1). Measurements of the length and width of these arrow points are given in Table 7.2. To calculate the average or mean for length and width for each of the three groups, add up the numbers in a column and divide by the number of observations (by convention, this is abbreviated as n = 6). For example, the sum of !Kung point length is 5.6 (Table 7.2); 5.6 divided by 6 is 0.93 cm, the average length for !Kung arrow points. The sum and mean value for each column are shown at the bottom of Table 7.2. It is clear from the mean value that the !Kung arrow points are more than 1 cm shorter than the !Xo and G/wi points on average.

Median values are used for ordinal or ratio scales of measurement. The median defines average by locating the exact middle number of the ordered values. Median values are often whole numbers. They are sometimes preferred with ratio scale data if there are extreme values affecting the mean. Test scores, for example, are often reported as median values. To calculate the median value for the !Kung arrow point lengths in Table 7.2, we have to put them in rank order from smallest

www.mhhe.com/pricearch1

For a Web-based activity on statistics, please see the Internet exercises on your online learning center.

descriptive statistics Numbers that are used to condense information in order to summarize and compare different sets of data.

inferential statistics Numbers that are used for making decisions about *data* and describing relationships among variables.

range A measure of the spread of values using the minimum and maximum.

mean The average for ratio scale data calculated by dividing the sum by the number of observations.

median The exact middle number of the nominal or ordinal values.

to largest: 0.7, 0.8, 0.8, 0.9, 1.2, 1.2. Because there is an even number of values, the median value is the middle value, halfway between the two middle numbers 0.8 and 0.9, or 0.85. If there were an odd number of values, the median would be the number in the exact middle.

Nominal data are simply classes of unrelated objects, but counts of those classes have some meaning. If we counted the different colors of flint in a Paleolithic assemblage of stone tools, the most common color would be the **mode**, or modal color. The mode is simply the most common category of number in the set or the highest peak in the histogram of the data. A set of values can have more than one mode, but only one mean and median. The values for the length of !Kung arrow points have two modes, one at 0.8 and another at 1.2; each of these values occurs twice in the six length measurements.

Range, Variance, and Standard Deviation

Range is a simple measure of the spread of a set of values using the highest and lowest values. Range requires two numbers to define the spread. The range for the !Kung arrow point lengths is from 0.8 to 1.2, the lowest (minimum) and highest (maximum) values.

Variance is a single measure of spread or range in data, an index of dispersal. The variance of data is a measure of spread that will take into account both the deviations of the values (away from the mean) and how frequently these deviations occur. By definition, the variance (V) is the sum of the difference between the mean and each data point squared divided by the number of observations. The variance for the !Kung arrow point lengths is calculated in Table 7.2 as 0.05. Variance is not often used in basic descriptive statistics.

Variance is important, however, because it is the basis for calculating the standard deviation. The **standard deviation (s.d.)** of the observations is simply the square root of the variance. Therefore it measures both the deviation from the mean and the frequency of this deviation. Standard deviation is normally used instead of the variance. The value of the variance tends to be large because it is squared. The value of the standard deviation is in the same scale and unit of measurement as the original data.

Standard deviation is measured as the average difference between all the values and the mean. In other words, you subtract the mean from the value of each observation and square each result. Sum the total of the squared values and divide that value by the number of observations minus one (here we are at the variance again) and take the square root of that number to get the s.d. Because standard deviations can be both less than and greater than the mean, the values are positive or negative and are sometimes written as ±. It's a tad tedious to calculate by hand, but computers can do the job easily.

Standard deviations are useful for comparing sets of information. Let's look again at the arrow points from southern Africa (Table 7.2). We know from the mean values that the !Kung arrows are noticeably shorter than the two other sets, which have a similar length. The mean length is a measure of average, of the central tendency in these data. But what about the spread of values? We can calculate the standard deviation of point length. The standard deviation is the difference between the observed value and the mean squared and summed, then divided by the number of observations plus one. The sum of the squared deviations for the points is 0.2334 (Table 7.3). That value divided by n − 1 (6 − 1 = 5) is 0.047 and the square root of that number is 0.22, the standard deviation. These values for the standard deviations for all the point groups are shown at the bottom of Table 7.2. A difference in the standard deviations between the sites would mean that there was more or less variation among the points that were measured. As you can see in Table 7.2, the standard deviation for the length of !Kung points is a good bit less than for !Xo or G/wi points, meaning that there is less spread in the value, less variation.

mode The most common category in nominal or ordinal data or the highest peak in ratio scale data.

variance A single measure of spread or range in ratio data.

standard deviation (s.d.) The square root of the variance, a single measure of spread.

normal curve The standard, or normal, shape of measured values plotted in a frequency diagram.

TABLE 7.3 Calculation of standard deviation for !Kung arrow points.

Point	x (observed value)	(x-xbar)	(x-xbar)^2
A	1.2	1.2 – 0.93 = 0.27	0.0729
B	1.2	1.2 – 0.93 = 0.27	0.0729
C	0.8	0.8 – 0.93 = –0.13	0.0169
D	0.9	0.9 – 0.93 = –0.03	0.0009
E	0.8	0.8 – 0.93 = –0.13	0.0169
F	0.7	0.7 – 0.93 = –0.23	0.0529
Sum			0.2334

The Normal Curve

The **normal curve** is an important concept involving the shape or distribution of the values of a quantitative, ratio scale variable. The normal curve (or bell-shaped curve) describes the standard, or normal, shape of measured values on virtually any variable. That sounds hard to believe, but it is true. Take height, the stature of the individuals in a class of ten people. A graph of the heights might look something like Fig. 7.20. The measured heights are on the bottom line or x-axis, and the number of students in each interval of height are indicated on the vertical axis in the histogram. The graph shows no clear pattern.

But if we measured the height of all the individuals at the school, say 2500 students, the graph would look very much like a normal curve (Fig. 7.21). This is true for most things we can measure as long as we can measure them fairly accurately and as long as we are measuring a simple variable. This is true for project point length, pottery rim diameter, distance between mounds, height of rock

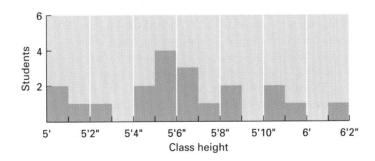

Fig. 7.20 Histogram of class height.

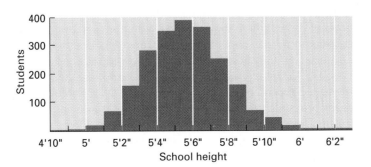

Fig. 7.21 Histogram of school height.

Fig. 7.22 The mean, standard deviation, and areas under the normal curve.

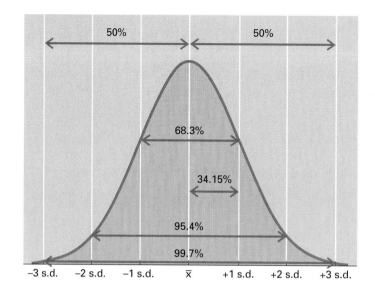

carvings, size of cave, *ad infinitum.* Continuous variables usually show a normal curve when enough measurements are plotted on the graph. A normal curve, or distribution, of data means that most of the measured samples are close to "average," while a few occur at one extreme or the other.

Just two statistics are needed to define the normal curve: The mean marks the midpoint of the curve; the standard deviation describes the dispersal (flatness or peakedness) of the curve. The curve looks like a round-topped hill or mountain (Fig. 7.22). It can be flat and wide or tall and thin or anywhere in between. The mean of the data set is always the middle value on the x-axis. The standard deviation determines the dispersal of the curve. A small standard deviation makes a tall, thin curve; a large standard deviation makes a low, flat shape.

The importance of the normal curve lies in the area within the curve itself (i.e., under the line). If we think of the area inside the curve as 100%, then by definition, half of the samples are greater than the mean value and half of the samples are less than the mean value. Standard deviations define areas under the curve: +1 standard deviation to the right of the mean contains 34.15% of all the observations; within plus and minus (±) 1 s.d., there are 68.3% of all the samples. Within ±2 s.d. 95.4% of the cases, and within ±3 s.d. are 99.73% of all the samples.

There are lots of uses for the normal curve. Inferential statistics often employ the properties of the curve. For the moment, however, it serves as a model of variation to keep in mind when thinking about how archaeological evidence changes over time and space. In terms of time, think of the x-axis of the curve as the passing years and the y-axis as the number of artifacts or features of a certain style each year. An item appears, peaks in popularity, declines, and disappears. In terms of geography, imagine the mean as the place of origin or manufacture for an idea or an item. Imagine the normal curve as three-dimensional, a kind of upside-down ice cream sundae glass. Ideas or objects are created at the central point of origin where they are most common, and spread in all directions in decreasing number. These are heuristic (an approximation to help explain) models, of course, but they help to understand how ideas, objects, and people act.

Fig. 7.23 shows an archaeological example of the normal curve. In this case, the values represent the lengths measured on 175 arrowheads. The mean length of the projectile points is 5 cm and the standard deviation for this set of values is 0.5 cm. The values for length range from 3.5 to 6.5 cm, and 95.4% of the measurements fall between 4.0 and 6.0 cm. A histogram of the values (Fig. 7.23) closely follows the shape of the normal curve for these measurements.

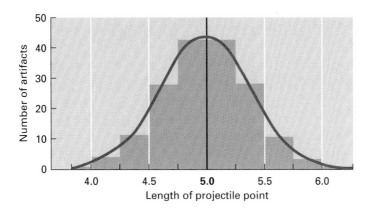

Fig. 7.23 A histogram of 175 projectile point lengths matched to a normal curve. The mean length is 5 cm and the standard deviation is 0.5 cm.

Chi-Square and Contingency Tables

It is often the case in archaeology that we have information about two groups of things—artifacts, sites, structures, and the like—and we want to compare the groups. Usually the information that we have is nominal scale, simple categories. For example, let's say we have excavated a cemetery with sixteen graves of males and females, adults and children, and various artifacts in the graves. One question would concern gender differences—are males and females buried with the same kinds of grave offerings? **Chi-square** (χ^2) is a statistical test that can help us answer that question. Chi-square compares what we observe in the data to what we would expect if there were no differences between the two groups. Chi-square is used only with nominal scale data. These are discrete data that come from counting, not measuring.

Table 7.4 contains information on the graves. The sex of the two children (C) is marked as unknown because it is difficult to determine at a young age. It shows the known sex of individuals and the approximate age group of each—young adult (Y) = 18–30, adult (A) = 30–50, mature (M) = >50. The table also shows individuals were buried with a grinding stone or some projectile points but not both.

A 2 × 2 table is the basic arrangement for calculating a chi-square test. We can count the number of males or females with projectile points or grinding stones and put the numbers in a table (Table 7.5). The question we want to answer is whether there are differences in the contents of male and female graves. Because the answer is not obvious, we will use chi-square to help make this decision.

Does the observed distribution of points and grinding stones show a difference between males and females, or is the distribution what we might expect by chance? To answer this, we compare the observed to the expected situation (chance or random patterns). A chance or random pattern would mean that there was no difference among the graves. A chi-square distribution is the chance or random pattern for a specific set of numbers, so we have to calculate a value for chi-square.

To calculate chi-square we can use the following notation for our table (7.6).

For a 2 × 2 contingency table, then, the chi-square statistic is calculated by the formula

$$\chi^2 = \frac{(ab-bc)^2(a+b+c+d)}{(a+b)(c+d)(b+d)(a+c)}$$

In the example above with gender and grave goods, the values are plugged into the formula and a value of 1.08 is calculated for chi-square:

$$\chi^2 = \frac{(20-6)^2(5+3+2+4)}{(8)(6)(7)(7)} = 1.08$$

chi-square (χ^2) A statistical test of association for nominal scale information.

TABLE 7.4 Data on the graves used in chi-square example.

Grave	Sex	Age	Projectile Points	Grinding Stone
1	M	YA	x	
2	?	C	x	
3	F	A		x
4	M	A	x	
5	F	Y	x	
6	F	YA		x
7	M	A	x	
8	M	A		x
9	F	YA	x	
10	F	A		x
11	?	C		x
12	F	A		x
13	M	YA	x	
14	M	M		x
15	F	A	x	
16	M	M	x	

TABLE 7.5 Summary of information in Table 7.4. Association of male or female burial with projectile point or grinding stone, including row and column totals.

	Male	Female	Total
Projectile Point	5	3	8
Grinding Stone	2	4	6
Total	7	7	14

TABLE 7.6 General notation for a 2 × 2 contingency table.

	Variable 1	Variable 2	Total
Category 1	a	b	a + b
Category 2	c	d	c + d
Total	a + c	b + d	a + b + c + d

This observed value for chi-square has to be compared to the known value expected if the distribution of observations were possible by chance. These known values are listed in most statistics books. For a simple 2 × 2 table, that value is always 3.84 to be 95% confident that we are correct. Since our calculated value does not exceed the expected value, it means that there is no statistical relationship between gender and grave goods. We cannot say that males and females get different gifts in their graves.

bar graph Visual display of *data;* basically a tally sheet with bars instead of tally marks, used to display nominal or ordinal scale data.

histogram A graph of the number of measurements in interval form.

Chi-square and other statistics are usually more complicated than in the simple example provided here. Appropriate use of these statistics will require more information and study than can be covered in this introductory text.

Visual Display of Information

There are several ways to display information. A table is a standard method for listing information and works fine if the amount of information is low. But as the amount of information increases, a table becomes less and less informative. One very good way to approach a lot of information is to use graphs. A graph is a visual display of information; it is a picture of data. Graphs consolidate large amounts of information, usually numbers, into a form that is easier to comprehend. To paraphrase a cliché, a graph is worth a thousand numbers.

Graphs provide a way to see relationships in the information you have collected. There are several kinds of graphs—stem and leaf plots, bar graphs, histograms, pie charts, box and whisker plots, and scatterplots—that can help to condense information and reveal patterns in data. There are of course many other kinds of graphs for displaying data. An excellent source for thinking about the graphic description of information is Edward Tufte's 2001 book *The Visual Display of Quantitative Information*.

Stem and Leaf Plots

One simple way to record information is to use a tally sheet (Fig. 7.24). The number of items in each interval between 10–20, 20–30, 30–40, and 40–50 has been counted and tallied in this example. The length of the group of tally marks in each interval provides a measure of the number of observations. The interval between 40 and 50 has the most tallies. These data might show, for example, the number of potsherds per room in forty-seven rooms at a Pueblo site in Arizona.

Another way to construct a tally sheet and show more information in the graph is to use a stem and leaf plot that displays the numbers themselves to form the diagram. Consider the following data, sorted in ascending order:

2,2,2,3,5,5,11,13,16,18,20,21,21,22,24,27,29,30,31,35,35,36,37,38,40,
42,43,44,48,52,52,56

These numbers might represent the number of sites found in each square kilometer of survey in a large valley in Mexico. Draw a vertical line. A stem and leaf plot of these data can be constructed by writing the first digits (i.e., from the tens digits) in the first column, then writing the second digits (i.e., from the ones digits) of all the numbers in that range to the right of the vertical line. Use zero or the first number on the left side of the line and the second number on the right side of the line (Fig. 7.25). The list of numbers on the right side gives a dimension to the number of observations, and the actual numbers are present for evaluating the data.

Bar Graphs and Histograms

A **bar graph** is basically a tally sheet with bars instead of tally marks. A stem and leaf plot is another form of a bar graph. A bar graph is used to display nominal or ordinal scale data—counts or ranked data. A **histogram** is a bar graph for ratio scale information and shows how measurements are spread over their range of values. A histogram is a picture of the number of measurements in each interval that you define.

A simple bar graph appears in Fig. 7.26, showing the number of houses at ten different sites. The x-axis with five categories, or intervals, shows how many houses are present at a site, from zero to four in number. The y-axis shows the number of sites in each category. This graph makes it clear that there are three

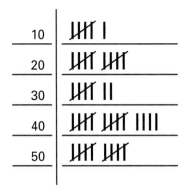

Fig. 7.24 Tally count of the number of sherds in 47 excavated rooms at a hypothetical Pueblo site in Arizona.

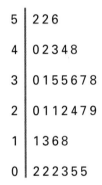

Fig. 7.25 Stem and leaf plot of the numbers listed in the text.

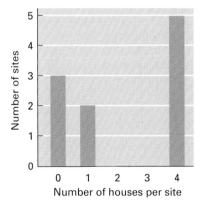

Fig. 7.26 A bar graph showing the number of houses at ten different sites. For example, it can be seen that two of the sites have only one house and five sites have four houses. There are five intervals in this graph.

kinds of sites in this set, those with no houses, those with one house, and those with four houses.

To construct a histogram for ratio scale data, it is necessary to determine the number of intervals to be used and to calculate the width of the interval. The first step is to determine the maximum and minimum values in the data set and calculate the difference between them. Divide that value by the number of intervals you think will best show you the distribution of values. Ten to fifteen intervals is a common number to use.

A very good rule of thumb is to construct a histogram whenever you calculate a mean. Archaeologists often report mean values of the things they measure—points, houses, fireplaces, amount of phosphate, or length of bone, for example—but in some cases they may be measuring two different things and combining them into one descriptive statistic. This problem is described in the next paragraphs.

Here are two sets of data: both have the same mean value (25). Let's say these values represent the size of house floors in square feet at two different archaeological sites.

A	B
27	8
15	25
31	11
38	33
23	14
25	34
26	16
10	36
30	18
18	38
20	24
40	43

Now look at a histogram of each data set (Fig. 7.27). The house floor sizes from site A have a clear peak around 25 and decrease in both directions from the

Fig. 7.27 A histogram of the two data sets for house floor size at sites A and B. The numbers on the y-axis indicate how many houses fall in each interval.

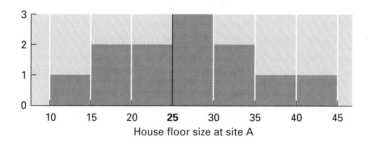

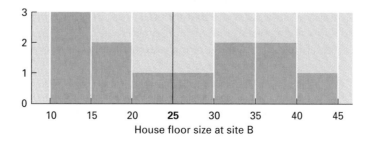

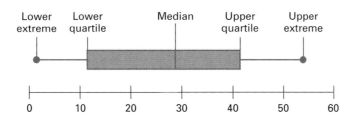

Fig. 7.28 A box and whisker plot showing the components, five different statistical measures displayed in one graphic.

mean. Site B has two clear peaks (modes) with a gap or valley in between. Clearly, two different sizes or areas are being measured in B. In this situation, it is necessary to rethink the analysis, break up the two sizes at site B into two groups and provide a mean to describe each group.

One advantage to the stem and leaf plot over a histogram is that the stem-and-leaf plot not only displays the frequency for each interval, but also displays all of the individual values within that interval. On the other hand, only one size interval is possible and for this reason histograms with variable interval sizes are more commonly used. Histograms are also easier to compare.

Box and Whisker Plots

A histogram uses bars to show the spread of values in a set of data. A box and whisker plot is the name for a graph that shows five summary measures in a single figure. It is also very useful for comparing these measures among two or more sets of data. The five summary measures include the median, the quartiles, and the minimum and maximum values in the distribution. With these values, the box and whisker plot immediately shows the center, spread, and overall range of the values. To construct a box and whisker plot, you need to draw a line with equal intervals from the minimum to maximum value. The data from the stem and leaf plot (2, 2, 2, 3, 5, 5, 11, 13, 16, 18, 20, 21, 21, 22, 24, 27, 29, 30, 31, 35, 35, 36, 37, 38, 40, 42, 43, 44, 48, 52, 52, 56) above are used in the example in Fig. 7.28.

Calculate the quartiles, four groups of equal size among the ordered numbers, starting with the lowest number. There are thirty-two numbers so each quartile will contain eight numbers from lowest to highest. The first quartile contains 2, 2, 2, 3, 5, 5, 11, and 13; the second quartile contains the next eight numbers, 16, 18, 20, 21, 21, 22, 24, and 27; the third quartile includes 29, 30, 31, 35, 35, 36, 37, and 38; the fourth quartile has 40, 42, 43, 44, 48, 52, 52, and 56. Draw a box from the lowest number in the second quartile to the highest number in the third quartile. Draw the statistical median (28) as a horizontal line in the box. Now extend the "whiskers" to the farthest points that are not outliers (more than 1.5 times the one quartile range from the end of the box). Draw a dot for any outlier beyond the extremes. That's a box and whisker plot.

Pie Charts

A pie chart shows the distribution of information as slices of a circular pie. It is another useful technique for condensing information and providing a quick glimpse at a large body of information. The width of each slice of the pie is determined by the proportion of each item in the whole.

In the example shown in Fig. 7.29, pie charts are used to display the contents of human feces (**coprolites**) preserved at archaeological sites in the western United States. A series of dry caves around an ancient lake have provided archaeologists with a rich harvest of dry human coprolites. These sites have been occupied over the last 9000 years. Analysis of tiny pieces of bone, seeds, and fiber in these coprolites reveal some of the components of past diet. In this arid region, the resources of the lake (fish, birds, tubers) were an important part of the diet. The contents of the coprolites are summarized in the pie charts for each site and show how diets differed in various parts of the region.

coprolites Preserved ancient feces.

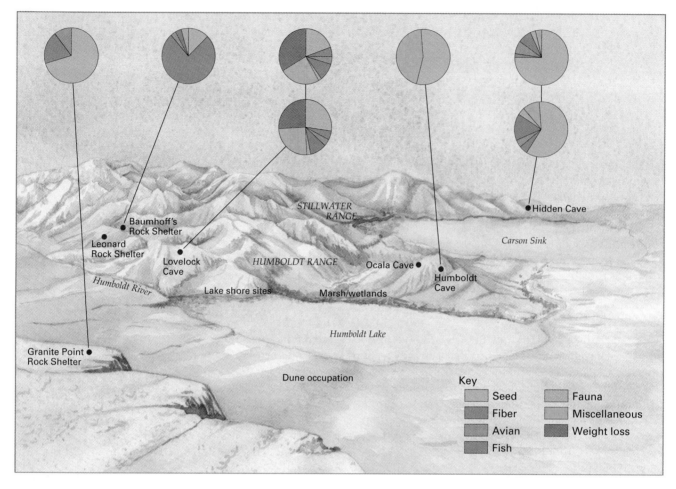

Fig. 7.29 A graphic with pie charts showing the contents of prehistoric coprolites (fossil human feces) from caves in ancient Nevada. The information in the pie charts reflects what people were eating in different areas of the region.

Scatterplots

A **scatterplot** is a graph that allows you to look at two sets of numbers simultaneously. Each dot on the graph represents one sample and one pair of measurements. Usually these two sets are two measurements on the same sample, for example, length and width measurements on projectile points, or size and elevation of a series of sites, or the number of copper and chert knives at sites.

Making sense of what the pattern in the dots means requires some thought. Fig. 7.30 shows a scatterplot of chert knives and copper knives at sites in a fictitious area. In this case, we learn from the scatterplot that sites either have a lot of copper knives and only a few chert knives, or have a lot of chert knives and a few copper knives, but not a lot of both. This pattern may reflect which of the two raw materials, copper or chert, is closer to the sites in the study area.

Scatterplots provide a great deal of information on both the measured variables and the samples. There are three patterns to look for in such plots: random, linear, or clustered (Fig. 7.31). A random pattern means there is no relationship indicated in the plot; the scatter of points looks like a shotgun target.

A linear pattern means that a clear relationship is present. The dots more or less line up on the graph. This is known as **correlation**; the two values are changing together. A positive trend, from lower right to upper left, means that as one item increases so does the other; a negative trend, from upper left to lower right, indicates that as one characteristic increases the other decreases.

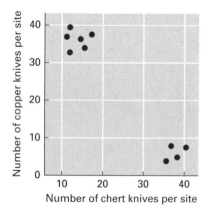

Fig. 7.30 Number of chert knives per site plotted against the number of copper knives per site. It is clear from the graph that sites with many copper knives have fewer chert knives, and vice versa. The two clusters of dots on the graph reveal that there are two different kinds of sites present.

A clustered pattern with distinct groups of dots in the plot tells us about the relationship between the measured variables. **Association** means that there are closely related groups, or subsets, within the sample that have similar values. The groups that follow a positive, linear trend from lower right to upper left reflect correlated values; that is, the values of both variables increase together. In this situation with two groups, one group will have high values for both variables and one group will have low values for both measured variables. The second example, where the two groups show a negative, linear relationship from upper left to lower right, shows that the values of the two variables behave in opposition. As one increases, the other decreases. Thus, one group has high values of variable 1 and low values for variable 2; the second group has low values for variable 1 and high values for variable 2. Both kinds of information—positive and negative relationships—are useful.

An example of this clustering can be seen in Fig. 7.32—a scatterplot with both linear patterns and clusters. This example comes from an ethnoarchaeological study of pottery-making in modern villages in Mexico. The study was undertaken to determine if the chemistry of the ceramics could be used to distinguish where they were made. The scatterplot clearly shows that this is possible. The amount of calcium, strontium, and barium in sherds from each village was measured. A ratio of strontium to calcium was plotted against a ratio of barium to calcium. Three distinct groups show up on the plot, corresponding to pottery from the three villages. Within each of the three groups, there are linear patterns that indicate that strontium and barium are strongly associated in these ceramics.

CONCLUSIONS

This chapter is about classification and data, important concepts for the analysis of archaeological materials. Archaeological projects produce enormous amounts of material in the form of artifacts and information. The artifacts must be cleaned, conserved, and cataloged to create order before the major portion of the analysis begins. The information from the excavation must be checked, studied, analyzed, and archived as the record of the excavations and their results.

The analysis of the artifacts and other materials from the excavations is a major undertaking. A variety of specialists identify and evaluate the stones, sherds, bones, plant remains, and many of the other items that can come from an archaeological site. Analysis usually begins with classification, the identification and sorting of the materials into related sets and subsets. For example, stone artifacts are sorted into flaked or ground stone; flaked stone tools are separated into intentionally shaped tools or waste material; intentionally shaped tools are grouped into defined types—projectile point, scraper, drill, and so on. Plant and

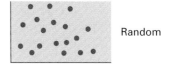

No pattern

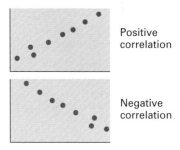

Random

Linear patterns

Positive correlation

Negative correlation

Clustered patterns

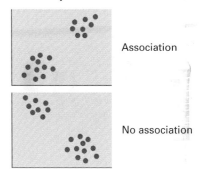

Association

No association

Fig. 7.31 Different kinds of scatterplots showing no pattern (random relationships), positive and negative linear correlations, and positive and negative clustered associations.

Artifacts themselves are not important—it's the information they can provide about cultures and about people.

—H. Marie Wormington, archaeologist

Fig. 7.32 Scatterplot of barium and strontium in pottery from modern villages in Mexico. The plot shows clearly that these two elements can be used to distinguish the pottery from the three villages. The values are ratioed to calcium to make them comparable. The three colors represent the three different villages; each dot is a pottery vessel from a village.

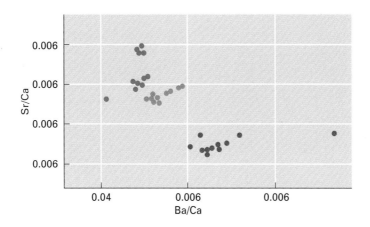

scatterplot   A single graph combining two sets of numbers simultaneously.

correlation   A measure of association between two sets of numbers.

association   A statistical term referring to related groups, or subsets, within a sample that have similar values. The members of the group are said to be associated.

animal remains must be identified and classified according to known species. Human remains are classified according to the various bones in the skeleton.

After the classification has been done, the analyses continue as more detailed studies of the materials take place. These studies take many directions but usually include measuring the artifacts and ecofacts, chemical tests, dating materials, sourcing exotic artifacts, and comparing the finds with other known materials. All of these analyses produce more information about the materials and the site, and further analysis and interpretation is necessary as new questions arise.

A lot of archaeological information takes the form of numbers—counts, percentages, parts per million, length, thickness, weight, and more. These numbers need to be summarized so that comparison can be made and descriptions of the artifacts can be simplified by using measures of average and spread. The scale of measurement used in recording data is important. Information occurs at three common scales—nominal scale, ordinal scale, or ratio scale. A lot of information in archaeology is nominal scale (e.g., color, species, type). Ratio scale information—real numbers—is the most useful because a variety of statistical tests can be applied. Both for analysis and for publication, visual displays of information provide helpful summaries and can condense many numbers into a few lines.

At the end, the materials and information from the project are given to a museum or appropriate storage facility to be archived and kept in perpetuity. Archaeological materials are stored because they have been moved from their original context. Careful and well-organized storage allows others to study the collections in the future. Reports are published and the discoveries and interpretations from the project are available to the community of archaeologists and to the public.

A ROOM IN THE PUEBLO

Grasshopper Pueblo is a large multiroom ruin in the highlands of east-central Arizona. The pueblo was built during the thirteenth century and occupied for approximately 125 years. The University of Arizona conducted archaeological training courses (field schools) at the site for many years, uncovering a large number of rooms (Fig. 7.33). Most rooms had a fireplace, storage areas, and other indications of residence and activity (Fig. 7.34).

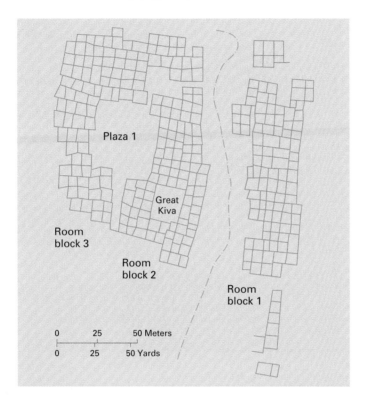

Fig. 7.33 Plan of Grasshopper Pueblo in the highlands of east-central Arizona, excavated by the University of Arizona for many years. The pueblo is a multiroom, multistory series of compounds built around open plazas. Rooms are individually numbered on the plan.

Fig. 7.34 A room at Grasshopper Pueblo in the course of excavation by the University of Arizona field school.

TABLE 7.7 Room number, age, room size, and hearth size from a sample of 20 rooms at Grasshopper Pueblo.

Room Number	Date	Room Size (m²)	Hearth Size (cm²)
1	early	17.3	1864
2	early	16.4	1350
18	early	22	2937
28	early	18.1	1564
146	early	15.7	1665
3	late	18.6	838
5	late	13.7	589
6	late	15.8	1860
7	late	21.3	1440
11	late	12.9	1456
13	late	14.4	800
205	late	17.7	1004
216	late	17.5	761
218	late	22.4	1435
319	late	23.4	1444
349	late	16.1	1386
359	late	25.9	1140
371	late	15.3	1013
398	late	12.4	870
425	late	12.6	1534

Data from Ciolek-Torello, R., and J. J. Reid. 1974. Change in household size at Grasshopper. *The Kiva* 40:39–48.

Hundreds of rooms were excavated and recorded over the years. You have available a random sample of information from 20 of these rooms (Table 7.7). These rooms should be representative of the whole pueblo. The information in the table provides the room number assigned during the excavations, the estimated age of the room based on ceramic finds, the size of the room in square meters, and the size of the hearth in the room in square centimeters.

Using the information in the table and the methods discussed in this chapter, answer the following questions.

1. What is the average room size at Grasshopper?

2. What is the average hearth size at Grasshopper?

3. Is there a relationship between room size and hearth size at Grasshopper?

4. What is the average room size for early rooms?

5. What is the average room size for late rooms?

6. Is there more or less variation in the size of the later rooms compared to the early ones?

7. Make a pie chart of the proportion of early and late rooms at Grasshopper.

8. What would you conclude about the relationship between time and room size at Grasshopper Pueblo?

STUDY QUESTIONS

1. What is the role of conservation in archaeological research?

2. What is the purpose of classification in archaeology?

3. What kinds of information about the past can be learned from the use of types in archaeology?

4. What are some of the basic statistics used in archaeology?

5. Scatterplots can provide a great deal of information about the relationship between two variables. What are some of the things that can be learned?

www.mhhe.com/pricearch1

For more review material and study questions, please see the self-quizzes on your online learning center.

REFERENCES

Banning, E. B. 2000. *The Archaeologist's Laboratory: The Analysis of Archaeological Data.* New York: Kluwer.

Bettinger, R. L., R. Boyd, and P. J. Richerson. 1996. Style, function, and cultural evolutionary processes. In *Darwinian Archaeologies,* edited by H. Maschner, 133–164. New York: Plenum.

Conkey, M., and C. Hastorf, eds. 1990. *The Uses of Style in Archaeology.* New Directions in Archaeology. Cambridge: Cambridge University Press.

Drennan, Robert D. 1996. *Statistics for Archaeologists.* New York: Plenum.

Hegmon, M. 1992. Archaeological Research on Style. *Annual Review of Anthropology* 21:517–536.

Lock, Gary. 2003. *Using Computers in Archaeology: Towards Virtual Pasts.* London: Routledge.

Sease, Catherine. 1994. *A Conservation Manual for the Field Archaeologist.* 3rd ed. Los Angeles: Los Angeles Institute of Archaeology.

Wiessner, P. 1983. Style and Social Information in Kalahari San Projectile Points. *American Antiquity* 48:253–276.

www.mhhe.com/pricearch1

For Internet references related to this chapter, please see the chapter links on your online learning center.

8

Dating

INTRODUCTION: FRAMEWORKS FOR MEASURING TIME

The funerals of Viking kings and queens that took place more than 1000 years ago in Norway were rich and spectacular. The ceremony sometimes involved the burial of the body and treasure of the ruler along with a complete ship under a huge mound of earth. One of the most famous of these is the Oseberg (*OSS-eh-bear*) ship burial, excavated in 1904, long before methods of accurate dating were available in archaeology. At the time of the excavation, the queen's burial was estimated to date sometime after AD 850, based on changes in the styles of Viking art. In 1959, samples were taken from the wooden burial chamber on the ship and scientifically dated to between AD 780 and 960, apparently confirming the estimate from the art styles.

In recent years, however, a master sequence based on tree rings in old oak timbers has been assembled for southern Scandinavia, using a technique known as **dendrochronology**. This sequence of tree rings, taken from old farm buildings, churches, prehistoric artifacts, and the like, extends back several hundred years before the Vikings. Tree rings from timbers in the burial chamber on the Oseberg ship were matched to the master chronology and provided a new date, one earlier than the stylistic estimates and more precise than the radiocarbon measurement. The entire tree ring sequence from the Oseberg timbers involved twelve samples spanning 299 years from AD 536 to 834 (Fig. 8.1). The year of cutting, AD 834, was the last ring on the five samples with sapwood remaining. The presence of sapwood indicates that the latest growth rings from the tree are present. The burial chamber must have been constructed in that year or shortly thereafter.

Two of the most important questions in archaeology are when and where. Time and location are critical pieces of knowledge about the past. Accurate dating is essential to document changes in human behavior over time. It is necessary to be able to place things and events in a framework of time and geographic space to know what happened, when, where, and the sequence of events—the order in which things happened. That time framework is called a **chronology**, a dated sequence of events in the past. Chronologies exist for sites, regions, and continents. *Where* is of course often answered by the place where sites and artifacts are found. The answer to *when* is more difficult, and it is only in the last 50 years that archaeologists have been able to answer this question with some accuracy. A variety of methods have been developed for determining the age of archaeological materials, and several of the most important of these techniques are discussed in this chapter.

Archaeologists use a number of different terms and abbreviations for dates. Dates older than 10,000 years ago are usually described in years before the

dendrochronology The study of the annual growth rings of trees as a dating technique to build *chronologies.*

chronology A framework of time to show the order of events, a dated sequence of events in the past.

Fig. 8.1 The dendrochronological measurements for the 12 grave chamber timbers on the Oseberg Viking ship burial from Oslo, Norway. The latest date of felling on the timbers, recorded where bark or sapwood was present (blue), coincided with the year AD 834. Many of the timbers were more than 200 years old, providing some indication of the value of the wood.

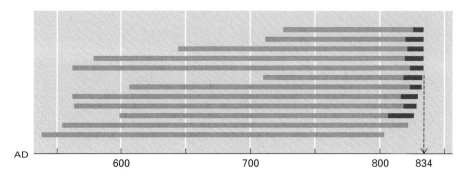

AD 600 700 800 834

Chronology is the backbone of archaeology: not the entire skeleton, but nothing less than the backbone.
—Sir Mortimer Wheeler, archaeologist

Time is nature's way of keeping everything from happening at once.
—Woody Allen, writer

www.mhhe.com/pricearch1

For preview material for this chapter, please see the chapter summary, outline, and objectives on your online learning center.

www.mhhe.com/pricearch1

For a Web-based activity on dating techniques, please see the Internet exercises on your online learning center.

relative dating   Method of dating that determines whether an object or layer is older or younger than another.

absolute dating   Method of dating that can provide an age in *calendar* years.

present (BP) or in millions of years ago (m.y.a.). Dates younger than 10,000 years ago are often given in calendar years before Christ (BC) or anno Domini, "in the year of the Lord" (AD). Classical archaeologists and some historical archaeologists may use BCE (before the Common Era) instead of BC. In this book, the terms bp (before 10,000 years ago) and BC/AD (after 10,000 years) are conventionally used.

This chapter is intended to introduce you to methods for recording and measuring time, to consider the primary techniques archaeologists use for determining the age of prehistoric materials. Techniques for dating items from the past are either relative or absolute in terms of the age they provide. **Relative dating** methods can determine whether an object or layer is older or younger than another, but only **absolute dating** methods can provide an age in calendar years. The primary absolute methods are dendrochronology, radiocarbon dating, and radiopotassium dating. There are a number of other techniques in use or under development as well, but they are not as reliable and are less commonly applied. Thermoluminescence dating is described in this chapter as an example of one of these experimental procedures.

RELATIVE DATING METHODS

Until about 1950, there was almost no way to reliably determine the age of the remains of early humans and their artifacts. Before that time, several techniques were used to estimate the antiquity of bones and stones or to connect artifacts to historical chronologies such as the Egyptian calendar. But, in general, it was not possible to establish the absolute age of a layer or artifact in calendar years. It is also important to remember that until the middle of the nineteenth century few people believed that the earth had much of an antiquity. Christian doctrine decreed that the earth was created in 4004 BC.

Stratigraphy, the study of layers of deposits at archaeological sites, was the basis for dating many early finds. The basic principle of superposition—deeper layers are older than higher layers in a sequence—describes the relative age of the layers. Study of the stratigraphy of sediments at an archaeological site provides a better understanding of the processes that create and enclose the deposits. The law of superposition applies and can be used to help date finds and features from various contexts at the site. Different episodes of activity can sometimes be seen in the stratigraphy, usually best in a cross-section view (known as a section or profile) in the wall of the excavation. Because archaeological sites were often places of human activity, including digging and deposition, the stratigraphy of layers and deposits requires careful attention and recording.

Dating was often done by association and the dates were relative (for example, younger than or older than), rather than absolute (for example, 3000 years old). Relative dating methods often use stratigraphic relationships to order older and younger materials. Stratigraphic sequences provide a relative chronology of geological layers from older at the bottom to younger at the top. Excavations in caves and sites with many layers revealed a sequence of levels, each one older than the one above. A deeply stratified deposit may allow the archaeologist to determine a temporal sequence for a number of different periods. Comparison of these layers and their artifact contents among different sites provided a means for determining the relative age of the materials found at the sites. A relative chronology makes it possible to study changes in the artifacts through time and observe temporal trends of change. Ordering artifacts in a relative chronology based on stratigraphy is a big step towards establishing a temporal framework. However, a relative chronology does not provide the actual age for an object and it cannot tell us how much time is involved in calendar years. Stratigraphy is discussed in more detail in Chapter 9, "Geoarchaeology."

One of the best examples of dating by association involves the establishment of the antiquity of humans. The bones of extinct animals, such as elephants in France, found with stone tools were clear evidence that the artifacts were as old as the elephants, even if the exact age was uncertain. In North America in the later part of the nineteenth century, there was great debate about how long the American Indians had been present and whether there was any substantial antiquity to the presence of humans in the Americas. Remember that at the time of Darwin's treatise *On the Origin of Species* in 1859, the generally accepted date for the creation of humans was around 4000 BC. In the 1920s, the discovery of fluted projectile points associated with skeletons of an extinct bison at sites in New Mexico (Fig. 5.3) finally convinced archaeologists that human populations had entered the New World much earlier than the previously accepted date for this event.

Another example of dating by association is described below using smoking pipes from the seventeenth and eighteenth centuries to date parts of an historic archaeological site.

 EXAMPLE ~~~~~~

PIPE STEMS

It may be surprising to learn, but historical records rarely tell us much about the lives of the people who were alive at that time. Upper-class individuals may appear in written documents, but everyday citizens are usually not described and underprivileged or minority groups are rarely mentioned. Historic archaeology is able to fill in some of the gaps in the story of past societies, their technology, their architecture, and their lives. The concerns of historical archaeology include industrial archaeology, maritime archaeology, military archaeology, the archaeology of slavery, and other matters.

The archaeology of slavery has received substantial attention in recent years with the excavation of cabins and cemeteries in both the North and the South of the United States. An example at Poplar Forest, Virginia, was described at the beginning of Chapter 1. A fascinating look at the archaeology of war comes from the Custer Battlefield National Monument, where survey and excavation revealed the locations of intense fighting and the course of the battle at Little Bighorn, also discussed in Chapter 1. Another example of battlefield archaeology from World War I Belgium is discussed in Chapter 17, "Responsibilities."

Historical archaeologists also classify and organize the materials they excavate. Accurate dating is even more important in historical archaeology in order to match up with known dates in historical documents. Various keys to times past have been developed on the basis of rapidly changing technology. Information from coins, bottles, nails, and pipes is among the most useful in this area. Coins, of course, are marked with dates and provide a temporal endpoint for a find. Archaeological remains found with a coin should not be younger than that coin. Iron nails were common in construction in the historic era and changed rapidly as technology moved from handmade to machine production. The chronology of the changes in nails is known and can be used to assign an approximate date.

One of the more interesting keys to historic time comes from the classification of clay smoking pipes. Hundreds of stem and bowl fragments of these pipes can

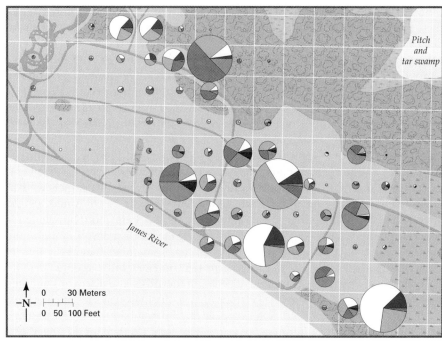

Key

■ 1580–1620	■ 1710–1750	□ River	■ Brush
□ 1620–1650	■ 1750–1800	▨ Tidal wetlands	▨ Forest
▨ 1650–1680	◉ Pipe era	▨ Field	▨ Cotter grid
▨ 1680–1710		□ Lawn	

Fig. 8.3 A plan of New Town, Jamestown Island, and the distribution of pipe fragments from 1580 to 1800 in six time intervals shown as pie graphs. The size of the circle represents the number of pipes found while the size of the slices shows the proportion from each interval on the time scale.

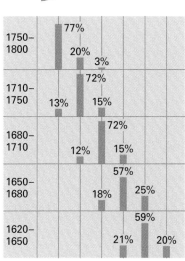

Fig. 8.2 A diagram showing the changes in pipe stem hole diameters in the century between 1650 and 1750.

sometimes be found at historic sites. The pipes were fragile and often broken. Moreover, pipes were shared in public places like taverns and each new smoker broke off a piece of the stem to have a fresh bit.

Clay pipes for smoking tobacco were produced by the thousands in the seventeenth and eighteenth centuries AD. These pipes were made by pouring a clay soup into brass molds. When the pipe casts were dry as leather they were removed from the mold and a fine wire was used to make a hole through the stem from the bit to bowl. The size of the wire and thus the diameter of the whole became finer over time. Pipes with a hole diameter of 4/64 or 5/64 of an inch date from the 1700s. Pipes with larger holes are usually earlier (Fig. 8.2). The shape of the pipe bowl also changed over time from small and round to large and funnel shaped. The combination of characteristics that are found in a pipe can thus be dated fairly precisely.

These changes allow different areas in an excavation to be dated accurately. Fig. 8.3 shows the early colonial settlement of New Town on Jamestown Island, Virginia. The pie charts show the age of the pipe fragments found in every 100-sq-ft grid unit at the settlement. (Pie charts are discussed in Chapter 7, "Classification and Data.") The size of the pie indicates how many fragments were found and the colors indicate their age. The blue and white colors are earlier; the orange and green colors are later. The chronology of the centers of activity and growth in this small town is clear from the location, number, and estimated age of the pipe fragments. Activity at the site seems to have shifted from a few focal points to a more regular pattern of use. This information helps greatly to understand the location and growth of the community and to interpret some of the features of the houses.

RECKONING TIME

The Gregorian calendar, used officially in many parts of the world today, was installed by Pope Gregory in AD 1582. This calendar was originally created for religious purposes to calculate the dates for the moveable feasts of Christian ritual. Although Christmas has a fixed date, a number of observances, such as Easter, are on variable days.

The Gregorian calendar is a solar calendar based on a cycle of 400 years of 146,097 days; each year has an average of 365.2425 days. The 12 months of the year have a fixed order and an unequal number of days. Years are counted both forward (AD) and backward (BC) from the birth of Christ. There are two types of years: A common year is 365 days; a leap year of 366 days occurs once every four years with a few exceptions. Our Gregorian calendar accumulates an error of one day in approximately 2500 years.

> 30 days hath September,
> April, June, and November;
> All the rest have thirty-one
> Except February —
> That's the weird one.

A **calendar** is a system for organizing time into repeatable and predictable units. Calendars operate in both the past and the future for recording history and scheduling activities. A day is the smallest unit of calendrical time; the measurement of fractions of a day is referred to as timekeeping and involves hours and minutes.

There are approximately forty different calendars in use in the world today. All of these are originally based on observations of movements of the sun, moon, planets, and/or stars, which cross the night sky with regularity and provide a reference for the passage of time. Astronomy was one of the very first sciences, responsible for recognizing and recording these recurring celestial events. Time likely was important in early human societies for agricultural and ritual purposes.

The earliest evidence for an awareness of time comes from 15,000 years ago during the Upper Paleolithic when seasons of the year and perhaps the phases of the moon were recorded in art and systems of notation. By 3000 BC, the Sumerians in Mesopotamia were using a lunar calendar that divided the year into 30-day months and split each day into twelve equal periods.

The first Egyptian calendar was based on the moon but was revised with the realization that the star Sirius rose next to the sun every 365 days, often coinciding with the onset of the annual Nile flood. The Egyptians began their 365-day calendar in 3100 BC and recorded the history of Egypt and its kings for several thousand years. The Romans divided their days into two parts, day and night, each with 12 hours. Since days are shorter in the winter, the length of these hours varied during the year. The Chinese calendar is based on the sun and moon. Months of 29 or 30 days begin on a new moon, and an extra month is added every two or three years. This calendar is used by Chinese people all over the world for traditional festivals and agricultural activities.

Maya Calendar

Most of the known calendrical systems have minor errors or inaccuracies, requiring some correction. The Maya, however, appear to have developed an extremely exact system of time. The Mayan calendar is based upon two cycles: a 260-day sacred year and the 365-day solar year. The 260-day sacred cycle consists of the complete sequence constructed by using thirteen numbers with twenty named days (Fig. 8.4). After 260 of these numbered and named days have passed, the cycle begins again. For the Maya, each day involved certain characteristics of

calendar   A system for organizing time into repeatable and predictable units.

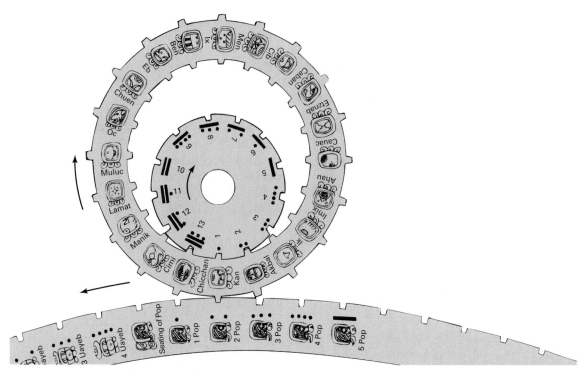

Fig. 8.4 A schematic representation of the Maya calendar of two major cycles, the sacred cycle and the solar cycle. These cycles are like wheels, and their units are cogs on the wheels. The two upper wheels are the numbers and names of the sacred cycle. The large lower wheel is the solar calendar of 365 days. The combination of these two cycles repeated every 52 years; longer periods of time were recorded using a more detailed long count.

a particular god, a bit like astrology. Some gods were benevolent, some destructive, others were in control of vital forces like fertility and rain.

A complete date in the Maya system involves both the ritual year and the solar year. The named and numbered ritual day is combined with a day in the solar year. The solar year consisted of 18 months of 20 days each, plus a short month of 5 unlucky days at the end of the year. The Maya priest-astronomers made minor corrections in their calendar on a regular basis. When the Spanish conquered this area, the Maya calendar was reported to be more accurate than the European one.

The Maya combination of the ritual and solar cycles, begun at the same time, can account for approximately 52 years (18,980 days) before repeating. In order to account for longer periods of time and historical dates, the Maya used a long count to distinguish the cycles. The long count reports the number of each kind of count and cycle in the calendar and the number of days in the current cycle to express a specific date in time. An arbitrary starting date of 3113 BC was chosen for the Maya long count. The first written historical date using the long count is on a monument at the site of Tikal, dating to July 6, AD 292 in the Gregorian system. The Maya calendar is still in use in some remote highland regions of Mexico and Guatemala.

ABSOLUTE DATING METHODS

Absolute dating methods are used to assign a specific, calendar age to an object in years bp, BC, AD, or another conventional system. For example, the end of construction on the great Egyptian pyramid of Khufu at Giza dates to around 2500 BC. The White House was completed in AD 1800. Those are absolute dates. Absolute doesn't mean the date is perfect; it means the date is in years according to our calendar. Dating in calendar years is possible if artifacts can be related to historical events or documents. However, a large part of the archaeological record is older than historical records or coinage and cannot be dated using such information.

There are many methods of dating in use in archaeology; some are reliable and commonly used and others are experimental. There are four major groups of

It is only in appearance that time is a river. It is rather a vast landscape and it is the eye of the beholder that moves.

—Thornton Wilder, writer

TABLE 8.1 Methods of absolute dating in archaeology, indicating the kinds of sample material, the dating range of the technique, the basic principles, and the limitations.

Method	Materials	Range in Years	Principle	Limitations
Dendrochronology	Tree rings in preserved logs and lumber	8000	Matching of annual tree growth rings	Region specific
Radiocarbon	Wood, charcoal, bone, carbonate, and others	100–40,000	Radioactive decay	Contamination, calibration
Radiopotassium	Volcanic rocks or minerals	Older than 500,000	Radioactive decay	Appropriate samples are rare
Uranium series	Coral, mollusks, travertine	30,000–300,000	Radioactive decay	Few labs, technical problems, contamination
Geomagnetism	Undisturbed sediment or volcanic rocks	Unlimited but approximate	Alignment of particles with pole reversals	Few labs
Archaeomagnetism	Intact hearths, kilns, burned areas	2000	Alignment with changes in location of earth's magnetic pole	Few labs, calibration
Thermoluminescence (TL)	Pottery, heated stone, calcites	500,000	Accumulation of TL in crystals	Environmental irradiation rate, few labs
Electron spin resonance	Heated crystalline stones, calcites, bone, shell	1,000,000	Accumulation of unpaired electrons in crystals	Few labs, experimental technique
Obsidian hydration	Obsidian artifacts	8000	Accumulation of weathering rind	Requires local calibration
Fission track	Volcanic rocks, crystalline materials	100,000–1,000,000	Radioactive decay leaves microscopic tracks in crystal	Materials rare in archaeological contexts

absolute dating techniques more commonly used in archaeology, based on the principle of the method: accumulation of layers, radioactive decay, trapped charges, and magnetism. Each of these methods is used with specific kinds of materials to obtain a date. For example, radiocarbon dating works only with substances containing organic materials; dendrochronology requires wood samples with preserved annual growth rings. Most of these methods can be used to obtain dates within a specific range of time. For example, radiocarbon can date materials a few hundred years old to approximately 40,000 years old; dendrochronology, on the other hand, can rarely be applied to specimens older than 10,000 years ago. Each of these techniques also has certain constraints that limit archaeological applications. Some of the more common methods are listed in Table 8.1 along with some information regarding materials that are used, the dating range of the technique, the basic principle involved, and some of the limitations. The approximate ranges for these techniques are schematically shown in Fig. 8.5. Four of these methods—dendrochronology, radiocarbon dating, radiopotassium dating, and thermoluminescence dating—are described in some detail in this chapter.

Accumulated layers take several forms. Annual layers, or growth rings, form in trees and provide the basic data for dendrochronology, described below. Annual layers known as **varves** form in lake bottoms in arctic and subarctic regions and provide a kind of calendar of past climates, but these layers are rarely related directly to archaeology. Obsidian, a black volcanic glass used for making stone tools, accumulates a layer of weathering, known as hydration, which becomes thicker over time. **Obsidian hydration dating** is based on the assumption that the rate of accumulation is constant.

varves Annual layers of deposits in cold-water lakes.

obsidian hydration dating A dating technique which relies on the accumulation of a hydration (weathering) layer on the fresh surface of obsidian objects.

Fig. 8.5 The range of various absolute dating techniques.

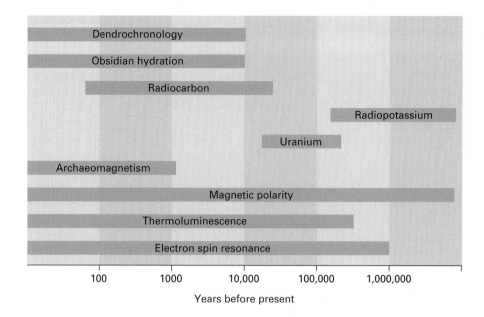

The principle of radioactive decay is well known. Radioactive forms of elements like carbon, argon, and uranium decay over time into nonradioactive states. The rate of decay, or half-life, is well known so that it is possible to determine how much time has passed since the material began to decay. **Radiocarbon** and **radiopotassium** dating are discussed in detail below as common techniques used in archaeology. **Uranium series dating** is not as common in archaeological use.

Trapped charge techniques involve the principle of the accumulation of charges or records of events in material. If the rate of accumulation is known, the number of years elapsed during accumulation can be determined, providing the age of the artifact. **Thermoluminescence** (TL), for example, is a form of radiation trapped as light energy in crystalline materials. TL is used today to date artifacts in situations where other methods of dating are not applicable and is described in more detail below. **Electron spin resonance** (ESR) is another trapped charge technique used for dating tooth enamel. Ninety-six percent of enamel is made up of the mineral hydroxyapatite. Once formed, this hydroxyapatite begins to accumulate radiation in the form of electrons that can be counted. Again, if the rate of accumulation is constant, elapsed time since the formation of the enamel can be determined.

There are two kinds of magnetic dating techniques used in archaeology, involving changes in the position of the earth's magnetic pole. The earth's magnetic field is produced by the iron core of our rotating planet. **Archaeomagnetism** relies on the continual shifting of the location of the North Pole over the last several thousand years (Fig. 8.6). This shifting, or polar wandering as it is known, is probably a result of movements in the earth's crust. When certain materials like clay or clayey soil are heated, either intentionally or accidentally, the iron compounds in the clay realign themselves and point to the position of the north pole at the time of heating. The orientation of the iron particles can be measured and an approximate date determined.

The second kind of magnetic dating—**magnetic polarity**—relies on reversals in the placement of the earth's magnetic pole. It is the case that the north pole on occasion shifts suddenly from the northern hemisphere to the southern, from the Arctic to the Antarctic. These magnetic reversals have been dated and are known to have occurred in a regular fashion. Determination of the location of the pole (whether north or south) in a sample of material that has been heated (usually volcanic deposits) can indicate during which period the material formed and provide an approximate age for very old materials. Reversals have been found

radiocarbon A radioactive *isotope* of carbon (^{14}C, carbon-14); an important dating technique in *archaeology.*

radiopotassium, or potassium-argon, dating Dating technique for old samples that is based on *half-life* for decay of potassium into argon in new rock.

uranium series dating An isotopic dating method based on radioactive decay of uranium.

thermoluminescence (TL) dating Technique for *absolute dating* based on the principle of the rate of accumulation of TL after heating, used with burned *flint* and *clay.*

electron spin resonance (ESR) A dating method based on trapped electrons in tooth enamel, assuming the accumulation rate is constant.

archaeomagnetism A dating technique based on the migration of the earth's north pole, known for the last 1000 years.

magnetic polarity A dating technique based on shifts in the location of the earth's magnetic pole.

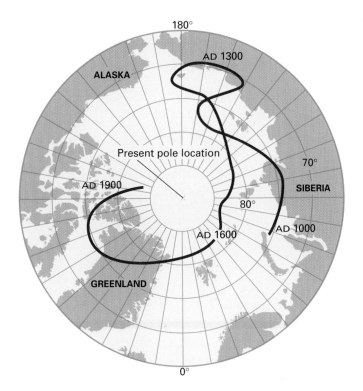

Fig. 8.6 Archaeomagnetic dating is based on the meanderings of the earth's magnetic north pole over time. This diagram shows the present location of the magnetic north pole relative to Great Britain and the projected location of the pole over the last 1000 years.

more than 300 million years ago. Since that time, there has been a magnetic reversal approximately every 700,000 years, with the most recent 780,000 years ago. So this technique is useful only for very old human materials.

Dendrochronology

One of the first methods to be used for absolute dating was based on the annual growth rings in trees. We have all seen a section cut from a large old tree with specific years and historical events marked on the rings (Fig. 8.7). Trees grow by building a new ring each year at the outer edge of the trunk. When a tree is cut, the stump, or cross section, reveals this sequence of rings from the core to the outer edge. Each ring has a darker and lighter part, marking the slower and faster growth of the tree during the year.

These annual growth rings are the key to one of the most accurate dating methods used in archaeology, dendrochronology. This technique is based on the principle that the width of the annual growth rings varies with temperature and rainfall. In general, wider rings are produced during years of good rainfall. Thus, every tree has a sequence of wider and narrower rings reflecting the climatic conditions during the period of its growth. All of the trees of that species in a particular region will exhibit a similar sequence of wider and narrower growth rings.

If one special tree had lived for thousands and thousands of years, it would have been possible to have the set of rings from that single tree. But of course trees don't live so long. To create such an extended sequence, it's necessary to find a series of trees and old wood whose lives overlapped one another. Scientists drill a small core from trees and old wood that provides a look at the sequence of tree rings. Because the width of individual rings varies with each year of growth, part of the distinctive sequence of rings from one tree can be overlapped with all or part of a sequence from another tree. By connecting older and older timbers and trees to this sequence, the string of years can be extended back in time (Fig. 8.8). Newly discovered wood or wooden artifacts can then be matched to the chronology that has been established.

Fig. 8.7 A cross-section through a Douglas fir showing approximately 50 years of annual rings. One annual ring includes both a dark and a light layer.

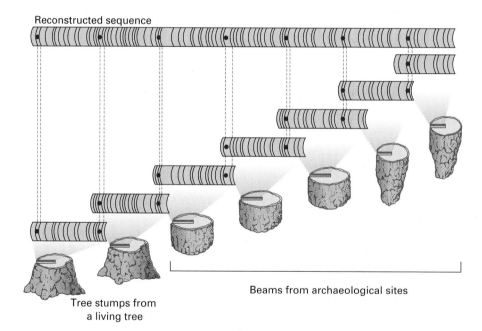

Reconstructed sequence

Tree stumps from a living tree

Beams from archaeological sites

Fig. 8.8 Building a dendrochronology using wood and timber in surviving structures. Three cores from a living tree, a church, and an old mill can be matched by overlap and used to build a longer chronology. In addition to the chronology, information on climate is also available from the annual growth rings.

Dendrochronology can only be used in areas where substantial timbers and trees are preserved. The inventor of tree-ring dating, A. E. Douglass (1867–1962) and his colleagues at the University of Arizona worked with the ancient timbers used in construction of prehistoric pueblo sites in the American Southwest, where arid conditions allowed their preservation. They established a continuous tree-ring chronology for the Colorado Plateau going back several thousand years. Dendrochronological sequences have also been established in the Aegean region, northwestern Europe, Central Europe, and elsewhere.

Two examples of the use of dendrochronology are described below. The first example comes from the American Southwest and the ruins of Pueblo Bonito. The second example is provided by the Neolithic lake dwellings of Central Europe where wooden timbers have been preserved under cold lake waters for more than 6000 years.

 ## EXAMPLE ～～～～～～～～～～～～～～～～～

PUEBLO BONITO

Chaco (*CHOCK-oh*) Canyon lies in the arid mountains of northwestern New Mexico. Today this is an isolated region, but between AD 1 and 1300 there was a substantial population present. The sequence of changes here in terms of human settlement and subsistence is fascinating. The first sedentary sites were small clusters of **pithouses** as maize farming was combined with hunting and gathering for subsistence. Settlements moved from the plateau above the canyon to the canyon floor after AD 500, and population expanded into larger communities of 50–100 pithouses. After AD 700, residences were built of timber and stone above ground while the shared communal structures continued to be large pithouses. After AD 900, the population congregated into larger, apartmentlike complexes of adjacent rooms known as pueblos. There were at least nine large towns of several hundred rooms each in Chaco Canyon at that time. The largest and most impressive of these was Pueblo Bonito (*bo-KNEE-toe*). This town was a huge, D-shaped complex of more than 800 rooms in several stories covering an area of more than two soccer fields (Fig. 8.9).

The occupation of Pueblo Bonito has been precisely dated using dendrochronology. Based on the work of A. E. Douglass and his successors, a continuous tree-ring chronology for the Colorado Plateau has been established back more than a thousand years. Tree-ring dates obtained from preserved wooden beams place the earliest building at Pueblo Bonito at AD 919; construction apparently was finished by AD 1115. Thus, this great apartment complex and town was erected, occupied, and abandoned in a period of approximately 200 years.

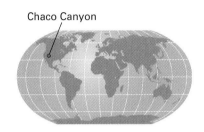

Chaco Canyon

Fig. 8.9 Pueblo Bonito in Chaco Canyon, New Mexico.

～～～～～～～～～～～～～

pithouse A dwelling constructed over a hole in the ground; semisubterranean structure; structure built on a semisubterranean foundation.

EXAMPLE

FRENCH NEOLITHIC LAKE DWELLINGS

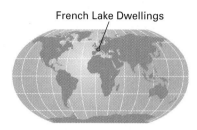

French Lake Dwellings

In Central Europe, because of the good preservation of fallen oak trees in wetlands and watercourses, a tree-ring sequence has been established going back to about 7000 BC. In a few cases, the very fine time scale provided by dendrochronology provides some remarkable information. One such example is from the Alpine region of France where a series of Neolithic settlements have been found. Originally described as **lake dwellings**, these settlements were thought to have stood over the water on raised pilings (Fig. 8.10). It is clear today, however, that the lake levels are higher now than during the Neolithic. These villages, once along the shoreline, were submerged sometime after their abandonment as the lakes grew in size and depth.

French archaeologists were able to date a series of settlements along an ancient lakeshore precisely using the tree-ring sequence from the well-preserved construction timbers in the lake sediments. The faunal and botanical remains at the sites can then be dated to specific decades, depending on the age of the layer in which they occur. The layers are precisely dated by the tree rings in the construction timbers. These data provide a fascinating glimpse of well-dated changes in population, environment, and subsistence usually not available in archaeology (Fig. 8.11).

The French data tell us about land use and degradation and the response of the population to crowding, and about rapid changes in human population numbers in the period between 3180 BC and 2950 BC. The number of villages increases from 2 to 9 by 2980 BC and then shows a clear decline to 5. Study of the bone refuse revealed meat consumption declined substantially during the period and the proportion of wild animals increased with the size of the human population. Hunting appears to have been the solution to more mouths to feed. The increase in elm twigs identified at the sites during the period of human population increase likely is related to feeding the domestic animals. The decline in the elm twigs is matched by an increase in the use of fir branches. Fir was a secondary fodder and grew only at higher elevations. This pattern suggests that the primary sources of winter fodder for the herded animals (elm, ivy, and ash) had been exhausted. Changes in pottery types suggest two separate groups of immigrants arrived during this period. Curiously, pigs were more important than cattle in the diet following each arrival.

Fig. 8.10 Timber pilings from a French Neolithic lakeside settlement exposed during low lake levels in the nineteenth century.

lake dwellings   Archaeological remains of settlements once thought to have stood over the water on raised pilings, but now known to have been situated along former shorelines, now submerged.

radioactivity   The process of decay of unstable *isotopes* over time through the spontaneous emission of radiation from the nucleus of an atom.

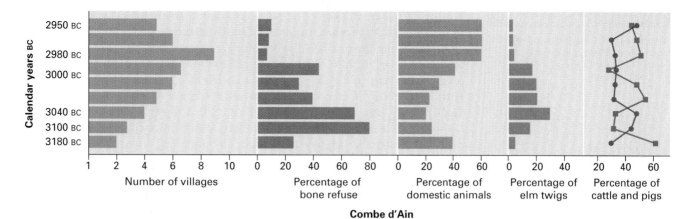

Combe d'Ain

Fig. 8.11 Results of the study of several French lake dwelling settlements during a period of approximately 250 years from 3180 BC to 2950 BC. Each row in the graph summarizes the information for a period of 15–80 years. Thus, the French data document a rapid rise in population (number of villages) around the beginning of the third millennium BC, associated with immigration, degradation of the landscape, and an increasing emphasis on hunting. Perhaps in response to the reduced productivity of the environment, population declines during the later decades of this period.

Radiocarbon Dating

The Manhattan Project was the most secret and expensive weapons development effort of the U.S. government during World War II. Laboratories in Chicago, New York, Tennessee, New Mexico, and elsewhere, employed thousands of scientists and technicians to create the first atomic bomb. Many of the unknowns of **radioactivity** were discovered for the first time during this work. One spin-off was the realization that some radioactive elements could be used to measure the age of various materials. Willard Libby, a physicist at the University of Chicago and a participant in the Manhattan Project, announced the first age determinations from radioactive carbon in 1949 and received the Nobel Prize for his discovery (Fig. 8.12).

The key to this procedure involves the principle of radioactive decay. Carbon (abbreviated as C) is a chemical element, a member of the periodic table of elements like gold, uranium, oxygen, and more than 100 others. These elements exist as atoms and make up the world around us. Some elements like carbon occur in several different forms, called isotopes, with slightly different atomic weights. There are three isotopes of carbon. Two of these isotopes are stable over time. One of them is carbon-12 (^{12}C), by far the most common isotopic form, making up 98.89% of the total carbon on earth. The other, carbon-13 (^{13}C), makes up about 1.1% of all carbon. The unstable, or radioactive, form is carbon-14 (known as ^{14}C or radiocarbon); it makes up only 0.000001% of the total carbon on earth. Unstable radioactive isotopes in various materials decay into stable isotopes over a known period of time. The unstable, radioactive isotope of carbon is produced in the atmosphere as a result of cosmic radiation. This ^{14}C is a very rare commodity and only 6 kg (13 lb) are produced each year. That's about two big handfuls. There are just 60 tons of ^{14}C on earth at any one time.

^{14}C is distributed evenly in the atmosphere (but not in the oceans, see below) and combines with oxygen in the same way as normal carbon-12 to form carbon dioxide. All living things absorb both stable carbon (primarily ^{12}C) and its radioactive isotope (^{14}C) throughout their lifetime (Fig. 8.13). Plants incorporate carbon dioxide through photosynthesis and animals eat plants or other animals.

Fig. 8.12 Willard Libby on the cover of *Time*, August 1955, five years before he was awarded the Nobel Prize for the discovery of radiocarbon dating.

Time has been transformed, and we have changed; it has advanced and set us in motion; it has unveiled its face, inspiring us with bewilderment and exhilaration.

—Kahlil Gibran, poet

For a Web-based activity on the use of radiocarbon dating , please see the Internet exercises on your online learning center.

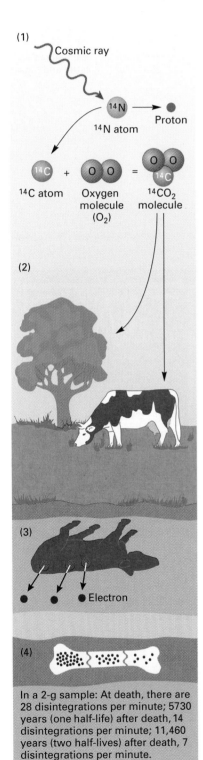

(1)

Cosmic ray

^{14}N → Proton

^{14}N atom

^{14}C atom + O O Oxygen molecule (O_2) = O O $^{14}CO_2$ molecule

(2)

(3)

Electron

(4)

In a 2-g sample: At death, there are 28 disintegrations per minute; 5730 years (one half-life) after death, 14 disintegrations per minute; 11,460 years (two half-lives) after death, 7 disintegrations per minute.

The proportion of ^{12}C and ^{14}C remains constant in an organism, as in the atmosphere, until its death when the intake of fresh carbon stops.

Following the death of the organism, radioactive carbon begins to decay and the ratio of ^{14}C to ^{12}C begins to decrease at a constant rate. The rate of decay for ^{14}C has a **half-life** of about 5730 years. This means that a sample which contains 20 grams of ^{14}C has only 10 grams after a period of 5730 years; after 11,460 years only 5 grams remain, and so on (Fig. 8.14). Thus, the amount of ^{14}C left in ancient plant or animal remains may be used to determine the time elapsed since death. The difference between the original amount of ^{14}C and the present amount is used to calculate the age of the sample in calendar years. After approximately eight half-lives, there is so little ^{14}C left in a sample that it cannot be accurately counted. Thus, the limit of radiocarbon dating is around 40,000 years ago.

There are a number of minor corrections that are made to radiocarbon dates to improve their accuracy. Because of potential errors in counting radiocarbon, dates are always given with a plus/minus value (±) to indicate that the actual date probably falls within the range indicated. The plus/minus value represents one standard deviation of the estimated years before present. A radiocarbon measurement of 2250 ± 50 years means that there is a 68.3% probability (a roughly two out of three chance) that the date of the object falls between 2200 and 2300 years ago. All radiocarbon dates before present are calculated from AD 1950 by convention. Thus, the calendar year date for a radiocarbon date of 2250 years ago is 300 BC.

Living organisms, composed of organic material, contain lots of carbon as part of the chemical composition of their tissues. A variety of organic materials can be assayed using radiocarbon dating, including wood, bone, shell, charcoal, antler, and more. ^{14}C often survives best at prehistoric sites in the form of charcoal, and this material has been most commonly dated by the radiocarbon method. However, wood charcoal can come from very old trees and may not date the actual archaeological material accurately. If charcoal from the inner rings of a large, old tree is used, a ^{14}C date for when the tree actually died may be off by several hundred years. For more reliable dates, plants other than trees should be used. Materials with a short life, such as nutshells, corncobs, and small twigs, are preferred over wood charcoal.

Accelerator Mass Spectrometer (AMS) Dating

Determining the amount of ^{14}C remaining in prehistoric materials is not an easy task. It's something equivalent to finding a specific piece of gravel in a full dump truck. Careful laboratory procedures and expensive scientific equipment are needed to measure the amount of ^{14}C in a sample. Until recently, a sample of known weight was carefully cleaned and then burned to create a pure gas of carbon dioxide. The radioactive carbon isotopes in that gas were then counted. In simple terms, a **Geiger counter** was used to record individual radioactive decay events or emissions from the gas. Several grams of organic material were normally required to produce enough gas for counting.

In the last two decades, however, technology has greatly improved in radiocarbon dating. **Accelerator mass spectrometers (AMS)** have replaced the Geiger counter method (Fig. 8.15). AMS are very large instruments that use magnets and sensitive counters to separate and count individual carbon atoms by measuring their weight, a much more accurate process. Much smaller samples can be measured with AMS dating (Fig. 8.16). Less than 0.01 g of sample is needed and indi-

◀ **Fig. 8.13** The basic principles of radiocarbon dating involve the creation of radiocarbon in the atmosphere through bombardment of nitrogen atoms by cosmic rays and ingestion of carbon dioxide by plants and animals. At death, radiocarbon begins to decay and disappear in organic material at a known rate. Counts of remaining radiocarbon provide the age estimate of the death of the sample.

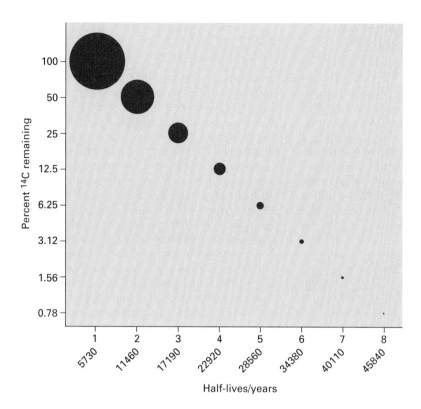

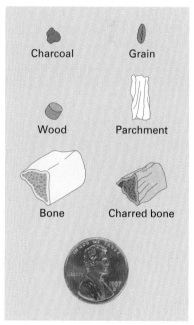

Fig. 8.14 A schematic diagram of the amount of radiocarbon left after a number of half-lives or years. The size of the dot represents the percentage of radiocarbon remaining.

Fig. 8.15 The AMS facility at Aarhus University in Denmark. The photo shows the instrument itself. Note the scientist standing by the instrument rear center of the photo for scale.

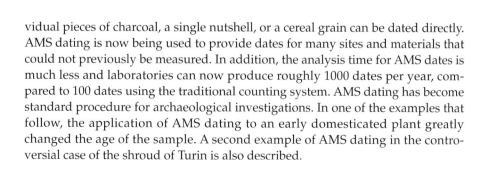

Fig. 8.16 Size of sample needed for AMS dating compared to a U.S. penny. Before AMS dating, a cupful of charcoal was needed.

vidual pieces of charcoal, a single nutshell, or a cereal grain can be dated directly. AMS dating is now being used to provide dates for many sites and materials that could not previously be measured. In addition, the analysis time for AMS dates is much less and laboratories can now produce roughly 1000 dates per year, compared to 100 dates using the traditional counting system. AMS dating has become standard procedure for archaeological investigations. In one of the examples that follow, the application of AMS dating to an early domesticated plant greatly changed the age of the sample. A second example of AMS dating in the controversial case of the shroud of Turin is also described.

half-life   Conventional rate for radioactivity based on the time period for the decay of half the unstable *isotopes* in a known quantity of material.

Geiger counter   A device for measuring radioactive emissions.

accelerator mass spectrometers (AMS)
Huge scientific instruments used for sorting and counting *isotopes*. AMS dating allows much smaller samples to be used in *archaeology*.

Absolute Dating Methods   **229**

Early Agriculture

A useful example of the development of radiocarbon dating comes from an archaeological project in the 1970s and 1980s. Archaeologists working near the Nile River in southern Egypt discovered a few grains of barley in a fireplace at a Late Paleolithic site called Wadi Kubbaniya (*coo-BAA-knee-yah*). Conventional radiocarbon dates were made on charcoal from the site and indicated the startlingly old age of 18,240 to 17,130 years ago. This date almost doubled the antiquity of the earliest known evidence for domesticated plants. The news provided the

TABLE 8.2 Original radiocarbon dates from the Wadi Kubbinaya, Egypt.

Laboratory	Sample Number	Dated Material	Years Before Present
SMU	591	Charcoal	18,240 ± 290
SMU	592	Charcoal	17,850 ± 200
SMU	595	Charcoal	17,130 ± 200

cover and lead article for the prestigious journal of *Science* in September 1979.

These new dates stirred up a great controversy. Until that point, the earliest evidence for farming had been found in the Near East and was believed to have appeared about 9000 years before present. By 1982, the University of Arizona had acquired a new scientific instrument, an accelerator mass spectrometer, capable of actually counting the atoms of radiocarbon rather than the decay emissions. Since smaller samples were used in the new instrument, it was possible to date the actual grains of barley that were found at Kubbaniya. The AMS date for one of the pieces of barley from the site came out as 4850 ± 150 years before present. This new date conclusively demonstrated that the site was mixed, that the barley at Kubbaniya was later in time and did not provide evidence of early plant domestication. The original date had come from a piece of much older charcoal buried close by. The application of new science in the form of AMS technology resolved a controversial discovery and removed the Kubbaniya material as a candidate for the earliest evidence for plant domestication.

 EXAMPLE

THE SHROUD OF TURIN

The Shroud of Turin is a religious relic that many people believe was used to wrap the body of Christ. The linen shroud—a piece of cloth 4.5 m (14 ft) long and 1.1 m (3.5 ft) wide—bears detailed front and back images of a bearded man who appears to have suffered whipping and crucifixion (Fig. 8.17). It was first displayed in France in the fourteenth century AD and eventually came to Turin, Italy, where it was housed in the cathedral in 1694. Every 20 years or so, the shroud is put on display. At the last showing in 1998, some 3 million people viewed the linen cloth.

The authenticity of the shroud has been examined on a number of occasions. Traditional radiocarbon dating could not be used on the shroud because a large sample of the cloth would have been destroyed in the process. With the advent of AMS dating, however, laboratories at Arizona, Oxford, and Zurich were invited by the Archbishop of Turin in 1987 to date samples of the shroud. A small strip of cloth was removed from one side and divided into three postage stamp–sized pieces. One piece of the shroud, along with three control samples of known age, was given to each lab. At two of the laboratories, the scientists did not know which of the four specimens came from the shroud.

The control samples were pieces of ancient cloth of known date to be used to validate the results from the different labs. One of the control samples was a piece of linen from a tomb in Nubia. Islamic embroidery and Christian inscriptions on the cloth suggested a date in the eleventh or twelfth century AD. A second control sample was taken from the linen wrappings of the mummy of Cleopatra in the British Museum. This cloth had been dated using traditional radiocarbon methods between 110 BC and AD 75, around the time of the birth of Christ. The third control sample consisted of threads removed from the cloak of a French saint who lived during the reign of King

What then is time? If no one asks me, I know what it is. If I wish to explain it to him who asks, I do not know.
— Saint Augustine, philosopher

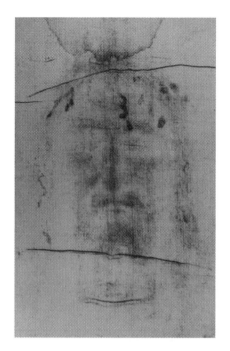 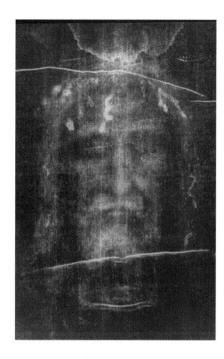

Figure 8.17 The face from the Shroud of Turin. Two depictions of the same view are shown here; one is black and white and the other is reversed. The linen cloth of the shroud is believed by some to have recorded an image of the body of Jesus. The head region is argued to show bloodstains resulting from a crown of thorns.

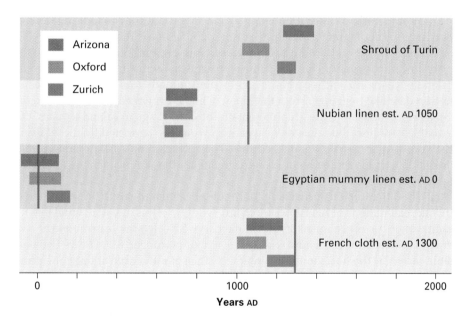

Fig. 8.18 Average radiocarbon dates with ±1 standard deviation for the Shroud of Turin and three control samples. Three laboratories measured the same samples, Arizona, Oxford, and Zurich. The vertical lines mark the estimated age of the control samples. AMS measurements showed the shroud to date to AD 1260–1390, with at least 95% confidence.

Phillipe IV, AD 1290–1310. The dating results from the three control samples matched previous radiocarbon measurements and/or historical dates and supported the accuracy of the dates from these labs.

At the three laboratories, the shroud samples were cleaned and treated following standard procedures to remove contaminants. The samples were then combusted to gas and their radiocarbon content was measured in an accelerator mass spectrometer. The almost identical AMS measurements at the three laboratories provided a calendar age range of AD 1260–1390 (Fig. 8.18). The AMS dating provides conclusive evidence that the linen for the Shroud of Turin was not made until some 1300 years after the death of Christ.

Of course whenever science and religion meet, there are controversies. That is certainly the case with the shroud. A heated debate continues today. One of the scientists, perhaps in exasperation, declared that anyone who believed the shroud was genuine was a "flat-earther." The shroud supporters raised hundreds of questions about the validity of the AMS results, claiming that burned cloth was dated, that there was varnish on the cloth, that the samples came from later repairs to the shroud, that mold growing on the cloth produced a younger date, among many others. Scientists pointed out that any contaminants would have had to be present in amounts three times the weight of the sample to cause such an error. The AMS dating of the shroud is reliable, but at the same time it is clear that no matter what evidence is brought to bear, true believers will continue to venerate this cloth and not question its authenticity.

Calibration

Radiocarbon dating was originally based on the assumption that there had been no changes in the amount of ^{14}C in the atmosphere over time. However, the radiocarbon dating of tree rings of known age (based on dendrochronology) has shown that this assumption was incorrect and that radiocarbon dates slightly underestimate the actual age of a sample. To make up for this error, dates in radiocarbon years are now corrected, or calibrated, to calendar years using a graph, a formula, or computer program available on the Web. **Calibration** is necessary for all radiocarbon dates.

To understand calibration using a graph, you can think about this correction in terms of diagram a. in Fig. 8.19. A horizontal line is drawn from the y-axis on the left of the graph (radiocarbon years before present) out to the right to the wavy line on the graph. This wavy line represents the actual relationship between calendar years and radiocarbon years as determined from dating samples of known date like tree rings. From that point, a line is drawn vertically down to the x-axis at the bottom of the graph to obtain the correct age in calendar years. For example, a radiocarbon date of 995 years bp would be corrected to AD 930 using the graph, as shown by the dashed line. The corrected date is known as a calibrated date and is a more accurate age estimate for the sample than the measured radiocarbon years bp.

The situation is as usual a bit more complicated and has to do with the fact that the calibration curve is not smooth but "wiggly." Thus, the horizontal line for radiocarbon years can in fact intercept the curve for calendar years in one or several places depending on how wiggly it is at that point. Fig. 8.19 shows two possible cases: (a) the horizontal line intersects the smooth curve at only one point resulting in a single high probability calendar date, or (b) the horizontal line intersects the wiggly curve at several points, resulting in several possible calendar

Fig. 8.19 Two possible cases of calibrating radiocarbon dates depending on the shape of the calibration curve. If the curve is straight and steep with few wiggles (a), the calibrated date is precise and straightforward with high probability. If, on the other hand, the curve is more horizontal and has several points of intersection (b), there will be several possible dates and the probability of being correct is lower. The probability is shown by the height of the curve on the x-axis of the graph; the higher the curve, the greater the probability that the date is correct. Both dates have the same standard deviation.

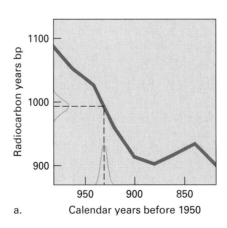

a.

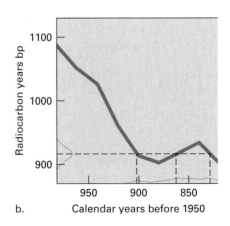

b.

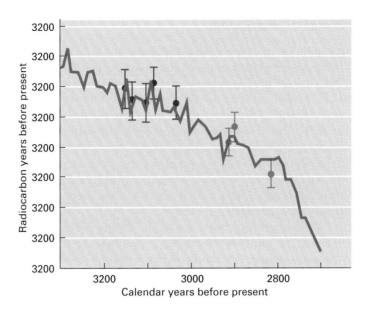

Fig. 8.20 The use of wiggle-matching can provide very accurate dates in archaeology. Two sets of dates (red and green) from a site are matched to the calibration curve for radiocarbon dating. The eight dates are shown with measured radio-carbon years (circle) and standard deviation (vertical line).

year dates with a lower probability of being correct. Some portions of the radio-carbon curve are wigglier than others, so there are some time periods when it is harder to get a really accurate date.

That's the bad news. The good news is that these wiggles in the curve can be used to fit a series of dates from a sequence of related samples to a specific point in time, using a technique known as **wiggle matching**. By matching the position of the sequence of dates to the wiggly curve, the exact dates for the samples may be obtained (Fig. 8.20). In this example, a series of buried logs from the southwestern United States were dated, but the individual determinations were difficult to calibrate since they fell in a flat part of the curve. Since the logs were known to be close together in age, the series of dates could be plotted directly against the radiocarbon curve. The close fit or wiggle match between the measured dates and the curve indicate that these dates can be calibrated at the positions of intersect with the curve.

There is another correction that must be made for samples of certain kinds of plants or marine organisms. Calculation of the amount of radiocarbon in a sample is based on the ratio of radiocarbon (^{14}C) to a stable isotope of carbon (^{12}C). As noted earlier, there is a third stable isotope of carbon (^{13}C) that occurs in small proportions in nature (ca. 1.1%). The deeper waters of the earth's oceans are older and are slightly depleted in ^{14}C compared to the atmosphere. This older water mixes with surface waters and reduces the amount of ^{14}C present. Thus, organisms living in the oceans, or eating marine foods, will have less ^{14}C than expected. Radiocarbon dates calculated from marine-related samples can be older than their actual calendar age by 400 years or more. This problem is known as the marine reservoir effect. The error can be fixed by measuring the ratio of ^{13}C to ^{12}C in the sample and correcting the date to the known ratio for terrestrial organisms.

There is one further complication in that certain kinds of grasses and other tropical plant species use a metabolic process that incorporates more ^{13}C in their tissues. Some of the plants are important human foods (e.g., corn, sorghum). Thus, plants and animals that eat those plants (either directly or from the herbivores that eat those plants) also have a ratio of ^{13}C to ^{12}C that is higher than expected and must be corrected. The error is about the same as the marine reservoir effect and the correction is done in the same fashion. These variations with stable carbon are the basis of an important method for studying past human diets described in Chapter 15, "Archaeometry."

Time is the longest distance between two places.
—Tennessee Williams, playwright

calibration Correction of *radiocarbon* dates for the difference between *calendar* years and *radiocarbon* years.

wiggle matching A technique for finding precise dates using a series of *radiocarbon* dates and the irregularities in the calibration curve.

Radiopotassium Dating

Radiopotassium, or potassium-argon, dating is of crucial importance for determining the age of the earliest human remains. This technique can date most of the earth's history and has been used to measure the age of the oldest rocks on our planet, as well as samples of moon rocks. The technique was developed by Garniss Curtis, a professor of geology at the University of California-Berkeley (Fig. 8.21). The first potassium-argon dates from the lava at the base of Olduvai (*OL-due-vie*) Gorge—1.75 m.y.a.—startled the scientific community in the 1960s. The human fossil remains were almost one million years older than previously believed. Bones and artifacts are not themselves directly dated; rather, newly formed volcanic rocks or ash deposits that lie directly under or over the prehistoric materials are analyzed.

The technique is based on the following principles. Potassium (chemical symbol = K) is found in abundance in granites, clays, and basalts in the minerals of the earth's crust. Potassium occurs in several stable forms and has one radioactive isotope, ^{40}K, with a half-life of approximately 1.3 billion years. Because this isotope has such a very long half-life, it is generally not possible to date materials that are younger than 500,000 years or so, as too little decay has taken place to measure.

The radioactive isotope ^{40}K decays into argon (^{40}Ar), an inert gas, and calcium (^{40}Ca). About 11% of ^{40}K becomes ^{40}Ar as it decays. The materials generally dated by the $^{40}K/^{40}Ar$ technique are limited to rocks, volcanic ashes, and other substances that contain radioactive potassium and trap the argon gas that is produced. The molten state of the rock permits the release of trapped gas in the parent rock and resets the argon reservoirs in the new rock to zero. ^{40}Ar begins to accumulate as soon as a rock is formed. By measuring the amount of ^{40}Ar to ^{40}K remaining, it is possible to determine how much ^{40}K has decayed and thus the amount of time that has elapsed since the rock was created. Measurements are done with sophisticated counters that record the amount of radioactivity remaining.

Advances in radiopotassium dating in recent years have greatly improved the method. One of the problems with the potassium-argon method was that the sample to be dated had to be split into two parts to measure each of the elements. Minor differences between the two parts caused inaccuracies in the measurements. Today a technique called argon-argon dating is used to measure the proportion of ^{40}Ar to ^{39}Ar. Using this method, the stable isotope of potassium ^{39}K is converted to ^{39}Ar by neutron bombardment in a nuclear reactor. Both argon isotopes can then be measured from the same sample. In addition, much smaller samples can be used. The improved precision of this technique allows samples younger than 100,000 years to be dated. In one recent study, an argon-argon date of AD 73 was obtained for the eruption of Vesuvius that buried the Roman town of Pompeii in AD 79. Another example is described below for a site with very early evidence for human activity in East Africa.

Fig. 8.21 Garniss Curtis, developer of the potassium-argon dating method. A sample is being heated to extract gases for measurement of the isotope ratio.

We almost cried with sheer joy, each seized by that terrific emotion that comes rarely in life. After all our hoping and hardship and sacrifice, at last we had reached our goal— we had found the world's earliest human.

—Louis Leakey, archaeologist

Laetoli

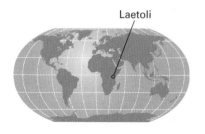

◉ EXAMPLE 〜〜〜〜〜〜〜〜〜〜〜〜〜〜

LAETOLI—OUR FIRST STEPS

All of the evidence for our early ancestors before 2 million years ago comes from Africa. New fossils have pushed back the age of the earliest known hominins and have considerably modified our understanding of their behavior and appearance. Until 1970, there was relatively little evidence for the earliest human ancestors other than a few skulls and pieces of bone. The human characteristics of upright posture, large brain size, and tool use were thought to have evolved simultaneously as large primates moved out from the forest into the savannah. In the last 30 years or so, however, discoveries in Central and East Africa have reshaped and redefined our family tree.

Current information indicates that the first recognizable remains of our human ancestors began to appear in East Africa shortly before 6 million years ago. The brain size of these earliest human relatives from the Miocene was not larger than that of the modern apes, nor had their teeth changed significantly from those of their earlier ape ancestors. They also did not use stone tools. What was different, however, was a new form of movement. The earliest human ancestors show definite indications of habitual **bipedalism**—walking on two feet rather than four.

The most dramatic evidence for this new posture comes not from the fossil bones, however, but from actual footprints at the site of Laetoli (*lay-TOE-lee*) in Tanzania, discovered by Mary Leakey in 1976 (Fig. 8.22). An active volcano near Laetoli covered the area with a layer of volcanic ash. Following a rain shower, various animals moved across the damp layer of ash. A chemical reaction between rainwater and the ash quickly hardened the surface so that even the impressions of the raindrops are preserved at the site. Hares, birds, extinct elephants, pigs, buffalo, rhinos, a saber-toothed tiger, and lots of baboons left their tracks along with three humans. The numerous sets of footprints do not often overlap one another, suggesting that this layer was quickly buried by more ash, resulting in its preservation.

Radiopotassium dating was used to measure the age of the two ash layers. Eight potassium-argon dates were obtained from a volcanic tuff (hard ash) layer above the footprints with an average date of 3.6 ± 0.2 m.y.a. Two dates from the tuff below the footprints gave a date of 3.8 ± 0.1 m.y.a. The best estimate for the Laetoli footprints then lies between these dates.

We had been working really hard that day and were heading back toward camp when one of our team decided to liven things up by slinging elephant dung at the rest of us. He aimed one at me, and I had to dive out of the way. I ended up flat on my face. I started to rise and saw marks in the ground. I realized they were fossilized raindrops. Then I looked around and saw ancient animal footprints all over the place. We had passed over that ground so many times before that evening, but none of us had noticed a thing. But once we saw the first prints, we could see them everywhere: fossilized tracks of rhino, elephants, antelopes, all sorts of animals.

—Andrew Hill, paleontologist

Fig. 8.22 The very ancient human footprints preserved in volcanic ash at Laetoli, Tanzania.

bipedalism The human method of locomotion, walking on two legs; one of the first human characteristics to distinguish the early *hominins*, as opposed to quadrupedalism, walking on four legs.

The Laetoli Footprints

Dr. Mary Leakey originally excavated the site during 1978–1979, recorded the footprints using various techniques, and then reburied the footprints. Because of the extraordinary finds at Laetoli, it was named a UNESCO World Heritage site in 1979 as part of the Ngorongoro (*IN-gore-oh-gore-oh*) Conservation Area. Unfortunately the area has seen the growth of acacia trees and the spread of tree roots into the zone of footprints. Because of this threat to the site, the Getty Conservation Institute of Los Angeles, in collaboration with the Tanzanian Department of Antiquities, undertook the conservation of the Laetoli trackway. The Getty Conservation Institute (GCI) works around the world to advance the field of conservation through scientific research, field projects, education, and public awareness.

The GCI team traveled to Tanzania in 1995 and 1996 to reopen the site, remove the tree roots, record and study the tracks, and conserve the footprints in situ. The final step in the conservation process involved the careful reburial of the entire area, with steps taken to inhibit the return of vegetation. The reburial of the footprints was determined to be the only means of ensuring their protection. While the site is not accessible to the public, the GCI team has made reproductions of the trackway for museum display at Olduvai and at the National Museum in Dar es Salaam. The Tanzanian authorities are regularly monitoring the site today.

www.mhhe.com/pricearch1

For a Web-based activity on thermoluminescence, please see the Internet exercises on your online learning center.

Thermoluminescence Dating

Thermoluminescence (TL) dating is a still experimental, but promising, technique for determining the age of samples too old for radiocarbon and too young for potassium-argon. Researchers can use it to date samples up to 500,000 years old, and it can be used to date burned flint and other burned materials that are common at archaeological sites. A disadvantage with TL dating is the large error factor associated with the dates because of uncertain assumptions in the method.

The term *thermoluminescence* is the name for the light or glow that a mineral produces when heated. For a specific mineral, the amount of light emitted is a known quantity that varies with temperature. Although a large number of crystalline materials exhibit thermoluminescence, the minerals normally dated for geological and archaeological applications are quartz, feldspar, and flint.

All buried materials are constantly exposed to radiation from naturally occurring radioactivity and from cosmic rays that pass through the earth. A small portion of this radiation is trapped as energy in crystalline materials in the form of thermoluminescence. In a sense, the crystal retains a memory of how much radiation it has absorbed. If the rate of exposure is constant, then the amount of time that the crystal has been in the ground is recorded in the amount of TL that has accumulated.

Heating essentially erases the TL accumulated inside the crystal, so crystalline archaeological materials heated to more than 400°C in association with past human activity can be used as a kind of TL stopwatch, in which the last date of heating is the starting point for TL accumulation. Ceramics, burned flint, bricks, hearths, slag, and heating stones are all candidates for TL dating. When heat is reapplied to the crystalline material in the laboratory, the energy in the crystal is released in the form of light, causing the material to glow (Fig. 8.23). The amount of TL released is measured and used to calculate how much time has passed since the last heating.

Thermoluminescence is often used to authenticate certain art objects; modern samples have very little accumulated TL indicating that an object is not old. As mentioned, the technique is also being used more frequently in situations where radiocarbon and potassium-argon dating cannot be applied. An example comes from two caves in Israel where very early remains of modern humans, *Homo sapiens,* have been found. Chronology here is critical in order to understand

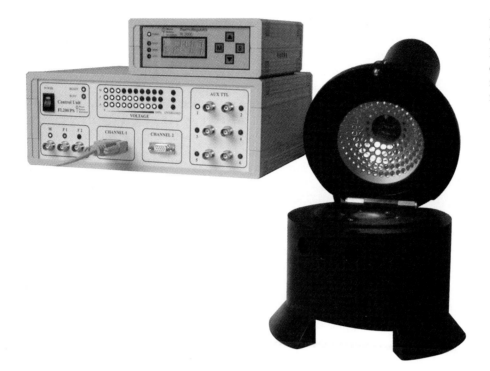

Fig. 8.23 Thermoluminescence dosimeter for measuring emitted light from TL samples. Sample chamber for heating samples and measuring TL (right); control and recording equipment (left).

the spread of fully modern humans and the disappearance of Neanderthals. This transition takes places at a point in time beyond the limits of radiocarbon dating, and the evidence is not associated with volcanic deposits suitable for potassium-argon dating. TL dating of burned flint in association with Neanderthal bones provided an age of 60,000 bp. TL measurements on burned flint found with the modern human remains gave a date of 90,000 to 100,000 bp. These determinations indicate that fully modern humans were present in the Near East prior to the arrival of Neanderthals. This new date emphasizes the antiquity of *Homo sapiens* in Southwest Asia and documents their contemporaneity with Neanderthals for many millennia.

CONCLUSIONS

Dating techniques fall into two general categories, relative or absolute. Relative dating methods provide an indication of the age of an item in relation to other materials. These methods rely on stratigraphic position or association—context—to determine that an object is of approximately the same age or younger or older than another. Stratigraphic superpositioning is an important part of relative dating for materials from the Stone Age. Deep deposits in caves formed the primary evidence for much of the Stone Age during the early years of investigations. The stratigraphic position of the finds documented the younger materials above and the older materials below. Such sequences of relative dates provided the initial means of sequencing various periods of time.

Association is another form of relative dating in archaeology in which an object of unknown age is dated by association with an object of known age. The basic principle involves archaeological context, the set of objects, features, layers, and sediments in which an item is found. Dating by association is probably the most obvious way to determine the age of an object. An example would be the presence of a glass bottle with a known year of manufacture found in a pit with animal bones and some burned bricks. Although we do not know the age of the bones and bricks, it is very likely they are no older than the glass bottle and we can thus date these unknown items by this association. The principle applies as well in situations without dated artifacts. Certain species of animals are known to have lived during a specific period of time. For example, mastodons, an extinct relative of the elephant, left what is now Wisconsin approximately 10,000 years ago. Stone artifacts found in Wisconsin in association with the bones of these mastodons are very likely older than 10,000 years.

Absolute dating methods provide a real, calendar age in years and are the most useful kinds of dates to have. The most common methods for absolute dating include radiocarbon for the last 40,000 years, potassium-argon dating for materials older than 500,000 years or so, dendrochronology for the last 10,000 years, and thermoluminescence for samples up to 500,000 years ago. In spite of the usefulness of these techniques, there are still limitations. There is a degree of error or uncertainty in the principles and calculation of absolute dates so that they are usually reported with a plus/minus (±) error factor. Radiocarbon dating requires preserved organic materials with carbon; so only bone, shell, and charcoal are commonly dated with this method. Potassium-argon dating requires deposits of volcanic rock or ash in association with archaeological remains for dating. Dendrochronology requires preserved wood with tree rings. Another absolute dating technique uses the principle of thermoluminescence (TL) to measure the accumulation of radiation in heated stone or clay.

Dating is a fundamental aspect of archaeology. There are many methods for dating archaeological materials, some more reliable and applicable than others. It is essential to be able to determine the age of objects and places. Without reliable dating methods, it is impossible to track changes or to talk about the relationships among different objects or places. If we want to understand the course of human prehistory, we must be able to date the remains of that past.

Time is in fact the hero of the plot. . . . Given so much time, the "impossible" becomes possible, the possible probable, and the probable virtually certain. One has only to wait: time itself performs the miracles.
—George Wald, physicist

kurgans   Burial *mounds* in the steppe region of eastern Europe.

DATING A SCYTHIAN TOMB

North of the Himalayas and Caucasus Mountains lie the vast rolling steppes of Central Asia, an area of grassland extending thousands of miles from China to the Ukraine. This area has been homeland to nomads for several millennia. The Scythians (*SITH-ee-ins*) were a great pastoral group occupying this region in the first millennium BC. The Greek historian Herodotus wrote that the Scythians ruled from the Don River in southern Russia to the Carpathian Mountains in central Europe in the fifth century BC (Fig. 8.24).

The **kurgans**—burial mounds—of the Scythians dot the steppe landscape. The deceased was usually placed in an extended position in a log tomb with the head to the east. The tomb was then buried under an earthen mound. For Scythian aristocrats, these tombs were made large and filled with astounding wealth. The body was usually embalmed and placed in a special coffin made from the trunk of a tree. The noble was buried with sacrificed retainers and attendants, horses and chariots, riding and military equipment, along with silk cloth, metal mirrors, and gold jewelry. These tombs and their contents are the primary evidence for the Scythians. The chronology of the tombs is also critical to understanding Scythian society and its relationships with other groups in Asia and Europe.

A new tomb has recently been discovered in the steppes. Although the tomb was heavily looted many years ago, a number of the timbers have survived, along with several important artifacts. Samples of the wood from six timbers have been sent for both radiocarbon and dendrochronological measurements, and the data are starting to come in.

There are three parts to this project: (1) work with the radiocarbon measurements; (2) work with the dendrochronology information; (3) compare the results of the two dating methods.

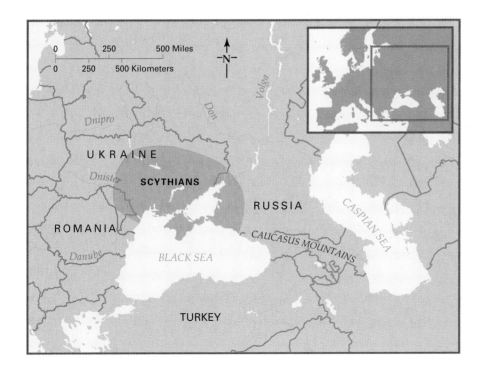

Fig. 8.24 Location of the Scythians in eastern Europe. The main concentration of Scythian materials, dating to the first millennium BC, comes from an area north of the Black Sea, largely in the modern country of the Ukraine.

TABLE 8.3 Radiocarbon dates bp for wood samples from the Scythian tomb.

Sample No.	Material	¹⁴C Years bp	Standard Deviation	Calibrated Date BC
1	Wood	2500	±18	617
2	Wood	2418	±20	473
3	Wood	2505	±21	617
4	Wood	2453	±22	503
5	Wood	2533	±22	598
6	Wood	2468	±21	586

1. The radiocarbon data arrive first. You receive a list of the radiocarbon years before present (bp) for each of the six samples (Table 8.3). These dates have been calibrated—corrected to actual calendar years BC—so that you can compare them with the dendrochronological dates. What do the calibrated radiocarbon dates tell you about the age of the tomb? What do the dates tell you about radiocarbon dating? What is the most likely date for the tomb based on these radiocarbon dates?

2. There is a problem with this time period in terms of radiocarbon dating. As you can see from the curve of radiocarbon ages in Fig. 8.25, the time period between about 770 and 400 BC is flat and wiggly. These years are hard to separate with radiocarbon measurements because a radiocarbon date of 2460 ± 40 bp could come from several different calendar years in the flat part of the curve (Fig 8.25). Because of these problems, the dendrochronology dates will be very useful in determining the age of the kurgan.

3. The dendrochronology data consist of measurements of ring widths for four timbers. Only one of the timbers had remaining bark and sapwood while the outer rings of the other four were missing. Use the ring-width data in

Fig. 8.25 Curve of radiocarbon dates for the period 800 to 350 BC. The horizontal line shows the radiocarbon date of 2460 years before present. The seven vertical red lines show where the horizontal red line intersects the blue calibration curve. There are seven possible calendrical dates for the one radiocarbon date, between 2500 and 2750 years before present, shown where the vertical red lines intersect the x-axis.

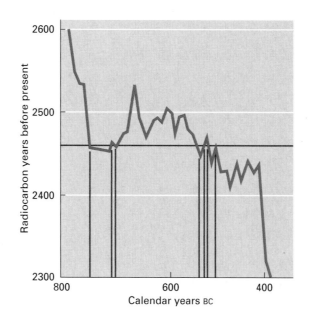

TABLE 8.4 Tree-ring data from the Scythian tomb.

Ring#	Timber 1	Timber 2	Timber 3	Timber 4
0	3	2	3	5 (Sap)
1	4	5	5	B
2	B	3	4	B
3	4	5	1	B
4	B	4	B	2
5	3	1	B	5
6	B	B	3	3
7	B	B	4	5
8	2	3	B	4
9	B	4	4	1
10	3	B	B	B
11	4	4	3	B
12	B		B	3
13	3		B	4
14	B		2	
15	4		B	
16	2		3	
17	5		4	
18	2		B	
19	5		3	
20	B			
21	B			
22	3			
23	B			
24	4			
25	5			
26	4			
27	B			
28	3			
29	2			
30	B			
31	3			
32	B			
33	5			
34	5			

Table 8.4 to determine the age of the tomb. To do this, you will need to compare the widths of the rings from the four timbers to the master tree-ring chronology for this area (Fig. 8.27).

Plots of the tree-ring data for the four timbers are shown in Fig. 8.26. Each vertical line represents one tree ring; the length of the line shows the width of the tree ring. Each block on the graph paper represents 1 mm. Note that there are a number of rings missing and that is why there are gaps in the tree-ring graph.

To determine the age of the timbers, you compare the plots of the timbers to the master chronology. The master chronology is shown in Fig. 8.27 and covers a 150-year period between 575 and 425 BC. Hopefully your timbers will belong to this period of time.

You need to fit the plot for each timber to the master chronology. You might want to copy this page and cut out the individual timber plots. Then

Fig. 8.26 Tree-ring graph paper.

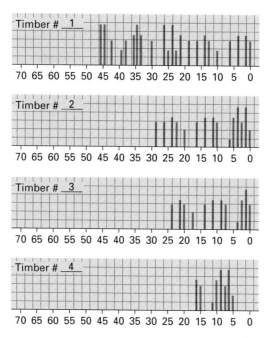

Timber # __1__
70 65 60 55 50 45 40 35 30 25 20 15 10 5 0

Timber # __2__
70 65 60 55 50 45 40 35 30 25 20 15 10 5 0

Timber # __3__
70 65 60 55 50 45 40 35 30 25 20 15 10 5 0

Timber # __4__
70 65 60 55 50 45 40 35 30 25 20 15 10 5 0

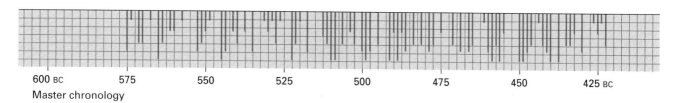

600 BC   575   550   525   500   475   450   425 BC

Master chronology

Fig. 8.27 Master tree-ring chronology.

you can slide each plot back and forth until the series of lines best match up. A close match should appear that fits the sequence of each timber to the known years of the master chronology. The plots for the different timbers will overlap on the master chronology.

Once all the timbers have been matched to the master chronology, look at the youngest sample you have with sapwood and see what calendar year on the master chronology this youngest ring corresponds to. That should be the year of felling for the youngest timber and should provide the best tree-ring date for the tomb. Fill in this date here: _____.

4. Now let's see if your radiocarbon results and your dendrochronology dates are comparable. Please answer the following questions.

a. What are the two estimates for the age of the tomb?

The best radiocarbon estimate is _____.

The best dendrochronology estimate is _____.

b. Are the estimates the same? Identical? If not, what does the difference mean?

c. Which estimate is correct?

d. What does this exercise tell you about dating in archaeology?

STUDY QUESTIONS

1. What is the difference between relative and absolute dating?
2. Why is accurate dating important in archaeological research?
3. What kinds of information are present in tree rings?
4. What are the important principles of radiocarbon dating?
5. What are the advantages of AMS dating?
6. What method could be used to date wood older than 100,000 years?
7. What are the limitations and range for radiopotassium dating?
8. What parts of prehistory are not accurately dated?

www.mhhe.com/pricearch1

For more review material and study questions, please see the self-quizzes on your online learning center.

REFERENCES

Baillie, M. G. L. 1995. *A Slice through Time: Dendrochronology and Precision Dating.* London: Batsford.

Bowman, S. 1990. *Radiocarbon Dating.* Berkeley: University of California Press.

Fleming, S. J. 1979. *Thermoluminescence Techniques in Archaeology.* Oxford: Clarendon Press.

Nash, Stephen Edward, ed. 2000. *It's about Time: A History of Archaeological Dating in North America.* Salt Lake City: University of Utah Press.

Stokes, Marvin A., and Terah L. Smiley. 1996. *An Introduction to Tree-Ring Dating.* Tucson: University of Arizona Press.

Taylor, R. E., and M. J. Aitken. 1997. *Chronometric Dating in Archaeology.* New York: Plenum.

www.mhhe.com/pricearch1

For Internet references related to this chapter, please see the chapter links on your online learning center.

EUROPE
UKRAINE
BLACK SEA
ASIA
Mediterranean Sea
AFRICA

RUSSIA

UKRAINE

Sea
of
Azov

Crimea

MOLDOVA

Ryan and Pitman
study region

ROMANIA

B L A C K   S E A

Ryan and Pitman
study region

Ballard
study region

BULGARIA

Core site

Shipwreck
sites

Sinop
Karasu
beach

Ikiztepe

Present-day
shoreline

Deepest
point
-7,365 ft
-2,245 m

Ancient
shoreline
(500-foot
contour)

TURKEY

Bosporus

Istanbul

TURKEY

Sea
of
Marmara

Bittium
reticulatum

Abra alba

Mytilus
galloprovincialis

Turricaspia
caspia lincta

Dreissena
rostriformis
var. distincta

Geoarchaeology

INTRODUCTION: GEOLOGY AND ARCHAEOLOGY

The Black Sea, lying between Asia and Europe, is the second largest enclosed sea on earth after the Mediterranean. This great body of water—bounded by Russia, Georgia, Ukraine, Romania, Bulgaria, and Turkey—empties into the Mediterranean through the Bosporus (*BOS-per-us*) straits at Istanbul. This saltwater sea today is 1207 km (750 mi) long and 612 km (380 mi) wide, covering an area larger than the state of California, and it's more than 2000 m (7000 ft) at its deepest.

The illustration depicts some of the major aspects of what is known as the Black Sea Flood Hypothesis. The lower right is an artist's reconstruction of the proposed massive flooding of the Black Sea, with the waters of the Mediterranean pouring through the Bosporus straits. Upper right shows the change in mollusk shells that are used as evidence for a shift from fresh to salt water in the Black Sea. The illustration to the left depicts a core from the seafloor with changes in sediment that also are thought to reflect the flood. The small inset map in the center shows the location of the Black Sea between Europe and Asia.

In 1996, two marine geologists from Columbia University, William Ryan and Walter Pitman, published the Black Sea Flood Hypothesis. These geologists had spent 30 years studying the Black Sea and had repeatedly observed deposits of mussel shells at a depth of approximately 140 m (500 ft) on the sea floor. Because mussels normally live in shallow water, the presence of shells at 140 m caused the geologists to wonder. Radiocarbon dates from these mollusk shells were consistently around 6500 BC. The two geologists argued that the evidence pointed to a catastrophic change from a smaller freshwater lake to a large saltwater sea at that point in time. They suggested that the waters of the Mediterranean, gradually returning to their original levels with the warming of climate and the melting of continental ice following the end of the Pleistocene, reached a threshold at the Bosporus and broke through, killing the mollusks, quickly raising water levels, and flooding an enormous area of land around the borders of the freshwater lake.

Ryan and Pitman dramatically depicted this event—waters pouring over the Bosporus into the Black Sea with a volume 200 times that of Niagara Falls. They suggested this calamity was very likely the basis for the biblical story of Noah's flood. They argued that the flooding would have drowned a number of towns and villages around the shores of the former Black Sea with the water rising 15 cm (6 in) a day. They also hypothesized that the flood was probably responsible for the expansion of farming into Europe, as villagers from the former

www.mhhe.com/pricearch1

For preview material for this chapter, please see the chapter summary, outline, and objectives on your online learning center.

www.mhhe.com/pricearch1

For a Web-based activity on the Black Sea Flood Hypothesis, please see the Internet exercises on your online learning center.

shores of the freshwater lake moved inland. Ryan and Pitman's proposal was very popular, promulgated by the National Geographic Society and the media, and eventually involved underwater explorer Robert Ballard and millions of dollars in an unsuccessful search for submerged ancient communities on the Black Sea floor. It's a fascinating story.

It also appears to be wrong. A number of scientists who have worked in this region for years have examined the argument and pointed to various lines of powerful evidence to the contrary. Geologist Valentina Yanko-Hombach of the Avalon Institute of Applied Science points to thousands of samples that have been analyzed in detail and correlated with hundreds of isotope measurements. These data demonstrate that the depth of the Black Sea was much higher at the time Ryan and Pitman argue for the flooding.

Other geologists have examined marine sediments at the mouth of the Black Sea where it opens into the Mediterranean. This group found rich mud deposits that could only have come from the Black Sea. Their evidence documents continuous flow between the Black Sea and the Mediterranean for the last 10,000 years. Another team has examined the marine and coastal sediments along the Black Sea coast in northern Turkey. Their results indicate that the Black Sea was a freshwater lake prior to 6500 BC. The water level in this lake was 18 m (55 ft) below present but still far above the level of the outlet of the Bosporus at 35 m (110 ft) below sea level. The outlet is the level where the Black Sea and the Mediterranean meet underwater. This information reiterates the fact that the Black Sea was higher than the outlet and had been continuously flowing into the Mediterranean. It is likely that a change from fresh to salt water around the time of the proposed flood was responsible for the death of the mollusks, but a growing body of data suggests that Noah's flood did not happen in the Black Sea.

Geology is an essential aspect of the human past. Archaeological research concerned with geology and the earth sciences is called **geoarchaeology**. Geoarchaeologists work with archaeologists to examine the geological aspects of the archaeological record. Because archaeology is on and in the earth, the geological context of archaeological finds is very important. In addition, many of the raw materials used in the past came from geological deposits of stone, clay, and metal ores and these sources can be studied from the perspective of geoarchaeology.

Geoarchaeology is concerned with both regional (landscape) and/or local (site) scales of analysis. Many branches of geology are involved in geoarchaeology, for example, geomorphology (landforms), glaciology (glaciation), hydrology (bodies of water), pedology (soils), petrology (minerals), and sedimentology (sediments). In this chapter, emphasis is on geomorphology, stratigraphy, and micromorphology. Other aspects of the interface between geology and archaeology will be apparent in later chapters.

> *To find old sites, you must look in old dirt.*
>
> —Jonathan O. Davis, geoarchaeologist

geoarchaeology Archaeological research concerned with geology and the earth sciences.

geomorphology The branch of geology concerned with the study of the shape of the land; involves *classification*, description, origin, and change of land forms.

uniformitarianism Geological principle that the processes of erosion and deposition observed in action today also operated in the past.

GEOMORPHOLOGY

Geomorphology is a branch of geology concerned with the study of the shape of the earth's surface and involves the classification, description, origin, and development of landforms. The physical landscape is the place where past and present human activity takes place. Geomorphology tells us about the nature of that landscape and how it may have changed from past to present. Geomorphology can also tell us about the events that form, preserve, and destroy archaeological sites, those places on the landscape where human activities took place. Archaeologists need to know the basics of geomorphology in order to understand landscape and site contexts.

Geomorphological studies focus on deposition and erosion in building and changing the earth's surface. Geomorphologists follow the principle of **uniformitarianism**, that the processes of erosion and deposition seen today have always

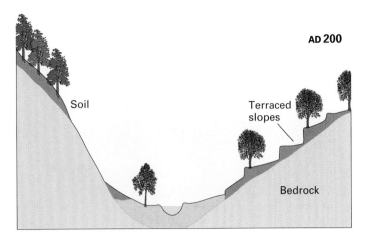

AD 200

Soil

Terraced slopes

Bedrock

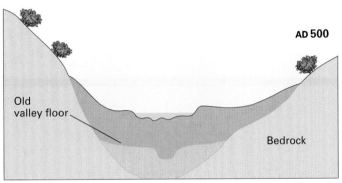

AD 500

Old valley floor

Bedrock

Fig. 9.1 A schematic reconstruction of the changing landscape of Roman Italy, with a typical Italian valley, in AD 200 (top) and in AD 500 (bottom). Intensive cultivation leads to erosion. Overgrazing and the need for wood for fuel and construction leads to deforestation. Eroded soils are deposited in the bottom of the valley, below the denuded slopes. The agricultural potential of the area declines steeply.

been at work. Thus, the present is the key to the past. Investigation of the present physical landscape is essential for the reconstruction of the prehistoric geography of a region.

Geomorphological changes over time will determine the survival of archaeological materials, in some cases destroying or deeply burying remains. Information on changes in the landscape allows archaeologists to evaluate the completeness of the archaeological record. Geomorphologists are interested in the dynamic landscape and changes over time. A dramatic transformation in a past landscape is schematically depicted in Fig. 9.1. The drawings show a typical Italian valley during the Roman period, ca. AD 200 (top) and AD 500 (bottom). Intensive agriculture, deforestation, and overgrazing resulted in the heavy erosion of soils in the valley, the eventual denudation of the landscape, and a dramatic loss in agricultural productivity. Moreover, much of the archaeological record of the area would be removed by the catastrophic erosion of the soils.

Fig. 9.2 is another geomorphological view of a landscape and depicts several important features. The illustration shows a meandering river building a **levee** across a relatively flat floodbasin. The river erodes and deposits soil—cuts and fills—along its channel, leaving a series of remnant and active features. The **oxbow lake** is an old meander in the river that was cut off and stranded, left as a lake when the river moved away. The series of **point bars** in the channel mark an area of active deposition. The river builds a levee, a raised bank, because regular flooding raises sediments out of the channel and onto the floodplain. The sediments grade from coarse to fine with distance from the river. The coarser sediments accumulate more rapidly, gradually building a raised levee. Changes in this basic pattern over time are a reflection of energy, climate, and other factors.

Sediment is an important term in geoarchaeology. Sediment is any particulate matter (clay, sand, silt, gravel, leaves, shell, and other materials) that can be

Daily it is forced home on the mind of the geologist that nothing, not even the wind that blows, is so unstable as the level of the crust of this earth.
—Charles Darwin, naturalist

levee   A raised bank created by repeated flooding.

oxbow lake   A stranded river meander left as a lake in a floodplain.

point bar   A low ridge of sand and gravel that forms underwater along the inner bank of a meandering stream.

sediment   Any particulate matter (*clay*, sand, silt, mud, leaves, shell, and other materials) that can be transported by water. Opposite of rock.

Fig. 9.2 Geomorphological views of landforms, sediments, and transport in an active, levee-building stream valley.

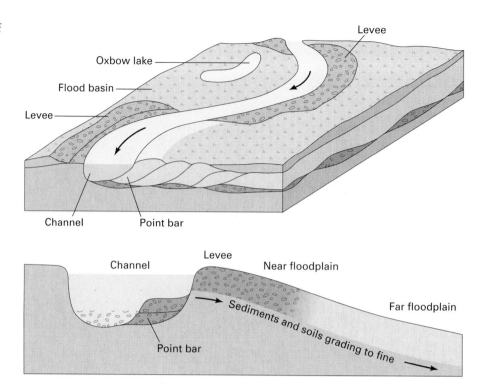

soil   Surface sediments weathered in situ.

weathering   Chemical and biological processes that break down and change the surface of the earth, altering its color, texture, or composition.

horizon   Layer or *assemblage* associated with geological strata or archaeological contents, e.g., usage includes a soil horizon, a cultural horizon; the geographic extent of similar artifacts and design in space.

pedologist   Soil scientist.

transported by water or other fluids. Sediments are eventually deposited as a layer of solid particles. They make up all of the earth's surface that is not water or rock. Virtually all buried archaeological materials are found in sedimentary deposits. Rocks take a long time to form and most archaeological materials are simply too young to end up in a rock layer. Volcanic eruptions can also bury prehistoric artifacts in lava, but that is an unusual situation.

Soil is a special kind of sedimentary deposit produced in situ by the weathering of the earth's surface. **Weathering** refers to the chemical and biological processes that operate to break down and change the surface of the earth, altering its color, texture, or composition. These processes include rainfall, frost, and plant and animal activity as major forces of change. Soils are not only found on the surface of the ground. Old soils can be buried by later deposits. Buried soils provide a useful marker of the location of former land surfaces.

Soils form on the surface of sediments and usually exhibit zones of weathering that reflect changes in the physical and chemical nature of the deposit. There are many different kinds of soils depending on the type of parent material and the conditions of weathering. Soils also vary with temperature, rainfall, and the type of vegetation present. Most soils, however, share common features related to the process of weathering and the solubility of the material, and most exhibit several strata or **horizons** that form during their development.

Pedologists (soil scientists) use a standard system to describe these horizons. The top of the soil is the organic or O horizon and contains dust, leaf litter, and other organic materials that accumulate on the surface. This horizon is normally dark in color from the decomposition of organic matter. The A horizon (a.k.a. topsoil) is also dark with organic matter and is a zone of generally loose and crumbly sediment. Water leaching through the topsoil dissolves various minerals and nutrients and moves them down through the ground into the B horizon or subsoil (Fig. 9.3). Most of the leached materials stop and accumulate in this zone. Subsoil is usually lighter in color, lower in organic material, and more densely packed. The C horizon is the transition zone where the breakdown of the parent

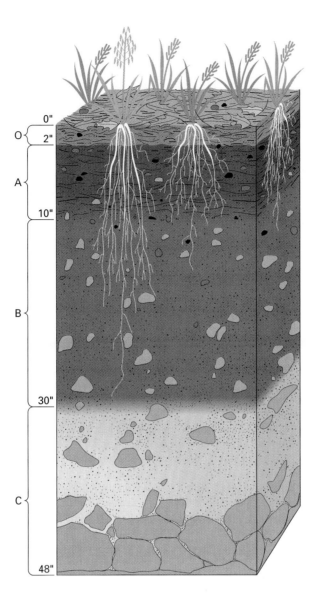

Fig. 9.3 A typical soil profile and the major soil horizons: O, organic horizon; A, topsoil; B, subsoil; and C, transition. Parent material (bedrock) is shown at the bottom as it gradually breaks down into sediment. The thickness of these horizons varies depending on the age of the soil, the kind of parent material, and the conditions of formation.

material is initiated. Beneath the C horizon is the unaltered parent material (bedrock or sediments). Soil chemistry and a variety of physical processes, along with plant and animal activities, dissolve and break down the parent material, changing rock into sediment.

Geomorphology is a complex science involving agents of change, sources of energy, time, climate, and how they affect the processes of landscape modification, such as weathering, erosion, transport, and deposition. The scope of geomorphology is enormous, ranging from continental scale events to very local phenomena, from oceans and glaciers, to raindrops and sand grains. Volcanic and tectonic forces create and mold the land surface. Weathering of the surface permits erosion and forms soils. Water, wind, and ice erode and transport sediments. Through time and geomorphological activity, the landscape changes and evolves. Such changes can be rapid and sometimes dramatic.

Geomorphology provides a means for archaeologists to understand the local landscape of a site or region and a way to investigate site formation processes and environmental change. The example of Troy described below illustrates this kind of study.

The violets in the mountains have broken the rocks.
—Tennessee Williams, playwright

EXAMPLE

GEOMORPHOLOGY AND HOMER'S TROY

www.mhhe.com/pricearch1

For a Web-based activity on Schlie-mann's excavations, please see the Internet exercises on your online learning center.

Homer's *Iliad*, the epic tale of the Trojan War—of Helen, Achilles, Agamemnon, of Priam, Hector, and Odysseus—is one of the more memorable sagas in human history. Elements of the story touch us all and celebrate the human condition. The lives and deaths of those ancient heroes are part of our heritage, and the Trojan horse is part of our vocabulary.

The authenticity of the story and the location of Troy, however, have been debated for centuries. The Greek author Homer wrote down this story several hundred years after it may have taken place. The manuscript was probably completed around 800 BC, while the Greeks who besieged the Trojans and finally tricked them into defeat lived around 1200 BC. Thus, the truth and accuracy of Homer's account is open to some question. Although later Greeks and the Romans never doubted Homer's account, by the beginning of the European Renaissance the location of Troy had been lost and the existence of the city denied.

Heinrich Schliemann was a German entrepreneur, treasure hunter, and self-proclaimed archaeologist. Schliemann went in search of Troy, in 1870, following the descriptions of Homer and the Roman author Strabo, excavating at the ancient tell of Hisarlik (*hiss-AR-lick*), 5 km (3 mi) inland from the coast of the Dardanelles in Turkey. Here the layers he exposed revealed a series of fortified cities and earlier towns going back 5000 years. Schliemann argued that this was Troy. Other scholars doubted that Schliemann had found Troy because the city was supposed to be on the coast; the Homeric and Roman descriptions of the place did not match the present-day setting of Hisarlik.

More recent excavations in the last 20 years have documented repeated attacks during the city's history and a major episode of destruction around the reputed date of the Trojan War. These excavations have also documented the fact that at the time of the Trojan War, Troy was a large city with an enormous citadel that controlled the waters between the Mediterranean and the Black seas. The fieldwork uncovered a lower city that covered about 75 acres and was surrounded by a U-shaped ditch cut into the limestone bedrock that was 4 m (12 ft) wide and 2 m (6 ft) deep.

Resolving the question of Troy's location is a good lesson in geoarchaeology. Geologist John Kraft of the University of Delaware and his colleagues studied this part of northwestern Turkey intensively for many years. To reconstruct the geological and environmental history of the area around Hisarlik, they made a series of deep borings to obtain samples of sediment and were able to produce a series of paleo-geomorphological maps showing the changes in topography and coastlines over time (Fig. 9.4). In addition, they used the descriptions of local geographic features in the writings of Homer and Strabo to locate reported places around the site.

Homer's *Iliad* describes the battle between the Greeks and Trojans at the Scamander River. The Trojans attack "on the swelling of the plain" near the Greek ships, but are driven back to the river by Achilles. "But when they came to the ford of the fair-flowing river . . . Achilles broke the Trojan line and sent half the enemy flying in rout across the plain toward Troy . . . the remainder were pinned back against the deep stream with its silver eddies . . . cowered below the overhang." Kraft and colleagues interpret this as a description of the upper and middle stretches of the river plain in front of Troy where the river would have been deep with cut banks and strong currents.

Kraft and his colleagues have documented dramatic geomorphological changes in the landscape since 3000 BC. At that time, a large bay of the sea opened to the north of Hisarlik and continued to the south another 5 km (3 mi) to the mouth of the Scamander River. The sea level was 2 m (6 ft) higher and the climate was somewhat warmer than today. Over the next 2000 years, this bay began to fill with sediments as the sea rose to modern levels. Deforestation of the region due to cultivation and the cutting of firewood resulted in the heavy erosion of soils, which washed into the bay. By the time of Homer's Troy, at least half the bay had filled and the coastlines were being reshaped by **tectonic** activity. The deep layers at Troy record a number of prehistoric earthquakes. By the time of Schliemann's visit, the bay was completely filled and Hisarlik was an inland site, quite a distance from the sea. The geoarchaeology of

Troy

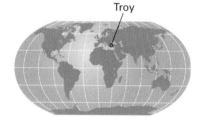

tectonic Geological forces that move and deform the earth's crust.

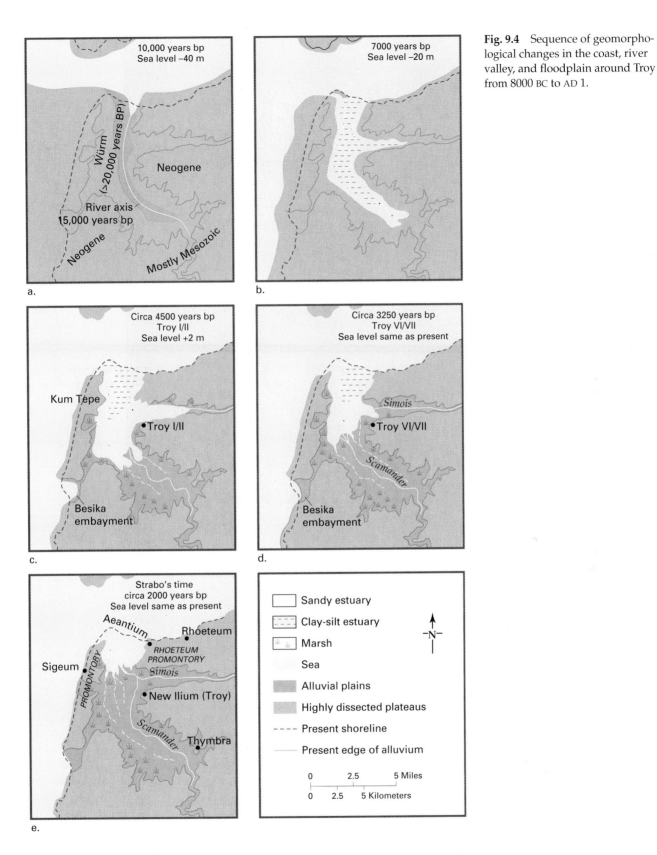

Fig. 9.4 Sequence of geomorphological changes in the coast, river valley, and floodplain around Troy from 8000 BC to AD 1.

Troy reminds us that the surface of the earth is a dynamic place, changing constantly through time. Schliemann must have had a notion of these changes when he selected the mound of Hisarlik for excavation.

Fig. 9.5 A computer graphic showing a hypothetical excavation in Great Britain with various layers containing a range of artifacts from the plastic bag at the top to Roman helmet and vase on the floor.

STRATIGRAPHY

Excavations open holes into the ground and reveal buried layers of earth (Fig. 9.5). Although it is artifacts that usually attract attention, these layers are also a key part of archaeological research. A layer, feature, or structure without artifacts may tell us a great deal about a site, but an artifact out of its stratigraphic context is of much less interest.

Archaeologists dig square holes so that the layers, and the relationships among them, will be more distinct (Fig. 9.6). The term *stratigraphy* is used for the sequence of layers, or strata, in the ground. Stratigraphy is often described as a kind of layer cake, but actually the analogy of a book lying on its side is more accurate. The layers are pages of information, one on top of the other, from the beginning of the story, or sequence, to the end.

Stratigraphy has been a fundamental basis for understanding the past in archaeology since its inception. It provided essential information about the chronological relationships of archaeological materials long before sophisticated dating methods became available. Archaeologists, like geologists and paleontologists, use stratigraphy to study the layers of earth, following the principle of **superposition**: the lowest layers are older and younger materials are higher. This simple obser-

stratigraphy   A sequence of layers in the ground.

superposition   Principle that governs the interpretation of *stratigraphy*—in a sequence the oldest layers are on the bottom and the youngest layers are on top.

Fig. 9.6 The dramatic black and white stratigraphy of the Swiss lake dwelling sites. These bands are alternating layers of dark cultural deposits and natural white lake deposits. Wooden posts can be seen in the sections, part of the construction for the lake dwellings. This area of lake deposits was drained so that the archaeologists could work under dry conditions.

vation allows scientists to study a sequence of events through time and to determine also that artifacts found in lower layers are older than artifacts found in upper layers. Such a sequence is the basis for chronology in archaeology. The ability to say that one type of object is older than or younger than another has allowed archaeologists to give chronological order to the past.

Understanding the way deposits accumulated to form the layers of an archaeological site requires an awareness of stratigraphy. Knowledge of stratigraphy is essential to understand the history of the site, the activities that took place, and the relationships among the archaeological remains that are present. This is the study of "strata," the accumulation of layers of soil, sediments, refuse, building debris, and other material in the ground.

The thickness of a layer is not determined so much by the length of time that it took to accumulate, but by the natural or human activities involved in the deposition of the materials. Heaps of shells from edible mollusks may accumulate very rapidly into high shell **middens**; the collapse of houses with earth or sod walls results in very thick layers; stone tool manufacture can produce extensive debris. On the other hand, the place where an animal was killed and butchered— a kill site—may leave almost no archaeological trace.

Archaeologists have traditionally recorded the layers they dig through in great detail, using drawings, photographs, and written descriptions. Drawings of stratigraphic sections take a great deal of time and study. Distinguishing different layers and features is not an easy task and yet the information is critical to understanding the archaeological site. Fig. 9.7 shows an elaborate section drawing from Gatecliff Shelter in Nevada. The cowboy at the top of the section is there to provide a sense of scale. Radiocarbon dates from different layers are shown to the right of the section drawing.

Each layer is numbered and described in terms of texture, color, moisture, contents, and so forth. Soil color is often recorded using a Munsell soil color chart, displaying many hues and colors that can be compared to the soil in a stratigraphic section (Fig. 9.8). Recording the color of the soil allows a more detailed description of the stratigraphy to be made.

Sediments in each layer are distinguished as to size. Gravel, sand, silt, and clay are the major categories of sediments. Gravel, sand, silt, and clay particles

> *Essentially, all life depends upon the soil. . . . There can be no life without soil and no soil without life; they have evolved together.*
> —Charles E. Kellogg, soil scientist

midden Any substantial accumulation of garbage or waste at a locus of human activity; archaeological deposits of trash and/or shells that accumulate in heaps and mounds. A shell midden is a specific type of midden composed largely of mollusk shells.

Fig. 9.7 Stratigraphic section drawing at Gatecliff Shelter, Nevada. Seven meters (22 ft) of deposits are shown in the drawing from 4000 BC to the present. The drawing is intended to show the details of the stratigraphy and the relationships and depths of the layers.

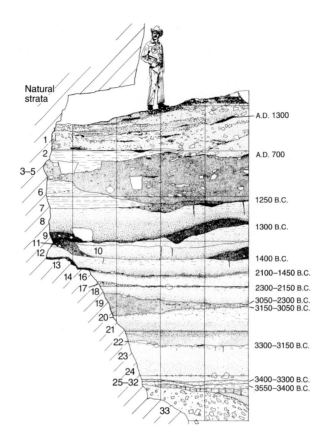

Natural strata

A.D. 1300

A.D. 700

1250 B.C.

1300 B.C.

1400 B.C.
2100–1450 B.C.
2300–2150 B.C.
3050–2300 B.C.
3150–3050 B.C.

3300–3150 B.C.

3400–3300 B.C.
3550–3400 B.C.

Fig. 9.8 The Munsell soil color chart. The colors in the book are compared to a handful of dry soil to select an appropriate tint and hue.

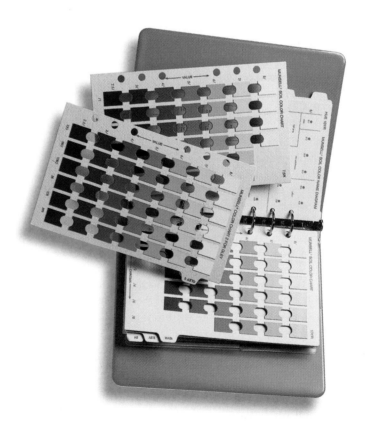

TABLE 9.1	Categories of sediments and size criteria.
Gravel	> 2.0 mm
Very coarse sand	2.0–1.0 mm
Coarse sand	1.0–0.5 mm
Medium sand	0.5–0.25 mm
Fine sand	0.25–0.10 mm
Very fine sand	0.10–0.05 mm
Silt	0.05–0.002 mm
Clay	< 0.002 mm
Pebbles	2–64 mm (U.S. quarter)
Cobbles	64–256 mm (baseball size)
Boulders	> 256 mm

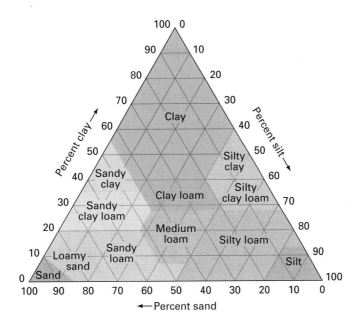

Fig. 9.9 The soil triangle. Terminology for soil types based on sand, silt, and clay proportion.

are defined by their size. The standard size ranges for these different kinds of sediments are provided in Table 9.1.

Soil texture refers to the mixture of sand, silt, and clay particles in a soil. Pedologists use the percentage of each component—sand, silt, and clay—to define the texture of soils. The diagram in Fig. 9.9—the soil triangle—shows the various terms, for example, sandy clay, loamy sand, that are used. The three sides of the diagram show the percent of the three components of sediments: sand, silt, and clay. For a particular sediment, the percentage of each of these three components is measured and plotted on the graph. The position of that point on the graph determines the designation of the sediment. For example, 30% sand, 10% clay, and 60% silt would be a silty loam.

In nature, the processes of deposition and erosion by ice, wind, water, and waves are largely responsible for the development of stratigraphic sequences. At archaeological sites, humans are a major force in the movement and redeposition of sediments, complicating the stratigraphy. Human activities at a site often

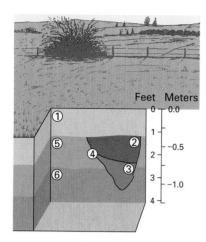

Fig. 9.10 A small excavation showing the stratigraphic profile with three major layers (1, 5, 6) and a buried pit (4) with two kinds of fill (2, 3). A basic description of the layers might be as follows. In the description, "sterile" means no archaeological finds. (1) Plow zone of red-brown, sandy humus; little archaeological material. (2) Dark brown silty sand with fine layers, windblown; sterile. (3) Yellow sandy clay, washed in; artifacts present. (4) Outline of pit—interface between pit fill and layers 5 and 6. (5) Brown sandy clay with soil formation; sterile. (6) Subsoil, dark sandy clay, water deposited, perhaps old lake deposit; sterile.

cut   Geomorphological term for erosion of *sediments,* also human digging.

fill   Geomorphological term for deposition of *sediments,* also human filling.

sterile   Containing no archaeological materials.

plow zone   The upper part of soil layers that has been disturbed by plowing.

plan view   A bird's-eye or top-down view of a *site* or *region.* A kind of map of the features and characteristics of a place. A standard representation of archaeological *sites* and areas.

profile   A cross-section of archaeological or geological deposits showing the *stratigraphy,* sequence of layers. Also, the cross-section of the walls of a *ceramic* vessel, a measure of shape.

micromorphology   The study of *anthropogenic sediments* at a *microscopic* level.

anthropogenic   Created or produced by human activity, e.g., anthropogenic soils are a result of human activity.

included digging, construction, burning, burial, and the like. Such visible changes in the ground at an archaeological site are called features. The terms **cut** and **fill** are sometimes used to describe human activities that modify the ground. Cutting is removing sediment, such as digging a pit; filling is adding sediment, such as filling a pit. The pit shown in the simple stratigraphic profile in Fig. 9.10 is one such feature.

This sequence shows a **plow zone** on top of a soil developed in former lake deposits. Artifacts in the plow zone (layer 1) indicate that the actual surface at the time of the prehistoric activity has been plowed through and mixed. The absence of artifacts and the soil development in layer 5 indicates this is a natural layer. Layer 6 is the underground, subsoil across the area. The pit (cut 4) was dug from a ground surface somewhere in the plow zone. The pit may have been used for storage, but after abandonment it gradually filled with washed-in sediments (fill 2). Eventually, blowing sand and silt covered the rest of the depression (fill 3). The top part of the pit has been plowed away.

An even more complex stratigraphy with many layers and features is shown in Fig. 9.11. Cuts (such as pits, ditches, postholes, or graves) disrupt the normal sequence of layers. However, superposition still works. The pit or ditch is younger than (and stratigraphically above) the layers through which it has been cut. The fill of the pit or ditch will be younger than the cut itself. A layer that covers both the fill and the surrounding soil will be more recent. These layers and features are observed from changes in texture, color, and content. They are recorded both in **plan view** (horizontal) and in **profile** (vertical section). Through the observation of episodes of soil removal and redeposition, construction, and superpositioning, it is possible to determine the sequence of deposits and thus the order of events at the site. Meticulous excavations are necessary to sort out such complex stratigraphy.

MICROMORPHOLOGY

Geoarchaeological studies span the scale from continental to the barely visible. Climate change and catastrophic events are visible on a global or regional level. Other evidence is found under the microscope. **Micromorphology** is a rapidly growing area of geoarchaeology involving the study of **anthropogenic** sediments at a microscopic level. These sediments usually come from past living surfaces where the almost invisible trash and dust of everyday life accumulates. Standard soil analysis techniques generally do not work well with anthropogenic sediments because of the inclusion of a variety of organic and artifactual material. Identification of the contents of ancient living surfaces and how they formed using micromorphology provides greater insight on past behavior.

Undisturbed blocks of sediment are removed from a site and taken to a laboratory. The block is embedded with polyester resin to harden it, and then a thin slice is cut and polished so that it can be examined at 20–200 magnification under a petrographic microscope. This instrument is made specifically for identifying minerals in sediments and stone.

Under the microscope, important observations include **composition** (the mineral and organic contents), **texture** (size and sorting of sediments), and especially the **fabric**—the geometric relationships—of the constituents. At the early Neolithic site of Catalhöyük (*sha-TALL-who-yuke*) in Turkey, for example, micromorphology revealed that some of the house floors had been plastered with a thin coat of clay at least fifty times. These layers of plaster incorporated many small finds of plant remains and other evidence. At Keatley Creek, examination of samples from the house floors revealed the compaction of the living surface and a variety of micro-artifacts. This research is discussed in the next section of this chapter.

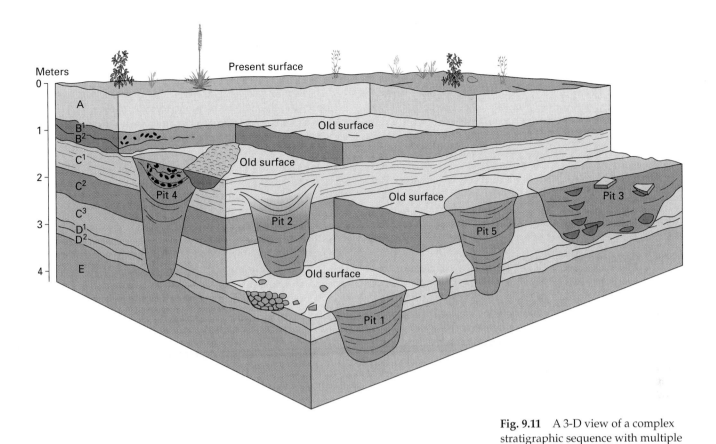

Meters
0 —
A
1 —
B¹
B²
C¹
2 —
C²
Pit 4
C³
3 —
D¹
D²
4 —
E

Present surface

Old surface

Old surface

Old surface

Old surface

Pit 2

Pit 5

Pit 3

Pit 1

Fig. 9.11 A 3-D view of a complex stratigraphic sequence with multiple cultural layers and pits.

 EXAMPLE ∼∼∼∼∼∼∼∼∼∼∼∼∼∼∼∼∼∼∼∼∼∼∼

KEATLEY CREEK

Keatley (*KEAT-lee*) Creek was a major focus of archaeological investigations directed by Brian Hayden of Simon Fraser University between 1986 and 1996. The site is an unusually large prehistoric village of hunter-gatherers located on the Fraser River in the interior of British Columbia, Canada. The site is visible today as a concentration of more than 100 large depressions or pits that mark the location of the houses of the former inhabitants (Fig. 9.15). Geoarchaeology was involved in various aspects of the investigations.

The main part of the site is about 4 hectares (10 acres) in area, the size of a large city block. The first house pits appear to have been dug shortly after 800 BC, but the major period of occupation ran from AD 300 to 1200 with some interruption. Population at that time is estimated to have been approximately 1200 people.

There were a total of 120 houses at the site. Measurement of the diameter of all 120 houses at the site reveals clear differences in their size. Fig. 9.16 shows a histogram of house size with three groups of houses, small, medium, and large. Small houses range from 4 m to 12 m (12–36 ft) in diameter; medium houses are 13 to 16 m (40–50 ft) in diameter; there are six large houses greater than 16 m (50 ft) in diameter. The largest of these house depressions are 18 to 21 m (more than 60 ft) in diameter, almost the size of a tennis court in area. These great structures were among the largest buildings in prehistoric North America.

The goal of the archaeological project was to examine the economic and social organization that made large villages and households possible prehistorically and to examine potential social and status differences among the households. In order to answer such questions, special attention was given to the houses and the sediments in and around the houses. The first step was to test a number of the house pits to determine which would be more suitable for excavation.

Keatley Creek

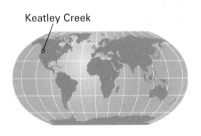

∼∼∼∼∼∼∼∼∼∼∼∼∼∼∼∼∼∼∼∼∼∼∼∼∼

composition The mineral and organic contents in a *petrographic* thin section.

texture The size and sorting of *sediments,* for example, in a *petrographic* thin section.

fabric The geometric relationship of the constituents in a *petrographic* thin section.

Micromorphology **257**

The Harris Matrix

The **Harris Matrix** is a method for describing intricate stratigraphy in a schematic way to reduce some of the complexity of drawings, photographs, and wordy descriptions. It is a kind of stratigraphic diagram or flow chart, showing layers, structures, cuts, and fills from more recent at the top to oldest at the bottom. It is not a realistic illustration like a traditional section drawing. The "matrix" is a chart of lines linking numbered boxes, which represent individual layers, deposits, features, and **interfaces** in the profile. Its purpose is to document the sequence of layers, features, and their connections at the site in time, not their physical characteristics.

Edward Harris was involved in the excavation of very complex historical, urban sites with multiple episodes of building, leveling, and rebuilding in London, England. Harris developed this method because he was unhappy with traditional archaeological techniques for recording stratigraphy, based on geological concepts. The Harris system emphasizes the kinds of stratigraphic elements that are found where people live: layers, features, and interfaces. Layers are the standard geological unit of analysis, based on the strata of rocks and sediments that form in nature. At archaeological sites, layers are sedimentary deposits that accumulate through cultural or natural processes.

Features, as we have seen, are the pits, burials, ditches, wells, walls, and the like that people make by digging and building and doing. Features can be created through removal or addition, through digging or depositing. Features can be vertical (e.g., graves, pits, postholes) or horizontal (e.g., middens, piles of rubble, soil removed from pits). These activities have few counterparts in nature. Features are thus an important component of the Harris system for recording stratigraphy.

An *interface* is the term Harris uses for surfaces at a site that were areas of activity before they were buried. Interfaces include living areas and the surface of features. Interface is a somewhat difficult concept, but it is basically a surface or place of use, in contrast to deposits that are not places of activity but places of fill. Since many sites contain lots of features, there are often more interfaces than layers.

Harris thinks of the matrix as a kind of calendar, a way of displaying the relative sequence (which came first?) of deposits in an archaeological site. In this way, as well, the Harris Matrix differs from traditional stratigraphic methods which invoke the law of superpositioning to indicate that each layer is older than the one above it. At locations of human residence or activity, with episodes of digging and filling at various locations at the site, superpositioning does not always apply since the sediment removed from a pit can be deposited on top of a later, younger layer.

Constructing a Harris Matrix involves boxes and lines and the relationships between them. Boxes are used to assign numbers to layers, features, and interfaces. A simple stratigraphic situation is depicted in Fig. 9.12 as both a standard section drawing and a Harris Matrix. In this case, there are two layers of sediments on top of the original subsoil along the outline of a pit (feature) that was dug down through the earth and later filled with two different sediments. Each of the layers, pit fills, and the pit cut (interface) is marked with a number. This simple profile exhibits the three major characteristics of stratigraphy: layer, cut, and fill. Level 1 refers to the topsoil or plowzone. Numbers 3, 4, and 5 are associated with pit; the boxes with these numbers are indented to indicate that the layers sit under 2 and in the subzone. Numbers 3 and 4 are layers of fill in the pit; number 5 is the outline of the pit that was cut or dug into the sublayer. Level 5 is the interface between the sublayer and the fill of the pit. Recording the interface between features and layers is an important aspect of the Harris system.

A more complex stratigraphic situation is shown in Fig. 9.13 with the remains of a buried wall. The traditional section drawing is shown in the upper left. The numbers 2 and 6 indicate interfaces in the stratigraphy. A Harris Matrix on the lower left shows all the relationships among layers, features, and interfaces indicated by connecting lines. In the middle Harris diagram, the redundant or duplicate lines have been removed. This is the normal way in which a Harris Matrix is published. The drawing on the right is a three-dimensional Harris Matrix and provides a clearer picture of the deposits and their relationships over time.

www.mhhe.com/pricearch1

For a Web-based activity on the Harris Matrix, please see the Internet exercises on your online learning center.

Harris Matrix A method for depicting intricate archaeological stratigraphy in a schematic way.

interface The term used in the Harris Matrix for surfaces at a site that were places of activity before they were buried—for example, the surface of a pit.

Test excavations were conducted at all of the large houses and at 18 of the medium and small house pits, approximately 20% of all the structures at the site. The testing indicated which of the houses had intact living floors and also provided good information on the chronology of the site. Major excavations followed the testing and uncovered one large, one medium, and three small house pits (Fig. 9.17).

Pithouses were still in use only a century ago in the area, so the construction techniques are well known. A circular hole with a flat bottom about 1 m (3 ft) deep and from 3 to 21 m (10 to 65 ft) in diameter was dug through the topsoil and into the glacial gravel that underlay the site. A conical roof frame was erected by bracing

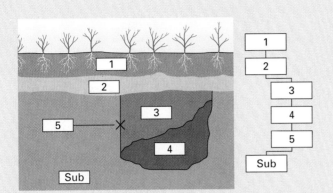

Fig. 9.12 A stratigraphy on one side of a square excavation unit. The drawing on the left is called a profile, or cross-section, of the layers. On the right is the Harris Matrix, which shows this sequence schematically.

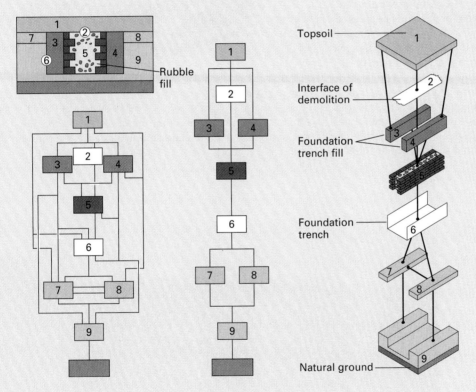

Rubble fill

Topsoil

Interface of demolition

Foundation trench fill

Foundation trench

Natural ground

Fig. 9.13 The stratigraphy of a buried wall. In a traditional stratigraphic drawing (upper left), numbers 2 and 6 indicate interfaces in the stratigraphy. A Harris Matrix on the lower left shows all the relationships indicated by lines. The middle diagram has the redundant or duplicate lines removed. The drawing on the right is a 3-D view of the Harris Matrix.

logs against the walls of the pit and binding them together at the top. This structure was covered with branches and then with either reed mats or the dirt that had been removed from the hole. A hole near the center of the roof was both a door and a chimney.

Excavation of the pithouses at Keatley Creek revealed the same kind of construction with some differences in the roofing material. The earlier houses at the site had a roof cover of mats, replaced in later periods by earthen roofs. The sequence of construction and abandonment could be determined from the stratigraphy of the earthen mounds left around the rim of the house pit (Fig. 9.18).

The Petrographic Microscope

Archaeologists use many different kinds of tools from trowels to brushes to atom accelerators and mass spectrometers. But an optical microscope remains one of the most useful pieces of equipment. Most archaeological laboratories have at least one microscope, usually binocular, and there is a growing interest in petrographic microscopes for micromorphology, ceramic analysis, and mineral identification.

A binocular microscope, with two independent microscope tubes focused on the same object, is designed to provide low magnifications of objects in three dimensions. The large, bright stereoscopic field of the microscope is ideal for examining a variety of materials, including plant remains, small artifacts, usewear, and cutmarks.

A **petrographic microscope** is a specialized version of a binocular microscope (Fig. 9.14). A petrographic microscope is specifically designed for the study of thin sections—slices of rock, pottery, or other materials—ground and polished to a thickness of only 0.3 mm. This slice, or section, is so thin that light passes through the material. Two kinds of light are used for viewing the contents of the thin section, normal and polarized light. Polarized light is light that is constrained to a single plane. Many minerals change color and brightness when polarized light passes through them. These changes are a useful way of identifying specific minerals in the thin section. The identifica-

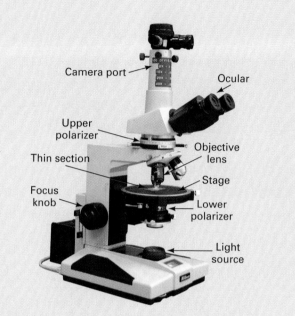

Fig. 9.14   A petrographic microscope with component parts labeled.

tion of the minerals and other materials allows the analyst to study the source and composition of the contents of the thin section.

Fig. 9.15   The site of Keatley Creek in interior British Columbia, Canada, along the Fraser River. The ancient housepits at the site are clearly visible.

petrographic microscope   A specialized version of a binocular microscope designed for the study of thin sections of rock or pottery.

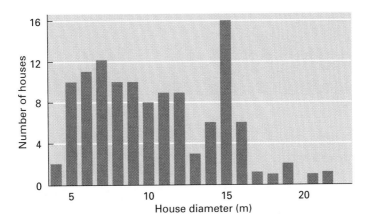

Fig. 9.16 Diameter of the house pits at Keatley Creek.

Fig. 9.17 Excavated floor of the larger house pit at Keatley Creek.

The living floors of these houses provided substantial information on both contents and context. Several techniques were used to study the house floors, including micromorphology and soil chemistry (described below and also in Chapter 15, "Archaeometry").

Paul Goldberg of Boston University did the micromorphology study. Fig. 9.19 is a slide from his investigations. Samples for thin sections were taken from different contexts at the site, including roof and floor deposits, hearths and ash layers, and the fill of pits. Sample thin sections were examined under a petrographic microscope using different kinds of light and magnification. Fig. 9.19 shows a thin section from a house floor as a dense, compact sandy silt in the lower part of the photo. Deposits associated with floors or occupation surfaces were generally richer in fine mineral matter, which produces the slightly lighter color of these layers. The amount of anthropogenic material—bone, ash, burned stones, or fine charcoal—in the thin sections of the house floors was surprisingly low. There was, however, usually a 1–2 mm thick deposit of salmon bones directly on top of the living surface of the floor. In addition, in this sample there was a gap or crack between the house floor and the upper deposits, likely left by the decay of vegetation, perhaps mats on the floor. During excavation, the upper deposits peeled away easily from the more compact house floor. Micromorphological studies revealed the nature of this house floor and the deposits

Fig. 9.18 The formation process involved in two cycles of construction and abandonment of a pithouse. These activities resulted in stratified deposits of sediments and refuse around the edge of the house pit. (a) Initial excavation of the house pit. (b) Construction of first house with mat roof and accumulation of midden around edges of house. (c) Abandonment and removal of timbers. (d) Construction of second house with earthen roof and more accumulation of midden. (e) Final abandonment and erosion.

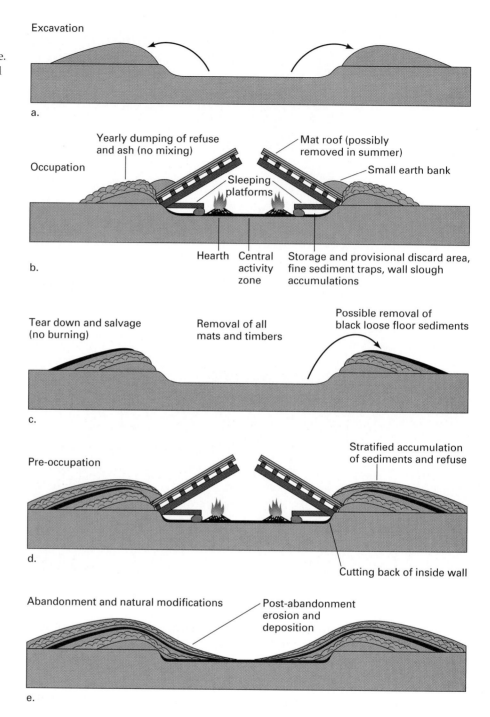

Excavation

a.

Yearly dumping of refuse and ash (no mixing)

Mat roof (possibly removed in summer)

Occupation

Small earth bank

Sleeping platforms

Hearth   Central activity zone

Storage and provisional discard area, fine sediment traps, wall slough accumulations

b.

Tear down and salvage (no burning)

Removal of all mats and timbers

Possible removal of black loose floor sediments

c.

Pre-occupation

Stratified accumulation of sediments and refuse

Cutting back of inside wall

d.

Abandonment and natural modifications

Post-abandonment erosion and deposition

e.

that accumulated on it, both during and after use. These studies helped with the identification of the floor construction and provided information on the distribution of different kinds of small waste material from different activities.

Excavations of this house revealed further details of its construction and artifacts (Fig. 9.20). The significant architectural features in the house include two sleeping platforms. These platforms are raised earthen benches where members of the co-residential group slept and did a variety of other things. The hearth and cache pit are two other important features. The hearth was the center of domestic activities, and specific work areas can be seen to the west and southeast of this fireplace. The cache pit is a storage facility beneath the house floor where various foodstuffs and supplies were kept. These areas can be detected in the soil chemistry study, which

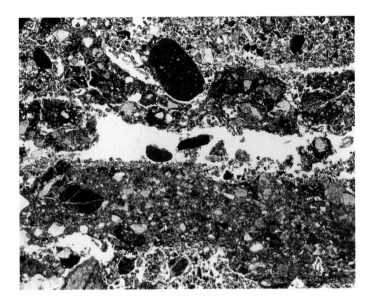

Fig. 9.19 Micromorphology slide of the house floor from Keatley Creek. The lower half of the photo shows the house floor as compact fine sediments covered by less compact material. Polarized Light; width of the photo is about 3.5 mm.

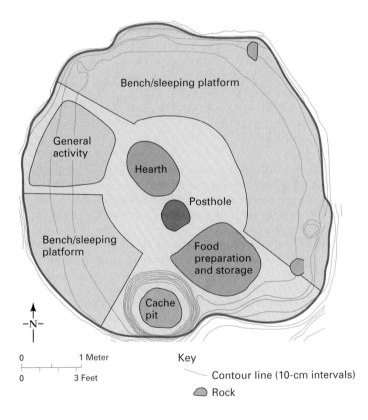

Fig. 9.20 Reconstruction of House 9 with major features of sleeping platforms, hearth, cache pit, food preparation and storage, and activity areas.

showed that the earthen benches and cache pit had very low levels of phosphorus compared to higher concentrations in the activity areas.

The excavations at Keatley Creek provided detailed information on the houses and differences among them. The larger houses belonged to elite families who lived with hereditary servants. The wealthy owners lived on one side of the large house, where the larger hearths, the bigger storage pits, and the better tools and ornaments were found, and their servants or poor relations inhabited the other side. The deer bones were largely from the rich side. The fish bones from the wealthy part of the house were mostly ribs and vertebrae from the best parts of the fish, while the tailbones were found on the poorer side.

The Chemistry of House Floors

A soil chemistry study of the Keatley Creek site was carried out by Bill Middleton of the Rochester Institute of Technology. Samples of sediment were taken from a 1-m (ca. 3-ft) grid on the floor of the house. The concentrations present were determined in parts per million for twelve different elements. Fig. 9.21 shows the outline of the house floor and the distribution of the element phosphorus. In this example, the northern half of the house has very little phosphorus while the southern half has substantially more with the exception of a small, circular area. Phosphorus levels are higher in areas of ash, food remains, and body wastes. Other elements in the study also showed distinctive patterning that coincided with the activity areas reconstructed for the house interior. More information on soil chemistry in archaeology can be found in Chapter 15, "Archaeometry."

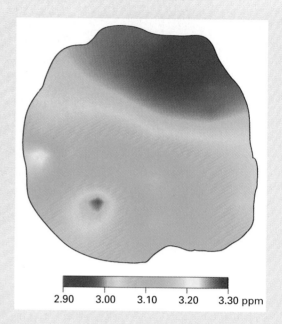

2.90   3.00   3.10   3.20   3.30 ppm

Fig. 9.21 The distribution of phosphorus in the sediments on the living floor of House 9, a small structure. Higher concentrations are shown in green, yellow, and red. In this example, the northern half of the house has very little phosphorus while the southern half has substantially more, with the exception of a small, circular area.

On the basis of the analysis of fish remains at the site, it appears that large households probably owned or restricted access to some of the more lucrative fishing and hunting areas. The wealth of these elite families was based on ownership of the best fishing places, but they also controlled the prime sites for hunting deer and collecting berries.

Elite families or individuals were also in control of long-distance trade and prestige goods in the region. The villages were in strategic locations to catch and trade large numbers of prime salmon for drying and exchange. Evidence of trade with the coast is abundant at the site, as well as evidence for ownership of resources, wealth accumulation, and hierarchical socioeconomic organization. Prestige technologies included crafted local materials (rare stone adzes, copper jewelry, and carved antler or bone) as well as raw materials obtained from long distances (such as coastal shells, whalebone, obsidian, and moose antler). The seashore was some 120 km (80 mi) west of Keatley Creek as the crow flies.

Geoarchaeology and environmental studies can also tell us about the demise of Keatley Creek. Climatic warming and environmental richness may have been associated with the rise of larger villages and social hierarchy in this region after AD 300. In the same vein, climatic deterioration is a possible cause of the disappearance of other sites throughout the area around AD 800. Another factor may have been a major landslide on the Fraser River that may have blocked salmon runs for years or decades, destroying the economy of these remarkable communities. Investigation of these factors continues.

Geoarchaeology played a big role in the study of Keatley Creek. The formation processes of the pithouses required detailed stratigraphic study. Micromorphology was used to analyze the house floors and their contents, and soil chemistry of the house floors was able to provide information confirming areas of specific activity within these structures.

Fig. 9.22 Two walls and the floor of a Maya house buried beneath almost 5 m (16 ft) of volcanic ash at the site of Joya de Cerén in El Salvador almost 500 years ago. The difference between the brown soils of the former land surface and the gray and white layers of volcanic ash is very clear.

CATASTROPHE

Major catastrophes are recorded in various ways in the archaeological record. Earthquakes, volcanic eruptions, floods, tidal waves, and major conflagrations usually leave stratigraphic and geomorphological traces. Some of these can be very dramatic. The site of Joya de Cerén was a small Maya village buried beneath almost 5 m (16 ft) of volcanic ash around AD 500 in El Salvador (Fig. 9.22).

Among other famous examples are the Roman towns of Pompeii and Herculaneum, buried by ash and lava from the August 23, AD 79, eruption of Mount Vesuvius near Naples, Italy. A number of enormous longhouses at the site of Ozette on the northwest coast of Washington state were buried under a great mudslide sometime around AD 1500. The story of the explosive eruption of the island of Thera in the Aegean in the middle of the second millennium BC is told in Chapter 13. The proposed Black Sea flood, related at the beginning of this chapter, is of course another possible example.

CONCLUSIONS

Geology and archaeology find common ground in the field of geoarchaeology—the application of geological methods to the solution of archaeological questions. Understanding the landscape and sediments in which archaeological materials are found is an essential part of explaining past human behavior. Geology has a variety of methods and theories about the formation of the earth that are useful in archaeology. Geomorphology is the branch of geology specifically concerned with the features found on the surface of the earth and the processes that create them. Changes in the landscape over time have significant effects on human life and must be documented. The example of Troy in this chapter provides a dramatic case of landscape changes, to the point that the ancient place no longer resembled the fabled battlefield of Achilles and Hector and debate about the location of the site raged for decades. The eruptions of Vesuvius and Thera wiped out large towns and killed thousands of people.

Stratigraphy is a fundamental aspect of archaeology, essential for documenting and understanding the context and relative age of buried materials. Stratigraphy

While the farmer holds the title to the land, actually it belongs to all the people because civilization itself rests upon the soil.
—Thomas Jefferson, president

refers to the strata, or layers, that make up the sedimentary deposits at all archaeological sites. The site stratigraphy provides information on the geological history of the site, the kinds of depositional and erosional events that took place, human activities that left traces of filling or cutting of deposits, as well as chemical and biological traces of human and natural activities at the site. Stratigraphic study has traditionally been done by detailed descriptions of layers accompanied by drawings and photographs. In recent years, a new system for depicting the sequence of layers at a site, known as a Harris Matrix, has come into use. This technique is used in combination with traditional methods to provide a more comprehensive record of layers and activities. The Harris Matrix emphasizes cutting as well as filling and records the interfaces between layers as an important aspect of the events that took place. In this way, the Harris system is better for defining human activities at a site than traditional methods.

Another method of geoarchaeology involves the microscopic study of small sections of anthropogenic or archaeological deposits. Study of the sediments that accumulated where people lived reveals the tiny fragments of food, artifacts, and construction material that was used and helps archaeologists to understand how those sediments accumulated. The geomorphological work at Keatley Creek helped in the definition of the house floors and revealed how those floors had formed.

A dramatic aspect of geoarchaeology involves the study of natural catastrophes in the past and their effect on human lives. A variety of events, including volcanic eruptions, floods, and earthquakes, struck human settlements in the past, just as they do today. Some of these events were enormous in scale and affected large communities and sizable regions. Well-known examples of this include the eruptions of Vesuvius and Thera, which wiped out large towns and killed thousands of people.

ROMAN STRATIGRAPHY

A drawing of site stratigraphy (Fig. 9.23) shows a sequence of deposits in the ground, involving several different episodes of human activity. This could be a Roman building along the Adriatic Coast of eastern Italy. Careful study and analysis of the layers make it possible to determine the sequence of events that took place there. The basal layer of sterile earth was first covered by a layer of shells and charcoal that accumulated as a pile or midden of garbage from eating food like clams or mussels. Note that a Greek coin dating to ca. 600 BC was found in this layer. This shell layer was then covered naturally by sandy clay, deposited by a river flood.

Later, a house was built on top of the sandy clay layer. The foundation trenches for the stone house walls were cut through the sandy clay and into the older midden beneath. The house was destroyed by fire; a dark layer of ash and burned rubble covered the area in and around the house. Subsequently, a sand storm buried the area completely in a thick layer. Next, the growth of vegetation created a layer of topsoil in the upper part of the sand layer. Most recently, a pit was dug into the topsoil, through the sand, the house remains, the sandy clay, and into the midden deposit. The pit was then filled with trash, including some beer cans, and topsoil.

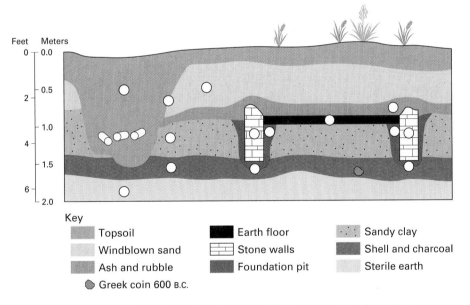

Key

▦ Topsoil	▪ Earth floor	⦂ Sandy clay
Windblown sand	▤ Stone walls	Shell and charcoal
Ash and rubble	Foundation pit	Sterile earth
⬡ Greek coin 600 B.C.		

Fig. 9.23 Drawing of a hypothetical section or profile from an archaeological site.

Harris Matrix

Number the layers and interfaces on the drawing. You might start with 1 for the top layer. Use your numbers to fill in the blank Harris Matrix (Fig. 9.24). Then answer the questions about this stratigraphic example. There are both multiple choice questions and short essay questions.

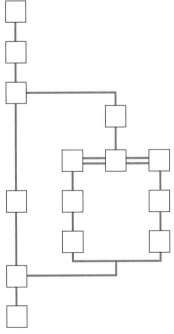

Fig. 9.24 Harris Matrix to be filled in.

Multiple Choice Questions

1. How big was the building shown in the section?

   a. 4 m wide

   b. 2 m wide by 4 m long

   c. 2 m wide or long

   d. 4 m wide or long

2. From what period does the Greek coin date?

   a. 4000 BC

   b. 600 BC

   c. AD 600

   d. Roman period

3. Where did the sediments in the sandy layer come from?

   a. windblown sand from the coast

   b. river clays that flooded the site

   c. natural soil formation

   d. all of the above

4. How many different episodes of human activity are recorded in this stratigraphy?

   a. one

   b. two

   c. three

   d. four

5. What is the best estimate for the age of the sandy clay layer above the sterile earth layer?

   a. younger than the Roman building

   b. older than the Roman building

   c. from 600 BC or older

   d. from 600 BC or younger

   e. from between 600 BC and the Roman period

Essay Questions

Prepare a one-paragraph answer to the following questions.

1. What is the reason for using the Harris Matrix?

2. How did the Greek coin get in this Roman site?

3. What are the major differences between the Harris Matrix and a traditional section drawing?

STUDY QUESTIONS

1. Why are archaeology and geology good partners?

2. The principles of stratigraphy are one of the foundations of archaeological research. State these principles in your own words.

3. Please describe the basic principles of the Harris Matrix for recording archaeological stratigraphy.

4. What were some of the geomorphological methods used in the investigations at Keatley Creek, British Columbia?

5. Are sediments or artifacts more important for understanding past human activity?

6. What kinds of catastrophes are recorded in the archaeological record?

REFERENCES

Brown, A. G. 1997. *Alluvial Geoarchaeology.* Cambridge: Cambridge University Press.

Courty, M. A., Paul Goldberg, and Richard MacPhail. 1989. *Soils and Micromorphology in Archaeology.* Cambridge: Cambridge University Press.

Goldberg, Paul, V. T. Holliday, and C. Reid Ferring, eds. 2001. *Earth Sciences and Archaeology.* New York: Kluwer/Plenum.

Harris, E. C. 1989. *Principles of Archaeological Stratigraphy.* 2d ed. London: Academic Press.

Holliday, V. T. 2004. *Soils in Archaeological Research.* New York: Oxford University Press.

Stein, J. K. 2001. A review of site formation processes and their relevance to geoarchaeology. In *Earth Sciences and Archaeology,* edited by P. Goldberg, V. T. Holliday, and C. R. Ferring, 37–51. New York: Kluwer/Plenum.

Waters, Michael R. 1997. *Principles of Geoarchaeology: A North American Perspective.* Tucson: University of Arizona Press.

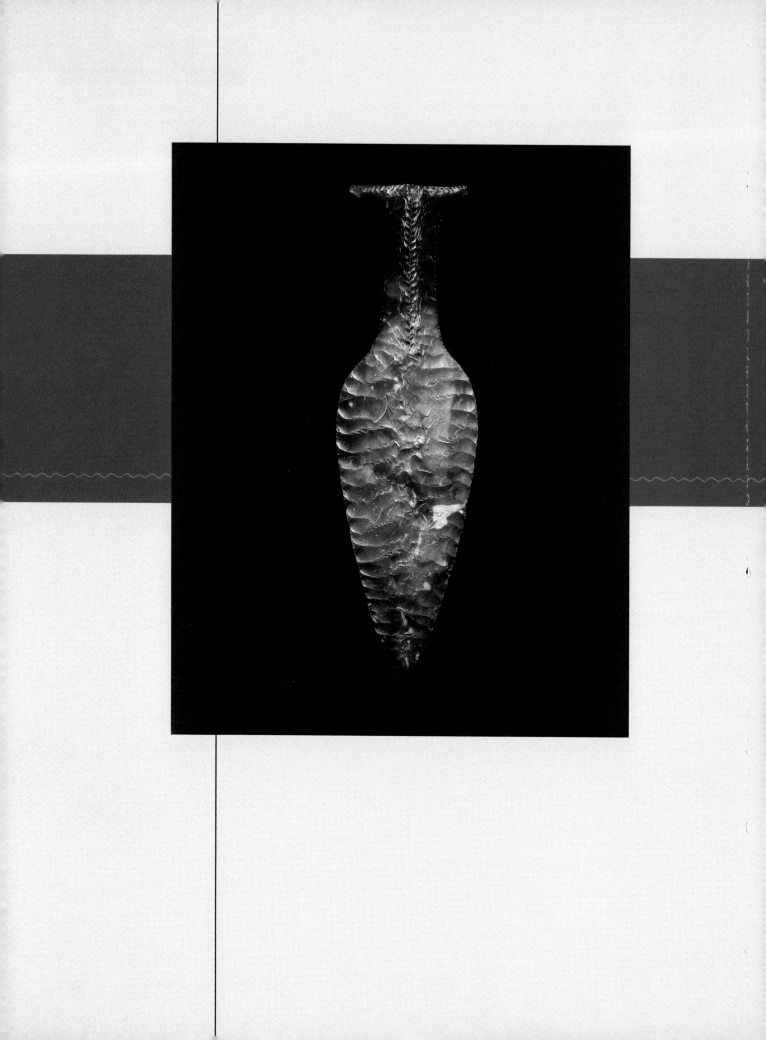

Lithic Analysis

INTRODUCTION: STONE TOOLS AND HUMAN BEHAVIOR

Simple stone tools are the earliest human artifacts that archaeologists study. Small cobbles were first broken to produce sharp edges in Africa between 3 and 2 million years ago, probably associated with the increasing importance of meat in the human diet. The edges of these sharp flakes and cobbles provide access to the carcasses of animals, enabling early humans to cut through tough skins and remove the meaty tissue—actions simply not possible without some kind of sharp implement. Stone tools provide useful cutting edges for a species that lacks both sharp teeth and claws for slicing meat, shredding plants, or digging. As Nicholas Toth of Indiana University puts it, "Sharp-edged stones became the equivalent of canines and carnassials (meat-cutting teeth) and heavier rocks served as bone-crunching jaws."

Prior to the introduction of cast metals about 5000 years ago, most tools with cutting edges were made of stone. Although many of the stone artifacts produced in the Stone Age were utilitarian and not particularly exciting to the nonspecialist, there are a number of very spectacular flint artifacts. Examples of such objects are known from a variety of times and places, but some of the more dramatic come from northern Europe.

The Bronze Age in Scandinavia saw the first introduction of hard-edged bronze tools, mostly daggers and axes, around 2500 BC. For a long time, however, these metal artifacts were rare and must have been very expensive. They are found only in the graves of the more powerful members of society. At the same time, daggers and axes of stone continued to be made in the area. As often happens when desirable commodities are rare, copies are produced in other materials. In the case of the daggers, Scandinavian flint smiths were able to produce remarkable replicas of the bronze originals. In the example shown here, even the casting seam from the production of a metal dagger is reproduced in the handle of the flint copy. These daggers were meant to be seen, not used. They document the fact that stone tools were also sometimes remarkable pieces of craftsmanship and important symbols of status.

Stone was, and still is, an important natural resource for human use. The simple action of striking one rock against another to knock off a small piece was a very successful invention, one that was used long after the discovery of metals. Sharp fragments of stone are perhaps the most common prehistoric artifacts on earth. The earliest worked pieces of stone have been found in East Africa dating to 2.6 million years ago. Our ancient ancestors may also have used pieces of wood or bone for tools, but these have not survived. The principal reason that early

Hello to all intelligent life forms everywhere . . . and to everyone else out there, the secret is to bang the rocks together, guys.
—Douglas Adams, author

humans banged rocks together was to have sharp edges for cutting. Evolution deprived us of the long claws or big fangs that other animals use to tear flesh or defend themselves. Early humans had to use their brains to create cutting edges from hard, round stones.

Stone can be shaped in a variety of ways, for example, flaking, cutting, grinding, polishing, pecking, and breaking. This chapter focuses on the intentional flaking of stone to make tools. Many different terms are used to describe prehistoric stone tools and the ways of making them. The technique for making stone tools by intentionally removing a series of flakes is called flaking or **knapping**. A **flake** is any piece intentionally removed in the process. The people who make stone tools today often call themselves flint knappers or rock knockers. Archaeologists often refer to shaped stone artifacts as **lithics**, or lithic artifacts.

This chapter is organized in several parts concerned with making and studying stone tools. Most stone tools were made by breaking rock. The first section considers the basics of manufacture, including fracture mechanics and raw material, the characteristics of a flake, and terminology. A second section on making stone tools concerns the different kinds of stone tools in the past and how they were made. The third section—"Making Sense of Stone Tools"—describes some methods for the study of lithic artifacts. The late Paleolithic site of Meer provides a case study in lithic analysis, the investigation of a small scatter of flint artifacts on a sand dune in Belgium for information on past human activity. Finally, stone tools made by pecking, grinding, polishing, and other methods are briefly discussed. Ground stone tools—made using these methods—are a second major category of lithic artifacts.

FRACTURE MECHANICS AND RAW MATERIAL

The key to making stone tools is to use a raw material that will break in a predictable way and produce a sharp edge. Stone is used because it is one of the hardest materials in nature and will hold an edge. **Fracture mechanics** is the concept used to describe how materials break. The best raw materials were brittle enough to break, and hard and smooth enough to provide a cutting edge. The stone also had to be fine-grained so that it would break in a predictable fashion, resulting in large flakes, rather than hundreds of shattered fragments.

Essentially this means that the makers of stone tools sought hard, fine-grained, crystalline rocks. The most common materials used were a form of **cryptocrystalline** quartz. This material has microscopic crystals formed from silica under pressure in marine deposits. There are many types of this material, varying in color, crystal size, banding, and other features. The rocks typically used for tools included basalt (a hard volcanic lava), obsidian (a volcanic glass), jasper, quartzite, chert, and flint, depending on local availability. A piece of raw material for making stone tools is usually called a **nodule** or **core**. Nodules are unworked pieces of stone; cores have some flakes already removed.

Flint, or **chert**, was the type of material most often used. Chert is a cryptocrystalline quartz with a slightly larger crystal size than other such quartzes and certain impurities that give it color and cloudiness. The term *chert* is commonly used in North America. Flint, according to its mineralogical status, is simply black chert. But the term *flint* is more commonly used for this material throughout the Old World (Fig. 10.1), perhaps coming from the deposits of black gunflint in England used for flintlock weapons during the period of European expansion in the sixteenth and seventeenth centuries.

Predictable fracture is the important characteristic of this material, so that desired shapes can be achieved by flaking. Perhaps the best way to visualize this process of fracture is to think about what happens when a pebble hits a window.

In many cases, a small cone of glass is knocked from the outside in (Fig. 10.2). This cone shows the plane of fracture in cryptocrystalline solids like glass

---

knapping Intentionally removing a series of *flakes*, working stone (a.k.a. *flaking*).

flake A type of stone artifact produced by removing a piece from a *core* by chipping or *knapping*. *Flakes* are made into a variety of different kinds of *tools* or used for their sharp edges (without further *retouching*).

lithics A generic term used for stone *artifacts* in *archaeology* and more specifically for flaked stone *artifacts*.

fracture mechanics The physics of how materials break.

cryptocrystalline Stone with microscopic crystals, formed from *silica* under pressure in marine deposits, such as quartz, *chert*, *flint*.

nodule Unworked pieces of stone, raw material for making stone *tools*.

core The stone from which other pieces or *flakes* are removed. Core *tools* are shaped by the removal of *flakes*.

flint A hard, siliceous stone that breaks in predictable ways to produce sharp *flakes*, common raw material for stone *tools* in *prehistory*.

chert A *cryptocrystalline* quartz with large crystal size and impurities that give it color and cloudiness.

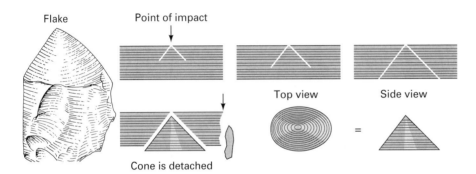

Flake   Point of impact

Cone is detached

Top view   Side view

=

Fig. 10.2 Fracture mechanics of cryptocrystalline solids like glass, obsidian, and flint. The large object on the left is a flake, showing the Hertzian cone or bulb of percussion.

and flint. The shape of the surface is described as **conchoidal** (shell-like), and the cone itself is sometimes called a **Hertzian Cone**. The removal of a flake from a larger piece of stone involves the same principles. A hard object strikes the flint, producing a cone-shaped fracture. Because the blow is aimed at the edge of the stone, only a portion of the cone is in the stone and the blow removes just a flake, not a complete cone.

   Because of fracture mechanics and the nature of the material itself, flakes have a number of distinctive characteristics, shown in Fig. 10.3. Orientation of the flake is essential for observing these characteristics. The top of the flake, the place where force was applied to remove the flake, is called the **striking platform**. The outer surface of the flake, which may have scars from flakes that have already been removed, is called the **dorsal surface**. The inner, fresh surface of the flake itself is called the **bulbar**, or ventral, **surface**. The edges of the flake, at the margins of the dorsal and bulbar surface, are normally sharp. The bulbar surface is so-called because of the **bulb of percussion** that appears near the top. This bulb is a remnant of the cone of percussion, visible as a slight bump or bulb on the stone material. The bulbar surface may also exhibit other features resulting from the forceful removal of the flake, including ripple marks and concentric rings. The bulbar scar may also show evidence of this force in a small fissure directly on the bulb.

   These characteristics can also be produced by some natural forces (falling rock, water-rolling, glacial ice), but examples are rare in nature. Thus, the combination of these distinctive characteristics and the discovery of a number of such

conchoidal fracture   Shell-like shape of the interior surface of a *flake;* the breakage pattern seen in flaking stone *tools.*

Hertzian Cone   Name for the bulb of force produced in fracture of *cryptocrystalline* materials.

striking platform   The flat surface of a *core* where a blow is struck to remove *flake*, visible at the top of the *flake.*

dorsal surface   The outer surface of a *flake.*

bulbar surface   (a.k.a. ventral) The inner, fresh surface of a *flake.*

bulb of percussion   A partial cone of fracture that is seen on the inner surface of *flakes* as a slightly rounded protrusion or bulb.

Fig. 10.3 Major characteristics of a flake.

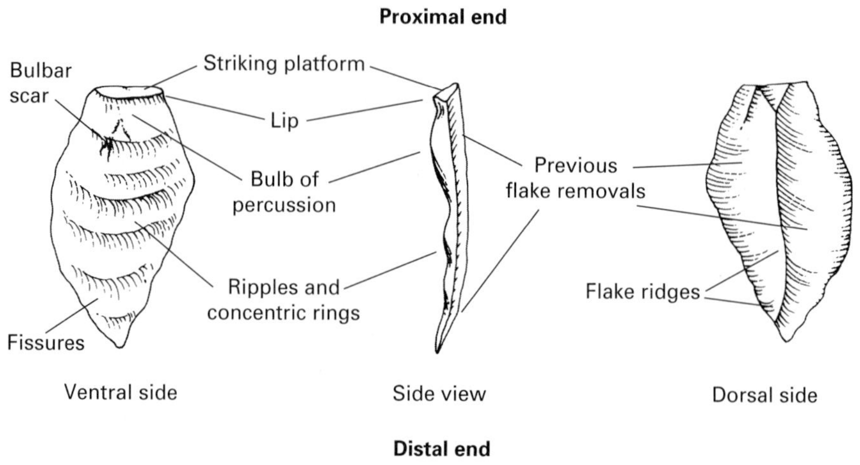

Proximal end

Bulbar scar
Striking platform
Lip
Bulb of percussion
Previous flake removals
Ripples and concentric rings
Flake ridges
Fissures

Ventral side · Side view · Dorsal side

Distal end

percussion flaking A technique for producing stone *artifacts* by striking or *knapping crystalline* stone with a *hard* or *soft hammer*. See also *pressure flaking*.

pressure flaking A technique for producing stone *artifacts* by removing *flakes* from a stone *core* by pressing with a pointed implement. See also *percussion flaking*.

hard hammer A *percussion* technique for making stone *tools* by striking one stone, or *core*, with another stone, or *hammer*. See also *soft hammer* technique.

hammerstone A stone used to knock *flakes* from *cores*; part of the toolkit of a *flintknapper*.

hammer and anvil A *hard hammer* percussion technique which involves striking the *core* (hammer) itself against a large rock in the ground (anvil) to produce a *flake*.

soft hammer A *flintknapping* technique that involves the use of a hammer of bone, antler, or wood, rather than stone. See also *hard hammer* technique.

punch A piece of antler, bone, or wood used as a pointed object between the hammer and the *core* to assist the removal of the *flake*, a kind of chisel for *flintknapping*.

flintknapping Chipping or flaking stone to make *tools* and other *artifacts*.

tool Any equipment, weapon, object intentionally modified by humans to change the *environment* around them.

waste A term referring to all the pieces of *shatter* and *flakes* produced and not used when stone *tools* are made; also called *débitage*.

débitage (French) A term referring to all the pieces of *shatter* and *flakes* produced and not used when stone *tools* are made; also called *waste*.

blade A special kind of elongated *flake* with two parallel sides and a length at least twice the width of the piece. The regular manufacture of blades characterized the Upper Paleolithic, with an efficient way of producing mass quantities of cutting edges.

unifacial A term describing a flaked stone *tool* in which only one face or side is retouched to make a sharp edge. See also *bifacial*.

bifacial A term describing a flaked stone *tool* in which both faces or sides are retouched to make a thinner *tool*. See also *unifacial*.

projectile point Generic name for the range of shapes and materials used to make a sharp end on weapons such as spears, darts, javelins, arrows, and the like (synonym: arrowhead, spearhead).

flakes in a single location are very good evidence of human involvement in the production of the flakes.

In some time periods in various parts of the world, low-quality cherts were heated to improve their flaking qualities. Gradual heating of some cryptocrystalline materials changes the properties of the stone including an increase in luster and often distinctive changes in color. In addition, the material becomes easier to knap, producing long and thinner flakes. This heat treatment of stone for flaking probably began in the Upper Paleolithic period.

MAKING STONE TOOLS

A flake can be removed from the parent stone, or core, by either a blow or pressure. The technique of striking stone to remove a flake is called **percussion** (Fig. 10.4); **pressure flaking** is the term used to describe removals made by pressing a point into the edge of a core. There are variants of both these methods.

Percussion can be done using a **hard hammer**, hammer and anvil, or soft hammer. The term *hard hammer* refers to the use of a hammer of equal or greater hardness than the core, usually called a **hammerstone**. The **hammer and anvil** method is a specialized hard hammer technique. It reverses the normal process of striking the parent rock with a hammer. In this method, the parent rock or core is held in the hand and struck against a rock fixed in the ground (the anvil) to remove a flake.

Soft hammer means the use of a hammer of lighter, softer material, usually antler, bone, or even wood, to remove flakes. While it may seem surprising that a soft hammer can be used to remove flakes from stone, it is the application of force that is important rather than the hardness of the hammer. The use of a soft hammer results in the removal of wider, thinner flakes.

Percussion can be direct or indirect. Direct percussion means that the hammer strikes the core directly; indirect percussion means that a piece of antler, bone, or wood is used as a pointed object called a **punch** between the hammer and the core to assist in the removal of the flake. Indirect percussion allows the flintknapper to have better control on the location of the removal.

Pressure flaking involves the use of a pointed tool, usually of antler or bone, to press on the edge of a core to remove very long, narrow flakes (Fig. 10.5). Copper was sometimes used for this pointed tool as well because the metal provided a good grip on the sharp edge of the core. Many of the finest flint tools were made by pressure flaking.

The goal of the prehistoric flintknapper was to make tools that could be used for various activities. Because **flintknapping** is a subtractive process, there is a lot

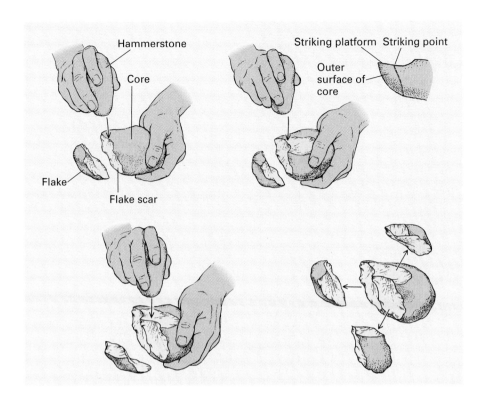

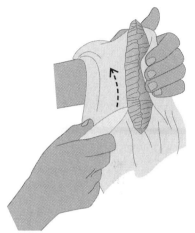

Fig. 10.4 The technique of flint-knapping involves the use of force against a stone core to produce a flake. Removal of a flake leaves a scar on the surface of the core. The striking platform is the place at which the blow is struck on the core. A series of flakes can be removed from the core. This example illustrates percussion flaking.

Fig. 10.5 Hand-held, direct pressure flaking using a pointed bone tool to remove regular, small, long, thin flakes from a biface.

of waste material produced, like the shavings and sawdust from woodworking. An important distinction is made between **tools**, which are the intentional product of the manufacturing process, and **waste**, which is the unused material that results from the process. The French word *débitage* (*deb-e-TAJ*) is often used to describe this waste material. This waste includes lots of flakes, blocks of flint, and shatter. *Shatter, chips,* or *debris* are terms used for the very small pieces of waste flint that are produced in working stone. All of these products—both the finished pieces and the waste—are artifacts, items made by humans.

Another useful distinction is made between flakes and blades, an invention from the late Paleolithic period. **Blades** are simply long, narrow flakes that can be removed sequentially from a prepared core in a manner akin to peeling a carrot. Blades are recognized both by their elongated shape and by the process for making them, which requires a specially prepared core. They can be produced by either direct or indirect percussion (Fig. 10.6). Less flint is required to make a lot of cutting edge; blades can be made into a variety of different kinds of tools, described below; the long, narrow shape of blades makes them more suitable for hafting than flakes.

Two kinds of blades can be identified, depending on the hardness of the tool used as a hammer. Hard hammer blades are struck directly with a stone hammer and have a wider striking platform, a pronounced bulb of percussion, and some crushing at the point of impact. Soft hammer blades are generally longer and thinner with a narrow striking platform and a thin bulb of percussion (Fig. 10.7).

Tools are often distinguished as core tools—a larger tool produced by removing flakes to shape it—or flake tools, tools made on flakes, or blade tools on blades. Another distinction is made between **unifacial** tools worked on one side, or face, or **bifacial** tools, worked on both sides. Bifacial tools are often pointed implements like **projectile points**. The generic term *projectile point* is used for the variety of artifacts that could be used as the sharp end of a spear, dart, or arrow. An arrowhead is one kind of a projectile point.

Tools are often intentionally shaped to a specific form by secondary flaking. The technique for further shaping flakes, blades, and other pieces into specific

Fig. 10.6 Removal of a blade from a prepared blade core using the indirect punch technique. In this case, a pointed antler punch is struck with a hammer stone to remove a long blade.

Fig. 10.7 Three views of a soft hammer blade. Blades are elongated flakes. The characteristics of a flake are visible on this artifact, including the bulb of percussion, ripple marks, and scars from previous removals. This soft hammer blade has a very narrow striking platform and a flat bulb of percussion.

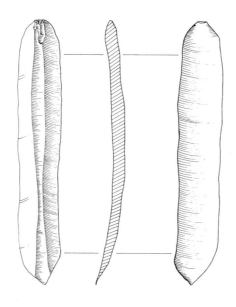

Fig. 10.8 Blades are useful preforms, or blanks, for making many other types of artifacts by retouching. Some distinctive types of blade tools that are known from prehistory are shown in this drawing. The darker edges of these artifacts show the results of retouching, in which a number of smaller flakes have been removed to shape the final tool.

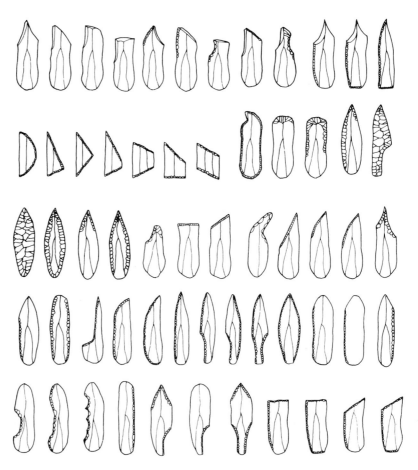

retouching   The shaping or sharpening of stone *artifacts* through *percussion* or *pressure flaking;* a technique of *flintknapping.*

preform   (a.k.a. blank) A basic piece or blank form used to make a specific kind of finished product. Term is used in lithic studies to describe early stages in manufacture of certain kinds of *tools* like *projectile points.*

forms is called **retouching**, the removal of additional flakes to modify the original piece. Sometimes this process is as simple as blunting one edge of a flake for a finger rest or resharpening the working edge of a tool. Sometimes the process is complex and involves a number of steps to produce a specific size and shape. Lots of secondary flakes and chips are created in the process. Blades are commonly retouched into a variety of shapes (Fig. 10.8). In this way, blades are a blank or **preform** for making a variety of other kinds of tools.

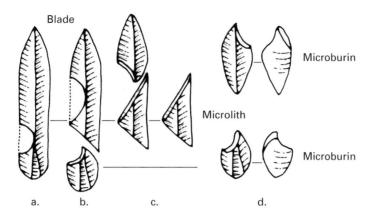

Fig. 10.9 The microburin process and products: (a) blade is notched by retouching; (b) snapped at the notch to produce (c) geometric microliths and (d) distinctive waste material known as microburins.

The **microburin** technique is a specialized process involving a series of steps to produce small, usually geometric-shaped projectile points (Fig. 10.9). A blade is used as a preform to make the final product (a). Two notches are retouched along the edge of the blade (b). The blade is then broken at the notches to create a geometric segment from the middle of the blade (c). This triangular or rhombic piece is then retouched along the broken edges to complete its geometric form. Because these pieces are often small in size, they are sometimes called geometric **microliths** (small stones). Such microliths are thought to have been used as projectile points. The term *microburin* refers both to the technique of snapping the blade on the notch and to the ends of the blade that are created as waste in this process (d). The presence of these microburins indicates that microliths were being made at a site.

MAKING SENSE OF STONE TOOLS

There are many ways to study the results of prehistoric stone tool production. Experimental studies are common; archaeologists make and use stone tools to better understand the process and the results. Replication of ancient shapes and techniques using different raw materials is a powerful learning process. There are also many techniques for studying how tools were made and used, discussed in this section.

Typology is the conventional approach to classifying stone tools. Knowledge of the types of lithic artifacts is essential for the local archaeologist. Studies of the process of making stone tools, both the finished tools and the waste that is produced, often involve a concept or method known as the **chaîne opératoire** (*chan oh-PAIR-ah-twar*), involving all the stages of manufacturing and use. *Refitting,* or conjoining, is the term used to describe the re-assembling of the original parent cores and tools that were used and broken on a site. The horizontal location of these refitted pieces is very informative. Microwear analysis is one of the more effective techniques used for studying how lithic artifacts were used. This analysis involves microscopic studies of damage and polish on the edges of stone artifacts, which reveal the materials that were worked. These aspects of lithic analysis are discussed below.

After the stone artifacts have been cleaned and numbered, the process of sorting, classifying, measuring, and analyzing begins. The initial sorting is often based on the simple technological types of core and flake and tools, but a variety of other criteria are considered, including raw material, heating or burning, **patination**, and more. Patination is a weathering process that gradually changes the surface appearance of flint from shiny to dull, and often from one color to another, over time.

Another distinction is sometimes made based on the presence of the outer surface of the stone nodule. The surface of a nodule of chert or flint is often weathered and patinated, but older surfaces have **cortex**, a heavily weathered rind on

www.mhhe.com/pricearch1

For a Web-based activity on the Chaîne Opératoire, please see the Internet exercises on your online learning center.

microburin   (1) A technique for making segments of *blades* into small geometric pieces (*microlith*); (2) waste products of the microburin process are also called microburins.

microlith   Small *blades* and geometric forms of stone *tools,* usually associated with the Mesolithic period in the Old World.

chaîne opératoire   (French: *sequence of production*) The different stages of production from the acquisition of raw material to the final abandonment of the desired and/or used objects.

patination   A weathering process that gradually changes the surface appearance of *flint* from shiny to dull, and often from one color to another over time; the new surface is described as a patina.

cortex   A heavily weathered rind on the outside of *flint* or *chert nodules.* The presence of this cortex is the criterion for a *cortical flake.*

Fig. 10.10 Three-dimensional depiction of a bifacial artifact from Texas. This image was created using a combination of 3-D laser scanning and close-range photogrammetry.

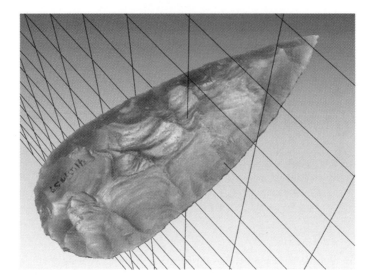

the outside of the stone. The presence of this cortex is the criterion for a cortical flake. The proportion of **cortical flakes** in an assemblage of stone artifacts is an indication of the size of the nodules in use at the site—the more cortical flakes, the smaller the nodules.

It is often necessary to draw stone tools in order to illustrate the characteristics of the artifact and the details of manufacture and use. Such illustrations are sometimes real works of art, and a great deal of talent, skill, and experience is needed to make such illustrations. The handaxe shown in Fig. 10.11 is the product of an illustrator's talent.

Today, however, the combination of laser and photo technology is replacing the artist's hand and eye to record the details of prehistoric artifacts (Fig. 10.10). This technology, using 3-D laser scanning and close-range photogrammetry, can record objects of almost any size from architecture to artifacts with remarkable accuracy and clarity.

Typology

Archaeologists categorize and count the lithic artifacts recovered in an excavation. These categories are usually the result of a long process of recognition and identification of distinctive types developed by several generations of researchers. Typology is the study and definition of types of artifacts, whether made of stone, ceramic, bone, metal, or whatever. A **type list** is the set of types of artifacts for a specific area. The goal of recording types is to have a standardized way of reporting the finds and comparing them with other sites. Types also carry important functional, stylistic, and chronological information.

For example, a **handaxe** is a distinctive type of artifact. It is a large, bifacial core tool with a distinctive shape—pointed at one end, rounded at the other, retouched to a desired size, shape, and heft. Functionally, the handaxe was an all-purpose implement, probably used for cutting, sawing, digging, bashing, and boring large holes, among other things. Stylistically, there are distinctive types of handaxes that show regional differences in East Africa. Archaeologist Glynn Isaac suggested that the highly individual character of many of the artifacts at the site of Olorgesailie (*oh-lorg-ah-SIGH-lee*) might reflect the styles of individual bands of *Homo erectus*.

There is also an important development in handaxes that marks a change over time. During the nineteenth century, early prehistorians collected handaxes near the town of St. Acheul (*SANT ah-SHEWL*) in southern France. The name of

cortical flake A *flake* with some of the outer surface (*cortex*) of the stone *nodule* present.

type list The set of types of *artifacts* for a specific area.

handaxe The characteristic artifact of the Paleolithic: a large, teardrop-shaped stone *tool* bifacially flaked to a point at one end and a broader base at the other, for general-purpose use.

lithic assemblage The complete set of stone *artifacts* found at an archaeological *site*.

the town gave rise to the term *Acheulean*, used to describe a period in the Paleolithic. Crude handaxes with irregular edges and heavy flake scars on their surface were found on the higher, older river terraces. Handaxes from the lower, younger terraces had more symmetrical shapes with straighter edges. The introduction of soft hammer flaking resulted in the more regular handaxe shapes and a distinctive chronological marker for the later Lower Paleolithic. Handaxes made with the hard hammer method exhibit sinuous, or wavy, irregular edges (Fig. 10.11).

Single artifacts are usually collected as stray finds on the landscape, but stone tools and waste material are often found together at archaeological sites. The set of stone tools from a site is known as a **lithic assemblage**. Assemblages of lithic artifacts from a particular time period are characteristic of archaeological cultures. Types of lithic artifacts refer to specific kinds of artifacts.

Some artifact types from the Paleolithic are illustrated in Fig. 10.12. The Acheulean assemblages of the Lower Paleolithic are characterized by handaxes and their close relatives the cleavers, but also include a variety of other large flake tools, such as scrapers and notched pieces. The Middle Paleolithic assemblage is distinguished by a multitude of flake tools, scrapers, burins, points, along with a few handaxes and other bifacial tools. Blade technology characterizes the Upper Paleolithic, starting 40,000 years ago. More types of tools and new raw materials (bone, ivory, antler, and wood) are also known from this period.

There are striking differences between the artifact types in the New World and the Old World. Most of the well-made artifacts in the early prehistory of the

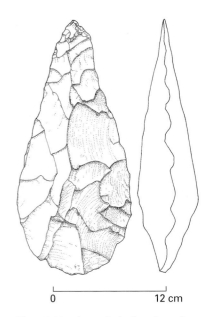

Fig. 10.11 An artist's drawing of a handaxe from the site of Olorgesailie in Kenya. Note that the edge is irregular, indicating hard hammer flaking.

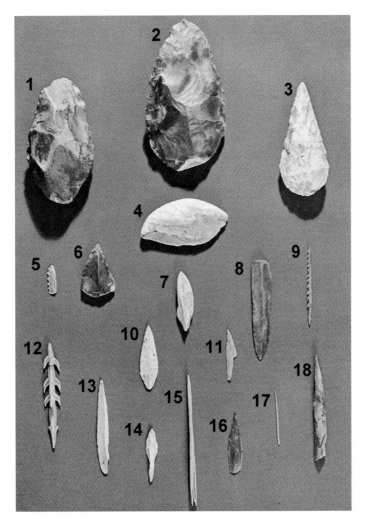

Fig. 10.12 Tools of the Paleolithic: 1–3. handaxes from the Lower Paleolithic; 4–6. side scraper, denticulated blade, and Levallois point from the Middle Paleolithic; 7–19. Upper Paleolithic tools: 7. flint point; 8. end scraper on blade; 9. barbed bone harpoon; 10–11. flint points; 12. barbed antler harpoon; 13. backed flint knife; 14. flint point; 15. bone point; 16. blade borer; 17. bone needle; 18. bone point.

www.mhhe.com/pricearch1

For a Web-based activity on Acheulean tools, please see the Internet exercises on your online learning center.

Fig. 10.13 Some of the basic types of stone tools common in many parts of the Old World: side scraper, end scraper, drill, projectile point, and burin.

www.mhhe.com/pricearch1

For a Web-based activity on Upper Paleolithic tools from France, please see the Internet exercises on your online learning center.

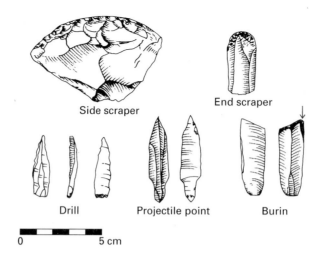

Side scraper End scraper

Drill Projectile point Burin

0 5 cm

New World were bifaces, largely in the form of projectile points for spears and later for the bow and arrow, which came very late to the Americas. Most of the unifacial artifacts from the Archaic and Woodland periods are irregular in appearance. Flakes also predominate in New World industries; blades were not of significance until the later periods of the prehistory of Central America and the Arctic region.

Some common artifact types in the Old World are shown in Fig. 10.13. These types include scrapers. A scraper is a flake or blade with a heavy, steep edge thought to have been used for working hide, bone, or wood. Both a side scraper on a large flake and an end scraper on a blade are shown in the illustration. A drill, or borer, on a blade was used for making holes in various materials. The projectile point in the illustration is stemmed or tanged for hafting and is typical for the latest Paleolithic in northern Europe. The **burin** is a distinctively edged tool with a 90° shaving edge and an oblique angled working edge. Burins are thought to be cutting and engraving tools for hard material like bone. The small arrow on the drawing of the burin shows where a spall or small flake of flint was removed to create the distinctive edges.

In North America, typologies of stone tools are often dominated by projectile point types. Most states or regions have a typology of points for local collectors to use to identify the time period to which different sizes and shapes belong. One example of such a typology for the northwestern plains of the United States is shown in Fig. 7.8.

Chaîne Opératoire

The study of the production of stone tools provides substantial information on technology, the life history of artifacts, and human behavior. The French term *chaîne opératoire* (operational sequence) refers to the steps in the process of production. It is a particularly useful concept for prehistoric activities like stone tool or pottery manufacture. The chaîne opératoire is defined by the different stages of production from the acquisition of raw material to the final abandonment of the desired and/or used objects. While typology focuses only on the end product, studies of the chaîne opératoire look at the entire production and use sequence. Such studies focus on the waste material, refitting, human motor abilities and skills, knowledge, and experience as well as the end products of the process (tools).

Reconstruction of the operational sequence reveals the choices humans make in each step of the process. This reconstruction provides a biography or life history of an artifact. The life history of a lithic artifact involves four major stages: the procurement of raw material, the technology used to make the tool, the use of

burin A distinctively edged stone *tool* combining a 90° edge and an oblique angled working edge.

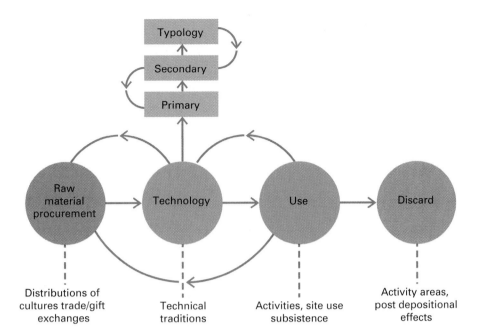

Fig. 10.14 A diagram of the chaîne opératoire showing four major stages: raw material procurement, technology, use, and discard. Technology, or manufacture, is investigated at three levels: primary reduction, secondary reduction, and typological variation.

the tool, and the discard of the tool. Roger Grace of the University of Essex, England, has graphed this sequence in Fig. 10.14. In this graph, technology is divided into primary reduction, secondary reduction, and typology. In addition, listed at the bottom of the graph are some of the kinds of archaeological information that these components of the chaîne opératoire can provide.

Another advantage of studying the operational steps is that it provides more awareness of the relationship among the components in the sequence. Choices that are made in one stage affect decisions in another. Availability of a specific raw material may limit the kinds of tools that can be produced. A desire to produce a specific type of tool may require certain raw materials and technology.

The intended use of an artifact has major consequences for all other steps in the sequence. A useful distinction between expedient and curated tools, proposed by Lewis Binford, helps to understand this relationship. **Expedient tools** are quickly made, used, and discarded. Raw material for this manufacture is more generic, technology fairly simple, production fairly rapid, use more general purpose, and discard immediate. Expedient tools are more common in lithic assemblages, and their spatial distribution is more homogeneous across a site living area.

Curated tools, on the other hand, are often special-purpose implements that require specific raw materials and substantial time and labor in manufacture. Curated tools are intended to be used for a long period. They can often be repaired or recycled and are normally discarded only when exhausted. Thus, curated tools are usually rare in lithic assemblages although they may be very important in human activity.

Assemblages of lithic artifacts are the result of human activity and interaction with the environment. The application of the chaîne opératoire concept helps the archaeologist to understand this dynamic process involved in the production of stone tools and other artifacts.

Refitting

Another kind of lithic analysis involves the investigation of the horizontal distribution of artifacts by **refitting**, or conjoining, as many as possible of the broken pieces back together (Fig. 10.17). Refitting these pieces into their original cores and parent rock requires skill and patience. It is like trying to solve a three-dimensional

expedient tools Implements that are quickly made, used, and discarded. The *technology* is fairly simple, production fairly rapid, use more general purpose, and discard immediate. Contrast with *curated tools.*

curated tools Special-purpose implements that require specific raw materials and substantial time and labor in manufacture. Curated tools can often be repaired or recycled and are normally discarded only when exhausted. Contrast with *expedient tools.*

refitting A technique for reassembling the scattered pieces of stone, *pottery,* or bone at an archaeological *site* to study patterns of manufacture and disposal.

Stone Tools and Hunter-Gatherers in Western Nevada

Stone tools often survive the destructive forces of time and nature and provide a major piece of the evidence for past human presence in most places in the world. Archaeologists also depend on stone artifacts for information on the behavior of prehistoric hunter-gatherers. The shape and use of stone tools is thought to reflect the activities of hunter-gatherers. At the same time, this information is difficult to obtain because there are various factors involved in the manufacture of tools. These factors include style, function, and raw material, all of which play important roles in the finished artifact. Style involves traditional or cultural ways of how things are done. It may reflect subconscious ethnic or individual differences or be intentionally added to identify an artifact. Function concerns the intended purpose of the artifact, and raw material affects how stone can be worked and shaped, and its final appearance.

Robert Kelly of the University of Wyoming looked at the stone tools of prehistoric hunter-gatherers in the Carson Sink region of western Nevada. He assumed that the patterns of stone tool technology would provide information on the nature of settlement and the annual cycle of hunter-gatherers in this area. Kelly was specifically in-

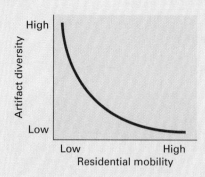

Fig. 10.15 The theoretical relationship between residential mobility (how often a group moves) and artifact diversity (the number of different kinds of tools that are present at a site).

terested in the relationship between stone tools and human mobility. Archaeological sites occur both at low elevations on the valley floor and at higher elevations in the surrounding mountains. Hunter-gatherers often moved seasonally to take advantage of changing resource abundance and availability in these zones. Be-

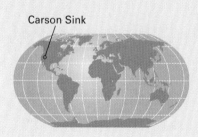

Carson Sink

TABLE 10.1 Artifact production in the valley and mountains of Carson Sink. Counts of artifact types by production category; percentage is shown in parentheses.

Location	Sites (n)	Recycled/ Bipolar	Simple Flake	Rough Bifacial	Fine Bifacial	Total
Valley floor	40	478 (39)	589 (47)	36 (3)	132 (11)	1235
Mountains	24	45 (5)	257 (36)	116 (17)	277 (40)	695

jigsaw puzzle with no picture and many missing pieces. The work takes a great deal of time. But the reassembled objects provide a great deal of information about the site and past human activities. Refitting is done with a variety of archaeological materials, but most commonly with lithics, pottery, and bone.

The information that is obtained from refitting and studying the sequence of flaking or breakage is useful for a number of reasons. The horizontal distribution of pieces reveals where activities were taking place and the extent of the area that was in use. The presence of pieces from the same original parent in different concentrations provides a good indication of association and contemporaneity between concentrations. Pieces from the same original object found close together suggest that there has not been much post-deposition disturbance of the site. Missing pieces from the refitted original indicate what kinds of tools were made and removed from the site. Study of the sequence of removals and flaking from the refitted assemblage of cores reveals much about the techniques of stone tool manufacture and the chaîne opératoire at the site.

cause mobile people have to take their possessions with them, the tools they carry must be carefully chosen.

There is in fact a clear relationship between the length of time that a site is used and the number and kinds of tools that are present. Long-term occupations have a greater diversity of artifacts and tool types. This relationship is schematically graphed in Fig. 10.15 based on data from ethnographically-known groups of hunter-gatherers.

Kelly examined this relationship using the information from western Nevada, and he focused on the artifacts known as "bifaces"—tools that have been retouched on both sides (or faces) into a specific form. Kelly argued that bifaces were of two kinds, either cores for obtaining flakes, or long-lasting cutting tools that could be resharpened.

Kelly then counted the artifacts and noted the raw material types from a series of sites in Carson Sink region. The surrounding mountains had abundant sources of raw material compared to the valley floor. Table 10.1 shows the differences in artifact production between the two areas. The numbers in parentheses show the percentage of the artifact types in each area. From this evidence, it is clear that bifacial artifacts are made and used primarily in the mountains and simple flake tools are more common on the valley floor: Some 47% of the tools on the valley floor are simple flake artifacts; 57% of the tools in the mountains are bifaces.

At the mountain sites, there was a clear difference between sites where bifaces were made or repaired and used as tools and sites where bifaces were used as cores. This difference can be seen in a comparison of the numbers of utilized flakes from bifaces (evidence of core use) and flakes from knapping bifaces (production or sharpening) in Fig. 10.16. Kelly argues that bifaces were used as tools at residential sites and used as cores at short-term hunting and collecting camps. This distinction fol-

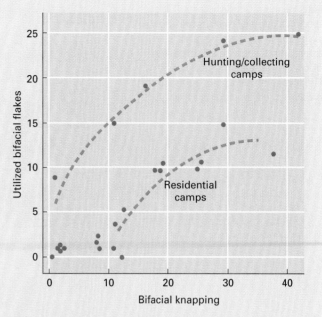

Fig. 10.16 Observed patterns of utilized bifacial flakes and evidence of bifacial knapping distinguish residential camps and extraction camps.

lows the dichotomy between curated and expedient tools that was discussed earlier. Bifacial tools would be used for a long time and curated, while the flakes removed from bifacial cores were expedient tools to be quickly used and discarded.

Kelly's study documents the use of stone tools as a source of information about prehistoric hunter-gatherers. Kelly was able to recognize different kinds of sites—residential vs. hunting or collecting sites—in the mountains of western Nevada based on the use of bifacial artifacts.

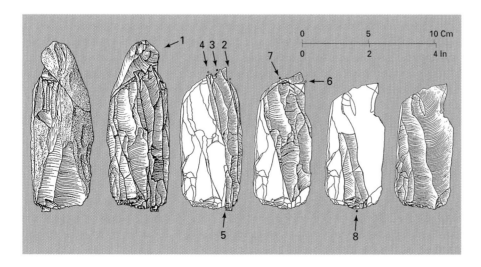

Fig. 10.17 A refitted sequence of débitage and tools from Paleolithic Egypt.

Fig. 10.18 The distribution of stone artifacts on the floor of the late Paleolithic site of Sitra in northwestern Egypt. The lines show connections between refitted pieces. Three specific examples of refits are shown in the corners of the site plan. The colored lines show these three specific refits on the living floor at Sitra. The legend in the upper right shows symbols used for different tool types.

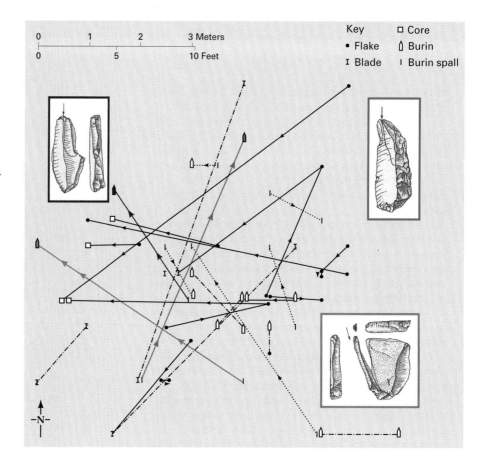

A distribution of refitted artifacts is shown in Fig. 10.18. This example comes from the late Paleolithic site of Sitra (*SEAT-trah*) in northwestern Egypt, studied by Erwin Cziesla and Rudolph Kuper. The plan of the site shows the distribution of various types of artifacts, including flakes, blades, cores, burins, and burin spalls. Burin spalls are the small slivers that are removed when burins are made. The various lines show the refit of pieces together at the site. It is clear that the artifacts are connected across this site. Three specific examples of refits are shown in the corners of the site plan. These are tools with refitted broken working edges or burins with the burin spalls. The colored lines show the refit of these pieces. The broken edge or burin spall likely lies where the tool was used, while the tool itself was discarded elsewhere.

The vertical distribution of refitted pieces is also very useful information for learning about formation processes and the reliability of site stratigraphy. Artifacts that fit into the same original parent core are assumed to be contemporary. Their horizontal distribution marks an activity area where flint knapping was done. Their vertical spread should be very limited since the objects would have lain on the same living surface. Post-depositional movement of the artifacts by animal disturbance or bioturbation would produce differences in their vertical distribution at the site.

Microwear Analysis

One of the primary questions about prehistoric stone tools concerns how they were used. Archaeologists tend to name the things they find. Many types of stone tools have been given names that imply a certain kind of use: handaxes, scrapers, arrowheads, for example (Fig. 10.20).

How Many Layers?

An example of refitting and site formation process comes from the Lower Paleolithic site of Terra Amata (*TARE-ah ah-MOT-ah*) on the Mediterranean coast of France. Stone artifacts and animal bones were found in a series of layers of fossil dunes and beach sand. Fig. 10.19 lists the many different layers of dune, beach, and lower sands at the site, distinguished by alphanumeric labels. At the time of the excavation, these different layers were thought to represent many different episodes of human activity at this 250,000-year-old beach site. However, painstaking refitting of the lithics from the site by Paola Villa of the University of Colorado revealed a pronounced vertical distribution of the conjoined pieces. The short horizontal lines in Fig. 10.19 represent individual stone artifacts in a particular layer, and the vertical lines indicate that the pieces fit together. In several cases, a number of vertical and horizontal lines are grouped, indicating a number of refits from the same parent core. Based on the refitting study, it appears that there were only two to three periods of activity possible at the site, rather than many as originally thought.

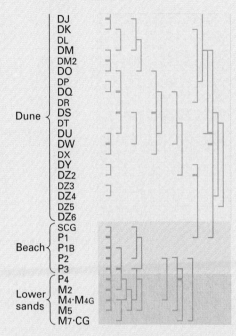

Fig. 10.19 A schematic view of the distribution of stone artifacts in the various layers at Terra Amata. The individual layers that were recognized in the excavations are designated by combinations of letters and numbers. The sets of vertical and horizontal lines to the right show where refits of stone artifacts were found, crossing the separate layers. The fact that refitted pieces of the same artifact or core are found at different depths and in different layers is convincing evidence that the artifacts have moved vertically after their original deposition.

Terra Amata

But, in fact, the actual uses of many implements are unknown. The term *handaxe* comes from a French word implying that it was an axe held in the hand, but this hallmark of the Paleolithic was likely used for many purposes, a kind of Stone Age Swiss army knife. For example, the point could be used for digging or gouging, the edges for cutting, and the heavy butt end for chopping or hammering. Scrapers are usually somewhat heavy tools with a thick, curved edge. The name implies that they were used for scraping, and their use for cleaning animal hides is often assumed. However, these tools may have been used for a range of purposes in addition to scraping. *Arrowhead* is a generic name for pointed lithic artifacts, but, in fact, many so-called arrowheads in North America were more likely mounted at the working end of darts and spears or used as knives.

Because of these problems in understanding the function of stone tools, researchers have developed new methods for learning about how these implements were used. One of these techniques is **microwear analysis** and involves the use of microscopes to study the edges of stone tools. This kind of analysis started in the second half of the twentieth century as the Russian Sergei Semenov began the detailed study of the edges of artifacts. The technique was enhanced with the use

microwear analysis Microscopic studies of damage and polish on the edges of stone *artifacts* to reveal the materials that were worked.

Fig. 10.20 Possible functions for some Paleolithic stone tools. Most of the listed uses are assumed rather than known.

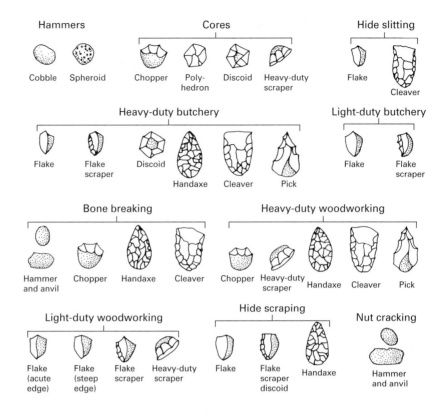

Hammers
Cobble   Spheroid

Cores
Chopper   Poly-hedron   Discoid   Heavy-duty scraper

Hide slitting
Flake   Cleaver

Heavy-duty butchery
Flake   Flake scraper   Discoid   Handaxe   Cleaver   Pick

Light-duty butchery
Flake   Flake scraper

Bone breaking
Hammer and anvil   Chopper   Handaxe   Cleaver

Heavy-duty woodworking
Chopper   Heavy-duty scraper   Handaxe   Cleaver   Pick

Light-duty woodworking
Flake (acute edge)   Flake (steep edge)   Flake scraper   Heavy-duty scraper

Hide scraping
Flake   Flake scraper discoid   Handaxe

Nut cracking
Hammer and anvil

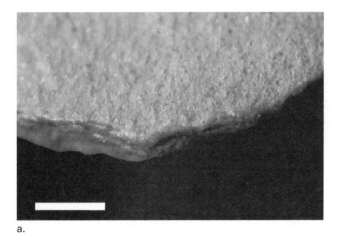

a.

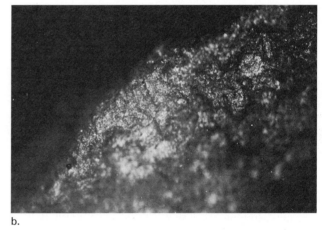

b.

Fig. 10.21 Microwear analysis and curated tools from an Upper Paleolithic site in Austria. (a) Clear edge rounding under low magnification (30×). Bar for scale = 1 mm. (b) Same location on edge at 200× magnification, showing rough polish and striations.

of high-powered microscopes and the recognition of distinctive polishes on the edge of tools, introduced by Lawrence Keeley of the University of Illinois-Chicago (Fig. 10.21). Experimental studies, using stone tools on known materials like dry hide, meat, wood, and plant fibers, allowed researchers to characterize polishes specific to certain kinds of materials and activities.

"Blind" tests have been an important part of this research. Microwear analysts have followed a protocol in which they identify polishes on a series of samples they have not seen before. The origin of each polish is known to the person handling the samples, but not to the analyst. The identification of polishes is difficult, and learning to distinguish different varieties is time-consuming. Researchers who can identify these polishes "blindly" demonstrate their knowledge and skill.

Many stone tools were probably used in a range of activities, limiting how much we can learn from microwear studies. It is also the case that stone tools were

Stone Tools and Food

Microwear studies have provided important clues about the use of stone tools. Keeley used a high-powered microscope to examine the edges of stone artifacts from the 1.5-million-year-old site of Koobi Fora (*COO-bee FORE-ah*) in East Africa. His experimental work had demonstrated that different materials left different kinds of traces in the form of polish on the edges of stone tools. At a magnification of 400 power, Keeley observed microscopic polish and wear, indicating the cutting of meat, the slicing of soft plant material, and the scraping and sawing of wood, on about 10% of the flakes. Two of the flakes with evidence of meat butchering were found within 1 m (3 ft) of a large herbivore bone exhibiting cutmarks. Such an association supports the use of these stone artifacts as butchering tools. The evidence for woodworking suggests that wooden tools were also being made, perhaps crude digging sticks for finding roots and tubers. This indirect information is the only evidence that exists for the use or consumption of plant materials at this early point of human prehistory.

often used to make other tools of bone, antler, wood, and other materials. It was these implements that were the primary interface with the environment, making it more difficult to investigate human activity beyond toolmaking. Nevertheless, microwear studies offer one of the only ways to reliably understand the use of stone tools.

 EXAMPLE

THE CAREFUL FLINTKNAPPER

Many of the late Paleolithic and Mesolithic sites of northwestern Europe are represented today by nothing more than small scatters of flint tools and waste (Fig. 10.22). In some cases, charcoal pieces may also be preserved, but nothing more. These sites are a challenge to the ingenuity of archaeologists to learn something beyond their approximate age based on the kinds of tools that were found. Information on the number of inhabitants and the activities that took place at the site would be a breakthrough.

The site called Meer (*MERE*) is one such small scatter of flint in an area of fossil sand dunes in northern Belgium. The site dates to approximately 8000 BC and belongs to the very latest Paleolithic in this area. The excavation of the site was done carefully by Francis van Noten, and the exact find location of each artifact was recorded so that the site could be reconstructed and studied in detail. Four distinct clusters of artifacts were recognized on the occupation floor at the site.

Fortunately, the archaeologists (Daniel Cahen of the Royal Museum in Belgium and Lawrence Keeley) studying the materials from Meer worked long and hard to understand this site. One of the first questions to be answered was whether the artifacts came from a single episode of residence or if the location had been repeatedly visited. Repeated visits would likely smear any spatial patterns of activity. The distribution of the flint artifacts in the sand dune did not strengthen the case for a single visit. The artifacts were found over a vertical distance of 45 cm (15 in) in the sediments. However, after months of refitting the small bits of flint back together, a more coherent picture emerged. Pieces of flint from the top and bottom of the sand deposit could be put back together, demonstrating that the artifacts had moved vertically in the sand by natural processes after they had been deposited. Refitting documented the vertical and the horizontal integrity of the site and argued strongly for a single occupation at Meer (Fig. 10.23).

The archaeologists then focused on one small concentration of artifacts at the site, designated Concentration IV or CIV, roughly 3.5–4 m (10–12 ft) in diameter with

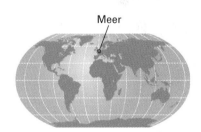
Meer

Fig. 10.22 Scatter of lithic tools, stones, and bones around two hearths at the late Paleolithic site of Pincevent in France. The use and distribution of such artifacts and scatters was the focus of study at Meer, but the bones were missing.

Fig. 10.23 The vertical distribution of the lithic artifacts at Meer. Refits between the top and bottom of the vertical distribution argue that the site represents a single episode of occupation, rather than a series of different visits. The vertical axis on the diagram shows the depth of artifacts at the site; the horizontal axis shows different sets of refitted artifacts.

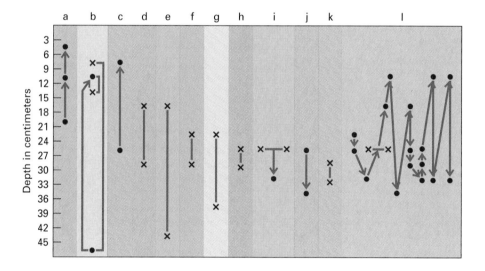

an area of 11 m² (the size of an average room). There was one small circular cluster of charcoal fragments in the northern end of CIV that was probably the remains of a hearth. The 1500 artifacts differed significantly from those in the other concentrations at the site. There were a large number of burins and drilling tools and very few projectile points or waste from making points. More than half of the flint material was very small flakes, many of which were from tool resharpening. These many small pieces suggest that activities using stone tools took place at this spot. A high proportion of the tools and waste in CIV could be refitted, another argument that they were made and used at this place (Fig. 10.24). This evidence also suggests that the activities probably took place over a short time, since the relationships among the artifacts have remained largely intact.

The archaeologists believe that Concentration I was a living area with more varied daily activities represented, in contrast to the specialized activities seen in CIV (Fig. 10.25). Microwear analysis and refitting have provided evidence to indicate that

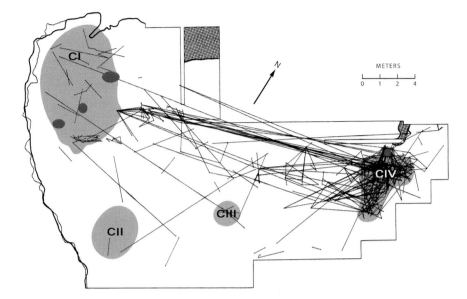

Fig. 10.24 The refits at Meer shown with lines connecting the refitted pieces. Four concentrations of stone artifacts (CI–CIV) are also shown on this drawing along with the four hearths at the site. This information, which took months to put together, helped the archaeologists understand what activities took place where at the site.

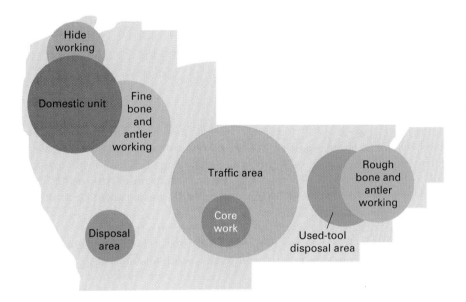

Fig. 10.25 Activity areas identified at Meer from the study of the lithic artifacts and their distribution. The various areas include a living area (domestic unit) and places for hide working, bone and antler working, stone tool making (core work), and refuse disposal.

CIV was focused on making bone and antler tools. The three major actions using stone tools were graving (cutting grooves), scraping (or planing), and boring. A difference between fine and coarse actions could be recognized in the tools. The investigators believe that this evidence indicates that the individuals working here cut out and shaped rough pieces (or "performs") of antler and bone before finishing them by smoothing and decorating.

The archaeologists then tried to determine how many individuals might have been working at CIV. The small size of the area would limit the number to no more than four persons, and it would be difficult for more than three to sit around the fire in the north end. In fact, the excavations had revealed two semicircular bands of flint artifacts around the hearth that suggest it would have been very crowded for three persons.

Next, Cahen and Keeley looked at the boring tools, which were twisted and turned to drill small holes into bone and antler. One set of these borers had been turned clockwise and the other counterclockwise. They argue that this pattern results from the handedness of the two individuals using these tools. Because the type of flint was distinctive, it was possible to look at how each of these individuals made their stone tools in CIV. The left-handed individual was careful, almost meticulous, in working the flint to produce very regular tools while the right-hander was impatient and rather careless in how the tools were made and used.

The detailed work of the archaeologists at Meer has provided an extraordinary insight into one of the small flint scatters that dot the landscape of northwestern Europe. The archaeologists concluded their study with a clever synopsis. They wrote:

"Once upon a time, 9,000 years ago in the Belgian Campine, a group of hunter-gatherers had established their camp on an old sand dune that rose above an area of marshes and woods. One day, a member of this group, a right-hander, walked a little way away from his habitation, built a fire, sat down beside it and began to make some tools. Some of these tools he made from blanks he had brought with him. He also brought along some cobbles of flint on which he prepared some platforms and struck from them a number of blanks which he retouched into tools. Using all of these tools, he began boring, graving and scraping bone and antler. While he was at work another member of the group, a left-hander, sat down beside him next to the fire. This left-hander had brought with him a previously prepared core from which he now struck several elegant blanks and retouched them into tools. He also began boring and graving bone. After working for some time the left-hander departed, taking his core with him. The right-hander also left, taking with him a few tools, some blanks and one prepared core. He walked back to his habitation perhaps because the light had failed, or perhaps because supper was ready and the family was waiting (or not waiting). There in due course he gave his bone objects their finishing touches and decoration."

~~~~~~

OTHER STONE ARTIFACTS

There were many uses of stone in prehistory and only some involved shaping stone by flaking to make a useful tool. A variety of other techniques were also employed to shape stone for other purposes. For example, blocks of stone—marble, travertine, and other building stone—were cut out of quarries using fire and water, saws, and other methods and shaped into blocks for construction, or carved by chisels into statuary.

Stone was also shaped into useful artifacts. The term *ground stone artifacts* is applied to the general category of portable lithic objects including figurines, bowls and other containers, grinding slabs, beads, weapons, and many other forms. Often a combination of techniques was used to make the final product—hammering, pecking, grinding, and/or polishing. Rough blocks of basalt were hammered and ground into a variety of shapes to provide grindstones to turn corn kernels into flour in ancient Mesoamerica (Fig. 10.26). Carnelian cobbles were heated and flaked, then ground and polished, to make the fine, long beads known from the Harappan civilization in South Asia (see Chapter 4, "Harappan Beads"). Large nodules of flint were flaked into rough form and then polished into beautiful axes in the Neolithic of Scandinavia. Studies of ground stone tools are common in the archaeological literature and several are listed in the bibliography of this book.

CONCLUSIONS

Stone lasts almost forever and worked pieces of stone are a prized material for archaeologists. Stone was used for many purposes in the past, not only for making tools but also for construction, containers, figurines and statues, grinding grain, or shaping other materials. Stone artifacts dominated the Stone Age and survive readily to the present. In most parts of the world, stone artifacts can still be found in agricultural fields and on exposed ground surfaces.

Fig. 10.26 A basalt metate, or grinding stone, from Central Mexico. Length 32 cm (13 in).

THE FAR SIDE® BY GARY LARSON

"So what's this? I asked for a hammer! A *hammer*! This is a crescent wrench! ... Well, maybe it's a hammer. ... Damn these stone tools!"

Tools provide an interface between humans and the environment, enabling us to manipulate and change our surroundings. One of the most remarkable things about stone tools is the investment they represent—a vision of the future, an anticipation of action. An object was made at one time and place, often intended to be used later elsewhere. Stone tools document that our ancestors were planning for the future.

1.0 kg of flint

From 1.0 kg of flint:

The pebble tool would have 5 cm of cutting edge.

The handaxe would have about 30 cm of cutting edge.

Middle Paleolithic flake tools would have about 90 cm of cutting edge.

Upper Paleolithic blade production would have up to 14 m of cutting edge.

Fig. 10.27 The amount of cutting edge from 0.5 kg of flint in different periods of the Paleolithic. A pebble tool had some 5 cm of cutting edge. One Lower Paleolithic handaxe would have 30 cm of cutting edge. Ten Middle Paleolithic flake tools would have approximately 90 cm of cutting edge. Forty Upper Paleolithic blades might have as much as 14 m of cutting edge in total.

Much of the archaeology of early humans concerns changes in stone tools. These changes are evident in a number of trends during the Paleolithic period. In general, tools became smaller in size and more specialized in purpose over time. There was also a dramatic increase in the efficiency of raw material use towards the end of the Paleolithic when blade technology was introduced as a kind of mass production technique. This efficiency of use can be considered in terms of what happened to a fist-sized piece of raw material (Fig. 10.27). One pebble tool with perhaps 5 cm (2 in) of cutting edge was made from that piece of stone 2 million years ago. One handaxe with 25–30 cm (10–12 in) of edge was made during the Lower Paleolithic. Some 15–20 flakes could have been produced during the Middle Paleolithic and shaped into various kinds of tools with 90–120 cm (30–40 in) of edge. The introduction of blade technology, however, meant that perhaps 100 blades with 10–14 m (30–40 ft) of cutting edge could be made from that same amount of stone, a huge increase in efficiency.

In this chapter, we have seen how stone tools are made and used. The basics of flintknapping involve striking cryptocrystalline stone with a hammer to produce flakes and blades. Retouching is used to shape these artifacts into finished tools of a wide variety of forms and functions. Archaeologists use a number of methods in the study of stone tools. Here we have discussed typology and the concept of chaîne opératoire as two approaches to classifying and analyzing lithic artifacts. The use of refitting provides important information about where tools were used and discarded as well as details of the formation processes operating at a site. Microwear studies use high magnification to study the modification of tool edges in order to determine the kinds of materials that have been worked and the function of the stone tools themselves.

It is important to remember that stone artifacts provided our most important tools for more than 2 million years. These artifacts are a hallmark of humanness as much as the space station or your computer. Stone tools, because they survive, also provide much of the information that is used to study the prehistory of our species. Archaeology courses on lithic analysis are taught in many universities. Most archaeologists are familiar with stone artifacts and know the basic features of these materials, a testament to their importance in our discipline.

STONE TOOLS AND THE AMERICAN BOTTOM

Four sites have recently been excavated in the American Bottom region of the Mississippi River. This area is one of the most fertile in the United States and has been occupied for many millennia. More information on this area is provided in Chapter 3 on the FAI-270 Project.

Prior research in the American Bottom and neighboring regions has established a number of facts that will help you answer the following questions.

1. During the Archaic period, people made large spear points, while during the Mississippian period people produced smaller points due to the introduction of the bow and arrow.

2. Experimentation and microwear analysis of edge damage of many tools has helped archaeologists determine production stages and assign general functions to a number of categories.

3. Study of the "hoes" has identified a distinct sheen due to being repeatedly forced into the ground. Hoe flakes were removed from the hoe but still retain the distinctive sheen.

4. We also know that two particular types of stone found at some of these sites come from different parts of the United States. The obsidian comes from the southwestern United States and the novaculite (a hard stone suitable for flaking) comes from southern Illinois.

5. Artifact categories such as chunks, cores, and cortical flakes are the result of the initial stages of stone tool production, where raw materials are converted to more usable pieces. Chunks are broken, but unworked pieces of raw material. Cortical flakes are pieces with some of the outer cortex or rind of the nodule present on the distal surface. Unused flakes and blades can be waste material or potential tools.

Table 10.2 shows summary counts of various chipped stone products at the four sites.

TABLE 10.2

	Crescent Hills	Dupo	Troy	Alton
Chunks	75	3	0	0
Cores	45	10	1	1
Cortical flakes	89	16	1	2
Used flakes	5	45	51	20
Unused flakes	97	30	12	4
Used blades	1	11	15	4
Unused blades	0	10	0	1
Small points	1	12	20	0
Large points	2	0	0	12
Hoe flakes	0	6	7	0
Total	315	143	107	44
Local chert	315	129	79	33
Novaculite	0	13	3	11
Obsidian	0	1	15	7

As a lithic analyst, you are asked to investigate the following issues:

1. The level of stone tool production at the site (either production or utilization).

2. The function of the tools and therefore the subsistence and economic orientation of each site.

3. The potential connections between each site and nearby regions.

4. The time period of each site (i.e., Archaic or Mississippian).

Based on the above data and background information, answer the following questions. Remember that archaeological data do not always support definitive conclusions, so simply present your best estimate. Your answers should be brief and to the point; most questions require only the name of the site for an answer. If you feel you need to justify your answer, use no more than two sentences.

1. Stone tool production

   What stages of tool manufacture and use seem to have been most prevalent at various sites? Identify the site(s) at which

   a. people were extracting raw material, shaping nodules into cores, but not using many tools at the site;

   b. people on the site seem to have been both making and using stone tools; and

   c. people were mainly using tools with very little evidence of production.

2. General site function (determined from the tool assemblages)

   Which site best matches each of the descriptions below? Consider both the numbers of artifacts and the kinds of tools present.

   a. Temporary hunting camp.

   b. Agricultural settlement with evidence for hunting.

   c. Station for preliminary flintknapping stages, probably close to a raw material source.

3. Inter-regional comparison

   Some of the artifacts at the above sites show links with other regions. Which sites have affiliations with neighboring regions to the

   a. southwest _____

   b. east _____

   c. both _____

4. Time period

   Some of these artifacts also indicate a temporal association with either the Archaic or Mississippian period. Which of the sites appears to be

   a. Mississippian.

   b. Archaic.

   c. Which site is difficult to place within one of these temporal phases and why?

STUDY QUESTIONS

1. Why is stone such an important material for making tools?

2. What kinds of information are present in stone tools?

3. What are the major trends in the evolution of stone tools?

4. How were stone tools used in the past?

5. How do archaeologists use stone tools to understand human behavior?

www.mhhe.com/pricearch1

For more review material and study questions, please see the self-quizzes on your online learning center.

REFERENCES

Adams, Jenny L. 2002. *Ground Stone Analysis: A Technological Approach.* Salt Lake City: University of Utah Press.

Andrefsky, W., ed. 2001. *Lithic Debitage: Context, Form, Meaning.* Salt Lake City: University of Utah Press.

Bamforth, D. B. 1986. Technological efficiency and tool curation. *American Antiquity* 51:38–50.

Bradley, B. A. 1975. Lithic reduction sequences: A glossary and discussion. *In Lithic Technology: Making and Using Stone Tools,* edited by E. Swanson. The Hague: Mouton.

Keeley, Lawrence H. 1980. *Experimental Determination of Stone Tool Use: A Microwear Analysis.* Chicago: University of Chicago Press.

Schick, Kathy, and Nick Toth. 1993. *Making Silent Stones Speak.* New York: Simon & Schuster.

Whittaker, J. C. 1994. *Flintknapping: Making and Understanding Stone Tools.* Austin: University of Texas Press.

www.mhhe.com/pricearch1

For Internet references related to this chapter, please see the chapter links on your online learning center.

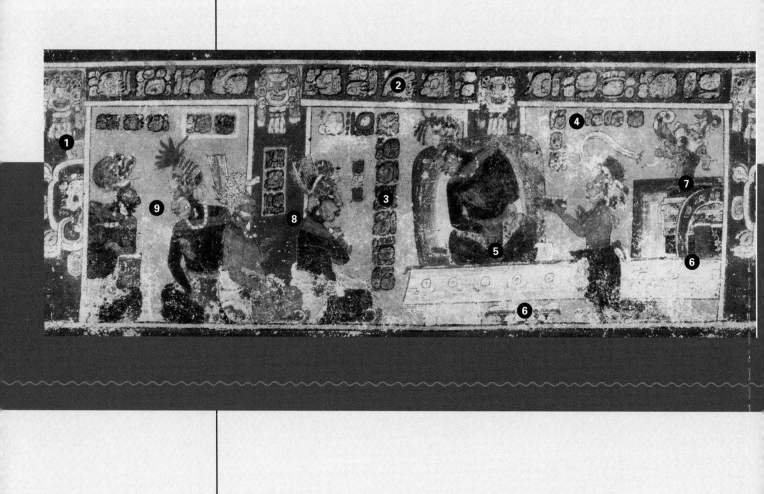

CHAPTER 11

Ceramic Analysis

INTRODUCTION: PREHISTORIC POTTERY

This photograph is a rollout of a spectacular painting in the round on a cylindrical vase from the Maya region, dating to approximately AD 720. Cylindrical vases are made using a slab technique, described in this chapter (Fig. 11.4). The place of origin of the vase is uncertain, but the story it tells is one of power, dominion, and life among the Maya nobility. There are thousands of these vases from the Maya area in museums and private collections. It is only in the last two decades, however, that advances in our understanding of the Maya hieroglyphic language and the chemical analysis of these ceramics have helped to decode their meaning, purpose, and origin.

The vase shows a complex scene depicting a Maya lord in front of three doors of a palace. The numbers on the painting refer to specific elements described here. To the left (1) are decorative designs on the red wall of the palace. Along the rim of the vessel above the three doors, the **lintels** are covered by **hieroglyphic** writing (2). There are additional inscriptions within the doors themselves. The hieroglyphs appear as a series of rounded rectangles, each different and each conveying the name of a person, a place, a date, or a verb. The date comes from the Maya calendar.

The inscriptions refer to specific individuals and important events. The words above the doors indicate this vase is the drinking cup of an artist and ballplayer (the Maya were hooked on a ritual game that involved a large rubber ball). His name was Chuy-ti Chan (*CHEWEY-tea CHAN*) and he was the son of a ruler, named Sak Muwaan (*SOCK MOO-ahn*), of an important center called Ik'. The text in the central doorway (3) commemorates the crowning of a Maya lord at another place. The glyphs in the room to the right (4) name the artist who made the vase, perhaps the individual shown below the text.

In front of the doorways sits the lord of this place on a raised platform (5), a huge pillow behind his back. A kneeling figure to the right, perhaps the artist himself, offers a dish of food. Other serving dishes are at his feet and to the right (6). A cylindrical vase, like this one, is shown with a lid and probably held a chocolate drink that was part of the feasting that took place at major ceremonies. Part of the costume and regalia of the lord can be seen behind and to the right inside the room, including a large headdress (7). To the left, four nobles are seated talking either to the lord (8) or to each other (9). All of the nobles wear elaborate headdresses and jewelry.

lintel   A horizontal beam of wood or stone that supports the wall above a doorway or window.

hieroglyph   Originally, the pictographic script of ancient Egypt; any depictive, art-related system of writing, such as that of *Mesoamerica*; may also refer to an individual symbol.

Fig. 11.1 Pottery can take many surprising forms. This example comes from the Jomon culture of Japan and dates to approximately 3000 BC. The earliest known pottery vessels in the world are from Japan and China and date to almost 12,000 years ago.

www.mhhe.com/pricearch1

For preview material for this chapter, please see the chapter summary, outline, and objectives on your online learning center.

sherds   Broken pieces of *pottery*.

ceramic   Fired *clay*.

pottery   *Ceramic* container or vessel.

Although the place where this vase was found is unknown, there are several clues about its origins. Analysis of the elemental chemical composition of the ceramic paste, in combination with study of the stylistic composition of the painting, suggests that the vessel was not made at Ik' or at other sites in the vicinity. The chemistry of the pottery points in fact toward a site called Maan (MAHN), approximately 150 km (100 mi) to the south of Ik'. Interpretation of the vessel suggests that it was given as a gift to the son of the ruler of Ik' when he attended the inauguration festivities of the new lord at Maan.

Such vases contain multiple messages—given as gifts, used for drinking sacred and expensive chocolate mixtures, depicting and authenticating the lives of the aristocrats of Maya society. As such, they are priceless archives of Maya history, as well as fascinating works of art.

Pottery often had multiple functions in the past and played an important role in human life. Ceramics in the form of abundant **sherds** and occasional vessels are also one of the more common archaeological materials to survive over the last 10,000 years or so. Ceramic analysis, then, is a key part of many archaeological investigations, and the subject of this chapter.

Ceramic is a remarkable material; it's basically a rock made by people. Firing soft clay to create a hard ceramic was an important discovery permitting the invention of containers—cooking and storage vessels—and other objects. The earliest known use of fired clay is for small human and animal figurines dating from about 25,000 years ago in the Upper Paleolithic in Europe. The first ceramic containers, actual **pottery**, appeared around 12,000 years ago in Japan and China.

There are many different kinds of pottery, depending on the kinds of clay used, the firing temperature, and other factors. Most early pottery is a form of earthenware, rather porous and fired at relatively low temperature, usually buff, red, or brown in color. Pottery containers are fairly fragile and normally have a short life. Broken pieces of pottery (known as sherds), however, are largely indestructible and found at many archaeological sites.

Pottery is a useful material for archaeologists because it is made in a regular way according to cultural patterns (Fig. 11.1). People made decisions about what kinds of clays to use, what size and shape pot to make, how to fire the pottery, how to decorate the vessel—decisions that leave distinctive traces in the ceramics. These patterns help archaeologists to understand the technology, activities, and interaction of different groups of people. Changes in pottery size, shape, color, and design over time also provide important chronological indicators.

This chapter provides an overview of prehistoric pottery, how it is made, how archaeologists analyze ceramics, and how archaeologists use pottery to study human behavior. These topics are considered in the next two sections—titled "Making Pottery" and "Studying Pottery." The composition of pottery is also an important characteristic, and several techniques have been developed to examine the physical and chemical makeup of ceramics, also discussed in this chapter.

MAKING POTTERY

There are a number of steps in the manufacture of ceramic vessels, including the collection of raw materials, the preparation of the paste, shaping the vessel, decoration, and firing (Fig. 11.2). Each step imparts distinctive characteristics to the final vessel that archaeologists study as part of ceramic analysis.

Collecting Raw Materials

The primary material used to make ceramics is **clay**. Clay becomes plastic when mixed with water and will hold a shape; it becomes hard when heated. These properties are essential for the production of pottery. Pottery-making peoples collect clays from nearby natural sources, usually within a few kilometers of their residence. Clay is any very fine-grained sediment, deposited in water and usually found in the area of a former lake or in stream deposits. Clay in the ground is usually moist and can be dug out of its source. Raw clay must sometimes be cleaned and prepared for the next step of making a paste.

Preparing the Paste

Natural deposits of clay are rarely suitable for making ceramics. A mix of clay and other materials called a **paste** is normally used to make pottery. These "other" materials are added to the clay, either intentionally by the potter or accidentally during preparation. For example, straw, seeds, and other materials were often rolled up in the paste as it was prepared on the ground. **Temper** is a nonplastic substance intentionally added to clay in order to reduce breakage caused by

clay   A very fine-grained sediment, deposited in water and usually found in former lake or stream deposits; raw material for making *pottery.*

paste   Mix of *clay* and other materials used to make *pottery.*

temper   A nonplastic substance intentionally added to *clay* in order to reduce breakage caused by shrinkage and firing.

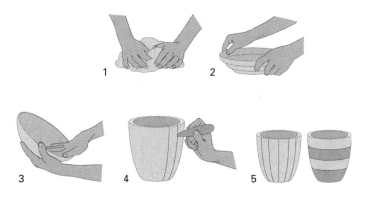

Fig. 11.2   Some of the basic steps in the making of pottery: 1. preparing the paste; 2–3. building the vessel; 4. decorating the pot; 5. finished vessels.

Fig. 11.3 Two common ways of making pottery vessels—hand and wheel.

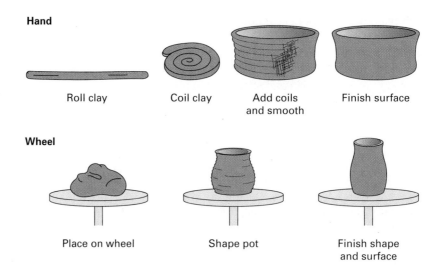

Hand

Roll clay Coil clay Add coils and smooth Finish surface

Wheel

Place on wheel Shape pot Finish shape and surface

shrinkage and firing. Prehistoric ceramics are typically about 70–80% clay and 20–30% temper. The temper allows a more even distribution of heat during the firing process. A variety of materials can be and have been used as temper, including sand, shell, volcanic ash, pulverized sherds (known as grog), bone, or rock, and even organic materials such as grass and other fibers. The type of temper used in pottery is often an important characteristic for archaeological studies and may be distinctive of certain places or groups of people.

Shaping the Vessel

Once the paste is prepared, the potter can begin to shape it into a vessel. There are three major techniques for forming pottery—using the hands, a mold, or a wheel. The most common methods in the past were coiling by hand or throwing on a wheel (Fig. 11.3). Each technique leaves distinctive marks that can be identified. Handmade ceramics are more irregular and idiosyncratic, as hand crafted objects tend to be.

Handmade ceramics were commonly made in one of three ways, using a coil, or paddle-and-anvil, or slab technique. In the **coil** method, long ropes of clay are rolled out and used to build up the walls of the vessel, pinching and pressing the coils together so that they disappear on the surface of the vessel (Fig. 11.3). Sherds of pottery made in this way often reveal the shape of the coils in their broken edges. The **paddle-and-anvil** method involves the use of tools to shape a lump of paste into a vessel. The anvil can be a small round stone or other hard object held on the inside of the pot while the paddle (stone, wood, or other material) is used on the outside to press against the anvil and flatten and spread the clay material to shape the vessel. The two techniques can also be used together—a coil-built vessel finished with paddle and anvil.

Another hand technique for making pottery involves rolling a **slab** of clay into a cylinder or fitting slabs of clay together to make a cube (Fig. 11.4). The two edges of the slab are joined neatly so that the seam is not visible and a base is fitted to one end of the cylinder. This technique for making vases is known from only a few areas. Some forms of Maya pottery were made in this manner, including the example discussed at the beginning of this chapter.

Molded ceramics are produced by pressing clay into prepared molds, carved in stone, wood, or made from ceramic. The paste casts are then removed and the object is fired in a kiln to harden it. In some cases, pottery vessels are made from two or more castings that must be joined before firing. Molded ceramics can also be made by pouring liquid clay into a mold. The mold technique

coil technique *Pottery* vessel made by ropes of *clay* used to build up the walls of the vessel.

paddle-and-anvil technique Use of two *tools* to press and shape the walls of a *ceramic* vessel.

slab technique *Pottery* vessel made by rolling a single sheet of *clay* into a cylinder and attaching a base.

molded *Pottery* produced by pressing *clay* into prepared molds.

Slab

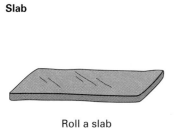
Roll a slab

Shape slab

Smooth join

Finish surface

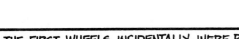

Fig. 11.4 Sequence of steps in the making of pottery using the slab technique. The finished product in this illustration is a cylindrical vase.

From *Cartoon History of the Universe* by Larry Gonick. Copyright © 1990 by Larry Gonick. Used by permission of Doubleday, a division of Random House, Inc.

results in virtually identical products and allows them to be made quickly. Molds were used to make figurines and elaborate ceremonial ceramics in Mesoamerica and other parts of the world. The famous Moche portrait vessels from Peru were made in this fashion (Fig. 2.3).

Wheel-thrown ceramics appear relatively late in time, around 3000 BC in Southwest Asia. The new method permits faster, more efficient production. A lump of paste on a spinning potter's wheel can be turned into a ceramic vessel in a matter of a few minutes compared with the much longer time required to build up a **hand-thrown** vessel. Wheel-thrown vessels often have horizontal circular bands on the inside or even outside of the vessel as a result of the manufacturing process. Wheel-thrown pottery is usually associated with state-level societies and specialized production facilities.

Decoration

Once a pottery vessel is formed into its intended shape, it may be decorated. There are many different ways to decorate the surface of ceramic vessels. Most forms of decoration are applied to the soft clay of the vessel before firing. Some techniques served to enhance the use of the vessel. Smoothing or **burnishing**, for example, improves bonding between coils. Decoration also functioned to signal individual or group identity as a social or ethnic symbol. In some cultures, decorations were used to tell stories and record events, myths, and legends.

The decoration of pottery involves modifying the surface of the vessel in some way. The surface can be burnished with a flat stone or similar object. This burnishing results in a shiny surface on the finished pot. The surface can be **brushed**, or roughened, before firing to give it a distinctive appearance.

wheel-thrown *Pottery* produced on a wheel with distinctive manufacturing characteristics.

hand-thrown *Pottery* made by hand.

burnishing Decorative technique for *pottery* involving smoothing or polishing of the surface.

brushing Decorative technique for *pottery* involving roughening of the surface.

Fig. 11.5 Various punctate and impressed decorations made with sticks, bone, cord, quills, and scalloped shell. These examples come from South Africa, but similar patterns are known in many other areas.

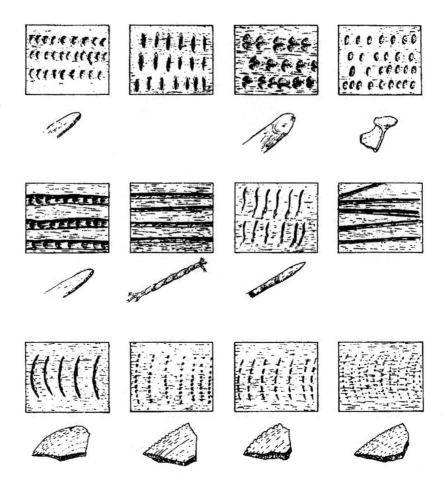

impressing Decorative technique for *pottery* involving impressions or incisions made with various small *tools*.

incising Decorative technique for *pottery* involving cutting or carving lines and other designs in the surface of the *clay*.

cord-marked Decorative technique for *pottery* involving impressions of cord-wrapping in the *clay*.

punctate Decorative technique for *pottery* involving impressions of circular depressions in the surface of the *clay*.

appliqué Decorative technique for *pottery* involving the addition of *clay* pieces to the original *clay* vessel.

slip A coating of the surface of a *ceramic* vessel for decorative or functional reasons.

glaze A metallic or glass mixture used to change the surface of the *pottery* vessel for decorative purposes.

resist A decorative technique for *pottery* involving materials which disappear on firing and leave a negative color on the surface of the vessel.

kiln Fire for making *pottery;* can be open or closed, updraft or downdraft.

waster *Pottery* that broke or warped in the process of firing.

A common technique in many areas involved some form of **impression** or **incision** in the soft clay of the unfired pot. Impressions were made with many different tools including fingernails, sharp sticks, combs, rollers, shells, or small paddles covered with cord or textiles (Fig. 11.5). **Cord-marked** pottery is one of the more common types of decoration in the past and is found on every continent. A string or cord was wrapped around a stick and pressed into the surface of the clay, leaving an impression of the string and any knots or features in it. Nets or fabric were sometimes pressed into clay vessels, leaving their own distinctive impressions.

Incising involves cutting designs into the soft clay of an unfired vessel. Lines could be carved into the clay with a sharp stick, bone, or flint using a stab and drag technique. Incised decorations usually include rows or patterns of straight lines that are arranged in zones. Incising can produce low relief designs, depending on the depth of cutting. Small round sticks were sometimes pressed into the clay to leave a series of circular depressions in a technique known as **punctate**. Designs were also stamped or rocked into soft clay using toothed tools like a short comb or the scalloped edge of a shell (Fig. 11.5). These tools could also be used in a stamp and drag technique to carry the pattern across the surface of the clay. Incised and impressed designs are somewhat limited in the varieties that can be produced, and similar kinds of designs are seen in various parts of the world where these techniques were employed.

Another form of decoration involved adding clay to the outside of the vessel. Pieces of clay could be attached to the basic pottery form, a technique known as **appliqué**, to add decoration to the rim or body. Lugs or handles were another form of appliqué, for practical or decorative reasons.

Slips and **glazes** involve coating the surface of the unfired vessel with a liquid clay or another mixture that leaves a thin layer on the pot. Slips and glazes can be applied by dipping, brushing, or wiping. Slips usually are added to change the color of the surface of the pot and perhaps to reduce permeability. Glazes are mixtures of metallic chemicals or glass, brushed or washed onto the surface of a pot to produce a distinctive finish. Firing a glaze produces a hard and shiny surface distinct from the original clay material. The earliest use of glaze on pottery is found in China ca. 1500 BC. A **resist** is an unusual technique in prehistory involving the use of a wax or another material to prevent a slip or glaze from covering a portion of a vessel.

The use of paint for decoration allows the clay to be a canvas for design. A great range of colors and designs were painted on pottery in the past (Fig. 11.6). Painted pottery was not made everywhere and usually appeared later than other types of decoration. Spectacular painted vessels, normally found in graves or as offerings or ritual objects of some kind, were often produced by craft specialists. Painted pottery is defined by the application of pigments. Painting was usually done on the dry clay of a vessel before firing. Both mineral and organic pigments were used to create a variety of colors. Colors were usually black, white, red, or orange and were produced from a variety of metallic oxides and oils. Paints were applied in various ways but usually with a brush or swab.

Firing

After the pot is thrown and decorated, it is allowed to dry for some time to remove water and stiffen the shape before firing. Temperatures required for hardening clay are around 800°C and higher. Firing can be done in an open fire or a **kiln**, a specialized oven or furnace for firing pottery. Temperatures are more controlled and higher in a kiln than in an open fire. A wide variety of kilns have been used in the past. One important distinction among them is whether they are open or closed. Pottery that is fired in an open kiln is said to be produced in an "oxidizing atmosphere," that is, one in which oxygen is continuously available. Open kilns reach temperatures around 900°C, sufficient to oxidize the pottery.

Pottery in a closed kiln, without fresh air, is fired in a "reducing atmosphere," one that is lacking oxygen. A closed kiln, which is a kind of oven, can reach temperatures for vitrification, up to 1000°C or more. Vitrification fuses the clays in the pottery and makes it waterproof. Oxidizing atmospheres produce pottery with dark, black cores, while reducing atmospheres produce ceramics with lighter, reddish interiors. A special type is the updraft kiln. This kiln takes in air at the bottom to feed the flames and fire pottery in the upper part of the structure (Fig. 11.7).

Kilns are usually straightforward to identify at archaeological sites. The remains are distinguished by an area of massive burning often associated with reddish discoloration of the surrounding earth and quantities of ash. Sometimes the structural remains of the kiln itself can be observed. Ceramic **wasters** are another good piece of evidence. Wasters are the pieces of pottery that broke in the process or did not fire correctly and were discarded around the kiln.

STUDYING POTTERY

Most of the pottery that archaeologists find is broken in pieces, or sherds. Whole vessels are rare and usually found in graves and other special situations. Archaeologists use pottery sherds to try to understand what the complete vessels looked like, how they were made, how they were used, what they contained, and how far they may have been moved. There are three basic levels of analysis in ceramic studies: the visual identification of macroscopic features, the microscopic identification of petrographic characteristics, and instrumental identification of chemical characteristics. These levels of analysis are discussed in the following sections of this chapter.

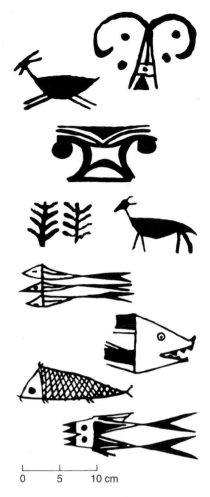

Fig. 11.6 Examples of black-painted zoomorphic and geomorphic designs painted on Yangshao pottery from China.

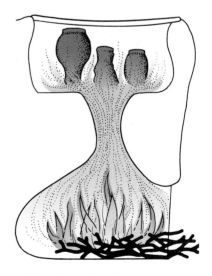

Fig. 11.7 Updraft kiln reconstructed from the Neolithic site of Ban-po-'tsun in China.

Fig. 11.8 Excavations at large sites can produce thousands and thousands of potsherds. The sorting and classification of this material is an enormous job.

The initial steps in analysis deal with sorting through the different kinds of pottery found at a site and the classification of pottery types. Archaeologists have developed ceramic typologies for most time periods and many places. Chapter 7, "Classification and Data," provides additional information on typology. Typological categories are usually based on characteristics such as surface treatment, temper, paste, color, and decorative techniques. Pottery typology provides geographic and chronological information based on the types that are present at a site.

More detailed analyses of prehistoric pottery focus on form, function, and style. Each of these is examined in this chapter. In addition to typology and investigations of form, function, and style, ceramics provide substantial information on group interaction and social organization.

Initial Sorting

Archaeologists normally study pottery sherds, the fragmentary remains of the original ceramic containers and vessels. Whole vessels rarely survive. Sherds are simply broken pieces of pottery; the term *shard* is common in classical archaeology, but is not used in prehistoric archaeology. The sherds from an excavation or survey are usually washed and sometimes numbered to identify their provenience, or place of discovery. These sherds are then initially sorted using several criteria, like color, thickness, and decoration (Fig. 11.8).

An important distinction is made between **rim sherds** and **body sherds** (Fig. 11.9). Rim sherds include part of the rim or mouth and can tell a lot about the vessel. Rim sherds indicate how the pot was finished and how big the vessel was. Rim pieces often are more heavily decorated than body sherds. Body sherds are rimless pieces of the pot that are useful, but less informative.

A variety of terms are used to describe a pottery vessel in addition to rim and body. The **base** of the pot provides a good indicator of the overall shape. Bases are usually flat, rounded, or pointed. The **shoulder** of the vessel is the transition zone where the shape changes as the body ends and the neck begins. The shoulder of the vessel is the place where the angle of the wall profile distinctly changes. This shoulder zone is a very visible part of the pot and often decorated. The **neck** is the zone between the shoulder and the rim. A **collar** is sometimes added to the

---

rim sherd Fragment of broken *pottery* that includes part of the rim of the vessel.

body sherd Fragment of broken *pottery* that does not include the rim of the vessel.

base The lower part of a *ceramic* vessel.

shoulder The transition zone where the body ends and the neck begins on a *ceramic* vessel.

neck The upper zone on a *pottery* vessel between the *shoulder* and the rim.

collar A vessel rim with added *clay* material.

orifice The opening or mouth of a *ceramic* vessel.

profile A cross-section of archaeological or geological deposits showing the *stratigraphy*, sequence of layers. Also, the cross-section of the walls of a *ceramic* vessel, a measure of shape.

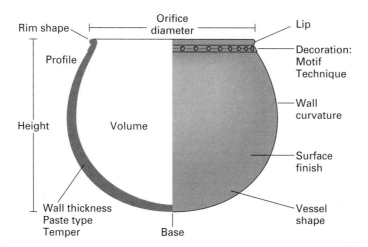

Fig. 11.9 Some common metric and nonmetric attributes of a ceramic vessel.

rim of the vessel, providing a more pronounced edge around the opening of the vessel. The collar is an area around the rim that is present only if additional clay has been added to this area to make it thicker.

Attributes of Form and Function

One of the goals of ceramic analysis is to reconstruct the size and shape, or form, of the original vessel. This information can tell us about the possible function of the vessel and provide additional information on manufacture and style. There are specific techniques for the analysis of the **orifice** or opening of the vessel, the thickness of vessel wall, and the **profile** of the vessel. The term *profile* refers to the cross section of the wall of the pot. This profile defines the shape of the vessel.

Fig. 11.10 is a diagram for determining the type of vessel based on the angle of the profile. Jars, bowls, dishes, and platters are distinguished using this scheme. Vases would be another category with more vertical, parallel walls. Other forms are also found archaeologically, including cups, bottles, and pitchers.

Another important attribute is the orifice. The diameter of the orifice is a good indicator of the overall size of the pot, and this value is often used to estimate the volume of the vessel. Orifice can be determined from a rim sherd using a series of measured circumferences as a diameter key (Fig. 11.11). With this information, vessel volume can be estimated.

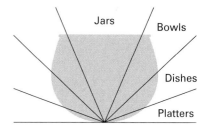

Fig. 11.10 A diagram for determining vessel type by angle of walls, measured from the center of the base to the rim. The pot shown here is a bowl.

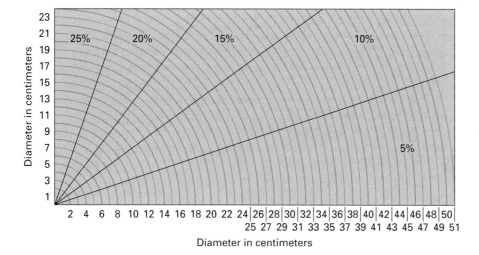

Diameter in centimeters

Fig. 11.11 A chart for determining orifice diameter from a rim sherd. The curve of the rim is placed on the chart to match one of the lines, and the diameter of the vessel is read from the x- or y-axis of the diagram. The percentages indicate the proportion the rim sherd is of the entire circumference of the vessel. Note that this illustration is not to scale.

Fig. 11.12 Measurement and recording of various attributes is an important part of ceramic analysis.

Ceramic as a class of material was used for a variety of purposes in prehistory. The term *ceramic* refers to any object made of fired clay; the term *pottery* refers specifically to ceramic containers. Ceramic was used for figurines, musical instruments (flutes and whistles), sling ammunition, and cooking "stones," in addition to containers.

Pottery also had many functions in the past—for storage, cooking, serving, drinking, straining, washing, and other purposes. The contents of the containers varied in these contexts. Some pottery clearly had several purposes. The Maya vase described at the beginning of this chapter, for example, was a container for a chocolate drink and a gift, as well as a status item.

These uses are important indicators of past human activity, but determination of the function of prehistoric pottery is often difficult. Small potsherds do not usually exhibit obvious indicators of the contents or function of the vessel. Several different kinds of information are used to investigate how ceramic containers were used—form, context, residues, use wear—and these are described below.

Function follows form in the study of the use of pottery. Size and shape provide clues about the use of a vessel. For example, large pottery containers were probably used for storage for liquids or bulk materials. They would not have been suitable for cooking. Cooking vessels are small or medium in size and have traces of burning on the outside or cooking on the inside of the vessel. Serving vessels are often bowl- or plate-shaped without other indications of use. Most pottery contains little indication of how it was used. Context—the location where the pottery was found (provenience) and the kinds of things found with it (association)—provides some of the best indications of how a container was used. The discovery of huge jars in underground storage rooms alongside bins for storing grain, for example, offers strong evidence that these jars were for storage, probably for olive oil or wine (Fig. 11.13).

Residues on pottery are found in several forms and can reveal both use and contents. Charred cooking residues sometimes are found inside vessels, adhering to the surface of the sherd. These residues first of all indicate use for cooking; in some cases, even the contents of the residue can be determined. An example of such a case from Denmark is discussed below.

An invisible residue can also be recovered in some cases from the interior clay of the pottery itself. Chemical residues, fragments of the fat and protein molecules of the contents, bond to the clay minerals of the vessel walls and can be extracted and sometimes identified using organic chemistry. Organic residues are discussed in more detail in Chapter 15, "Archaeometry."

Fig. 11.13 Large pithos, or storage jars, at the palace of Knossos (*KAH-know-sows*), Crete, approximately 2 m (6 ft) high, found in the storerooms in the basement of the palace.

Finally, some indication of use can be seen in the wear and damage to a vessel. Cooking pots may also show thermal spalling and oxidation from repeated heating. Washing of cooking vessels or stirring may leave distinctive marks or physical traces on the inside of a vessel. The absence of wear marks may indicate the use of the vessel in less active contexts or for display.

Attributes of Style

Most people know what style is, but would have a hard time defining the concept. The same is true in archaeology. Style is what is left when you take away function. Style appears in the choices that humans make in the way that they do things. As we have seen, stylistic variation is important in archaeology for studying changes in artifacts over time and space. Changes in the ways that people do things are the hallmarks of culture history, of the temporal and geographic description of the human past.

Stylistic attributes in pottery are those characteristics that reflect choices that the potter made in raw material, shape, design, decoration, and firing. It is that kind of style reflected in design elements and decoration that is most frequently the focus of analysis in archaeology. One way to visualize stylistic variation is to consider a series of pottery vessels from a particular area and time span. Fig. 11.16 shows a series of reconstructed pottery vessels from the Mississippian period in the Midwestern United States. There are a variety of vessels from each of the five phases, differing in size, shape, and decoration. The changes in the pottery take place over approximately 350 years, from bottom to top.

Clearly, a range of functions is represented in these assemblages. There are bowls, jars, pitchers, and plates intended for different purposes as indicated by their size and shape. Beyond the function of the vessels, however, there are clear differences in shape and decoration that represent choices that were made, styles that were incorporated, in the manufacture of the pottery. Distinct changes over time can be seen in the pottery with more surface decoration in the Moorehead and Sand Prairie assemblages and a clear decline in diversity at the end of the

What's Cooking?

Tybrind Vig is a remarkable underwater archaeological site in Denmark, dating from the Mesolithic period, approximately 4500 BC. Although the inhabitants were hunter-gatherers, they also made and used distinctive pointed-base pottery vessels. Rather heavy ceramic vessels with large pieces of temper were used for cooking and storage.

Because of the quality of preservation at this underwater site, traces and residues from heating and cooking were preserved on some of the pots. Soot or burn marks on the outside of the vessel were one indication of use for cooking. Other residues, known as food crusts, were the result of the burning and charring of food in and on the vessel. Fig. 11.14 shows where traces of cooking appeared on these vessels from Tybrind Vig, both on the inside and outside. The heaviest traces were on the outer lip and neck, likely from boiling over during cooking.

A second area of concentrated food residues was found on the inside bottom of the pot, where heavy charred remains can be observed (Fig. 11.15). In the food crust on some of the sherds, there were visible traces of fish scales and small fish bones, likely from cod species. Under a microscope, thin, grass-like stalks could be seen in the food crusts.

Several radiocarbon (^{14}C) dates were obtained from the food crusts in these vessels providing an accurate date for the pottery. The laboratory also measured the stable carbon isotopes (^{13}C, ^{12}C) in the samples. The ratio of these two isotopes (see Chapter 15, "Archaeometry") indicated that the charred contents of the vessels were largely from terrestrial, rather than marine, foods. This information contradicts the evidence from the codbones and may suggest that the biggest portion of the contents of the pot were vegetables rather than fish. A few charred potsherds can provide a great deal of information on the use of prehistoric pottery.

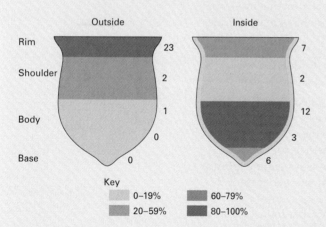

Fig. 11.14 Cooking traces and residues on the inside and outside of Mesolithic pottery from the site of Tybrind Vig, Denmark. The numbers along the right side of the pot show how many times evidence for cooking was observed on pottery at the site. The shading shows the percentage of occurrence of these traces. Most of the cooking traces on the outside are near the rim from boil over; most of the traces on the inside are on the bottom from overcooking and charring.

Fig. 11.15 A potsherd from the Mesolithic site of Tybrind Vig, Denmark, showing fish scales and seed impressions in the food crusts on the bottom of the pot. The enlargement shows a bone likely from cod embedded in the food crust. The potsherd is approximately 7 cm (3 in) high.

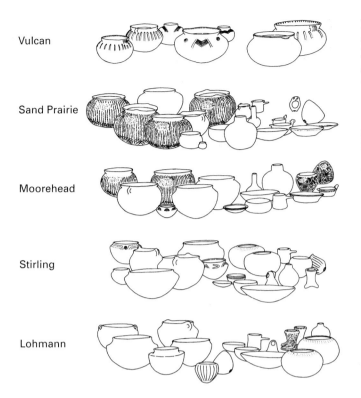

Vulcan

Sand Prairie

Moorehead

Stirling

Lohmann

Fig. 11.16 Mississippian pottery from the U.S. Midwest. Five chronological phases are shown, covering approximately 350 years from 1050 to 1400 BC, from bottom to top.

www.mhhe.com/pricearch1

For a Web-based activity on the site of Tybrind Vig, please see the Internet exercises on your online learning center.

sequence. These stylistic differences could be used to date the pottery and to examine its geographic distribution.

These differences between function and style in pottery are illustrated in Fig. 11.17. The drawing shows four different types of ceramic water vessels and the way they are carried in four areas of Guatemala. The function of all the vessels is the same—to hold and transport water. The manner of transporting water reflects local traditions or styles; the location and number of handles on the vessels is a stylistic difference, but it is also functional since the vessels are made to be held in a certain way. Obviously, form and function are related to style and tradition.

Fig. 11.17 Four different styles of water jars and transport in the highlands of Guatemala.

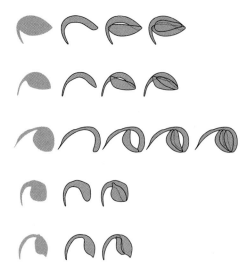

Fig. 11.18 The same design motif, a curved leaf, painted by five different ceramic artists from the village of San José in Mexico.

In addition to the information on time and geographic space present in stylistic variation, there are patterns that reflect identity, social organization, and ideology. Style in pottery can reflect individual or group choices, and these choices may be intentional or instinctive. Individual styles reflect personal choice or group conventions. Margaret Hardin studied individual variation among Mexican potters in the village of San José and found substantial differences among the artists in producing a single design motif (Fig. 11.18).

Ceramic design and style provides a major source of information about the past. James Deetz (1930–2000) was one of the first archaeologists to try to connect ceramic styles with past social organization. Deetz was interested in "how relationships perceived in the designs and forms of different sets of artifacts relate to organizing principles which tie a whole society together, and how over time these shift." Deetz believed that artifacts could provide key insights into the people of the past.

Deetz focused on a large assemblage of pottery from three time periods (1690 to 1720, 1720 to 1750, and 1750 to 1780) at a large Arikara Indian site in South Dakota. Deetz defined and recorded the presence or absence of more than 150 different traits, or attributes, on 2500 sherds from these three periods at the site. He then studied the associations among the attributes, which ones occurred together—either rarely or frequently. He noted that the total number of different attributes increased over time (more stylistic differences in the youngest period), but that the number of attributes regularly found together decreased (pottery styles were more mixed and diverse).

Based on other information from this region, Deetz assumed that women had made the pottery. He argued that women taught female children to make pottery and to decorate it. Thus, older women taught younger women to make pottery in the same way, using the same attributes, over generations. Where this practice was stable and consistent, there should be strong associations among the stylistic elements involved in the decoration of ceramics. Thus, Deetz suggested that the decrease in attributes that occurred together in the youngest period at the Arikara site likely reflected changes in the social organization of the group.

European contact and disease impacted the Arikara during the latter half of the eighteenth century and this may well have led to a breakdown in society. Deetz suggested that there was a shift in marital residence—individuals marrying and moving to a new place and community—over time. The two most common types of marital residence changes are matrilocal and patrilocal. Matrilocal marriage is a practice whereby the groom moves to the community of the bride; patrilocal residence rules send the bride to the home place of the groom. Deetz

In the beginning, God gave to every people a cup, a cup of clay, and from this cup they drank their life. They all dipped in the water, but their cups were different. Our cup is broken now. It has passed away.
—A chief of the Digger Indians to James Deetz

coefficient of stylistic variability A statistical measure of the strength of association among stylistic attributes.

Iroquois Pottery

Ceramic analysis often focuses on the relationship between pottery styles and human social organization. In pottery, elements of style can be seen in attributes of decoration and shape. These stylistic attributes of the pottery are usually recorded as present or absent. Robert Whallon of the University of Michigan recorded the presence or absence of a number of stylistic elements on prehistoric pottery from New York State. This pottery came from a series of sites spanning a 400-year period that ended at approximately 1500 AD. The earlier sites belong to the Owasco period while the latest sites he studied are Iroquois. Stylistic elements that Whallon recorded included rim profile, collar shape, rim orientation, neck form, design technique, and design motif (Fig. 11.19).

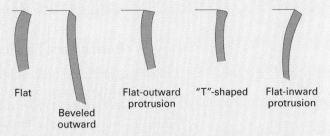

Fig. 11.19   Typical Owasco pottery rim profiles.

Archaeologists often use the co-occurrence of stylistic elements as a measure of social interaction. Communication and interaction between groups of people introduces new elements of design, new techniques of manufacture, new shapes. New patterns mean less association along stylistic elements. The opposite is also true; the more frequently the same elements occur together, the less social interaction between groups was taking place. This is the basic concept that Deetz used to study the Arikara ceramics.

The question is how to measure the strength of co-occurrence of stylistic elements. Whallon used a statistic that provided a summary measure (a single number) of the strength of association among the stylistic attributes at each site. This **"coefficient of stylistic variability"** varies between zero and one; the higher the value, the stronger the co-occurrence among the attributes and the more homogeneous the pottery.

Whallon calculated this statistic for pottery rim sherds from the New York sites. Fig. 11.20 shows a graph of the coefficient for the stylistic characteristics of rim profile, one kind of stylistic element. Rim profile is the shape of a cross-section through the rim sherd. Association, measured by changes in stylistic variation, is clearly increasing over time and higher at the more recent Owasco sites. This greater homogeneity in the pottery likely reflects a decrease in social contact among villages; fewer new patterns were introduced into the Owasco pottery. With the onset of the Iroquois period, variability gradually decreased.

This pattern corresponds well with other archaeological data from the area. It is known, for example, that fortifications appeared for the first time and then expanded during this same Owasco period. In addition, population—estimated from the total number of sites—was also increasing. It is likely that these two events are closely related; as population grew, there was increasing conflict and—based on the ceramic analysis—fewer interactions among the villages.

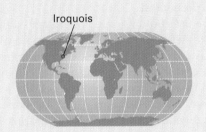

Iroquois

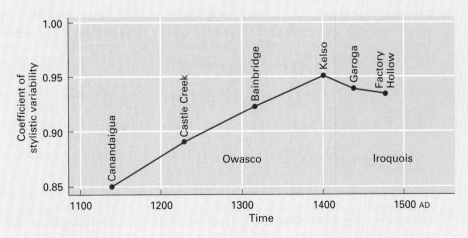

Fig. 11.20   A graph of the coefficient of stylistic variability for rim profile from Owasco and Iroquois ceramics between AD 1100 and 1500. The peak in variation occurs at the end of the Owasco period, ca. AD 1400.

argued that the changes in the pottery reflected a change from matrilocal residence during the older period of occupation at the site to patrilocal residence during the last phase of occupation. Such a practice would have brought women from different villages together into the same settlement and resulted in a greater mix of stylistic attributes and less association.

Provenience Studies

Another important kind of ceramic study involves the investigation of provenience, or source, of pottery. Determination of the place of origin of ceramics allows researchers to understand various aspects of social interaction, trade and exchange, and economy in the past. Several types of information can be used to investigate provenience. The kind of temper, vessel shape, or design motif can sometimes provide clues as to place of origin. More commonly, archaeologists use studies of the composition of the pottery—clays and tempers—to determine possible source areas. Three levels of analysis are available for studying composition: visual studies of distinctive tempers, petrographic studies of clays and inclusions in pottery, and compositional studies of ceramic using instrumental methods such as neutron activation or spectrometry. Visual inspection of ceramic tempers by eye or using a magnifying glass can sometimes reveal the kind of material used for tempering, such as shell, sand, bone, and so on. Petrographic and compositional studies are more complicated and are described in detail in the next sections.

Ceramic Petrography

Ceramic petrography is a useful microscopic technique to identify the physical composition of pottery sherds. The analyst makes a slide for study by sawing the edge of sherd to create a flat surface and then sawing a narrow slice from the same edge to create a thin section of the sherd (Fig. 11.22). Grinding and polishing this section to a thinness of 0.3 mm makes it translucent (light passes through), and the components of the sherd can be seen in a petrographic microscope. Various inclusions (foreign bodies) in the pottery—temper and other components of the paste—are of primary interest to the analyst.

A petrographic microscope uses both normal and polarized light to view the inclusions in the pottery paste (see section on the petrographic microscope in Chapter 9, "Geoarchaeology"). The way that light passes through the inclusions is the key to identifying the contents. Polarized light shows different aspects of the inclusions. The analyst is trained to recognize a variety of different minerals and other materials under different light conditions. The microscope can also be used for counting and measuring inclusions so that density and size become additional information on the components. These components vary from potter to potter, among types of pottery, and from region to region. Information on the identity, size, and quantity of the components is useful for determining the place of origin of the pottery and studying interaction among prehistoric communities. A study applying ceramic petrography to materials from the site of Icehouse Bottom is described here.

EXAMPLE

ICEHOUSE BOTTOM

Icehouse Bottom in Tennessee is a village settlement from the Hopewell period, dating to approximately AD 175 (Fig. 11.21). Hopewell is one of the most fascinating and enigmatic periods in the prehistory of North America. It is best known from a series of huge earthworks and mounds from across the Midwest. Hopewell is sometimes

ceramic petrography Microscopic technique for study of the mineral composition of *pottery*.

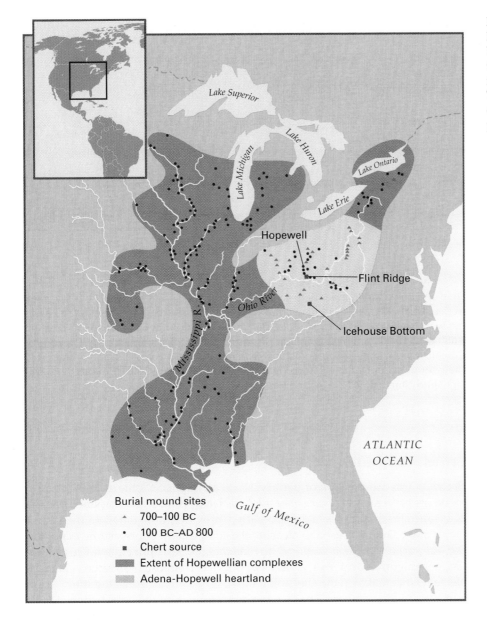

Fig. 11.21 The distribution of Hopewell materials in the eastern United States. The lighter area shows the concentration of Hopewell sites in the central Ohio River Valley. The darker color shows the location of sites with Hopewell materials present.

described as an "Interaction Sphere" because of the dramatic evidence for long-distance trade that is present. Hopewell culture is centered in southern Ohio, where burial sites include materials such as **obsidian** from Wyoming, copper from Lake Superior, and conch shells from the Gulf of Mexico.

Icehouse Bottom was excavated in the early 1970s in an area eventually flooded by a new dam. The site is important for several reasons and contains a number of chert blades from a source in south-central Ohio, more than 400 km (250 mi) distant. Such evidence reflects the participation of the people of this settlement in exchange over a broad area.

Petrographic studies of pottery from the site document other exchanges. James Stoltman of the University of Wisconsin-Madison examined twenty-nine thin sections of pottery sherds from the site. Twenty-six of the ceramic sherds were tempered with local sand or limestone, which could be readily identified under the petrographic microscope. The sand grains were particularly diagnostic, made up of distinctive minerals and of very small size. Three sherds in the sample of twenty-nine were different, with a distinctive decoration, and suspected to have been imported from elsewhere. Microscopic analysis of these three sherds revealed that one contained only local sand temper, while the other two were tempered with an exotic grit of coarsely crushed granite (Fig. 11.22).

www.mhhe.com/pricearch1

For a Web-based activity on ceramics from North America, please see the Internet exercises on your online learning center.

obsidian A glassy rock produced from sand in volcanic conditions, used for making stone *tools* in the past.

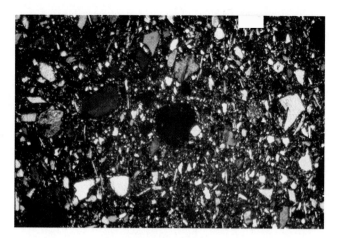

Fig. 11.22 Thin-section photomicrograph of a sherd from Icehouse Bottom at 10× under polarized light. Scale: Largest grain = 1.8 mm.

Stoltman also studied sherds from the central Hopewell region in southern Ohio and noted that temper here was typically crushed granite, identical to that seen in the two sherds from Icehouse Bottom. Among the sherds from Ohio that he studied were several with the same distinctive sand temper seen at Icehouse Bottom. Such evidence is not observable in the visible attributes of the sherds. The petrographic evidence thus documents the exchange of ceramic vessels (and presumably their contents) between western Tennessee and southern Ohio, providing new insight into "interaction" during the Hopewell period.

www.mhhe.com/pricearch1

For a Web-based activity on analyzing elements found in pottery, please see the Internet exercises on your online learning center.

Pots are about something other than use; they are not abstract in the way that art can be but belong in a context, they are not disengaged, but are about being with people and engaging with them.

—Jane Hamlyn, potter

Ceramic Composition

The chemical composition of pottery is also an important clue as to its place of origin, its provenience. A variety of methods have been used to measure chemical composition. Chapter 15, "Archaeometry," provides more detail on the instruments and techniques used to measure the composition of prehistoric materials. For our purposes here, it is enough to note that the basic principles of such studies are straightforward. Every piece of pottery is composed of various chemical elements that make up the clay and temper, for example, iron, aluminum, manganese, and many others. The chemical composition of the pottery depends on the mix of clay and temper and is often distinctive to the place where it was made. Most studies have looked at a series of elements to obtain a reliable indicator of the provenience of the pottery. The example on the following page concerns such a study in the southwestern United States.

CONCLUSIONS

Ceramic is an extraordinary material that first appeared in the archaeological record around 25,000 years ago as figurines, and again 12,000 years ago in the form of pottery. Virtually all societies today use ceramics in one form or another for a variety of purposes. Prehistoric pottery is largely known from the sherds, or pieces of broken pottery, that litter the surface of many sites. Complete ceramic vessels are rare in the archaeological record and are usually found only in special circumstances. Fig. 11.26 shows the ceramic assemblage from the early city of Mohenjo Daro (*moe-HIN-joe DAHR-oh*) in Pakistan, dating to approximately 2500 BC. These examples, shown whole, were pieced together from sherds found during the excavations.

Pottery is used primarily as a container, but has important roles as an art medium and status symbol. Prehistoric pottery was made initially by hand, often

polychrome Several colors; polychrome *pottery* is painted with at least two colors.

Salado Polychromes

Salado polychrome, distinguished by black and red designs painted on a white background, was one of the most common types of pottery in the American Southwest between AD 1275 and 1450. **Polychrome** refers to the presence of at least two colors on the same pottery vessel (Fig. 11.23).

There are three recognized groups of this Salado polychrome, distinguished by different designs and arrangements of the colors. The heartland of this pottery was in the Tonto Basin of central Arizona. Salado polychrome was widely distributed, however, and has been found hundreds of kilometers to the north, south, and east of the Tonto Basin (Fig. 11.24). It is found in adjacent culture areas—Hohokam, Mogollon, and Anasazi—as well as the "core" Salado region.

Both decorated and undecorated pottery was made and used in the Tonto Basin. Undecorated pottery was made using the paddle-and-anvil technique and comprises about 75% of the pottery. Decorated ceramics were made using the coil method and were then scraped and polished. Vessel sizes and shapes ranged from small to very large bowls and jars. Both kinds of pottery (decorated and undecorated) were used for various storage and food preparation tasks. Some of the storage vessels had a capacity of 200 to 250 liters (50 to 60 gallons—a keg of beer holds 30 gallons). Ceramic human and bird effigies were also produced.

In addition to Salado polychrome, a variety of "foreign" pottery was found in the Tonto Basin from the surrounding cultural areas of the Hohokam, Mogollon, and

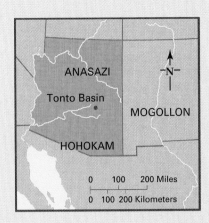

Fig. 11.24 Distribution of Salado materials in the American Southwest. The pottery is found hundreds of kilometers from the central Tonto Basin in Arizona, New Mexico, and northern Mexico. The approximate areas of Anasazi, Hohokam, and Mogollon are shown as well. For scale, the border between Arizona and New Mexico is about 700 km (400 mi) long.

Anasazi. This mix of many different pottery types is unusual and raises a number of questions about where the different types were being made, how they were distributed, what they contained, what the interregional connections in the Southwest were like at the time, and whether the interaction changed through time (Fig. 11.25).

Fig. 11.23 Painted pottery from the southwestern United States with geometric designs made using black and red pigments.

Continued

Salado Polychromes (continued)

There are two possible sources for the Salado polychromes. Either the pottery was made in many different places, which would be unusual because the places were so dispersed, or it was centrally produced in the core area and exported long distances, which also seems unlikely because the pottery is so common. Arelyn Simon, James Burton, and David Abbott tried to resolve these questions. They located sources of clay and temper throughout the Tonto Basin and adjacent areas in order to identify the raw materials being used in the production of Salado pottery. Then they examined the mineral and chemical composition of Salado pottery from a number of other places where it had been found outside the core area.

Simon, Burton, and Abbott were able to show that the mineral and chemical composition of the pottery was related and could be used to identify the geographic area where the raw materials were available. That information allowed them to determine where the pottery was made. One of the very interesting patterns they found was that the early Salado polychromes were made elsewhere and brought into the Tonto Basin from the east and north. The later Salado pottery was made in the Tonto Basin and exchanged outward toward the west. This change happened during a time of major growth in the size and population of sites in the Tonto Basin, probably associated with the arrival of new peoples from the north and east. Thus, the answer to the earlier question about where the pottery was being made is both locally and in the central area, depending on the time period.

Detailed studies of pottery provide substantial insight on community and social relationships in Arizona 800 years ago. These beautiful ceramic vessels document a highly integrated network of exchange and communication that connected the prehistoric communities of central Arizona. It is possible both to determine connections among groups and to see the movement of people into new areas. In addition, the information makes it clear from the relationship between pottery and people that there is a great deal more to learn from ancient ceramics.

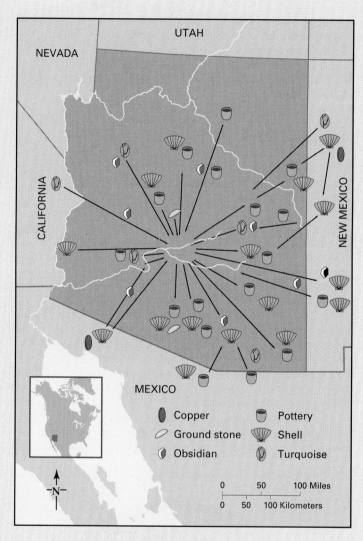

Fig. 11.25 Distribution of certain trade goods in Arizona, western New Mexico, and southeastern California. These exchange networks peaked between AD 800 and 1100.

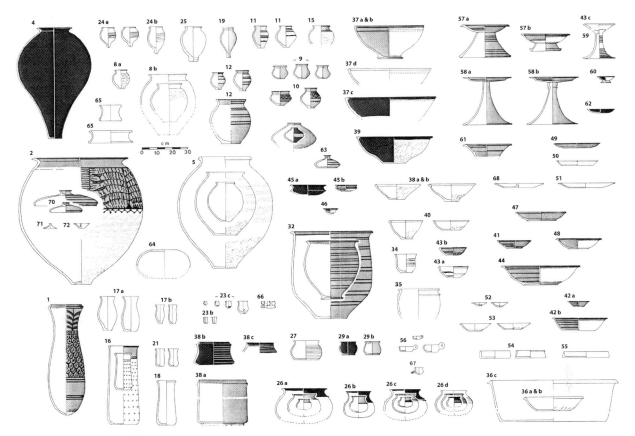

Fig. 11.26 The ceramic assemblage from Mohenjo Daro contains a variety of forms, shapes, and sizes with many different functions and designs. The set includes jars, vases, bowls, plates, pedestaled platters, and cups for cooking, serving, or storing a variety of materials.

using a coil or paddle-and-anvil technique, and later on a wheel as mass production became an economic necessity. Raw materials for making pottery include the clay itself and the temper that is used to prevent cracking during drying and firing. Ceramics are decorated using a wide range of techniques ranging from scratched or impressed designs to painting and glazing. Design and decoration are often the most distinctive features of ceramics and are used by archaeologists to sort pottery types in time and space.

The study of prehistoric pottery begins with the cleaning and cataloging of sherds. This material is sorted on the basis of shape and design using attributes of form, function, and style. Vessel shapes range from flat plates to vertical-walled vases, with a variety of bowls and other forms in between. Characteristics of function are features like size and shape that archaeologists measure using various techniques for estimating the original vessel form. Rim sherds are the most valuable piece of the pot for such studies.

Attributes of style are abundant on prehistoric pottery, found in all aspects of manufacture but more obvious in design elements and modes of decoration. Archaeologists use the information present in style to study both time and the geographic location of the prehistoric cultures that made the pottery. Styles in pottery and other forms of material culture change with time and distance. Stylistic variation also is informative with regard to the organization and interaction of societies. James Deetz studied Arikara ceramics to learn about changes in marital residence and the disruption of Native American society by European contact and disease. Robert Whallon used design elements to study interaction among Owasco and Iroquois villages in New York state.

Pottery provenience is another important area of ceramic studies. The petrographic and chemical composition of ceramics are two primary ways to determine the makeup of pottery and identify its place of origin. Petrographic analysis involves the use of a microscope to record the physical and mineral components of a sherd. Distinctive recipes for ceramic pastes can be identified in this way and used to determine local vs. exotic origins for pottery. James Stoltman used petrographic analysis to study the pottery from Icehouse Bottom in Tennessee to determine that some of the vessels were crossing long distances in the eastern United States.

Instrumental measurement of the elemental composition of pottery sherds is another major technique for ceramic analysis. A series of elements can provide a distinctive signature for the place of manufacture. Investigations of Salado polychrome pottery in the American Southwest, for example, used composition to identify the source and movement of this specific type of pottery and documented long-distance trade of these vessels and their contents.

MEAN CERAMIC DATING

Archaeologist Stanley South of the University of South Carolina is an innovator who has raised the visibility of historical archaeology in the Americas during his career. He has studied both the early Spanish and English colonies in the southeastern and eastern United States, respectively. Among his many contributions to the field is a new technique for dating historical sites and deposits based on the occurrence of different types of pottery.

South knew, as do most archaeologists, that material items usually exhibit a similar pattern in their popularity. Objects like music, hairstyles, clothing, dishes, and the like are fashionable—that is, they are rare and unusual when they first appear; if they catch on, their popularity grows and grows until the trend declines and the style becomes rare and disappears. South showed that this principle of popularity could be used to determine the age of an historical site when several fashionable pottery styles are present.

South pointed out that if you know the time of manufacture for different styles of pottery, then a formula based on changing fashions could be used to date a series of different types from an archaeological site—to determine a "mean ceramic age" as South called it. One of the advantages to the archaeology of history is that there are a variety of documents that provide information on events in the past. For example, there are documents providing the years of manufacture for many styles of ceramic plates and dishes made in the last several hundred years. Table 11.1 provides a list that South compiled with this information

TABLE 11.1 Ceramic types, type numbers, median manufacture date, and range of dates for selected historic pottery from the Eastern Seaboard of the United States.

Type	Type Abbreviation	Median Date of Manufacture	Years of Manufacture
Late Ming Chinese porcelain	MCP	1609	1574–1644
Blue decorated Rhenish stoneware	BRS	1668	1650–1725
Embellished hohr gray Rhenish stoneware	HRS	1700	1690–1710
North Devon gravel-tempered ware	DGW	1713	1650–1775
Overglaze enamel Chinese export porcelain	ECE	1730	1660–1800
Underglaze blue Chinese porcelain	BCP	1730	1660–1800
Refined red stoneware	RRS	1733	1690–1775
British brown stoneware	BBS	1733	1690–1775
Lead-glazed slipware	LGS	1733	1670–1795
Slip-dipped white salt-glazed stoneware	SWS	1745	1715–1775
Molded white salt-glazed stoneware	MWS	1753	1740–1765
"Clouded" wares	COW	1755	1740–1770
White salt-glazed stoneware plates	WSS	1758	1740–1775
Jackfield ware	JW	1760	1740–1780
English porcelain	EP	1770	1745–1795
Plain Delft wash basin	DWB	1775	1750–1800
Creamware	CW	1791	1762–1820
Overglaze enamel Chinese trade porcelain	ECT	1808	1790–1825
Canton porcelain	CP	1815	1800–1830
Underglaze polychrome pearlware	UPP	1830	1820–1840
Ironstone and granite china	IGC	1857	1813–1900
Whiteware	WW	1860	1820–1900+

for various types of historic pottery. Obviously, this kind of information is not available for most periods of archaeology.

An important concept in this scheme is the median date of manufacture. This is the year when the manufacture of this type of pottery peaked. Median means that half of the vessels were made before this date and half after this time. Thus, the median date of manufacture should approximate the maximum popularity of the style. The last column in Table 11.1 shows the range of dates of manufacture: when the type first appeared and when it stopped being made.

Now, if several of these types were present at a site, South was able to calculate a date for the site based on the number of sherds of each type and the median year of manufacture. South derived a mathematical formula to do this calculation. Essentially, the formula finds the average year of manufacture for different kinds of pottery based on their frequency of occurrence at the site.

The formula for the mean ceramic date (MCD) for a site is

$$MCD = \frac{\Sigma(d_1 f_1)}{\Sigma f_1}$$

In other words, to calculate the mean ceramic date, multiply the number of sherds of each type (f_1) times the median date of manufacture (d_1) for that type and add all the products. Divide that number by the total number of sherds to determine the MCD.

Now you try it. The historic house of Wilma Willoughby in the town of Beaufort, South Carolina, was excavated in the 1950s before the area was turned into a textile-importing center. Fortunately, the archaeologists counted all the artifacts and types of pottery found in a trash dump behind the house. This information is listed below in Table 11.2. The archaeologists were not able to determine the age of the dump or the house because little was known about when the pottery had been made. Then, in 1977, Stanley South published his method of mean ceramic dating and a list of manufacturing dates for various types of historic pottery. You can use his method to calculate a date for Willoughby's house.

TABLE 11.2 Pottery types and frequency of occurrence per meter square in the trash dump near the Wilma Willoughby House, Beaufort, South Carolina.

Type	Sq 1	Sq 2	Sq 3	Sq 4	Total
RRS	25	40	10	15	90
BBS	66	34	20	15	135
SWS	5	2	2	1	10
COW	200	140	80	30	450
WSS	10	60	60	20	150
JW	12	13	15	20	60
EP	8	4	7	6	25
DWB	325	175	60	140	700
Totals	651	468	254	247	1620

1. Use the excavated data and the formula for MCD to calculate an estimated age. Show your work.

2. What is your calculated estimate for the age of the trash dump?

3. Is this a good estimate for the age of the house?

4. Is there a better way to state the age of the house?

5. What are some of the possible problems with this method?

6. What about the issues of longevity and heirlooms?

Mean ceramic dating illustrates several aspects of pottery and archaeology. The concept of changing fashions and the appearance, increase in popularity, decrease in popularity, and disappearance is a typical pattern in the uselife of many objects and behaviors. Pottery is a very good example of this pattern because it breaks easily and often, is thrown away, survives in the ground, and different types are readily distinguished. The historic pottery in this example also documents the extent of global trade in the beginning of the industrial era with pottery from England, Holland, Germany, and China in use in the English colonies and during the early years of the United States.

Stanley A. South, *Method and Theory in Historical Archaeology*. Academic Press, 1977, pp. 210–212.

STUDY QUESTIONS

www.mhhe.com/pricearch1

For more review material and study questions, please see the self-quizzes on your online learning center.

1. What are the primary raw materials used to make ceramics?

2. How is pottery made? What are the different methods that have been used?

3. What are some of the different uses of ceramics in prehistory?

4. What are the important features of pottery?

5. Pottery decoration is an important source of information in archaeology. What are some of the major techniques used to decorate pottery?

6. What kinds of information from pottery do archaeologists use to help understand past human behavior?

7. What can prehistoric pottery tell us about the past?

REFERENCES

Arnold, D. 1985. *Ceramic Theory and Cultural Process.* Cambridge: Cambridge University Press.

Barnett, William, and John Hoopes, eds. 1995. *The Emergence of Pottery: Technology and Innovation in Prehistoric Societies.* Washington, D.C.: Smithsonian Institution Press.

Hardin, Margaret Friedrich. 1970. Design structure and social interaction: Archeological implications of an ethnographic analysis. *American Antiquity* 35.

Rice, Prudence. 1987. *Pottery Analysis: A Sourcebook.* Chicago: University of Chicago Press.

Shepard, A. O. 1956. *Ceramics for the Archaeologist.* Washington, D.C.: Carnegie Institution of Washington.

Sinopoli, Carla M. 1991. *Approaches to Archaeological Ceramics.* New York: Plenum.

Skibo, J. 1992. *Pottery Function: A Use-Alteration Perspective.* New York: Plenum.

www.mhhe.com/pricearch1

For Internet references related to this chapter, please see the chapter links on your online learning center.

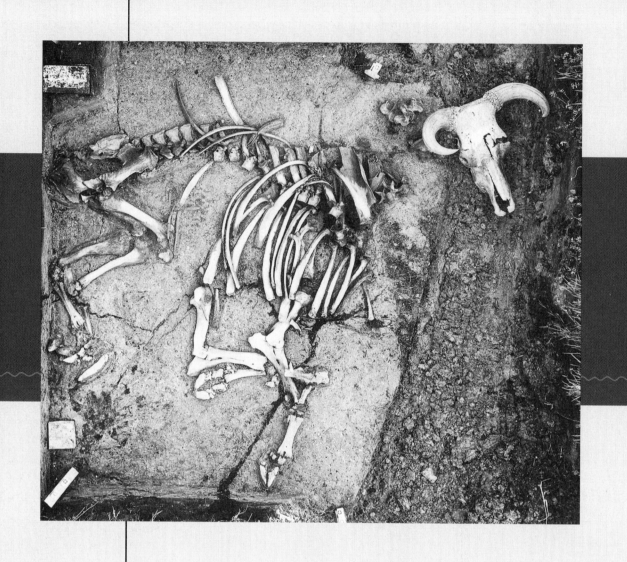

Archaeozoology

INTRODUCTION: ANIMAL REMAINS AND ARCHAEOLOGY

Sometime in the late fall of the year 6460 BC in eastern Denmark, an old wild bull, or **aurochs**, broke through the forest edge and painfully made his way to the shore of a small lake. The huge animal, some 1.85 m (6 ft) at the shoulder and weighing almost a ton, was mortally wounded. At least a dozen arrows had struck him as he fled the small group of hunters that pursued him (Fig. 12.1). The dying bull staggered into the cool waters to escape both the hunters and the torment of his wounds. Some time later, the body of this animal slowly sank to the bottom of the lake and lay there hidden from both the hunters and the elements. Over time, the lake sediments gradually covered his body and the arrows that had slain him. His bones and the stone arrow tips remained undisturbed for more than 8000 years.

In the year AD 1983, a Danish farmer was digging a ditch to help drain a wet part of his land. His shovel struck the great skull of that old aurochs in the bottom of his ditch. Aurochs were wild cattle, much larger than today's domestic cows, and they became extinct in Denmark around 3000 BC. The farmer called the Zoo-

Fig. 12.1 An artist's reconstruction of the aurochs bull. Mortally wounded by a flock of arrows in his back, the animal looks toward the salving waters of a small lake.

aurochs   Wild cattle.

323

Fig. 12.2 Selection of bone fragments from screening of sediments at an archaeological site. Species include pig, sheep, and cow.

It may come as a surprise to some that most of the behavioral ideas regarding our ancient past are dependent on the interpretation of faunal remains and depositional context—not . . . stone tools.
—Lewis Binford, archaeologist

archaeozoology   The study of animal remains in *archaeology.*

faunal remains   The animal ecofacts found in *archaeological contexts,* including bone, teeth, antler, ivory, shell, scales, and the like.

genus   A taxonomic group containing one or more related *species* (plural: genera).

species   A taxonomic group whose members can interbreed.

logical Museum in Copenhagen and a team went out to examine the find. It was clear that more bones lay in the ground. An excavation was mounted and exposed the complete skeleton of this huge creature. Because the work was done carefully and the sediments were screened, the excavators also found many small flint projectile points in the back and rear of the animal.

The aurochs skeleton is a well-preserved example of the remains of these huge, extinct Pleistocene bulls and a classic case in **archaeozoology**. It's also a poignant reminder of a specific moment in the past, of one that almost got away.

Archaeozoology is the study of the animal remains from archaeological sites—bone, teeth, antler, ivory, hides, hair, scales, and shell. Animal ecofacts in archaeology are also known as **faunal remains** and archaeozoologists are sometimes called faunal analysts. Archaeozoologists are interested in the relationship between humans and animals in the past. They study all kinds of animals, including mammals, birds, fish, reptiles, and amphibians, as well as mollusks and other invertebrates. Bones are not always present at archaeological sites, depending on conditions of preservation, and only some bone or some parts of bone may be well enough preserved that an archaeozoologist can study them (Fig. 12.2).

Archaeozoologists answer questions about whether animals were scavenged, hunted or herded, about how animals were butchered, about how much meat contributed to the diet, when animals died, and the process of domestication. Archaeozoologists are trained to identify the **genus** and **species** of animal from small fragments of bone, as well as to determine the age and sex of the animals, how bone was fragmented, and how many individual animals are represented in the bone assemblage (Fig. 12.3).

In identifying animals, scientists regularly use the scientific, or Latin, names for animals in archaeozoology so that they know they are dealing with the same genus and species in their communications. Faunal studies can show what animals were hunted and eaten and in what proportion. Faunal analysis can also provide an estimate of the ratio of adult to juvenile animals and of male to female animals. A predominance of certain age groups in a species such as deer may indicate that seasonal or selective hunting was practiced. For example, a site that

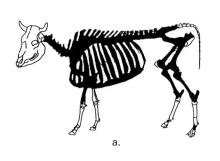

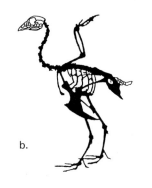

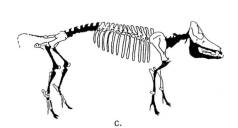

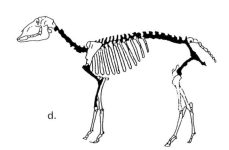

Fig. 12.3 Common faunal remains from a historic site in Dallas, Texas (not to scale). The black color indicates those bones which were found at the site: (a) *Bos taurus* (cow); (b) *Gallus gallus* (chicken); (c) *Sus scrofa* (pig); and (d) *Ovis aries /Capra hircus* (Sheep/goat).

contained a large proportion of three- to six-month-old deer would suggest the animals were killed primarily in the fall since deer are born in the spring.

The presence or absence of certain parts of the animal skeleton may indicate the way animals were butchered, and whether the animal was dismembered at human settlements or killed elsewhere and select steaks and chops brought back to the place of residence. Fracture patterns in long bones may reveal intentional breakage to remove marrow. Analysis of cutmarks on bone can provide information on butchering techniques. Not all animals were necessarily hunted for food. Nonfood items, such as antler, fur, bone, and hides, were also important materials that were used to make tools and equipment.

Archaeozoologists deal with a variety of questions concerned with the human use of animals. This chapter provides an introduction to some aspects of archaeozoology and focuses on identification and comparative collections, age and sex determination, seasonality studies, and taphonomy. Examples of archaeozoological studies are provided from several different contexts, including the extinction of many species at the end of the Pleistocene, the domestication of animals, the investigation of sedentism in the Preneolithic of Southwest Asia, seasonality and meat provision at the Mesolithic site of Star Carr in northern England, and menus and butchery patterns in Olduvai Gorge and Gold Rush Sacramento.

IDENTIFICATION AND COUNTS

An archaeological site is a kind of garbage dump where people leave their waste in piles (**middens**), or pits, or simply spread across the surface of the site. Animal parts from meals and other activities have been butchered, burned, broken and mixed with other sorts of trash, and then scattered by dogs and other scavengers. The difficulties involved in sorting and identifying this material are great.

The archaeozoological work begins with cleaning, cataloging, and conserving the faunal remains recovered from fieldwork. The bones are usually numbered so that information on their original provenience at the site is recorded. Initial sorting of the animal remains often is based on size and type of bone. For

www.mhhe.com/pricearch1

For a Web-based activity to learn more about archaeozoology, please see the Internet exercises on your online learning center.

midden   Any substantial accumulation of garbage or waste at a locus of human activity; archaeological deposits of trash and/or shells that accumulate in heaps and mounds. A shell midden is a specific type of midden composed largely of mollusk shells.

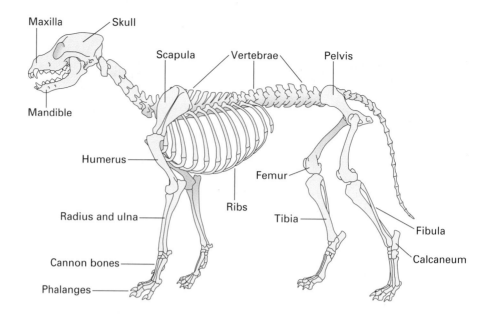

Fig. 12.4 Some of the major bones in the skeleton of a dog. Similar skeletal parts are found in most vertebrate animals.

Bones are documents as are potsherds and demand the same scrupulous attention both on the site and in the laboratory.
—Mortimer Wheeler, archaeologist

www.mhhe.com/pricearch1

For a Web-based activity on issues relating to zooarchaeology, please see the Internet exercises on your online learning center.

Fig. 12.5 Faunal remains from the Rich Neck Slave Quarter, located about one mile outside of Williamsburg, Virginia. Highly fragmented beef, pork, and mutton bones probably represent one-pot meals. The meat in the diet was diverse and included domesticated mammals, chicken, fish, turtle, wild birds, and wild mammals.

NISP The number of identified specimens, the number of bones from a *species* that has been identified.

MNI The minimum number of individuals, which is based on counts of the number of distinctive body parts from a particular *species*.

example, fish bone is quickly separated from mammal bone. The individual bones of the skeleton are identified whenever possible (Fig. 12.4).

A second pass at sorting moves toward the species level, but many bones cannot be identified beyond categories such as large mammal, medium rodent, and the like, if at all. A bone generally must retain several diagnostic characteristics to be assigned to a species.

Archaeozoologists are notorious for collecting and defleshing dead animals in order to build up a set of animal skeletons for comparison with archaeological materials. These comparative collections are an essential component in the process of identification. In addition, there are a number of published guides and keys that provide help in identifying various species of animals.

The species list is an important step in faunal analysis involving the identification of the finds. This list contains the names of the different kinds of animals present in the faunal remains at a site. A great deal of work is required to produce this list because of the difficulties involved in identifying species from fragmentary bones (Fig. 12.5). Many bone fragments cannot be identified, or can only be

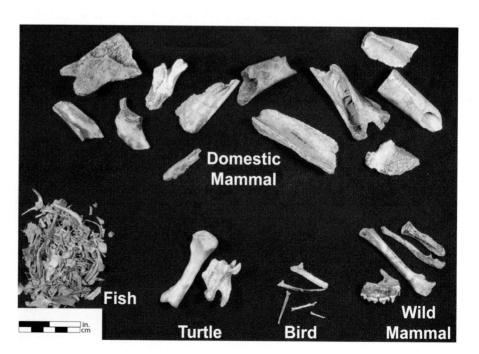

determined to the genus or family level. As a very general rule of thumb, archaeo-zoologists can usually identify between 5% and 40% of the faunal remains at a site. This percentage depends on the conditions of preservation, fragmentation, and deposition.

A second step in the analysis is to work out the number of individuals of each species that are present to get some idea about the relative importance of different animals. Because the faunal remains are only pieces of animals, not whole animals, it is difficult to know how many individual animals are represented for each species present. Archaeozoologists have defined techniques for counting the animal remains at a site. One measure is **NISP**—the number of identified specimens—that records the total number of bones from a species that have been identified. More useful, and more difficult to determine, is the **MNI**—the minimum number of individuals—which is based on counts of the number of a unique skeletal part (e.g., lower jaw, left femur, or lower right canine tooth) from a particular species. This count should represent the minimum number of individuals of that species present in the faunal assemblage. For some species, like fish, the number of bones that are found can be extraordinary (Fig. 12.6) and analysis can be very time-consuming. Measures like NISP and MNI are only estimates because of the fragmentary nature of the archaeozoological record.

Fig. 12.6 A small portion of fish bones from water screening. The original photograph is 10 cm in width.

◉ EXAMPLE ∿∿∿∿∿∿∿∿∿∿∿∿∿∿∿∿∿∿

EXTINCTION IS FOREVER

In various places around North America—the La Brea tar pits in Los Angeles, the caves of the Grand Canyon, the bone beds of eastern Missouri—the remains of very large animals that once roamed North America have been found and have attracted a great deal of attention. Many of these animals were large carnivores and herbivores that wandered the continent over the last 2 million years (Fig. 12.7). By the end of the Pleistocene, however, some thirty-five genera (more than one genus) of large land mammals, nearly half the total number, became extinct in North America.

The identification of the bones of these extinct creatures is an important step in understanding why they disappeared. Species such as giant sloth and giant beaver, the horse, camel, mammoth and mastodon, cheetah, and short-faced bear, all much larger than their modern counterparts, became extinct by 10,000 years ago (Fig. 12.8). The giant sloth was about the size of a giraffe and weighed up to three tons. Caves in the Grand Canyon have preserved many examples of softball-sized giant sloth dung. The giant beaver in the Great Lakes area weighed as much as 140 kg (300 lb). A similar, though not as complete, pattern of extinction in large mammals occurred at the close of the Pleistocene in Europe and Asia, where mammoth, woolly rhino, cave bear, cave lion, and other species also became extinct.

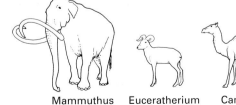

Mammuthus   Euceratherium   Camelops   Navahoceros   Equus   Equus asinus   Stockoceros

Fig. 12.7 Some of the large animals that became extinct in North America by the end of the Pleistocene. The mammoth (*Mammuthus*) is slightly larger than a modern African elephant. Drawings are not to scale.

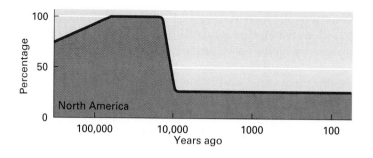

Fig. 12.8 The percentage of species in existence and the years before present in North America. The end of the Pleistocene at 10,000 years ago marks a period of major extinction for many animal species. The cause of this extinction, whether natural or human, is still debated although the evidence favors changing environments rather than hunting.

Overkill proponents have argued that these animals would still be around if people hadn't killed them and that ecological niches still exist for them. Those niches do not exist. Otherwise the herbivores would still be there.
—Donald Grayson, archaeologist

What caused the demise of so many animals in such a relatively short period of time? Scientists, archaeologists, paleontologists, climatologists, and others have considered this question for decades. Two major scenarios have been proposed: climatic change (a natural cause) and hunting overkill (a human cause).

Each side of the argument has a set of facts and conjecture that appears to contradict those of the other. For example, proponents of hunting overkill argue that very similar climatic changes during earlier periods did not result in the extinction of species, such as the mammoth, which are adapted to a broad range of environments. Also, the widespread appearance of Paleoindian hunters around 11,000 years ago coincides closely with the demise of a number of the extinct species. Spear points have been found in association with the bones of extinct mammoth, mastodon, horse, tapir, camel, and bison, suggesting that Paleoindian hunters, with easy access to animals virtually ignorant of human predators, quickly eliminated the species of large animals they encountered.

Those who doubt the role of human hunters in the disappearance point out that a number of extinct species are never found at archaeological sites. There is, in fact, no direct evidence of human predation on animals such as the giant sloth and beaver. Other, nonmammalian species also suffered extinction at the end of the Pleistocene. For example, almost 45% of the genera of birds in Pleistocene North America disappeared by 11,000 years ago. There is little reason to suspect human intervention in the extinction of these species.

New evidence for increasing aridity at the end of the Pleistocene and its effect on animal populations argues against the role of human hunters as the sole factor in the extinctions. This climatic change caused a shift in the distribution of small species, and perhaps caused the extinction of many large animals. Larger animals require more food and more space to live and thus, as a group, are more vulnerable to changes in their environment. Large animals are also found in lower numbers than smaller ones; the loss of a few individuals in an area may have serious consequences during mating season, making it difficult to find a member of the opposite sex. Larger animals, too, have a longer generation length than smaller ones, so that genetic changes move more slowly through the population, making larger animals more susceptible to extinction.

AGE AND SEX

Another stage in the analysis of faunal remains is the determination of the age and sex of animal remains. In many cases, this will be done only for the most abundant species or in situations of special interest. An example where information on the sex and age of goats is critical for determining the role of herding is discussed below. Age and sex information can also be very useful in examining questions of site seasonality. An example from the site of Star Carr in England documents this kind of study.

Determination of age and sex in animal skeletons is similar to the methods used for humans. There are specific indicators that archaeozoologists look for in the bones and teeth. Sex distinctions are found both in the size of animals and in cer-

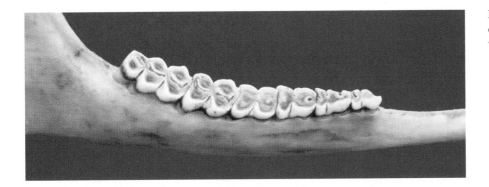

Fig. 12.9 The tooth wear patterns on the mandible of a 6½-year-old whitetail deer.

a.

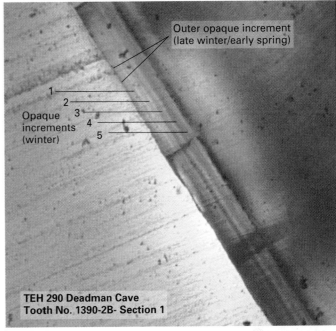

Outer opaque increment
(late winter/early spring)

Opaque
increments
(winter)

1
2
3
4
5

TEH 290 Deadman Cave
Tooth No. 1390-2B- Section 1

b.

Fig. 12.10 (a) Archaeozoologist Chris O'Brien uses a microscopic digital imaging system to analyze a thin section of an animal tooth. The monitor displays the image from the microscope for observation. (b) Deer tooth section from site of Deadman Cave in northeastern California, dated to approximately 1500 BC. The five increments document a 5½-year-old animal that died in the late fall. Labels have been added to micro-photograph to indicate the bands.

tain bones and teeth in the skeleton. Many species of animals exhibit considerable **sexual dimorphism** so that male and female remains show significant size differences. In some cases, sex-specific skeletal parts such as antlers in some species of **cervids**, members of the deer family, can be used to distinguish males and females.

Age determination is more difficult in animals, in part because many species are rather short-lived compared to humans. Animal lives are often calculated in months rather than years. A few species of animals have clear age markers, seen in the timing of the formation of antler, or certain teeth, or a regular increase in size with age.

Tooth development is a commonly used indicator of animal age. A number of techniques rely on tooth eruption and/or wear to calculate the age. Wildlife managers and ecologists have developed systematic ways for aging animals using these criteria in order to understand population trends for purposes of game management. Tooth wear is assumed to be fairly constant in a given species so that patterns of tooth wear should be a reliable indicator of age (Fig. 12.9).

Another common and reliable method for determining animal age is the study of annual growth rings. Probably the best technique for determining age in large herbivores is the study of **cementum annuli** in teeth (Fig. 12.10). These are annual deposits of cementum around the base of teeth. Cementum is bone tissue

sexual dimorphism   Size difference between the males and females of the same *species*.

cervids   Members of the deer family.

cementum annuli   Annual deposits of cementum around the base of teeth.

Animal Domestication in Southwest Asia

Herded animals show certain changes in size and body parts that provide direct evidence for domestication. For example, domesticated species are generally smaller than their wild ancestors. Also, the shape of horns often changes in the domestic form of a species, and the microscopic structure of bone undergoes modification in domestic animals. Other traits may be selected and changed by herders to increase yields of milk, wool, or meat. However, because it can take many generations for such biological change, the earliest stages of domestication may not have been recorded in the bones and horns that remain.

Mindy Zeder of the Smithsonian Institution and Brian Hesse of the University of Alabama, Birmingham, found another way. They identified the age and sex of animals that had been killed at a pre-farming site in the Zagros (*zah-GROSS*) Mountains of western Iran. They used this information to study whether hunting or herding was practiced. The basic principle of their study relies on the fact that herded animals are slaughtered when the herder decides; for most species, this means that the average age of death for domesticated animals is younger than for wild animals (Fig. 12.11). Hunted animals are taken by chance encounter and the proportion of adults is higher in such a situation.

The ages of animals are most frequently determined by an assessment of tooth eruption and wear, along with information about changes in bone. All of the known sites in the Zagros Mountains from before 10,000 years ago show similar slaughter patterns for wild sheep and goats, and red deer. These sites contain bone assemblages of primarily adult animals, indicating that all were hunted in the wild. However, a number of sites from the period after 10,000 years ago contain assemblages of bones that are dominated by the bones of younger animals. In each case, the younger groups of animals are sheep or goat, in a proportion higher than in a normal wild herd. This evidence likely documents the beginnings of animal domestication in the area.

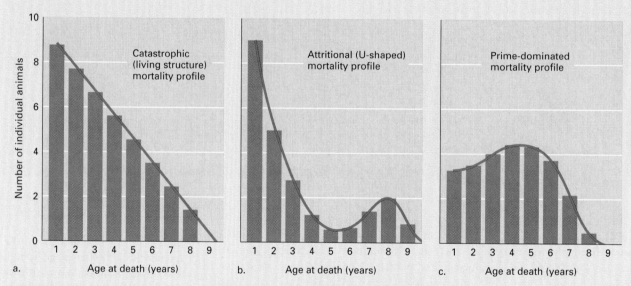

Fig. 12.11 Three hypothetical age profiles for animal populations showing age of death on the x-axis and number of animals in each year of age on the y-axis: (a) a catastrophic situation in which all animals in the herd die simultaneously; (b) a natural, attritional pattern in which animals are more likely to die when young or older; and (c) a profile in which animals die more often in their prime, as is the case when humans control the herd and select the animals to die.

that forms around the roots of teeth in concentric bands similar to tree rings. Thin sections made through the animal teeth reveal the annual layers of growth as distinct light-dark bands. In many species, winter is a period of food stress and changes in diet that are reflected in the darker, slower-forming parts of the cementum band. By counting the number of bands, and determining the part of the band where growth ceased, it is possible to establish the age of the animal at death.

SEASONALITY

Animal remains provide the best evidence for determining season of residence at the settlements of nonsedentary populations. This information is particularly important during the Paleolithic and Mesolithic periods, when hunter-gatherer groups were thought to be largely mobile, utilizing different parts of the landscape at different times. Determination of the season of site occupation or documenting year-round utilization is an important part of understanding the larger pattern of settlement and subsistence that hunter-gatherers followed.

Information on **seasonality** comes from a variety of evidence. Some species of animals are present only during certain times of the year; for example, migratory birds might be summer-only visitors. A number of species of deer lose their antlers at known times of the year and replace them some months later. Recovery of dropped antlers or antlers attached to the skull at an archaeological site is an indicator of the season of human presence. The age of animals is often used to determine season by calculating the number of months from the season of birth. Many species of animals have fixed and known seasons of birth; for example, reindeer calve in May and June. An animal that died at an age of eighteen months must have been killed in the late fall of the year.

Analysis of faunal and floral remains at a Mesolithic site called Smakkerup Huse (*SMOCK-er-roop HOOS-ah*) in eastern Denmark, dating from approximately 4500 BC, produced a number of seasonal indicators and provides an example of some of the kinds of information that can be used (Fig. 12.12). Deer antlers from two different species provide evidence for any of the seasons but spring. Tooth eruption in wild boar provides an animal age in months that can be used to indicate human activity at all times of the year except mid-winter. Small fur-bearing animals are likely taken in cooler months when fur is prime.

Seasonal indicators for spring are less common or visible in most faunal assemblages. Migratory fish are present in the summer, and oyster collecting is normally done in the winter and spring. One of the advantages of the archaeological materials from Smakkerup Huse is the availability of additional seasonal information from wood and plant remains. The presence of hazelnuts and hawthorn fruits indicates autumn activities. Also, hazel poles were cut in the spring and fall of the year. Information on the cutting of hazel in the spring fills in that missing season and suggests a year-round occupation at the site.

> *In the central blinds of bone, as they stand in their natural order, there are certain curious marks, curves, hollows, and ridges, whereby some whalemen calculate the creature's age, as the age of an oak by its circular rings. Though the certainty of this criterion is far from demonstrable, yet it has the savor of analogical probability.*
> —Herman Melville, author

Month/indicator	J	F	M	A	M	J	J	A	S	O	N	D
Red deer antler development	■	■							■	■	■	■
Red deer juvenile ontogeny					■	■						
Roe deer antler development				■	■	■	■	■	■			
Wild boar tooth eruption			■	■	■	■	■	■	■	■	■	
Otter/beaver prime fur	■	■									■	■
Hazel branch cutting			■	■					■	■		
Hazelnut harvesting									■	■		
Hawthorne fruits										■	■	
Migratory fish					■	■	■	■				
Oyster collecting	■	■	■	■							■	■

Fig. 12.12 Seasonal indicators at Smakkerup Huse based on animal bone, tooth, and antler development and other assumptions. Shading indicates likely presence or use.

seasonality   The time of year a *site* was occupied, part of an annual cycle, usually related to *hunter-gatherer* settlement patterns.

EXAMPLE

STAR CARR

Star Carr

The site of Star Carr (*star CAR*) lies in northeastern England, some 8 km (5 mi) west of the coast. The site dates to the early part of the Mesolithic around 9000 BC. Excavations were carried out there from 1949 to 1951 by Grahame Clark of Cambridge University. The excavations exposed an area of almost 350 square meters (the size of a basketball court) and recovered a vast array of archaeological materials.

The settlement was located on the south shore of a narrow peninsula that extended into a small lake. Preservation in the waterlogged organic sediments was excellent. Star Carr contained approximately 17,000 flint artifacts, shale and amber beads, and lumps of hematite and iron pyrite. The finds also included numerous barbed antler points, many animal bones, and a wide range of wood and bone tools. Numerous animal species were represented, especially red deer, roe deer, elk, aurochs, and wild pig. No fish bones were found, despite the proximity of the site to a lake.

Star Carr is interesting for a number of reasons, including the insights it provides on questions of site seasonality and food yields. These insights have helped fuel a long debate in archaeology about the time of year that people lived at Star Carr and the kind of site it was.

Clark, the original excavator, suggested the site was a base camp for three or four families during the winter months of the year. "The site was evidently occupied by a small hunting band which supported itself during the winter by the culling of red deer stags, supplemented by hunting elk, aurochs, and other game, and which took advantage of a period of settled existence to replenish the equipment needed during the course of the year."

Clark's interpretation has been questioned by others. Star Carr has been variously described as a specialized location for hide and antler working used over several seasons, as a hunting camp and butchering place used repeatedly for short episodes by a small group, or as only a small dump area for a much larger settlement on the adjacent peninsula. Clearly, the same evidence has been used in a variety of conflicting interpretations.

The original evidence for seasonality was taken from the presence or absence of antler attached to the skulls of red deer, roe deer, and elk. For example, the antlers of red deer are fully grown and attached to the skull from October through March. The antlers are shed in April and grown through the summer. Further, the stage of antler development can be determined readily by examination. Roe deer and elk exhibit similar cycles in the growth and loss of their antlers. A graph of the antler finds from Star Carr (Fig. 12.14) indicates all seasons of the year. Clark's argument for a winter occupation was based largely on the abundance of red deer antler at the site and the assumption that red deer could have been hunted most readily in the winter.

Re-examination of the antler, teeth, and other remains in the 1980s revised Clark's interpretation and suggested possible year-round residence at the site, but with a clear emphasis on the summer months. Examination of charred reed remains and other organic clues, for example, indicated that the site was most likely occupied from late March/early April until June or early July. Thus, while members of the group may have been at Star Carr either permanently or intermittently during the year, it seems that there was more activity at the site in the warmer months.

A study in 1998 used a new technique to age the red deer jaws and determined that the deer mandibles indeed indicated a winter presence at Star Carr. Thus, in the 50 years since the excavations the season of occupation at Star Carr has gone from a winter residence, to year-round, to a late spring and summer extraction site, and back to some occupation in the late fall and winter at a short-term camp. This frequent revision of the interpretation of the site points to several things: (1) The site was well excavated and finds have been curated so that reanalysis is possible; (2) determining the seasonality of site occupation is a difficult undertaking; and (3) the variety of conclusions about the season of occupation suggests that Star Carr was probably used at different times for different purposes.

Based on the abundance of antler and bone from red deer, Clark argued that the hunters of Star Carr primarily focused on this animal. However, it is important to

Fig. 12.13 Red deer antler frontlet from the site of Star Carr modified to be used as a mask or headdress.

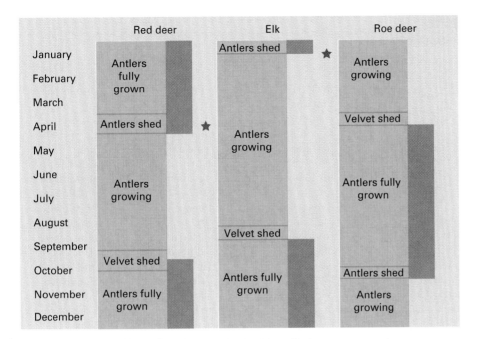

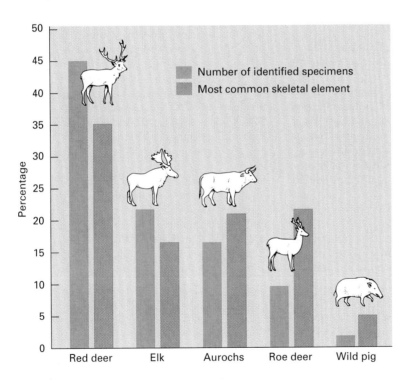

Fig. 12.14 The seasonality estimates for the site of Star Carr, England, based on antler presence and absence in three species of deer. These data suggest a season of occupation between January and April.

★ Indicates times at which site must have been occupied

▨ Indicates period during which animals could have been obtained

Fig. 12.15 Estimates of the percentages of individual animals and their meat weight from five species of prey at the Mesolithic site of Star Carr, England.

consider not only the number of bones at a site, but also the relative meat yields of the species present. Relative meat yields reflect the size of the animal and how much food could be obtained. Fig. 12.15 shows both the number of bones found per species (as a percentage of all the bones found) and the percentage of total meat weight the animals would have provided. It is clear that the bones of red deer are most common, but it is also clear that more meat came from the bigger aurochs and the European elk together than the red deer.

Seasonality in the Preneolithic

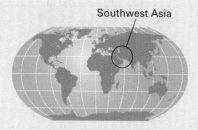

Southwest Asia

Our ancestry as food collectors, consuming the wild products of the earth, extends back more than 6 million years. Nevertheless, at the end of the Pleistocene around 10,000 BC, some human groups began to domesticate wild plants and animals, to grow their food rather than hunt and gather it. And in the process, they achieved what was perhaps the most remarkable transition of our entire human past. This was the origin of agriculture.

The earliest known domesticates—rye, wheat, barley, peas, lentils, pigs, goats, sheep, and cattle—first appeared in Southwest Asia around 9000 BC. Neolithic farming villages with permanent houses are found at this time in a mountainous region paralleling the eastern shore of the Mediterranean across the countries of Israel, Lebanon, Syria, and Turkey.

The period just before agriculture, roughly 11,000–9000 BC, is referred to as the Preneolithic. In this period, there was a distinct increase in the use of plant foods. Particularly noticeable is the range of equipment for processing plants: sickle blades, along with grinding stones, storage pits, and roasting areas for preparing wild wheat. Sites were often located in areas of cultivable land but depended on wild cereals such as wheat and barley. Hunting continued, and more immature animals were killed, including gazelles and wild goats. Settlements were composed of a number of circular houses with stone-wall foundations (Fig. 12.16). Graves were found inside and outside the houses.

One of the changes that occurred, as hunters became farmers, was a shift to **sedentary** settlement—permanent residence—rather than regular movements during the year to different resource locations. An important question for understanding the origins of agriculture is, just when did sedentism appear? To answer this question, it is necessary to determine if Preneolithic residential sites were occupied seasonally or year-round.

Archaeozoology can provide insight on this issue. In the temperate and arctic regions of the world, the evidence for site seasonality is often available from information on the season of death or the availability of plants and animals. In the subtropical and tropical regions of the world, seasonality is less pronounced and evidence for the period of site occupation more difficult to come by. This is the case for Southwest Asia and the sites dating to the time of the origins of agriculture. However, insight on the question of human mobility in this area can be obtained from study of gazelle teeth. Teeth are the hardest tissue in the skeleton and often well preserved at archaeological sites.

Daniel Lieberman of Harvard University studied growth rings (*cementum annuli*) in the base of these teeth. Examination of a section cut across the root of a tooth under a microscope can reveal the number and pattern of these annual bands of cementum. Each year is represented by a pair of bands, one clear (fast growth = summer) and one opaque (slow growth = winter). The total number of pairs of bands corresponds to the years of age of the animal, and the outermost band marks the season of death.

Fortunately, gazelle have a very distinct seasonal pattern, even in Southwest Asia, and the growth rings show up clearly (Fig. 12.17). Lieberman examined more than 300 animal teeth from twenty different cultural layers dating from the Upper Paleolithic (45,000–11,000 years ago) and the Preneolithic (11,000–9000 years ago). By sectioning teeth and counting the bands, he was able to determine when these animals died (when cementum stopped forming). A very clear difference emerged. Upper Paleolithic sites showed a distinct pattern of single-season animal kills, from either the spring/summer dry season or the winter rainy season. Preneolithic gazelles show a clear multiseason pattern with roughly equal numbers of animals exhibiting dry and wet season bands at death.

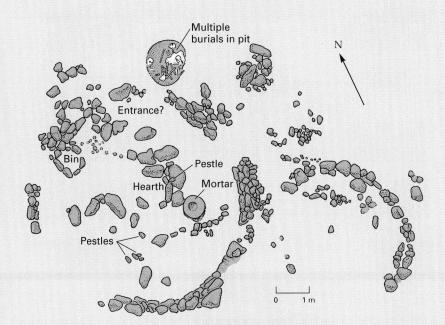

Fig. 12.16 Plan of a small part of a Preneolithic site in Israel with round houses with rock-wall foundations, storage pits, hearths, and multiple burials. The site is approximately 12,000 years old and predates the origins of agriculture.

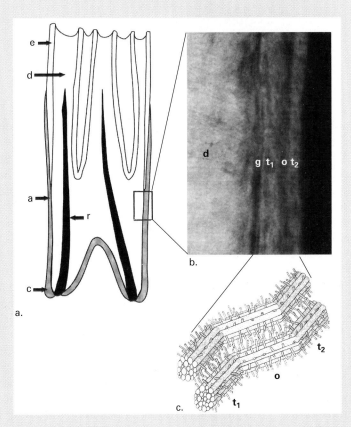

This evidence means that the animal skeletons found at Preneolithic sites accumulated over both seasons of the year.

Other archaeozoological evidence confirms permanent residence at these sites. Studies of the age (not season) of death of the gazelle at one of the Preneolithic sites indicated that they were hunted year-round. Another study has identified migratory birds from both the winter and the summer in the same cultural layer. Finally, several Preneolithic sites have human **commensals** found among the faunal remains, including the house mouse, house sparrow, and the house rat. Commensals are species in a symbiotic relationship in which one species is benefited while the other is unaffected. The presence of these commensals indicates long-term human residence at these sites.

Thus, new techniques and fundamental archaeozoological data document a shift from mobile to sedentary residence in the Preneolithic period, 2000 years before the origins of agriculture. Now we can ask a rhetorical question, was sedentism a necessary prerequisite for the origins of agriculture?

Fig. 12.17 (A) Schematic cross-section of a gazelle tooth showing location of cementum (c), dentine (d), and enamel (e). (B) Section through the cementum showing increments in transmitted polarized light. (C) Drawing of the annual growth rings showing translucent bands (t) which form in the warmer, dryer summer season and opaque bands (o) which form in the cooler, wetter winter months.

sedentary Permanent or year-round settlement.

commensals *Species* in a symbiotic relationship in which one *species* is benefited while the other is unaffected.

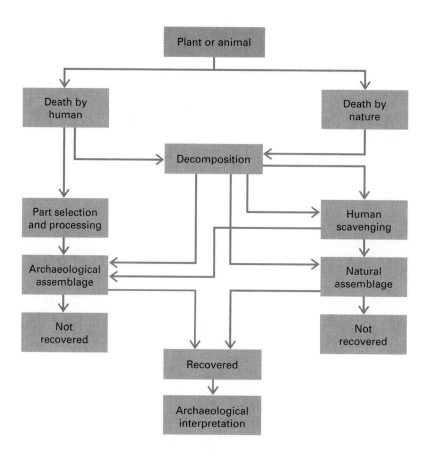

Fig. 12.18 Some of the processes that modify the plants and animal remains found at an archaeological site.

TAPHONOMY

Taphonomy is the study of what happens to an organism after its death, and it includes decomposition, postmortem transport, burial, and a variety of other biological, physical, and chemical changes that take place. Taphonomic analysis attempts to reconstruct the postmortem processes that have produced a faunal assemblage. The study of the taphonomic changes in archaeological bone is useful for understanding site formation processes, the paleoenvironment, and the nature of the sample of prehistoric animals.

Fig. 12.18 is a diagram of the general taphonomic processes that affect plant and animal remains between death and archaeological recovery. A bone or plant fragment can take a variety of courses, from a natural or human-related death, removal of some pieces by humans or animals or other processes, through decomposition and alteration, to inclusion in an archaeological or natural assemblage. Remains can be archaeologically recovered and analyzed, but most prehistoric materials either disintegrate in the ground or are never found or excavated.

A number of indicators can be observed on the surface of bone that document various taphonomic processes. Abrasion, rounding, and fragmentation are the result of physical processes of water rolling, trampling, or exposure. Weathering of bone exposed on the ground results in cracking and flaking of the surface. The loss of the outer surface gives the bone a fibrous appearance. Various animals, insects, and other organisms begin to consume bone after it is exposed, so that **bioerosion** is another aspect of the weathering process to be considered (Fig. 12.19). Tooth marks and gnaw marks from various animals testify to this bioerosion that takes place. Bone that remains unburied for extended periods of time can also become bleached white by the sun. Accidental or intentional exposure of bone to fire results in charred and burned bone; repeated exposure or very hot

taphonomy The study of what happens to an organism after its death, including decomposition, postmortem transport, burial, and the biological, physical, and chemical changes.

bioerosion Changes in the exterior surface on bone that indicate conditions of deposition.

Fig. 12.19 A scatter of bones from a number of different species found at a modern hyena den in Jordan. The animals represented in the natural assemblage of faunal remains included camel, dog, sheep, goat, horse, donkey, gazelle, badger, and various birds.

temperatures produce hard, white calcined bone. Burned bone feels sticky to a wet finger or tongue. Evidence of heat exposure may indicate cooking or other preparation of the animal carcass.

The largely invisible physical and chemical changes that take place in bone after burial are known as **diagenesis**. Diagenesis involves the loss or absorption of a variety of chemical elements and the addition of various foreign materials such as sediments into the bone. In the very long term and under appropriate conditions, bones will mineralize and turn into fossils. This process rarely affects archaeological bone because it takes so long. Dramatic changes in bone can take place under certain conditions of burials. Knowledge of these changes is essential in order to evaluate the reliability of the sample for certain kinds of analyses.

BUTCHERY

Butchery is another taphonomic process that animal bones undergo after death and prior to burial. Animal carcasses were often cut up in certain ways to obtain the most meat possible and to make portions transportable. By identifying the size and shape of butchered parcels, scientists can determine the cuts of meat that were most sought. Taphonomic analysis can provide information regarding the types of tools used to obtain these portions because the process of cutting and butchering often leaves distinctive traces or cutmarks on the bones themselves. Two examples of studies of butchery marks and practices are described below— one concerns early human ancestors in Africa and the other deals with California gold miners.

 EXAMPLE ~~~~~~~~~~~~~~~~~~~~~~~~~~~~~~~~~~~~~

CUTMARKS AND EARLY HUMANS

Questions about the diets of our earliest ancestors in Africa several million years ago are difficult to answer because the remains of meals are generally not preserved. Thus, the relative importance of fruits, nuts, and other plant foods in the diet is unknown. The wild plants of East Africa probably provided a ready source of food, but plant materials do not survive in the archaeological record from this period.

Bones do sometimes survive on these sites and document meat eating at that time. But how did these early humans obtain meat? Another controversial issue is

diagenesis Physical and chemical changes in bone after burial.

a.

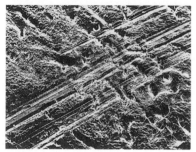

b.

Fig. 12.20 (a) Photomicrograph of round-bottom grooves made by hyena teeth on modern bone. (b) Photomicrograph of a v-shaped cutmark left on modern bone by a stone tool.

the question of scavenging versus hunting. Some archaeologists believe that the first humans were primarily scavenging the kills of lions and other predators, taking the morsels that remained, and competing with hyenas and vultures. These scholars argue that the hunting of large animals is a relatively recent development in human prehistory. Another school, however, contends that early humans were in fact hunters—stalking, killing, butchering, and eating large animals. The evidence is limited and open to debate.

Evidence from a number of sites suggests that early humans brought animal parts to a common location and removed meat and marrow with stone tools. In one case, the large leg bone of an antelope-size creature had been broken into ten pieces, in the same way that modern hunters obtain the nutritious and tasty marrow. On this same bone, tiny scratches made were also visible. Such **cutmarks** resulted from the use of stone tools that were used to remove larger pieces of meat from the bone (Fig. 12.20).

This evidence may indicate that early humans were hunters with access to the better cuts of meat from their prey. But Richard Potts and Pat Shipman have observed that such cutmarks are sometimes found on top of the marks left by the teeth of carnivores, suggesting the scavenging of animal carcasses. Teeth and tools leave distinctive marks that can be recognized (Fig. 12.21). Recent studies of marks on bones from Olduvai Gorge suggest a sequence of cuts that include marks made by large carnivore teeth, cuts by stone tools, and smaller carnivore tooth marks that overlay the stone tool cuts. Such a pattern suggests that the animal was killed by a large carnivore, scavenged by humans, and then eaten by smaller animals.

The specific parts of animals that were brought to certain locations by early humans also provide some clues about how food was obtained. Scavengers can more easily get access to limb bones than other parts of a carcass. These are the larger, harder bones of the skeleton that often remain after predators have abandoned a kill. Limb bones are also rich in marrow. At several sites, complete skeletons of small animals were present, but larger animals were represented primarily by limb bones. This evidence suggests that early humans may have hunted small game but scavenged the carcasses of large game.

Fig. 12.21 Schematic drawing of the traces left on bone by tooth and stone tool. Pointed teeth leave a smooth, v-shaped groove while stone tools often leave a more rounded, jagged trail.

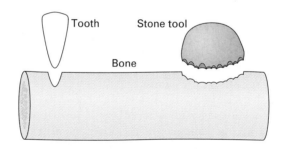

○ **EXAMPLE** ～～～～～～～～～～～～～～～

GOLD RUSH MENUS

Historical archaeology is the branch of archaeology that deals with the recent past, largely with existing nations and the archaeology of the industrial era, basically the last 400 years. Although this is not so long ago and the societies of the time were literate, there are still very few written records of many of the everyday aspects of life. It is in this unknown space that archaeology can contribute to the knowledge of our own society.

Archaeozoology can be applied to any aspect of the past where faunal remains have been preserved. Excavations in the center of historic Sacramento, California,

Sacramento

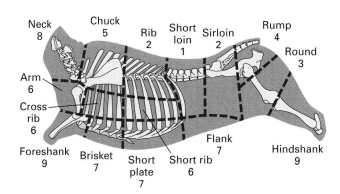

Fig. 12.22 Cuts of meat consumed in different areas of Sacramento during the gold rush in the 1850s. The numbers from 1–9 indicate the relative value of the cuts, with 1 the most expensive.

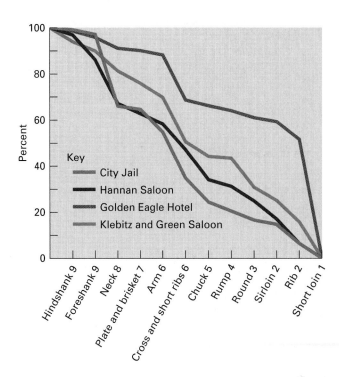

uncovered a series of buildings dating from the early settlement of the city. In the two years following the discovery of gold in 1848, more than 90,000 people made their way to California. By 1854, more than 300,000—one of every 90 people living in the United States—had gone West to join the 49ers. This was really the birth of California as a state. Sacramento was the destination of this migration, the gateway to the gold in those hills.

The archaeological excavations uncovered four buildings of particular interest: the jail, a low-class saloon, a more prosperous bar, and a hotel for well-to-do visitors to the city. Newspapers from the time provide some information on these establishments, but very little on the real nature of the places. Archaeozoologists cleverly examined the cattle bones that were found at all four sites to get some idea of the quality of the meat that was being consumed at each place. More than 1500 beef bones were recovered in the excavations. The kind of bone found revealed the cut of meat that was popular at a particular place.

The archaeologists, Peter Schulz and Sherri Gust, examined newspaper accounts from the period to determine the approximate cost of different cuts of meat. Using that information, they established the value of various cuts from cheap shank and neck bone cuts to very expensive steaks, ribs, and short loin (Fig. 12.22). They plotted the percentage of each kind of cut on a graph using a cumulative curve. This kind of graph plots the percentage of each cut added to the next from expensive to cheap, resulting in a final value of 100%. The line is drawn from right to left, beginning with the percent of short loin in the assemblage. If short loin is 5% and the next item (ribs) is 10%, the two values are summed and a point plotted at 15% on the graph. This process continues until all the different cuts have been added to the total to make 100%. In essence, each line on the graph shows the amount of different cuts of meat used in the hotel, saloons, and the jail.

For example, looking at the plot for the Golden Eagle Hotel, it is clear that loin, ribs, and steak cuts accounted for more than 50% of the beef bones found at the place. The City Jail, on the other hand, has a much higher proportion of cheaper cuts, lots of soup bones with little meat, for the poorly fed prisoners. The two saloons can be distinguished as well by the quality of meat they served. Much of the meat they served was at free lunches to attract customers and consisted of easy to cook and serve roasts. Diet was clearly a sign of social status in the gold rush period of Sacramento, as it is today.

Archaeologists formerly used bones to say what the environment was. . . . [T]hey did not view bones as carrying information because they were not manufactured by humans. . . . [With studies of] the dynamics of the breakage and discarding of bones . . . we could look at a site in a different way, with a different reference. It was a Rosetta Stone.
—Lewis Binford, archaeologist

cutmarks Scratches and cuts on bone indicating the use of stone *tools* for butchering.

SECONDARY PRODUCTS

Most discussions of animals in archaeology focus on these creatures as a source of meat and protein for human hunters and herders. It is, however, important to remember that domestic animals in particular provide a number of other products, both food and nonfood materials and energy. These other uses and materials are sometimes referred to as **secondary products**, after the primary emphasis on meat. For example, several animal species serve as draft animals for humans—best known are horses, oxen, and camels, even elephants in some areas of the world. Milk is taken from cows, sheep, goats, and other species to be consumed directly or turned into a variety of dairy products including cheeses and a wide range of soured milk products. Blood is taken from live animals and consumed in some societies. Sheep, goats, alpacas, and other species provide wool as a fiber for making yarn and textiles. Hair and fur from horses and other animals has been used for products in the past. Many animal species provide their skins for leather. And finally, the bones, horns, and antler of both wild and domestic species are a useful raw material for many kinds of implements.

WORKED BONE

Such nonfood resources from animals as bone, antler, ivory, teeth, and horn have been used by humans at least since the Upper Paleolithic and probably earlier. Raymond Dart, a South African paleoanthropologist, argued that some of our earliest human ancestors had used **osteodontokeratic** tools, a wonderful word meaning bone, tooth, and horn. Dart was probably correct that early humans picked up the heavy and sharp animal parts lying about the landscape and used them for various purposes. The problem is that early humans did not modify these items, they simply used them as they were. In that context, the bones, teeth, and horns technically are not tools since they have not been shaped by humans. Moreover, it is impossible to prove that these objects were used since they are unchanged.

Bone, horn, antler, and teeth can be shaped in a variety of ways into a range of tools. Bone tools are modified by intentional breakage, cutting, drilling, groov-

Fig. 12.23 Finely decorated antler weapon with shafthole and lethal point from the Early Mesolithic in Denmark.

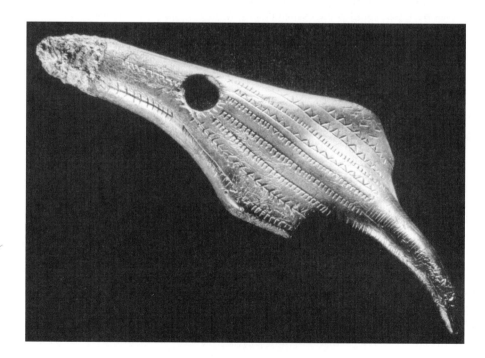

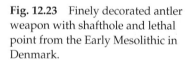

secondary products Both food and nonfood materials and energy that come from domestic animals in addition to meat.

osteodontokeratic "Bone-tooth-horn," a term coined to describe what might have been the earliest *tools;* lack of modification makes them impossible to identify.

ing, grinding, or polishing (Fig. 12.23). Bone was often used in the Upper Paleolithic and Mesolithic because it is tough and flexible, and less likely to break than tools of flint. Moreover, it can be shaped into new forms. Needles, disks, plaques, hoes, weapons, and many other artifacts were crafted from bone. In fact, bone was used for some tools until the industrial era. Bone and antler were made into hair combs and long pieces of polished bone were used for ice skates in some places in Europe and North America at the beginning of the twentieth century. Bone and ivory are still used in jewelry, and salad forks made of horn are quite fashionable. Animal teeth were once used as jewelry too, sometimes perforated in the root and worn as pendants and bangles.

SHELLS AND SHELLFISH

In addition to bone, tooth, antler, and horn, there are other remains of animals occasionally preserved in archaeological sites. Feathers, hoofs, hide, and shell also occur in conditions of good preservation. Shell is a particularly important category in many places. Shellfish—such as oysters, clams, mussels, scallops, limpets, and many others—are an important category of foods eaten both today and in the past, and the shells of these animals are often found in archaeological sites. Evidence for the consumption of shellfish dates back several hundred thousand years in human prehistory. Shellfish are a plentiful and easily collected source of protein and essential trace elements, such as iron, copper, and magnesium.

Shellfish belong to the biological group of species known as mollusks, animals with a shell and a foot. Univalve mollusks have one shell and include many species of snails, conchs, and others. Bivalve mollusks have two shells and include clams, scallops, and oysters. There are many species of mollusks and both freshwater and saltwater varieties. In addition to their use as food, shells were often used to make beads, fishhooks, and other objects. Crushed shells have been used as a source of lime, for pottery temper, and as construction material. In some areas, such as the South Pacific, shells of species like the cowrie have been traded as valued items over long distances and even used as money.

Large heaps of shells, known as shell middens, representing the refuse of thousands of meals can be found on coasts and riverbanks in various parts of the world. These shell middens can be hundreds of meters long, tens of meters wide, and up to 15 m (50 ft) high. For example, the Emeryville shell mound in San Francisco Bay (see Chapter 16) was 100×300 m in size (the area of six football fields) and more than 10 m high (equivalent to a three-story building).

In addition to information about diet, shells at archaeological sites also can tell us about the local habitat, climate, and the seasonality of site occupation. Different species of shellfish live in different depths of water and prefer different temperatures, salinity, and amounts of current. The proportions of shellfish at a site reflect the local water conditions. Shells are composed of calcium carbonate ($CaCO_3$), which is a molecule of calcium, carbon, and oxygen. The exact ratio of oxygen isotopes in shell depends on the temperature of the water in which the shell formed. Determination of that ratio in the shell allows scientists to study changes in water temperature (correlated with air temperature) over time in the study of climate.

Site seasonality can be assessed using the shells of certain mollusks with growth rings. A growth ring is a layer of shell that a mollusk adds every year. The time of year that a shell was harvested can be determined from these rings, documenting when humans both harvested the shell and occupied the area. Fig. 12.24 shows an oyster with several annual rings or layers of shell growth. Careful preparation and study of these shells can also help determine how old the creatures were when they were harvested.

Fig. 12.24 Annual growth rings on a mollusk shell. Four years of growth are visible in the cross section of the shell.

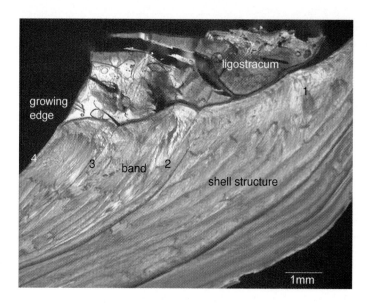

CONCLUSIONS

There are a number of things to remember about archaeozoology. Animal remains, largely in the form of bones and teeth, are not found at many archaeological sites. Faunal evidence is present only under good conditions of preservation. Bones are a valuable source of information and can answer many questions.

The list of the species represented at a site says a great deal about subsistence (e.g., hunting, farming, fishing, shellfish collecting), the kinds of environments that human groups were exploiting (e.g., mountains, deserts, lakes and streams, sea coasts, deep water, shallow water), and technology (e.g., net vs. line vs. spear fishing). Counts of the various species present can indicate the importance of different foods in the diet and document the local environment. Age and sex of the animals that are represented in a bone assemblage tells us about hunting or herding activities and how humans interacted with animal species. A number of indicators in bones and teeth can tell us about the time of year that animals were killed, which in turn tells us about the seasonality of site occupation or if places were occupied in a more permanent way. Cutmarks and butchering information are indicators of how meat was prepared and cooking preferences. All of these cultural practices are reflected in faunal remains.

Faunal remains also provide important evidence on some of the big questions in archaeology. For example, the broken and fragmentary bones of early human sites in East Africa help us to understand how our ancient ancestors obtained meat via scavenging or hunting. Evidence from archaeological and paleontological assemblages from the end of the Pleistocene tell us about the extinction of a variety of species at that turning point in time and provide the evidence to evaluate hypotheses of hunting vs. extinction. Faunal remains from both the domesticated species and their ancestors, also help answer the question of why humans domesticated animals at the origins of agriculture. Status difference in diets within human societies—an indicator of the presence of social inequality—is another important issue for faunal analysts.

The secondary products of animals were of great significance in earlier societies. Antler, ivory, skin, horn, hoofs, and hair have all been used in the past as raw material for tools and other equipment. Bone was also a useful raw material. Even broader questions regarding changes in human diets can be addressed in studies of animal bone from various times and places.

The History of every major Galactic Civilization tends to pass through three distinct and recognizable phases, those of Survival, Inquiry, and Sophistication, otherwise known as the How, Why, and Where phases. For instance, the first phase is characterized by the question "How can we eat?" the second by the question "Why do we eat?" and the third by the question "Where shall we have lunch?"

—Douglas Adams, author

SITE SEASONALITY

One of the major issues in archaeozoological research is the determination of the season of site occupation. Three archaeological sites and their contents are described below. Excavations at these sites uncovered a variety of ecofacts that provide information on human subsistence and site seasonality. There is also a description of the various plants and animals that were found by water screening (Fig. 12.25) and information on their seasonal availability. With this background, you should be able to determine the time of year that these sites were occupied and get some idea about human diet.

On the chart provided in Table 12.2 (page 352) list the species of plants and animals found at each site. Then draw a line across the months in the table when that species should be available. The completed chart will provide an overview of species seasonality from which you can infer the times when people were exploiting the resources of the region and living at these sites (see also Fig. 12.2). You may also want to list the names of the species present at each site on the map of the area (Fig. 12.26).

Sites

Harley site: This site is in the foothills of a mountain range and close to a wide expanse of grasslands (Fig. 12.26). Excavation at the site revealed fifteen rock-lined fire hearths. Seven of the hearths were found approximately one foot below the modern ground surface. The other eight hearths were at depths of nearly three feet below the modern ground surface. Several thousand charred nutshells of hickory were found in many of the hearths. Adjacent to the two groups of hearths, the excavators found a variety of faunal remains. These remains included 13,927 bones and 129 skulls with mature antlers of deer, and 12,297 bones of one-to-two-month-old mountain sheep. There were 24,376 bones and 324 skulls with immature (velvet) antlers of antelope. There also were 8,529 bones of adult bison. Finally, the excavators found more than three dozen human coprolites that contained many small seeds of blackberry. The excavators also recovered several

Fig. 12.25 Faunal remains recovered in the water screening.

Fig. 12.26 Site location for the three sites in this problem.

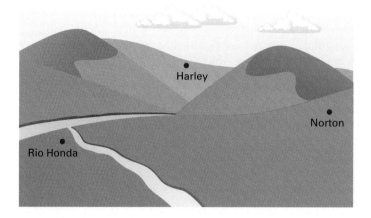

chipped stone knives, spear points, and scrapers, along with several hundred flakes of chipped stone.

Rio Honda site: This site is located on relatively level ground at the confluence of two rivers. All of the archaeological remains at this site were found in a single cultural layer about 30 cm (1 ft) thick over an area of approximately one-half acre. Above the cultural layer was a 30-cm (1-ft) thick layer of flood-deposited soils. Below the cultural layer were naturally deposited flood soils of an unknown depth. Within the cultural layer were several thousand flakes of obsidian, some obsidian chipped stone tools, and several bone fishhooks. Mixed among these artifacts were thousands of bones and scales of salmon and 31,239 clamshells. On virtually all the mollusk shells, the final growth rings were identified as being complete to nearly complete, wide, incremental rings. Also in the cultural layer were more than 13,650 bones of swan and several hundred fragments of eggshells of pigeon.

Norton site: This site is located along a stream on a terrace high above the floodplain. The site is huge and covers an area of about 25 acres. Excavations uncovered numerous house floors (some with the stumps of charred wood posts still in the foundations), fire hearths, and storage pits. Among the various artifact types were thousands of pottery sherds representing six different vessel forms and displaying eight different painted designs. Excavators recovered hundreds of chipped stone arrow points, scrapers, knives, and drills. Among the numerous bone tools were awls, fishhooks, harpoons, and needles. Within many of the pit features were thousands of grains of wild rice. Some of the pit features also had hundreds of seeds of grass and the charred nutshell fragments of hickory. Charred hickory nutshell fragments were also found in some of the hearths, along with some bones and scales of trout and remains of flat turtle (an extinct species about which you have no behavioral information). On the periphery of the site was an extensive midden area containing 37,697 bones and 638 skulls with mature antlers of antelope. Excavation of the midden also yielded more than 18,000 bones and 397 skulls with mature antlers of deer. The midden also yielded thousands of jawbones of seven-to-eight-month-old pike and 8,013 bones of duck.

TABLE 12.1 Information on fauna and flora.

Fish

Salmon:	A migrating fish that schools to spawn in the rivers in late May and early June.
Pike:	The young of this fish are hatched in October.
Trout:	Fish that spawn in rivers during July and August.

Shellfish

Clam:	A freshwater clam; its shell exhibits seasonally alternating growth rings; wide growth rings represent growth during warm months, a period that begins in May and is completed by mid-September; narrow growth rings represent arrested growth from late September to the end of April.

Mammal

Deer:	A deer that sheds its antlers by late March; antlers are covered with velvet from mid-July to October; mature antlers last from late October to mid-March.
Mountain sheep:	A mountain sheep with an early March to early April birth season.
Antelope:	An antelope that sheds its antlers in late September; the antlers of this species are covered with velvet from early December to early April; mature antlers last from late April to early September.
Bison:	A prairie bison that migrates through the region in the spring and again in the fall.

Bird

Duck:	A migratory species available locally in March and November.
Swan:	A migratory species that inhabits the area from June to September.
Pigeon:	A local species that nests and incubates its eggs from May to early June.

Plant

Grass:	A wild grass that has edible seeds during late August and September.
Hickory:	A tree with nuts that ripen in late September and early October.
Wild rice:	An aquatic grass that produces ripe grain from early August into early September.
Blackberry:	A shrub that produces edible berries in September.

TABLE 12.2 Seasonality chart.

	Jan	Feb	Mar	Apr	May	Jun	Jul	Aug	Sep	Oct	Nov	Dec
Harley species:												
Rio Honda species:												
Norton species:												

Questions

Using your seasonality chart in Table 12.2 and knowledge from evaluating the site data and other information, describe as accurately as possible the time of year (season, seasons, or months) that each site was occupied. Is there any evidence that indicates how many times people may have occupied a site? If so, identify that evidence and speculate on how many times people may have lived there. What are the problems involved in making estimates of site seasonality? Are there other factors that could make your results less reliable? Please limit your answers to two pages.

STUDY QUESTIONS

www.mhhe.com/pricearch1

For more review material and study questions, please see the self-quizzes on your online learning center.

1. What are the arguments for and against a human role in the extinction of large game animals at the end of the Pleistocene?

2. What are the indicators of domestication in the first herded animals?

3. Site seasonality is an important aspect of hunter-gatherer settlements. What kinds of evidence provide information on site season of occupation?

4. What is taphonomy and why is it important in archaeozoological studies?

5. Why is bone a useful material for making tools?

REFERENCES

Binford, Lewis R. 1981. *Bones: Ancient Men and Modern Myths.* New York: Academic Press.

Davis, Simon. 1995. *The Archaeology of Animal.* New Haven: Yale University Press.

Dincauze, D. 2000. *Environmental Archaeology.* Cambridge: Cambridge University Press.

O'Connor, Terry. 2000. *The Archaeology of Animal Bones.* College Station: Texas A&M University Press.

Rackham, James. 1994. *Animal Bones.* London: British Museum Press.

Reitz, Elizabeth J., and Elizabeth S. Wing. 1999. *Zooarchaeology.* Cambridge Manuals in Archaeology. Cambridge: Cambridge University Press.

Rowley-Conwy, P.A., ed. 2000. *Animal Bones, Human Societies.* Oxford: Oxbow Books.

www.mhhe.com/pricearch1

For Internet references related to this chapter, please see the chapter links on your online learning center.

Archaeobotany

INTRODUCTION: THE STUDY OF ARCHAEOLOGICAL PLANTS

Corn, or maize, is one of the most remarkable domesticated plants on earth, an important staple food for people and animals almost everywhere. The great diversity of modern maize, which grows under a variety of environmental and topographic conditions, is an indication of its adaptability and genetic versatility. This diversity is evident in the photograph of different types of maize shown here.

Maize is one of many species of plants and animals that humans have tamed over the last 10,000 years. The story of corn is also a saga of **archaeobotany**, the study of archaeological plant remains. One of the primary questions in archaeology and archaeobotany concerns the origins of agriculture and the identification of early domesticated plants. The pursuit of the ancestors and timing of the domestication of corn has proven difficult. There is still argument today about the ancestor of modern corn, this after more than 100 years of debate. Most favor the wild Mexican grass known as **teosinte** (*tea-oh-SEEN-tay*); others, however, insist that there is a wild maize plant that gave rise to corn and has since disappeared as a hybrid of the domesticated variety (Fig. 13.1). Genetic information from modern maize suggests that its closest ancestors are in fact the teosinte that grows in the highlands of western Mexico.

Determining the antiquity of domesticated maize is also difficult. The dates for this event have changed several times. Once thought to be several millennia earlier, maize is now argued to have been domesticated around 4200 BC, somewhere in southwestern Mexico. There are few archaeologists who think that date and maybe the place as well won't change. Dates given for the earliest corn in South America are sometimes earlier than the dates in Mesoamerica. This is not possible if teosinte is the ancestor, since teosinte does not grow south of Panama.

The search for the origins and antiquity of domesticated maize continues. This story contains many elements of archaeobotanical research: the identification of plant remains, the study of human diet, dating, plant genetics, the origins of agriculture, and fieldwork. This chapter is about archaeobotany, its goals and methods, and its contribution to our knowledge of the past.

The remains of plants that archaeobotanists study can vary in size from microscopic fragments to large pieces of timber or even complete trees. Some scholars use the word *paleoethnobotany* for this branch of archaeology, but that term refers to a larger domain of plant use by both living and prehistoric peoples. *Paleobotany* is another term, but it refers specifically to fossil plants and is more

www.mhhe.com/pricearch1

For preview material for this chapter, please see the chapter summary, outline, and objectives on your online learning center.

archaeobotany (a.k.a. *paleobotany, paleoethnobotany*)   The study of archaeological plant remains.

teosinte   Wild Mexican grass, probable ancestor of corn.

paleoethnobotany   The study of plant use by both living and prehistoric peoples.

paleobotany   Study of fossil plants.

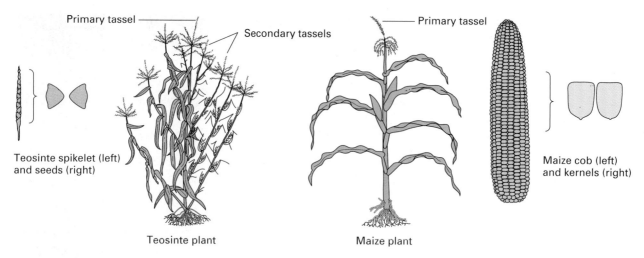

Primary tassel

Secondary tassels

Primary tassel

Teosinte spikelet (left)
and seeds (right)

Teosinte plant

Maize plant

Maize cob (left)
and kernels (right)

Fig. 13.1 Corn, or maize, and its
ancestor teosinte.

akin to **paleontology**. I prefer the term *archaeobotany* because it fits well with archaeozoology and relates directly to archaeology. Archaeozoologists study faunal
remains; archaeobotanists study **floral**, or botanical, remains.

We humans have used plants as long as we have been human. Plants are
important for food, of course, but they fill many other needs as well, for tools,
clothing, bedding, medicine, and construction materials. The preservation of
plants at archaeological sites, however, is generally poor. Plant remains—fragile
organic materials—are one of the first things to decompose. Sites that are extremely arid or extremely wet may have suitable conditions for the preservation
of floral material. In other situations, plants that have been burned or carbonized
are sometimes preserved as charred pieces. In both cases, the plant remains are
often fragmentary and identification is difficult.

Archaeobotanists want to know what plants are present at a site. That involves separating plant remains from the other materials found in excavations,
sorting through the floral specimens themselves and identifying what is there.
Plants provide useful information on the seasonality of site use. For example, nuts
ripen and are harvested in the fall of the year; the presence of nutshell in the
botanical remains means that people collected nuts at that time. Other major questions in archaeobotany concern the use of plants in diet, for medicinal or hallu-
cinogenic purposes, as tools and raw material, and in terms of domestication—the
origins of agriculture. With the introduction of agriculture, humans began to modify and use plants in a variety of new ways.

Botanical remains also tell us about the natural environment around a site
and about human choices that were made in the selection of plant resources. Special growing requirements and other characteristics of certain plant species may
reflect climatic conditions or specific local situations, like a grassland versus a
forested environment. Preserved seeds, grain, fruit stones, and nutshells can provide information about diet, land use, climate, storage, and ritual. Wood, fibers,
and charcoal can tell us about tools, structures, fuel, forests, and textiles.

Two general categories of plant remains are recognized, **macroscopic**—visible
to the naked eye—and **microscopic**—visible only with magnification. Macrobotanical remains from an archaeological site may include seeds, nutshells, leaves,
pieces of wood and the like, depending on the quality of preservation. Microscopic materials may also be present and include things like pollen, phytoliths,
diatoms, and starch grains, again depending on the conditions of preservation. Special techniques are needed to isolate and identify these microscopic
specimens.

DNA testing has become common practice in more and more areas of science and medicine. Archaeobotanists are now extracting and studying ancient

paleontology   Study of fossil animals.

floral   Plants, botanical materials, in contrast to
fauna, or animals.

macroscopic   Visible to the naked eye.

microscopic   Visible only with magnification.

wattle-and-daub   A construction technique that
involves standing posts and interwoven horizontal
branches (wattle) that are covered in mud (daub) to
make a wall.

flotation   An archaeological technique for recovering charred plant remains using water and density
differences between heavy and light materials in
sediments. Dry sediments are stirred into water and
the lighter plant remains float to the top.

flot   The lighter, carbonized plant remains that
"float" in the flotation methods of recovering plant
remains.

DNA (aDNA) in plants. Information from aDNA helps not only with the identification of species but also in terms of genetic relationships among different varieties of a species and questions of domestication.

The remainder of this chapter deals with various aspects of archaeobotany, beginning with macrobotanical remains. Flotation and wet sieving are the techniques used to obtain these samples in archaeological deposits. Sorting the samples leads to the process of identification, often involving the use of a binocular microscope and collections of comparative modern specimens. The Incinerator site from the Late Woodland period in Ohio provides an example of the study of macrobotanical remains for information on seasonality and diet.

The origin of agriculture is a fundamental concern in archaeobotany. The section dealing with this issue is followed by a description of the early Neolithic site of Abu Hureyra in Syria. Abu Hureyra contained evidence for the earliest domesticated plants in the world and is a good example for archaeobotanical methods of analysis. Wood and charcoal identification is another important part of the study of floral remains, and this section has an exciting example from the Aegean island of Thera, which exploded around 1650 BC. Microbotanical studies focus on pollen and phytoliths, and these are the subject of the next sections of this chapter. Changes in the types of pollen through time can be used to reconstruct the vegetational history of the area and to provide a record of climatic changes. An example of pollen analysis involving the famous elm decline in northern Europe is discussed.

Fig. 13.2 Macrobotanical remains from the flotation process include a variety of seeds and grains.

MACROBOTANICAL REMAINS

Macrobotanical materials are visible remains like seeds, nutshells, and other plant parts that are likely to be present at a site due to direct human contact or utilization (Fig. 13.2). Identification of these remains indicates what species of plants were present, whether they were wild or domestic, and in what context they were found. It is important to study the context of these remains to know how the plants were used. Plants may be collected for food, but they may also be used for construction; for the production of textiles, mats, and baskets; for making poison for arrowheads; or as drugs, for example.

In addition to the preserved whole or charred remains of seeds, stems, nutshells, and other plant parts that are found at archaeological sites, there is other evidence. Casts of plant remains in ceramics and accidentally fired clay sediments provide remarkable reproductions of the appearance of the plant remains. Casts of wheat grains in pottery from the Early Neolithic in Denmark permit identification of the species that were present. Construction techniques are sometimes revealed in the remains of burned structures. Evidence for **wattle-and-daub** buildings can clearly be seen in the fired mud or daub from the walls of houses and other structures that burned (Fig. 13.3). Impressions of the wattle-and-timber framework remain permanently in the fired clay daub.

Flotation

Preserved plants are rare in archaeological sites unless the remains have been carbonized, generally through burning or oxidation. Such burned plant materials can be recovered through a process called **flotation**. In its simplest form, flotation involves drying excavated sediments and then pouring them into a bucket or tank of water. The lighter, carbonized plant fragments (the "**flot**") rise to the top and float, while the heavier sediments fall to the bottom. A filter or screen can be used to skim the flot from the surface of the water. There are several different commercial models of flotation equipment available that use pumps, multiple tanks, and sieves to speed up and improve the process (Fig. 13.4). More complex flotation techniques involve heavy liquids and the separation of different classes of material and are usually done in the laboratory.

Fig. 13.3 Burned daub fragment from an historic Spanish mission in Texas. This piece retains impressions of the wattle and the grass that was mixed with the clay to strengthen it. The fragment is approximately 5 cm (2 in) high.

Macrobotanical Remains **351**

Fig. 13.5 An archaeobotanist begins the long process of sorting the charred material obtained from flotation of sediments at an archaeological site. The round screens contain different sizes of material.

Fig. 13.4 Flotation equipment in action. Water is pumped through a series of tanks and the lighter fraction of the sediments, largely charcoal and charred plant remains, rises to the top. Heavier sediments drop to the bottom of the tank. Sorting and identifying the "flot" material that is recovered is a time-consuming job.

Sorting and Identification

The majority of the identifiable macrobotanical remains that come from archaeological sites are recovered during wet screening and flotation. This material is taken to laboratories where drying facilities, good lighting, and microscopes are available. It is important to remember that most plant remains survive at archaeological sites because they have been carbonized or charred by exposure to heat. Identification of these remains is complicated by the charring. They survive largely as fragments of charcoal that have shrunken from their original size and are often warped by the heat of the fire. In unusual waterlogged or extremely arid conditions, plant remains may survive in their original form, but this is a rare situation.

The macrobotanical remains are first sorted by size and shape and identifiable pieces (Fig. 13.5). Some of this sorting can be done by eye, but most of it requires low power magnification using a binocular microscope (see Chapter 9, "The Petrographic Microscope"). The majority of the sample material will lack diagnostic features and cannot be identified. Wood and nonwood specimens are separated in this process. Much of the material will be burned wood or fuel from heating and/or cooking fires. Wood identification, described later in this chapter, can provide information on the species used for fuel and construction at a site. A small proportion of the remains will be identifiable charred seeds, nutshells, stems, and other parts of edible plants.

The identification of this material is a major task for the archaeobotanist. As in other situations, the use of a comparative collection of reference materials is essential. Most major universities and natural history museums house **reference collections** of modern plant parts in herbariums, and there are numerous regional plant catalogs and guides that illustrate plant structure and parts. In addition, archaeobotanists often build their own collections of plant remains that are intentionally charred to simulate the archaeological material and assist in the identification of prehistoric remains (Fig. 13.6). Identification is a demanding job; recognizing distinctive features on hundreds of specimens and assigning the proper genus and/or species takes both experience and time.

Fig. 13.6 The cast of a wheat spikelet in a fired clay lump from the 9000-year-old site of Jarmo in northern Iraq (left) compared to a modern spikelet of the same species (right).

The result of the sorting and identification process is a list of the species present and counts of their abundance at the site (see, for example, Table 13.1). This information allows archaeobotanists to answer questions about the environment surrounding an archaeological site, the types of plants that people ate and used, seasonal use of species, and possible human manipulation of the vegetation. The example below from the Incinerator site provides a good case study of what can be learned in archaeobotanical investigations.

 EXAMPLE ~~~~~~~~~~~~~~~~~~~~~~~~~~~

THE INCINERATOR SITE

Fort Ancient is the name for a time period and archaeological culture in the eastern United States, dating from the first half of the second millennium AD (ca. AD 1000–1500). Fort Ancient communities were focused on a narrow range of food resources. Such societies are subject to repeated, short-term seasonal shortages that can be ameliorated through storage practices. This pattern is seen at sites of the Fort Ancient culture.

Fort Ancient people were maize farmers, relying on a few plants and animals for most of their food. Deer, elk, and black bear supplied 80% of the meat. Carbon isotope ratios in human bone (Chapter 15) indicate a diet of approximately 80% maize. Maize was supplemented by hickory nut, black walnut, and domesticated beans and **chenopod**. The settlement pattern was structured to optimize this diet. Residential groups gathered in larger villages of permanent houses in the spring and summer. During the fall and winter, family groups dispersed to hunting camps, leaving a small contingent behind in the permanent village.

Studies of the botanical remains from the Incinerator site in southern Ohio provide substantial insight on the use of plant remains. The site was occupied for only a short period, perhaps 15–20 years, around AD 1250. The circular site was designed and laid out around a huge timber pole in the very center of the site. This center point is a solar alignment pole thought to mark the winter solstice, as well as the approximate planting and harvesting dates of April 20 and August 20. The circular site is fortified at its margin by a stockade. Within the stockade walls is a concentric row of houses and associated storage and trash pits (Fig. 13.7). The central area of the circle is generally open with a few large pits and thought to be the central plaza for the settlement, as seen in the reconstruction (Fig. 13.8). Along the northern edge of the plaza are a series of graves marking a burial ground.

The site provides excellent information on plant and animal utilization because preservation is good and the many pits provide discrete sets of remains. Many of the pits were used for food storage, as indicated by their size and shape and the discovery of charred grass linings and stacked cobs of maize. These pits were filled with trash when they could no longer be used for storage.

Almost forty of these pits could be assigned to a season of use based on the presence of the mandibles (lower jaws) from young whitetail deer. The tooth wear and eruption pattern on these jaws allows determination of the time of year that the pits were filled with trash. Six of the pits were filled in the spring (April–June), seventeen in the summer (late May–September), and sixteen in the winter (October–April). Note that only three seasons can be distinguished at this site, based on the variation in the deer mandibles. Winter includes the fall and runs from October through April.

There are fewer deer bones in the pits from the colder months, possibly reflecting a smaller population at the site in the winter. Several lines of evidence suggest that the trash pits were filled quickly and were probably used for no more than one season. Thus, identification of the charred macrobotanical remains in the pits allows determination of the diet for each season (Table 13.1).

Pits from the different seasons of the year contained the same kinds of plant foods. The most common plant remains—maize, hickory, black walnut, sumac, and

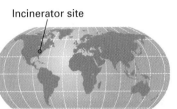
Incinerator site

Cattails (Recipe)
Get the roots of the cattails. Peel away tough leafy layers to the tender core, about ½ inch in diameter and maybe 12 inches long. This can be eaten raw, like celery, or sliced into a salad. Or, cover the cores with boiling water and simmer about 10 minutes. You may pick the green bloom spikes of the cattails, remove sheathes, and boil in water until tender, and eat like corn-on-the-cob.
—Elias and Dykeman,
Edible Wild Plants: A North American Field Guide

~~~~~~~~~~~~~~~~~~~~~~~~~~~

reference collections Collections of modern plants, animal bones, human skeletal material, and other items to be used in the process of identification of archaeological remains. Prehistoric items are compared to modern to find the closest match.

chenopod A variety of weedy herbs belonging to the goosefoot family, which includes spinach, beets, and pigweed.

Fig. 13.7 A plan of the Incinerator site showing the circular shape, the outer palisade, the houses along the inside of the palisade, the distribution of storage pits, and the interior plaza and cemetery area. Only about one-half of the site was excavated.

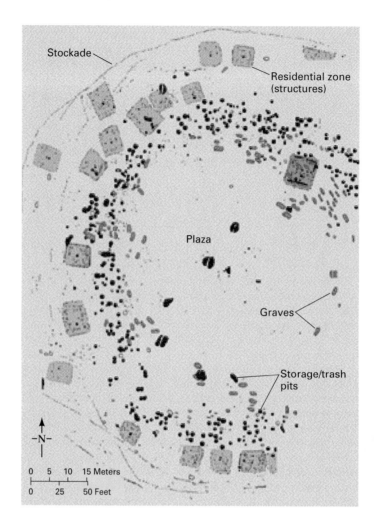

Stockade

Residential zone (structures)

Plaza

Graves

Storage/trash pits

-N-

0 5 10 15 Meters
0   25   50 Feet

▼ **Fig. 13.8** A modern reconstruction of the Incinerator/Sunwatch site, showing the stockade, interior row of houses, and the large post in the center of the site.

TABLE 13.1 Floral remains[a] from the seasonally identified pits at the Incinerator site.

Taxa	Spring	Summer	Winter
Domesticates			
Maize (*Zea mays*)	77	126	169
Common bean (*Phaseolus vulgaris*)	—	4	2
Tobacco (*Nicotiana* spp.)	—	1	—
Chenopod (*Chenopodium berlandieri*)	—	1	1
Wild and weedy plants			
Sumac (*Rhus* spp.)	50	24	18
Purslane (*Portulaca* spp.)	13	8	22
Bramble (*Rubus* spp.)	5	7	2
Panic grass (*Panicum* spp.)	4	3	3
Nightshade (*Solanum* spp.)	3	3	8
Chenopod (*Chenopodium* spp.)	2	4	2
Smartweeds (*Polygonum* spp.)	2	3	4
Groundcherry (*Physalis* spp.)	1	—	—
Unidentified grasses (Poaceae)	4	3	1
Little barley (*Hordeum pusillum*)	—	—	1
Maygrass[b] (*Phalaris caroliniana*)	(1)	—	—
Foxtail grass (*Setaria* spp.)	1	—	—
Unidentified legumes (Fabaceae)	—	—	3
Tick-trefoil (*Desmodium* spp.)	—	1	—
Grape (*Vitis* spp.)	—	1	—
Hackberry (*Celtis* spp.)	1	—	2[c]
Hawthorn (*Crataegus* spp.)	1	—	—
Vervain (*Verbena* spp.)	1	—	(1)
Sedge (*Scirpus* spp.)	—	2	—
Wood sorrel (*Oxalis* spp.)	1	—	—
Spurge (*Euphorbia* spp.)	1	—	1
Unidentified seeds	18	9	13
Unidentifiable seeds	30	16	25
Total identified wild/weedy seeds	91	59	68
Flotation samples (N)	11	13	13
Features (N)	3	6	7
Dirt floated (liters)	62.5	32.0	33.0

[a]The count was of all seeds from all size fractions. Figures in parentheses are uncertain identifications.
[b]May be a cultigen.
[c]One storage/trash pit (F22/76) contains a cache of 261 hackberry seeds that may be uncarbonized and are of questionable age.

purslane—are present in all the pits. Sumac and purslane are weedy plants that produce lots of small, edible seeds. The only unusual pattern is the increase in fruit seeds in the spring pits. As might be expected, evidence for burning is most pronounced in the winter (maize cobs and nutshell were burned in addition to wood) when heat was essential.

The botanical evidence from the Incinerator site provides a remarkable insight into plant storage and use in the past (Fig. 13.9). The information indicates that plants

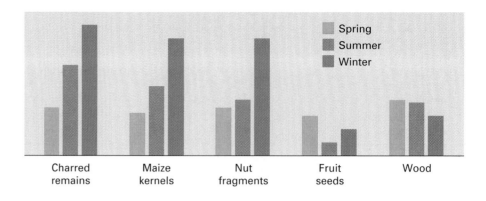

Fig. 13.9 The relative amounts of various categories of plant remains at the Incinerator site during the three seasons of the year. For example, charred remains—evidence of burning—are most common in the winter months; fruit seeds are more frequent in the spring; and maize and nut fragments dominate the winter months. Plants were consumed year-round at this site, testament to the efficient drying and storage techniques that were practiced.

Charred remains	Maize kernels	Nut fragments	Fruit seeds	Wood

Legend: Spring, Summer, Winter

were essentially available year-round to the inhabitants—that drying and storage techniques were sufficient to provide these foods throughout the year. Even fruits, normally eaten fresh, were dried, stored, and available in the spring. There is no evidence for a shortage of plant foods at any time.

Agriculture provided the lever for the extraordinary development that subsequent human societies experienced.
Bruce Smith, archaeologist

Fig. 13.10 Increase in seed size between wild (left) and domesticated (right) varieties of marsh elder (top), sunflower (middle), and squash (bottom). Plants from larger seeds grow faster and produce more food.

Origins of Agriculture

The origin of agriculture is one of the really big questions in archaeology. Agriculture represents one of the major changes in the evolution of human culture and is an important focus of archaeobotany. We would like to know when, where, what, and why people began to control the plants and animals around them.

An important distinction in agricultural plants is made between **seed crops** and **root crops**. Most of the evidence for early domesticated plants comes from seed crops. The best known early domesticates are the cereals—the grasses that produce large, hard-shelled seeds—which are nutritious kernels of carbohydrate that can be stored for long periods. The hard cereal grains, and occasionally the stems of these plants, were often burned during preparation or cooking in the past and thereby preserved to the present.

Root crops such as potatoes, yams, manioc, and taro may also have been domesticated early. But root crops are not well documented in the archaeological record because they lack hard parts that are resistant to decay. In addition, because they reproduce asexually from shoots or cuttings, it is difficult to distinguish domesticated varieties from their wild ancestors. Asexually reproducing plants may maintain exactly the same genetic structure through many generations, because a piece of the parent plant is used to start the daughter. Such plants may also exhibit great variation within a species, making domestication difficult to recognize.

Archaeologists have started to identify root crops from prehistoric sites only recently. One of the more important developments in archaeobotany has been the use of the **scanning electron microscope** (SEM). This instrument, capable of very high magnifications, has enabled researchers to identify minute scraps of charred plant remains, especially roots and tubers, which would otherwise be missed at archaeological sites.

Seed crops remain the focus of most research on the origins of agriculture. One of the important hallmarks of plant domestication is an increase in the size of the seeds or grains of the plant. Humans select for more productive plants with larger seeds. Fig. 13.10 shows three species of plants—marsh elder, sunflower, and squash—that were domesticated in the eastern United States around 4000 years ago. There is a pronounced difference in the size of the seeds of the

Sunwatch Indian Village/Archaeological Park

The Incinerator site was named because of its location amid landfill, dumps, and sewage treatment facilities on the edge of Dayton, Ohio. The place was originally intended for the expansion of wastewater treatment, but the importance of the site was recognized in time. Because of the extraordinary finds, the Incinerator or Sunwatch site, as it is now called, was declared a National Historic Landmark and protected for the future. Archaeological ethics dictate the protection of cultural and historical remains whenever possible.

The site is now property of the Dayton Society of Natural History and has become the Sunwatch Indian Village/Archaeological Park. There are five reconstructed buildings and a partially reconstructed stockade, as well as a museum and gift shop. Sunwatch is one of the more popular attractions in the Dayton area, with 25,000 visitors annually, half of whom are schoolchildren. Sunwatch is now protected for the future and provides a place for education and participation in the area's significant past. To learn more, check out www.sunwatch.org.

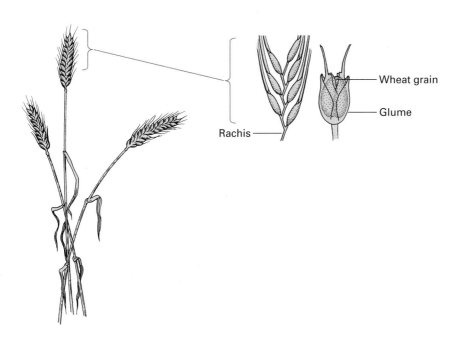

Fig. 13.11 Major characteristics of wheat.

www.mhhe.com/pricearch1

For a Web-based activity on the domestication of maize, please see the Internet exercises on your online learning center.

domesticated varieties. Interestingly, domestic animals are usually smaller than their wild counterparts.

In addition to the size, other morphological changes in the plant often are related to seeding mechanisms. According to the late Hans Helbaek, an expert who worked on the issue of plant domestication, the most important characteristic of a domesticated species is the loss of its natural seeding ability. The plant comes to depend on human intervention in order to reproduce. This change also permits humans to select more directly the traits of those plants to be sown and harvested, leading to preferred characteristics.

The changes in wheat from wild to domestic clearly document this modification of the seeding mechanism. Wheat is an annual grass with a large seed grain that concentrates carbohydrates inside a hard shell. Grain at the top of the grass stalk is connected by the **rachis**, or stem (Fig. 13.11). Each seed is covered by a husk, or **glume**. The major features that distinguish wild and domesticated wheat are found in the rachis and glume. There is little size difference between wild and domestic forms. In wild wheat, the rachis of each seed cluster is brittle, to allow natural seed dispersal by a mechanism known as **shattering**. The glumes

seed crop Plants that reproduce sexually by making and dispersing seeds.

root crop Plants that reproduce asexually from shoots or cuttings.

scanning electron microscope (SEM) An electronic (not optical) instrument for very high magnification of microscopic structures. The SEM uses electrons instead of light to form an image.

rachis The stem that connects the grain seed to the main plant stalk in cereals.

glume The husk that covers and protects cereal grains.

shattering Seed dispersal mechanism.

TABLE 13.2 Common food plants in the Early Neolithic Near East.

Einkorn wheat, wild and domesticated forms
Emmer wheat, wild and domesticated forms
Rye, wild and domesticated forms
Barley, wild and domesticated forms
Oats, wild and domesticated forms
Flax, wild and domesticated forms
Chickpeas, domesticated form
Field peas, domesticated form
Lentils, wild and domesticated forms
Common vetch
Bitter vetch
Horse bean
Grape, wild and domesticated forms
Caper berries
Prosopis (mesquite)
Fig
Hackberry
Turpentine tree
Wild pistachio

covering the seeds are tough, to protect the grain until the next growing season. These two features, however, are counterproductive for effective harvesting and consumption by humans. Because of the brittleness of the rachis, many seeds fall to the ground before and during harvesting, making collection difficult. The tough glume must be roasted so that it can be removed by threshing.

Domesticated wheats exhibit the reverse of these characteristics: a tough rachis and a brittle glume. These changes enable the seed to stay on the plant so that it can be harvested in quantity and the glume can be removed by threshing without roasting. These changes also mean that the wheat is dependent upon humans for seeding and therefore, by definition, is domesticated.

Another major change in domesticated plants is the human removal of plants from their natural habitat to new environmental zones. New conditions of growth obviously select for different characteristics. Some varieties do very well when moved to a new setting. For this reason, an important consideration in the study of plant domestication is the original distribution of the wild ancestor of the domesticate. Are the early domestic varieties found within the zone where the wild ancestors grow, or are domesticates the result of being introduced into a new habitat?

The ancient Near East was the home to a variety of domesticated plant species (Table 13.2). Two varieties of wheat (emmer and einkorn), two-row barley, rye, oats, lentils, peas, chickpeas, and flax were originally cultivated very early in this region. The wild forms of several of these species are common today, as they were in the past. Wild emmer wheat has a restricted distribution in the southern Levant. Wild einkorn wheat is relatively widespread in the northern and eastern sections of the Near East. Einkorn was probably domesticated in southern Turkey, while emmer may have been first cultivated in the Jordan Valley. Wild barley grows throughout the **Fertile Crescent** (Fig. 13.12). All of these wild grasses grow well in disturbed ground around human settlements. Further evidence for the domestication of plants comes from the excavation and analysis of archaeobotanical materials at Abu Hureyra in Syria, described below.

Fertile Crescent The arc-shaped zone of wetter uplands in Southwest Asia that stretches from the Mediterranean coast through the mountains of southeastern Turkey, to the mountains of southwestern Iran. The ancestral homeland of many species that were domesticated.

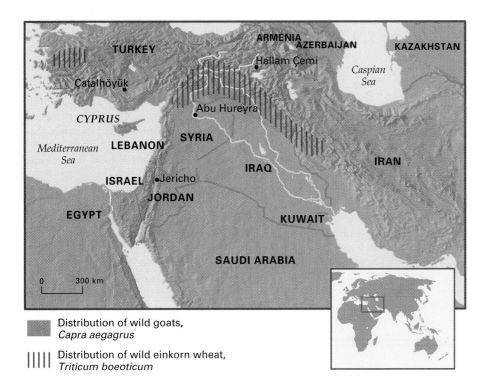

Fig. 13.12 The location of the Fertile Crescent, important sites, and the distribution of wild goats and wild einkorn wheat in the Near East.

 Distribution of wild goats, *Capra aegagrus*

||||| Distribution of wild einkorn wheat, *Triticum boeoticum*

ARCHAEOLOGICAL THINKING

Domesticating Plants

A fascinating question about the origins of agriculture concerns how long the process of plant domestication takes. How much time is required for wild wheat to become domestic wheat? There is a problem in identifying plants early in the process of domestication. Archaeologists will never find the spot where the first wheat or barley was domesticated. Moreover, it is necessary to observe changes in grain size and other characteristics on the plants themselves. Domesticated varieties cannot be distinguished from wild types without actual plant parts or grain impressions in clay bricks or pottery. So, answering the question of the length of time for domestication is difficult.

Archaeobotanist Gordon Hillman, of the University College, London, took a different route to answer this question. Hillman studied wild einkorn growing today in the Near East and conducted a number of experiments involving sowing, harvesting, and storage. Hillman observed that simple harvesting had no major impact on the genetic structure of the wheat (Fig. 13.13). Only when selective harvesting and other cultivation techniques were involved could changes in the morphology of the seeds be observed. Such an observation means that certain characteristics of domesticated wheat and barley, which show definite morphological differences from the wild ancestral forms, must have been intentionally selected, not accidental. Results from Hillman's experimental studies further suggest that the change from wild to domesticated wheat may have occurred in a brief period, perhaps less than 300 years, perhaps no more than 25 years. Experimental archaeology is an important part of archaeological thinking and can provide powerful insights on processes in operation in the past.

Fig. 13.13 Harvesting of wild wheats in Turkey. These experiments demonstrated that wild cereals were abundant, nutritious, and available.

ABU HUREYRA

Abu Hureyra

www.mhhe.com/pricearch1

For a Web-based activity on Abu Hureyra, please see the Internet exercises on your online learning center.

In 1974, the site of Abu Hureyra (*AH-boo who-RAY-ruh*) in northern Syria was submerged beneath the waters behind a new dam on the Euphrates River. Fortunately, in 1972 and 1973, before the water level in the reservoir rose and flooded the area, rescue excavations uncovered parts of this site, one of the largest early Holocene communities in Southwest Asia. A. M. T. Moore, of the Rochester Institute of Technology, and his colleagues, conducted the excavations.

Abu Hureyra was a large **tell**—an accumulated mound of occupation debris from human activity—that covered some 11.5 ha (30 acres) with deposits from the Preneolithic and the early Neolithic, up to 8 m (25 ft) high in some places. One million cubic meters (1.3 million cubic yards) of earth were removed during the excavations. The primary component of the tell was the decayed mud from the generations of houses that had been built there, along with the artifacts and food remains left behind by the inhabitants. The layers contained an uninterrupted occupation of the mound from approximately 10,500 BC to 6000 BC, through the Preneolithic and the Neolithic periods. Abu Hureyra thus contains one of the best records of the changes that took place as farming and herding first began.

The mound lies at the edge of the Euphrates River, with the river floodplain on one side and dry steppe on the other. The area today receives approximately 200 mm (8 in) of rainfall per year, and cultivation is difficult without irrigation. During the Preneolithic occupation of the site, however, the climate was warmer and wetter. An open forest of oak and pistachio trees grew on the steppes nearby with dense stands of wild grasses among the trees. These grasses, probably no more than 1–2 km (about 1 mi) distant, included wild wheats, rye, and various pulses (lentils and legumes).

The settlement may have been placed here originally adjacent to the Euphrates River along the migration route of gazelle herds. These animals were killed in great numbers during the spring migration. The Preneolithic settlement consisted of small, circular pit dwellings dug into the original ground surface. These structures had a framework of wooden posts supporting the wall and roof. Almost 1 m (3 ft) of debris accumulated during this first phase of occupation, between approximately 10,500 and 9000 BC. The population of the site is estimated to have been between 200 and 300 inhabitants at that time.

It is clear that the bulk of their food came from wild plants, some of which were staples. The plant remains at the site indicate a year-round occupation in both the Preneolithic and the Neolithic periods. The excavators used flotation techniques at Abu Hureyra to recover more than 500 liters (140 gallons) of plant remains. From the Preneolithic levels, there was evidence for wild lentils, hackberry fruit, caper berries, and nuts from the turpentine tree, related to pistachios. Most intriguing, however, were the remains of wild wheat, barley, and rye.

Around 10,000 BC, the climate became cooler and drier and the nearby stands of wild cereals retreated more than 100 km (62.5 mi) to the higher elevations of the Fertile Crescent. Local vegetation around the site appears to have changed from moist, woodland steppe to dry, treeless steppe. Fruits and seeds of drought-sensitive plants from the oak-pistachio open woodland disappeared at Abu Hureyra as the steppe expanded. At the same time, wild wheats continued to be consumed at the site in spite of the fact that their habitat had been eliminated. The excavators believe that the Preneolithic inhabitants of Abu Hureyra cultivated wild cereals before the changes in the glume and rachis brought about by domestication were evident.

Domestication may have resulted from the cultivation of these cereals in this area, after the natural habitat had been eliminated. The earliest known domesticated plant, rye, appeared at this time. Grinding stones and milling equipment at the site also point to the importance of cereals in the diet during this period. Shortly after the initial domestication of rye and the probable cultivation of wild wheats, lentils, and legumes reappeared in the deposits and increased. By 8500 BC, the range of domesticated plants included rye, lentils, and large-seeded legumes, and domesticated wheats. Clearly, plant domestication began in the Preneolithic period at Abu Hureyra, perhaps in response to the disappearance of the wild stands of these important foods.

tell An accumulated mound of occupation debris; man-made living mounds of earth and trash that accumulate from the decomposition of mud brick, common in Southwest Asia and Southeast Europe.

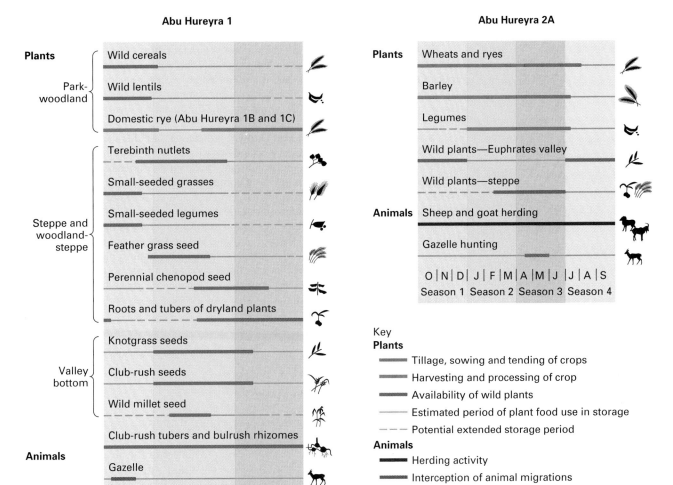

Abu Hureyra 1

Plants

Park-woodland
- Wild cereals
- Wild lentils
- Domestic rye (Abu Hureyra 1B and 1C)

Steppe and woodland-steppe
- Terebinth nutlets
- Small-seeded grasses
- Small-seeded legumes
- Feather grass seed
- Perennial chenopod seed
- Roots and tubers of dryland plants

Valley bottom
- Knotgrass seeds
- Club-rush seeds
- Wild millet seed

Animals
- Club-rush tubers and bulrush rhizomes
- Gazelle
- Onager
- Wild sheep
- Hare

A|M|J|J|A|S|O|N|D|J|F|M
Season 1   Season 2   Season 3

Abu Hureyra 2A

Plants
- Wheats and ryes
- Barley
- Legumes
- Wild plants—Euphrates valley
- Wild plants—steppe

Animals
- Sheep and goat herding
- Gazelle hunting

O|N|D|J|F|M|A|M|J|J|A|S
Season 1 Season 2 Season 3 Season 4

Key
Plants
- Tillage, sowing and tending of crops
- Harvesting and processing of crop
- Availability of wild plants
- Estimated period of plant food use in storage
- Potential extended storage period

Animals
- Herding activity
- Interception of animal migrations
- Hunting of non-migratory wild animals
- Estimated period of stored meat use

Fig. 13.14 The seasonal availability and use of plants and animals at Abu Hureyra during the Preneolithic and the Neolithic. During Abu Hureyra 1, ca. 12,000 years ago, there were no domesticated plants or animals and a wide variety of species contributed to the diet during all seasons of the year. In the Early Neolithic (Abu Hureyra 2a), ca. 10,500 years ago, domesticated plants and herded sheep and goats played an important role in subsistence. Wild plants remained important and the seasonal hunting of wild gazelle continued to supplement the food provided by herds of domestic sheep and goats. In later periods, the wild species decline in importance.

Two tons of animal bone, antler, and shell also were recovered during the excavations. Shells from river mussels, fish bones, and fishhooks made from bone indicate that the inhabitants obtained food from the Euphrates River as well as from the surrounding hills. Gazelle bones dominate the lower layers at Abu Hureyra and constitute 80% of all animal bones. By the beginning of the Neolithic, however, sheep and goats had been domesticated and were being herded. After 7500 BC, the number of gazelle bones dropped sharply and sheep and goats became much more important in the diet (Fig. 13.14). During the subsequent phases of the Neolithic at Abu Hureyra, domesticated cattle and pigs were added to the larder.

Abu Hureyra grew quickly in the Neolithic to become the largest community of its day, with 2000 to 3000 inhabitants. Houses were rectangular with mud-brick walls that were plastered and whitewashed. Plaster also was used to make heavy rectangular containers. Clay was used for beads and figurines, but pottery was not present. The importance of this town is documented by the quantity and variety of exotic materials that arrived there through trade and exchange: cowrie shells from the Mediterranean or Red Sea, turquoise from the Sinai peninsula, and obsidian, malachite, agate, jadeite, and serpentine from the mountains of Turkey. These rare stones were made into large, thin "butterfly" beads, often found in burials.

By 6000 BC, Abu Hureyra was abandoned. A similar pattern is seen at other Neolithic sites in the Levant at this time. It seems likely that increasingly arid conditions reduced agricultural productivity and made herding a more viable enterprise. It may be at this time that nomadic herding became the dominant mode of life, perhaps the start of the pastoralists who still roam parts of Southwest Asia with their herds of sheep and goats.

In sum, the evidence from Abu Hureyra indicates that cultivation began in the ancient Near East in a small sedentary village of gatherer-hunters around 10,500 years ago during a period of environmental change. The disappearance of the habitat for wild plant species coincided with the early domestication of rye and eventual cultivation of wheat, lentils, and legumes. However, the transition from wild, gathered foods and hunted animals to a dependence on domesticated varieties took 2500 years. The evidence suggests that not all families in the settlement were initially involved in farming and that the number increased over time. The first sheep and goat husbandry appeared around 7500 BC, followed by cattle and pigs. This pattern of a gradual transition from food collection to food production is typical of most parts of the world. The general sequence often involves settlement in villages, followed by plant cultivation and subsequent animal herding.

Wood and Charcoal Identification

Charcoal is the term that archaeologists use for heavily burned fragments of wood and other plant tissues. Charcoal is technically an inorganic material, impure carbon produced by heating wood or other organic matter in the absence of air. Because it is largely inorganic, it will preserve when other organic materials disappear. On the other hand, it is fragile and bioturbation can turn charcoal to powder in the soil.

Charcoal is useful for several reasons. Charcoal often retains the original structure of the plant tissue and can be identified as to species. It is thus possible to determine the kinds of woods that were intentionally or accidentally burned at archaeological sites. This information is useful for reconstructing environments and learning about cultural differences in the selection of wood for various purposes. A case study in wood charcoal identification from the island of Thera in the Aegean is discussed below.

Because the anatomy of the wood is retained in charcoal, identification at the genus or even species level is possible. In those unusual cases where the wood itself is preserved, the same procedures are used for identification. Because the diagnostic structures in the wood are very small, a microscope is used at magnifications between 40× and 400× to examine specific characteristics.

In addition to the identification of seeds, nuts, fruits, and tree species, the investigation of charred plant remains has recently advanced to the other tissue. In particular, SEM (scanning electron microscope) studies have been able to identify charred **parenchymous tissues**. Parenchyma (*pahr-in-CHI-mah*) is the most common plant tissue and makes up the bulk of the primary plant body, including the leaves, flowers, roots, the pulp of fruits, and the pith of stems in woody plants. The thin-walled parenchyma cells have large empty spaces and distinctive intercellular areas (Fig. 13.15).

Parenchyma is a relatively unspecialized tissue commonly found in roots and tubers. Roots and tubers were often a source of carbohydrates for prehistoric groups, but because of problems with the identification of these plant organs, they have been almost invisible in the charred plant remains recovered from archaeological sites. Now with the development of SEM analysis, compendiums of

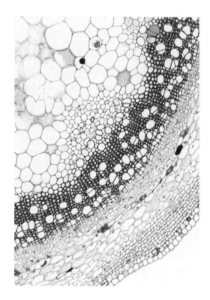

Fig. 13.15 Scanning electron microscope (SEM) photo of parenchyma tissue (thin-walled cells with large empty spaces) in modern *Sambucus* (Elderberry) stem.

parenchymous tissues   Parenchyma is plant storage tissue, commonly found in roots, tubers, rhizomes, and corms.

The Scanning Electron Microscope

The scanning electron microscope (SEM) is widely used in archaeology to obtain high-resolution images of artifacts and other materials (Fig. 13.16). The SEM can provide detailed three-dimensional images at magnifications hundreds of times greater than most optical microscopes and reveal features of materials like plant remains or stone tools that are otherwise invisible (see Fig. 13.15).

The SEM creates magnified images using electrons instead of light waves. A sample is placed inside the vacuum column and the air is evacuated. An electron gun shoots a beam of high-energy electrons at the sample. This beam passes through a series of magnetic lenses that focus the electrons on a very small spot. At the point of focus, scanning coils move the electron beam back and forth. As the electron beam hits the sample, secondary electrons are knocked loose from its surface. The detector counts and amplifies these signals for the computer, which uses this information to compose an image of the sample surface on a monitor.

Fig. 13.16 A SEM in action at the Department of Scientific Research in the British Museum. Major components include the computer and monitor where images are generated, the sample vacuum chamber, the electron source, and the detector.

reference material, and keys for parenchymous tissue identification, new plant foods are being added to descriptions of past diets.

In much of the Pacific, for example, root crops such as **taro**, **cassava**, and the sweet potato are rarely found in archaeological excavations because they quickly decompose. Taro (*Coloscia esculenta*) is sometimes called the potato of the tropics and a staple for many people across the Pacific Ocean. Taro is slightly toxic and must be cooked to be eaten. The root of the plant is a large starchy bulb that is boiled, baked, or roasted or ground into flour. Cassava (*Manihot esculenta*) is a woody shrub with an edible root, growing in tropical and subtropical areas of the world. Also known as manioc, the starchy roots can be stored for up to two years in the ground and powdered, boiled, or eaten raw.

Sweet potatoes are well known. The sweet potato (*Ipomoea batatas*) is of particular interest archaeologically because of questions about its antiquity and its spread across the Pacific. The sweet potato is an important crop in eastern Polynesia (Hawaii, Easter Island, and New Zealand) and the highlands of New Guinea. Yet the original home of the sweet potato is in South America.

The sweet potato spread to the Pacific prior to the arrival of European explorers who collected herbarium specimens of the plant when they first visited

taro Tropical root crop with slightly toxic potato-like tuber.

cassava Tropical root crop with starchy roots (a.k.a. manioc), source of tapioca.

New Zealand and other islands. But direct archaeological evidence for pre-European sweet potatoes has been lacking. In 1989, however, excavations at a deep rockshelter in the Cook Islands, smack in the middle of the South Pacific, recovered charred plant remains dating to AD 1000, long before the European voyages of discovery. Several diagnostic features observed with the scanning electron microscope confirm a number of these specimens as sweet potato. The remaining question, of course, is how the plants got there. Did the Polynesians sail to the coast of South America returning with sweet potatoes, or did people from South America venture into the Pacific?

 **EXAMPLE** ～～～～～～～～～～～～～～～～～～～～～～～

www.mhhe.com/pricearch1

For a Web-based activity on Akotiri, please see the Internet exercises on your online learning center.

WOOD CHARCOAL FROM THERA

Thera (*THERE-a*) is one of many islands in the Aegean Sea (Fig. 13.17). It is of volcanic origin, an accumulation of magma, lava, and ash that gradually rose from the sea floor as the island originally formed millions of years ago. In 1700 BC, Thera was a volcanic cone, some 10–15 km (6–10 mi) in diameter at the base, rising perhaps 600 meters (almost 2000 ft) in elevation. The volcano must have been relatively stable at that time since its lower sides were heavily inhabited. A large town, Akrotiri (*ACK-ro-TIER-ee*), stood on its southern flank just at the coast.

Today, most of the island is gone—the volcanic cone has disappeared and only remnants of its coast stand above sea level. These 300-meter-high (930 ft) cliffs are a layer cake of the ash and lava that accumulated as the volcano grew. Akrotiri is located at the edge of these cliffs and is buried beneath many meters of ash.

Fig. 13.17 Map of the Aegean with the location of Thera, Knossos, and Mycenae, ca. 1500 BC.

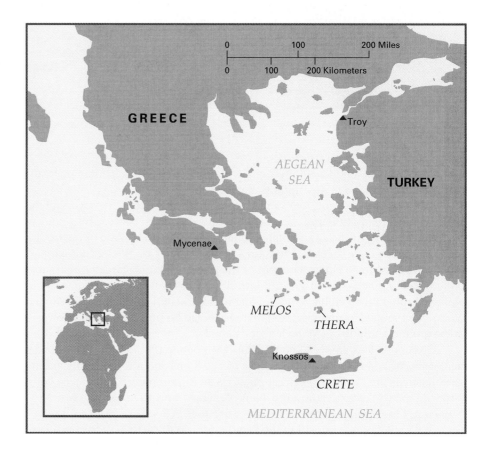

Fig. 13.18 Excavations at the site of Akrotiri on the island of Thera have removed tons of volcanic ash to expose the buried town. Large parts of the site are protected under a roofed shelter.

Thera erupted around 1500 BC with enormous energy, spewing rock, cinders, and ash over much of the eastern Mediterranean. The initial volcanic activity must have lasted some days as the town of Akrotiri was abandoned and the inhabitants fled the island. Then, perhaps suddenly, when the mountain had spewed out most of its insides, the cone collapsed into the sea with what must have been a humongous explosion as hot magma fell into the seawater. The mountain blew apart, leaving only the crescent of small islands that mark its former outline. Large parts of the town of Akrotiri had been buried in ash prior to the explosion and thus survived the blast (Fig. 13.18). Archaeologists have been removing this ash for many years, and the site now is a prominent tourist attraction on the island.

The environmental picture of the Aegean during the Bronze Age when Akrotiri was inhabited has been rather limited. Pollen studies from Greece and the Near East have been used to suggest that the Aegean islands were arid. Although conditions for vegetation might have been slightly better than today, Thera was thought not to have supported substantial tree and shrub vegetation because of a lack of rainfall. This information has been difficult to verify because pollen does not survive well in the rocky, volcanic soils of the islands.

A recent study of wood charcoal from the site of Akrotiri, however, has provided dramatic new evidence on the availability of various kinds of trees, as well as the cultivation of some species, and the import of exotic timber to the island. Archaeobotanist Eleni Asouti of the Institute of Archaeology at University College, London, has examined almost 800 charcoal specimens from three levels at the site, corresponding to the early, middle, and late Bronze Age (ca. 3200–1500 BCC). She uses a scanning electron microscope (SEM) in her studies to obtain a view of the high detail of the wood structure (Fig. 13.19). Her results show a surprising variety of species present and an abundance of material.

The list of species that Asouti identified is shown in Table 13.3. The general picture she draws from the analysis strongly contrasts with earlier views of vegetation on the island. Olive is the most abundant charcoal, in more than half the samples, and must have been used for fuel as well as for its fruit. Pine and another species, either cypress or juniper which are very hard to distinguish, were also common and must have also provided firewood. The simple fact that the people of Akrotiri are burning so much wood suggests that trees must have been widespread on the small island.

Several other typical Mediterranean species were also identified including deciduous and evergreen oaks, strawberry-tree, honeysuckle, thorn or wild pear, and pomegranate. The pomegranate is the earliest example known from the Mediterranean islands and was probably cultivated for its fruit. Other scrub vegetation represented in the charcoal included tamarisk, caper, and buckthorn.

Three of the species identified were a major surprise. Cedar, yew, and beech are strong, fragrant woods popular for use in construction and tool manufacture.

Fig. 13.19 Scanning electron microscope pictures of pomegranate wood charcoal.

TABLE 13.3 Wood identifications from Akrotiri showing species, number of samples, and number and percentage of identified specimens, for the early, middle, and late Bronze Age.

	EBA (late 4th–3rd millennium BC)		MBA (early 2nd millennium BC)		LBA (up to mid-2nd millennium BC)	
	N = 5	%	N = 11	%	N = 7	%
Pinus (pine)	48	36.4	93	17.8	9	7.0
Cedrus libani (cedar)			14	2.7		
Cupressaceae (cypress/juniper)	10	7.6	29	5.6	9	7.0
Taxus baccata (yew)			61	11.7		
Olea (olive)	57	43.2	221	42.3	87	68.0
Punica granatum (pomegranate)	1	0.8	4	0.8	2	1.6
Arbutus (strawberry-tree)			7	1.3	3	2.3
Maloideae (pears/hawthorns)	1	0.8				
Quercus deciduous (oak)	4	3.0	56	10.7	7	5.5
Quercus evergreen (oak)	2	1.5	10	1.9	5	3.9
Fagus (beech)			2	0.4		
cf. Rhamnus (buckthorn)			9	1.7		
cf. Tamarix (tamarisk)	2	1.5	8	1.5		
cf. Capparis (caper)					4	3.1
Lonicera (honeysuckle)			1	0.2	1	0.8
Fabaceae (legume undershrubs)	6	4.6	1	0.2	1	0.8
Lamiaceae (mint family)	1	0.8	5	1.0		
Poaceae (reeds?)			1	0.2		
Indeterminate	119		315		106	
Total	251	100	837	100	234	100
Total (-Indeterminate)	132		522		128	

None of these three species are known to have ever grown in the southern Aegean. The clear implication of their presence in the Bronze Age levels at Akrotiri is that they were imported to the island. Known sources for this wood are Turkey, Lebanon, Cyprus, and North Africa. Extensive trade in bulky materials such as timber documents large-scale shipping and trade in the western Mediterranean Bronze Age.

In sum, the wood charcoal analysis provides a new picture of the vegetation of Thera. Far from being treeless, the island appears to have had a relatively moist and cool climate. The evidence suggests pine forests and open oak woodlands in some areas and substantial variety of plant life. Cultivation of olives and pomegranates is documented from at least the early Bronze Age. The import of timber from large trees in mainland Asia, Africa, or Europe marks the position of Thera as a center of sea trade in the Bronze Age of the eastern Mediterranean. All of this of course ended when the volcano exploded.

MICROBOTANICAL REMAINS

There are several different kinds of microbotanical remains, or plant microfossils, used for studying past vegetation and environments. **Spores** and **pollen** are the coverings of the gametes of terrestrial plants that are released in sexual reproduc-

spore Microscopic gamete of nonflowering plant.

pollen Covering of the gametes of flowering plants released in sexual reproduction.

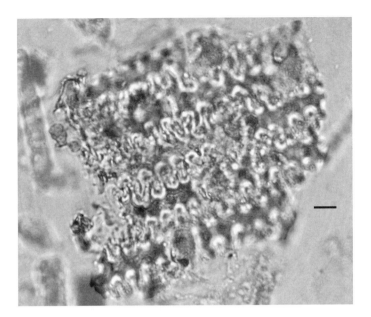

Fig. 13.20 A photomicrograph of a phytolith from a wheat husk, Catalhöyük, Turkey. The size is somewhat smaller than a dust particle.

tion. They tend to survive in the earth for very long times and to be common in archaeological contexts. Different kinds of plants produce these two fossils. Spores are known from the Silurian period of geological time onward, while pollen appears in the Early Cretaceous with the appearance of flowering plants. Both spores and pollen are distinctive at the genus and sometimes the species level. Spores are somewhat larger than pollen, having a flattened and oval, circular, or triangular shape. Pollen grains are very small and often spherical in shape.

Phytoliths (*FIE-toe-liths*) are another microscopic form of evidence for plants. Phytoliths ("plant rocks") can survive under conditions in which pollen disappears (Fig. 13.20). Phytoliths form inside the structure of the plant. The nutrients that enter and feed plants through their roots include monosilicic acid. The silica (SiO_2) in this acid cannot be absorbed and instead is deposited between the cells of the plant. Phytoliths are present in many terrestrial plants, particularly grasses. When the plant dies (or is cooked), these mineral deposits survive intact, potentially for millions of years. Phytoliths thus are microfossils of the plant.

Phytoliths come in various three-dimensional shapes (e.g., "dumbbells," "saddles," "bowls," "boats," and "pyramidal"). These shapes can be used to identify the kinds of plants that produce phytoliths, although they are usually not diagnostic to the genus or species level. Analysis of phytoliths from cultural and natural contexts provides information on both plant use by people and the natural vegetation of an area. The study of phytoliths in archaeology is relatively recent, and most of the work to date has focused on the archaeology of South America.

Diatoms are another useful plantlike microfossil that can be identified at the species level under a microscope (Fig. 13.21). Diatoms are aquatic unicellular plants, a microscopic algae, and the most abundant single source of oxygen producers in the biosphere. There are perhaps 100,000 different species of diatoms that occupy varied marine and freshwater environments. The silicate shells of diatoms accumulate in huge numbers in lake and marine sediments.

The grains of starch that certain species of plants produce are another microfossil of interest (Fig. 13.22). **Starch** is a complex carbohydrate, insoluble in water, used today in cooking and stiffening clothing. It is found in seeds, bulbs, and tubers of plants like arrowroot, cassava, barley, maize, millet, oat, potato, rice, sage, sweet potato, taro, wheat, and yam. Starch grains can be long-lived in certain depositional contexts and can be identified under a microscope at the genus, and sometimes species, level. The diagnostic information for identification of starch

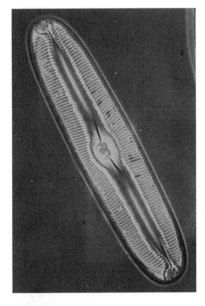

Fig. 13.21 Elongated diatom, a microbotanical form of algae.

phytoliths Genus-specific silicate bodies inside plants.

diatom Silicate shells of microscopic algae.

starch Microscopic grains of a complex carbohydrate found in certain species of plants.

Fig. 13.22 Archaeological maize starch (ca. 500 BC) at high magnification. Peruvian specimen collected by Don Ugent at the Paracas Necropolis.

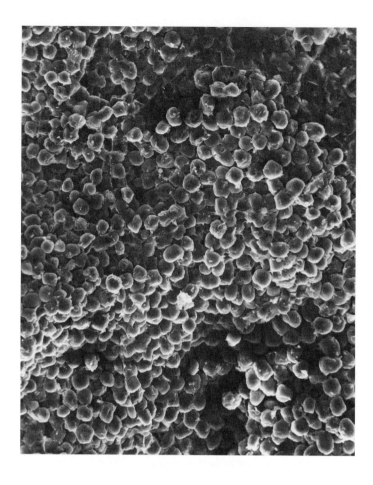

And here was cabbage, here
were beets, their foliage extending
*   wide;*
And fruitful sorrel, elecampane too
and mallows here were flourishing
*   and here*
was parsnip, 'leeks indebted to
*   their head*
for name, and here as well the
*   poppy cool*
and hurtful to the head, and
*   lettuce too,*
the pleasing rest at the end of
*   noble foods.*
And there the radish sweet doth
*   thrust its points*
well into th'earth and there the
*   heavy gourd*
has sunk to earth upon its belly wide.
*   —Virgil, Roman poet*

includes size, shape, as well as certain optical and chemical properties. Starch grains have been found on prehistoric stone tools and pottery. A number of the plants—particularly tropical root crops—that are good starch sources produce little pollen or phytoliths; as a result, starch is important for their identification. As in the case of pollen and phytolith analyses, the study of fossil starch grains can help the archaeobotanist to better understand the diet and environment of ancient human cultures.

Archaeobotanists study specific kinds of microfossil remains depending on what they want to know and what is preserved. Spores generally are used for species of plants in deposits that are much older than the human presence on the planet. Diatoms are very useful for studies of seas and lakes and often provide excellent climatic information for comparison with the archaeological record. Starch grains are a relatively recent focus in archaeobotanical research and only a few applications have been reported. Phytoliths are an intriguing microfossil and have been employed to argue for early agriculture in South America. Pollen is a record of past vegetation and can also be found in direct association with archaeological remains. Pollen is the most commonly studied of these different microfossils and, for these reasons, will be the focus of the discussion here.

Palynology

Although the vagaries of preservation normally remove the stems, flowers, fruits, and other bits and pieces of plants from archaeological sites, the pollen those plants produce often survives. Pollen is a microscopic particle (the male gamete) produced by many seed-bearing plants and released to fertilize a neighbor. Wind or insect pollination is common to most trees, shrubs, grasses, and flowering plants. Plant pollen is very, very small and weighs almost nothing. Pollen "rain"

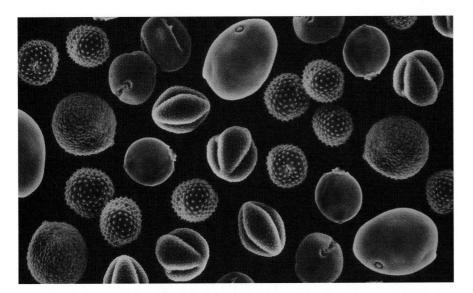

Fig. 13.23 Microphotograph of different types of pollen: ragweed (yellow), sage brush (brown), timothy (light green), scotch broom (purple), alder (dark green), and poplar (orange), magnified 3000 times. Colors have been added to the photograph to show the different types. Because the size and shape of the grains is distinctive to individual species, they can be used to identify the plants that were present in an area in the past.

is carried everywhere as sufferers of hay fever know well. Some types of pollen can be transported hundreds of kilometers and high up into the atmosphere. Tree pollen generally travels farther than that of flowering plants. Pollen is produced in enormous quantities by plants and can be found in densities reaching several thousand grains per cubic centimeter of soil.

In spite of their miniscule size, pollen grains are protected by a hard shell that is impervious to water and most soil acids. As long as sediments protect the pollen grains from oxidation, they will be preserved for thousands of years under most conditions. Pollen is also preserved in coal and has been found in rocks that are 500 million years old.

Types of pollen are very specific in shape and size and can be identified to the genus or even species of plant that produced it (Fig. 13.23). The pollen that accumulates in the sediments around an archaeological site can be used to provide a picture of past vegetation, climate, and environmental conditions. Such study is called **palynology**, or pollen analysis.

In the field, samples of sediment for pollen analysis are taken every few centimeters from a stratigraphic column. Deposits in lakes and bogs often provide the best pollen records, but many types of sediments will preserve these grains.

In the laboratory, pollen grains must be removed from sediment and examined under a microscope. It is essential that there is no contamination by modern pollen, so scientists try to use a closed room and air filtration system. Some modern pollen will always be present in a sample, but its effect can be determined by a glycerine-coated slide left out in the work area. Regular examination of this slide will reveal the amount and types of modern pollen present in the laboratory.

The palynologist uses a high power microscope to identify the species present and counts the grains of pollen of each type that are found. It takes some months to become adept at recognizing pollen species, and even experienced palynologists use a reference collection to diagnose difficult specimens. Several hundred grains are identified and counted to produce a list of the pollen species that are present and their relative proportions. Each species is recorded in a graph known as a pollen diagram, which summarizes both the species and proportion of the various groups of plants found in each sample (Fig. 13.24). The pollen diagram shows a series of curves, one for each species, with changes in percentage through the layers where the samples were taken.

Pollen analysis can be applied to the reconstruction of local vegetation, to regional maps of plant distributions, or to the study of climatic change. For example, the ratio of tree (**arboreal pollen**, or AP) to non-tree (**non-arboreal pollen**,

palynology The study of pollen from plants for information on species, environment, and climate.

arboreal pollen (AP) Pollen from trees.

non-arboreal pollen (NAP) Pollen from plants other than trees.

or NAP) specimens provides an indication of the density of forest and even precipitation in a given area (i.e., the more trees, the greater the rainfall). Certain marker species or changes in the pollen record may aid in the recognition of prehistoric settlements or cultivation practices. For example, the beginning of agriculture in northern Europe is often recognized by the appearance of cereal pollen, a reduction in tree pollen, and tiny pieces of charcoal from wood burning found in the pollen samples. An example of pollen analysis from northern Europe concerning a remarkable decline in elm trees is described below.

 **EXAMPLE** 〜〜〜〜〜〜〜〜〜〜〜〜〜〜〜〜〜〜〜〜〜〜〜〜

THE ELM DECLINE

Pollen analysis began in northern Europe where lake and bog deposits with lots of pollen were abundant. Scientists made pollen diagrams of the vegetation for the last 10,000 years. A clear pattern of changes showed up in these diagrams that reflects a succession of species over time.

Southern Scandinavia was originally covered by glacial ice during the late Pleistocene. This ice began melting with the warming climate beginning about 15,000 years ago and eventually retreated completely from this area. The new landscape was sequentially colonized by a series of plants and animals, initially subarctic and eventually temperate. The pollen diagrams document that these changes from cold-tolerating, pioneer species of plants such as willow, birch, and pine were gradually replaced by hazel, elm, lime, beech, and oak. In the period from approximately 15,000 to 7000 years ago, southern Scandinavia went from a fresh and barren land surface to open coniferous woodlands, to a dense, dark forest of deciduous trees.

One of the striking patterns observed in the pollen diagrams from this period was a precipitous decrease in elm pollen around 4000 BC (see Fig. 13.24). The cause of this "elm decline" has been the subject of debate since its recognition more than 50 years ago. The elm decline takes place just at the time of the arrival of agriculture in northern Europe. A number of reasons for this decline have been suggested, in-

Fig. 13.24 A simplified pollen diagram from northern Europe showing the dramatic elm decline at 4000 BC. The width of the curve for each species shows the percent of pollen for that species at a given point in time. Note that other species also change when elm declines. For example, grass and plantain (a pasture plant) show clear increases.

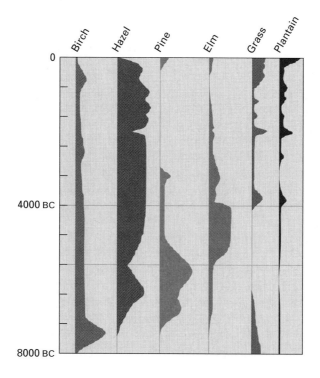

cluding climate change, soil depletion, human exploitation, expansion of agricultural fields, or disease. However, there is little evidence for climatic change at this time and the elm decline was likely not caused by new weather patterns. Soil depletion also remains a hypothetical and unlikely factor.

Human interference with elm was a popular explanation for many years. Suggestions included both tree felling for field clearance and the clipping of elm branches to use for animal fodder, resulting in an absence of pollen. A number of studies have been done to evaluate these suggestions. It is hard to imagine that field clearance would affect only elm trees and not others. In addition, pollen studies of the early Neolithic have revealed that cultivation was a minor activity. Investigations of elm branches as fodder have revealed that this practice was in use in the Neolithic. However, detailed analysis of domestic animal coprolites (preserved feces and cowpies) in both Switzerland and Denmark has demonstrated that elm was only one of many species used for fodder.

New information obtained in the last decade or so may have resolved this issue. Mapping of the spread of vegetation across Europe at the beginning of the Holocene indicates that the elm decline spread at a rate of approximately 4 km/year (2.5 mi/year), comparable to known statistics for elm disease. Studies of pollen in deep lake sediments with annual layers in England and Sweden demonstrate that the elm decline actually took place within a very short time, perhaps a decade or two. It is difficult to imagine that human interference could cause the decline of elm over most of northern Europe within a period of 20 years. Finally, discovery of beetle tunnels in elm wood from the time of the elm decline has confirmed that bark beetles were present. These insects carry the fungus that is responsible for Dutch elm disease. In all probability, the rapid disappearance of elm trees across northern Europe was caused not by climate or humans, but by beetle-borne disease.

~~~~~~

CONCLUSIONS

Archaeobotany is a branch of archaeology concerned with the study of plant remains. Plants almost never survive in the archaeological record except in charred and fragmentary form. There are of course exceptionally wet or dry contexts where plant parts can survive largely intact, but these situations are very unusual. There are two general classes of plant remains based on size. Macrobotanical remains include nutshells, seeds, and wood, and are generally identifiable by eye or a low magnification. Macrobotanical remains are usually collected through the flotation technique or the careful wet sieving of site deposits.

Microbotanical remains are microscopic in size and include things like pollen, phytoliths, starch grains, spores, and diatoms. Microbotanical remains normally come from cores or small sediment samples taken from lakes, wetlands, or sites themselves. The microscopic remains are usually extracted using wet chemistry.

Macrobotanical remains are identified and counted to determine the presence and proportion of different species present in an archaeobotanical assemblage. This information is of great use in answering questions about human diet, season of occupation, and the environment of the site. The study of floral remains at the Incinerator site provides an excellent example. Climatic information may also be available in the plant data. The presence and number of species within the floral remains are also useful in the investigation of questions concerning the origins of agriculture, where the proportion of wild vs. cultivated species tells us about beginnings of plant domestication. Studies at Abu Hureyra documented significant changes in the plants, related to the beginnings of cultivation. Wood identification at Akrotiri provided some remarkable information on both the environment of the island of Thera and the long-distance import of wood and timber for construction in the Bronze Age Aegean.

Microbotanical remains can tell us about the presence of species in association with human activities, but say little about the proportions of various vegetal foods in the diet. Microbotanical remains such as pollen, diatoms, and phytoliths in a deep deposit can tell us about the timing of the appearance of certain plants, information useful in the study of the beginnings of agriculture or climatic change. Such remains are most useful for information on environmental and climatic change since these samples usually are studied from a stratigraphic sequence. Evidence for the elm decline in Europe, for example, comes almost exclusively from pollen records.

Archaeobotany continues to advance with the development of new methods. Ancient DNA in Neolithic wheats and barleys is the subject of several large research projects in Europe. In the New World, the genetics of corn are providing detailed information on both the sequence of changes that the plant underwent and the probable location of those changes. As more archaeologists are trained in the procedures of archaeobotany, we can expect these new discoveries and advances to continue.

THE ORIGINS OF AGRICULTURE

In the following hypothetical situation, we will suppose that an archaeologist is undertaking the study of the origins of agriculture in Southeast Asia. She selects a coastal region in which to conduct a survey for sites and to make a few small excavations. The coast has a number of lagoons and estuaries, which contain a variety of shellfish such as oysters and mussels. Inland from the swampy zone, the land rises rapidly to a series of hills. The entire study region is drained by a small river.

The study of modern plants in the area has been done by a botanist. This study resulted in a map showing the distribution of two economically important species of wild plants (Fig. 13.25). Wild rice occurs only at higher elevations in the hills (north of the dotted line on the map). Wild beans grow at the higher elevations as well as lower down, almost to the edge of the swamps (all of the area north of the dashed line). The wild rice and wild beans are the ancestors of the most important domesticated plants in the area today. Because geological evidence indicates that there have been no significant climatic changes here since 10,000 BC, it is assumed that the distribution of wild species has not shifted in that time.

Archaeological survey involved systematically walking back and forth over the entire area looking for artifacts on the ground. The archaeologists were able to make a map of the distribution of prehistoric sites. By analyzing the pottery from these

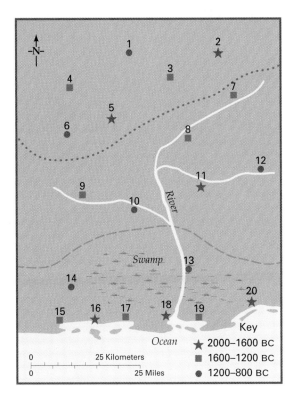

Fig. 13.25   The study area. The symbols show the earliest date of settlement for each site.

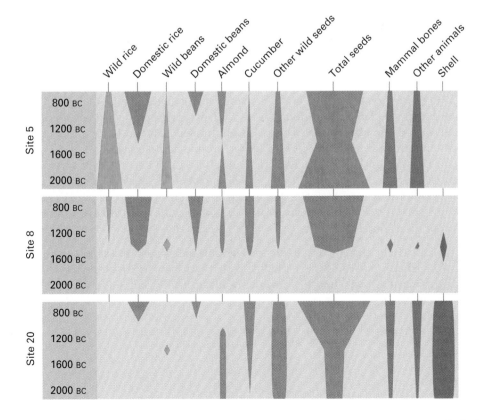

Fig. 13.26   Percentage graphs of different species in use at different sites through time.

TABLE 13.4 Artifacts at the excavated sites.

Site	Period	Artifacts
5	1200–800 BC	Flake and chopping tools, fragments of slate, much pottery
	1600–1200 BC	Flake and chopping tools, a few potsherds
	2000–1600 BC	Flaked stone tools, small chopping tools, charred bamboo projectile points
8	1200–800 BC	Flake and chopping tools, much pottery
	1600–1200 BC	A few potsherds, a slate knife, flake and chopping tools
20	1200–800 BC	Flake and chopping tools, pottery, grooved pebbles, fishhooks, shell pendants
	1600–1200 BC	Flake and chopping tools, shell fishhooks
	2000–1600 BC	Flaked stone tools, small chopping tools, grooved pebbles, fishhooks

sites and using radiocarbon dating, it was possible to assign the sites to various chronological stages. Several sites (indicated by stars) have been occupied continuously from 2000 to 1600 BC. Intermediate period sites (indicated by squares) have been occupied since 1600–1200 BC. Other sites (indicated by circles) have been occupied from 1200 to 800 BC. All of the sites seem to have been sedentary, year-round occupations and all are about the same size.

Following the survey work, sites 5, 8, and 20 were excavated, and the paleobotanical and archaeozoological information recovered in those excavations is summarized in the graph (Fig. 13.26). The data are arranged in frequency polygons to show the relative quantities of plant and animal remains through time. The total seeds column in the graph is a summary of all the plant remains at the sites. All of the plant remains found were wild, except the cultivated beans and rice. All of the small mammals were wild and hunted. Table 13.4 provides additional information about the types of artifacts found at these sites.

The purpose of this exercise is to locate and explain the origins of agriculture in this hypothetical area. Please answer the following question using the information above and the accompanying table, graph, and map. Be sure to explicitly state any assumptions you make. You can include other tables or graphs in your discussion if you like.

1. Discuss the changes in subsistence over time in this area. You should identify the major food sources in each time period and show how food sources changed through time. Present your results to justify your interpretation of the changes.

STUDY QUESTIONS

1. What is the difference between macrobotanical and microbotanical remains?
2. What is the difference between root crops and seed crops? What are some examples of each?
3. What is the evidence for the domestication of plants in the ancient Near East?
4. Why is wood identification an important part of archaeobotany?
5. What kinds of information can be obtained from pollen, from phytoliths, from starch grains?

www.mhhe.com/pricearch1

For more review material and study questions, please see the self-quizzes on your online learning center.

REFERENCES

Brothwell, D., and P. 1998. *Food in Antiquity. A Survey of the Diet of Early Peoples.* Baltimore: Johns Hopkins University Press.

Dimbleby, G. W. 1985. *The Palynology of Archaeological Sites.* Orlando: Academic Press.

Evans, J., and T. O'Connor. 1999. *Environmental Archaeology, Principles and Method.* Stroud: Sutton.

Hoadley, R. Bruce. 1990. *Identifying Wood: Accurate Results with Simple Tools.* Newtown, Conn.: Taunton Press.

Pearsall, Deborah M. 2000. *Paleoethnobotany. A Handbook of Procedures.* 2d ed. San Diego: Academic Press.

Reitz, E. J., L. A. Newsom, and S. J. Scudder, eds. 1996. *Case Studies in Environmental Archaeology.* New York: Plenum.

Smith, Bruce D. 1998. *The Emergence of Agriculture.* 2d ed. New York: Scientific American Library.

www.mhhe.com/pricearch1

For Internet references related to this chapter, please see the chapter links on your online learning center.

14

Bioarchaeology

INTRODUCTION: THE SKELETAL EVIDENCE

This photograph shows the reconstructed face of a five-year-old boy who died in Denmark around 7500 years ago. The cause of death is unknown. His body was wrapped in an animal skin and placed in a shallow grave. A flat stone was set beneath his head, perhaps as a pillow. **Ochre**, a reddish mineral powder, was sprinkled on his corpse. Over time, as with us all, his body returned to the earth.

When the grave was discovered and excavated in 1992, only parts of the skeleton and the ochre remained. The face in the photograph is a **forensic reconstruction**, based on the shape of the skull. In this case the skull was scanned and a copy made in plastic. That copy went to a specialist in England who has studied the facial tissue of more than 200 children in order to reconstruct the face of the living person from the bones of the skull that remain (Fig. 14.1). The reconstruction has not been painted and remains the brown color of the plasticine used to mold the features. This is one of the stories of **bioarchaeology**, the study of human remains in archaeological contexts.

Biological anthropology is one of the four major branches of anthropology, along with archaeology, linguistics, and cultural anthropology. Biological anthropology, sometimes called physical anthropology, is concerned with the biological characteristics of humans and their closest relatives among the other primates (apes and monkeys). These scientists study a wide range of subjects in both modern and past peoples and primates, including anatomy, blood groups, demography, evolution, genetics, forensics, and many others. One branch of biological anthropology concerns the identification and analysis of human bones, from prehistoric through modern. Modern skeletal material is usually the provenience of forensic anthropologists, working with the police to solve crimes.

Human bones are frequently found at archaeological sites (Fig. 14.2). *Bioarchaeology* is the term for the study of those remains, usually undertaken by an individual trained in biological anthropology. *Human osteology* is another term to describe the study of human skeletal remains, but it also used for modern and forensic investigations. Bioarchaeologists use the information from their studies to learn more about the human species.

The human skeleton is much more than a structural framework for supporting our bodies. An enormous amount of information about both the deceased individual and her or his society is stored in the human skeleton (Fig. 14.3). For example, information on the age and sex of the deceased individual is recorded in the skeleton. The length and thickness of bone provide an indication of an

ochre   A red iron mineral sometimes found in prehistoric graves.

forensic reconstruction   *Restoration* of the facial tissues on human skulls, both past and present.

bioarchaeology   The study of human remains from archaeological contexts.

human osteology   The study of human skeletal remains for information on past biology and behavior.

Fig. 14.1 Caroline Wilkinson at work reconstructing the face of the boy from Nivå.

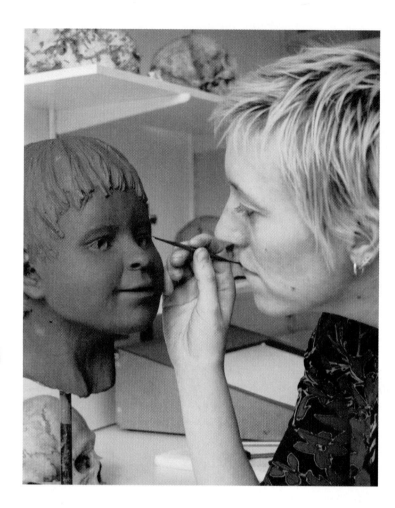

www.mhhe.com/pricearch1

For preview material for this chapter, please see the chapter summary, outline, and objectives on your online learning center.

Fig. 14.2 The mass grave at Talheim, Germany, from the Early Neolithic.

Fig. 14.3 The skeleton is a storehouse of information. The following lists some of the information that can come from the human skeleton. (1) Lesions on the skull suggest scalping at the time of death. (2) Flattened ribs and a fused breastbone result from corsets of the eighteenth century. (3) Badly twisted and eroded joints are evidence of arthritis. (4) Bone spurs appear on the knees of riders who spent too much time in the saddle. (5) Bone cells, or osteons, are denser in middle age (right) than in adolescence (left). (6) Shortened and deformed foot bones document the practice of foot binding in the China of previous centuries. (7) Osteoporosis, a loss of bone density, is more common in the elderly (bottom) than the young (top). (8) The female pelvis is wider than that of the male, for giving birth. (9) More robust femurs are evidence of a diet higher in meat; thin bones suggest a protein-deficient diet. (10) Bumps and irregularities in bone show improperly healed fractures and injuries. (11) Indentations and grooves in the teeth are found among fishermen and wool spinners, who used their teeth for cutting thread.

individual's size and strength. Evidence of disease or illness is also embedded in bone. It is often possible to determine age at death, cause of death, sex, a history of disease or accident, occupation, and nutritional status from the analysis of prehistoric human bone. Diet, too, may be reflected in the chemical composition of bone. In addition, the chemical and genetic composition of bone provides more information on genealogy, diet, and life history. These topics are discussed in the following pages.

FIELD RECORDING

Bioarchaeologists are concerned with the identification and analysis of human remains. Because human skeletons are often poorly preserved and fragile, information can be lost when the remains are removed from the ground. In addition, the position and relationships of the individual bones provide evidence on burial posture and condition. For this reason, studies of human skeletal remains usually begin in the field. Information is recorded on the size and shape of the burial chamber, the contents of the grave, and the location, position, and identity of the bones in the grave. This information is normally recorded in a computer database and in photographs and drawings.

An initial distinction is made in the treatment of the corpse between **cremation** and **inhumation** (burial of the body). Bodies can be buried, either intentionally or accidentally, in a variety of positions (Fig. 14.4). Intentional inhumation usually involves an extended burial with the body laid out in a natural position. Burial posture is important information. Burial position for extended burials can

cremation A funereal practice involving immolation of the corpse. Cremation burials usually consist of ash and a few fragments of bone and teeth, and are often found in urns and small pits. Contrast with *inhumation*.

inhumation Burial of all or part of the corpse; contrast with *cremation*.

Fig. 14.4 Excavation of one of the victims of the eruption of Vesuvius that covered the Roman city of Pompeii in meters of ash in AD 79. This individual lies where she died, beneath the ash.

be on the back (supine), on the side, or on the stomach, an uncommon position. The orientation of the long axis of the body and the direction the head is facing are important to record and may be a result of religious or ceremonial beliefs.

Burials may be primary or secondary (Fig. 14.5). **Primary** burials were interred as a complete corpse, while secondary burials were moved some time after death, following defleshing, burial at another site, or the like. Primary burials are articulated, i.e. the bones are present in their correct anatomical position. They are usually either extended or flexed (Fig. 14.5 a, b). Flexed burials were often placed in a semifetal position with the legs folded up over the chest. **Secondary** burials are usually disarticulated; that is, the bones are not in the correct anatomical position and have been moved or sometimes lost during the handling of the remains (Fig. 14.5 c, d). A *bundle burial* is the term used for a disarticulated group of bones buried in a clump, probably tied in a bundle or wrapped in a skin or cloth before burial. The wrapping rarely survives. The burial on top of scaffolding shown in Fig. 14.5c might end up as a scatter of bones on the surface of the ground or the remains might be reburied in a secondary fashion.

PREPARATION AND SORTING

Since the time of the Neanderthals, the human species has buried its dead. As a result, intact human skeletons are sometimes preserved in isolated graves or in cemeteries. Bioarchaeologists spend hours carefully uncovering and removing

primary inhumation   Burial of the complete corpse after death.

secondary inhumation   Reburial or burial of partial or skeletal human remains often missing some parts.

bundle burial   A disarticulated group of bones buried in a group, probably tied in a bundle or wrapped in a skin or cloth.

cortical bone   Hard, dense bone tissue commonly found in limbs and supporting structure of the skeleton.

trabecular bone   Spongy bone tissue found in the interior of bone.

Fig. 14.5 Types of burials: (a) primary extended; (b) primary flexed; (c) scaffold burial; (d) secondary bundle burial.

these skeletal remains from the ground. Bones and teeth are taken to the laboratory, where a surprising amount of information can be obtained from the observation and measurement of various features. Examination of a group of burials from a single cemetery can provide useful information on an entire population, including demography, life expectancy, and genetic inheritance.

After the bones and teeth are taken to the laboratory, they must be prepared for analysis. This preparation involves cleaning and, in some cases, restoration or reconstruction. For example, the skull is frequently broken or damaged during burial and is usually restored by refitting and gluing prior to further analysis. Teeth are often loose or out of socket and can be restored in place or kept separate. Other broken and damaged bones may also be reconstructed if necessary. Each individual skeleton is placed in a separate box or container, and the bones are often numbered in order to catalog and inventory the burial.

Not all bones of the skeleton always survive or are present. In secondary burials, not all the bones were always interred. In other situations, some bones survive while others do not. Tooth enamel is the hardest part of our skeleton and often preserves in even harsh burial conditions. Bone is more susceptible to decomposition. The distinction between cortical and trabecular bone tissue is an important one in understanding the survival of skeletal parts (Fig. 14.6). Most bones are made of both kinds. **Cortical** bone is the hard, dense bone that provides support and strength in the skeleton, and is more common in the limbs. **Trabecular** bone is the spongy bone tissue that makes up the interior of ribs, vertebrae, pelvis, and other bones. Trabecular bone provides less structural support in the skeleton but has an important role in metabolism. Because of the more porous and softer nature of trabecular tissue, it is usually the first type of bone to decompose during burial. The proportion of cortical and trabecular bone varies in the different bones of the skeleton .

You go to come,
You sleep to wake,
You die to live.
　　　　—Funereal inscription,
　　　　　Egypt, 2160 BC

THE HUMAN SKELETON

Our skeleton is the rigid, internal structure that holds our body up and, along with our muscular system, allows us to move. Our skeleton also protects the vital organs inside it from damage. In addition, our skeleton manufactures blood cells in the marrow and stores various nutrients and elements needed for tissue maintenance and repair.

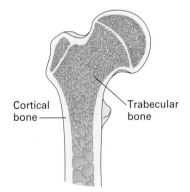

Cross section of bone

Fig. 14.6 Appearance of trabecular and cortical bone in a cross-section of human vertebra.

Fig. 14.7 Major bones in the human skeleton.

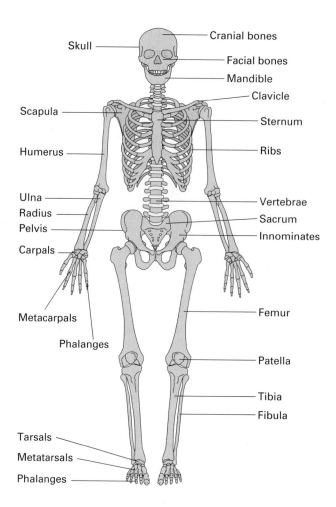

Skull — Cranial bones
— Facial bones
— Mandible
— Clavicle
Scapula — — Sternum
Humerus — — Ribs
Ulna — — Vertebrae
Radius — — Sacrum
Pelvis — — Innominates
Carpals —
Metacarpals — — Femur
Phalanges —
— Patella
— Tibia
— Fibula
Tarsals —
Metatarsals —
Phalanges —

Identification of skeletal remains requires a detailed knowledge of human anatomy. At birth, the human skeleton consists of 270 different bones. As your body grows, some of these bones—such as the skull and wrist and anklebones—fuse together, leaving a total of 206 bones in the average adult body (Fig. 14.7).

One way to simplify learning skeletal anatomy is to divide the bones into two groups, the **axial skeleton** (the trunk and head) and the **appendicular skeleton** (the limbs). The axial skeleton includes all the bones of the head and neck, the vertebrae, ribs, and sternum. The appendicular skeleton consists of the clavicles, scapulae, bones of the pelvis, and the upper and lower limbs, including the hands and feet.

Another way to think about the human skeleton is according to the shape of the bones. There are four major shapes of bones, not including the skull and mandible: long bones, short bones, flat bones, and irregular bones. Long bones have a tubular shaft and an **articular** (contact) surface at each end. The larger appendicular bones of the arms and legs are long bones, including the pairs of femurs, tibia, and fibula in the legs, and the pairs of humeri, radii, and ulnae in the arms. The short bones also have tubular shaft and articular ends but they are much smaller. The short bones include the bones of the hands and feet (metacarpals, phalanges, metatarsals) and the pair of collar bones (clavicles). The flat bones are thin with broad surfaces and include the paired pelvis bones (innominates), the shoulder blades (scapulae), the twenty-four ribs and the sternum. The irregular bones are variable in size and shape and found throughout the skeleton, including the vertebrae, the carpal and tarsal bones, and the paired knee caps (patellae).

axial skeleton The trunk and head (all the bones of the head and neck, the vertebrae, ribs and sternum).

appendicular skeleton The limbs (the clavicles, scapulae, bones of the pelvis, and the upper and lower limbs, including the hands and feet).

articular The portion of the bone that touches another bone, usually a surface at the end or edge of a bone.

Bioarchaeologists usually keep several human skeletons in their lab for reference and comparison studies. Holding an unknown bone next to a known example is a great help in identification. During the process of identification, unusual features or changes in the bone are often noticed. In the example below, indications of burning and breakage of certain bones indicate that these individuals had been cooked and eaten.

 ## EXAMPLE 〜〜〜〜〜〜〜〜〜〜〜〜〜〜〜〜〜〜〜〜〜〜

CANNIBALISM

Cannibalism is an old and emotionally charged topic in human society. Because of strict cultural taboos against cannibalism in our culture, many people do not want to believe it was practiced in spite of the fact that there are a number of reports of cannibalism from various places around the globe over the last century.

There are also a number of examples in archaeology, often controversial as well, from the Paleolithic to the recent past. At the cave of Krapina (*CROP-ee-nah*) in Croatia, the bones of at least thirteen Neanderthal individuals were found mixed with those of various herbivores and other animals. The human bones had been burned, split to extract marrow, and treated just like the other animals that provided the meals for the inhabitants of the site. Whether such practices may represent rituals for the consecration of the dead or individuals from enemy groups that were added to the larder is unclear. On the other hand, it can be argued that these bones may have been accidentally burned and broken by later inhabitants at the sites.

The Aztecs of ancient Mexico were reported by the Spanish conquistadores to have killed, butchered, and eaten thousands of their enemies as sacrificial victims (Fig. 14.8). Some scholars have attributed these reports to exaggeration by the conquering Spanish, but the evidence is incontrovertible. Fragments of small, broken, and weathered human bones were found by archaeologists throughout the temple precinct of the Aztec capital.

Another example of cannibalism comes from the Southwest United States. A 1999 book entitled *Man Corn: Cannibalism and Violence in the Prehistoric American Southwest* by Christy and Jacqueline Turner of Arizona State University stirred great controversy. The Turners examined skeletal remains from seventy-six sites in the prehistoric Southwest and found indications of cannibalism at more than forty. Many people refused to believe the vivid evidence that was presented, preferring instead a politically correct view of the Pueblo Indians as peaceful and ecological. In fact, a growing body of data suggests warfare and violence were rife in this region during certain periods in the past.

One example of the evidence for cannibalism comes from the Mancos Anasazi (*MAN-kos ahn-ah-SAWS-ee*) Pueblo ruin in southwestern Colorado. Analysis of the skeletal remains by Tim White of the University of California-Berkeley revealed that nearly thirty men, women, and children were butchered and cooked there around AD 1100. The remains of these individuals were scattered and discarded in various rooms of the pueblo. Comparison of the human remains with those of animals that were eaten revealed skinning, dismembering, cooking, and fracturing of the human bones.

In spite of the evidence, detractors have argued that there are other possible explanations for the appearance and location of the bones, including the disturbance of earlier burials or the killing and dismemberment of witches in Pueblo society. The thorny question was whether these individuals had really been eaten or not.

The science of archaeology struck once again. A group of investigators, led by Brian Billman of the University of North Carolina, searched for the answer to this question. At another site where the skeletal material indicated cannibalism had taken place, a human coprolite (preserved feces) was found in an abandoned fireplace. The coprolite apparently resulted from a meat meal, as no plant remains were observed. A series of biomolecular tests were undertaken to identify the contents. A distinctive protein, human **myoglobin**, was found in the coprolite. Myoglobin is a protein found

> *Societies that do not eat people are fascinated by those that do.*
> —Ronald Wright, author

Mancos Pueblo

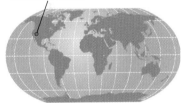

〜〜〜〜〜〜〜〜〜〜〜〜〜〜〜〜〜〜

myoglobin   A *protein* found in human tissue, its presence in human feces is used as evidence for cannibalism.

Fig. 14.8 Removal of the heart of a sacrificial victim atop an Aztec pyramid. The Spanish reported that the bodies of these victims were then thrown down the steps of the pyramid to be butchered and distributed to the populace.

only in human skeletal and cardiac muscles, where it carries oxygen to the energy-producing components of cells. The presence of the myoglobin proved that human tissue had been eaten.

The question still remains as to why cannibalism was practiced. Several suggestions have been made. Cannibalism might have been intended to terrorize enemies or perhaps was borrowed as a ritual practice from Mexico. Another idea emphasizes periods of starvation during a long drought. An invasion by violent outsiders might also explain the practice. The investigators themselves proposed that cannibalism was associated with violent conflict between Anasazi communities in the mid-1100s, concomitant with a long period of drought. They note a sharp increase in evidence of cannibalism between AD 1130 and 1150, followed in each case by site abandonment, and then a decrease in the practice during the 1200s as rainfall increased.

There are in fact four kinds of cannibalism recorded in archaeological remains: (1) survival cannibalism in cases of extreme starvation; (2) ritualized, sacrifice-related cannibalism, such as that associated with the Aztecs; (3) reverential funerary cannibalism; and (4) warfare-driven cannibalism, such as that perhaps seen among the Anasazi Indians. There is evidence for cannibalism in almost every society and time period in prehistory.

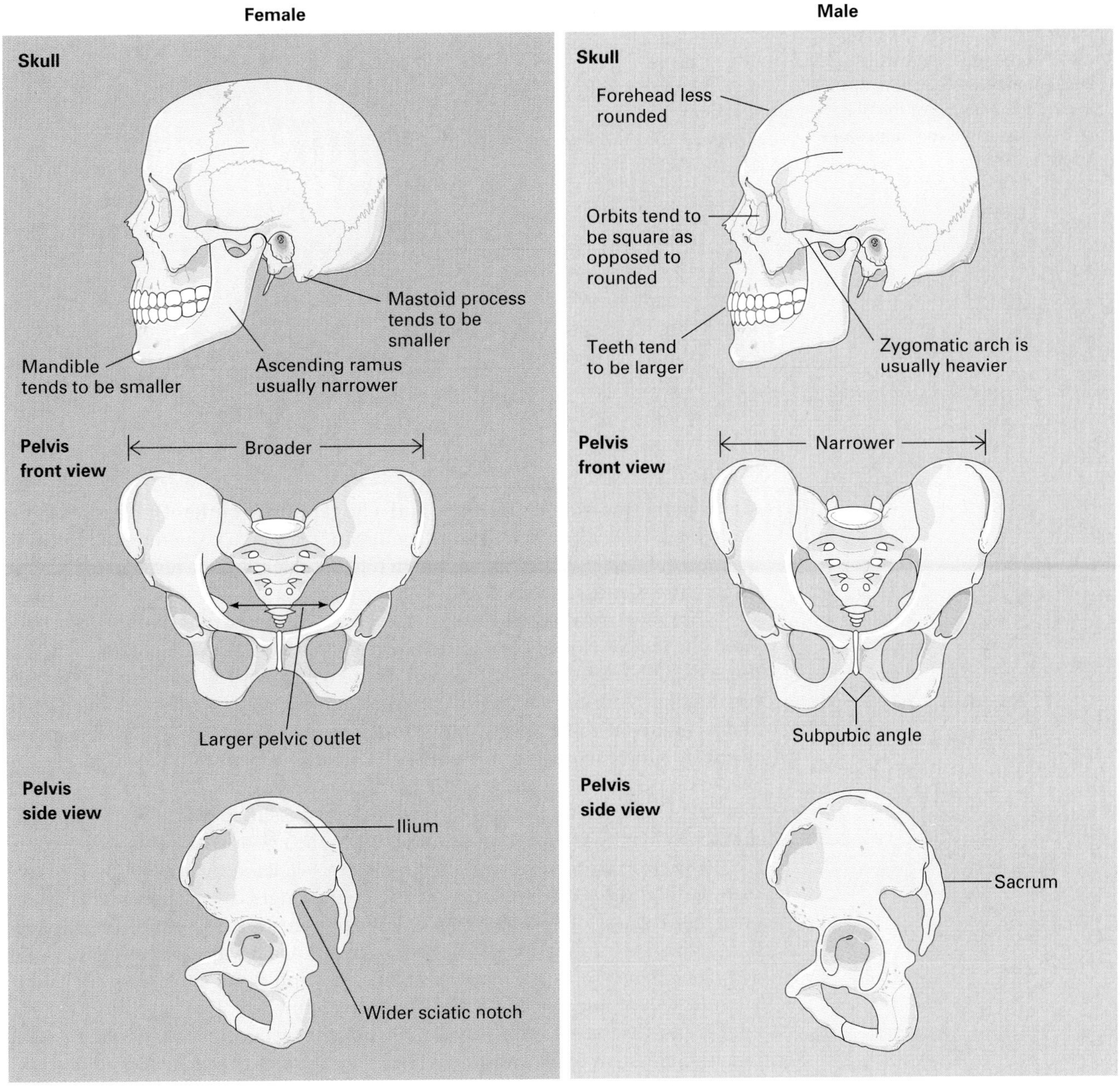

Female

Skull

Mandible tends to be smaller

Ascending ramus usually narrower

Mastoid process tends to be smaller

Pelvis front view

Broader

Larger pelvic outlet

Pelvis side view

Ilium

Wider sciatic notch

Male

Skull

Forehead less rounded

Orbits tend to be square as opposed to rounded

Teeth tend to be larger

Zygomatic arch is usually heavier

Pelvis front view

Narrower

Subpubic angle

Pelvis side view

Sacrum

Fig. 14.9 Major indicators of sex in the skull and pelvis of the human skeleton.

SEX, AGE, AND STATURE

Determination of the sex and age of human skeletons provides valuable information on both the individual and the group in terms of the demography of the population. Information on life expectancy, infant mortality, and sex ratios provides useful measures of adaptation. It should be noted that sex, age, and stature data from the skeleton are only estimates and that these determinations have some uncertainty.

The major diagnostic sites are in the pelvis and skull (Fig. 14.9). The sex of the skeleton can usually be estimated by examination of the size and shape of the pelvis and the skull. Adult males are generally taller than females with more robust bones, but in most cases these criteria alone are not sufficient to determine sex. Several features of the pelvis are most useful for sexing skeletal remains. The female pelvis is broader than the male and slightly different in shape, with a wider

Fig. 14.10 Changes in the long bone epiphyses with aging. The diagram shows the change from cartilaginous tissue to bone from infant to adult, along with the fusing of the bone ends (epiphyses) to the main shaft of the bone.

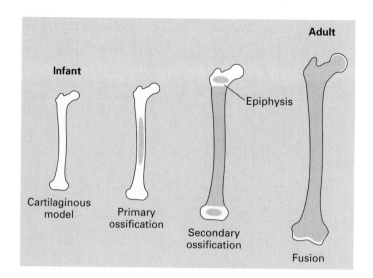

sciatic notch and subpelvic notch, and a larger pelvic outlet. Differences in the skull (Fig. 14.9) include smaller teeth and mandible and a more rounded forehead in females. In males, the zygomatic arch (Fig. 14.9) tends to be heavier and the eye orbits more square than round.

The age of death can be estimated by the eruption sequence and wear of the teeth, the fusion (closing) of sutures between bones of the skull, and the fusion of the ends of the limb bones to the shaft. There will always be some error in age estimates due to normal variability in the growth and aging process. Tooth eruption and wear are the most reliable indicators. The age of children and adolescents is relatively simple to determine from teeth. The **deciduous teeth** of children are replaced by permanent teeth, and the timing of the eruption of permanent teeth is well known. For example, most 6-year-olds are missing their two front teeth. We also speak of a twelve-year molar, referring to the age at which this tooth erupts.

The size and condition of the bones of the skeleton can also be used to estimate age at death. Body size, as indicated by the length of long bones, is of course one clue. The age of **epiphysis** (joint ends of bones) fusion varies for different bones, and this information can be used to determine the age at death (Fig. 14.10). Most long bone shafts (the diaphysis) have an epiphysis at either end. All lengthwise growth of bone occurs at the epiphyseal juncture. During childhood and adolescence, as the skeleton grows and hardens, the ends of long bones are separate from the shaft to allow growth. However, at puberty and during adolescence the epiphyses harden and unite with the shaft to become a single bone, terminating growth. Most long bone epiphyses unite by around the age of 20, but there is substantial variation. Fusion occurs in women about 2 years before men on average. Fig. 14.11 provides a summary of information on the age of epiphyseal fusion in different bones of the skeleton.

By the early twenties, the development of teeth and bones is largely complete in humans. Less precise indicators must be used to estimate the age of death from the skeletal material. Skeletal features used for adult ages include the pelvis and skull, and degenerative changes in bone tissue. These estimates are usually only reliable within 5 to 10 years. In adulthood, certain bones continue to join together. For example, the sutures where the individual bones of the skull join together begin to close in young adulthood. The **pubic symphysis** is the most reliable indicator of age. This area, where the two innominates (halves of the pelvis) join, changes in a predictable pattern from a heavily contoured face, to one marked by a rim for a person in the mid-30s, to a surface marked by increasing porosity for someone 40 years of age or older. This method is generally accurate for ages 17 to 50.

deciduous teeth   The first set of "baby" teeth that are lost when the permanent teeth come in.

epiphysis   Joint ends of bones where growth occurs.

pubic symphysis   The "face" of the pelvis where the two halves join, important area for age determination in the skeleton.

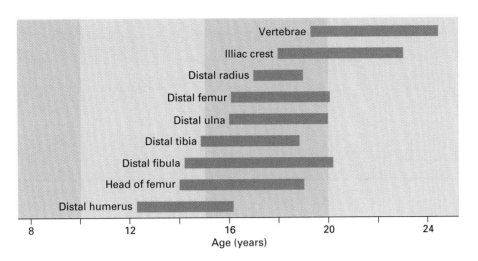

Fig. 14.11 Range of age of epiphyseal fusion for various bones in the human skeleton for European males. Age of fusion varies by sex and ancestry. Age at fusion is shown along the bottom of the graph.

TABLE 14.1 Age categories for estimates from human skeletal remains. Because of the difficulties in determining age at death for older human individuals, the number of age categories is higher in the younger range and fewer in the mature range. Depending upon the conditions of preservation, age estimates can be more precise.

Category	Age Range
Fetal	Conception to birth
Infancy	Birth to 2 years
Early childhood	3–5 years
Late childhood	6–12 years
Adolescence	13–24 years
Adult	25–49 years
Mature adult	50 years or more

Because the indicators that can be used are not completely accurate, bioarchaeologists estimate age of a skeleton within a range of years rather than at a specific age. One example of these ranges is shown in Table 14.1. Other systems are used by bioarchaeologists as well, depending on the quality of the evidence for age in the skeleton. Estimates are more reliable in well-preserved, complete skeletal material.

Stature can be estimated from measurements of the long bones of the arm or leg. Table 14.2 presents a formula and constants for estimating living stature from the measured maximum length of the femur in millimeters. The result is in inches. More specific information can be found in various reference tables. For example, a femur from a female of European ancestry that is 400 mm in maximum length would result in an estimated height of 5 feet ± 2.4 inches, using the formula

$$[a(mm) + b] \pm c$$

In the calculation below, a, b, and c are constant values taken from a reference table (Table 14.2) for European white females:

$$[0.11869(400) + 12.43] \pm 2.4$$
$$[47.48 + 12.43] \pm 2.4$$
$$59.91" = 5' \pm 2.4"$$

TABLE 14.2 Calculation of stature from femur length for American males. These values are approximate. For precise estimates, refer to published tables.

Ancestry	a	b	c
European male	0.10560	19.39	±2.8
European female	0.11869	12.43	±2.4
African male	0.08388	28.57	±4.0
African female	0.11640	11.98	±2.4

An intriguing application of stature estimates appeared recently in a study entitled "The Biological Standard of Living in Europe during the Last Two Millennia" by Nikola Koepke and Joerg Baten. The two authors used estimates of stature from archaeological and historical skeletal material from the last 2000 years in Europe. The sample they used included 2938 female and 6539 male stature estimates. Different formulas were used to estimate height for each sex.

One of the summary charts from the study is shown in Fig. 14.12. Several patterns are evident. Male and female heights generally follow the same trends over time, but there are differences. Females tend to vary more than males; that is, females show greater divergence from the average. Peak periods in male stature occurred during the middle centuries of the two millennia, while peaks in female stature were centered on the fifth and sixteenth centuries. Modern stature is not plotted on the graph and would be much higher than in any previous period. The authors of the study also looked at the factors statistically related to the changes in stature and found that population density had substantial effect, as did climate, social inequality, and gender inequality to a lesser degree.

Fig. 14.12 Average stature by sex in Europe by century for the last two millennia. Values for male height are shown on the left. Values for female height appear on the right. The two lines have been placed together for easier comparison. 170 cm is approximately 5'7" tall; 160 cm is approximately 5'3" tall. Data for females are missing for the eighteenth and nineteenth centuries.

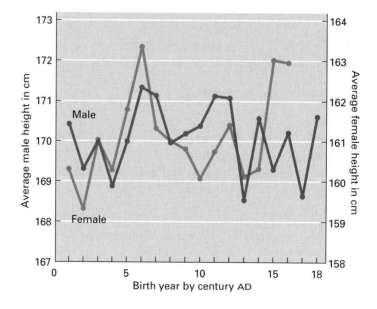

STRESS, DISEASE, AND TRAUMA

Paleopathology is the study of medical disorders and injury in human skeletal remains. It involves the nature and incidence of trauma that affects the skeleton, which can provide important information on the health status of past populations. Diseases and injuries studied by paleopathologists include bone fractures, arthritis, and periodontal diseases. Nutritional problems may be reflected in

paleopathology The study of medical disorders and injury in human skeletal remains.

Maya Stature

The Maya civilization was one of the most remarkable in the world in the centuries between the birth of Christ and the arrival of the Spanish. Spectacular cities, pyramids, and monuments characterized this region of Guatemala, Belize, and the Yucatan peninsula of Mexico beginning around AD 1. Yet when the Spanish arrived in this area in AD 1524, it was depopulated; the civilization of the Maya had disappeared. The collapse of the Maya remains one the mysteries of archaeology. What happened to the societies who built those monuments?

This question is also discussed in some detail in Chapter 16, "Explanation in Archaeology," but an important piece of the evidence comes from the human skeletal remains. Part of the answer may lie in diet and nutrition. William Haviland reported some years ago that

individuals buried in stone tombs (i.e., elite burial places) at the site of Tikal (*tea-CALL*) were taller and more robust than those buried in simple graves. He argued that this difference was due to a nutritional advantage for the elite. Information on stature among the Maya is shown in Table 14.3 for men, women, and elite burials. Measurements are given for both commoners and elite males, identified by the nature of the burial, whether simple grave or elaborate stone tomb. In addition, the average height of modern Maya in this region is also given.

The hypothesis was that stature declined among the Maya until the collapse around AD 800, due to reduced yields from exhausted agricultural fields and a decline in nutrition. The actual data, however, do not support this hypothesis. Common people were often smaller than the nobility, almost certainly due to differences in diet. Stature did fluctuate over time, but the pattern is different for men and women. Males are tallest ca. AD 500 and decrease from that point to the present. Women are the shortest in that same time period. In addition to the decline in stature in males, other evidence in the skeletons indicates that disease and malnutrition were common. The fact that the modern Maya are the shortest of all suggests that these patterns continue today and are not directly related to the collapse of the Classic Maya.

Maya Region

TABLE 14.3 Stature of common males, females, and elite males at the Maya site of Tikal over time. There are insufficient measurements on elite females and no information on early Tikal or modern elite Maya. Stature of common males clearly declines at the end of the Classic Maya period around AD 800 but females become taller.

	Tikal Pre AD 300	Tikal AD 500	Tikal AD 800	Modern Maya
Common Male	164.5 (5′5″)	167.0 (5′6″)	157.4 (5′2″)	155.0 (5′1″)
Common Female	146.8 (4′10′)	142.3 (4′8″)	149.0 (4′11″)	148.5 (4′10.5″)
Elite Male	—	172.0 (5′8″)	163 (5′4″)	—

poorly developed bones and a low average height for a population. Cultural practices like cranial deformation or dental mutilation, practiced in prehistoric America and elsewhere, also are recorded in the skeletal remains.

Cause of death can be determined in only a small percentage of burials, but violence is not infrequently reflected in the human skeleton. A variety of injuries produce broken bones and infection can leave traces in bone as well. Indications of conflict in human society can be seen in cuts or weapon fragments in bone, cranial fractures, and other damage. A **parry fracture**, for example, is a distinctive break in the right or left forearm usually resulting from the defensive action of raising an arm to protect oneself from a blow.

Some examples of violence in the past are both dramatic and disturbing. Fig. 14.13 is a drawing of the mass grave from Talheim, Germany, dating to

parry fracture A distinctive break in the forearm resulting from a blow to an arm raised in protection.

Fig. 14.13 The mass grave at Talheim shown in three views. The first drawing (a) shows the location of adult males in the mass grave, the second view (b) shows adult females, and the third view (c) shows subadults.

a.   b.   c.

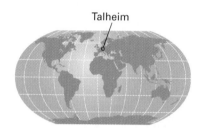

Talheim

approximately 4850 BC and belonging to the Early Neolithic period. The thirty-four individuals were buried in a square pit 3 m on a side (10 ft × 10 ft) and include nine men, seven women, two adults of unknown sex, and sixteen children.

All of these individuals bear evidence of a violent death. Twenty of the victims were killed by a massive blow to the left back of the head, as if they had been bound, placed on their knees, and struck from behind. The shapes of the wounds match closely the cross-sections of two different types of heavy stone axes used in this period. The remains are of a single massacre, possibly the residents of a single village. Other mass graves from this period show patterns of skull fragmentation caused by a heavy wooden club (Fig. 14.14).

Stress during one's lifetime is also revealed in the skeleton. Malnourishment in childhood causes the disruption of bone growth, which shows up in the skeleton as a series of distinct features, known as **Harris lines**, in the ends of long bones. Tooth enamel also reflects childhood stress and malnourishment in an irregular series of lines, a condition known as dental **enamel hypoplasia**. Various diseases and other health problems also are reflected in bone. Arthritis is one of the most common pathological conditions in the bones of adult individuals, resulting in an accumulation of bone tissue around an afflicted area. Syphilis, tuberculosis, and other infectious diseases may result in bone loss and pitting or the deformation of the skull and other bone surfaces. Anemia and parasitic infections are sometimes recorded in pitting and thickening of the eye sockets in the skull, a condition known as **cribra orbitalia** (Fig. 14.15).

Fig. 14.14 Experimental creation of skull fractures caused by a blow from a heavy club.

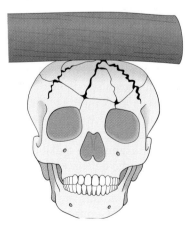 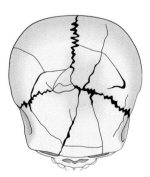

Harris lines   Interruption of growth evidenced in a skeleton by darker bands in the ends of long bones.

enamel hypoplasia   Irregular lines in tooth enamel resulting from childhood stress or malnutrition.

cribra orbitalia   Pitting and thickening of the eye sockets in the skull caused by anemia or parasitic infections.

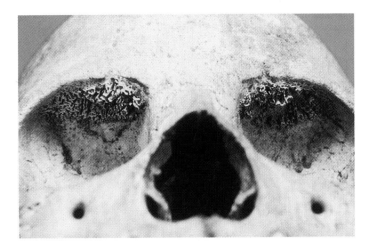

Fig. 14.15 Cribra orbitalia from an individual from Amelia Island, Florida.

 EXAMPLE ～～～～～～～～～～～～～～～～

ABU HUREYRA

The site of Abu Hureyra lies along the Euphrates River in northern Syria. The ancient settlement is one of the oldest farming villages in the world. Houses changed over time from pit dwellings and timber and reed houses in the Preneolithic level to clusters of mud-brick houses in the Neolithic layers around 10,000 years ago. The site is described in some detail in Chapter 13, "Archaeobotany."

Thousands of artifacts, tens of house foundations, and many burials were found during the excavations. The burials contained 75 children and 87 adults, including at least 44 females, 27 males, and 16 of indeterminate sex. The skeletons of these individuals were carefully examined by a bioarchaeologist, who found the health of the inhabitants to have been quite good. However, there were signs of unusual disease or wear seen in the skeletal material. One of the indications of stress was seen in enlarged neck vertebrae, suggesting the inhabitants had carried heavy loads on their heads. Other bone deformities included collapsed vertebrae and arthritic big toes seen only among the young and adult women at the site (Fig. 14.16). These problems were likely caused by the preparation of the plant foods like wheats and rye. Kneeling at a grinding stone, or quern, pushing and pulling a heavy stone, for several hours a day for many years could have produced these injuries, also associated with heavy muscular development in the upper arms.

The roughly ground grain had a damaging effect on the inhabitants' teeth. Teeth were often fractured and heavily ground down. In addition, many people lost their teeth at an early age. These problems were likely related to the coarse grain they were eating and the presence of small stones and grit in the grain that came from grinding and a failure to sift the flour they were preparing. Several of the individuals also exhibited unusual worn grooves on the front teeth often associated with working fibers when making baskets. Others had heavily developed jaw musculature that has also been observed among individuals who use their teeth to chew plant stems to make fiber string and rope. The first indications of tooth decay appeared in the Neolithic levels at the site as carbohydrates became more common in the diet.

The evidence at Abu Hureyra demonstrates the kinds of new insights provided by detailed investigation of human bones and teeth on the health and activities of the inhabitants of this early farming village. Clearly the preparation of food from domesticated plants was a demanding and time-consuming task. Better health, it seems, was not a result of the Neolithic revolution.

www.mhhe.com/pricearch1

For a Web-based activity on the site of Abu Hureyra, please see the Internet exercises on your online learning center.

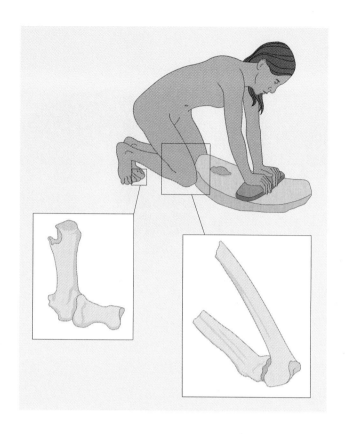

Fig. 14.16 Paleopathology of female skeletons from the early Neolithic site of Abu Hureyra, Syria. Bone problems included collapsed vertebrae, changes in the knees, and arthritic big toes likely caused by kneeling at a grinding stone, or quern, pushing and pulling a heavy stone, for several hours a day for many years preparing cereals.

◉ EXAMPLE

RAISING THE DEAD: THE MARY ROSE

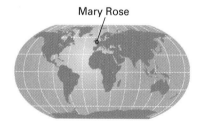

Mary Rose

The Mary Rose, pride of King Henry VIII's fleet, sank at the beginning of a naval battle against the French, within sight of land and the king, on July 19, 1545, in the Selton estuary, near Portsmouth, on the south coast of England (Fig. 14.17). A major catastrophe for the English, the sinking was probably due to a combination of causes, including a sudden wind, which tipped the ship so that the sea flowed in through the gun ports and sank her.

The Mary Rose was one of the first ships built intentionally as a warship to carry heavy guns. Her length at the waterline is estimated to have been 38.5 m (120 ft) and her draught was 4.6 m (14 ft). The height of the ship was 13 m (40 ft) and her weight was 700 tons when she sank. The Mary Rose appears to have been constructed with a hold and four decks. Over time, the sunken hull on the sea floor broke apart. One-half was buried in the muds and clays on the sea floor while the other parts disappeared. The shipwreck was discovered in 1967 and finally raised in 1982.

Most of the crew of 415 individuals lost their lives; only 35 men escaped from drowning. One or two of the deceased are known by name; the rest are anonymous seamen who served the crown. The evidence for their lives comes largely from the skeletal remains that were recovered within the remaining hull of the ship. Many human bones were found during the excavation of the ship, often scattered and jumbled between the decks. A few individual skeletons were found under cannons or other heavy objects.

The study of these human remains was a major undertaking, particularly since the mixed-up bones had to be sorted by individual before further analyses could be undertaken. The sorting took months but eventually the scientists were able to determine that approximately 179 individuals were represented among the skeletal

Fig. 14.17 An early drawing of the Mary Rose.

TABLE 14.4 Age distribution of the Mary Rose crew as determined from the skeletal remains (number of individuals=82).

Age Category	Number
10–13-year-old juveniles (preadolescent)	2
Adolescents (13–18 years of age)	17
Young adults (18–30 years of age)	54
Middle-aged adults (30–40 years of age)	15
Old adults (more than 40 years of age)	1

remains, a little more than 43% of the 415 men on board the ship when it sank. This was determined by counting the numbers of intact skulls and lower jaws without matching skulls found in the shipwreck. The other individuals either washed away from the sunken ship or remain buried in the sea floor.

Only 92 skeletons were fairly complete; all of them were male. These individuals were used for the determination of age of the members of the crew. Age estimates are normally based on tooth eruption and bone development, but growth stops around age 25 making the determination of age more difficult. Thus, tooth wear and markers in the pelvis and on the ends of ribs were used to age older individuals.

The investigators determined the number of individuals in each of five age categories on board the Mary Rose. Table 14.4 shows the results of the study. In this study, adult ages were estimated for the categories 18–30 (young adult), 30–40 (middle age), and greater than 40 (old).

Other information on the physical attributes of the crew was also recorded including stature and bone strength or robustness. The average member of the crew was a young man in his late teens or early 20s about 5 ft 7 in in height, strong, with several cavities in his teeth.

Beyond these basic statistics, the bones provided a great deal more information on the health and activities of the crew because the shape and condition of bone change with disease, injury, and use, leaving permanent records in the skeleton. For example, some of the skeletal remains suggest the presence of several deficiency diseases, including rickets (vitamin D), scurvy (vitamin C), and anemia (iron). In addition, 7% of the individuals exhibited the lines of enamel hypoplasia in their teeth, evidence of childhood dietary deficiency or stress. The members of the crew suffered from various fractures, but there was little evidence of infectious diseases. Most of the fractures were to the lower skeleton, perhaps reflecting the slippery surfaces aboard ship. In general, the health of the crew was good and they appear fairly well fed.

Skeletal evidence for activity among the remains of the crew is particularly interesting. This evidence reflected the specialized occupations of the sailors. In one example, an unusual deformity of the shoulder blade appears in almost 20% of the individuals. This pattern is almost certainly associated with the lifelong use of a heavy English longbow as a weapon. Almost half of the crew was made up of soldiers, many of whom would have been archers. Some 250 bows and thousands of arrows were listed in the ship's stores. A thirteenth-century law in England required all males to be proficient with the longbow. This heavy yew bow probably had a draw weight of 150 pounds, demanding a great deal of strength. The English practice of pushing the bow away from the body to release the arrow meant that the left shoulder bore much of the strain of shooting for right-handed archers. More than half of the shoulder-blade deformation was on the left side of the body.

In addition, a number of individuals exhibited changes in the vertebrae of their spine that must reflect activity. The vertebrae of the young men of the crew of the Mary Rose closely resembled vertebrae of much older males. The distinctive pattern of pits and bone formation lesions reflect the heavy labor that would have been involved in shipboard activities and particularly may be associated with gun crews and the movement of heavy cannons on the confined decks of the Mary Rose.

GENETIC INFORMATION

Life is defined by an ability to reproduce, to make a copy of one's self. This ability depends on genetic material present in living tissue. The tissue of most organisms is made up of different kinds of cells—skin cells, brain cells, sex cells, and the like. These cells carry the genetic material, or **DNA** (deoxyribonucleic acid). DNA is a long molecular chain of **nucleotides**, each made up of one of four base units (adenine, cytosine, guanine, or thymine). These long chains of molecules are called

Fig. 14.18 The sources of DNA in the cell: chromosomes in mitochondria and the nucleus.

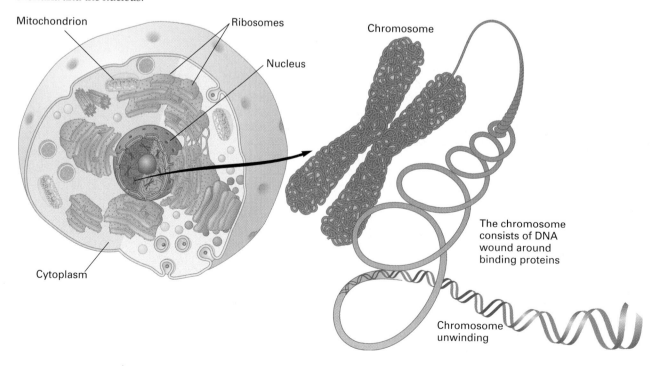

Mitochondrion
Ribosomes
Nucleus
Cytoplasm

Chromosome

The chromosome consists of DNA wound around binding proteins

Chromosome unwinding

The Mary Rose Today

The story of the sinking, discovery, and excavation of the ship is a well-known one in Britain. Today the ship is on display in the Mary Rose Museum at the Historic Dockyard at the home of the Royal Navy in Portsmouth, England. A trust was established to oversee the museum, artifacts, and remains. Restoration of the ship is taking place, including treating the wooden timbers and other artifacts with polyethylene glycol to preserve the objects.

The museum provides an extraordinary visual and virtual tour of the ship and the lives of those who died onboard. None of those who died could be specifically identified among the remains nor ascribed to any descendants. Out of respect, the Mary Rose Trust does not display any human remains in the exhibits. At the same time, the scientific value of the skeletal material cannot be ignored and it is for this reason that the Trust remains their custodians. The human remains are carefully kept at the museum and are available for genuine research investigations.

The Mary Rose Trust has a Code of Practice that includes the treatment of human remains and provides a model for many such situations in other places around the world.

Extract from Mary Rose Trust Code of Practice:

4.0 *Human Remains.*
The collections of the MRT include human remains recovered from the ship. None of these can be identified and one individual was buried in Portsmouth Cathedral with ceremonies which included a Requiem for all who died on the *Mary Rose*.

The scholarly study of these elements of the collections is an essential part of the MRT archive. They contribute a unique corpus of information relating to our understanding of seafaring men of the period.

There are few collections of sixteenth-century comparative human bone material in the world, and none as well preserved as this group.

The MRT recognises, however, that all such material must be utilised with dignity and respect for the feelings of others. The staff and its consultants will therefore

4.1 use these remains only for the furtherance of legitimate research,

4.2 make the material available only to qualified researchers and never to the merely curious,

4.3 endeavour to accomplish the work with dignity and respect,

4.4 exercise the same care in documenting and handling this material as with the other elements of the collection,

4.5 secure and store these remains in a proper manner in accordance with the policies relating to the remainder of the collection,

4.6 reject any attempt to use the material in a public exhibition or to allow it to feature in the popular press or television,

4.7 ensure that all anthropological studies undertaken shall be in accordance with the code of ethics accepted within the discipline.

---

chromosomes and are found in both the nucleus of the cell and cell structures known as mitochrondria (Fig. 14.18). The individual genes that determine the growth and characteristics of offspring are segments of DNA molecules. There are an estimated 50,000 genes in the DNA of a single human being.

Two general kinds of studies—on either modern or **ancient DNA**—are being carried out to investigate the human past and are described below.

Modern DNA

Living populations today are studied to identify genetic differences and the time at which groups of people diverged in the past. These studies generally use DNA in blood, saliva, or other cells to determine genetic similarities or differences between various groups of people. These studies have been used, for example, to examine the spread of Neolithic farmers into Europe. Genetic differences among living people in Europe have been assumed to be due in part to the arrival of new people from Southwest Asia, bringing domestic plants and animals and the accoutrements of farming for the first time more than 8000 years ago.

Evidence from genetic studies of living peoples can also provide some information on the point in time when humans became a species distinct from an

DNA The blueprints for life; hereditary material; a long molecular chain of molecules called chromosomes found in both the nucleus of the cell and in cell structures known as mitochrondria.

nucleotides Basic building blocks of DNA, each made up of one of four base units (adenine, cytosine, guanine, or thymine) that together make up the long molecules of chromosomes.

ancient DNA (aDNA) Genetic material preserved in archaeological or *paleontological* remains.

Neanderthal Genealogy

One of the more remarkable discoveries in the last decade was the presence of ancient DNA in the bones of Neanderthals. The Neanderthals are one of the more intriguing branches of the human family. These individuals lived in Europe and the Near East from approximately 200,000 years ago and completely disappeared after 30,000 years ago, replaced by fully modern humans (FMH), *Homo sapiens*. Neanderthals (*Homo neanderthalensis*), classified as our close relatives, were robust, with heavy bones, thick skulls, and larger teeth than our own (Fig. 14.19). Neanderthals lacked the bulging forehead and chin of modern humans, as well as the spectacular specialized tools, art, and notation that appeared after 30,000 years ago. A great deal has been written and debated about their relationship with us and about why they disappeared.

The fate of these Neanderthals is open to question. Were Neanderthals violently replaced by modern humans, or did they interbreed and simply disappear in the mix? The archaeological evidence concerning our relationship is equivocal and quite different between Europe and the Near East.

Current evidence from the Near East suggests that the first modern-looking humans appeared in this area about 100,000 years ago. At several sites, the bones of *H. sapiens* are found in layers with Neanderthal stone tools, dating to 90,000 years ago. At other sites, Neanderthal skeletons have been found between 75,000 and 45,000 years ago. So it appears that modern-looking humans co-existed with Neanderthals in the Near East until around 45,000 years ago. Importantly, there is no direct association between Neanderthal and Middle Paleolithic

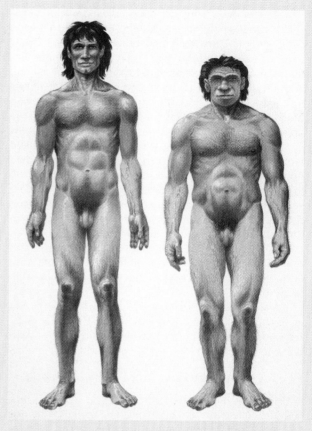

Fig. 14.19 Artist's reconstruction of *Homo sapiens* (left) and *Homo neanderthalensis* side-by-side.

www.mhhe.com/pricearch1

For a Web-based activity on mitochondrial DNA, please see the Internet exercises on your online learning center.

mitochondrial DNA (mtDNA) Modern genetic material taken from the mitochondria, inherited only through the maternal line.

apelike ancestor or reached fully modern status. Biological scientists have developed a "molecular clock" that estimates the time at which different species or groups separated from a common ancestor in the past. The mechanism for this clock is change over time in the amino acids which make up DNA. Known as nucleotide substitutions, these changes are observed as mutations or mismatches in the genetic material of two species. The number of mismatches in the chromosomes of two species correlates closely with the evolutionary distance and time between them. Our closest relatives are the chimpanzee and gorilla. Comparison of amino acid sequences in humans, chimps, and gorillas indicates that the three species diverged between 6 and 4 million years ago—a date very close to that for the earliest fossils of our human ancestors.

There is also intriguing modern genetic evidence regarding the evolution of *Homo sapiens sapiens*, or fully modern humans. This evidence comes from studies of **mitochondrial DNA** (mtDNA), genetic material that is assumed to mutate at a relatively rapid and constant rate. Because this type of DNA is inherited directly through the maternal line, it provides a continuous trail back into the past. The number of different mutations between two individuals should be a function of how far back in time they shared a common maternal ancestor. Based on the num-

tools and between FMH and the Upper Paleolithic humans. Modern-looking humans before 45,000 years ago used Middle Paleolithic technology.

In Europe, the transition is less clear and the evidence for the first modern-looking humans is much later. Neanderthals are known in Europe by approximately 200,000 years ago. The earliest bones of modern-looking humans do not appear in this area until after 46,000 years ago. It is entirely likely that the Neanderthals found in the Near East between 75,000 and 45,000 years ago moved there from Europe during a period of intense cold. The disappearance of Neanderthals and their replacement by modern-looking humans in Europe appears to take place between 46,000 and 41,000 years ago, from east to west. Several pieces of evidence suggest that this was a gradual process.

The question of the fate of the Neanderthals remains unsolved. Why did they disappear? Several possibilities have been suggested in both scientific and popular literature. Were Neanderthals simply conquered and slain by advancing groups of technologically superior *Homo sapiens*? The stone tool evidence does not readily support such a suggestion. Two recent discoveries of human skeletal remains suggest some interbreeding among Neanderthals and modern humans.

On the other hand, there is genetic evidence to the contrary. Did Neanderthals disappear into the gene pool of modern-looking humans, as smaller numbers of Neanderthals interbred with larger numbers of *Homo sapiens*? Ancient DNA extracted from several Neanderthal bones from Germany and several other places in Europe and western Asia suggests that there was little genetic relationship, and little or no mating, between the Neanderthals and the fully modern humans who replaced them. A total of eight Neanderthal skeletons have provided ancient DNA so far. The samples look very much alike and very different from *Homo sapiens* (Fig. 14.20). Based on this evidence, the end of the Neanderthals may have been more violent than romantic. However, those who argue for interbreeding among Neanderthals and modern humans argue that the geneticists throw out results that show modern genes because of possible contamination. In fact, the genetic evidence is far from conclusive as yet and the jury is still out in this scientific trial.

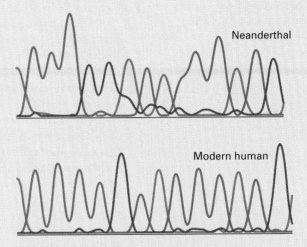

Fig. 14.20 Differences in the ancient DNA of Neanderthal and modern humans.

ber of accumulated mutations in the mtDNA, researchers concluded that *Homo sapiens* first appeared in southern Africa between 130,000 and 170,000 years ago. Similar studies of DNA in the Y-chromosome, present only in males, have argued for a roughly similar date of appearance, around 200,000 years ago.

Ancient DNA

The second kind of study of genetic material involves ancient DNA in the nucleus of cells, extracted from archaeological plants and animals. Discovery of DNA preserved in prehistoric human bone was first reported in 1989. Since that time, numerous studies have looked for and found DNA in ancient materials. Samples from human bone, for example, can provide information on the sex or genealogy of an individual. In many cases, however, molecules of ancient DNA have been badly degraded by decay over time and are found often only as short segments of the larger molecules. This breakdown of the molecule makes it more difficult, but not impossible, to reconstruct the original genetic information.

Analysis of ancient DNA has been greatly enhanced by the development of the technique known as the **polymerase chain reaction (PCR)**, which results in

polymerase chain reaction (PCR) Technique in genetic studies to increase quantities of *DNA* sample by rapid cloning.

the cloning of large quantities of material for analysis even when only a very small original sample is available—often the case with archaeological remains. Theoretically, even a single molecule, as well as badly degraded segments of molecules, can be analyzed with the help of the PCR technique.

Contamination is a significant problem. Since only small amounts of ancient DNA are present in samples, any contamination from living humans during excavation or laboratory analysis can mask or hide the prehistoric evidence. Researchers must use great caution when removing and preparing samples for such analyses.

MORTUARY ANALYSIS

www.mhhe.com/pricearch1

For a Web-based activity on funerary equipment, please see the Internet exercises on your online learning center.

Most of what archaeologists usually find has been intentionally discarded or accidentally lost. Human burials, on the other hand, are purposeful deposits of materials placed together in a grave for specific reasons—a statement about the deceased. The study of graves, including the human skeletal remains, the contents, and the pit or chamber, provides substantial information on both the living and the dead. Various attributes and relationships that characterized the deceased individual in life may be restated in the grave, such as social status, age, sex, religious beliefs, and vocation. Most archaeological remains refer only to groups of people or households. Graves refer directly to individuals and provide a more personal perspective on the past. **Mortuary analysis** is the study of graves and their contents to learn about past societies and individuals.

Grave goods, the items buried with individuals at death, are an important source of information about the social organization of prehistoric groups. A person's status during life is generally reflected at death; elaborate burials and grave goods may be associated with people of high status, but little or no special contents often mark low-status individuals. In addition to grave contents, the location and simple or elaborate nature of a tomb or grave are important attributes for mortuary analysis. Larger, more complex societies with marked social differentiation usually have a greater degree of mortuary variation than less hierarchical groups (Fig. 14.21).

One important characteristic that may be determined from mortuary analysis is the kind of status relationships operating in a society. Tomb contents, structure, and location, relative to the age and sex of the interred individual, may indicate whether a person held **achieved status**, earned through personal accomplishments, or **ascribed status**, inherited at birth. Some archaeologists have argued that graves of infants or children with an unusually rich array of grave goods are indicative of ascribed status since these individuals would not have been able to achieve high status on their own. Ascribed status is an important indicator of more complex, ranked or stratified societies. State-level societies often have several distinct classes of citizens that may be distinguished in a study of burials.

Mortuary analysis today frequently includes **human taphonomy**, the study of the placement and decomposition of the body in the grave in order to better understand the treatment of the dead. Bioarchaeologists must be present in the field to examine burials firsthand in order to determine the processes at work that changed the body of the deceased into a fragmentary human skeleton. Human taphonomy is a variety of forensic anthropology aimed at learning more about the rituals and activities involved in the placement of the body. Some of the important issues in human taphonomy include soft-tissue decomposition and disarticulation, the potential movement of interred skeletal elements, and the influence of gravity and the space in which decomposition takes place. Bioarchaeologists examine the location and orientation of the human skeleton in the grave to deter-

mortuary analysis   Study of graves and their contents to learn about past societies and individuals.

grave goods   Food and/or other goods, often valuable, sometimes buried with deceased individuals.

achieved status   Earned position of prestige in society determined by skills, abilities, and effort.

ascribed status   Inherited position of prestige in society determined by birth.

human taphonomy   Study of the placement and decomposition of the corpse in the grave.

Fig. 14.21 This extraordinarily rich grave from Varna, Bulgaria, dating to around 4000 BC, contains an adult male buried with a large number of copper and gold weapons and jewelry. This individual was undoubtedly an important member of society and likely a member of the elite. This is one of the earliest known examples of the use of gold in prehistory.

mine how the body was originally placed and in what condition. The effects of empty space and walls in the grave are considered in relation to the movement of bone during the process of decomposition. Studies of human taphonomy have been able to suggest the presence of wrapping or coffins in graves where these materials have long since vanished.

Several examples of mortuary analysis are described below, including a cemetery from the early Neolithic in Central Europe, the burial of a Melanesian chief and his relatives and retainers in the South Pacific, and the graves of the inhabitants of Moundville, a major center in Alabama 600 years ago.

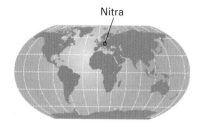

Nitra

EXAMPLE

LBK CEMETERY AT NITRA

The Linearbandkeramik (LBK) is the name given to certain archaeological materials that suddenly appeared across Central Europe in the Early Neolithic between 5500 and 5000 BC. The LBK period is known for small farming settlements of longhouses found on distinctive silt sediments from Hungary to Poland and from France to the Ukraine. The term *Linearbandkeramik* specifically describes the very homogeneous, banded pottery that is found at these settlements and associated with the period. These sites often have burials either among the houses or in adjacent cemeteries (Fig. 14.22).

The LBK settlement of Nitra (*KNEE-tra*) is one of the earliest, found in the country of Slovakia and dating to ca. 5500 BC. The cemetery accompanying the settlement is typical. Men, women, and children were buried in shallow graves usually on their back or sides and often facing to the east. Grave goods are limited and include materials such as heavy stone axes and spondylus shell bracelets or ornaments. **Spondylus** is a large mollusk with a pearl-like shell interior that lives in the Mediterranean Sea, some 500 km (300 mi) from Nitra. This shell must have been highly prized jewelry during the LBK.

Some information from the mortuary analysis at Nitra is presented in Fig. 14.23. The chart is a way of summarizing a lot of information, depicting the age and sex of each buried individual along with the contents of their grave. Each box represents one individual and the age classes are shown in five- or ten-year intervals on the vertical axis. Remember that an accurate estimate of the age of individuals over 20 years old from skeletal remains is difficult. Sex is indicated in the diagram, with women on the right and men on the left. The sex of children under age 15 cannot be reliably determined from the skeleton.

From the chart, it is possible to see that there are twenty-three males and twenty-one females over the age of 15, and twenty-one children under 15. That is an even distribution. It would seem that all members of the society were buried when they died. No one lived past 60 years of age. Most of the males died between 40 and 50, and most of the females died between 30 and 40. The life expectancy for females was substantially less than for males. Most of the children died between birth and 5 years of age, and there were a surprising number of deaths between 5 and 15. Burial goods were almost exclusively the property of the males. Older males were often buried with axes and shell jewelry, and all but one member of the oldest group of males was buried with both. In contrast, only one female was buried with a shell arti-

Fig. 14.22 LBK graves from France.

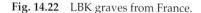

spondylus   Species of large marine mollusk with a prized shell.

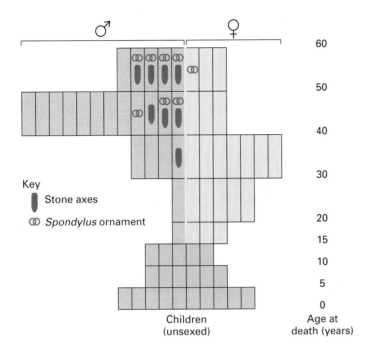

Fig. 14.23 A schematic representation of the age, sex, and grave goods in the Linearbandkeramik cemetery at the site of Nitra, Slovakia, ca. 5500 BC.

Key
▮ Stone axes
◎ *Spondylus* ornament

♂ ♀

60
50
40
30
20
15
10
5
0

Children
(unsexed)

Age at
death (years)

fact and no grave goods were placed with children. The data from the Nitra cemetery suggest that there was no ascribed status in this population. It does appear that while these groups may have been egalitarian, older males clearly had some achieved status signified by the axes and jewelry.

◉ EXAMPLE

ROY MATA

Retoka (*re-TOKE-ah*) (or Hat Island) is a small coral atoll some 2 km (1.2 mi) long and 600 m (1/3 mi) wide. It is heavily wooded and lacks surface water. Today, the atoll is uninhabited and has been for many generations, certainly since the burial there of a chief named Roy Mata around AD 1265. A taboo was placed on the island at that time, and it is still said to be dangerous to spend the night there and fatal to touch the grave. Roy Mata is considered the greatest hero of the region. He brought peace between warring tribes in the New Hebrides Islands of Melanesia in the South Pacific during the thirteenth century. He also established a number of mechanisms for organizing the people and polities of this area, including the dispersal of chiefs, various celebratory and alliance feasts, and inauguration ceremonies.

The living oral history of the people on a neighboring island says that Roy Mata was buried with several members of his court on the island of Retoka and that representatives of different clans volunteered to be buried with him. Other individuals were interred after being sacrificed. There is an historical account of the death of another chief reporting that his wives, at least those without children, were buried with him to keep him company and that one wife's body was buried under her husband in a perpendicular position. There are also reports of a powerful sedative or poison being used to put men to sleep before they were buried. Reports say that women were strangled or buried alive, but were not given the sedative.

In the mid-1960s a French archaeologist, José Garanger, conducted excavations at the island to find the grave of this famous chief. Several standing stones at

Retoka

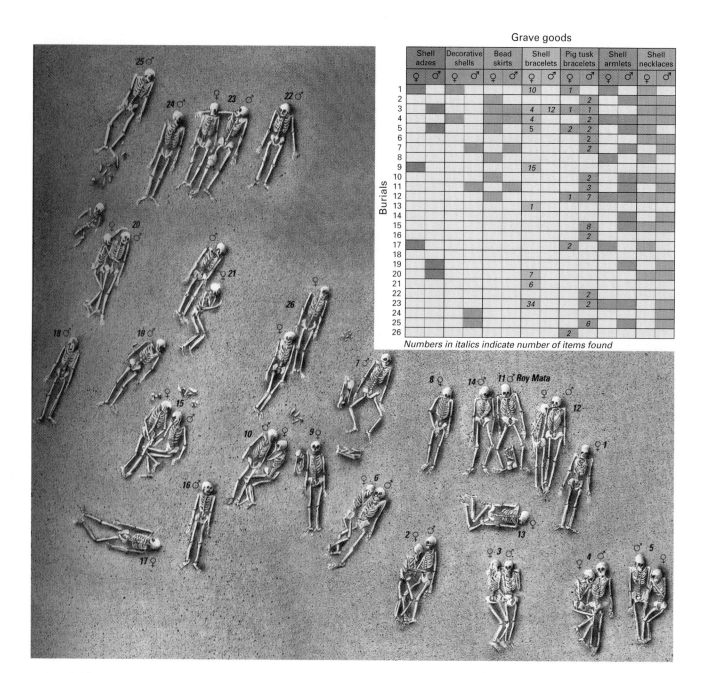

Grave goods

Numbers in italics indicate number of items found

Fig, 14.24 The burial ground of Roy Mata and company on Retoka Island, Melanesia. The chart lists the contents of the graves.

the base of a very large tree still marked the burial area. Excavations revealed that the burial area had been dug down to a depth of 30 cm (1 ft) over an area of more than 100 m^2 (a large room) before the graves and tomb were put in place (Fig. 14.24).

There was one large tomb on the east side of the area, some 30 cm (1 ft) below the floor of the burial area. This collective tomb contained several individuals, including Roy Mata in the center along with a male–female couple to his left, a man to his right, and a very young woman at his feet buried at a right angle. There is also a secondary, bundle burial between the legs of the chief.

After the filling of the tomb, a funeral ceremony appears to have taken place at the site. The ground had been heavily trampled, there were a number of fireplaces, and pig bones were scattered about. After these rites, more than thirty-five individuals were buried in some twenty shallow graves to the west and north of the tomb of Roy Mata, as part of his funeral entourage.

Many of these graves contain a male and a female. The men are usually buried on their back in an extended position; the women are usually on their side and turned toward the male, slightly flexed, often holding his arm, waist, or neck. The women's fingers and toes sometimes were found in a clenched position. It is impossible to tell how these women actually died. One young female, in grave 15, seems to have tried to get out of the ground; her head is raised in the earth. In addition to the couples, there are several secondary or partial burials present. A total of twenty-nine individuals could be identified as to sex, sixteen males and thirteen females. These were all adults with the exception of one adolescent girl.

The grave goods of jewelry are of interest. Small, disk-shaped shell beads were used to make necklaces, armbands, and waistbands. Most of the individuals wore these necklaces, with various added beads and pendants. Half of the men wore shell armbands, while only 13% of the women were so adorned. Individuals wearing waistbands were found in or adjacent to the tomb. Shell bracelets were worn largely by women, nine of ten individuals, and again were found in or adjacent to the tomb. Pig tusk bracelets are particularly interesting because they are related to the killing of large pigs at feasts and a known sign of wealth. Nine of fifteen men wear these bracelets on both arms and the other six on one arm only. Only a few women have these tusk bracelets.

The archaeological results from Retoka tallied very closely with the legends and oral history from the area. It seems clear that Garanger found the tomb of Roy Mata on the island and that the other burials and grave goods confirm what is known of the event. The archaeological materials from Retoka are now on permanent display in the National Museum and Cultural Centre on Vanuatu Island.

 EXAMPLE

MOUNDVILLE

Some 800 years ago, Moundville was one of the largest communities in North America. The site itself, along the Black Warrior River in central Alabama, covered 150 ha (370 acres) and had a population of perhaps 1000. The focus of the site is a set of twenty large platform mounds placed symmetrically around a huge 30-ha (75-acre) plaza (Fig. 14.25). These mounds provided a dramatic foundation for temples or elite residences, erected high above the surrounding landscape. The largest of the mounds, almost 20 m (60 ft) high, is a steep pyramid with two ramps. The site contains a

Moundville

Fig. 14.25 The site of Moundville, Alabama, on the Black Warrior River. The center of the site is enclosed by a palisade and contains a number of large mounds arranged in a circular fashion.

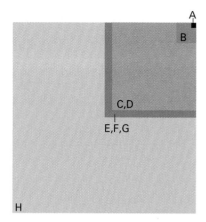

Fig. 14.26 A schematic view of the relative size of different groups of the burial population at Moundville. The letters correspond to Table 14.5. The small black square in the upper right corner represents the 7 individuals buried in the central mounds with copper axes and other wealth.

TABLE 14.5 Burials and grave goods at Moundville, Alabama.

Burial Group	Number of Individuals	%	Sex	Primary Grave Goods	Location of Burial
A	7	0.4	Male	Copper axes	Central mounds
B	110	5.6	Both	Copper ear spools, bear teeth, galena	Mounds, adjacent cemeteries
C	211	10.7	Both	Effigy vessels	Cemeteries
D	50	2.5	Both	Projectile points, discoids	Cemeteries
E	125	6.3	Unknown	Bowls and jars	Cemeteries and in village area
F	136	7.4	Both	Water bottles	Cemeteries and in village area
G	70	3.5	Male	Sherds	Village area
H	1256	63.6	Both	None	Retainers in mounds, isolated skulls, cemeteries, village area

surprising quantity of imported luxury goods, such as copper, mica, galena, and marine shell. Highly skilled craftspeople at Moundville produced pottery, stonework, and embossed copper artifacts, also found at the site.

Government-sponsored excavations in the 1930s, employing more than 100 workers during the Great Depression, uncovered more than 3000 burials in the mounds, under house floors, and in the general area of the town. This is a huge number of burials from an archaeological site. Mortuary analysis clearly reveals evidence of social inequality and ascribed status among the Moundville graves.

The burials were originally divided into eight groups, designated as A–H based on the location and content of the graves. Table 14.5 provides the number and percentage of burials in each group, the grave goods associated with the group, and the location of the burials in the group. The higher-status individuals belonged to groups A and B. A second group of middle- to high-status individuals composed C and D. The lower-status individuals at the site fall into groups E–H. Fig. 14.26 schematically shows the proportionate size of the respective groups.

The highest-status individuals in Group A, 7 in total, were always buried in or near the mounds with rare and valuable artifacts, including copper axes and pendants, and many shell beads, some covered with copper. These burials appear to have been all males and they were probably chiefs. Group B, a second set of elaborate burials (110 individuals, about 6% of the population), included both children and adults; these graves also were placed in or near the mounds. This group was interred with copper ear spools, stone disks, bear-tooth pendants, oblong copper **gorgets**, and decorated artifacts. Each mound also contained lower-status graves from Group H, often without any grave goods. These simple graves may have been those of servants or retainers sacrificed and buried to accompany the higher-status individuals.

Another group of high-status interments (about 13% of the population) included individuals of both sexes and all ages, buried in cemeteries near the mounds, accompanied by shell beads, oblong copper gorgets, and galena clubs (groups C and D). Since rare and exotic items were buried with individuals of both sexes and all ages, it appears that status at Moundville must have been ascribed rather than achieved.

The vast majority of the population (groups E, F, G, and H), ca. 81%, was buried in the residential areas of the town or in cemeteries, away from the central mound group. These male and female graves usually contained only a few sherds or one or two ceramic vessels, if anything. More mundane grave goods were distributed very

*And nothing can we call our own
but death,
And that small model of the barren
earth
Which serves as paste and cover to
our bones.
For God's sake, let us sit upon the
ground
And tell sad stories of the death
of kings.*
 —William Shakespeare, author

gorget Jewelry worn on the chest.

Moundville Archaeological Park

Today, Moundville is an archaeological preserve, part of the University of Alabama museums, and an important tourist attraction in west-central Alabama. The 300-acre park contains more than two dozen mounds, the Jones Archaeological Museum, and a boardwalk nature trail. The museum, opened in 1939, houses archaeological materials and interpretive exhibits with information on more than 60 years of archaeological investigations at the site. In addition, there is a reconstructed Indian Village and several pavilions in the park. The pavilions serve as outdoor classrooms and demonstration areas for Native American artists-in-residence. Every year in September, the Moundville Native American Festival is held on the grounds.

differently than the ornate items associated with high-status burials. In the lower-status graves, the distribution of goods corresponded more closely with differences in age and sex. Graves of older adults generally contained pottery vessels, bone awls, flint projectile points, and stone pipes. Such other items as deer bones, bird claws, and turtle bones were found exclusively with adults, while children and infants were sometimes accompanied by small vessels and clay toys. Stone ceremonial axes were found only with adult males, while **effigy** pottery vessels were associated with adults of both sexes. The different grave goods indicate that status for commoners was determined according to sex and age. While high or low status in general was a result of birth, ranking within each group seems to have depended partly on individual achievement or role.

CONCLUSIONS

There is a fascination with buried human skeletons that has little to do with the morbid. The fragile nature of our existence is nowhere more obvious than in the remains of the dead. Moreover, human skeletons hold an encyclopedia of information about the past. Graves and human burials are one of the richest sources of archaeological information. The contents are protected, the corpse and accompanying goods are placed intentionally and intact in the ground, conditions for preservation are improved.

Bioarchaeology is the study of human skeletal remains from archaeological contexts. It combines the anatomical investigation of the skeleton with the archaeological study of graves and their contents. Bioarchaeologists obtain information on the demography of past populations (such as age, sex, and stature), as well as their paleopathology (including stress, disease, trauma, violence, and occupation). Beyond the visible, anatomical characteristics of the skeleton, there are numerous chemical and molecular signals in the skeleton that can tell us about diet, migration, and genetic relationships. Bioarchaeology tells us, for example, that cannibalism was not unusual in many past times and places. The evidence from the U.S. Southwest and elsewhere is incontrovertible. Studies of stature from bioarchaeologists can tell us about a basic individual characteristic—height—but also much more about changes in nutrition, economic conditions, and climate over long periods of time.

Mortuary analysis is the study of the practices, rituals, and traditions of burial, the cultural aspects of funerary behavior. Scientists conducting mortuary analysis focus on the contents, architecture, and arrangement of graves and tombs. The burial practices of a society, as seen in cemeteries or sets of burials, can reveal a

effigy An object or construction in the shape of a plant, animal, or human figure.

great deal about values and ideals, about trade and exchange, and about social organization. Examples used in this chapter included a cemetery of village farmers at Nitra in Slovakia, where only older males were buried with axes and shell jewelry. Another example was the burial ground of Roy Mata in Melanesia, which vividly documents the authority of this individual in the accompanying sacrifices that were made of his relatives, retainers, and slaves. The final example of the multitude of graves from Moundville, Alabama, provides an unusual insight into social organization, in which a class-structured society allowed relatively few to exploit the labor of many.

It is also important to remember that disturbing the dead is a sacrilege to certain groups of people. Digging up ancestors may violate ethical concerns and/or legal statutes. In the United States, there are strict laws regarding the excavation of human remains, both recent and ancient. Since 1990, universities and museums have been required to return human skeletal remains to their descendants in an attempt to resolve the wanton excavation of graves in earlier times. These issues are discussed in more detail in Chapter 17, "Responsibilities."

MORTUARY ANALYSIS

The practice of human burial involves both biological and cultural remains that are intentionally placed together in the ground. Burials are a storehouse of information on human activity, organization, and belief. Because burial is intentional, artifacts are usually complete, not discarded when broken or exhausted, and skeletons are intact, not isolated single finds of bone. All aspects of burial information have potential meaning, and archaeologists are very careful in the excavation and recording of graves.

This problem in bioarchaeology involves a group of human burials found in graves, along with the objects and materials interred with them. Mortuary analysis of this evidence provides information on demography, health, activity, social organization, and other aspects of past human behavior. This exercise was developed by Paul Mullins of Indiana University–Purdue University Indianapolis and is used with his permission.

Discovery

A hypothetical Neolithic site somewhere in Eurasia contained at least fifty graves. As far as we can tell, the graves are roughly contemporary, within a 150-year span of time, dating to around 4000 BC. The graves do not appear to have been disturbed by later activities and the excavators believe they found most of the graves at the site. Archaeological analysis follows discovery and it is directed by the questions we are trying to answer. In this case of mortuary analysis, the research questions that define the problem can be listed. Read the description of the project completely before beginning your work.

1. What was the health status of the population?
2. How did people die?
3. What was the life expectancy?
4. Is there evidence for a sexual division of labor?
5. Were there status differences within this society?
6. If status did exist, was it achieved or ascribed, or both?
7. Is health status related to sex or social status?

Burial Data

The list of burials (Table 14.6) contains various kinds of information: burial number, the age and sex of each individual, the provenience of the grave (i.e., location), body posture (i.e., literally how the body was positioned in the grave), and grave goods (i.e., the things buried with the deceased).

Each burial number is a unique, sequential identifier assigned to an individual; the burial numbers were designated as the graves were found and should have no significance in your study except to distinguish the burials. Most of the graves contained a single interment. A few graves with multiple burials are noted parenthetically in the comments in the grave goods column in Table 14.6. For instance, Burial 16 (infant) was found with Burial 15, a 20–24-year-old adult female, and is denoted in the grave goods column as "(w/B15)."

Regarding gender, the table only contains information on adults because sex cannot be determined in the skeletons of infants and children. Sex information is coded as M for males, F for females, and U for unknown. Infants are designated as those less than 1 year old; children range in age from 1 to 14 years old.

TABLE 14.6 Burial data for project.

Burial	Sex	Age	Prov	Post	Pathology	Grave Goods
1	M	20–24	M	F		ChPt, ChKn
2	U	<1	C	E		2CoBr, AmBe, PaCAn, PaCPo
3	F	20–24	M	F		UnCAnFi
4	M	40–44	M	F	Dental decay	2 ChPt, ChKn
5	M	30–34	M	F		ChPt, 2ChKn
6	M	20–24	M	F		ChKn, ChNo
7	M	15–19	M	F	Arthritic big toe	ChPt
8	U	1–4	M	F		None
9	U	1–4	M	I		None
10	U	5–9	M	F	Enamel hypoplasia	UnCBifi
11	F	15–19	M	F		UnCBo
12	M	15–19	M	F	Enamel hypoplasia	ChPt, ChKn, UnCBo
13	F	35–39	C	E	Arthritic big toe, dental decay	CoBr, 12CoBe, AmPe, 3PaCBo, PaAnFi, BuBa (w/B20)
14	M	35–39	C	F		ChPt, ChKn, UnCbBo
15	F	20–24	C	E	Axe wound to skull	CoBr, 4CoBe, CoPe, 4PaCBo, AmFi (w/B16)
16	U	<1	C	E		CoBr, 6CoBe, PaCBo (w/B15)
17	F	15–19	M	F	Point in pelvis, no skull	UnCBiFi
18	U	1–4	M	F		None
19	F	20–24	M	F	Dental decay	UnCBo, BuWh
20	F	25–29	C	F		UnCJa
21	M	45–49	M	F	Axe wound to skull; parry fracture	ChKn, 3ChPt, UnCBo (w/B13)
22	M	50–54	M	E		2CoBr, CoPe, 3ObKn, 5PaCJa, BuWh (w/B27)
23	U	5–9	M	F		ChKn
24	U	1–4	M	I	Enamel hypoplasia	None
25	F	15–19	M	F	Harris lines	3UnCBe

Adults are defined as individuals older than 14, and specific age ranges are estimated for each adult burial. Age is reported in Table 14.6 in a range of years (e.g., 10–14) or as U (unknown).

The burials were discovered in one of two locations. A few individuals were found in a *cemetery,* a discrete location specifically for interment of the dead, while the majority of graves were in a *midden* (a refuse area or garbage dump) containing common household refuse as well as mortuary remains. Provenience is coded as M for midden and C for cemetery.

TABLE 14.6 (continued)

Burial	Sex	Age	Prov	Post	Pathology	Grave Goods
26	U	<1	M	I		None
27	U	<1	M	I		None (w/B21)
28	F	60+	M	F	Arthritic big toe	3UnCBo, ChKn, UnCBe, BuBa
29	F	30–34	M	F		GrSt, BuBa
30	M	25–29	M	E	Parry fracture	4ObBl, CoBr, CoNC, 2PaCJa, 2ObPt, ChPt (w/B49)
31	U	1–4	M	I		UnCBiFi
32	M	15–19	M	F	Dental decay	ChBl
33	F	40–44	M	F	Dental decay, Harris lines	2UnCBo, GrSt, BuBa
34	U	<1	M	F		None (w/B35)
35	U	<1	M	I		None (w/B34)
36	U	<1	M	I		None
37	U	<1	M	F		None
38	U	<1	M	I		None
39	F	25–29	M	F	Harris lines	None
40	F	15–19	C	F	Dental decay	CoPe
41	M	30–34	M	F	Axe wound to skull	ChPt, ChSi, UnCBo
42	M	25–29	M	F	Obsidian point in rib	None
43	U	5–9	C	E		3AmBe, AmBr, PaCBe, BuWh
44	U	10–14	C	E		2CoBr, 2ObKn, PaCBo, BuWh
45	U	<1	M	I		None
46	F	25–29	M	F	Arthritic big toe	UnCBo, BoSi
47	F	20–24	M	F		5UnCBe
48	U	1–4	M	F		None
49	M	60+	M	F	Dental decay	2ChBl, ObPt, UnCBo, UnCJa w/ BuBa (w/B30)
50	F	45–49	M	F	Arthritic big toe	2UnCPo, 8ShBe, ShPe, GrSt, BuBa

Body posture describes how individuals were placed in the grave, in an extended position (laid out flat), or flexed (either partially or fully curled with knees near or at the chest), or uncertain. Coding for burial posture is listed in the table as E for extended, F for flexed, and I for indeterminate.

Information on paleopathology observed on the skeletal remains is also recorded in the data table. A variety of conditions related to health, nutrition, activity, and trauma are reported though cause of death is only occasionally recorded in the skeleton and disease and age-related fatalities usually could not be determined. Traumatic injuries include axe blows to skull, points in bone, and parry fractures. Parry fractures are usually healed breaks in the ulna caused by a blow to the forearm raised in defense. Nutritional pathologies in the table data include tooth decay as a result of starchy foods in the diet, and Harris lines and enamel hypoplasia, which result from nutritional deficiencies or malnutrition. Arthritis also falls under the pathology category. Arthritis often is caused by heavy use of particular joints. In this table, arthritic big toes are recorded. Such toes have been observed in individuals spending long periods on their knees grinding grain, for example, at Abu Hureyra in Syria.

Grave goods are the material objects buried with the dead. In most egalitarian societies, lacking status differentiation, individuals are generally buried with similar graves and goods. Graves tend to be very simple and the contents are often utilitarian items if anything. In more hierarchical societies with various forms of social inequality, position and status in life are sometimes reflected by the grave and its contents. Mortuary goods were frequently used to symbolize the activities the deceased performed in life. In some prehistoric societies, for example, the deceased might be buried with medicine bundles that reflected their role as a **shaman**, or curer, in life; a craftsperson might be buried with the products of his or her work. Small symbols used in burial ritual or public display are often intended to convey a much larger set of associated concepts known to the members of the society. For example, in our own society largely useless or wasteful status symbols like Hummer SUVs can convey a great deal of information about their owners. Rare or valuable goods are not buried by accident with a human body; scarce objects reflect an intentional statement about the deceased's role in that society.

In more hierarchical societies, positions of power are determined by lineage and inheritance, so there are some children born to positions of ascribed status. This status may be displayed in the grave if these individuals die during infancy or childhood. In a society with achieved status, infants would not typically merit lavish burial rituals.

There are five kinds of grave goods in the cemetery data in Table 14.6. The first is several types of *nonlocal stones*—obsidian, amber, and copper—that were rare and could be acquired only through long-distance trade. The second grave good is a local stone, *chert*, which could be quarried nearby and was available to all members of the group. The stone tools made from both exotic and local materials include "knives," a multipurpose cutting tool; "points," archaeological shorthand for projectile points used in hunting and warfare; "sickles," blade tools designed for cutting vegetation; and "grinding stones," which are used in the preparation of grains such as barley and wheat. The third grave good category is *undecorated ceramics*, which were produced by local craftspeople and were relatively common. The fourth type of grave good is *painted ceramics*, which were more costly to produce and less common than the undecorated wares. Both painted and unpainted ceramics are found as "bowls" (primarily associated with food preparation), "jars" (primarily associated with storage), "decorative figurines," and "beads." A few burials also contain some plant or animal remains, such as barley seeds or pig bones.

The information on grave goods is coded in the following way: Am = amber, An = animal, Ba = barley, Be = bead, Bi = bird, Bl = blade, Bo = bowl, Br = bracelet, Bu = burned, C = ceramic, Ch = chert, Co = copper, Fi = figurine, Gr = grinding, Ja = jar, Kn = knife, NC = neck collar, No = nodule, Ob = obsidian, Pa = painted, Pe = pendant, Po = pot, Pt = point, Sh = shell, Si = sickle, St = stone,

shaman Specialist in ritual and healing, seers of the future in *hunter-gatherer* and *subsistence* farming societies.

Un = unpainted, Wh = wheat. The presence of more than one object is indicated by the number in front of the code.

Analysis

There are several ways to approach this problem. Keep in mind the questions that are being asked about status and activity differences among age groups and between sexes. Information on a number of different variables (age, sex, posture, provenience, grave goods) is provided. Your job is to find patterns or relationships among these variables that may answer the questions. This takes some time, thought, and effort.

It's a lot of information, both visual and numerical. It would be a good idea to try to condense this information in various ways to make it easier to find patterns. You could change the counts of some of the categories into percentages. Take the number of individuals in each category and divide by the total in all categories. For example, if there are fourteen males, sixteen females, ten children, and ten infants, the percentage of children is $10/50 = 20\%$. You could also use tally charts or bar graphs to indicate the relative amount of each category. For example, Fig. 14.27 shows a simple tally chart for men, women, children, and infants.

It will also be useful to know more about the different kinds of grave goods. Were some of these items highly valued? You might want to tabulate how rare or common the various grave goods were to get a sense of how important they might have been in this society. Again, a tally chart might provide some information. You may also want to group some kinds of grave goods together to see if a pattern emerges (for example, wealth vs. nonwealth, or food preparation vs. nonfood preparation).

To find relationships between the different variables, you need to look at co-occurrence (items found together frequently or rarely). A contingency table is a useful tool for cross-tabulating information such as this burial data. Set up the table with the variables of interest (for example, sex and provenience) and then count the cases where the categories of sex are found in different proveniences (shown in Fig. 14.28). These contingency tables can be constructed for any between-variable pairs. You can also calculate percentages in the table boxes by dividing the tallied number by the row or column total.

	Female	ǀᕼᕼ ǀᕼᕼ ǀᕼᕼ ǀ
	Male	ǀᕼᕼ ǀᕼᕼ ǀǀǀǀ
	Child	ǀᕼᕼ ǀᕼᕼ
	Infant	ǀᕼᕼ ǀᕼᕼ

Fig. 14.27 Example of a tally chart.

Sex

Location		Male	Female	Sum
	Cemetery	ǀǀǀǀ 4 (13.3%)	ǀ 1 (3.3%)	5 (16.7%)
	Midden	ǀᕼᕼ ǀᕼᕼ ǀǀ 12 (40%)	ǀᕼᕼ ǀᕼᕼ ǀǀǀ 13 (43.3%)	25 (83.3%)
	Sum	16 (53.3%)	14 (46.7%)	30 (100%)

Fig. 14.28 Example of a contingency table.

Interpretation

Now the analysis is done and it's time for some interpretation. What are your ideas about the information and patterns you have found in the data? Can you provide answers to the research questions that initiated this project? Please answer each of the following questions with a one-paragraph response. Be as specific as possible and provide examples to bolster your argument.

1. What was the health status of the population? What kinds of nutritional or disease indicators appear in the skeletal remains? What is the proportion of individuals with paleopathologies? Is this a normal population?

2. What were causes of death? How did people die? How many individuals exhibit probable-cause-of-death evidence? Was disease a problem in this region?

3. What was the life expectancy for adults? For males? For females? How did you calculate these values? Do these numbers seem comparable to other societies? If there are differences between males and females, what is responsible?

4. Is there evidence for a sexual division of labor? Did males and females undertake the same activities? Were children involved in labor? What kinds of activities are represented in the skeletal remains?

5. Were there status differences within this society? What kinds of evidence provide information on status differences? Is the location of burial (provenience) related to status? How confident are you in your answer to this question?

6. If status did exist, was it achieved or ascribed, or both? What is the evidence to support your answer?

7. Is health related to sex or social status? What are some of the patterns or associations you noted?

8. Do you have any particular observations or comments you would like to add that did not appear in your previous responses?

STUDY QUESTIONS

1. What are the primary criteria for determining the age of a skeleton?

2. There is significant debate about the prevalence of cannibalism in the human past. What is your opinion and why?

3. What kinds of evidence provide information on paleopathologies?

4. Ancient DNA is a promising new technology for studying human genetic relationships in the past. How does it work and what are some of the problems?

5. Mortuary analysis combines the study of human skeletal remains and the cultural practices associated with burial. What kinds of information can be obtained in such studies?

www.mhhe.com/pricearch1

For more review material and study questions, please see the self-quizzes on your online learning center.

REFERENCES

Aufderheide, A. C. 2003. *The Scientific Study of Mummies.* Cambridge: Cambridge University Press.

Bahn, Paul G., ed. 2003. *Written in Bones: How Human Remains Unlock the Secrets of the Dead.* Richmond Hill, Ontario: Firefly Books.

Grauer, Anne L., ed. 1995. *Bodies of Evidence: Reconstructing History through Skeletal Analysis.* New York: Wiley.

Katzenberg, M. A., and R. G. Harrison. 1997. What's in a bone? Recent advances in archaeological bone chemistry. *Journal of Archaeological Research* 5:265–293.

Larsen, C. S. 2000. *Skeletons in Our Closet: Revealing Our Past through Bioarchaeology.* Princeton: Princeton University Press.

White, Tim D., and Pieter A. Folkens. 2000. *Human Osteology.* 2d ed. Orlando: Academic Press.

Wilkinson, Caroline. 2004. *Forensic Facial Reconstruction.* Cambridge: Cambridge University Press.

www.mhhe.com/pricearch1

For Internet references related to this chapter, please see the chapter links on your online learning center.

Archaeometry

INTRODUCTION: ARCHAEOLOGY IN THE LABORATORY

A *kouros* (Greek: youth) is a stone statue of a nude, muscular young male, carved during the classic period of Greek civilization between the sixth and third centuries BC. A *kouros* (*KURH-oss*) was an artistic manifestation of the Greek worldview that emphasized youth and male beauty. The poet Simonides may have been referring to a *kouros* in the late sixth century BC when he wrote, "In hand and foot and mind alike foursquare/fashioned without flaw."

The statue in the photo is 2.25 m (6 ft 9 in) in height and has several characteristic features. The hands are balled into fists and are held along the body; the hair is arranged in a regular grid of vertical and horizontal lines; and the feet are placed with the left foot forward. Its face and those of other *kouroi* like it are very distinctive and appear to depict individuals in lifelike portraits, not as a generic human. The eyes are wide open and the mouth is formed in a serene, closed-lip smile. Such statues have been variously identified as gods, warriors, or victorious athletes. There exist only a dozen examples of these figures in good condition. When the opportunity to obtain such a piece came to the J. Paul Getty Museum in California in the late 1980s, excitement was high.

The statue was accompanied by documents that indicated its origin and authenticity. The museum checked with the governments of Greece and Italy to be sure that the statue had been legally obtained. The Getty also requested samples of stone from the statue for analysis. Preliminary studies pointed to the island of Thasos (*THOSS-os*), an ancient quarry site, as the source of the marble. Moreover, the surface chemistry of the stone revealed a calcite crust that was thought to require a long period of time to form.

The Getty then purchased the *kouros* for approximately $8,000,000 and put it on display while experts—art historians, conservators, archaeologists, and archaeometrists—studied the piece. Opinions regarding its authenticity were divided. Why was it in such good condition and why so white? Also, experts noted that the styles used to depict the hair and feet were different: The wiglike hair is normally found around 600 BC, while the arrangement of the feet should date to 525 BC. Would an ancient sculptor combine several styles in a single piece? Was the quarry at Thasos in operation when this statue was purported to have been made?

The debate regarding the statue intensified when in the early 1990s evidence came forth indicating that the authenticating documents were forgeries. Moreover, a clearly fake marble torso very similar to the Getty *kouros* was found. New

kouros   Ancient stone statue of a nude Greek youth.

www.mhhe.com/pricearch1

For preview material for this chapter, please see the chapter summary, outline, and objectives on your online learning center.

www.mhhe.com/pricearch1

For a Web-based activity on the site of the Getty kouros, please see the Internet exercises on your online learning center.

archaeometry   The measurement of the chemical or physical properties of an artifact in order to solve problems of chemical composition, *technology, chronology,* etc. Sometimes described as "instrumental" archaeology.

molecular archaeology   Sometimes used to refer to the organic component of archaeological chemistry and particularly to the investigation of ancient DNA in plant and animal remains, including humans. Sometimes called biomolecular archaeology.

archaeological science   A generic term that includes noninstrumental areas such as faunal analysis, *paleoethnobotany,* and *human osteology.*

archaeological chemistry   A part of archaeometry, the investigation of inorganic and organic composition, *elements* and *isotopes, molecules* and *compounds* in archaeological materials.

neutron   Particle in the core of an atom with no electrical charge; part of the nucleus of an atom.

proton   Particle in the core of an atom with a positive electrical charge.

element   Building blocks of matter, different atoms by weight.

atomic number   The number of protons in the nucleus of an atom.

isotopes   Slightly different atoms of the same element with the same *atomic number,* but different numbers of neutrons.

ion   Electrically charged atoms that have lost or gained electrons.

molecule   A combination of atoms held together by chemical bonds.

compounds   Combinations of elements in either organic or inorganic molecules in nature.

tests were then done on the museum piece as well as the forged torso. The torso was shown to have been treated in an acid bath to simulate aging. Furthermore, the Getty *kouros* and the torso had different surfaces. Analysis revealed that the surface of the Getty *kouros* was a complex compound (calcium oxalate monohydrate), not a simple calcite (calcium carbonate), with characteristics that could not be duplicated in the laboratory.

The story of the Getty *kouros* is a classic example of archaeometry in action, where art and science meet. There is no doubt that the Getty statue is a *kouros.* To most viewers, it is beautiful, it is art. The question is whether it is ancient art or a more recent forgery. While most art historians and archaeologists believe the statue is a fake, the scientists involved believe it to be authentic. The status of the Getty *kouros* remains a mystery. The information plaque with the statue at the museum today reads "Greek, 530 BC or modern forgery." The story of the *kouros* also raises an important issue of ethics in archaeology. Should museums purchase artifacts and monuments that are part of the heritage of other nations or peoples? This question of who owns the past is addressed further in Chapter 17, "Responsibilities."

This chapter is an introduction to **archaeometry,** the application of chemical and physical methods to the study of archaeological materials. This is hard science in archaeology. In addition to marble statues, archaeometrists study a wide variety of materials, including ceramics, bone, lithics, soils, dyes, and organic residues. Some of the methods and techniques for these studies are described in the following pages.

Archaeologists are often found in the laboratory. There are laboratories for studying faunal remains, laboratories for archaeobotany, laboratories for spreading out artifacts for analysis. There are also laboratories where archaeologists and physical scientists investigate the chemical properties of remains from the past. These are wet labs with chemical hoods and a variety of scientific instrumentation. The science of archaeology in these technical laboratories is called archaeometry. There are several other terms for this kind of archaeology as well.

Archaeometry technically includes dating methods, remote sensing, and ancient DNA but these fields tend to pursue a separate identity. Physicists are usually responsible for dating laboratories and geneticists are the experts on DNA. The phrase **molecular archaeology** is sometimes used to refer to the organic component of archaeological chemistry and particularly to the investigation of ancient DNA in plant and animal remains, including humans. **Archaeological Science** is a more general term that includes non-instrumental areas such as faunal analysis, paleoethnobotany, and human osteology. **Archaeological chemistry,** a part of archaeometry, involves the investigation of the inorganic and organic composition—elements and isotopes, molecules and compounds—of archaeological materials.

All matter is composed of atoms. Atoms have three major components: neutrons, protons, and electrons. **Neutrons** and **protons** make up the core of an atom and have about the same weight. Neutrons have no electrical charge, and protons have a positive charge. Electrons spin around the core of neutrons and protons with a negative electrical charge and a very small mass. Atoms vary in the number of protons and neutrons they contain, so they also vary in weight. These different weights make up the ninety-two chemical **elements** in nature.

The **atomic number** of an element reflects the number of protons in the atom's nucleus. **Isotopes** are slightly different atoms of the same element. They all have the same atomic number, but different numbers of neutrons. **Ions** are electrically charged atoms that have lost or gained electrons.

Every substance on earth is made up of combinations of some of these ninety-two elements. A **molecule** is a combination of atoms held together by bonds (e.g., the water molecule is H_2O—two atoms of hydrogen bound to one atom of oxygen). **Compounds** are combinations of elements in either organic or inorganic materials in nature. **Organic compounds** make up the tissues of living organisms and have the element carbon as a base. **Inorganic compounds** do not normally contain carbon.

Archaeometry is primarily concerned with (1) identification—determining the original material of an unknown item, (2) authentication—verifying the antiquity of an item, often associated with works of art, and (3) characterization—measuring the chemical composition of a variety of prehistoric materials. Much of archaeometric research involves elemental and isotopic analyses of inorganic materials or compound identification in the case of organic specimens. Through such research we can learn about subsistence and diet, exchange and trade, residence, demography, status, and many other aspects of prehistoric human behavior and organization. As with other areas of archaeological study, the goal of archaeometry is to learn more about the human past.

Archaeometry is still a young field—although one with a significant history. Early studies focused on one or a few elements to resolve problems of chronology, authenticity, or source characterization. One of the early and most famous examples involved the Piltdown discovery in England in the early part of the twentieth century, described in Chapter 1. A human skull and ape jaw were made to appear ancient and passed to experts as the "missing link" between apes and humans. It took almost 40 years for new techniques to expose the deceit. Kenneth Oakley (1911–1981) and his colleagues at the British Museum of Natural History reanalyzed the Piltdown materials in the late 1940s. They used a new **fluorine absorption** test and measured concentrations of flourine as well as iron, nitrogen, collagen, organic carbon, organic water, radioactivity, and crystal structure in the samples.

The level of fluorine absorption in a bone sample can provide a kind of relative age for the sample. Teeth and bones absorb fluorine from groundwater during burial. The fluorine reacts with phosphate **hydroxyapatite** (*HI-drock-see-AP-a-tite*) (the mineral component of teeth and bones) to form fluorapatite. The rate of this reaction varies over time, depending on local conditions of burial. Thus, the amount of fluorine present in the fossils from the same locality should be the same if they were deposited at the same time. Oakley's work showed different levels of fluorine in the skull and jaw from Piltdown man. They published their results in 1953 and Piltdown was finally removed from the list of our ancestors. Later radiocarbon determinations indicated that the skull was medieval and the jaw fragment, identified as belonging to an orangutan, was approximately 500 years old.

Over the last 50 years, a multitude of new ideas, instruments, and procedures have been added to the tool chest of what is now called archaeometry. Part of this expansion comes from the evolution of both methodology and instrumentation in quantitative chemistry, which has permitted more detailed descriptions of the composition of a variety of materials, including the geological, biological, and archaeological. Today, a number of innovative approaches and techniques provide exciting new information about the past.

This chapter is an introduction to archaeometry and offers some information on instrumentation and laboratories, the questions asked in archaeometry, and examples of interesting studies. A description of major types of instruments is followed by a profile of the Laboratory for Archaeological Chemistry as an example of an archaeometric facility. Various aspects of archaeometry are then described in sections on elemental analyses, isotopic analyses, and organic analyses. Several examples are included. Obsidian sourcing in the Near East and soil chemistry in Maya Honduras provide case studies using elemental analyses. Isotopic studies are documented by examples of the diets of early Greenlanders and the birthplace of a Maya king. Various kinds of residues are the focus of most organic chemistry in archaeometry, and a discussion of them concludes the chapter text.

The fluorine content of every available bone and tooth from Piltdown has now been tested by Dr. C. R. Hoskins in the Government Laboratory. All those of undoubted Lower Pleistocene (Villafranchian) age proved to contain 2–3 per cent fluorine, while all those which are certainly of later date showed less than 1.6 per cent fluorine. The Eoanthropus material [Piltdown], including all the cranial fragments, the mandible, the isolated canine tooth, and the remains of the second [344] skull found 2 miles away, showed extremely little fluorine (average 0.2 per cent).

—Kenneth Oakley, archaeologist

organic compounds The molecules of living organisms with the element carbon as a base.

inorganic compounds Molecules that do contain carbon.

fluorine absorption An archaeometric test for *relative dating* based on the assumption that fluorine accumulates at a constant rate in buried bone.

hydroxyapatite The mineral component of bone.

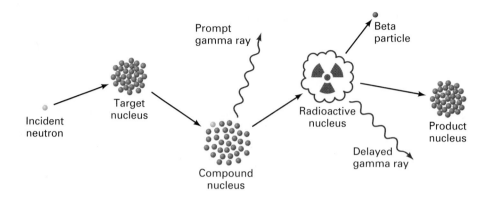

Fig. 15.1 The reaction involved in neutron activation. The neutron is captured by the target nucleus and prompt gamma rays are released, making the nucleus radioactive. The radioactive nucleus decays by emitting a beta particle and delayed gamma rays at a rate determined in part by the half-life. The delayed gamma rays are detected and the number counted is proportional to the concentration of the element present in the sample.

INSTRUMENTATION

Archaeometry laboratories utilize a wide range of instruments and equipment. Four commonly used instruments are described in this chapter, each based on different principles: **neutron activation analysis** (NAA), **inductively coupled plasma-mass spectrometer** (ICP-MS), **X-ray diffraction** (XRD), and **gas chromatograph-mass spectrometer** (GC-MS). Another instrument used in archaeometry, the scanning electron microscope (SEM), is discussed in Chapter 13. These instruments examine and measure the composition of various materials. Each technique has advantages and disadvantages, and they are described below.

Important concerns in instrumental analysis are the condition of the sample, the requirements for preparation of the sample, and whether the technique of analysis is destructive or nondestructive. Rare or valuable artifacts and materials should not be damaged by analytical methods, but many instruments analyze samples in the form of a powder or liquid, which means destroying the intact form of the sample. For example, sample preparation involves powders for NAA and XRD, liquids or solids for ICP-MS, and gas for GC-MS. Only certain instruments with larger sample chambers can perform nondestructive analyses.

Neutron Activation Analysis (NAA)

Neutron activation analysis is an instrumental method for measuring elemental concentrations in a wide variety of samples. The technique determines many elements simultaneously. Ceramics and various kinds of stone are common archaeological materials analyzed using NAA. Once a sample is powdered, it is exposed to a burst of neutrons that causes many elements to become temporarily radioactive. These radioactive elements decay into stable ones by giving off gamma rays. The NAA instrument measures these gamma rays that have energy levels specific to different elements. The energy and intensity of the emissions provides the identity of the element and the amount present.

The most common type of nuclear reaction used for NAA is shown in Fig. 15.1. About 70% of the elements have properties suitable for measurement by NAA. Normally about thirty-five elements are measured quantitatively in 5 to 100 mg samples of archaeological and geological materials. The lower limit of detection is on the order of parts per million or parts per billion depending on the element.

A source of neutrons, instrumentation for detecting gamma rays, and information about the reactions that occur when neutrons interact with nuclei are the basic requirements for NAA. Although there are several possible sources for neutrons (reactors, accelerators, and radioisotope neutron emitters), nuclear reactors with high fluxes of neutrons from uranium fission offer the best sensitivities for most elements. For this reason, facilities for NAA are somewhat limited in number and accessibility. In addition, problems with waste disposal have led to the closing of some research reactors.

neutron activation analysis (NAA) *Archaeometric* technique using *neutron* bombardment to release detectable element-specific gamma rays in samples.

inductively coupled plasma-mass spectrometry (ICP-MS) *Archaeometric* technique in which samples introduced to a plasma source are ionized and elemental mass and concentration are measured.

X-ray diffraction (XRD) Archaeometric method for measuring mineral and elemental composition of most solids using distinctive patterns of X-ray scattering.

gas chromatography-mass spectrometry (GC-MS) *Archaeometric* technique for organic materials in which samples in gas state separate in a column and exit sequentially to a detector that produces a spectrum of the weight and amount of the molecules.

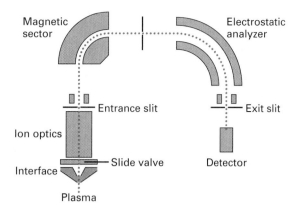

Fig. 15.2 Basic components of ICP-MS. Samples are ionized in the plasma and moved through an entrance slit and toward the detector by a magnetic field that separates the atoms by weight. The detector counts the atoms of different weights that arrive.

Fig. 15.3 The ICP-MS in the Laboratory for Archaeological Chemistry, University of Wisconsin-Madison.

Inductively Coupled Plasma-Mass Spectrometry (ICP-MS)

ICP-MS is a widely used technology that employs a superheated **plasma** source to generate ions and a **mass spectrometer** to determine the mass of the ions that are carried to the target (Fig. 15.2). The combination provides an efficient and general-purpose instrument for the analysis of a wide variety of materials. ICP-MS is a standard technique for the measurement of trace elements, recording elemental concentrations to ppb (parts per billion). The method is destructive, but almost anything that can be put into solution can be analyzed by ICP-MS. The addition of a laser as an ion source allows the analysis of solids.

A wide range of archaeological materials have been analyzed by ICP-MS including bone, ceramics, stone, metals, and glass. In a typical application, samples are placed in solution by digestion in acid. The solution is sprayed into a flowing stream of inert argon gas and carried to a torch that is heated to 6000°C, the temperature of the surface of the sun. In this plasma, the gas and sample are ionized to their atomic constituents. In the ICP-MS instrument, positive ions in the plasma are magnetically focused through a mass spectrometer to a collector that records their mass. The amount of most elements present in the original material can be measured in just seconds, even at low concentrations (Fig. 15.3).

plasma   The gaseous state of hot ionized material consisting of *ions* and electrons used as a source for ions in spectrometry.

mass spectrometer   Any analytical instrument that records components of a spectrum by weight.

X-ray Diffraction (XRD)

X-ray diffraction is an important technique used to obtain structural and compositional information from **crystalline** materials (Fig. 15.4). Solid matter can be distinguished as either amorphous, with the atoms arranged in a random way (e.g., glass), or crystalline, where the atoms are arranged in a regular pattern. About 95% of all solids are crystalline. In archaeology, XRD has been used largely for ceramics, rock, and sediment samples to identify the mineral constituents.

When X-rays are directed at crystalline materials, they are scattered in a systematic pattern by the regular arrangement of the atoms in the material (Fig. 15.5). Different kinds of material with different arrangements of atoms produce distinctive scatter, or **diffraction**, patterns. XRD directs an X-ray source at a powdered

Fig. 15.4 The instrument for X-ray diffraction analysis. This equipment contains the sample tray and the X-ray generator and is connected to a computer for operation and calculations.

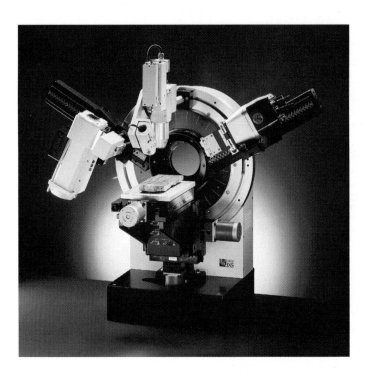

Fig. 15.5 The diffractometer beam path and detector.

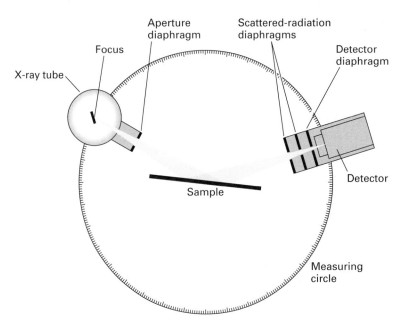

crystalline Materials with atoms arranged in a regular geometric pattern, used in *XRD* analysis.

diffraction Principle of X-rays being scattered when striking a crystal, used in X-ray diffraction analyses.

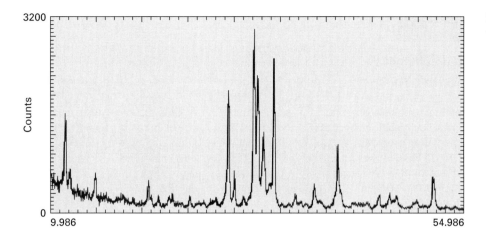

Fig. 15.6 A graph of peak intensities produced by XRD analysis.

sample and measures the pattern of diffraction that results. That pattern is compared to a large database of patterns from known materials to identify the sample. XRD can be applied to determine the crystal structures of metals and alloys, minerals, inorganic compounds, polymers and organic materials, as well as to obtain information such as crystal size and orientation and chemical composition.

The results of XRD analysis are displayed in a plot of peak intensities (Fig. 15.6). The peaks identify the scatter of the diffraction pattern while the height of the peaks reveals the concentration of the material present. One of the advantages of XRD is that portable instruments are now available, making studies possible in museums and the field.

Gas Chromatography-Mass Spectrometry

The use of a gas chromatograph-mass spectrometer (GC-MS) instrument has become standard practice in the analysis of organic compounds (Fig. 15.7). The gas chromatograph separates the hundreds of molecules present in a gaseous form of the sample in a long column containing a solid that slows some of the gas molecules more than others. The molecules then exit sequentially from the chromatograph and pass into a mass spectrometer with a detector that registers a peak for each type of molecule. The GC-MS produces a spectrum of the weight and amount of the various molecules present. These spectra are compared with known materials in order to make identifications.

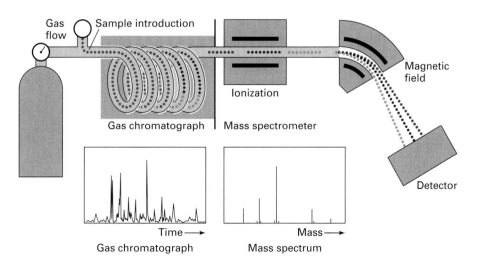

Fig. 15.7 A gas chromatograph-mass spectrometer (GC-MS), basic components and output. Sample is converted to gas and introduced into a gas chromatograph, which separates molecules by weight. Molecules are ionized and sent through a magnetic field to separate them by weight, which is measured by a detector. Output graphs below show the results of the gas chromatography and the mass spectrometry.

The Laboratory for Archaeological Chemistry

The Laboratory for Archaeological Chemistry at the University of Wisconsin-Madison, founded in 1987, is a center for research and training in the chemical analysis of archaeological materials, one of very few such facilities in the United States. Dedicated instrumentation provides the focus of analytical procedures, involving the elemental and isotopic characterization of prehistoric materials.

The Laboratory for Archaeological Chemistry occupies several rooms in the Department of Anthropology. There are two large rooms for research: a **wet lab** for sample preparation and an analytical lab housing instrumentation. The sample preparation area is dedicated to processing samples and includes a **fume hood**, furnaces, a system for deionized water, balances for delicate weighing, drills and grinding equipment, and necessary glassware and chemical supplies.

The primary instruments in the lab are two inductively-coupled plasma (ICP) spectrometers. The older instrument is an atomic emission spectrometer (ICP-AES) capable of quantitatively analyzing approximately six dozen elements at parts-per-million levels. Since beginning operation, more than 30,000 archaeological samples have been analyzed on this equipment. The newer instrument is a high-resolution, magnetic sector, ICP-mass spectrometer (ICP-MS) for elemental and isotopic analysis of liquid samples to the parts-per-billion level (Fig. 15.3).

The laboratory has two full-time staff members and employs several graduate and undergraduate students as laboratory assistants (Fig. 15.8). Funding for the lab comes largely from the National Science Foundation and the University of Wisconsin-Madison. Students are constantly in and out of the lab as their own research often involves the facilities and expertise of the staff. The laboratory is also a center of training in archaeometric research, and students and professionals from other universities around the world spend weeks and months in the lab learning theory and methods. The staff also regularly teaches a lecture and lab course on archaeological chemistry.

Fig. 15.8 Kelly Knudson preparing enamel samples in the Laboratory for Archaeological Chemistry.

Research in the laboratory usually involves the study of the composition and source of different kinds of materials to answer archaeological questions about past human behavior. Research methods involve the trace element and isotopic analyses of bones, ceramics, and sediments and have expanded to include lithics, pigments, and other materials. Research questions include past diet, human migration, raw material sources, interaction and trade, and the identification of activity areas on prehistoric living floors. The Laboratory for Archaeological Chemistry has active research projects on five continents. Collaborative projects have included bone assemblages from Ireland, ores and gemstones from South Asia, soils from Alaska, and reindeer antler from Germany. Collaborative activities include projects in Peru, Ecuador, central Europe, Iceland, India, the Yucatán, Oaxaca, and Veracruz in Mexico, Europe, Turkey, and the United States.

Major discoveries in archaeology in the coming years will be made more often in the laboratory than in the field.
—T. Douglas Price, archaeologist

wet lab   A chemistry facility with lab tables, equipment, and running water.

fume hood   A ventilation system for removal of toxic gas in a chemistry lab.

ELEMENTAL ANALYSES

Elemental analysis is a major part of archaeometric research and is used for a variety of studies, including authentication and characterization. The elemental composition of a material is often a specific signature that can be repeatedly recognized. Thus, the elemental composition of archaeological items has been used for years as a tool to determine provenience. A variety of materials have been studied in terms of their elemental composition. Stone, metal, ceramics, and sediments are some of the more common materials. Lithic, ceramic, and anthropogenic sediments studies are described below.

Lithic Analysis

The geological sources of a variety of materials (lead, silver, obsidian, copper) have distinctive elemental signatures. Finds of these materials at sites some distance from their sources provide a means for examining trade and interaction among early peoples if the sources can be determined. An example of such a study involves obsidian sources and trade in the ancient Near East.

 EXAMPLE ~~~~~~

OBSIDIAN SOURCES AND TRADE IN THE ANCIENT NEAR EAST

Obsidian is a translucent, hard, black or dark green glass, produced during volcanic eruptions. Molten **silica** sometimes flows out of a volcanic core and hardens into this material, which was highly sought by prehistoric makers of stone tools. Obsidian, like glass and flint, fractures easily and regularly, creating very sharp edges (Fig. 15.9).

In the past, obsidian was often traded or exchanged over long distances, hundreds of kilometers or more. It is available from only a few sources, limited by proximity to volcanic terrain and the chance formation of a silica flow. Most volcanic sources for obsidian are known because they are rare and the material is unusual.

It is possible to fingerprint different flows of obsidian through minor differences in the chemical composition of the material, allowing pieces found elsewhere to be traced to the places where they originated. This procedure relies on what is known as the **provenience postulate**—chemical differences within a single source of material must be less than the differences between two or more sources of the material. In principle, this means that if a source is chemically distinct, pieces removed some distance from their source share that same chemistry and can be identified. That is to say, the **provenience**, or place of origin, of the piece can be determined. The provenience postulate must be true for the study of sources of raw materials. This principle has been applied to a variety of archaeological materials, including obsidian, pottery, turquoise, tin, and many others. The chemical composition of some materials, such as chert in North America, varies greatly within a single source and different sources cannot be distinguished. Chert, and other materials that don't comply to the provenience postulate, cannot be used for studies of place of origin.

Neutron activation analysis (NAA) is commonly used in studies of obsidian. The sources of obsidian in Southwest Asia, the Mediterranean, North America, Mexico, and elsewhere have been examined using NAA. Most of the obsidian in Southwest Asia comes from sources or outcrops either in the mountains of Turkey or in northern Iran, both outside the Fertile Crescent. The graph below shows the results of the NAA measurement of the elements iron (Fe) and scandium (Sc) in obsidian in Southwest Asia (Fig. 15.10). Samples were also taken from the original outcrops. There are clear differences among most of the sources.

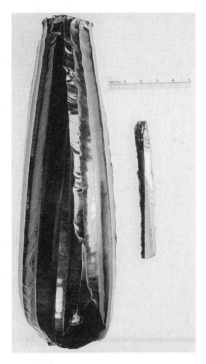

Fig. 15.9 An obsidian core and blade. This glasslike stone produces very sharp edges and was a highly desired raw material in prehistory.

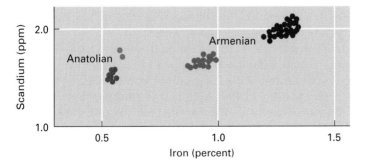

Fig. 15.10 Elemental characterization of obsidian sources in Armenia and Anatolia, Turkey. The graph plots the percent of iron vs. the parts per million (ppm) of scandium to show how the amounts of these two elements distinguish the sources of obsidian.

~~~~~~

obsidian A glassy rock produced from sand in volcanic conditions, used for making stone *tools* in the past.

silica The mineral component of sand.

provenience postulate States that if differences within a source of material are less than differences with other sources, then it is possible to distinguish individual sources, or *provenience*.

provenience The place of discovery or origin. Where an item is from (a.k.a. provenance in *classical archaeology*).

Fig. 15.11 The location of obsidian sources and samples in the early Neolithic of Southwest Asia. Two major sources are shown in Anatolia and two in Armenia. The distribution of obsidian from these sources is seen at settlements across the area. The distributions are largely separate with the exception of one site where obsidian from both source areas is found. Note also the Anatolian obsidian found on the island of Cyprus.

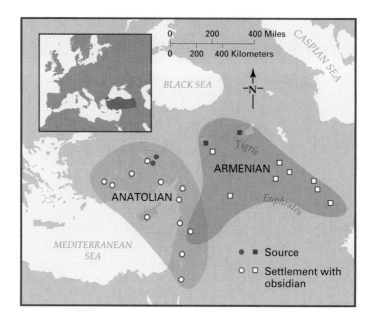

The identity of the sources of obsidian found at early Neolithic sites provides information on both the direction and intensity of trade (Fig. 15.11). Sites along the Mediterranean coast generally obtained obsidian from Anatolia, while sites in the eastern part of the region used the Armenian material. The percentage of obsidian in the total flaked stone assemblage at these sites indicates that places closest to the sources used a great deal of obsidian, while those farthest away had only a small amount available. At the site of Jericho, for example, 700 km (400 mi) from the Turkish sources, only about 1% of the stone tools were made from obsidian.

Ceramic Analysis

In addition to obsidian and other stones, a wide variety of archaeological materials are subjected to elemental analyses, including ceramics, metals, bone, and many more. Ceramic analysis often involves elemental characterization to examine the composition and potential sources of raw material for the pottery. NAA or ICP spectrometry is normally used for such analysis. The chemical characterization of ceramic composition provides information on manufacturing locations, trade and exchange, and more general economic patterns. A variety of major, minor, and trace elements have been investigated in ceramic compositional studies. The specific elements of interest have depended largely upon local geochemistry, manufacturing techniques, and/or available instruments.

A simple example can provide an introduction to ceramic analysis in archaeometry. In order to evaluate the utility of elemental analyses for the study of variation in ceramics, James Burton of the Laboratory for Archaeological Chemistry undertook an experiment using modern pottery from three Mexican villages. Each village used different sources of clay for raw material and different recipes for their paste. Potsherds were obtained from each village and analyzed by ICP spectrometer. A plot of several elements in the pottery, combined using a statistical technique known as **discriminant analysis**, produced results which almost exactly matched the three sets of modern pottery made in the three different villages (Fig. 15.12)—the chemistry mimicked human behavior. Such results

discriminant analysis Statistical technique for classifying a set of observations into predefined classes based on new measurement.

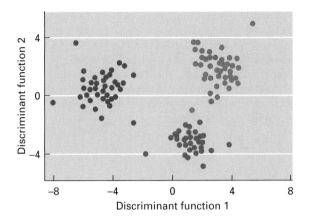

Fig. 15.12 Plot of two discriminant functions (a statistical summary of several different elements) that separate the modern pottery from Mexico into three distinct groups belonging to the three different potters.

convey confidence in elemental studies of prehistoric ceramics. Another ceramic provenience study can be found in Chapter 11 in the example involving the Salado polychromes.

Anthropogenic Sediments

The analysis of **anthropogenic** sediments is potentially one of the more informative aspects of archaeological chemistry. The basic principles of such studies are related to the fact that different human activities in the past involved different kinds of materials. The decomposition of those materials at archaeological sites should leave chemical traces in the sediments. These traces remain in the soil for long periods of time, depending on circumstances of deposition and conditions of preservation.

A variety of elements in sediments (phosphorus, calcium, potassium, iron, magnesium, copper, and zinc) have potential significance as indicators of human activity. Soils from prehistoric occupations may contain information on site extent, boundaries, activities, chronology, resource availability, or past environments. Phosphorus is the best known element in anthropogenic soils and results from accumulations of organic wastes such as bone, refuse, and human excrement.

Studies of earthen living floors today in Mexico, Turkey, and elsewhere have confirmed these assumptions and document elemental signatures for different activities. Sediments are normally analyzed using NAA or ICP-MS instruments. One example of anthropogenic soil chemistry was discussed in Chapter 9, "Geoarchaeology," for a house floor at the site of Keatley Creek. Another example is given below for a large plaza at the Maya site of El Coyote.

 EXAMPLE ～～～～～～～～～～～～～～～～～～

EL COYOTE

The site of El Coyote (*KOY-oat-tay*) in northwestern Honduras was an important Classic Maya center between AD 600 and 1000. The site covers about one-quarter of a square kilometer (several city blocks) with at least 250 visible structures. There is a core of monumental buildings with 28 platforms and pyramids arranged around 6 plazas. The main plaza is a flat, limestone-plastered surface, roughly 100 by 50 m in size (like a football field).

One of the unanswered questions about the large plazas at Maya sites concerns their use. Christian Wells, of the University of South Florida, designed a project to

El Coyote

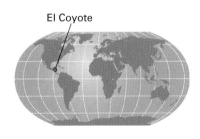

~～～～～～～～～～～～～～～～～～～～

anthropogenic   Created or produced by human activity, e.g., anthropogenic soils are a result of human activity.

Instrumentation   **425**

investigate this question at El Coyote. A series of forty 2 × 2 m (6 × 6 ft) units were excavated across the plaza area down to the original plaster floor. These excavations revealed fragments of large bowls and cooking jars, grinding stones for preparing corn, and a variety of flaked stone tools, concentrated in the southeast quarter of the plaza. Wells interpreted these finds as evidence of large-scale preparation and consumption of food and beverages. Midden deposits outside the plaza behind the buildings contained evidence for craft manufacturing activities in waste material from making stone tools, bark beaters for making bark cloth or paper, and grinding equipment for

Fig. 15.13 The monumental center of El Coyote and the large plaza. The shading shows concentrations of phosphate, with darker shading representing higher levels. The lighter areas within the plaza likely reflect repeated cleaning of this area during the period of occupation. The location of the three sediment types is also shown on the plan with Roman numerals. These types are described in the text.

food or pigments. Thus, the artifactual evidence suggests that the plaza was used for feasting and craft production, perhaps as a market area.

The artifacts that were found were not in their original places of use, having been swept and dumped to the corners to keep the plaza clean. In order to learn where these activities had taken place on the plaza, Wells turned to soil chemistry, assuming that different kinds of activities would produce different chemical signatures. Wells analyzed more than 500 sediment samples from the plaza and surrounding area using ICP spectrometry. The concentration of twelve different elements was measured in each sample, and these values were compared to baseline levels for natural soils sampled at some distance from the site.

Statistical analysis and mapping of the elemental concentrations revealed three patterns of use in and around the large plaza (Fig. 15.13). Type I areas were characterized by manufacturing waste and higher levels of iron and titanium, which may come from the preparation of pigments and were likely used for craft activities. This type was found to the north outside the large plaza. Type II soils were found in the main plaza and the ballcourt area. Artifacts in these areas included ceramic vessels for foods, grinding stones, and censers (used for burning incense). Soils had high concentrations of potassium, phosphate, calcium, and sodium, perhaps reflecting the presence of food remains in these areas. These activities would appear to result from feasting and ceremonial activities. Type III sediments were found in residential areas to the east and south of the plaza. The artifacts and chemical signatures suggest that typical domestic food preparation and household maintenance activities were practiced in these areas.

~~~~~~

ISOTOPIC ANALYSES

Isotopes are atoms of the same element that have different masses—alternate states of the element with the same number of protons, but a different number of neutrons. Three isotopes of carbon, 12, 13, and 14, have already been discussed in Chapter 8, "Dating," along with potassium (^{40}K) and argon (^{40}Ar). Radiocarbon dating relies on the ratio of ^{14}C to ^{12}C to determine the age of archaeological materials. ^{14}C is a radioactive isotope, unstable and subject to decay within a known period of time. The majority of isotopes are stable and not subject to radioactive decay.

An important distinction is also made between light and heavy isotopes. The lighter elements (primarily carbon, nitrogen, and oxygen in archaeological studies) **fractionate**. That means that the proportion of different isotopes present can be changed by processes in nature involving heat, **photosynthesis**, **enzymes**, and the like. Heavier isotopes (with a mass greater than 40) do not fractionate under normal conditions. Isotope analyses are normally reported in ratios of one isotope to another in order to standardize the results for different kinds of materials and varying original isotope amounts.

Isotopes of several elements are used in applications in archaeology other than dating. Lead isotopes have been used to study the provenience of silver, lead, and other ore deposits. Carbon isotopes have been used for the determination of sources for marble and other stone composed of marine sediments. The example of the Getty *kouros* statue from Greece was described at the beginning of this chapter. Carbon, hydrogen, and oxygen isotopes have been measured in phytoliths to assess the environmental conditions when these plant silicates were formed. The light isotopes of carbon and nitrogen have been used extensively to study human diets in the past and are described in the next section. Heavy isotopes of strontium and lead along with the light isotopes of oxygen have been used to look at human migration and provenience. This subject is discussed in the following pages along with an example from the Maya site of Copan.

fractionate   Process through which the ratio of *isotopes* in a material can be changed by heat, *photosynthesis*, *enzymes*, or other natural mechanisms.

photosynthesis   Process in plants for manufacture of carbohydrates and oxygen from carbon dioxide and water in the presence of chlorophyll with sunlight as the energy source.

enzyme   A protein that catalyzes a chemical reaction.

Fig. 15.14 Schematic representation of human diet involving both maize, a tropical grass with a less negative $\delta^{13}C$ value, and wheat, with a more negative $\delta^{13}C$ value. Human digestion fractionates the carbon isotopes so that there is a difference of about +5‰ between diet and collagen values.

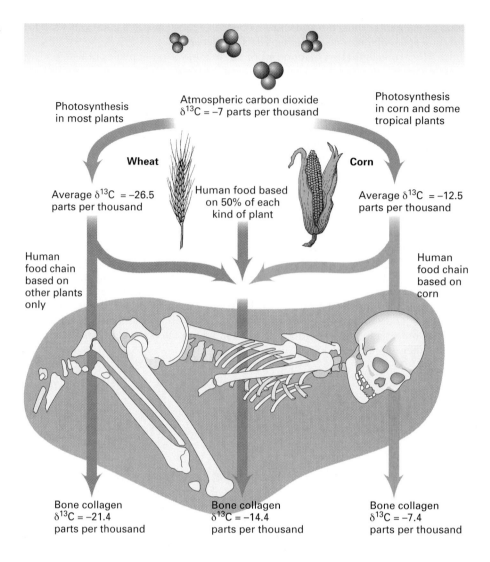

Photosynthesis in most plants

Atmospheric carbon dioxide $\delta^{13}C = -7$ parts per thousand

Photosynthesis in corn and some tropical plants

Wheat

Average $\delta^{13}C = -26.5$ parts per thousand

Human food based on 50% of each kind of plant

Corn

Average $\delta^{13}C = -12.5$ parts per thousand

Human food chain based on other plants only

Human food chain based on corn

Bone collagen $\delta^{13}C = -21.4$ parts per thousand

Bone collagen $\delta^{13}C = -14.4$ parts per thousand

Bone collagen $\delta^{13}C = -7.4$ parts per thousand

collagen   The *protein* that makes up the organic portion of bone.

Bone Chemistry and Prehistoric Diet

The primary use of isotopes in archaeology, outside of dating, has been in research on past diet. A basic principle of such studies is that "we are what we eat." Carbon and nitrogen isotopes from the food we eat are deposited in our tooth and bone. Human bone is a remarkable material, composed of organic and mineral compounds and water. Isotopic studies of the composition of bone utilize the organic portion, primarily the protein known as **collagen**.

The isotopes of carbon ($^{13}C/^{12}C$) and nitrogen ($^{15}N/^{14}N$) are measured in collagen using a mass spectrometer. While the level of these elements in bone is under strict metabolic control, the ratio of stable isotopes reflects the ratio in the diet. These isotope ratios are reported in parts per thousand (‰) and as a difference (delta or δ) between the measured ratio in the sample and a known standard. Convention thus dictates that carbon is reported as $\delta^{13}C$ and nitrogen as $\delta^{15}N$.

Values for $\delta^{13}C$ in human bone collagen range between approximately -5‰ and -25‰. The numbers are negative because observed ratios are lower than the standard. There are two primary sources of variation in ^{13}C in human diet and bone collagen—different ratios in the kinds of plants we eat and different ratios

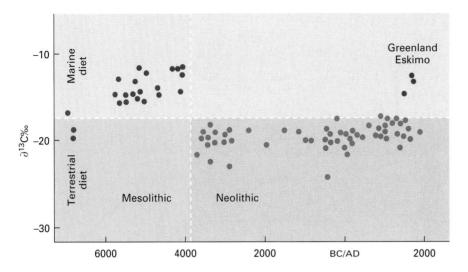

Fig. 15.15 The carbon isotope ratios for human bone collagen from the Mesolithic and Neolithic in Denmark. The y-axis shows the difference between marine and terrestrial diets. The x-axis shows calendar years. There is a clear shift from a more marine diet to a more terrestrial diet at the time of the transition to agriculture at the beginning of the Neolithic. The modern Greenland Eskimo values are shown in the upper right of the diagram.

between terrestrial and marine foods. ^{13}C is more abundant in certain kinds of tropical plants, such as corn, and in the oceans.

People who eat certain tropical grasses like corn have higher ratios of carbon-13 isotopes in their bones. Changes in this isotope ratio in prehistoric bone can indicate when corn becomes an important part of the diet. Fig. 15.14 shows the results of a diet involving both a tropical species such as corn and a temperate species such as wheat. Studies of corn have been done both in Mexico to ascertain when this crop was first domesticated and in North America to record when this important staple first arrived. Analysis of carbon isotopes from human bone from Mexico indicates that a heavy dependence on corn began sometime before 4000 BC.

Marine plants, and the marine animals that consume those plants, exhibit carbon isotope ratio values ranging between -5 and -18 $\delta^{13}C$. Values less negative than $-16‰$ to $-18‰$ indicate a predominance of marine foods in the diet, while more negative values reflect the primary consumption of terrestrial plants and animals. Henrik Tauber of the National Museum of Denmark measured carbon isotope ratios in the bones of human skeletons from the Mesolithic and Neolithic in Scandinavia and historic Greenland (Fig. 15.15). The Greenland Eskimo are known to have consumed marine foods extensively—perhaps as much as 70 to 90% of their diet—and a similar dependence on seafoods may have characterized the diet of the Mesolithic. The ratios from the Mesolithic are close to values for Eskimo skeletal material. Neolithic bone collagen, however, shows a sharp decline in carbon isotope values, indicative of an increase in the importance of terrestrial foodstuffs among the early agriculturalists.

Nitrogen isotopes are used in archaeometry in much the same way as carbon isotopes, but they provide different information about diet. The ratio of nitrogen 15 (0.37% of all nitrogen in nature) to nitrogen 14 (99.63% in nature) is used in paleodiet studies. Nitrogen is reported as $\delta^{15}N$ and values in human bone range from approximately +5‰ to +20‰. This nitrogen ratio is measured in bone collagen using a mass spectrometer.

Fig. 15.16 provides a summary look at carbon and nitrogen isotope ratios in nature. Variations in nitrogen isotope ratios are largely due to the role of **leguminous plants** in diet and the **trophic level** (position in the food chain) of the organism. Atmospheric nitrogen ($\delta^{15}N = 0‰$) is isotopically lighter than that in plant tissues; values in soil tend to be even higher. Non-nitrogen-fixing plants, which derive all of their nitrogen from soil nitrates, can thus be expected to be

leguminous plant (legume) One of thousands of *species* with seed pods that split along both sides when ripe; more common legumes include beans, lentils, peanuts, peas, and soybeans; plants that absorb nitrogen from the atmosphere rather than from soil.

trophic level Position in the food chain, e.g., herbivore, carnivore, bottom-feeder.

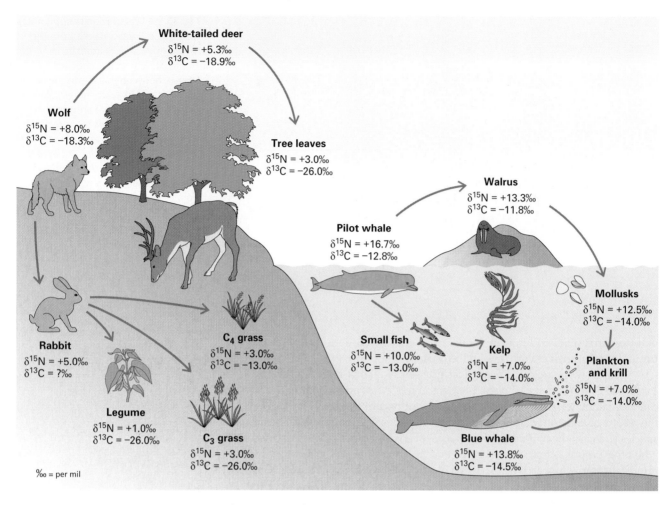

Fig. 15.16 A schematic view of carbon and nitrogen isotope ratios in marine and terrestrial systems.

isotopically heavier than nitrogen-fixing plants, which derive some of their nitrogen directly from the atmosphere.

These values in plants are passed through the food chain accompanied by an approximately 2–3‰ positive shift for each trophic level, including between mother and nursing infant. Grazing animals exhibit ^{15}N enrichment, and more positive $\delta^{15}N$, compared to the plants they eat; predators show enrichment relative to their prey species. There are also differences in nitrogen isotope ratios between marine and terrestrial sources of food that can be used in the study of past diets. Human consumers of terrestrial plants and animals typically have $\delta^{15}N$ values of 6–10‰, while consumers of freshwater or marine fish, seals, and sea lions usually have $\delta^{15}N$ values of 15–20‰. Nitrogen isotope ratios may also vary with rainfall, altitude, and other factors. The nitrogen system is in general less well understood than that of carbon isotopes.

The composition of past human diet is one of the most important questions in prehistoric research. The quest for food directly affects many aspects of human behavior and society, including group size and social organization, residence patterns, technology, and transportation. The use of carbon and nitrogen isotopes in tandem provides a powerful means for determining the sources of food in the human past. Fig. 15.17 shows the various kinds of plants and animals that can be identified using carbon and nitrogen isotopes. The values from human bone col-

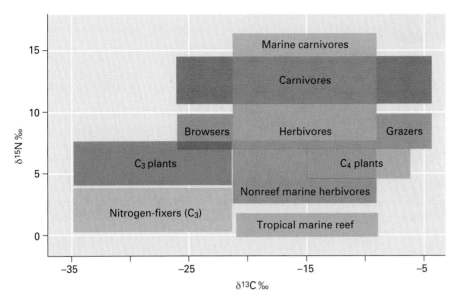

Fig. 15.17 Carbon and nitrogen isotope ratios for various marine and terrestrial species. Sources of variation are discussed in the text.

lagen placed on this graph would provide an indication of diet and trophic level. An example of the application of isotopes to human diet is provided in the next section on the Vikings in Greenland.

Human Provenience and Migration

One of the core questions in archaeology concerns changes in material culture. A new kind of projectile point appears, domestic plants and animals are found for the first time at a site, a new burial practice spreads across a region. New things are innovations and they represent what is called **culture change**. The question then arises, from where did these new things come? Was culture change introduced by new people coming to the area, or did local people independently invent these things or simply borrow foreign ideas and artifacts? This is a question of invention vs. diffusion and is one of the more difficult to answer.

The difficult part is determining if people moved around in the past. We can usually identify **exotic** artifacts, but cannot determine how the artifacts came to be in that place. Imagine finding a coke bottle in Botswana in southern Africa in 1900. Was the bottle brought by foreigners or was the concept copied by local peoples? Iron and horses were absent in North America until the Europeans arrived. But after their arrival, iron hatchets and domesticated horses spread across western North America long before the Europeans who brought them reached that part of the continent. The axes were popular trade items among Native American groups; the horses came from the earlier Spanish colonists in the Southwest. Artifacts and other objects are often used as markers of groups of people in archaeology, but such objects can be traded, borrowed, or stolen and are not necessarily carried directly by the people who made them. This may seem self-evident, but it's not.

Until recently archaeologists have not been able to determine directly if people themselves moved. However, the application of isotopic tracers has made it possible to provenience human skeletons. The principle is straightforward. Tooth enamel forms during infancy and does not change during life. Bone, on the other hand, is constantly rebuilding itself as part of the body's maintenance plan. The

culture change In *archaeology*, innovations or modification in *technology* or *material culture*.

exotic Foreign, unusual; in *archaeology* refers to artifacts and other materials from nonlocal sources.

Climate, Isotopes, and People

Columbus arrived in the Caribbean islands in 1492 as we all learn in elementary school. But the first Europeans to set foot in the Americas came almost 500 years earlier and they were not Italian but Scandinavian—the Vikings, also known as the Norse people.

Their daring voyages across the North Atlantic were made in a series of shorter trips from Norway, Sweden, and Denmark to the Western Isles (Britain and Ireland) and then to the Faeroe Islands, Iceland, Greenland, and eventually to Newfoundland in eastern Canada (Fig. 15.18). The Vikings conquered parts of Britain and Ireland by AD 800 and occupied many of the island groups in the northern British Isles, including the Shetlands, Orkneys, and Hebrides. As explorers and colonists, they were the first people to settle on the Faeroe Islands and Iceland (AD 874). However, on Greenland and in North America

the Eskimos and American Indians had already been present for thousands of years.

The story of the Viking exploration of the North Atlantic is an incredible saga of many tales. One chapter concerns the colonies on Greenland, their success and their failure in the light of major climate change. A group of Icelandic farmers led by Erik the Red founded the Eastern Settlement in southwest Greenland around AD 985. Another group from Iceland went farther north along the west coast of Greenland and colonized the Western Settlement. These Viking groups took domesticated cereals and animals with them and successfully cultivated these crops and fed their herds. The North Atlantic climate entered a particularly good phase—known as the Medieval Warm Period—around AD 900. Temperatures were 1–2°C warmer than today on average and the growing season

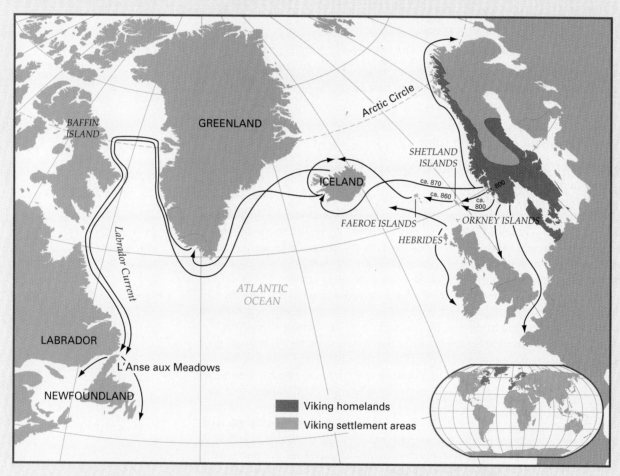

Fig. 15.18   The homelands, settlements, and routes of the Vikings in the North Atlantic.

was longer. The Viking population of Greenland soon expanded to between 4000 and 5000 people. However, after AD 1300 those numbers began to decline and by the middle of the fifteenth century Greenland was completely abandoned by the Norse.

The present icecap on Greenland provides some evidence as to what happened. This ice sheet is more than 2 km (1.2 mi) thick, made up of layer upon layer of ice and frozen snow in a stratigraphy of the last several hundred thousand years. Borings deep into this ice provide information on past climate on Greenland and show a steady decline in maximum temperature during the 500 years of the Viking occupation. This cold period between AD 1300 and 1850 has been designated as the Little Ice Age and its effects were dramatic in the North Atlantic.

Isotopic studies of the tooth enamel from Norse burials from Greenland document these changes in climate. Oxygen isotopes—a reflection of atmospheric temperature—in tooth enamel show a clear increase in cold during the period of settlement (Fig. 15.19). Carbon isotopes in the enamel, on the other hand, indicate a marked increase in the proportion of marine foods in the diet over time, from less than 20% when the Vikings arrived to something like 80% at the end of their time on Greenland. It appears from the evidence that as temperatures

and growing season declined and shortened, the Viking people of Greenland ate more seals and fish. A long summer was necessary to grow hay to store and feed their cows and sheep through the spring, when the Norse could hunt seals on the ice. If the crop failed, the cattle and sheep died before the seals arrived and the Norse would starve.

Archaeological evidence corroborates this scenario. Excavations at Norse houses from the later period of the settlement have revealed the skeletons of cattle that died in their stalls during the winter. Other bioarchaeological information suggests a clear decline in human nutrition. There are indications of a decline in stature in the Greenland Vikings over time, and a number of the later skeletons exhibit evidence of disease and malnutrition.

Changes in climate played a major role in Viking history. The Medieval Warm Period provided better growing conditions in Scandinavia and supported expanding population that may have forced the exploration and colonization of new land. Several hundred years later, as the Little Ice Age took hold, the growing season declined, and the Viking way of life collapsed. At the same time, colder conditions on Greenland increased the herds of seal and reindeer and the Greenland Eskimo hunters farther north flourished.

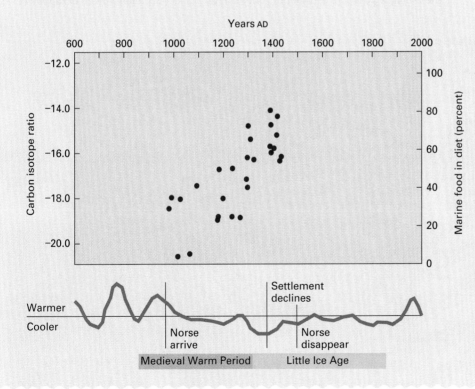

Fig. 15.19 Climatic changes over the last 1400 years revealed in Greenland ice cores document periods of warmer and colder conditions than today. The temperature curve on the bottom of the diagram is based on oxygen isotopes, a proxy for atmospheric temperature. The Medieval Warm Period witnessed the expansion of the Vikings across the North Atlantic while the Little Ice Age documents a time of cooler conditions and declining harvests. The carbon isotope evidence from human tooth enamel in the upper part of the diagram shows a shift from terrestrial to marine diet during this period.

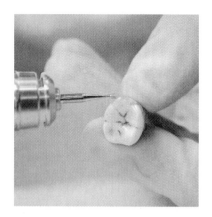

Fig. 15.20 Taking a sample of dental enamel from a prehistoric tooth using a dental drill.

composition of our tooth enamel then is made up of the things an individual (and his or her mother) ate during infancy. The composition of bone is a product of the nutrients consumed during the last years of life.

Certain isotopes in the foods we eat are geographically distinctive. Isotopes of strontium and oxygen are particularly good signatures for the place of residence. Strontium isotopes vary among different types of rock and go into the body through the food chain, from rock to soil to plant to animal to human. Oxygen isotopes enter the body in drinking water, which comes from rainfall. Isotope ratios in rainfall vary with temperature and latitude. Rain that falls in warm areas close to the sea has a high oxygen isotope ratio while rain that falls more inland and at higher elevations and latitudes has a lower ratio.

These isotopes can be measured in the enamel and bone of a human skeleton (Fig. 15.20). The isotope ratios in tooth enamel come from the place of birth; the isotope ratios in bone come from the place of death. If the ratios in the enamel and the bone of the same individual are different, that person must have changed their place of residence—she or he must have moved. In some cases it is possible to determine not just that a person moved, but also to suggest from where he or she may have come. Isotopic ratios are measured using a mass spectrometer.

 EXAMPLE ～～～～～～～～～～～～～～～～～～

THE FIRST KING OF COPAN

Fig. 15.21 An artist's reconstruction of the acropolis at Copan, Honduras, showing several of the burial structures and tombs.

One example of human proveniencing comes from the Maya area in Mesoamerica. The site of Copan (*CO-pahn*) is located in Honduras, in the southwestern corner of the Maya region. The central part of this huge site is dominated by an **acropolis** cov-

Fig. 15.22   The primary burial under the acropolis at Copan, Honduras, probably the tomb of Yax Kuk M'o.

ered with temples, buildings, and inscribed stone **stelae** and altars (Fig. 15.21). This was the civic and ceremonial focus of the site and the residence and burial place of its rulers.

In the 1990s, Robert Sharer of the University of Pennsylvania and a team of archaeologists began to tunnel into the artificial hill of the acropolis to see what lay inside. This huge, terraced mound had been built in stages, each new level burying the previous architecture under layers of clay and gravel. Their tunnel revealed earlier temples and altars that had been left intact and were preserved almost perfectly with their brightly painted facades. At the bottom of the earliest level of the acropolis, they uncovered a series of graves and human burials around a large central tomb (Fig. 15.22). It seems that the mound was initially built to mark the burial place of one of the early rulers, but which one? There were sixteen kings listed in the dynasty at Copan.

Ancient Maya hieroglyphic inscriptions abound at Copan and often refer to the important events in the lives of these rulers—birth, marriage, conquest, and death. A number of inscriptions described Yax Kuk M'o (*YASCH-kook-moe*), the first king of Copan. He was apparently quite a warrior, having won a number of major battles. He was said to have come to Copan from the north in AD 427 to found the dynasty at what was then a simple village. Was this deep tomb at the base of the Copan acropolis the grave of Yax Kuk M'o? This first king was also sometimes depicted wearing a costume typical of the major Mexican center of Teotihuacán, almost 1200 km (750 mi) to the northwest near modern Mexico City. Did he come from that distant center?

Isotopic proveniencing was used to answer these questions. Bones and teeth from the central tomb and several of the adjacent graves were analyzed. This information was compared with isotope ratios from modern local animals and human bone from other parts of the Maya region. The combination of strontium and oxygen

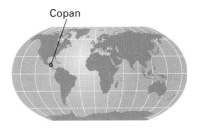

Copan

acropolis   Refers to the citadel or upper part of ancient cities in the classical world or Maya region.

stelae   A stone monument, carved and/or painted with designs and/or inscription, common in the Maya region (sing.: stela).

isotopes in the tooth enamel from the central tomb burial pointed to a place of birth to the north, perhaps somewhere around the site of Tikal. This individual most definitely did not come from Teotihuacán, though the regalia he wore was likely intended to emphasize symbolic connections with that important center.

The individual in the central tomb was an older male, between 50 and 60 years of age, and his skeleton showed a number of old breaks and lesions that were probably the result of conflict and warfare. Certainly the age of the individual, the wounds he had suffered, and the probable place of birth correspond with what we know of Yax Kuk M'o. This is likely his tomb and skeleton at the base of the Copan acropolis.

ORGANIC RESIDUES IN ARCHAEOLOGY

The food and many raw materials that humans use are organic—meat, fish, fowl, vegetables, fruits, wood, hide, bone, antler, thatch, fur, and more—and come from living things. These materials were once abundant at the living places of prehistoric people. The bad news is that in most cases this "biological" component of the past is very susceptible to decomposition and does not survive to the present. Fungi and bacteria feed on carbon-based materials and eventually consume them. The good news, however, is that biological materials sometimes leave traces in and on artifacts and sediments which can survive for thousands of years. For instance, organic compounds from the interior of a potsherd have been dated to more than 6000 years before present.

Trace organic compounds are distinguished from visible organic residues such as charred food on pottery or other macroscopic organic remains. Analysis of trace organic compounds, which have adhered to or been absorbed into the structural matrix of archaeological materials, can provide information about past artifact function, diet, and other aspects of prehistoric societies. This branch of archaeometry is sometimes referred to as molecular or "biomolecular" archaeology.

A variety of archaeological materials may contain trace organic compounds, including ceramics, stone tools, grinding stones, cooking slabs, plaster, fecal material, soil, and sediments. The best preservation seems to be in artifacts such as pottery that have absorbed trace organic compounds into their structural matrix, thus preventing, or at least reducing, the introduction of "contaminants" from handling or **diagenesis**, and the oxygen-induced degradation that can interfere with the identification of the original parent material.

Trace compounds come from things like blood, tissue, food residues, oils, fats, and grease, pitches, tars, and resins. A variety of molecules make up these compounds, including **proteins**, **lipids**, **nucleic acids**, **amino acids**, and **hydrocarbons**. Lipids have been the focus of most investigations of organic residues to date. Lipids are a generic category of compounds that are constituents of living tissues. Lipids appear to survive better than other organic compounds in archaeological contexts and are amenable to sensitive methods of analysis such as gas chromatography/mass spectrometry. There are many different forms of lipids. Certain kinds of lipids differ greatly not only between plants and animals, but among the various families and genera of plants and animals. The most important in archaeological studies are **fatty acids** and **sterols**. Their identification in archaeological contexts provides a means of distinguishing the original biological materials.

Sterols are widely distributed in animals (zoosterols) and plants (phytosterols). They are often species specific, and scientists can use them to discriminate different classes of plant and animal. Because of their potential to identify organic traces to the species level, sterols may be more useful in some archaeolog-

diagenesis Physical and chemical changes in bone after burial.

protein Complex organic macromolecule composed of more chains of *amino acids* containing carbon, hydrogen, oxygen, and nitrogen; fundamental components of all living cells and many substances such as enzymes, hormones, and antibodies.

lipids A generic category of greasy compounds including fats, oils, waxes, sterols, and triglycerides, that are constituents of living tissues.

nucleic acid Compounds found in all living cells and viruses, composed of purines, pyrimidines, carbohydrates, and phosphoric acid.

amino acid Simple organic compounds containing carbon, hydrogen, oxygen, nitrogen, and in certain cases sulfur. Twenty amino acids are the building blocks of proteins.

hydrocarbon One of many *organic compounds* that contain only carbon and hydrogen.

fatty acid Organic compound in animal and vegetable fats and oils, made up of saturated or unsaturated fats.

sterol Unsaturated solid alcohol, such as cholesterol and ergosterol, present in the fatty tissues of plants and animals.

ical studies than fatty acids. For example, there are a number of lipid compounds specific to fecal material, including some sterols, bile, and others that can be found in either soils or coprolites. One byproduct of these sterols is a compound known as 5β stanol, produced in the gut of animals and a distinctive marker of the presence of animal feces. The presence of this compound in prehistoric agricultural fields has been used as evidence of intentional fertilization.

Although the analysis of trace organic compounds has great potential in archaeological research, a number of problems remain, largely due to postdepositional changes in the molecules through either contamination—the addition of new materials to the matrix—or the breakdown of the original molecules into small, unidentifiable components. There are in fact a relatively small number of both reliable and useful studies that have been done to date.

Most of the effort, and success, in the organic analysis of archaeological residues has been in characterizing specific organic molecules retained in potsherds. Highly specific residues from fruits, milk, wine, olive oil, and cedar wood oil have been identified in various studies. Other potentially diagnostic compounds recovered from potsherds include proteins, some of which are diagnostic of certain animal foods. No doubt as scientific instrumentation becomes more sensitive to the identification of ancient compounds and as these instruments become more accessible to archaeology, studies of trace organic compounds will become a larger part of archaeometry.

CONCLUSIONS

Archaeometry is the branch of archaeology concerned with the instrumental analysis of ancient materials. It includes areas such as dating methods, remote sensing, and ancient DNA, but the core of the field lies in inorganic and organic chemistry—the elemental and isotopic characterization of archaeological materials and organic analyses. Archaeometric studies are intended to identify unknown materials, to authenticate the antiquity of pieces of questionable origin, and to characterize the chemical composition of various raw materials and finished artifacts. A large part of archaeometric research has to do with determining provenience, or place of origin, in order to investigate questions of exchange or movement in the past.

Archaeometry involves many more methods and materials than are discussed here. This chapter presented some information about the goals of archaeometry and about instrumentation and laboratories. The major techniques of elemental and isotopic analyses and organic chemistry were a point of focus for the chapter, and a discussion of the elemental characterization of obsidian provided information on source and exchange. Element analysis of soil samples from the plaza at the Maya site of El Coyote is an example of how archaeologists can use anthropogenic sediments to gain insight on the characterization of activity areas from earlier times. In other examples of archaeometry in action, isotopic studies of prehistoric Greenland reveal changes in diet associated with climatic deterioration. In addition, isotopic investigation of human mobility in the Maya region documents the origin of the first king of Copan to the north, probably in the Peten (PAY-ten) region of Guatemala.

Archaeometry has expanded dramatically in the last two decades. One way to consider this is to look at the meetings and publications that appear each year. The number of symposia that focus on archaeometry at the annual meetings of American archaeologists has grown to more than thirty sessions (about 10% of the total number of sessions) each year. At the same time, the number of journals focused on archaeometry also has grown steadily to more than twenty-five (about 20%).

Along with this expansion, archaeometry has become a particularly interesting branch of archaeology for many scientists because its new approaches can help archaeologists tackle new questions and areas of research. Exciting technological developments in the field are simply revolutionizing the way archaeology is done. Archaeometry is also a fascinating area of archaeology because it combines the sciences and humanities, the quantitative and qualitative, and the objective and subjective in solving problems concerning our human past.

BONE CHEMISTRY

Now it's your turn. You are an isotope archaeologist. You have been sent a large batch of bones for analysis, but the labels on the bones have fallen off and you cannot tell which is which. All you know is that there are bones from four different places in the box: the Northwest Coast of North America, Pecos (*PAY-koss*) Pueblo in the southwestern United States, Archaic Ontario, and St. Catherine's Island off the coast of Georgia.

You decide to go ahead and analyze the samples in spite of the problems of identification. Most of the samples appear to be reasonably well preserved, and the carbon:nitrogen ratios you measure seem to confirm the quality of the collagen in the bone (Table 15.1). The carbon:nitrogen (C:N) ratio of pure, fresh collagen is 3.21. A carbon:nitrogen value between 2.9 and 3.6 is considered necessary for a sample to be reliable.

You measure both stable carbon and stable nitrogen ratios in the collagen extracted from the bone samples using a mass spectrometer. It takes a while. Table 15.1 lists your measurements.

Now it's time for some analysis. You may want to refer to the discussion of data and numbers in Chapter 7. First, look at the number to see if you notice any patterns or relationships. It's hard because there is a lot of variation. Also try to see if there are any values that appear aberrant or out of range. You may have entered a number incorrectly or perhaps there was an error in the spectrometer. These things happen all the time. Aberrant data should be deleted from the study.

Histograms

You need to draw three histograms, one for each set of data in the table: the carbon:nitrogen ratio, the carbon isotope ratios, and the nitrogen isotope ratios. Determine the range of values for each data set, the maximum and minimum numbers. Subtract the minimum from the maximum in each set to get the numerical distance. Now you need to determine how many intervals you want to see in your histogram. There is no fixed rule for this but fifteen intervals might be a good place to start. If you don't like the fifteen intervals, use another number.

Now divide the numerical distance of the range in your data set by fifteen, or the number of intervals you choose. That will give you the range of each interval. Draw a horizontal line on the graph paper and mark the left end of the line with a vertical line and write the minimum value in the data set under it. The first interval will be the minimum value in the data set plus this interval range. The second interval will be this new value plus the interval range. Continue this until you have all of your intervals marked across the line. The value on the right end of your line will be the maximum value in the data set.

Now look at each value for the data set in the table and put a mark in the interval on the line where it belongs. If you make all your marks the same size, they become a picture of your data. Stack tally marks on top of one another where there is more than one value in a single interval. The tally marks provide a visual summary of all the information in the data set.

It is important to look also for what is missing in the graph, for gaps between bars, or for significant differences in the lengths of the bars. Peaks and valleys in the graph show that there may be groups in the data. If you find groups, what do they represent?

TABLE 15.1 Measurements of bone collagen isotope ratios for carbon and nitrogen, and the carbon:nitrogen ratio for thirty-nine samples of bone.

Sample Number	C:N	$\delta^{13}C$	$\delta^{15}N$
1	3.1	−21.9	12.8
2	3.2	−12.3	10.2
3	2.9	−17.6	14.0
4	3.0	−13.8	18.2
5	3.3	−13.0	18.6
6	3.4	−14.2	17.4
7	3.2	−7.9	9.4
8	3.0	−22.1	12.6
9	2.9	−7.6	9.5
10	3.1	−22.0	12.1
11	3.5	−18.0	13.9
12	3.0	−12.8	18.2
13	3.1	−19.2	12.3
14	3.2	−12.5	18.1
15	3.3	−19.4	13.5
16	3.5	−13.1	10.1
17	3.0	−21.8	11.0
18	3.2	−21.4	10.8
19	3.3	−12.3	18.2
20	3.2	−7.7	8.6
21	3.1	−17.6	13.5
22	3.5	−12.1	18.3
23	3.6	−7.9	9.9
24	3.0	−7.4	8.4
25	3.3	−21.5	14.0
26	3.2	−7.1	10.3
27	3.4	−7.5	9.1
28	3.1	−14.2	11.1
29	3.3	−19.8	11.2
30	3.4	−14.3	10.1
31	3.0	−4.4	13.9
32	3.3	−16.3	10.0
33	3.1	−13.8	9.5
34	3.5	−7.5	9.5
35	2.9	−6.9	10.2
36	3.5	−19.5	11.6
37	3.1	−7.8	9.6
38	3.2	−13.9	9.2
39	3.2	−19.4	12.1

Scatterplots

Now you need to make some scatterplots of the data, comparing two variables simultaneously. Draw two lines on the graph paper, one horizontal and one vertical. The vertical line should rise from the left end of the horizontal line. The horizontal line will be the carbon isotope values. Mark the left end of the line with the minimum value in the data set and the right end of the line with the maximum value. You will need to indicate some of the values for the grid lines between the minimum and maximum values to make it easier to plot the bone samples. Now do the same thing for the nitrogen isotope values along the vertical line. Minimum value at the bottom; maximum value at the top. Put values on some of the grid lines in between.

Now you are ready to make a scatterplot. Look at the first sample; read the value for carbon isotopes and find this point on your horizontal line. Now read the value for the nitrogen ratio for the same sample. Find this point on your vertical line. Now draw an imaginary horizontal line from your nitrogen value and an imaginary vertical line from your carbon value. Mark a dot or small circle at the point where those two imaginary lines cross. Now you have reduced two numerical values to a single point on the graph. Continue this process for the rest of the bone samples. You should end up with one dot on the graph for each sample.

Now think about this—it's time for interpretation. What does this scatterplot of isotope data tell us? Do you see distinct clusters or linear patterns? If so, what do these mean?

Back to the Start

You received a box of bones with mixed-up labels indicating they came from four different places: the Northwest Coast of North America, Pecos Pueblo in the U.S. Southwest, Archaic Ontario, and St. Catherine's Island off the coast of Georgia. We know a bit more about these places from the archaeology that has been done. The Northwest Coast Indians were hunter-gatherer-fisher people living on the Pacific Coast of Washington state and British Columbia. Seafood was an important part of their diet and salmon were captured in huge numbers in the summer and fall. They also ate land mammals and some plants. The Pecos Pueblo site in New Mexico was occupied in the fifteenth century AD; corn, beans, and squash were major components of the diet along with some meat. Corn is a tropical plant introduced from Mexico and has a less negative carbon isotope ratio than most temperate area species. Archaic Ontario refers to groups of hunter-gatherers living in the temperate forest and lake regions of Ontario, a very long distance from the sea. These groups date from a time before agriculture and would have subsisted on wild game and plants and fish from the Great Lakes. St. Catherine's Island along the coast of Georgia is a sea island on the Atlantic shore with a Spanish mission dating to around 1700. Excavations at the site uncovered the graves of many Native Americans and a few Franciscan friars who were buried there. Their diet probably included a predominance of corn and seafood as well as a variety of wild plants and animals.

Given your analysis of the isotope data and this information on the sites, what sense can you make of the data in your scatterplot? Please answer each of the following five questions in a brief paragraph.

1. Did you find any aberrant data in your measurements? What did you do?

2. What did you see in the histograms you made? Were there any clear patterns?

3. Did you find any linear relationships? Please describe any linear patterns in terms of the specific points on the line and its location.

4. Did you find any clusters or groups in your scatterplot? How did you distinguish groups? Please describe the groups in terms of the range of values and the number of members of each group.

5. Can you make a reasoned guess about which of the four places that you know are present can be distinguished in the groups that you found?

If you want to know more about bone chemistry and isotope studies, you might take a look at the article by Schoeninger and Moore (1992) listed in the Bibliography.

STUDY QUESTIONS

1. What kinds of materials are studied in archaeometric laboratories?

2. Elemental analysis is one of the primary methods of archaeometric research. What methods are available to measure elemental composition?

3. How do archaeologists and archaeometrists learn about past human diets?

4. Discuss three isotope ratios and how they are used in archaeometry.

5. Organic residues are a potentially important but difficult to analyze source of information about the past. Discuss these materials and techniques for analysis.

www.mhhe.com/pricearch1

For more review material and study questions, please see the self-quizzes on your online learning center.

REFERENCES

Brothwell, D. R., and A. M. Pollard, eds. 2001. *Handbook of Archaeological Sciences.* Chichester: Wiley.

Henderson, J. 2000. *The Science and Archaeology of Materials: An Investigation of Inorganic Materials.* London: Routledge.

Jones, Martin. 2003. *The Molecule Hunt: Archaeology and the Search for Ancient DNA.* New York: Arcade Publishing.

Lambert, J. 1997. *Traces of the Past: Unraveling the Secrets of Archaeology through Chemistry.* New York: Addison Wesley Longman.

Wisseman, S. U., and W. S. Williams, eds. 1994. *Ancient Technologies and Archaeological Materials.* Amsterdam: Gordon and Breach Publishers.

www.mhhe.com/pricearch1

For Internet references related to this chapter, please see the chapter links on your online learning center.

PART 4

INTERPRETATION

The third and final stage of archaeological research involves the interpretation of the results of discovery and analysis, efforts to describe and explain past human behavior. This is in fact the most challenging part of archaeology and sometimes the most exasperating. We find artifacts and sites; we measure their size and chemical composition; and we record their shape and note design elements. But translating such basic information into behavior is a big step. Theory and method provide some bridges between facts and interpretation, but there is still a very large chasm to be crossed before the story of the past surfaces. It is important to remember that most archaeological interpretation is speculative, often raising more questions than it answers. That's frustrating, but the new questions lead us to seek out more answers, resulting in an ever-expanding knowledge base. It is also difficult to know if an interpretation is correct. That of course depends in large part on what it is you want to know—and that question is at the heart of research and of interpretation.

This fourth section of the book is an introduction to archaeological interpretation, to understanding the past beyond discovery and analysis. Archaeological theories are statements of archaeological thought; Chapter 16, "Explanation in Archaeology," looks at different schools of thought and the current status of archaeological theory. This chapter includes several case studies, portraying how various perspectives on the past can view the archaeological record.

Chapter 17 concludes this volume with a consideration of ethics and responsibility in archaeology, how archaeologists behave in and contribute to the larger sphere of our society and our world. Ethics and responsibility have the last word because they are an important part of what archaeologists do, and a part of our perspective on the past.

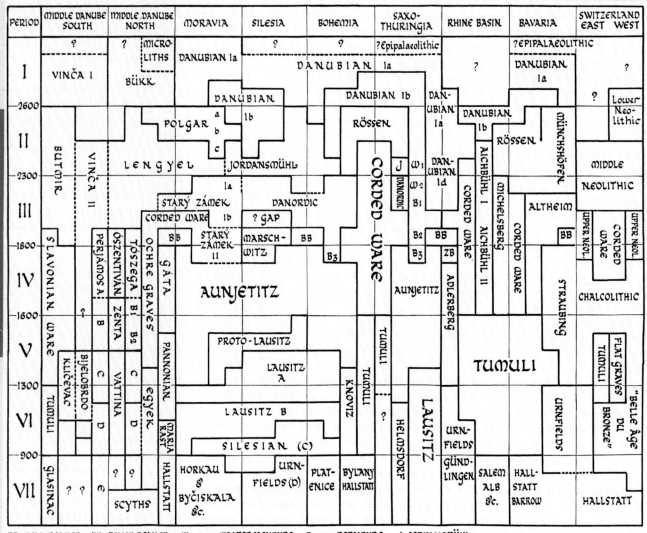

PERIOD	MIDDLE DANUBE SOUTH	MIDDLE DANUBE NORTH		MORAVIA	SILESIA	BOHEMIA	SAXO-THURINGIA	RHINE BASIN	BAVARIA	SWITZERLAND EAST WEST	
I	? VINČA I	? BÜKK	MICRO-LITHS	DANUBIAN Ia	? DANUBIAN	? Ia	?Epipalaeolithic	?	?EPIPALAEOLITHIC DANUBIAN Ia	?	?
−2600				DANUBIAN a b c Ib	DANUBIAN Ib	DANUBIAN Ib RÖSSEN	DAN-UBIAN Ia	DANUBIAN Ib	MÜNCHSHÖFEN	?	Lower Neo-lithic
II	BUTMIR	VINČA II		POLGAR LENGYEL	JORDANSMÜHL		J W₁ DANORDIC W₂	DANUBIAN Id RÖSSEN AICHBÜHL I		MIDDLE	
−2300								CORDED WARE	MICHELSBERG ALTHEIM	NEOLITHIC	
III			OCHRE GRAVES	STARÝ ZÁMEK CORDED WARE Ia Ib	DANORDIC ? GAP		B₁	AICHBÜHL II		UPPER NEOL.	UPPER NEOL.
−1800	SLAVONIAN WARE	PERJÁMOS A	TÓSZEG A	BB STARÝ ZÁMEK II	MARSCH-WITZ BB	B₃	B₂ BB B₃ ZB	CORDED WARE	CORDED WARE BB		CORDED WARE
IV			B₁ GÁTA B₂	AUNJETITZ			AUNJETITZ	ADLERBERG	STRAUBING	CHALCOLITHIC	
−1600		?	ZENTA								
V			VATTINA C	PROTO-LAUSITZ LAUSITZ A		TUMULI	TUMULI	TUMULI	FLAT GRAVES TUMULI		"BELLE ÂGE DU BRONZE"
−1300	TUMULI	BIJELOBRDO KLIČEVAC C	PANNONIAN egyek D			KNOVIZ			URNFIELDS		
VI			D	LAUSITZ B SILESIAN (C)			? HELMSDORF	LAUSITZ URN-FIELDS GÜND-LINGEN			
−900			MARIA RAST		URN-FIELDS (D)	PLAT-ENICE	BYLANY HALLSTATT				
VII	GLASINAC	? ? e	HALLSTATT SCYTHS	HORKAU & BYČISKALA &c.				SALEM ALB &c.	HALL-STATT BARROW	HALLSTATT	

BB = BELL-BEAKER   ZB = ZONED BEAKER   W₁ etc. = WALTERMENBURG   B₁ etc. = BERNBURG   J = JORDANSMÜHL

TABLE GIVING CORRELATIONS OF THE SEVERAL CULTURES IN TIME AND SPACE

Explanation in Archaeology

INTRODUCTION: INTERPRETING THE PAST

Sometimes a picture is not worth many words. When it was devised in the 1920s, this almost incomprehensible diagram was intended to show the prehistory of Central Europe from the beginning of the Neolithic to the Iron Age. There are seven major time periods, designated with Roman numerals, and speculative calendar dates from approximately 3000 BC to AD 600, arranged vertically. The geography of Central Europe is laid out horizontally, left to right from east to west. The various blocks in the diagram indicate archaeological cultures in time and geographic space and the relationships among them. Such frameworks were one of the primary goals of archaeology until the middle of the twentieth century. Today, the when and where of archaeological materials remains essential information, but questions usually focus more on human behavior and social change. It was the sterility of the descriptive particularism of the former culture history approach that gave rise to the new perspectives that direct archaeological research and explanation today. At the same time, archaeologists continue to pursue an understanding of chronology and geography, a basis of understanding that is necessary before other questions can be pursued.

This chapter is concerned with interpretation in archaeology, how we explain the things that we discover and analyze. The archaeological record, the artifacts and features that have survived from the past, are static, material objects. That is the information we have. We want to know about the dynamics of human behavior in the past. How do we get from static material to dynamic behavior? How do we explain the archaeological record in terms of humans and society?

This chapter, then, is about explanations and the role of theory in archaeology. Theory is an essential part of any scientific discipline that attempts to explain cause and effect relationships. A theory in science does not mean a guess or a hunch it means a generally accepted explanation of how things work. Without theory, archaeology would just be dusty rooms full of artifacts and data. Theory determines what questions are asked, what information is collected, how analysis is done, and what kinds of interpretations are made. Theories define what is knowable and what answers are acceptable.

A theory is a kind of lens for looking at the world, and the archaeological record, and for explaining our observations. Different lenses provide different views. A rose-colored lens concentrates certain kinds of light. 3-D glasses give some films a completely different look. A magnifying glass provides a close-up view. Like lenses, there are a number of different theories in archaeology today.

447

Related theoretical views can be grouped into schools of thought. A school of thought is basically a set of people with similar perspectives. This chapter will consider the schools of processual archaeology, post-processual archaeology, evolutionary archaeology, and gender archaeology. The two major schools are processual and post-processual; gender archaeology is sometimes considered a component of the post-processual school. Evolutionary archaeology is less mainstream, but offers an alternative to the two major theoretical groups.

This chapter also discusses archaeological case studies from these theoretical schools. Two studies—Bronze Age mounds in Denmark and the collapse of the Maya state—reflect processual views of the past. A study of the rock art of Scandinavia provides an example of post-processual interpretation. In another section, a discussion of resource depletion among the hunter-gatherers of the California coast documents the perspective of evolutionary archaeology. The selectionist aspect of evolutionary archaeology is portrayed in a study of the spread of horses and snowmobiles in North America. Finally, the role of women in the economy of the Aztec state is considered in the section on gender archaeology. After each of these case studies, I have added a discussion—under the theme of "Archaeological Thinking"—to point out some of the aspects of the case study that define the theoretical school the authors follow and, in some cases, a few questions that arise. It is probably important to note at this time as well that the same archaeologist could easily follow a different school of thought in another study at another time. In fact, a number of archaeologists have switched theoretical allegiances during their career. The chapter concludes with some mention of emerging new directions in archaeology.

One significant aspect of these new directions is that the previous tension between the processual and post-processual groups has largely dissipated; and most archaeologists believe that each perspective has contributions to make. Thus, archaeology is today largely an amalgam of theoretical views, working together to expand our understanding of the past.

SCHOOLS OF THOUGHT

Explaining human behavior in the past and changes in society and **culture** over time is a major goal of archaeology. One aspect of this quest lies in beliefs about what is knowable. In 1954, the late British archaeologist Christopher Hawkes proposed a "ladder of inference" to describe the objectives of archaeology and what can be known. Hawkes argued that technology was at the bottom of the ladder and the foundation of what is knowable about the past. Technology, according to Hawkes, determines everything that derives from it—economy, social organization, politics, and symbolism. Hawkes' ladder went from more knowable aspects of technology and economy to the less knowable components of social organization and ritual. Hawkes believed that some things were simply unknowable and that archaeologists should concentrate on what can be learned.

Today, most archaeologists believe that most things in the past are knowable in one way or another. The limitations on knowledge proposed by Hawkes are gradually being overcome by new methods and new ideas. What seems more important today is not what we can know, but how we should explain what it is that we do know.

Explanation is not an easy task. How we explain the things we observe depends on several factors, including what we know, our past experience, and how we view the world. Wilfred Sellars (1912–1989), an American philosopher, distinguished manifest and scientific views as two different ways of understanding what kinds of things exist and how they change. In the manifest view, interpretation and explanation are done according to how we understand the motivations of people today. Actions and change are thought to be caused by intentions, be-

But the "theory" side of what we do—using tiny scraps of information thus gained to tell us about the human past in all its richness and complexity—must be at least equally difficult as these "practical" tasks. In fact, it must be one of the most intellectually demanding tasks we as a species have ever set ourselves.

—Matthew Johnson, archaeologist

culture   A means of human adaptation based on intelligence, experience, learning, and the use of tools; the general set of behaviors and knowledge that humans use to survive and adapt.

liefs, and desires. From a scientific view, however, the personal is ignored in favor of the natural and physical forces that drive the dynamics of physical systems. Explanation in science is a description of how these forces work in objective or mathematical terms. These two contrasting views also dominate archaeological perspectives on the human past.

Much of the theoretical dissonance in the social sciences and archaeology comes from a related distinction involving structural vs. functional views of the world. Explanations of past human behavior in archaeology have oscillated between these two views. Structuralists argue that human thought processes are the same in all cultures, that the structure or organization of the human mind provides a commonality for all societies. Many structuralists understand the organization of the human mind in terms of binary oppositions, or pairs, such as hot-cold, raw-cooked, male-female. These pairs determine how humans view the world and how they structure the world around them, including their society. In this view, the institutions of society cannot be explained by themselves, but rather as parts of a meaningful whole that is determined by the structure of the human mind. Structuralism assumes that there are shared human thought processes that can explain the underlying meaning of cultural phenomena.

Functionalists, on the other hand, see the social world as objectively real and observable with the right instruments and methods. This positivist view of social science assumes that the investigator's values will not bias observations and interpretations. Functionalists examine the components of society to determine the purpose those parts play in maintaining the whole, how social institutions satisfy the needs of society and its members.

For example, a functionalist might look at a group of arrowheads from a site in Wyoming and try to understand how they were made, used, and discarded. A functionalist's interest would be more in technology and subsistence, how things worked to ensure survival. A structuralist might look at the same group of arrowheads and focus on their similarities and differences, to try to understand what these arrowheads meant to the people who made them and how the designs might reflect human traditions or identity. That structuralist would emphasize the organization and ideological aspects of human existence in an analysis of the artifacts.

These basic divisions in ways of thinking are reflected in how archaeologists interpret the past. Archaeological explanations are basically ideas about human behavior in the past. Groups of theories or explanations define schools of thought or related perspectives in archaeology. The emphasis in this chapter is on four major schools (processual, post-processual, evolutionary, and gender archaeology). Processual and evolutionary archaeology tend to be more functional and scientific in orientation; post-processual and gender archaeology tend to be more structural and manifest.

These four major schools have distinctive identities. Each has recognized founding members, specific methods, and separate goals; each also has its own particular concepts and vocabularies. These special words and views are like passwords or secret handshakes that identify participants. Employing the terms, methods, and goals sets the members of each school apart. While these schools are sometimes antagonistic, in practice most archaeologists take advantage of the best aspects of each in their pursuit of the past.

Processual Archaeology

Processual archaeology emerged in the 1960s as a reaction to the descriptive and staid nature of the culture history perspective that had dominated archaeology during the first half of the twentieth century. Although this processual movement was presaged by W. W. Taylor's (1913–1997) book *A Study of Archaeology* in 1948,

Humanists must cease thinking that ecology dehumanizes history, and ecologists must cease to regard art, religion, and ideology as mere "epiphenomena" without causal significance. In an ecosystem approach to the analysis of human societies, everything which transmits information is in the realm of ecology.
—Kent Flannery, archaeologist

There is far greater continuity between processual and post-processual archaeology than the various proponents, opponents, or commentators on these approaches have yet admitted.
—Philip Kohl, archaeologist

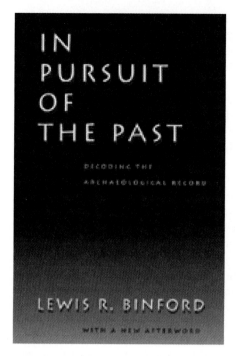

Fig. 16.1 *In Pursuit of the Past,* a major statement by Lewis R. Binford, a leader of the processual school of archaeology from 1983.

"One might venture that this is the most important archaeological work for twenty or thirty years."
THE TIMES LITERARY SUPPLEMENT

Fig. 16.2 *Analytical Archaeology,* written by David L. Clarke, a major proponent of the new archaeology, in 1968.

Until we as archaeologists begin thinking of our data in terms of total cultural systems, many prehistoric "enigmas" will remain unexplained. . . . Such a change could go far in advancing the field of archaeology specifically, and would certainly advance the general field of anthropology.

—Lewis Binford, archaeologist

the leaders of what is also called the "new" archaeology were Lewis Binford of Southern Methodist University and David Clarke (1937–1976) in England. The new archaeology wanted to know not just what, but why. New archaeologists wanted to *explain,* not just describe, cultural change over time in a scientific manner. The processual archaeologists asked new questions about change, about the evolution of culture, about the nature of social organization, and about the ways in which past societies adapted to their environment, how food and the other necessities of life were obtained.

Processual archaeologists questioned what all the dry facts assembled by culture historians meant. They argued that facts must be interpreted in light of theories. The dissatisfaction of the new archaeology with the old rose from the belief that that archaeology should be more scientific and more anthropological. This new archaeology is often described as formulated around logical **positivism,** a philosophy that everything can be understood using logical reasoning and empirical experience. Some of the hallmarks of processual archaeology include an emphasis on cultural evolution, a systems approach to the past, objective and scientific methods, the search for cultural process and generalizations, and the importance of the environment to cultural systems. Processual approaches to the past focused not on the artifact per se, but on the components of cultural systems, such as subsistence, settlement, technology, social organization, population, and environment.

As part of the scientific revolution that took place in the United States following World War II, the development of new instruments and especially computers led to an emphasis on the measurement and quantification of data. Statistics were introduced in archaeology as a way of dealing with large quantities of numbers and to assist in decision making using confidence levels and probability. They also provided an objective means for avoiding bias. Similar developments were changing all the social sciences.

positivism A philosophical view that the application of science and the evaluation of empirical evidence allow one to be objective.

Processual archaeologists promoted **systems theory** as an approach to explaining past human societies. Systems theory began as a way of explaining the physiology of biological organisms as physical systems and was adopted by archaeologists and other scientists seeking a way to define the operation of human societies. Systems theory is intended to explain the interaction of different variables within an organism or organization. It has allowed archaeologists to view the archaeological record in a new way by examining past human behavior in terms of its basic system components.

The new archaeology thus redefined culture as a system, a network of attributes or entities forming a complex whole, exchanging energy, information, and matter with the environment and other societies. Culture became another natural system that could be explained in mathematical terms. And just as in other systems, mechanisms like positive and negative feedback were assumed to operate in culture. Feedback means that an increase in one part of the system causes a corresponding increase (positive) or decrease (negative) in another part of the system.

Systems theory produces a flow chart of the feedback operation in terms of some aspect of human society or behavior. Systems explanations tend to be static, rather than dynamic, and **synchronic**—dealing with a moment in time—rather than **diachronic**—dealing with change over time. One of the consequences of this approach was an emphasis on "multivariate" causality; that is, a move away from the notion that a solitary or "prime" event or reason explains change and toward the recognition that several factors may operate to bring about change.

In the example shown in Fig. 16.3, a number of factors are involved in the relationship between a growing population and decreasing mobility among hunter-gatherers. The model here explains a shift to sedentary settlement. In the context of randomly scattered resources, decreasing mobility causes increasing use of lower-value resources and the storage of food, requiring more labor, increasing fertility, and growing population. The system is a spiral of increasing population and results in longer stays in one place (sedentism).

"New" archaeologists argued that archaeology's status as a science depends on what is called "middle range theory"—a series of methods, assumptions, and ideas to connect static archaeological data to the dynamics of past human behavior. This term was introduced by Lewis Binford. Low Range Theory was used to explain a single feature of a specific culture, such as the use of an artifact or a farming system. A **Middle Range Theory** was used to describe a cultural system outside of a specific cultural context, for example, agriculture. An Upper Range Theory explained any cultural system in general terms. Processual archaeologists use a variety of means—ethnoarchaeology, experimental archaeology, computer simulation, and more—to develop middle range theories to understand how artifacts and the archaeological record encode past human behavior.

Processual archaeology has produced many important studies and greatly expanded the questions that archaeologists ask of the past. Significant contributions include a focus on behavior, rather than artifacts, and the use of more scientific methods. Processual questions continue to provide an objective foundation for much of archaeological research. Processual archaeologists have investigated the origins of agriculture, the emergence of inequality, and the rise of the state, as well as marriage and kinship in prehistoric society. In the examples below, objective studies of two different archaeological cultures and two different questions are described. "A Crossroads of Barrows" documents the analysis of the location and contents of Bronze Age burial mounds in Denmark. Focus is on quantitatively identifying the centers of wealth and power in Denmark ca. 1500 BC. The second example concerns the collapse of Maya states in Central America and covers a series of systemic models that relate environment and climate to the social, political, and religious components of Maya society to understand why these rich and powerful states disappeared.

systems theory A method to explain the interaction of different variables within an organism or organization.

synchronic Dealing with a moment in time, a single time period.

diachronic Dealing with change over time, comparing two or more time periods.

Middle Range Theory Used to describe a cultural system outside of a specific cultural context.

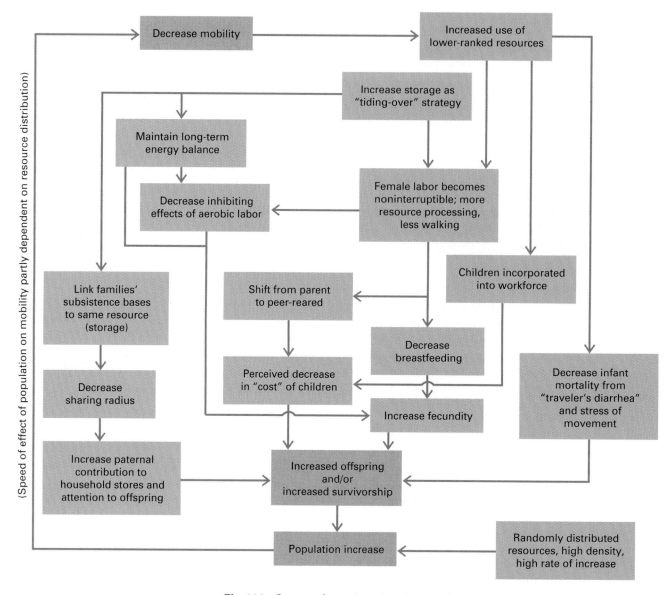

Fig. 16.3 Systems theory in action: A general systems model for increasing sedentism among mobile hunter-gatherers. In essence, population increase leads to decreasing mobility, which causes increasing use of lower-ranked resources and storage, requiring more labor, increasing fertility, and growing population.

EXAMPLE

A CROSSROADS OF BARROWS

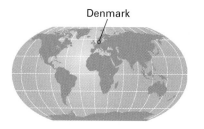

Denmark

Bronze objects began to appear in graves and cemeteries of farming settlements north of the Alps after 2000 BC. The Bronze Age in Denmark and southern Sweden was spectacular in terms of the quantity of fine metal objects buried in many funerary mounds and caches. In fact, much of what is known about the Bronze Age comes from large **barrows** as well as caches of metal objects hidden in the ground; relatively few houses or settlements have been discovered or excavated. Such information provides a limited, but spectacular, view of a small, wealthy segment of Bronze Age society north of the Alps.

Bronze Age barrows dot the landscape of southern Scandinavia (Fig. 16.4). In only a handful of cases have the contents of these barrows survived both the ravages of time and the greed of tomb robbers, to provide a glimpse of the elite of Bronze Age society in northwestern Europe. Bronze Age barrows were built for the wealthier members of society and placed near where the living had died. Most barrows in Denmark are located in areas of productive farmland, evidence of the important relationship between wealth and the control of agricultural resources.

The amount of bronze and gold in these burials provides some indication of the wealth of the deceased individuals. All bronze and gold in southern Scandinavia had to be imported because the ores are not indigenous. Gold was more valuable; only 1 g (0.04 oz) of gold is found for every 1000 g (2.2 lb) of bronze. There are pronounced differences in buried wealth between the sexes and between individuals. For example, male graves are more abundant than female graves, and they contain more wealth. Also, some individuals were buried with a great deal of bronze and gold and some without any, suggesting that social differentiation was pronounced.

The distribution of thousands of such barrows in Denmark offers information on the use of the landscape and the organization of early Bronze Age society. Fig. 16.5 shows the distribution of Bronze Age barrows in the southwestern corner of Denmark. The distinct linear arrangements of the barrows are shown. This figure also shows the location of gold finds in the barrows, indicating distinctive nodes where wealth was concentrated. These high circular burial mounds were placed dramatically on the horizon to emphasize the importance of the buried individuals. The lines of barrows almost certainly lie along routes of movement and communication in the area, and the major intersections must have been at the residences of the wealthy. An elite segment of the population must have controlled most of the resources as well as the trade.

Fig. 16.4 Two Bronze Age barrows dominate the skyline above a fjord in northern Denmark.

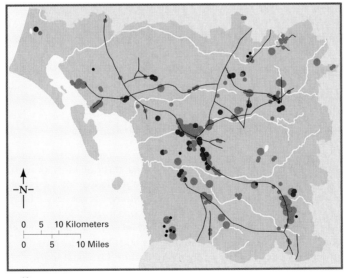

Key

● Minor/unspecified gold artifacts

Fig. 16.5 The distribution of Bronze Age barrows, or burial mounds, in southwestern Denmark. The locations of the individual mounds mark prehistoric trails or roads in this area. The contents of the mounds reflect the wealth of the interred individual. Larger circles mark greater burial wealth, shown in the form of bracelets and armbands at the bottom of the illustration. Wealth is clearly concentrated at a few strategic crossroads and locations in the area.

barrows   Earthen burial *mounds.*

Barrows in Denmark

The study of the distribution, alignment, and contents of Bronze Age barrows in southwestern Denmark is a fascinating investigation of diverse kinds of information (Fig. 16.6). The study follows a processual approach to the past, using empirical data such as site size, geographic location, and the quantitative measure of wealth to interpret the distribution of these tombs. The barrow study follows a scientific method which explicitly evaluates the ideas that the barrows were placed along routes of communication in the Bronze Age and that more important individuals in these tombs lived where these routes of communication intersected.

The archaeological questions in this study involve social inequality and the distribution of wealth in hierarchical societies. Although the general processes involved in the organization of Bronze Age society as a whole were not a focus, much of the direction and tone of the published study was pragmatic, working on the assumption that human behavior is patterned and can be revealed by analysis of the archaeological record. There was little attention given to the meaning of the finds. The symbolic aspects of the barrows and their contents were not an issue in this study.

Fig. 16.6 One of the extraordinarily well preserved coffins and contents from a Bronze Age barrow in Denmark. The split and hollowed oak tree trunk contained the body of a young woman wrapped in sheepskin and wool blankets and buried in fine clothing, some of the earliest textiles in the world.

 EXAMPLE

THE COLLAPSE OF MAYA CIVILIZATION

Civilizations come and go. The historian Arnold Toynbee in his book, *A Study of History,* outlined the life cycles of civilizations, through birth, growth, crises, troubles, and death. Toynbee calculated that the average lifespan of a civilization was on the order of 400 years. Such societies achieve preeminence for only a brief period. Over the last five centuries, for example, only France was a world leader for more than 90 years.

Ancient civilizations also rose and fell. One of the most fascinating cases comes from the Maya region of Mesoamerica (Fig. 16.7). Much of the central part of this region today is covered by dense, uninhabited tropical jungle, but beneath the forest canopy lie the ruins of the cities, villages, farms, and fields of the Classic Maya. This literate culture spanned the centuries between AD 300 and AD 900. Yet by the time the Spanish conquistadores entered the area in AD 1525, almost no one was living there. Their disappearance, along with eerie images of abandoned temples overgrown by rain forest, has fostered the mystery of the Maya.

The Maya achieved many of the hallmarks of state-level society. Their culture was characterized by monumental stone architecture, great pyramidal temples, magnificent palaces and tombs, cities, roads and reservoirs, long-distance trade, accurate calendrical and numerical systems, a written hieroglyphic language used for record-

Maya Region

vides a limited, but spectacular, view of a small, wealthy segment of Bronze Age society north of the Alps.

Bronze Age barrows dot the landscape of southern Scandinavia (Fig. 16.4). In only a handful of cases have the contents of these barrows survived both the ravages of time and the greed of tomb robbers, to provide a glimpse of the elite of Bronze Age society in northwestern Europe. Bronze Age barrows were built for the wealthier members of society and placed near where the living had died. Most barrows in Denmark are located in areas of productive farmland, evidence of the important relationship between wealth and the control of agricultural resources.

The amount of bronze and gold in these burials provides some indication of the wealth of the deceased individuals. All bronze and gold in southern Scandinavia had to be imported because the ores are not indigenous. Gold was more valuable; only 1 g (0.04 oz) of gold is found for every 1000 g (2.2 lb) of bronze. There are pronounced differences in buried wealth between the sexes and between individuals. For example, male graves are more abundant than female graves, and they contain more wealth. Also, some individuals were buried with a great deal of bronze and gold and some without any, suggesting that social differentiation was pronounced.

The distribution of thousands of such barrows in Denmark offers information on the use of the landscape and the organization of early Bronze Age society. Fig. 16.5 shows the distribution of Bronze Age barrows in the southwestern corner of Denmark. The distinct linear arrangements of the barrows are shown. This figure also shows the location of gold finds in the barrows, indicating distinctive nodes where wealth was concentrated. These high circular burial mounds were placed dramatically on the horizon to emphasize the importance of the buried individuals. The lines of barrows almost certainly lie along routes of movement and communication in the area, and the major intersections must have been at the residences of the wealthy. An elite segment of the population must have controlled most of the resources as well as the trade.

Fig. 16.4 Two Bronze Age barrows dominate the skyline above a fjord in northern Denmark.

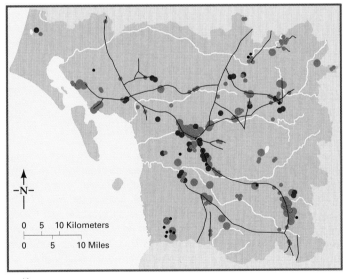

Key

• Minor/unspecified gold artifacts

Fig. 16.5 The distribution of Bronze Age barrows, or burial mounds, in southwestern Denmark. The locations of the individual mounds mark prehistoric trails or roads in this area. The contents of the mounds reflect the wealth of the interred individual. Larger circles mark greater burial wealth, shown in the form of bracelets and armbands at the bottom of the illustration. Wealth is clearly concentrated at a few strategic crossroads and locations in the area.

barrows   Earthen burial *mounds.*

Barrows in Denmark

The study of the distribution, alignment, and contents of Bronze Age barrows in southwestern Denmark is a fascinating investigation of diverse kinds of information (Fig. 16.6). The study follows a processual approach to the past, using empirical data such as site size, geographic location, and the quantitative measure of wealth to interpret the distribution of these tombs. The barrow study follows a scientific method which explicitly evaluates the ideas that the barrows were placed along routes of communication in the Bronze Age and that more important individuals in these tombs lived where these routes of communication intersected.

The archaeological questions in this study involve social inequality and the distribution of wealth in hierarchical societies. Although the general processes involved in the organization of Bronze Age society as a whole were not a focus, much of the direction and tone of the published study was pragmatic, working on the assumption that human behavior is patterned and can be revealed by analysis of the archaeological record. There was little attention given to the meaning of the finds. The symbolic aspects of the barrows and their contents were not an issue in this study.

Fig. 16.6 One of the extraordinarily well preserved coffins and contents from a Bronze Age barrow in Denmark. The split and hollowed oak tree trunk contained the body of a young woman wrapped in sheepskin and wool blankets and buried in fine clothing, some of the earliest textiles in the world.

 EXAMPLE

THE COLLAPSE OF MAYA CIVILIZATION

Civilizations come and go. The historian Arnold Toynbee in his book, *A Study of History,* outlined the life cycles of civilizations, through birth, growth, crises, troubles, and death. Toynbee calculated that the average lifespan of a civilization was on the order of 400 years. Such societies achieve preeminence for only a brief period. Over the last five centuries, for example, only France was a world leader for more than 90 years.

Ancient civilizations also rose and fell. One of the most fascinating cases comes from the Maya region of Mesoamerica (Fig. 16.7). Much of the central part of this region today is covered by dense, uninhabited tropical jungle, but beneath the forest canopy lie the ruins of the cities, villages, farms, and fields of the Classic Maya. This literate culture spanned the centuries between AD 300 and AD 900. Yet by the time the Spanish conquistadores entered the area in AD 1525, almost no one was living there. Their disappearance, along with eerie images of abandoned temples overgrown by rain forest, has fostered the mystery of the Maya.

The Maya achieved many of the hallmarks of state-level society. Their culture was characterized by monumental stone architecture, great pyramidal temples, magnificent palaces and tombs, cities, roads and reservoirs, long-distance trade, accurate calendrical and numerical systems, a written hieroglyphic language used for record-

Maya Region

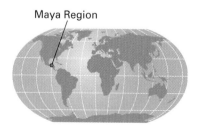

Fig. 16.7 The Maya region (shaded in green) of Mexico, Guatemala, Belize, and parts of Honduras and El Salvador, showing some of the major sites.

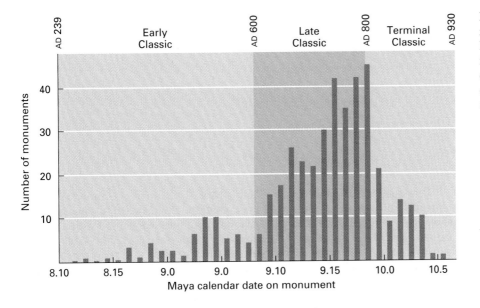

Fig. 16.8 A graph of the number of monuments erected over time in the Maya region. The monuments are inscribed with a date in the Maya calendar. It is clear that the erecting of monuments stopped gradually rather than abruptly after AD 800.

ing numbers, dates, and important events, astronomical observations, extraordinary art, endemic warfare, and a stratified social system dominated by powerful kings and priests. The population of the Maya region at its height must have been in the hundreds of thousands. Subsistence was based on agriculture, with corn, beans, and squash likely as the primary staples.

Several pieces of evidence, however, point to a rapid decline for the Maya. The Maya erected many dated monuments during their heyday, but around AD 800 the number declines dramatically (Fig. 16.8). At the same time, royal dynasties disappear from view and many major centers were abandoned without evidence of violence or destruction. Another indication can be seen in the radiocarbon dates from the area, showing a precipitous decrease in population after AD 800. However, the dates show a decrease, not a disappearance, indicating that some human presence continued in the area.

www.mhhe.com/pricearch1

For a Web-based activity on the Maya, please see the Internet exercises on your online learning center.

TABLE 16.1 Some explanations of the Maya collapse.

Elite collapse	Society Collapse
1. Peasant revolts	1. Demise of trade networks
2. Internal warfare	2. Ideological overkill
3. Foreign invasion	3. Earthquakes, hurricanes, or volcanic eruptions
4. Disruption of trade	4. Climatic change (drought)
	5. Epidemic human disease
	6. Exhaustion of agricultural lands

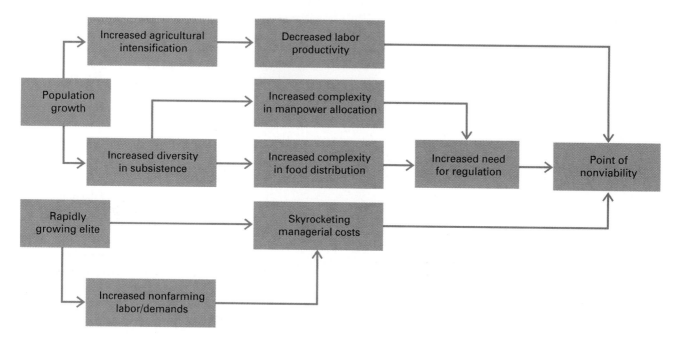

Fig. 16.9 John Lowe's model for the collapse of the Maya, based on excessive population and elite demand.

The question of what happened to the Maya—why their civilization and its inhabitants had largely disappeared by the time of the Spanish arrival—has intrigued scholars for decades. Many theories have been put forth concerned with either the demise of just the elite class or the collapse of the entire social system (Table 16.1). In the elite scenario, common folk continue to live in the region for some time, but eventually die out. Theories for the collapse of the entire society involve either short-term catastrophic events or long-term changes to explain the abandonment of the Maya region.

There are many ideas about the Maya collapse and relatively few hard facts. For example, arguments for catastrophic events are based on limited evidence. Major drought is suggested by some to have forced the abandonment of the Maya region, but climatic data show that excessive aridity was localized and short term at the time of the Maya collapse. There is evidence for environmental degradation from sediments from lake bottoms in the Maya area, which show that decreasing forests, more erosion, and higher sedimentation rates are associated with increasing population.

More realistic scenarios of the Maya collapse usually involve several factors. One of the more ambitious explanations appeared in 1985, involving a systems simulation of Maya society. John Lowe in a book entitled *The Dynamics of Collapse* considered a number of factors and argued that population pressure and a heavy burden imposed by too many elite in society caused the collapse of the entire system (Fig. 16.9).

David Webster in his 2002 book on *The Fall of the Ancient Maya* invoked more factors in the collapse. He focuses on the role of ambitious rulers, population growth,

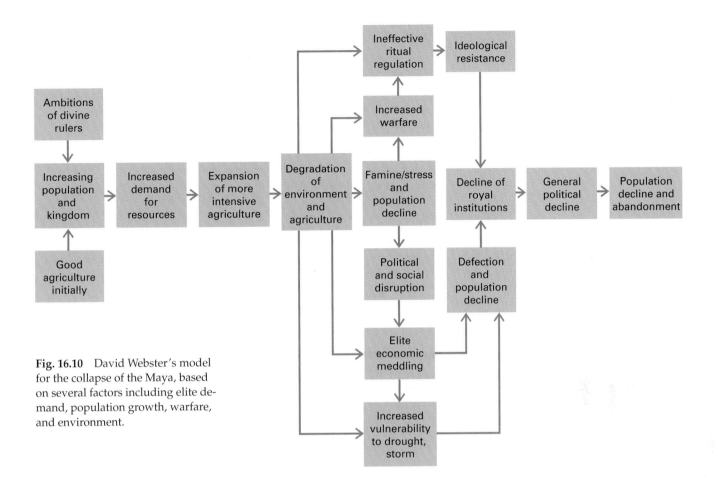

Fig. 16.10 David Webster's model for the collapse of the Maya, based on several factors including elite demand, population growth, warfare, and environment.

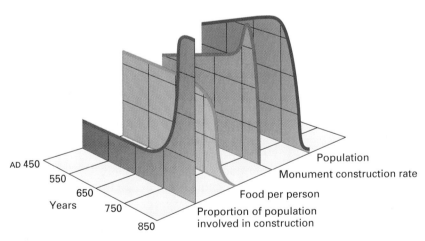

Fig. 16.11 The Hosler et al. model for the collapse of the Maya, based on monument construction, population, and available food.

warfare and competition, and environmental degradation in bringing about the end of the Maya (Fig. 16.10).

In another investigation of the Maya, Dorothy Hosler, Jeremy Sabloff, and Dale Runge created a computer simulation of the relationship among the factors of population, monument construction, per capita food intake, and proportion of population involved in construction instead of farming. They argue in essence that the growth of building and construction in the Maya region took labor from farming activities. As farming production declined, more construction was needed to placate the gods (Fig. 16.11). This destructive cycle, they argued, led to the rapid collapse of the Maya.

The End of the Maya

The case study discussed in the previous example is not the work of a single individual but an amalgam of opinions on the subject of the end of Classic Maya society after AD 800 or so. Most of the views that have been expressed are clearly processual, focusing on a variety of specific and objective causes. The emphasis on cause and effect and on multicausal explanation in this research is typical of the "new" archaeology. The flow charts used by Lowe and Webster are practically standard formats for explanation in processual archaeology and systems models of the past. These models, like computer programs, lead logically from one step to the next, taking us from cause to effect and from question to answer without the ambiguity that most solutions in the social sciences involve. At the same time, such models may oversimplify reality and run the risk of missing important factors in the system.

The emphasis on external, natural causes for social change (such as climate, catastrophe, disease, and overpopulation) reflects a processual approach as well, with less attention to internal social and ideological aspects of the Maya collapse. The focus on a quantitative formulation of the problem in the Hosler et al. model, using numbers of population, rates of monument construction, per capita food intake, and the proportion of population involved in construction, is also a consequence of the statistical and scientific approach of the processualists. The objective and quantitative tone of the argument reflects a belief in a logical and deductive methodology applied to a problem for which a solution must exist.

There are several problems with such processual approaches to the explanation of societal collapse. In particular, the emphasis on external factors in nature removes human behavior and decision making from consideration and makes issues of organization and ideology much less significant than environment, population, and technology. Quantification is a useful goal, but variables like the proportion of the population involved in construction are almost impossible to measure and the use of such estimates weakens these approaches. Processual approaches often emphasize factors that are important in modern Western nations where capitalism dominates the organization and operation of society. However, the nature and cost of labor likely had very different connotations in ancient Maya society. Such modern biases may obscure our chances of understanding the past.

None of these theories are fully satisfactory. The demise of Maya civilization is still not well understood. New theories arise and more data are collected; but the questions remain. What is clear is that civilizations, like people, are mortal and have a finite time on earth.

Post-Processual Archaeology

Every generation of archaeologists is likely to be critical of the methods of its predecessors.
—Glyn Daniel, archaeologist

A worldview known as postmodernism appeared in Europe in the late 1950s. This was a new way of academic thinking and critique in the humanities that initially focused on art and architecture and eventually migrated to the social sciences. Postmodernists are a group of critics rethinking concepts fundamental to modern scientists and humanists.

A major component of postmodernism is critical theory, a name given to an approach to the study of culture, literature, and thought that developed primarily in France. Critical theory is a perspective that encourages scholars to critically approach their assumptions about humanity and the world. Critical theory is ultimately a critique of capitalism and its goal is to transform society into a just, rational, and humane community. It examines how cultural institutions—like religion, science, academia, or the media—shape identities and determine what is acceptable, providing privilege to some and marginalizing others.

Another important aspect of the postmodern movement is **deconstruction**—a form of literary analysis that tries to expose the differences between the structure of a text and basic Western concepts about the meaning of reality. Deconstruction was intended to show how texts cannot simply be read as the message of the author, but must be understood within a given culture or worldview. A deconstructed text will reveal a multitude of different viewpoints, often in direct opposition with one another.

In archaeology, the term *post-processual* was substituted for *postmodern* to describe the reaction to the earlier processual school. The post-processual school,

deconstruction   A form of literary analysis used to show the differences between the structure of a text and basic Western concepts about the meaning of reality.

Fig. 16.12 Ian Hodder of Stanford University.

Fig. 16.13 *Archaeological Theory Today,* edited by Ian Hodder, one of the major proponents of the post-processual school.

led by British archaeologists Ian Hodder, Christopher Tilley, and Michael Shanks, reacted strongly to processual views (Fig. 16.12). Post-processual archaeology has also been described by the phrase "interpretative archaeologies," using the plural term to mark a diversity of approaches, encompassing structural, symbolic, Marxist, reflexive, gender, queer, and critical archaeology. We will consider these different "interpretative" archaeologies together as the school of post-processualism, but also take a more detailed look at gender archaeology.

From the perspective of relativism, some post-processualists argue that archaeology can never have an objective view of the past, that our own biases and perceptions determine what we see in the archaeological record. Interpreting the past is considered a political act, a reflection of the agendas and concerns of today rather than any reality in the past. Some post-processualists argue that archaeological interpretation must be hermeneutic (about ideas, meaning, and symbols) and not scientific, and that evaluation or testing is irrelevant since many interpretations are possible and acceptable. Some from this school do not believe that scientific methods can deal with human behavior—that many of the things that are most human (art, music, and literature) are not accessible to scientific study. They also argue that science is a Western ideology that has excluded minorities and women.

The post-processual school emphasizes that the individual is active in the formation of culture and that material culture is a text—that the meaning of artifacts is contextual, cultural, cognitive, or ideational. The statement that "material culture is meaningfully constituted" is one of the passwords of post-processual archaeology. The past is a code to be read.

The post-processual approach was a strong reaction to the processual school with its focus on the forces at work in the cultural, social, and ecological aspects of the human past (Fig. 16.14). Processualists, using systems models and quantification, were thought to have lost sight of the people behind the artifacts. Rather than seeking general laws, post-processualists argued for historical particularism—

Some very different intellectual developments have emerged in recent years, in general featuring the relativism characteristic of the "postmodern" school of thought seen most notably in anthropology and literary studies. In choosing to term their approach "post-processual" the leading practitioners of this trend in archaeology are pronouncing a judgement which some commentators have found to be a shade arrogant in its assumptions.
—Colin Renfrew, archaeologist

Theory is thoroughly subjective. It is not a technical product of a specialist but a delimited and localized production, arising from a specific contextualized interaction between individuals, the experiences of these individuals, the manner in which their life and work interacts, and the way in which the archaeologist manages to arrive at a specific picture of the past based on the scraps of contingent materials . . . and life experiences at his or her disposal.
—Michael Shanks and Christopher Tilley, archaeologists

Fig. 16.14 Processual and post-processual perspectives.

ACADEMIC SMACKDOWN!!

THE EMPIRICAL, MODERNIST ARCHAEOLOGISTS
They don't believe nothing they can't count!

VS.

THE INCOMPREHENSIBLE, FRENCH, PO-MO PHILOSOPHERS
So obtuse that they can't even understand each other!

"*Colonialist!*" "*Meshugge shikse!*"

THE MODERNISTS...

REALITY *exists. It's independent of our conceptualizations of it*
THERE *are objective facts & we can know them*
THINGS *have definite meanings*
PROOF *comes from scientific endeavor*
FIXED *canon guides research*
ACADEMIC *study*
BEHAVIOR *is patterned*
DISTANCE *from subject is desired*
ETHNOGRAPHY *is the product*
ANALYSIS *reveals structure*

THE POSTMODERNISTS...

REALITY *is a construct. It's a function of how we conceptualize it*
ALL *knowledge is relative*
THERE *are endless interpretations*
PROOF *is a fallacy, an illusion*
DIVERSE *approaches to research*
PRAXIS
BEHAVIOR *is variable*
PARTICIPATION *with subject is mandatory*
DECONSTRUCTION *is the goal*
ANALYSIS *reveals writer's presuppositions*

a detailed descriptive approach—and recognition of the importance of individuals and groups such as women and minorities. The post-processualists have rejected evolutionary arguments that suggest progressive change and they avoid generalization.

 EXAMPLE

THE ROCK ART OF NÄMFORSEN, SWEDEN

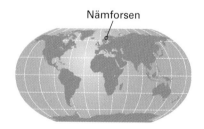

Nämforsen

Gustaf Hallström (1880–1962), a Swedish archaeologist, dedicated much of his life to discovering and documenting the Stone Age rock art of northern Scandinavia. Spending almost 40 years clambering around the isolated lakes and rivers of northern Sweden and once nearly drowning, Hallström published two major volumes on what he called the "monumental art of northern Europe." This phrase was intended to convey the magnificence of this art, in both quality and quantity.

A major focus of his research was at the site of Nämforsen (*NAHM-four-sin*), Sweden, one of the largest assemblages of rock art in the world. This art dates from the late Mesolithic through the Bronze Age periods—5000 BC to AD 500—and is found along both sides of a river and on several islands over a distance of 500 m (1/3 of a mile). This is an area of turbulent whitewater rapids (Fig. 16.15), and the many polished stone surfaces of the rock walls and banks of the river became a canvas for Stone Age artists (Fig. 16.16).

The figures of the Nämforsen rock art are pecked or "carved" on smooth stone surfaces along the river. There are approximately 2000 depictions of a variety of motifs, including moose (European elk), boats, humans, tools, shoes or feet, fish, and birds (Fig. 16.17). Most of the carvings are between 20 and 60 cm (8–25 in) in height.

Among all the motifs, the animals dominate in number, as seen in Table 16.2, but the spatial distribution of designs is variable. Elk and boats are most common

Fig. 16.15 The river rapids and rock art site at Nämforsen, Sweden.

Fig. 16.16 Rock carvings at Nämforsen. These examples and most of the depictions have been filled in with red paint to make them more visible.

Fig. 16.17 The major motifs at Nämforsen.

TABLE 16.2 Location, quantity, and percentage of motifs at Nämforsen.

Motif	Northern Shore		Southern Shore		Western Island		Eastern Island		Total
	n	%	n	%	n	%	n	%	
Elks	238	35	27	4	193	29	213	32	671
Boats	40	12	49	15	28	8	220	65	337
Humans	30	33	0	0	11	12	51	55	92
Fish	8	42	2	11	7	37	2	11	19
Birds	3	33	0	0	3	33	3	33	9
Feet	5	16	0	0	25	81	1	3	31
Tools	24	37	7	11	3	5	30	47	64
Total	348		85		270		520		1223
Total %	28		2		22		43		

and occur everywhere. Most of the figures were carved on the three large islands that command the rapids. Most of the other motifs appear on the islands as well. Only a small number of motifs appear on the southern shore, where boats predominate. Boats are most common on the eastern island. Humans are also most frequent on this island and are the third most common motif overall. Fish, birds, and feet are generally rare.

Christopher Tilley, a British archaeologist at University College, London, re-examined the Nämforsen rock carvings in the late 1980s using Hallström's published study. Tilley took exception to Hallström's conclusion that there was no conclusion to be made, that the carvings did not speak, and that their meaning would forever remain in the past. He described Hallström as a "pure empiricist subscribing to a rigid doctrine of atomistic particularism in which it is assumed that nothing is related unless it can be proved otherwise. . . ." Tilley suggested that in spite of the fine descriptions that Hallström produced, his "entire life's work ends without any conclusion. In this sense it is a complete failure." Tilley's strong words pierce both the archaeologist Hallström and the profession: "He exemplifies the tragedy of much contemporary archaeology—painstaking, almost masochistic effort, an immense labour, but a failure to disclose meaning."

Tilley then turned to extracting meaning from the art. His research questions were multiple: "What is to be made of these rock carvings? Since they are so utterly removed from contemporary experience, must our reaction to them always remain one of alienation? What is their meaning, significance, and value today? Our reaction may be one of fascination, but must this inevitably be reflected in interpretative incompetence, a dumb failure to discover meaning? Or can we hope to mediate them productively, reinscribe them into the present, open out the carvings to subjective experience once more?"

Tilley published his ideas in a 1991 study titled *Material Culture and Text: The Art of Ambiguity.* He regards the art of Nämforsen as text and decodes its meaning through the interplay of ideas and empirical data. "To read Nämforsen, unlike reading a book, is to write it. This reading is a process of translation, the movement from things to words, imagery to language." His first step was finding the rules of the grammar—a search for relationships among the carvings in terms of design, location, distribution, and association (Fig. 16.18).

Taking into account various patterns that can be identified in the rock art, Tilley then moved to the question of meaning. He presumed that sign systems, like the rock art of Nämforsen, have an inherent tendency to different sets of meanings. For this reason, in part, Tilley took three different paths across the landscape of meaning— three theoretical lenses in post-processual archaeology—structuralism, hermeneutics or cosmology, and Marxism. Each of these perspectives adds different layers of meaning to the rock art and to Tilley's interpretation of it.

Types of elk-boat associations from different carving surfaces at Nämforsen on which only elks and boats occur.

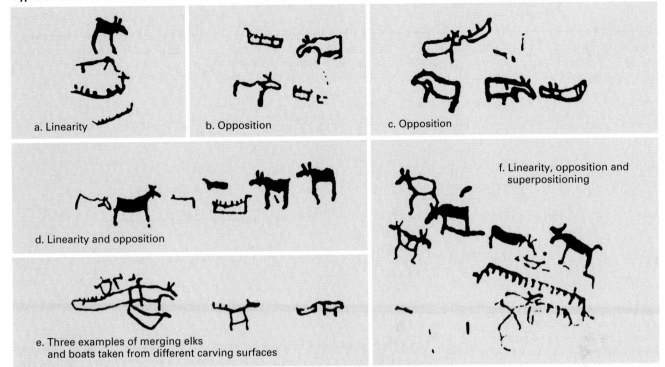

a. Linearity

b. Opposition

c. Opposition

d. Linearity and opposition

f. Linearity, opposition and superpositioning

e. Three examples of merging elks and boats taken from different carving surfaces

Fig. 16.18 Tilley's sets of elk and boat motifs found together at Nämforsen.

TABLE 16.3 Oppositional pairs in the structural logic of association at Nämforsen.

Outline Elk : Filled Elk

Double-line Boat : Single-line Boat

Outline Fish : Filled Fish

Feet : Elk Heads on Poles

Triangular Humans : Stick Humans

To simplify this account, we turn to Tilley's interpretation of the structural logic of the carvings. Through a series of arguments, Tilley suggested that the associations among the motifs at Nämforsen signify sets of social relations between the groups of hunter-gatherers who decorated these rocks. Ignoring the human figures, the six remaining motifs fall into two groups: natural (elk, fish, and bird) and cultural (feet, boat, and tool). A further structure is revealed within these sets—reiterating the categories—based on associations of place. Elk and feet are land, fish and boat are water, bird and tool are sky.

Tilley then provided the meaning: "Each of the motifs at Nämforsen signifies a different hunter-gatherer group visiting the place." Tilley and other researchers have noted that the human figures at Nämforsen take two forms: stick figures or triangular body figures. These figures almost always occur with elk or boats. Next, Tilley examined associations of different types of several motifs and noted the oppositional pairs listed in Table 16.3. These items rarely occur together.

On this basis, Tilley proposed an interpretation involving the kinship organization of the human groups who produced the rock art at Nämforsen. The two types of human figures seen in the rock art may represent two divisions (moieties or lineages) among the groups who visited Nämforsen. Sets of natural vs. cultural motifs may perhaps represent clans in each moiety as indicated by the motifs in each of the two groups. Two possible schematic representations of this structural logic are shown in Fig. 16.19.

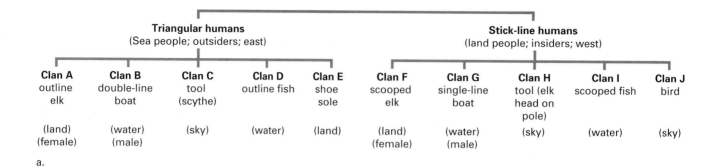

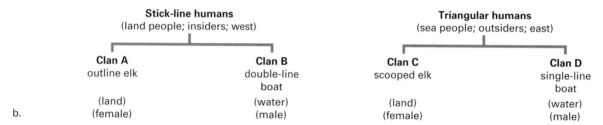

a.

b.

Fig. 16.19 Tilley's reconstructions of two possible kinship structures (a and b) for the hunter-gatherers who created the art at Nämforsen.

As Tilley recommends, you may evaluate his case for yourself and/or develop your own meaning of the rock art. Tilley concludes: "The point I am really trying to make is that these rock carvings invite a response from us, the infusion of our subjectivity. The carvings present a vocabulary, a cosmological thematics, which not only allows but necessitates a variety of readings. There is no fixed meaning and we must remember that images cannot in fact be reduced to words, 'read'. This 'reading' always results, is intimately linked, with textual production which both inevitably goes beyond the carvings themselves and yet simultaneously portrays a lack, a failure. I do not present a proper conclusion because it is an impossibility."

ARCHAEOLOGICAL THINKING

Text on Stone

Tilley's study of the rock art of Nämforsen, Sweden, is a classic example of the post-processual approach. It is a confounding and stimulating essay on archaeological approaches to meaning in the past and present. His ideas and words clearly reflect the major tenets of post-modernism. Tilley decries Hallström's fundamental study of the art because there is no conclusion. Tilley tells us that the art is text, to be read by archaeologists. Since reality is a construct, we can construct this art as we see fit.

Tilley takes several different approaches, exploring three branches of the post-processual school—structuralism, hermeneutics, and Marxism. Each perspective arrives at a different interpretation of the art. Ultimately, Tilley turns to a more objective examination of the asso-

ciations and relationships among the major motifs of the art, suggesting that these associations reflect different social groups among the peoples who visited the site.

Several elements of Tilley's study are discomforting. The rock art was produced over several thousand years and three major periods in European prehistory: the Mesolithic, the Neolithic, and the Bronze Age. That these motifs and their placement had constant and similar meanings to generations of artists does not seem likely. Tilley's failure to conclude—his decision that there is no fixed meaning but a variety of readings of the art—renders study of this material an exercise in individual perception and interpretation, and in fact he falls prey to his own stinging criticism of Hallström.

Evolution and Archaeology

There are two groups of archaeologists within the general school of evolutionary approaches. Both groups agree that "natural selection is the primary explanatory mechanism in scientific evolution," and both groups take a largely biological perspective on human behavior and change. Beyond this juncture, however, their views differ sharply. One group—the evolutionary archaeologists—follows a rather strict Darwinian approach to explaining the human past. This group is headed by individuals such as Robert Dunnell, Michael O'Brien, and Robert Leonard. A second group—the evolutionary ecologists—is concerned specifically with humans as part of nature and the environment. This group explains human behavior and the archaeological record in ecological terms. This group is headed by Eric Alden Smith, Bruce Winterhalder, James O'Connell, Robert Bettinger, and others. Relations between these two groups of evolutionists are frosty at best. Their two perspectives are discussed separately below.

Selectionist Archaeology

The evolutionary archaeologists, or **selectionists** as they like to be called, believe that cultural change in the archaeological record should be explained by natural selection and other Darwinian processes operating on inherited variation in artifacts and behavior (Fig. 16.20). Evolutionary archaeologists argue that other schools and explanations are unscientific and insist that natural selection, drift, and other evolutionary forces explain changes in the kind, characteristics, and number of artifacts at archaeological sites. Human choice and decision do not play a role in this process of change.

Selectionists claim that archaeologists can see "evolution in action" because some archaeological patterns reflect natural selection and others show that it is not operating. There are, however, few tangible examples provided by the selectionists. Gradual change over time is sometimes cited as a reflection of natural selection. Evolutionary archaeologists, for example, point to the relationship between population growth and evolution as a monitor of positive natural selection. However, empirical evidence has demonstrated that populations can grow, or shrink, without selection directly operating.

Selectionists often see evolution operating in situations where there is permanent, unidirectional change in archaeological evidence. They believe that artifacts (and other archaeological remains) are part of the human phenotype, controlled by our genetics, and thus operate under biological controls like evolution and natural selection. Functional characteristics in artifacts enhance the fitness of the user and are determined by selection; properties of artifacts that are not related to the fitness of the user are stylistic and considered selectively neutral.

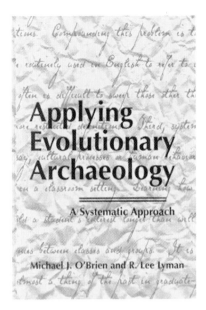

Fig. 16.20 *Applying Evolutionary Archaeology: A Systematic Approach,* by Michael J. O'Brien and R. Lee Lyman, a major statement by the selectionists.

⬤ EXAMPLE 〰〰〰〰〰〰〰〰〰〰〰〰〰〰〰〰〰

HORSES AND SNOWMOBILES

Ann Ramenofsky of the University of New Mexico has employed a selectionist perspective to explain major changes in transportation among Native American groups following European contact, specifically concerned with the adoption of the horse and the snowmobile. The story of the horse is a well-known one. Horses became extinct in North and South America at the close of the Pleistocene, some 11,000 years ago, along with a number of other species. The horse was reintroduced by the Spanish who conquered large areas of Central and South America and parts of North America, including what is now California, Texas, and Florida in the sixteenth century AD.

selectionist School of archaeological theory that believes culture should be explained by natural selection and other Darwinian processes.

The Pueblo Indians of the American Southwest used horses obtained from the Spanish for food and traded live animals to the Plains Indians for buffalo meat and jerky. These horses and riding skills gradually spread as the Plains Indians became the renowned mounted buffalo hunters of the American West. Very quickly, the horse became an integral and essential part of their culture.

Ramenofsky argues that the adoption of the horse is best understood in terms of an evolutionary perspective, that natural selection of cultural variation best explains the increase in the number of horses in use among the Plains Indians. Thus, in the selectionist view, horses became more common because they increased the adaptive fitness of the Plains Indians who used them. Adaptive fitness refers to reproductive success; individuals who used horses are assumed to have been more successful in obtaining food and to have produced more children than individuals who did not. Over several generations, individuals who used horses would become a larger proportion of the population (assuming that the children of horse users continued the tradition).

Ramenofsky then argues that the same mechanism operated among the Cree Indians in the boreal forests of eastern Canada when the snowmobile was introduced in the late twentieth century. In this area, snowshoe hunting was practiced until the arrival of the snowmobile. Ramenofsky suggests that when the first snowmobiles came into use, some hunters continued to walk while a few used the motorized transport. Snowmobile use resulted in a selective advantage in terms of greater hunting success and/or more free time, and this conferred reproductive success in the form of more children. Snowmobile use was passed on to these offspring and eventually became the common means of winter travel among the Cree.

There are several questionable aspects to such a perspective. Selectionist views remove human choice or decision from any role in cultural change. It is difficult to understand how artifacts, or behaviors for that matter, can directly confer a selective advantage without conscious decision making by individual members in society. One might also question whether a preference for "snowmobile use" is automatically passed on to one's offspring. As members of the evolutionary ecology school have pointed out, the Cree Indians adopted the snowmobile very quickly, within the time span of one generation. It would not have been possible for reproductive success to play a role in the change from snowshoes to snowmobiles.

Evolutionary Ecology

Evolutionary ecology in archaeology developed out of an earlier perspective known as cultural ecology, which focused on the dynamic relationship between human society and its environment, using culture as the primary mechanism of adaptation. Culture is a giant concept and hard to work with, so evolutionary ecologists emphasize human abilities to reason and to optimize their behavior. In this view, natural selection operates not on the artifacts themselves, but on the behavior of individuals. Evolutionary ecologists assume that natural selection designed organisms to adapt to local conditions in fitness-enhancing or optimizing ways.

One of the major tenets of this group involves a concept known as **optimal foraging theory**, borrowed from biology, to explain the food-getting behavior of humans—especially hunter-gatherers. Optimal foraging theory argues that the most efficient foraging strategies produce the greatest return in energy relative to time and effort expended. Optimal foraging assumes that humans make rational decisions based on economic efficiency.

Evolutionary ecologists examine the archaeological and ethnographic record looking for things like "optimization goals," "currencies," and "constraints," and apply ecological and mathematical models to explain human behavior. Perhaps the most comprehensive statement from this perspective has been

optimal foraging theory Evolutionary ecology perspective based on efficient *foraging* strategies.

Pots as Tools

In essence for selectionists, unidirectional changes over time in functional artifact characteristics are thought to document selection and evolution. There are few case studies, but a frequently cited example comes from a study of changes in pottery during the Woodland period in eastern North America. David Braun measured the thickness of the walls of pottery vessels used for cooking over a thousand-year period between 1000 and 2000 years ago. Because wall thickness affects the heating properties of the pot, it is a functional characteristic. Braun demonstrated from his measurements that wall thickness decreased substantially over time (Fig. 16.21). He argued that this change was brought about by a change in diet to more starchy seeds. His reasoning is based in part on the fact that the food value of starchy seeds is greatly in-creased if they are boiled at high temperatures for long periods of time. Pots with thinner walls are more efficient for cooking since thin walls better conduct heat and are more resistant to thermal shock. Thus, dietary change could be said to affect pottery characteristics.

There are several problems in using evolution to explain the changes in pottery in the prehistoric Eastern United States. First, the change in wall thickness as shown in Braun's measurements (Fig. 16.21) is not gradual as selectionists would argue, but rather sudden after 1600 bp. In fact, there is a slight increase in wall thickness over time between 2000 and 1700 bp. Also, small seeded plants were domesticated in the eastern United States more than 1500 years before this sudden change in the wall thickness of pottery is observed. In general, one of the problems with assumptions about the relationship between evolutionary forces and changes in artifacts is that a variety of factors may cause changes in artifacts, including fashion or style. There is, in fact, no obvious reason to invoke evolutionary forces for the change in wall thickness in pottery.

The major arguments against a selectionist view emphasize the absence of a mechanism for selection to directly modify material culture, that models are deterministic and teleological (requiring some grand design), that the biological ideas of Darwin cannot be applied to human behavior and culture, and that the concepts are largely sociobiological in approach. Sociobiology touts the biological basis of all social behavior and essentially argues that genes and evolution shaped both our bodies and our actions. In this view, culture and human choice are essentially denied a role in the development of human society.

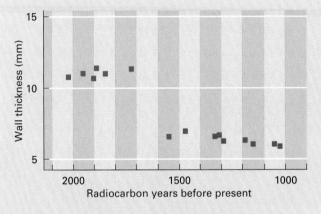

Fig. 16.21 Wall thickness for cooking pots in the Woodland period of the eastern United States.

the argument of Robert Bettinger of the University of California at Davis that the behavior of hunter-gatherers is determined largely by attempts to maximize their net rate of energy gain. An example of an evolutionary ecology approach is described below in a study of the Emeryville shellmound in California.

 EXAMPLE

THE EMERYVILLE SHELLMOUND, CALIFORNIA

One of the subjects of optimal foraging theory in recent years has been resource depression—declines in the sizes and numbers of animal species in response to human hunting. In essence, it is possible to examine the impact of hunter-gatherers on local resources and the consequences to fitness given a decline in availability of food. For example, societal responses to decreasing resources might include technological changes associated with using other foods, increases in violence and warfare, reduced stature and health, or the emergence of social hierarchies.

Emeryville
Shellmound

The Emeryville site, on the eastern shore of San Francisco Bay, provides a good example of the application of optimal foraging theory and change over time since the location witnessed repeated occupation by hunter-gatherers for almost 2000 years. The site was an enormous shell midden, measuring 100 × 300 m in area (like six football fields) and more than 10 m high (about the height of a three-story building). Radiocarbon dates from the layers of the midden show that it was in use from 600 BC to AD 1300. Excavations were conducted at the mound several times, and large numbers of animal bones were collected before it was leveled in 1924 to make way for a factory (Fig. 16.22).

Jack Broughton of the University of Utah identified and counted the wide range of mammal, bird, and fish bones that had been excavated from the site and stored in a museum. The largest species in the major classes of terrestrial mammal, estuarine fish, and waterfowl were the tule deer, white sturgeon, and geese, respectively. If a decrease in resources occurred during the occupation of Emeryville, the numbers of the large-sized prey should decrease relative to the smaller prey types, according to optimal foraging theory. Broughton's data demonstrated this to be the case using an index of the abundance of these species relative to others in the same class; each of the three largest species declined in abundance over time (Fig. 16.23). These trends are not associated with any known changes in the environment.

Fig. 16.22 The Emeryville shell-mound in San Francisco Bay, being removed by a steam shovel in 1924.

Fig. 16.23 A graph of the abundance of black-tailed deer and tule deer in eleven layers of the Emeryville shellmound. As black-tailed deer increase in the upper, younger levels, tule deer decrease in number.

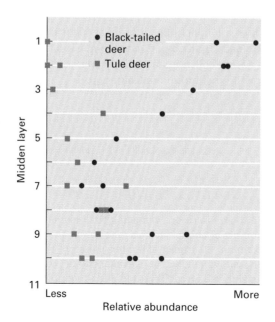

While tule deer, the largest species, declines, black-tailed deer—another large species whose preferred habitat extends far to the east of the mound—first declines in abundance, but then steadily increases over time. Broughton suggests that the rebound of black-tailed deer reflects a pattern of longer-distance hunting in response to local resource depletion. In the case of the Emeryville shellmound, long-distance hunting to increase the use of more distant large game (black-tailed deer) was one of the ways that hunter-gatherers solved the problem of a deteriorating local environment and behaved in an optimal foraging fashion.

Gender Archaeology

In the larger context of the rise of feminism, issues of gender in archaeology burst onto the scene in 1984 with the publication of an article by Meg Conkey of the University of California-Berkeley and Janet Spector of the University of Minnesota entitled "Archaeology and the Study of Gender." Prior to that time, archaeologists generally had regarded the identification of individuals in the archaeological record as difficult to impossible. The generic term "man" was often used for humanity and there was little consideration of the person behind the artifact. Since identification was difficult and often unverifiable, issues of gender had been largely avoided or ignored. Moreover, prior to the 1980s most archaeologists were male.

Initially, emphasis in gender studies was on finding women in the archaeological record. Patty Jo Watson and Mary Kennedy of Washington University in St. Louis, for example, in 1991 argued that women were likely responsible for the agricultural revolution as the persons who originally domesticated plants and animals. More recent investigations have gone beyond that search to important questions about the role of gender in the organization and development of society.

Feminist archaeology involves the belief that gender roles are culturally constructed rather than biologically determined, and that women, among others,

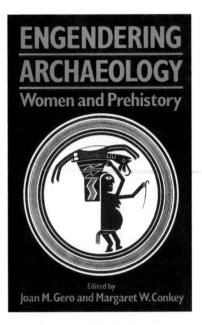

Fig. 16.24 *Engendering Archaeology* by Joan Gero and Meg Conkey, 1991, is an important volume for gender studies in archaeology.

 ARCHAEOLOGICAL THINKING

Optimal Species

Broughton's study comes from the ecological branch of evolutionary archaeology. The perspective of optimal foraging theory puts emphasis on resource use and efficiency. Broughton suggests that the trends in local resource depression and presumed declines in foraging efficiency led to increased stress for shellmound inhabitants and may have been associated with more intensive procurement of lower-ranked resources, which in turn increased disease, decreased body size and stature, and increased defense of territories and conflict.

In this way, evolutionary ecology tries to explain the general trend toward a broad-spectrum diet in the Holocene as an effect of the consequences of the optimizing decisions of hunter-gatherers in response to the declining availability of large-bodied animals. This argument resembles the flow charts of the processualists where one thing leads to another and neatly resolves the question. It also reflects an environmentalist perspective on the relationship between humans and nature in which humans disrupt the natural world around them.

The use of numbers, essential in archaeozoology where counting bones and estimating MNI and NISP are standard procedure, nicely fits the approach of quantitative ecologists who believe that much human behavior can be described in mathematical models. This ecological perspective appears to take a narrow view. According to this perspective, all changes are attributed to the relationship among numbers of people, technology, and the bounty of nature without consideration for human thought, flexibility, or organization. The argument that the shellmound inhabitants traveled farther and farther to obtain deer meat ignores the possibility that black-tailed deer moved into the niche opened by the overkill of the tule deer or that climate changed, expanding the habitat of the black-tailed deer.

have shared a long history of oppression in many societies. Feminist archaeology has pursued concerns regarding the examination of gender roles and inequality in the profession of archaeology, biases and assumptions made about ancient societies, and male-dominated construction of knowledge. Not all archaeologists involved in the study of gender, however, are feminists.

There is today among archaeologists a substantial interest in gender in the past. Gender studies have introduced important new perspectives in archaeology and have resulted in a richer and more "human" view of the past. The investigation of other social differences, including age, sexual orientation, ethnicity, and race have also received more attention as a result. Without question, the effects of sex and gender on behavior and production, on artifact manufacture and use, and on ritual and ideology, are important dimensions of variation in the archaeological record. Gender studies have emphasized the evolution of sex differences, the division of labor, social constructions of gender, the life cycle, the organization of hierarchy, and the social organization of activities. A study by Elizabeth Brumfiel of the role of gender in the political economy of the Aztec state is discussed below.

www.mhhe.com/pricearch1

For a Web-based activity on the Aztec, please see the Internet exercises on your online learning center.

◉ EXAMPLE

AZTEC WOMEN AND STATE ECONOMY

Liz Brumfiel of Northwestern University (Fig. 16.25) has focused on women in the economy of Aztec Mexico, using both archaeological and historical evidence. The Aztec ruled the Central Highlands in 1521 when the Spanish began the conquest of Mexico. Brumfiel examined artifacts used for cooking and weaving, which were primary occupations for women. The evidence for cooking came from specific kinds of pottery. Brumfiel argued that women were responsible for weaving based on written reports and drawings left by the Spanish (Fig. 16.26).

Archaeological evidence came from spindle whorls commonly found in women's graves. Textiles are made by spinning fiber into thread and weaving those threads into cloth. Spindle whorls are hemispherical ceramic or stone artifacts with a hole in the center. The whorl is attached as a weight on the end of a short wooden shaft (spindle) to maintain momentum as the shaft spins fiber into thread. The cloth that women wove was intended not only for their own household but also for exchange at markets and as tribute to the Aztec rulers.

Brumfiel studied the role of women in the production of cloth at three different sites both before and after the Aztec conquered the region. These sites varied in distance

Mexico City

Fig. 16.25 Liz Brumfiel, Northwestern University.

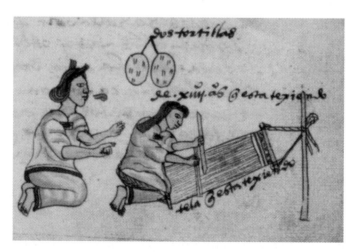

Fig. 16.26 A mother teaches her daughter to weave, from a Spanish document depicting Aztec society.

Gender and Government in Ancient Mexico

Brumfiel's research is a successful combination of processual and post-processual perspectives. In a post-processual vein, her study shows how a gender approach can provide new insights into past state-level societies. Brumfiel argued that ecological variables alone were unable to explain the rise of the Aztec state. Brumfiel's focus on women's labor emphasizes economic factors that were previously ignored. As part of the post-processual perspective, her findings are situated in the larger context of an Aztec state that increased demands on women's productivity. She demonstrates how Aztec women may have used different strategies to meet tribute demands by a powerful state. An engendered view thus provides a more "peopled" understanding of the past and a more detailed explanation of the operation of state societies.

At the same time, from a processual perspective, Brumfiel used various kinds of objective data to reach her conclusions, including information on artifact types and their geographic distribution. Brumfiel would argue that behavior is patterned, but that there are more factors involved in the patterning than archaeologists have normally considered. Brumfiel appears to view the archaeological record as rich with information about the past, rather than as a text to be read and interpreted.

from the Aztec capital and the quality of agricultural land surrounding them. The richest agricultural area was closest to the capital and the poorest land was most distant.

Brumfiel was able to draw several conclusions about the role of women in society and about how Aztec rule may have impacted those roles. She found that after the Aztec empire took control in this area, textile production as a whole was intensified, but it was less important at sites with high levels of agricultural productivity. Evidence for this came from the number of spindle whorls at sites in the agriculturally rich zone, which actually declined. Brumfiel surmised that households in the agriculturally rich area apparently were able to obtain cloth in the Aztec period, rather than make their own. The pottery evidence indicates that tortilla production increased in this region; tortillas are labor-intensive but are a highly portable food with a long shelf life. This pattern suggests that food preparation may have been for market exchange. Brumfiel suggests that the evidence points to an increase in food preparation by women living in agriculturally rich areas and an increase in women's spinning activities elsewhere, most likely to meet the tribute demands of the Aztec state.

www.mhhe.com/pricearch1

For a Web-based activity on Aztec women, please see the Internet exercises on your online learning center.

NEW DIRECTIONS

Ideas change and theoretical views evolve. New perspectives appear that may have an important influence on how archaeologists see the world in the coming years. We are now at the beginning of what has been labeled the century of biology, as biochemistry and genetic engineering unravel the fundamental chemistry of life. The remarkable discoveries of this research and the innovations that result will no doubt foster the rise of biological determinism as an explanation. Arguments that human behavior and social change can be explained by our genes are bound to gain ground in the short term.

Several other emerging perspectives include complexity theory, agency theory, and cognitive archaeology. One rapidly growing theoretical framework for studying stability and change focuses on complexity theory and the analysis of self-organizing systems in both natural and artificial worlds. This perspective is an outgrowth of systems theory and studies of artificial intelligence. Self-organizing systems are characterized by behaviors that arise as the result of nonlinear interactions among a large number of components. Systems that are large and complex, but not governed by hierarchical rules, are said to be self-organizing. Examples of such natural complex systems include multicellular organisms, insect societies, immune systems, and ecological regimes. Artificial systems with such properties include communication networks, computing systems, and evolutionary algorithms.

The study of self-organized, complex, adaptive systems focuses on the connections, interactions, and feedback loops among the parts of the system, known as agents. Agent-based approaches attempt to specify the rules of interaction between agents (individuals) to discover the properties of social systems—for example, how political actors and regions of shared culture can emerge from the repeated local interactions of autonomous agents operating through socioeconomic institutions. The agent-based study of complex cultural systems will likely result in a growing emphasis on individuals and households as agents in past human societies in the coming years.

Another recent direction in archaeology involves theories of agency and practice. The background for these related perspectives comes from the work of Anthony Giddens of Cambridge University, known for the theory of agency, and Pierre Bourdieu (1930–2002), who was involved with the theory of practice. Giddens argued that human agents act with intention and both are structured by and structure their social institutions and material surroundings. Agency studies have centered on individual motivations, intentions, and goals, and have emphasized individual behavior as strategic action.

The behavior of the actors, according to Bourdieu, arises from the interaction of biology and knowledge, what practice theorists refer to as **habitus**, common behavior and basic knowledge that constitute a practical cultural competence. Practice theorists in archaeology like Tim Pauketat of the University of Illinois believe that the traditional emphasis in archaeology on behavior and evolution is being supplanted by practice and history in explanation. Instead of looking at why cultures change, practice theorists focus on cultural practice—what people did and how they changed their own culture. This emphasis on practice requires historical, rather than evolutionary, explanations.

Cognitive archaeology involves the investigation of the development of human thought, the study of how humans think as inferred from the archaeological record. It is an approach to studying the past that employs recent breakthroughs in cognitive science. Cognitive science is an interdisciplinary approach to studying the mind, especially rational thought and behavior. Emphasis in archaeology is on the symbolic nature of human behavior and the role of ideology as an organizational force in society. Cognitive archaeology covers many aspects

We may not be able to establish what people thought; we can aspire to learn how they thought.
—Colin Renfrew, archaeologist

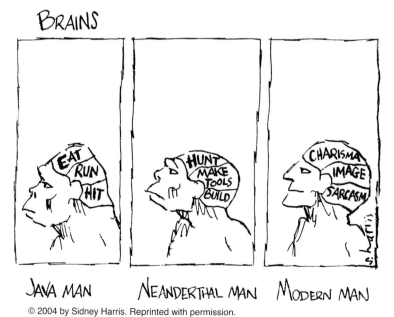

© 2004 by Sidney Harris. Reprinted with permission.

habitus Unthinking dispositions and basic knowledge that constitute a practical cultural competence.

of human thinking, including prehistoric art and symbolism, systems of weights and measures, planning and scheduling, and the structure and maintenance of social relationships. Cognitive perspectives also focus on the individual in society and the nature of human thought in structuring behavior and material culture.

CONCLUSIONS

New ideas circulate regularly through the social and natural sciences. Archaeology often evaluates these perspectives, absorbs some, declines others, and moves on. Theoretical tides in the discipline have ebbed and flowed over the past century. Four schools of thought in current archaeology have been described in this chapter—processual, post-processual, evolutionary, and gender archaeology—and examples have been provided of the kinds of investigations associated with each. These schools grew out of earlier perspectives in archaeology: A focus on culture history was supplanted with an emphasis on positivism in the post–World War II era. Then, processual or "new" archaeology arose in the 1960s as a response to the limitations of culture history and shifted focus to past human behavior and the search for regularities in the operation of human culture. That view was counterbalanced by an emphasis on introspection in the last decades of the twentieth century. Post-processual archaeology arose in the 1980s in response to the limitations of processual archaeology and has attempted to focus archaeology on the decisions, cognition, and symbols of the individual in the past. Evolutionary archaeology has followed two tracks, one Darwinian and one ecological, and has concentrated largely on the mechanisms of stability and change in human society. Evolutionary ecology concentrates on quantitative models of foraging behavior and human ecology. Darwinian evolutionary archaeology tries to fit the biological model of evolution to material culture and human society. Gender archaeology, as a branch of the post-processual school, has emphasized the role of women and minorities in prehistory and has pushed archaeology toward the study of individuals.

Processual and post-processual archaeology have dueled across the last several decades. Processualists were once more likely to be found in the United States, and post-processualists in Britain. But the actual theoretical leanings of many archaeologists are difficult to judge. Fortunately, a survey was done in 1994 with more than 2500 American respondents indicating the theoretical perspective that they followed. This information, although somewhat dated, is useful and is shown in graphic form in Figs. 16.27 and 16.28. Four possible schools of thought were given as choices in the survey form: culture history, cultural ecology, processual, and post-processual. The responses are plotted by the age of the archaeologist in Fig. 16.27. Culture historians clearly tend to be in the older segment of the archaeological population, and the popularity of this perspective among younger archaeologists was around 35%. Cultural ecology was rather evenly spread among the age classes, albeit with a slight tendency toward the older generations. Processual and post-processual archaeology were most popular among the young and least popular among older archaeologists.

More intriguing are the numbers in each perspective and by gender. Fig. 16.28 shows the percentage and number of male and female individuals claiming a particular archaeological perspective. It is probably worth noting that there is little distinction between culture ecological and processual approaches in the minds of many. Given that context, it is clear these two views were the most common among American archaeologists in 1994. By sex, males tend to favor processual and culture history approaches while females are much more likely to prefer post-processual approaches. The approximate numbers of survey respondents is shown in each bar of the graph. The total numbers of respondents for each category were culture history = 566, cultural ecology = 749, processual = 872, and post-processual = 400.

These survey data are now more than 10 years old and may not reflect current trends. At the same time, it is my impression that there is less contention among

Fig. 16.27 Percent of survey respondents by age in 1994 who claim a particular archaeological perspective.

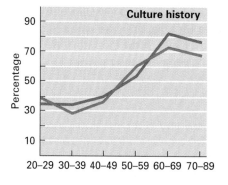

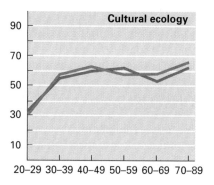

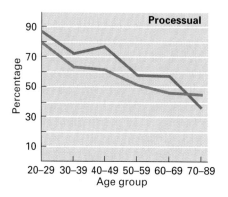

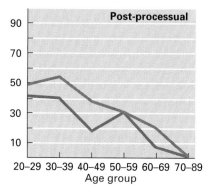

Fig. 16.28 Percent of survey respondents by sex in 1994 who claim a specific archaeological perspective. _____ is female; _____ is male.

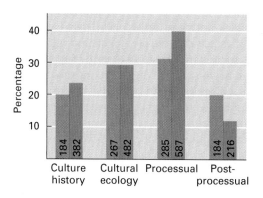

processual and post-processual schools of thought today, that a mingling of minds in archaeology has brought the best of both schools to current perspectives on the past. Issues of ethics and responsibilities appear to outweigh theoretical concerns at the moment, or perhaps it's a lack of new ideas to drive theoretical interests.

One of the reasons there are various schools of theory in archaeology is that explanation in the social sciences, and particularly in archaeology, is a difficult task. Archaeologists have to deal with a fragmentary, poorly preserved, and partial record of human material culture. Using that information, they attempt to understand past human behavior. Human behavior is difficult enough to understand in our own lives today.

Archaeology, along with the other social sciences, is not a predictive field of study—ambiguous results are often the norm. There are few laws and few predictable relationships in economics, sociology, archaeology, or political science. If these were exact sciences, then perhaps there would be no poverty, war, or crime. If the social sciences were like mathematics or physics, economists might be rich, political scientists would be elected, sociologists would be unemployed, and archaeologists would know all the answers.

equifinality A situation in which different initial conditions can lead to a similar end, making archaeological interpretation difficult.

One of the difficulties in dealing with human behavior and its products lies in the fact that several different behaviors may produce the same end result. For example, a cluster of stone tools, fireplaces, and animal bones might be the result of twenty people staying at a place for two nights in a row or ten people for four nights, or two people for twenty different nights over the course of a year. These initial conditions have very different implications for human behavior. Archaeological evidence—and many issues dealing with humans and their behavior—can be interpreted in different ways. This situation is known as **equifinality**—different initial conditions leading to a similar end, where it is difficult to determine which initial condition was important (Fig. 16.29).

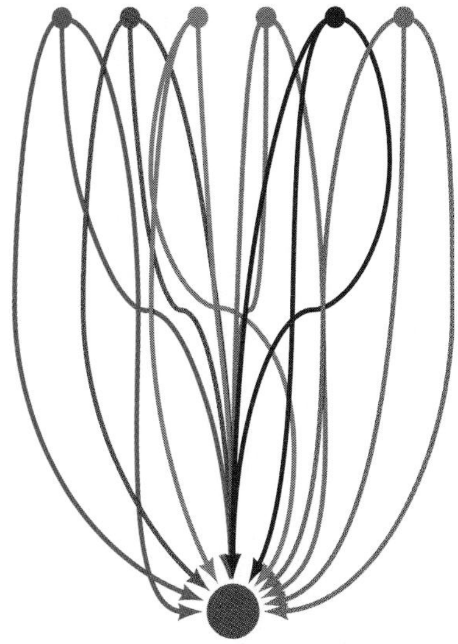

The archaeologist James Hill (1934–1997) remarked that there are many things we can never know with any degree of certainty—that one rarely finds proof of anything in science. Archaeology is not done by formula. Ideas and assumptions provide probable answers to questions, but ideas can be wrong, and assumptions can be off course. Determining the likely answer using the scientific method is something akin to a trial where the evidence is evaluated by a jury of peers (colleagues in archaeology). Answers are accepted or rejected based on the weight of evidence. There is no proof; truth is not an issue. Truth is a matter of individual belief; accepted answers are a matter of group consensus. These answers are often ambiguous. That uncertainty is frustrating, but it's a reflection of the real world.

This chapter has examined the subject of explanation in archaeology and what archaeologists want to know about the past. In sum, there are a variety of questions being asked in modern archaeology and a variety of perspectives to view our past. Variety is useful and important. New perspectives provide new information that informs us more fully about our ancestors. As Bruce Trigger noted in 1998 "… *multiple standpoints do not simply create multiple, incompatible archaeologies. They challenge all archaeologists, wherever possible, to use this multiplicity to create more holistic and objective syntheses. Their goal should be an archaeology that is more complete and less biased because it is informed by an ever-increasing number of viewpoints and constrained by more data.*"

Human activities

Archaeological evidence

Fig. 16.29 A schematic diagram of equifinality whereby different starting points, or initial conditions, of human activity can produce the same archaeological evidence.

STUDY QUESTIONS

1. What are the major differences between culture history and the "new" archaeology?

2. What are the major differences between processual and post-processual archaeology?

3. How does cultural ecology fit into the current scheme of schools of archaeological theory?

4. How would you characterize the approaches of evolutionary archaeology?

5. What are the primary tenets of gender archaeology?

www.mhhe.com/pricearch1

For more review material and study questions, please see the self-quizzes on your online learning center.

www.mhhe.com/pricearch1

For Internet references related to this chapter, please see the chapter links on your online learning center.

REFERENCES

Bell, J. A. 1994. *Reconstructing Prehistory: Scientific Method in Archaeology.* Philadelphia: Temple University Press.

Gero, Joan, and Margaret Conkey, eds. 1991. *Engendering Archaeology: Women and Prehistory.* Oxford: Basil Blackwell.

Hodder, I. 1985. Postprocessual archaeology. *Advances in Archaeological Method and Theory* 8:1–26.

Johnson, Matthew. 1999. *Archaeological Theory: An Introduction.* Oxford: Blackwell.

Peregrine, P. N. 2001. *Archaeological Research.* Upper Saddle River, NJ: Prentice Hall.

Praetzellis, Adrian. 2000. *Death by Theory: A Tale of Mystery and Archaeological Theory.* Lanham, MD: Rowman & Littlefield.

Preucel, Robert, and Ian Hodder, eds. 1996. *Contemporary Archaeology in Theory.* London: Blackwell.

Responsibilities

INTRODUCTION: ARCHAEOLOGY TODAY

Some years ago, the elders of the Squaxin (SQUAWK-sin) Island Tribe in the state of Washington decided to begin an effort to accurately record and teach the history of the Squaxin people. As part of this effort, they established a cultural resources department and a tribal museum, and began to educate the tribal staff in the management of cultural and archaeological sites and resources within the tribe's traditional territory. They also formed a partnership with the Anthropology Department at South Puget Sound Community College (SPSCC) to help meet their goals.

Today, the tribe's Cultural Resources Department (CRD) and the Anthropology Department at the college co-manage an excavation at an important site of an ancient culture on the shore of Mud Bay in south Puget Sound. At the site, the tribe provides cultural knowledge while the college faculty members provide scientific expertise. The excavations are run as a field school for training cultural anthropology and archaeology students, including tribal members, in field and laboratory methods. Although the tribe does not usually support the excavation of any archaeological site, the tribal members decided that the cultural and scientific training that could be provided at Mud Bay was an important enough reason to support this excavation.

The Mud Bay site is located directly on the Puget Sound shoreline and is dominated by a 100-meter- (300-foot-) long shell midden that includes a variety of stone and bone artifacts. Within the site area are evidence of the supports for a possible plank longhouse, a freshwater spring, a food-processing area, and an area of shell midden in front of the settlement. A portion of the midden area is waterlogged and contains excellently preserved wood, fiber, and other materials. One of the early artifacts excavated in this area is a roughly 60-square-foot section of gill net made of two-strand cedar bark string. Other excavated artifacts have included a carved harpoon shaft, basket fragments, fiber cordage, and wood chips dating 500 to 1000 years ago. Not far from the shell midden in the tidal flats of the bay are the remains of over 400 cedar posts from a wooden fishing weir recently C^{14} dated to 470 years ago.

The photo collage at the beginning of this chapter provides snapshots of some of the activities, finds, and developments at Mud Bay. Clockwise from the top are pictures of the field school with a welcoming pole in the background, excavations underway in the waterlogged part of the site, an exposed cedar pack basket, part of the cedar bark gill net, tribal basket weavers interpreting the just

www.mhhe.com/pricearch1

For preview material for this chapter, please see the chapter summary, outline, and objectives on your online learning center.

uncovered basket, the wooden posts of the fish weir, and the Squaxin Island Museum Library and Research Center. The Center was built to teach tribal members and the general public about the tribe's culture and to display artifacts and their interpretation from Mud Bay and other archaeological projects in the tribe's traditional area.

For the Squaxin Island Tribe, the site at Mud Bay is much more than just an archaeological excavation. It is a link to the tribe's centuries-old cultural history. The scientific methodology and study provided by archaeologists are one means of identifying and analyzing this ancient culture, but alone do not provide the complete picture. Therefore, the group incorporates into their work cultural information from the Squaxin Island Tribe to gain a more complete picture of the past, including the tribe's oral history, current tribal technologies and practices, and traditional beliefs. This cultural component is rarely included in typical archaeological work.

Today the tribe's Cultural Resources Department runs a program of cultural resource management (CRM) to identify, preserve, and protect all the various types of cultural resources that are of value to the community. This definition encompasses resources of the past (ancient and historical), the present, and the future. Archaeological sites and artifacts are only one type of cultural resource. Other types include such things as petroglyphs, sacred (community) and spiritual (personal) sites, burial sites and cemeteries, harvesting/gathering sites, traditional plants and animals, and intangibles, such as language, customs, traditional practices, songs, stories, dances, and oral history. At Mud Bay, the tribe and archaeologists look to see how all types of cultural resources were and are part of the site and the lives of the descendants of those who once inhabited the area. They also examine how the cultural information can be used to help interpret their lifestyles, and how these cultural resources can be preserved and protected.

CRM is about keeping a culture alive—in other words, supporting all activities of the tribe that are traditional. Squaxin Island members as well as members of other tribes who come to Mud Bay learn about the preservation and protection of their heritage, and receive technical training to become certified cultural resource technicians so that tribes can manage their own cultural sites and resources on reservation and can co-manage resources off reservation but in the local area. It is important for a tribe to manage its own cultural resources, as this strengthens their connection with their past, ancestors, and culture.

One benefit of the collaborative project at Mud Bay is the sharing of special knowledge and information that can take place between the tribal members and the scientists there. For example, tribal members quickly identified the gill net found at the site as intended for small species of salmon because of the size of the mesh openings and its similarity to nets in use today by tribal fisherpersons. In addition, hundreds of jaws of small salmon were found within the net, suggesting it may have been lost by accident before the catch could be removed.

Much has been gained from the collaborative effort at Mud Bay. The tribe and SPSCC today encourage such collaboration and have written about the importance of this cooperative approach.

> We believe we have shown an example of how a Tribe and an Anthropology/ Science unit can work together with a common goal, which is to support tribes who want to learn how to manage their resources, teach students how to work with the public and tribes, and embrace cultural resource preservation.
>
> We also believe that this cooperative approach demonstrates the general trend for American archaeology/anthropology for the future. With tribes involved with the management of cultural resources, anthropologists/archaeologists will more and more need to work directly with tribes in pursuing their own research interests. In the past, the non-Indian society who controlled the owner-

ship of cultural resources usually did not include in the management, study, and interpretation of those resources the people whose culture the resources pertained to. This minimized a comprehensive approach that would assist everyone in interpretation, understanding, and preservation of the resources.

Rhonda Foster—CR Director, Squaxin Island Tribe

Larry Ross—CR Specialist, Squaxin Island Tribe

Dale R. Croes—Professor, Anthropology, South Puget Sound Community College

This chapter is about archaeology today and the issues and concerns that are important in the present. These issues include the relevancy of archaeology to the present, the past as heritage and who owns our past, matters of ethics and responsibility, teaching archaeology to students and the public, and the destruction of cultural property. These are essential issues that will affect the prospects for archaeology as a discipline, as well as the future of the past.

Many of these issues involve interaction between archaeologists and the public. Public support of archaeology is an essential component of success in saving the past for everyone. Archaeology uses both private and public funding to finance research, and there is never enough money for the work that needs to be done. Archaeological materials are found on both public and private land, and the cooperation of owners and government is necessary to undertake investigations. An informed and interested public is an important goal of archaeology, and that requires an effort to tell people what archaeologists do, why it is interesting, and why it is worthwhile. One of the goals of this book is to inform a larger number of people about the fascinating field that is archaeology and how much we have to gain from learning about our common cultural heritage.

> *We have not inherited the earth from our fathers, we are borrowing it from our children.*
>
> *—Amish farmer*

THE RELEVANCY OF ARCHAEOLOGY

The importance of archaeology to the present and the future is inestimable. Knowing and understanding the past is essential to any comprehension of the future. According to its president and chairman Gilbert M. Grosvenor, the National Geographic Society publicizes and financially supports archaeology for two main reasons—because archaeological remains around the globe are part of our threatened environment and because the sites and artifacts that do survive are our sole source of information about the past. But beyond knowledge, aesthetics, and appreciation, archaeology has a great deal more to contribute.

In today's world of the twenty-first century, it seems that everything needs relevance to the present and to contribute to our quality of life. Some of today's important concerns include social inclusion, protection of the environment, and sustainable development. There is no question that archaeology also has significance and meaning in our modern world beyond its value in building human knowledge. Archaeology continually documents the diversity of our human past, while at the same time making clear that we are in fact all one, descended from our earliest human ancestors, mothered by an African Eve, passing through time together.

Archaeology also serves to document many of the environmental changes and problems that humans have faced over the millennia. It records climate changes and natural catastrophes and provides some insight on their frequency and severity. It also tells us what the human environment was like in the past and how changes have affected human societies. Information on terrain stability, flood hazards, changes in sea level, wildlife population dynamics, and the nature and distribution of plant and animal communities in the past are just some of the subjects of archaeological study, and this information has relevance to a variety of human endeavors. In the Netherlands, for example, archaeological studies of settlement and land use in prehistory have been an essential ingredient in the planning and construction of the dikes and drainage systems that enclose much of the country. Sea level change is also of great interest and relevance in today's era of global warming, and extensive archaeological records on the human use of coasts and changes in those coastlines over time provide information on how sea level change has affected humans. Climatic change and its effects on culture can be seen dramatically in some archaeological studies, including for example the consequences of the Little Ice Age for the inhabitants of Greenland, which are detailed in Chapter 15. In fact, catastrophic events in the past and their destructive nature are widely evidenced in archaeology—Pompeii, Akrotiri, and other sites document past volcanic activity and its effect on human settlements. Earthquakes of the past are also often recorded in archaeological sites and provide information on the incidence of these events. The sightings of celestial phenomena such as supernovas, comets, and eclipses have been found in the archaeological record too, providing an archive of the timing of such events.

Archaeology and archaeologists have helped in many areas of the world to develop places of great interest to travelers and tourists, bringing much needed moneys to parts of the developing world. Ecotourism is a growing aspect of globalization and archaeology provides one of its attractive cornerstones. One of the outgrowths of ecotourism has been the development of archaeological sites and museums in many places, which has fostered both local pride and international visits. Examples of such development include Sipán (Chapter 2) and Akrotiri and Sunwatch Indian Village (Chapter 13), among others.

Archaeologists are also involved in forensic investigations, contributing skills and knowledge to the study of crime scenes and the recovery of evidence from mass murders and other crimes. They have been employed, for example, in the recovery of human remains from soldiers missing in action in past wars and from mass graves in Kosovo and elsewhere. They have also participated in the recovery of human remains and personal effects from the World Trade Center in New York City following September 11, 2001.

Archaeology does have relevancy. The questions that are asked and the answers that are found can provide solutions to the problems of today. An example of the utility of archaeological research comes from the highlands of South America. This example is described below.

◉ EXAMPLE ~~~~~~~~~~~~~~~~~~~~~~~~~~~~

RAISED FIELDS OF TIWANAKU

Among the many cultures that took turns dominating the Andes mountains of South America the empire of Tiwanaku (*TEA-wah-NAH-coo*) was one of the largest between AD 500 and 950. The ancient city of Tiwanaku was an enormous ceremonial center of compounds and structures with beautifully carved stone walls, surrounded by the dwellings of perhaps 40,000 people. This capital was located along the shore of the highest navigable lake in the world—Lake Titicaca (*TIT-ee-COCK-ah*) on the border between Bolivia and Peru at an elevation of 3810 m (12,580 ft).

The key to the success of Tiwanaku lay in the engineering of a vast zone of swamps along the edge of the lake into richly productive farmland. The swamps were turned into fields by the construction of a series of carefully built canals 5 to 10 m (15 to 30 ft) apart and a meter or two in depth. Each canal had a gravel floor covered with clay. The soil from the canal ditches was piled up onto the land in between to create **raised fields** (Fig. 17.1). This system of agriculture was wonderfully suited to the high altitude and the crops of the region. The canals provided water for moisture in an area of unpredictable rainfall and were home to a large number of fish, also an important source of food. The water plants in the canals provided additional sources of food and served as a fertilizer for the fields. The water also acted as a buffer against the cold nights of a high-altitude land, protecting the crops against killing frosts. The

Lake Titicaca

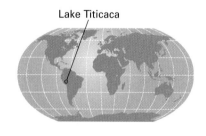

raised fields   A productive agricultural field system in wetlands using canals for water and built-up islands between canals for farmland.

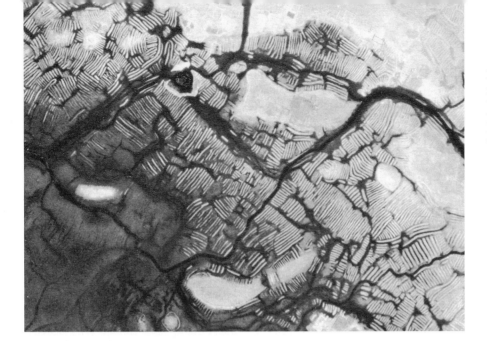

Fig. 17.1 An air photo of ancient raised fields and ditches in the Tiwanaku basin. Snow or frost highlights the depressions in this photograph.

Fig. 17.2 Part of rehabilitated raised field system in use along the shore of Lake Titicaca in Bolivia today. The reuse of an ancient technique has provided new productive farmlands for the inhabitants of the region.

fields were very productive, perhaps four times more so than traditional methods, and they fed a population of perhaps 120,000 people in the entire region.

Following the collapse of the Tiwanaku Empire by AD 1000, these fields were abandoned, the canals silted up, and the land returned to swamp—forgotten. In the last 30 years, however, archaeologists have discovered these ancient field systems and how they worked. In the early 1980s, archaeologist Clark Erickson of the University of Pennsylvania and Peruvian agronomist Ignacio Garaycochea realized that these ancient field systems had been an important part of highland agriculture. They were able to persuade local farmers on the Peruvian side of Lake Titicaca to rebuild a few of the raised fields, plant indigenous crops, and farm them using traditional methods. Across the lake at Tiwanaku, archaeologist Alan Kolata of the University of Chicago and Bolivian archaeologist Oswaldo Rivera were starting similar experiments. Reluctant village farmers near Tiwanaku first chased the pair away but later realized that there was a need to try something new as malnutrition and poverty are a rampant problem in this region.

The first crop in the new raised fields averaged about 20 tons of big potatoes per hectare (about 2.5 acres)—some were the size of grapefruit. Rich crops of the potatoes, cereals, and vegetables yielded almost sevenfold as much as normal dry farming in the area. Today, these rehabilitated ancient field systems are used by almost 1500 farmers, and villages around the lake continue to adopt the technique (Fig. 17.2).

www.mhhe.com/pricearch1

For a Web-based activity on the site of Tiwanaku, please see the Internet exercises on your online learning center.

The local food supply is improving dramatically with the produce from the rich fields and the fish and ducks from the canals. Thus, archaeology has helped the people of this region to improve their lot.

~~~~~~

THE PAST AS HERITAGE

Study the past if you would define the future.
—Confucius, philosopher

The Spanish American philosopher George Santayana wrote that those who cannot remember the past are condemned to repeat it. Certainly, there are lessons from the long span of our prehistory on earth and about the evolution of our species and our behavior. In terms of the vastness of geological or archaeological time, the role of humans on the planet is minuscule indeed. Yet the impact of our species is immeasurable.

Although relative newcomers in earth's history, we have an obligation and a responsibility toward all that is around us. Humans have tremendous destructive power as well as creative abilities. Through looting, careless development, and the wanton destruction of archaeological resources, we even have the potential to eliminate our abilities to reconstruct and understand our own past (Fig. 17.3). Such destruction is catastrophic since so much of human history oc-

Fig. 17.3 Before and after photographs of one of the massive statues of Buddha (58 m [180 ft] tall) destroyed near Bamiyan in AD 2000 by order of Molla Mohammad Omar, once the Supreme Leader of the Islamic Emirate of Afghanistan.

curred before the advent of written records and is largely retrievable through archaeological studies alone.

There is a note, rather a crescendo, of urgency in our quest for an understanding of the past. Protecting the past has been an important theme in this book and I have usually pointed to the positive aspects of preservation, showing how sites are being protected. But for every site that is saved, there are tens or hundreds that are being destroyed. The archaeological record, under attack from the expansion of increasing population and global economies, is rapidly disappearing in many areas. The growth of modern cities and transportation networks is covering the earth's surface with concrete, asphalt, and mountains of trash from our consumer society. The industrialization of agriculture results in deep plowing through the earth, mixing layers of soil, and lowering the groundwater table, destroying the organic component of the archaeological record. If we are to have archaeology in the future, it is essential that the fundamental information on our past that remains in the ground be recorded and protected before nothing is left for us to study. The urgency of this challenge should be a major focus of concern and action in the twenty-first century.

There are a number of ways to help protect the past. One of them is simply to learn more and to tell others of the importance of our archaeological heritage—public interest and awareness is needed to safeguard the past. Another way is to support local archaeologists. There are many avenues for such support. Contact your legislators in support of archaeological issues and the protection of historical and archaeological remains. Support local museums and archaeology programs at colleges and universities through donations of time and/or money. Participate in archaeological activities in your area and tell others about your interests and concerns.

Several organizations of archaeologists are working to increase public awareness and support. In the United States, the Society for American Archaeology is notably active in this effort. There are other organizations active to protect archaeological sites as well. Two of the larger ones are described below: the UNESCO World Heritage Site program and the Archaeological Conservancy. Both are worthy programs deserving public and private support.

 **EXAMPLE** ～～～～～～～～～～～～～～～～～～～～～

UNESCO WORLD HERITAGE

The United Nations Educational, Scientific and Cultural Organization (UNESCO) was chartered in 1972 to encourage the identification, protection, and preservation of cultural and natural heritage sites around the world considered to be of outstanding value. Cultural heritage refers to monuments, groups of buildings and sites with historical, aesthetic, archaeological, scientific, ethnological, or anthropological value. Natural heritage refers to outstanding geological formations, habitats of threatened species of animals and plants, and areas of scientific, conservation, or aesthetic value.

The mission of this program is described in Table 17.1. More than 750 sites have been inscribed in the program to date, including such archaeological localities in the United States as Mesa Verde, Mammoth Cave, Cahokia Mounds, and Chaco Canyon. The World Heritage program actively monitors the places under its protection and provides assistance for endangered sites, including training, technical cooperation, and assistance for information dissemination and for educational and promotional activities. Perhaps the most important part of the program is the encouragement it provides to countries all over the world to preserve their cultural and natural heritage.

TABLE 17.1 The mission of UNESCO's World Heritage program.

- Encourage countries to sign the World Heritage Convention and to ensure the protection of their natural and cultural heritage;
- Encourage countries to nominate sites within their national territory for inclusion on the World Heritage List;
- Encourage countries to set up reporting systems on the state of conservation of World Heritage sites;
- Help countries safeguard World Heritage sites by providing technical assistance and professional training;
- Provide emergency assistance for World Heritage sites in immediate danger;
- Support public awareness-building activities for World Heritage conservation;
- Encourage participation of the local population in the preservation of their cultural and natural heritage;
- Encourage international cooperation in conservation of cultural and natural heritage.

www.mhhe.com/pricearch1

For a Web-based activity on Egyptian kings, please see the Internet exercises on your online learning center.

PROTECTING THE PAST

Abu Simbel

One of the most famous rescue projects in archaeology was the removal and reconstruction of the temples of Abu Simbel in southern Egypt (Fig. 17.4). The two temples at Abu Simbel are among the most magnificent ancient monuments in the world. Built by Pharaoh Ramses II, the site is most famous for the four imposing statues of the seated pharaoh guarding the entrance to the temple. The seated figures of the pharaoh are more than five stories high! The statues and the cavelike temple behind them were carved into a sandstone cliff along the banks of the Nile more than 3000 years ago. Twice a year, during the spring and fall equinox, a shaft of sunlight reaches the interior of the cave and illuminates the innermost room of the temple.

The construction of the Aswan High Dam across the Nile in the 1960s meant that the temples at Abu Simbel would be flooded and eventually submerged by the rising waters behind the dam. A remarkable feat of engineering was then devised to move the temples up 60 m (185 ft) to higher ground by cutting the sandstone cliff into 950 large blocks and reassembling the structures at a higher level, above the encroaching water. An international effort was mounted, sponsored by UNESCO, involving more than fifty countries supplying the funding and manpower to accomplish this task. After four years of work, the temples were saved and have become one of the major tourist attractions of Egypt.

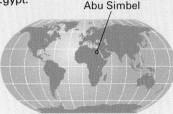

Abu Simbel

Fig. 17.4 The reconstruction of Ramses temple at Abu Simbel in the 1960s was an enormous, international effort to save these ancient monuments from the rising waters of the Aswan Dam.

THE ARCHAEOLOGICAL CONSERVANCY

The Archaeological Conservancy is the only national, nonprofit organization dedicated to acquiring and preserving remaining archaeological sites in the United States. Since its founding in 1980, the Conservancy, based in Albuquerque, New Mexico, has obtained through purchase or gift more than 285 archaeological and historical sites in thirty-eight states across America. These places range in size from a few acres to more than 1000 acres and include the earliest habitation sites in North America, a nineteenth-century frontier army post, and remains from nearly every major cultural period in between.

Every day, prehistoric and historic archaeological sites in the United States are lost forever—along with the precious information they contain. Modern-day looters use backhoes and bulldozers to recover artifacts for the international market (Fig. 17.5). Urban development, topsoil mining, and agricultural methods such as land leveling also destroy ancient sites. The Conservancy protects these sites by acquiring the land on which they sit, protecting them for posterity.

Conservancy purchases are varied. They include California's Borax Lake site, which encompasses 11,000 years of human occupation; the first mission established by the Spanish priest Father Kino in Arizona in AD 1691; several ancient Indian villages in Florida; major sites in Arkansas and Missouri, at least two of which Hernando de Soto visited in 1541; villages of the eastern lakeshore peoples in Michigan; ancestral sites of New Mexico's Pueblo people; Yellowjacket and Mud Springs Pueblos in Colorado, the two largest ruins of the Mesa Verde culture; and in the Northeast, two Paleoindian sites and a Seneca Iroquois village.

Some Conservancy sites have been incorporated into public parks, such as Petrified Forest National Park in Arizona, Chaco Culture National Historical Park in New Mexico, Parkin Archeological State Park in Arkansas, and the Hopewell Culture National Historical Park in Ohio.

Major funding for the Conservancy comes from its more than 23,000 members, as well as individual contributions, corporations, and foundations. Often the Conservancy raises money locally to purchase a specific site in a certain community. More information about the Archaeological Conservancy can be found at their website: www.americanarchaeology.com/aaabout.html

Fig. 17.5 Air photo of looters' holes at Slack Farm, Kentucky. Many of the graves at the site were completely destroyed before professional archaeologists were called to the scene.

WHO OWNS THE PAST?

One of the issues facing archaeology today is growing concern with questions about who owns the past. This issue involves both nations and individuals. When archaeology was just beginning and European empires controlled much of the known world, soldiers and merchants from the conquering nations returned home with many treasures, both ancient and modern, from the countries they had visited. For example, Napoleon returned from his invasion of Egypt with a number of marvelous ancient Egyptian artifacts and monuments.

A well-known example involving ownership of the past concerns the Elgin Marbles. These statues have a long and storied history. After defeating the Persians in 479 BC, the Greeks returned to Athens to resurrect their city, which was ruined during the war. Their leader, Pericles, rebuilt the city as an artistic and cultural center, with many wonderful structures including the Parthenon during the 30 years of his rule. The Parthenon took 15 years to construct and was finally dedicated in 432 BC as the temple of the goddess Athena, sitting on the acropolis above Athens as the pinnacle of Greek power and creativity.

Atop the Parthenon, just under the roofline, was a frieze of more than 400 human and 200 animal marble statues. The frieze has a maximum height of more than 2 m (approx. 7 ft) and total length of 160 m (about 500 ft) around the four sides of the temple. One of the marvels of antiquity, the frieze depicts the most important annual festival of ancient Athens. During the six-day celebrations, various music, poetry and other competitions were held, including beauty contests, track and field events, horse and chariot races, and regattas.

In AD 1801, Thomas Bruce, who was also Lord Elgin and the British ambassador to Constantinople (Istanbul), obtained permission to remove large portions of the Parthenon frieze. And so, from Athens the marble statues of the Parthenon were shipped to the British Museum in London, where the statues sit today, known as the Elgin Marbles (Fig. 17.6).

The Greek government has been petitioning the British government for many years for the return of these treasures, but to no avail. The United Nations,

Fig. 17.6 The Elgin Marbles at the British Museum.

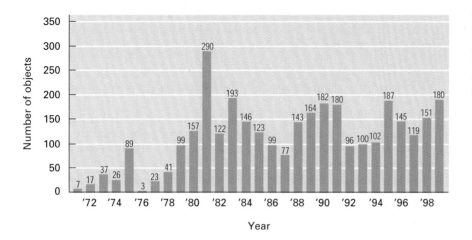

Fig. 17.7 The number of Maya artifacts sold in the United States by the auction house of Sotheby's since 1971. Although the largest auction to date was in 1981, the increasing trend over time is not a good sign.

the British populace, and world opinion support the Greek claim, but British authorities resist their return with statements about setting precedent for other museum treasures around the world. The British argue that the marbles were purchased legitimately from the Turks who controlled Athens at that time, that the marbles were removed in order to save them from destruction, and that the Greeks did not care at the time about the marbles. More recently the buildup of corrosive air pollution in Athens has been added to the argument against moving the marbles. One moral of such cases is that there are rarely easy answers to questions about ownership and/or the return of cultural heritage.

It is essential for us to recognize that no one owns the past, it belongs to all of us; important archaeological sites and artifacts should not be the property of individuals. Archaeological materials are valuable cultural resources and part of our human inheritance. It is therefore essential that we all understand their significance and work toward their care and curation. One of the means of caring for these resources is preventing their illegal sale. Though trading in antiquities or disturbing archaeological sites without permission is illegal in most states and punishable by fines and/or imprisonment, dealers in antiquities and the market they supply are ultimately responsible for the looting of hundreds of archaeological sites each year (Fig. 17.7). Enforcing existing legislation against the import and sale of antiquities is a large part of the battle to save the past.

The U.S. Congress recognized the importance of the historic and prehistoric past of the country in 1966 in the passage of the National Historic Preservation Act, which emphasized the importance of cultural resources and established the National Register of Historic Places and the legal framework for the protection of cultural resources. Because of growing public interest in the past and a substantial increase in looting and the illicit trade in antiquities, the U.S. Congress passed the Archaeological Resources Protection Act in 1979 (Public Law 96-95; 93 Stat. 712, 16 U.S.C. 470) to further help preserve archaeological resources on public and Indian lands. This law defined archaeological resources to be any material remains of past human life or activities that are of archaeological interest and are at least 100 years old. It also encouraged cooperation between groups and individuals in possession of archaeological resources from public or Indian lands with special permit and disposition rules for the protection of archaeological resources on Indian lands. The law further provided that information regarding the nature and location of archaeological resources may remain confidential (to prevent looting and disturbance), and it established civil and criminal penalties, including forfeiture of vehicles, fines of up to $100,000, and imprisonment of up to 5 years for second violations for the unauthorized appropriation, alteration, exchange, or other handling of archaeological resources with rewards for furnishing information about such unauthorized activity.

To archaeologists, the human past is owned by no one. It represents the cultural heritage of everyone who has ever lived on Earth or will live on it in the future. Archaeology puts all human societies on an equal footing.
—Brian Fagan, archaeologist

TABLE 17.2 Major stipulations of the Native American Graves Protection and Repatriation Act (NAGPRA) of 1990.

- Federal agencies and museums must identify cultural items in their collections that are subject to NAGPRA, and prepare inventories and summaries of the items.
- Federal agencies and museums must consult with lineal descendants, Indian tribes, and Native Hawaiian organizations regarding the identification and cultural affiliation of the cultural items listed in their NAGPRA inventories and summaries.
- Federal agencies and museums must send notices to lineal descendants, Indian tribes, and Native Hawaiian organizations describing cultural items and lineal descendancy or cultural affiliation, and stating that the cultural items may be repatriated. The law requires the Secretary of the Interior to publish these notices in the Federal Register.

An even more sensitive and contentious issue involves the disposition of ancient human skeletal remains. North American archaeologists have been excavating burials along with other cultural materials for many years. The Smithsonian Institution in Washington D.C., for example, housed the remains of more than 16,000 Native Americans collected over the years. By some estimates, more than 100,000 Native American graves have been excavated in the United States and the skeletons placed in museums. Because of growing concern about these remains and the desire of native peoples to take back these remains for reburial, the Congress passed the **Native American Graves Protection and Repatriation Act (NAGPRA)** in 1990.

NAGPRA provides a mechanism for museums and federal agencies to return certain Native American cultural materials—such as human remains, funerary and sacred artifacts, and objects of cultural patrimony—to lineal descendants, culturally affiliated Indian tribes, and Native Hawaiian organizations. The major features of NAGPRA are listed in Table 17.2. Items requested for return must be repatriated to a lineal descendant or related group. Several different lines of evidence are required to determine cultural affiliation, including geographic, biological, archaeological, linguistic, and anthropological evidence. The law also forbids trafficking in Native American cultural or human material and establishes procedures for notification and consultation with tribes for planned excavation or accidental discovery of cultural materials on tribal property. Because of NAGPRA and similar legislation, the Smithsonian has repatriated more than 4000 sets of human remains to native tribes for reburial, out of a total collection of some 16,000, since 1984.

The repatriation of human skeletal remains is not always a clear-cut issue, however, and this legislation has created several controversial situations. The case of Kennewick Man is described below.

 EXAMPLE ~~~~~~~~~~~~~~~~~~~~~~~~

KENNEWICK MAN

In the last 15 years, our picture of the first inhabitants of the New World has changed dramatically because of the discovery of a number of new sites and skeletons. Probably the most important of these is the human skeleton found near Kennewick

Native American Graves Protection and Repatriation Act (NAGPRA) Federal legislation intended to protect and return certain archaeological human remains and culturally significant artifacts to Native Americans.

(*KIN-eh-wick*) in the state of Washington. The Kennewick material has provided major lessons in both archaeology and human relations.

Spectators at a boat race on the Columbia River in 1996 came across a human skull washing out close to the riverbank near the town of Kennewick. Over the next month, other bones from the skeleton were found. By the end of August that year, a radiocarbon date of 7500 BC revealed that Kennewick was one of the earliest human skeletons found in the New World. Detailed reconstruction and study of the skull by James Chatters indicated that this individual was not typical of the ancestors of Native Americans (Fig. 17.8).

A local newspaper story about the find at the end of July prompted a series of ethical dilemmas, legal actions, court decisions, and several books that reflect the questions that arise from the discovery of prehistoric human remains in the United States. Five Native American tribes in the area claimed these remains for reburial, under the NAGPRA legislation. The Army Corps of Engineers took possession of the skeleton, which had been found on Corps lands, and agreed to return it to the tribes. Shortly thereafter, eight archaeologists and biological anthropologists filed an injunction to allow scientific investigation of this important find and to prevent the immediate return of the skeleton. The scientists argued that the remains were important and that they were not demonstrably Native American, questioning the legality of the tribes claim.

This issue was in the courts and the media for almost a decade. In 2002, a judge ruled that the "remains were so old, and information as to his era so limited, that it is impossible to say whether the Kennewick Man is related to the present-day Tribal Claimants." The judge also ordered that the remains be given over for scientific investigation. The tribes appealed this ruling, but a decision by the Appeals Court in 2004 upheld the judge's decision.

The ongoing conflict between science and belief is highlighted in such issues. The public battle over burial rights and the pursuit of knowledge about the past has both underscored and brushed aside the importance of the Kennewick find. This skeleton is important because of its antiquity and also because of the unusual nature of the remains. The questions raised by certain features of the skull demand further investigation to better understand the original inhabitants of the Americas. At the same time, the importance of learning more about the past of all of us is lost in the debate about who should control these remains and how they should be handled.

Kennewick is a special case, a very old skeleton with distinct and unusual characteristics. There are thousands of human remains that have been excavated in the United States that are not so old and not so unusual. These remains are by law to be given to identifiable ancestors who request their return. The issue of responsibility for human remains is one of the thorniest in archaeology. On the one hand, these materials are the remains of ancestors and significant, almost sacred, in many cultures. On the other hand, the bones and tissues of these ancestors hold an enormous amount of information about the individual represented and about our human past. As the Kennewick case shows, the issue is not easily resolved when diverse interests are at stake over control of such remains.

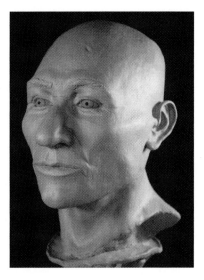

Fig. 17.8 A reconstructed face of Kennewick Man from the state of Washington.

ETHICS IN ARCHAEOLOGY

Ethics (Eth'ics) *n.* [Cf. F. *éthique*] The science of human duty; the body of rules of duty drawn from this science; a particular system of principles and rules concerting duty, whether true or false; rules of practice in respect to a single class of human actions; as, political or social *ethics.*

Ethics is an important and growing concern in modern life. Ethical behavior in archaeology is an increasingly complex subject, related to issues of heritage, native people, treatment of the dead, and the preservation of the past. Several new books

1. Stewardship. The archaeological record is irreplaceable and it is the responsibility of all archaeologists to practice and promote stewardship of the archaeological record.

2. Accountability. Responsible archaeological research requires a commitment to consult with affected group(s) to establish a working relationship that can be beneficial to all parties involved.

3. Commercialization. The buying and selling of objects contributes to the destruction of the archaeological record on the American continents and around the world. Archaeologists should discourage and avoid activities that enhance the commercial value of archaeological objects.

4. Public Education and Outreach. Archaeologists should work with the public to improve the preservation, protection, and interpretation of the record.

5. Intellectual Property. A researcher may have primary access to original materials and documents for a limited and reasonable time, after which these materials and documents must be made available to others.

6. Public Reporting and Publication. The knowledge that archaeologists obtain in their investigations must be presented to the public.

7. Records and Preservation. Archaeologists should work actively for the preservation of archaeological collections, records, and reports.

8. Training and Resources. Archaeologists must ensure that they have adequate training, experience, facilities, and other support necessary to conduct a program of research.

on the subject have appeared in the last decade, and panels on ethical issues are frequent at scientific conferences. In addition, national organizations have taken a stand and added ethical statements to their by-laws.

The major professional organization for archaeologists in the United States is the Society for American Archaeology (SAA). Founded in 1934, the society has more than 7000 professional archaeologists and students as members today. It is intended to stimulate interest and research in American archaeology, advocate and aid in the conservation of archaeological resources, encourage public access to and appreciation of archaeology, oppose all looting of sites and the purchase and sale of looted archaeological materials, and serve as a bond among those interested in the archaeology of the Americas.

The promotion of ethical behavior is an important aspect of the society's activities. The major principles of ethical practice have been set down by the SAA and are summarized in Table 17.3.

These principles encompass the major concerns of archaeology. Stewardship concerns the protection of our common archaeological and cultural heritage. Unless this heritage is protected, it will disappear. This principle of protection and preservation also extends to the collections and records that archaeologists accumulate. Accountability concerns archaeology's interaction with the individuals or groups who are involved with particular archaeological sites or materials. These individuals and groups include the landowners where archaeological projects may take place and Native American groups whose beliefs incorporate ancient artifacts and human remains. A third ethical principle regards the commercialization of the past, and particularly the illegal trade in antiquities that remains a major force in the destruction of the past by looters and thieves. It is the responsibility of an archaeologist to discourage and avoid such activities. For example, an archaeologist should not provide estimates of the value of antiquities to collectors and retailers.

Public education is an important role for archaeologists, intended to increase both interest and support. The more people who understand and appreciate the importance of the past, the better the job archaeology is doing. In addition, much of the financial support for research archaeology comes from government sources and ultimately from the public. A better-educated public, more appreciative of the importance of the past, will support greater funding for archaeology.

The ethical principles of the SAA also concern intellectual property—researchers are entitled to the copyright on original ideas and information that they produce. At the same time, it is essential that these materials become available to other scholars and the public through publication in various media. Archaeological finds—artifacts, photographs, reports, catalogs—should be stored under good conditions in perpetuity so that interested parties can study the evidence that has been recovered. Archaeological materials are normally stored in museums, university collections, and government facilities to provide a lasting record. The last ethical principle on the SAA list encourages archaeologists to have the training, resources, and support to be able to do their work at a high level.

Examples of recent ethical issues are discussed below to illustrate the dilemmas that confront modern archaeologists. One issue concerns contact with looters of archaeological sites and the other involves excavations on recent battlefields.

 EXAMPLE ~~~~~~

DONNAN AND SIPÁN

The royal tombs at Sipán, Peru, were the subject of Chapter 2, "Doing Archaeology." Ethical issues were a significant part of the Sipán story, and several different groups of individuals were involved in such concerns. The local looters and villagers who opened the tomb, while in dire straits and practicing an age-old tradition of robbing archaeological sites, were destroying their own heritage. The smugglers and buyers of Moche art in the United States and Europe are another group, one largely without ethical concerns. These individuals sell and buy the heritage of their own and other cultures for personal profit or pleasure. The ethics of protecting the past make it clear that these practices are unacceptable.

Another ethical aspect of the Sipán study concerns the archaeologists involved, in particular Christopher Donnan. While some of the artifacts were smuggled out of Peru shortly after their discovery, others remained in the hands of a private collector in Lima. Donnan visited this man and photographed some of the finds, as he had done with other collectors in Peru. Some of Donnan's photographs in fact appeared in a National Geographic article on the site.

Donnan's activities have been strongly condemned by some archaeologists who argue that professionals should have no contact whatsoever with looters and smugglers, that to do so validates their activities and gives them some legitimacy that they do not deserve. The president of the Society for American Archeology at the time criticized Donnan for his relationship with the collectors, saying, "I take a fairly hard line (with looted objects). If knowledge is lost, that's too bad." Donnan has responded that while he decries the looting, these objects would be lost to science unless he tracked them down, photographed, and recorded them for posterity.

It's a dicey argument without clear-cut answers. The Peruvian archaeologist Walter Alva has supported Donnan, and many other archaeologists accept that some archive should be made of these materials when possible before they disappear. At the same time, trafficking in antiquities is illegal and the individuals involved should be reported to the authorities, something Donnan did not do.

THE YPRES BATTLEFIELD

The domain of archaeology is enormous, as we have seen repeatedly in this book. An important part of this domain has been the study of warfare and conflict. Archaeologists have been involved in the excavations at the Little Big Horn—the site of the Custer Battlefield in Montana—with mass graves in Kosovo, and have sifted through the ashes of the World Trade Center. Our present world constantly reminds us of "man's inhumanity to man" (from "Man Was Made to Mourn," a dirge by Robert Burns) and the continual conflicts that plague our planet.

Archaeologists are also involved in the study of the twentieth century. For example, archaeologists spent more than a year diving in the South Pacific as part of a large project to find and record sunken military ships and planes from the Battle of Midway in World War II. Other archaeologists work in Southeast Asia, looking for those still missing in action from the Vietnam War.

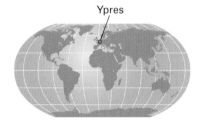

Ypres

Archaeologists are also digging in the battlefields of Western Europe, uncovering the trenches and tunnels of World War I (Fig. 17.9). It's dangerous work; unexploded military ordnance is still buried in the ground on these killing fields. It is also ethically challenging because of the human remains and personal belongings that lie buried.

Near the town of Ypres in Belgium, archaeologists have been excavating along the route of a planned motorway and have uncovered a series of military trenches from World War I (1914–1919). To do so, Belgian archaeologists are working hand-in-hand with military experts from Britain. Excavations have exposed a network of fortifications that were occupied by British, Australian, Canadian, and Indian soldiers between 1914 and 1918. Artifacts from the excavation filled a shipping container and included rifles, rum jars, newspapers, and a bugle (Fig. 17.10). In addition, the human remains of five individuals still in their uniforms have been removed from the excavations.

Several ethical issues surround the excavation of human remains and places of death on the battlefield. The first concerns the human remains themselves: How

Fig. 17.9 Excavation of trenches and fortifications with timber frameworks at the Ypres battlefield.

Fig. 17.10 One of the artifacts discovered during the excavations at the Ypres battlefield.

should these be treated and to whom do they belong? Soldiers from many different countries and different faiths died there. Second, who owns the artifacts? Some of the items recovered are personal belongings of the soldiers. Local people in the area have been searching the battlefields with metal detectors for years to find souvenirs and memorabilia to sell to collectors. Archaeologists regard this activity as looting. Do these materials belong to the finders—often the local people—to the archaeologists, to the nation, or to the descendants of the original owners? A third issue involves the preservation of the battlefield sites themselves. Are these places to be left as memorials, developed for tourism, or preserved for future archaeologists?

Today, the highway runs through the site. Bulldozers remodeled the landscape and destroyed the excavated zone. There was a campaign to save the area and reroute the highway, but unfortunately the entire region is covered with fortifications and unmarked graves. It seems it is impossible to save everything.

TEACHING ARCHAEOLOGY

Archaeology is taught at many different levels in the United States. There are exercises for elementary and middle schools as part of history and social studies. There are workshops and short courses taught by museums, community colleges, and a variety of other organizations. Field schools for various interests and abilities are an exciting opportunity to learn about the survey and excavation aspects of archaeology as well as to experience the social and educational benefits of such projects.

A number of educational and scientific organizations enable individuals to participate in archaeological investigations. Several organizations provide brief fieldwork opportunities for those who can afford them: the Earthwatch organization, the University Research Expeditions Program at the University of California, and the Smithsonian Research Expeditions. Some, such as the Crow Canyon Archaeological Center in Cortez, Colorado, or the Center for American Archeology in Kampsville, Illinois, offer participation at a variety of levels. As previously mentioned, many universities run field schools in the summer for undergraduate students.

Archaeology has been taught to students at the college and university level for many years, and a number of high schools around the United States offer a course or two in the subject. A variety of different programs exist, emphasizing different areas and aspects of the field. Basic courses are general introductions, area courses for specific regions, topical courses focusing on concepts and larger themes, methods courses emphasizing the analytical, field, and practical aspects of archaeology, and history and theory courses that cover the development and interpretative components of archaeology.

A few years ago, the Society for American Archaeology charged its Committee on Curriculum to develop a set of principles for teaching archaeology in the twenty-first century. That committee listed seven important concepts and suggested possible discussion topics for each (Table 17.4). These concepts emphasize some relevant aspects of education in general along with a focus on archaeology (e.g., stewardship of the past, basic archaeological skills). A number of these subjects have been discussed in *Principles of Archaeology.*

One example of how the teaching of archaeology is done today is presented in the example below in a description of classroom activity by Joe Ball of the San Diego State University in California. Professor Ball invites diverse interest groups into the classroom to discuss the question of who owns the past.

TABLE 17.4 Concepts and topics for teaching archaeology in the twenty-first century from the Society for American Archaeology.

1. Stewardship (taking care of the past). The archaeology curriculum fosters stewardship by making explicit the nonrenewable nature of archaeological resources and their associated documentation.
   Possible topics: looters and trafficking, conservation ethic, nonrenewable resources, law enforcement training, site management and protection.

2. Diverse interests. The archaeology curriculum makes students aware that archaeologists no longer have exclusive rights to the past, but that various publics have a stake in the past. Diverse groups—such as descendant communities; state, local, and federal agencies; and others—compete for and have vested interests in the nonrenewable resources of the past.
   Possible topics: different views of the past, partnerships (collaboration with many groups), public involvement (reporting results), political uses of the past (nation building).

3. Social relevance. If archaeology is to be justified as a discipline—in terms of both public support and interest—then we must effectively articulate the ways in which we can use the past to help students think productively about the present and the future.
   Possible topics: population dynamics, environmental history, systems of social inequality, warfare, health and disease, garbage.

4. Ethics and values. The articulation of ethics and values is seen as the sign of growth and maturation in the profession. The SAA principles of archaeological ethics are fundamental to how archaeologists conduct themselves in relation to the resources, their data, their colleagues, and the public. The linking of these principles to specific points within the curriculum will provide students with a basic foundation when establishing their interest in the study of cultural resources.
   Possible topics: principles of archaeological ethics, preservation law.

5. Written and oral communication. Archaeology depends on the understanding and support of the public. For this to occur, archaeologists must communicate their goals, results and recommendations clearly and effectively. Archaeology training must incorporate training and frequent practice in logical thinking as well as written and oral presentation.
   Possible topics: clear writing (implied clear thinking), clear speaking, public speaking, computer literacy.

6. Basic archaeological skills. Students planning on a career in archaeology must have mastered a set of basic cognitive and methodological skills that enable them to operate effectively in the field and laboratory contexts. These skills must span the range of basic professional responsibility: excavation, analysis, report writing, and long-term curation.
   Possible topics: observation skills, inferential skills, basic map skills, organize and assess data, knowledge of the law, technical writing.

7. Real-world problem solving. It is our public service responsibility as educators to demonstrate through examples and assignments a basic understanding of how business, politics and local community or bureaucracies work, as well as to foster an understanding of preservation laws and regulations.
   Possile topics: professional responsibilities and accountability, archaeopolitics, citizenship, how business works, legal and regulatory framework.

EXAMPLE ∿∿∿∿∿∿∿∿∿∿∿∿∿∿∿∿∿∿∿∿∿∿∿

THE OTHER SIDE OF THE STORY

Joe Ball is a professor of anthropology at San Diego State University (SDSU) where he teaches a variety of courses in archaeology. He is also a practicing archaeologist working in Mesoamerica. He conducts excavations at the Maya site of Acanmul in Campeche and is concerned with trade and interaction in prehispanic Mexico. Some years ago, he realized that an introduction to archaeology for college students should include ethical questions and concern professional responsibilities. Members of various interest groups in the San Diego area were invited to present their perspectives on who owns the past to archaeology classes. Professor Ball's description of these experiences follows:

Responsibility and Accountability. Two truly important words, but what do they really mean—especially to an archaeologist? I have been teaching archaeology for over 30 years now, and have been "doing" it for over 40. The question bothers me more now than ever, and I know that this has much to do with the ever more rapidly accelerating destruction of the remaining archaeological record, the increasingly common barring of archaeologists from access to ever more sites, and the growing disfavor with which American archaeologists are coming to be viewed. How did this come about, and why and what can we do as professionals and teachers to preserve what remains of the precious, nonrenewable physical record of past human activities, behavior, and history?

For the professional archaeologist, "responsibility" ultimately means the protection of the archaeological record. I began to appreciate this some years ago, and it was then that I decided that an ethically balanced introduction to archaeology for college students demanded intput from spokespersons from other parts of the real world that were equally aware of and affected by the archaeological record.

San Diego County borders Mexico, is the location of twenty-six separate Native American reservations—the largest number and concentration in the country—is home to Viejas Casino—one of the most successful tribal casinos in the U.S.—has the second highest housing costs in the nation, and has over sixteen active and viable cultural resource management companies currently in business. Each of these factors involves significant issues for archaeology and has relevance for many Americans. How do you balance these different needs and perspectives with the need to protect the archaeological record?

Some years ago the archaeology faculty at SDSU began inviting members of significantly affected nonarchaeological groups to visit and address our undergraduate and graduate classes in archaeology. The results have been interesting—on some occasions unexpected, discomforting, and disquieting—but always and inevitably provocative, producing a deeper appreciation of the significance and uses of the archaeological record. Far from being a "neutral" source of information about the past, our students have come to see the archaeological record as a means of exploring, revealing, and understanding modern human cultural and behavioral diversity. They also have come to appreciate how the record can be used to empower some, deny credibility to others, and be a basis for contentious debate among many different interest groups. How the record of the past is perceived, understood, and regarded with respect to present-day concerns is what training in "accountability" and "responsibility" really is all about, and that is why I have found it essential to address these issues in class.

I first recognized just how significant a divide can exist after inviting representatives from two local CRM firms to discuss their companies' objectives and policies. Both individuals were forthright, pragmatic, and earnest. One presented a "party line" adherence to county, state, and federal guidelines regarding identification, evaluation, and appropriate reporting and "management" of archaeological resources. The other individual described how some firms were consistently and predictably awarded contracts based on their record of overlooking archaeological resources. It disturbed the students to learn that real-life concerns—business and otherwise—can and sometimes do override the needs of history and science. For some of the

Fig. 17.11 Native American forensic anthropologist and graduate student Trish Mitchell discusses archaeological issues of repatriation, NAGPRA, and the future archaeological recovery and study of human remains with San Diego State University students in Anthropology 302 (*Principles of Archaeology*). Trish serves as a professional and advisor to a number of local bands of the Kumeyaay, the Office of the San Diego County Medical Examiner, and several CRM companies and building contractors.

students, this was seriously upsetting; for others, it was a wake-up call about the fragility of the archaeological record.

Most archaeologists are well aware that builders, contractors, public officials, the public at-large, and Native American groups hold divergent views as to the utility, value, and validity of the archaeological record. Students of archaeology deserve and need to be exposed to these perspectives in order to understand them, to form opinions, and to be able to address such issues.

Area builders, contractors, and county officials have discussed in class how archaeology can affect housing projects, highway improvements, and other development efforts either delaying, halting, or substantially (expensively) altering them and in the process adding thousands of dollars in costs to be passed on to the would-be home buyer or taxpayer. Students learned that anywhere from a few thousand to well over $10,000 of the median $470,000 cost of new housing units results from legally mandated archaeology-related expenses. These speakers have rarely been "anti-archaeology," but typically make an argument for careful, informed, and responsible action by those responsible for the archaeological record.

Representatives of the County Archaeologist, the State Park Service, the California Department of Transportation and other local agencies have addressed our classes on the demands and frustrations of arguing for the protection of archaeological resources to members of a largely uninformed public, housing developers, city councils and local planning groups, the County Board of Supervisors, and even Homeland Security. In 2005, nearly a score of important sites were destroyed during the construction of a 800-meter-wide "No Man's Land" barrier of concrete, steel, and razor wire along San Diego County's international border with Mexico. State and federal authorities carried out this construction without concern for the archaeological record. The Department of Homeland Security chose to ignore the reported cultural resources in this area in favor of rapid completion of the barrier. These are the kinds of real issues that archaeologists today face and will continue to face, and are examples of important issues of which students should be aware.

Native American guest-speakers have also provided varied perspectives on the archaeological record and its value. Our first speaker was an MA candidate in anthropology who had been ostracized by his band and extended family for his involvement with archaeology. Beginning class with a traditional prayer for blessings on the endeavor, he went on to explain the disdain and outrage of his people for the contempt for their oral histories that seemed apparent in scientific studies and legislated management of the archaeological record. These traditional histories have exactly and fully the same validity, weight, and sacredness for members of his people as Bible stories or those of the Koran for many of the Judeo-Christian and Muslim faiths. For many Native Americans, archaeology is one, last insult to their deepest cultural beliefs and traditions. For others, however, it is an important affirmation of their unwritten history, cultural heritage, and rights to their traditional lands.

We have also invited tribal council chairs, a traditional tribal singer, and members of various tribes throughout the region. These individuals have offered contrasting perspectives—that the archaeological record has no significance or utility, that its investigation is essentially an insensitive cultural and racial affront to Native American beliefs and history, or that the archaeological record is an important and priceless affirmation and validation of local Native American cultural roots and history that must be treated with appropriate respect and care in its recognition and preservation or recovery. These opposing views come from individuals and groups with a direct descendant interest. This debate remains an unresolved and contentious issue for many tribes throughout the United States. Students have found these sessions both informative and disturbing, and they have given them entirely a new appreciation of what it means to be an American archaeologist in the twenty-first century.

Without question, the most sensitive issue involves the recovery and treatment of human remains. Cultural norms in this regard vary greatly, no less among Native American groups and individuals. Over several years, we have invited tribal council members to describe the real and bitter pain that their peoples experience in seeing the remains of their ancestors boxed and shelved or displayed in local museums and universities. Their anguish and anger are genuine and palpable, and their demands for the expedient and respectful return of those remains and their burial accompaniments for culturally required purification and appropriate subsequent treatment are compelling. These arguments are not just strong, but sometimes seemingly impossible to counter.

To provide students with a balanced perspective, I asked one of our own graduate students, who is both a practicing physical anthropologist and of Native American descent, to discuss her work with human remains, her personal feelings and thoughts regarding this issue, and its effects on her relationship with other members of her family and larger ethnic community. Her experiences and thoughts have brought to our students some appreciation of the real issues, concerns, and areas of sensitivity that archaeologists must confront today.

Modern archaeologists need to recognize that other constituencies have legitimate agendas regarding the archaeological record and how it ought to be viewed and treated. Archaeologists need to develop awareness and sensitivity to the alternative perspectives of Native Americans, builders, CRM firms, public officials, and the general public, and to develop approaches that accommodate these in an ethically acceptable manner. If we do not, our own professional responsibilities to the past will only become increasingly more difficult to fulfill. Required today are genuine cross-cultural sensitivity, local socioeconomic and international political awareness, and overall adroitness and preparedness among those who are the stewards, custodians, protectors, preservers, and exploiters of that uniquely nonrenewable resource that is the archaeological record.

SDSU archaeologists aggressively enlisted the active input and participation of leading members of our local Native American tribal groups, county and state public officials, and the CRM industry in our classes. Almost all have responded enthusiastically and have provided speakers who express their own specific issues, concerns, and responsibilities involving the archaeological record. These encounters have consistently resulted in powerful and productive experiences. I cannot but strongly recommend similar efforts to others training future archaeologists at any academic level.

THE RESPONSIBLE ARCHAEOLOGIST

Historical archives may be studied over and over again, but archaeological sites are nonrenewable resources. Excavations involve moving the earth and all its contents from a site. Every excavation means the destruction of all or part of an archaeological site. It is for this reason, and a recognition that new methods and techniques in the future will be available to reveal more about the past, that archaeologists usually leave a substantial portion of a site undisturbed.

It is important to remember that archaeology is not a "do-it-yourself" activity. Amateur archaeologists in most cases work hand in hand with professionals. Most professional archaeologists have advanced degrees and have spent a great deal of time in the field and the classroom learning the many facets and skills of the discipline.

All that is left when an excavation is over are the finds themselves, the unexcavated parts of the site, and the samples, photographs, drawings, measurements, and other notes that the archaeologists made. Accurate notes and records of the layers, structures, and finds at a site are essential, not only for the investigator, but also to provide a permanent archive of information that is available to others.

In addition to keeping accurate records for a permanent archive, it is essential that archaeologists make their work public—known to other archaeologists and to the general public. Publication—making things public—in print or other media is part of the responsibility that archaeologists have to make their work and conclusions known so that the information can be checked and added to the general body of knowledge about the past. Books, articles in scientific journals, and reports are part of the permanent record that archaeology creates to document what is learned.

Beyond scientific publication, archaeologists try to make their discoveries known to the general public through magazines, newspapers, television, and the Web. Hardly a day goes by without the popular media mentioning a new discovery or revelation about the past. Keeping the public informed of what is being done is part of the responsibility of being an archaeologist as well. One of the popular means of keeping the public informed has been the creation of an Archaeology Week in most states (Fig. 17.12). This is an annual event when lectures, exhibitions, and other public activities are intended to provide more information to the public and raise awareness of the importance of archaeology.

Museums and monuments are of course another way in which the public has access to the past. Archaeological materials are displayed in exhibitions in museums around the world to document the activities and achievements of ancestors and former inhabitants of the area. Living museums like Williamsburg, Virginia, invite the visitor to partake of the past, walking among the architecture and activities of early America. National monuments in the United States and elsewhere also protect the remains of past societies in the form of living places, architecture, mounds, and other structures that mark areas of archaeological and historical interest. Museums and monuments serve both to inform the public of the past around them and to inspire more interest in the preservation and recovery of those former times.

CONCLUSIONS

This chapter began with the question "Who owns the past?" Hopefully by now the answer is crystal clear—we all do and it is our responsibility to protect and conserve the remains of that past for our children and future humanity. The illicit activities of looters and collectors alike only serve to damage our common her-

Fig, 17.12 The 1992 poster for Archaeology Week in Arizona, one of the first states to initiate this program.

itage and to take these important links to the past out of context and out of the public domain.

Archaeology is about responsibility, about sharing the remarkable story and items that have survived from antiquity, about caring for the past and the future, and about protecting our heritage. Archaeologists have a duty to themselves and to the public to protect and preserve the past and to share their knowledge of that past.

Archaeology is also about people. Archaeology tells about how humans, over thousands and millions of years, have survived and succeeded in the face of the difficult challenges of changing environments and competitive neighbors. Through archaeology, we learn how past societies dealt with issues such as environmental change, overpopulation, political competition, success, and failure. Maybe one of the most important lessons archaeology can teach us is that we are only building on what has gone on before.

And importantly, archaeology also allows us to see our place in the diversity of human societies and to gain some appreciation for how much we are all alike. Archaeology is the history of us. Perhaps more than any other field of study, archaeology tells us that we are all members of the human family, traveling together on a miraculous journey through time.

ETHICAL QUESTIONS

There are four hypothetical questions below that require decisions to be made in difficult archaeological situations. Considering what you have read in this chapter and the ethical guidelines of the Society for American Archaeology and your own moral standards, please write a two-paragraph response to each situation outlining your decision in each case and the reasoning behind it.

1. Permission from landowners is essential for archaeological fieldwork. Most people are willing to have archaeologists on their property, but problems sometimes arise. On one occasion a few years ago, a farmer reluctantly gave permission for fieldwork on his land. Excavations began at what became a very important site of regional importance. The farmer frequently visited the excavations, but seemed anxious about the project. After a week or two, artifacts began disappearing from the trenches. Keeping a night watch, the archaeologists caught the property owner removing conspicuous items. Confronted, the landowner told the archaeologists that he was worried that if anything of importance was found that his land would be taken by the government without sufficient compensation. How can this problem be resolved?

2. Excavations had gone on for 10 years at a major Maya site in the Yucatán of Mexico. The archaeologists had made a major effort to involve the local villagers and once took an injured child to a distant hospital. Toward the end of the last field season, an old man from the village came out to the site with a small bag containing a beautiful painted figurine. The figurine had been looted from the site some years before. It is a museum-quality piece, although its exact provenience at the site is unknown. The old man offers to sell the artifact to the archaeologists. The dilemma arises. Should the archaeologists pay the old man for the artifact, potentially encouraging others to loot the site for other valuable items? Or should the object be refused even though the old man will probably sell it to a tourist?

3. You are a professor of archaeology. During your field excavation season, you and your students visit a number of archaeological projects in California. At the excavations of another, well-known professor, you notice that the work is very sloppy, recording procedures are inadequate, and a number of important objects are being missed or ignored. The site is clearly significant based on its size and richness, but the excavations are below standard. You are new to the area and your job, while the archaeologist in charge of this excavation is well known and respected. What do you do? Speak to the archaeologist at the site, inform the state historic preservation office, or remain quiet?

4. Through the grapevine you hear a story about an archaeologist you know. It seems that a horde of valuable silver antiquities was found in Hungary and pirated out of the country to be sold to a collector in the United States. The Hungarian government eventually learned of this theft and sued the collector in a U.S. court. The collector denied that the items came from Hungary. Some of the evidence involved soil traces, still present on the artifacts, which were similar to the soils from the place in Hungary where the artifacts had been found. The defense lawyer for the collector paid an expert, the archaeologist you know, a large sum of money to testify that the tests for soil provenience were inconclusive. The court found for the collector. While it is technically true that soils are difficult to provenience, the evidence for Hungary as the place of origin was very good. What do you think about the behavior of the archaeologist? What should be done in a case like this?

STUDY QUESTIONS

www.mhhe.com/pricearch1

For more review material and study
questions, please see the self-quizzes
on your online learning center.

1. Why is archaeology important to society?

2. How can we protect the archaeological record?

3. Who owns the past?

4. The NAGPRA legislation has caused a great deal of conflict between the goals of archaeologists and Native American groups. How can this tension and disagreement be resolved?

5. What are the basic responsibilities of an archaeologist in today's world?

REFERENCES

Brodie, Neil, Jennifer Doole, and Colin Renfrew, eds. 2001. *Trade in Illicit Antiquities: The Destruction of the World's Archaeological Heritage.* Cambridge: McDonald Institute.

Carman, J. 2002. *Archaeology and Heritage: An Introduction.* London: Continuum.

King, T. F. 1998. *Cultural Resource Laws and Practice: An Introductory Guide.* Walnut Creek, Calif.: AltaMira Press.

Little, Barbara J. 2002. *Public Benefits of Archaeology.* Gainesville, Fla.: University Press of Florida.

Messenger, P. M., ed. 1999. *The Ethics of Collecting Cultural Property: Whose Culture? Whose Property?* 2d ed. Albuquerque: University of New Mexico Press.

Renfrew, Colin. 2000. *Loot, Legitimacy and Ownership: The Ethical Crisis in Archaeology.* London: Duckworth Publishing.

Zimmerman, Larry J., Karen D. Vitelli, and Julie Hollowell-Zimmer. 2003. *Ethical Issues in Archaeology.* Walnut Creek, Calif.: Altamira Press.

www.mhhe.com/pricearch1

For Internet references related to this
chapter, please see the chapter links
on your online learning center.

A Brief History of the Human Past

INTRODUCTION: WORLD PREHISTORY

World prehistory is a huge body of knowledge. There are libraries full of books, journals, reports, and articles about the human past. This appendix provides a brief overview of world prehistory from the first humans through the rise of Greece and Rome, along with some information on a few later societies and a bit of historical archaeology. It is intended to give you some background for the ideas and information presented in *Principles of Archaeology.*

   This appendix is also intended as a road map to help you find your way through prehistory. You many want to use the maps, charts, and text here for reference while reading the chapters in the book. Discussion of the methods and theories of archaeology in this book would be sterile without examples and case studies drawn from world prehistory, so many such examples and case studies have been provided throughout the text. Within this appendix, any sites that are discussed in the chapters are shown in **bold italics**, with the chapter number identified.

   Our prehistory starts a long time ago. It covers the last several million years of the earth's history and almost the entire planet. The saga of our human ancestors is an extraordinary one of expansion in numbers and geographic distribution, associated with increasing intelligence and the invention and development of technology. Much of our past takes place in the Old World—Africa, Asia, and Europe. And most of that took place in Africa. Our earliest ancestors emerged in Africa around 6 million years ago. It wasn't until 1½ million years ago that humans first began to spread into Asia and Europe. Three-quarters of our story then is about growing up in Africa. Humans didn't expand beyond the borders of the Old World until 50,000 years ago; eventually, by 10,000 years ago, our ancestors were living on every continent except Antarctica.

   So our human play takes place in many acts and several different theaters, Africa, Eurasia, the Americas, and the Pacific. The first farmers stepped onto the stage around 11,000 years ago—and nothing has been the same since. The domestication of plants and animals changed everything. This happens first in Southwest Asia, shortly thereafter in East Asia, and somewhat later in Africa. The first farming villages are dramatically different, technologically, socially, economically, and ideologically. Farming sets the stage for the rise of cities, and larger, more powerful political entities—states and empires—eventually arise. The archaeological evidence for these civilizations is spectacular as monumental architecture and human habitation in a variety of forms changed the landscape forever. Much of the fascination with archaeology lies in the romantic ruins of these ancient civilizations.

Humans moved to the New World sometime around 15,000 years ago when the first inhabitants walked across a former land bridge between Siberia and Alaska. The precise date of this event is unknown, but certainly by 13,000 years ago humans had occupied both continents of the Americas. The period between their arrival and the rise of farming villages is a time of successful hunting and gathering communities in many places. Domestication takes root in several areas of the New World as well. The earliest evidence for farming and herding comes from western South America by around 6000 BC; in Mexico, squash and then corn are put under cultivation by 5000 BC. The beginnings of agriculture are also witnessed in the eastern United States, where plants like sunflower and marsh elder were intentionally sown after 2000 BC. Village cultures quickly develop around these communities and political systems arise as well. Evidence of the long-distance exchange of rare and exotic items suggests that status differences drive the growth of political systems in these areas. Extraordinary states and empires eventually take hold in Central America and western South America—the Aztec, the Maya, the Inka, and many others—but are extinguished by the expansion of European empires following the end of the fifteenth century AD.

Time is a concept that is not easy to grasp. It is difficult to imagine the millions of years of our human presence on earth and the various periods of world prehistory. Two ways of looking at time—geological and archaeological—are described in the next section.

The remaining sections of this appendix provide a condensed prehistory of the world. A few notes on how this is organized may make it easier to follow. I focus initially on the Old World, first on our deep roots in Africa, then the expansion to Eurasia, and the transition from early varieties of our genus *Homo* to **Neanderthal** and modern forms. I then discuss a major flashpoint in our past: the creative explosion that followed the emergence of **fully modern humans**. Further geographic expansion and extraordinary technological and conceptual changes mark this period of time. A discussion of the origins of agriculture and the rise of states and empires concludes the geographic section on the Old World. The next section deals with the New World, its initial peopling, the rise of farming cultures, and the emergence of spectacular civilizations in Middle and South America.

The last two sections deal with the Pacific region—between the Old and New World—and historical archaeology, the last 500 years or so of recent time, including the Renaissance and the industrial era, where written records often provide supplementary data for archaeological research. A map and timeline for these sections provides geographical and chronological context.

GEOLOGICAL AND ARCHAEOLOGICAL TIME

Astronomers estimate the universe to be between 10 and 15 billion years old. Geologists estimate the earth to have been formed about 4.6 billion years ago. That's a long time. They futher divide up the earth's history into a multitude of eras, periods, and epochs. Fortunately, we humans came on the stage late in the day, between 6 and 7 million years ago, so that only those last few intervals of geological time are essential for an understanding of human prehistory. The Miocene, which dates from 24 million to 5.5 million years ago, witnessed the emergence of our first humanlike relative near the end of the epoch. The Pliocene is the next geological epoch when more human ancestors appeared, only some of whom survived. The Pleistocene, beginning about 2 million years ago, was marked by a series of major climatic fluctuations. Modern humans, indistinguishable from ourselves, appeared toward the end of this epoch. The Recent epoch—also called the Holocene—began only 11,000 years ago and witnessed the origins of agriculture, the first cities, the industrial age, and includes the present.

Archaeologists divide the time period of human existence into more manageable and understandable units, based on changes in artifacts and material cul-

Time has no beginnings and history has no bounds.
—Gordon Lightfoot, singer/songwriter

~~~~~~~~~~~~~~~~~~~~~~~~

Neanderthal An earlier human relative that lived largely in Europe from approximately 250,000 to 35,000 years ago, when it became extinct. *Homo neanderthalensis.*

fully modern humans (FMH) A synonymous term for *Homo sapiens sapiens,* first appearing more than 100,000 years ago in Africa.

bipedal The human method of locomotion, walking on two legs; one of the first human characteristics to distinguish the early hominins, as opposed to quadrupedalism, walking on four legs.

ture. This framework for dividing up the past was developed in the 1830s when an innovative three-age system with categories of Stone, Bronze, and Iron was used to organize museum exhibits. These three major divisions are still used in Europe and other parts of the Old World. The Stone Age was further divided in 1865 into the Paleolithic and the Neolithic. Flaked stone tools characterize the Paleolithic; the Neolithic is represented by polished stone tools and pottery. This distinction also marks the transition from hunting to farming in human prehistory. The Paleolithic as well as the geological interval called the Pleistocene came to an end some 11,000 years ago as Neolithic village farmers began to appear in various places around the globe.

In the New World, a different set of terms (Paleoindian, Archaic) is applied to the periods before the origins of agriculture. Regional terms are used for the time periods that follow the onset of village farming. A basic system in several areas includes the terms *Formative*, *Classic*, and *Postclassic* for the periods when more hierarchical societies emerge and states and empires follow. Outside of the states and empires in the Americas, hunting and village-farming groups continued, particularly in the northern two-thirds of North America and much of eastern South America, until the European conquest.

Another way to try to conceive of the vastness of time is to convert it into more comprehensible units. Imagine the 7 million years as a week. Each day in the week covers 1 million years, and each hour is 41,667 years. Our hypothetical week begins at midnight Sunday morning and continues until midnight Saturday night, as shown in the calendar in Fig. A.1. In this scenario, our earliest ancestors appear around midday on Sunday. The first members of our own genus, *Homo*, show up Thursday evening, and we begin to spread out of Africa early Friday morning. *Homo sapiens sapiens* arrives on the scene Saturday night after eight. The origins of agriculture take place in the final quarter of an hour of the week. Then, forty-five seconds before the stroke of midnight on Saturday, Columbus discovers the Americas.

OLD WORLD

This section covers the prehistory of the Old World—Africa, Asia, and Europe—from the first humans through the emergence of early civilizations. These states and empires rise in Mesopotamia, the Nile Valley, the Indus Valley, and China. The locations of most of the sites discussed in this and the following sections are shown throughout the appendix in the maps, along with timelines intended to give some indication of their chronological position. Fig. A2 shows the timeline and map for Old World sites.

Deep Roots in Africa

Although the evidence is fragmentary and hard to find, it is nevertheless possible to put together a picture of the evolutionary history of our earliest human ancestors during the late Miocene and Pliocene, from sometime before 6 million years ago (m.y.a.) to 2 m.y.a. Fig. A.3 provides a schematic summary of the major human fossil finds that have helped us build this evolutionary picture.

Many new varieties of African apes appeared in the late Miocene as the climate of this region became drier and the tropical rainforests shrank. Some of these ape species were becoming **bipedal**, and thus human ancestors, by the end of the Miocene. Only a very few examples of these Miocene creatures are known from fossils called *Sahelanthropus tchadensis*, *Orronin tugenensis*, and *Ardipithecus ramidus*. Their characteristics reveal a mix of ape and human features. These individuals

▶ **Fig. A.1** Human prehistory in a week. A condensed view of 7,000,000 years of humans on the planet, converted to a hypothetical week.

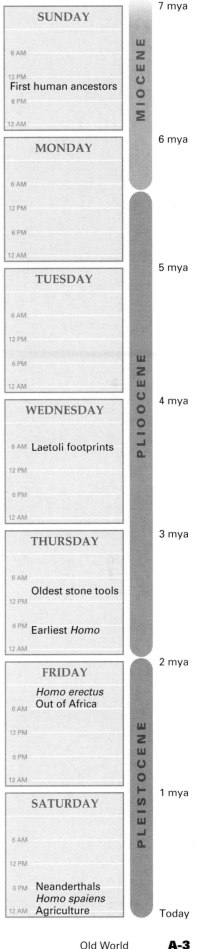

	7 mya
SUNDAY	
6 AM	
12 PM	
First human ancestors	
6 PM	
12 AM	
MONDAY	6 mya
6 AM	
12 PM	
6 PM	
12 AM	
TUESDAY	5 mya
6 AM	
12 PM	
6 PM	
12 AM	
WEDNESDAY	4 mya
6 AM Laetoli footprints	
12 PM	
6 PM	
12 AM	
THURSDAY	3 mya
6 AM	
Oldest stone tools	
12 PM	
6 PM Earliest *Homo*	
12 AM	
FRIDAY	2 mya
Homo erectus Out of Africa	
6 AM	
12 PM	
6 PM	
12 AM	
SATURDAY	1 mya
6 AM	
12 PM	
6 PM Neanderthals	
Homo spaiens	
12 AM Agriculture	Today

MIOCENE · PLIOCENE · PLEISTOCENE

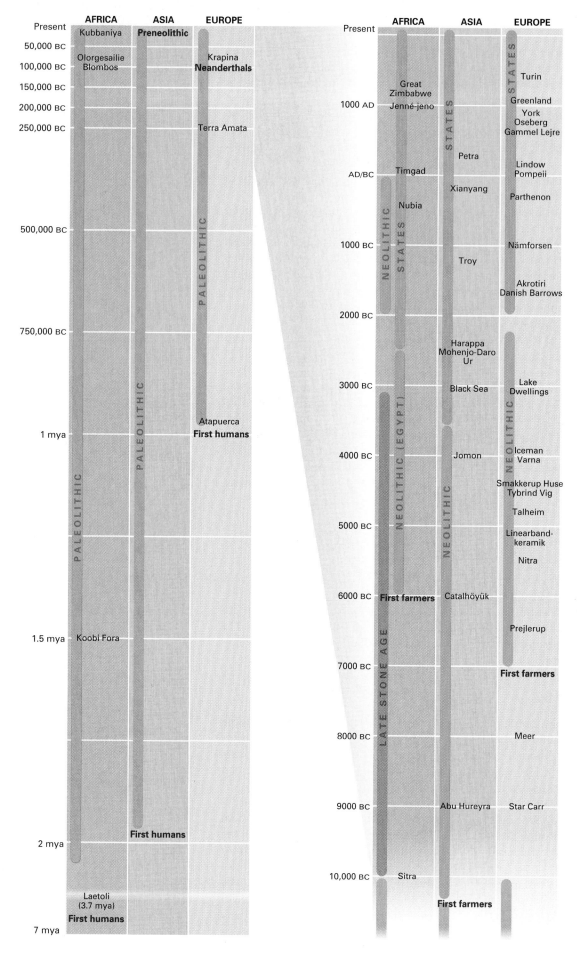

Fig. A.2 Map and timeline for the Old World.

Fig. A.3 A chart of the major human fossil forms, chronology, and characteristics. *Facultative bipedalism* means that the species occasionally walked on two legs; *obligate bipedalism* means that the species normally walked on two legs.

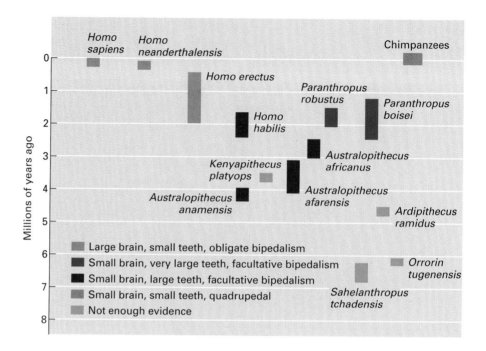

were generally small brained with large teeth. Bipedal locomotion is also well documented in these species, both in the fossil bones and especially in the remarkable footprints from the site of **Laetoli** (Chapter 8) in Tanzania, dating to 3.75 m.y.a.

Near the end of the Pliocene, sometime before 2 m.y.a., the first member of our genus *Homo* appeared: *Homo habilis.* This hominin was a curious species with a mixture of old and new traits. A noticeable increase in brain size is seen with the appearance of this species, almost one-third larger than earlier fossil forms. *Homo habilis* may also be responsible for the first stone tools that are found in Ethiopia around 2.5 m.y.a. These tools are remarkably simple, almost unrecognizable unless found together in groups. They were made by taking small round stones, the size of a large egg or tennis ball, and cracking them with another stone, creating sharp-edged pebble tools and the flakes that were broken off. Such stone tools provide useful cutting edges for creatures that lack both sharp teeth and claws for slicing meat, shredding plants, or digging.

Out of Africa

Homo habilis rather quickly gave rise to a new species by 1.9 m.y.a. This new species, called *Homo erectus,* was essentially human below the neck. The time period (1.9–0.2 m.y.a.) of *erectus* saw a doubling in brain size, reaching a maximum of three-quarters of modern size. The evidence from **Koobi Fora** (Chapter 10) provides some information on the activities of these early humans. *Olorgesailie* (Chapter 10), also in East Africa, marks an area of intensive human activity during this same period. *Homo erectus* groups undertook a dramatic geographic expansion, moving into Asia and Europe where they encountered a variety of new conditions. The earliest dates for the presence of humans outside of Africa are more recent than 2 million years ago, the beginning of the Pleistocene epoch. The Pleistocene, also known as the Ice Age, was a time of climatic extremes in many parts of the world. Repeated, pronounced changes in temperature, sea level, vegetation, and animal life characterize this time.

The harsh environments of the Pleistocene Old World were the places where our ancestors became more human, changing their habits, technology, and biology to adapt to new conditions. Their hands and simple tools had been sufficient to obtain the foods available in the benign warmth of Africa. But expansion out of the tropics required new skills and tools for surviving cold weather, where the lack of food or shelter could be fatal. It became necessary for our ancestors to change nature to fit their needs and enhance their survival. The first reliable evidence for the controlled use of fire, for systematic hunting, and for the use of wooden spears comes from this time. Sites like Atapuerca in Spain and *Terra Amata* (Chapter 10) in France document the early human presence in Europe.

It was a period of changes in stone tools as well. Archaeologists call this period when core and flake tools replaced pebble tools the Lower Paleolithic. The Lower Paleolithic extends from approximately 1.9 m.y.a. until about 200,000 years ago. The handaxe was invented as an all-purpose implement at this time, and it became the hallmark of the Lower Paleolithic. Flake tools also are common during this time period.

Neanderthal

The end of the Lower Paleolithic is followed by the Middle Paleolithic and the emergence of the *Neanderthals* (Chapter 14) in Europe and Southwest Asia. Conventional wisdom today generally regards the Neanderthals as a specialized human form that evolved from *Homo erectus* in the colder, more isolated parts of Europe sometime around 200,000 years ago. The skeletons of the Neanderthals differ somewhat from those of fully modern forms, although they had the same posture, dexterity, mobility, and comparable brain size. Neanderthal bones are generally described as robust; they had heavier limb bones than fully modern humans, suggesting greater muscular strength, and a more powerful grip.

The Middle Paleolithic is associated with Neanderthals and early *Homo sapiens* and is characterized by a predominance of flake tools in artifact assemblages. The period extends from about 200,000 to 40,000 years ago. Major changes in human behavior took place during this period. For the first time, our ancestors began to exhibit behaviors that were more than just practical activities, beyond the basic necessities for survival—that is, they became more human. In the Middle Paleolithic, these behaviors included the intentional burial of the dead, cannibalism, and the nurturing of the weak and elderly.

Beginning around 50,000 years ago, fully modern humans replaced Neanderthals in western Asia and then in Europe. The mechanism for this replacement is the subject of debate among archaeologists and physical anthropologists. The interaction between Neanderthals and modern individuals is thought to have been either violent or romantic—the modern humans either killed off the Neanderthals or mated with them and assimilated the species. There is evidence to support both theories and the question is not yet resolved.

The Creative Explosion

The earliest anatomically modern humans (*Homo sapiens sapiens*) have been found in East Africa and in South Africa, for example at the site of *Blombos* (Chapter 5) between 200,000 and 100,000 years ago. Lacking the robust frame, heavy brow ridges, and protruding jaw of the Neanderthals, the *H. sapiens sapiens* face sits almost directly under a bulging forehead. A chin reinforces the smaller, weaker jaw and the smaller teeth of this hominin. Its brain size is also fully modern, although its intellectual capacity is unknown.

By around 70,000 years ago, anatomically modern humans had moved into western Asia—as witnessed at the caves of *Qafzeh* and *Skhul* (Chapter 8)—and then to Europe by 40,000 years ago. These groups were responsible for most of the major advances in human culture prior to the invention of agriculture. Some of the innovations include new hunting equipment, such as the spearthrower and the bow and arrow; the domestication of the dog; the shaping of new materials

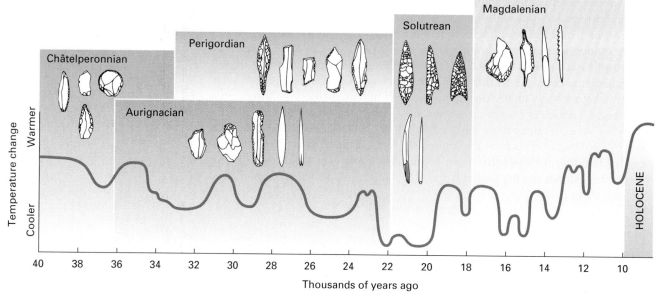

Fig. A.4   The major periods of the Upper Paleolithic with distinctive tool types. The blue line shows changes in temperature during this period and marks the Late Glacial Maximum cold around 20,000 years ago. The Holocene is the geological period that follows the Pleistocene, beginning 10,000 years ago. Solutrean leaf-shaped points are the upper three artifacts shown in the Solutrean section.

such as bone, wood, shell, and ivory into tools; the transport or exchange of raw materials such as flint over long distances; great diversity and specialization in artifacts; and the first art. This archaeological period between 40,000 and 11,000 years ago at the end of the Pleistocene is known at the Upper Paleolithic in Eurasia.

The Upper Paleolithic also represents an important phase in the geographic expansion of the human species. There were more sites in more places than ever before. Virtually all the earth's diverse environments, from tropical rain forest to arctic tundra, were inhabited during this period. Africa, Europe, and Asia were filled with groups of hunter-gatherers, and several continents were colonized for the first time. Modern humans spread into Australia and New Guinea (around 40,000 years ago) and into North and South America (perhaps by 15,000 years ago).

The archaeological materials of this period are best known from Europe, and especially from southwestern France, an important hub of archaeological activities during the twentieth century. Excavations over the last 100 years in the deep deposits of caves and rockshelters in this area have exposed layer upon layer of materials from the last part of the Pleistocene. These excavations and studies of the contents of the layers resulted in the recognition of a sequence of Upper Paleolithic subperiods, known as the Châtelperronnian, Aurignacian, Perigordian, Solutrean, and Magdalenian (Fig. A.4). In central and eastern Europe, the designation of subperiods is slightly different, with a period roughly equivalent to the Perigordian called the Gravettian. In general, the Upper Paleolithic was one of the coldest periods of the Pleistocene and the extreme of this climate is seen during the Solutrean.

The material remains left by these Upper Paleolithic societies reinforce the idea that by this time our species had indeed arrived as creative creatures. Blade manufacturing techniques and blade tools characterize the Upper Paleolithic. Stone blades are a special form of elongated flake, with a length at least twice its width, and sharp, parallel cutting edges on both sides. The site of *Meer* (Chapter 10) in Belgium provides an example of stone working in this period. *Sitra* (Chapter 10) in Egypt provides another example of late Paleolithic stone tool use.

Another distinctive aspect of Upper Paleolithic stone tool manufacture is the appearance of special flaking techniques during the Solutrean period, to make thin, beautiful leaf-shaped points in several different sizes. Some of these points were used for spears and some perhaps for arrows, while others may have served as knives. These tools are among the finest examples of the stoneworker's skill from the entire Paleolithic. At the end of the Solutrean, however, these flaking

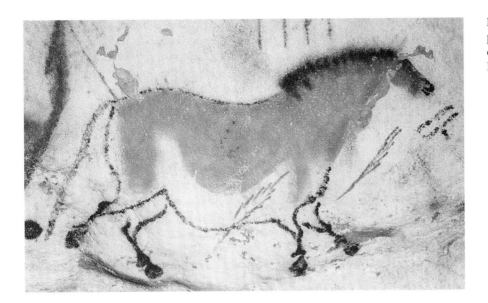

Fig. A.5 Upper Paleolithic cave painting of a Pleistocene horse with darts or spears from Lascaux, France.

techniques largely disappeared from the craft of stone tool manufacture, not to be used again for thousands of years.

Fine bone needles with small eyes document the manufacture of sewn clothing and other equipment from animal skins. Several categories of carved artifacts—buttons, gaming pieces, pendants, necklaces, and the like—marked a new concern with personal appearance, an expression of self, and the aesthetic embellishment of everyday objects. There is also compelling evidence for a celebration of the seasons and an awareness of time in the archaeological remains from the Upper Paleolithic. Finally, the suggestion of counting systems and the beginning of a calendar of sorts—at least a recording of the phases of the moon—may have appeared at this time.

This development was closely related to the appearance of decorative art. Figurines, cave paintings, engravings, and myriad decoration of other objects reflect the creative explosion that characterized Upper Paleolithic achievement. The artwork of the Upper Paleolithic can be divided into two major categories: mural art—paintings and engravings on the walls of caves, and portable art—carvings, figurines, and other shaped or decorated pieces that can be moved from place to place. Upper Paleolithic mural art is found primarily in France and Spain (Fig. A.5), although ancient examples have also been found in South Africa and Australia. The spectacular cave and rockshelter paintings of southern Africa are described in Chapter 5. Portable art from this time is found throughout Europe and much of the rest of the Old World.

The period in Europe following the end of the Paleolithic and before the arrival of Neolithic farming is known as the *Mesolithic* (Chapter 5), a time of hunter-gatherers in a climate much like today with rich forest and marine resources available. The site of *Star Carr* (Chapter 12) in England is an example of an Early Mesolithic lakeshore encampment. Other Mesolithic sites are known from the aurochs kill at *Prejlerup* (Chapter 12), the underwater site of *Tybrind Vig* (Chapter 11), and the coastal occupation of *Smakkerup Huse* (Chapter 12), all in Denmark. In Japan, the *Jomon* (Chapter 4) was a comparable period to the Mesolithic at approximately the same time.

The Origins of Agriculture

Roughly 99.9% of our past was spent as foragers, living off the land, scavenging, collecting, gathering, fishing, and hunting wild foods. The end of the Pleistocene, however, brought the most important changes in human behavior since the size increase of the human brain. Certain human groups began to produce food rather than collect it—that is, to domesticate and control wild plants and animals. The invention of agriculture was a remarkable, global phenomenon, documented in several different places on several different continents between 11,000 and 4000 years ago. This interval of time is the blink of an eye in the span of human prehistory. Yet the changes initiated during this interval were staggering in their consequences. As a species, we are still adjusting to this new way of life.

As mentioned, agriculture is a way of obtaining food from domesticated plants and animals. But the transition to farming is much more than simple herding and cultivation. It also entails major, long-term changes in the structure and organization of the societies that adopt this new way of life, as well as a totally new relationship with the environment. While hunter-gatherers largely live off the land in an extensive fashion, generally exploiting a diversity of resources over a broad area, farmers intensively utilize a smaller portion of the landscape and create a milieu that suits their needs. With the transition to agriculture, humans began to truly master the environment.

The domestication of both plants and animals may be related to the storage of food. Such cereals as wheat, barley, corn, and rice have hard outer coverings that protect the nutritious kernel for some months, permitting the seed to survive until the growing season and offering very good possibilities for storage. Meat can be stored in the form of living, tame animals that are always available for slaughter. As such, storage provides a means to regulate the availability of food and to accumulate surplus.

Primary centers of domestication in the Old World were in Southwest Asia, East Asia, and sub-Saharan Africa (Fig. A.6). The earliest known domesticates—including wheat, barley, peas, lentils, pigs, goats, sheep, and cattle—appeared in Southwest Asia, between the eastern Mediterranean Sea and Iran, at the end of the Pleistocene. Many other plants and animals—such as bread wheat, figs, olives, grapes, and flax—were gradually added to that list. Two of the examples in the book are relevant to this time. The *Preneolithic* (Chapter 12) is a period just before the beginnings of agriculture in Southwest Asia, found largely in the Levant region along the Mediterranean coast. *Abu Hureyra* (Chapters 13, 14) is a very early Neolithic site along the Tigris River in Syria. *Catalhöyük* (Chapter 9) is a large Neolithic town in central Turkey, dating to around 6000 BC, and it documents the rapid growth and aggregation of population that is witnessed following the origins of agriculture.

Agriculture was also invented in the Far East, perhaps in two or three different areas, sometime after 8000 BC. Rice was initially cultivated in South China, possibly as early as the eighth or ninth millennium BC, and somewhat later in Southeast Asia, before 4000 BC. Millet was first cultivated and pigs were domesticated in North China in early villages dating to roughly 5000 BC.

Plants such as African rice, sorghum, and pearl millet were domesticated in sub-Saharan Africa by 2000 BC. Cattle and goat herding had been practiced for several millennia in this area, prior to the appearance of the new domesticates. In addition, domesticated plants like wheat and barley spread from Southwest Asia to the Nile Valley in Egypt around 6000 BC. The site of *Wadi Kubbaniya* (Chapter 8) in Egypt is an example from the late Neolithic in this region.

Domesticated plants and animals begin to appear in Africa and Europe after 7000 BC. It is at this same time that the hypothetical *flood* took place, perhaps in the Black Sea, as discussed in Chapter 9. The archaeology of Europe changes dramatically with the arrival of agriculture and the Neolithic. Small farming villages began to appear in Greece and the Aegean after 7000 BC as domesticated plants and animals spread from their place of origin in Southwest Asia. From this initial beachhead, agriculture took two routes as the spread continued. One route was coastal, along the north shore of the Mediterranean. Many of the islands of the Mediter-

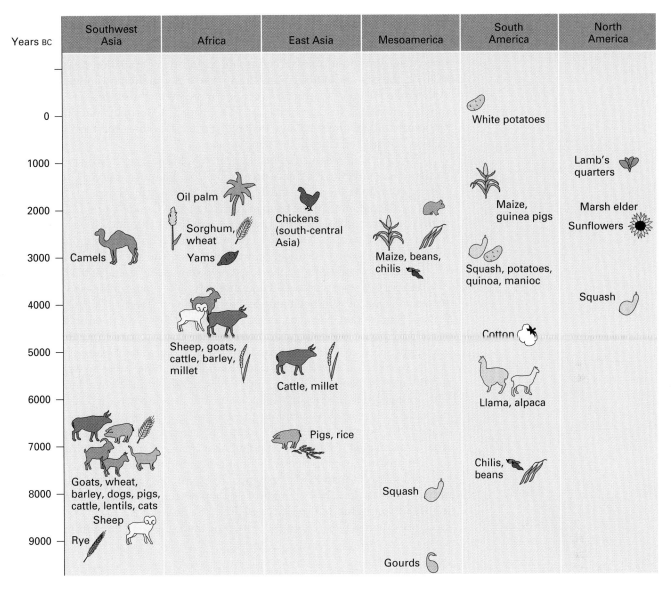

Fig. A.6 Primary centers of domestication, major species, and years BC.

ranean were colonized for the first time in this period along with the arrival of farmers on the coastline. A second route went inland through southeastern Europe.

The next step in the expansion of farming was movement into the interior from the coasts of the Mediterranean and into Central Europe from the Southeast. One of the more intriguing Neolithic cultures in this area was the Linearbandkeramik, named after a type of pottery, which spread from Hungary to Holland and northern Poland to the Ukraine in a period of 150 years or so. The burial evidence from the cemetery site of *Nitra* (Chapter 14) dates from this period. The mass grave at *Talheim* (Chapter 14) in Germany provides a stark contrast with the cemetery at Nitra. The French lake dwelling sites are another group of early farming villages in Europe in the area around the Alps. The frozen body of the *Iceman* (Chapter 5), found in the Italian Alps in 1992, also belongs to this period of the Neolithic. By 4000 BC, farming reached the northwestern fringes of Europe, arriving in the British Isles, Ireland, and Scandinavia and replacing hunter-gatherers across the continent to the limits of agriculture in northern Scandinavia. Neolithic cultures developed locally as sites increased in size and defensible locations became more popular.

States and Empires

The consequences of the origins and spread of farming were enormous. Sedentary village life and increased food resources meant a population could grow. By 6000 BC, the site of Catalhöyük in Turkey had a population estimated at 10,000. Among the villages of farmers, larger and more hierarchical societies developed quickly, and the first states in the world appeared in Mesopotamia (Iraq) during the fourth millennium BC. States are large, territorial polities and they incorporate villages, towns, and cities in the same society.

By 3500 BC, the first cities had appeared in Mesopotamia with monumental construction and elite residence areas. The Ubaid culture was centered around the city of Eridu to the south and Tepe Gawra to the north. Gawra has the earliest monumental planning: three temples carefully placed around a central courtyard with symmetry and balance. *Ur* (Chapter 3) at its height around 2100 BC was home to some 35,000 people. The inner city was dominated by a large mound surrounded by a massive fortification wall of bricks. The site of *Petra* (Chapter 6) was founded around 600 BC in the desert of Jordan as the capital of the Nabateans.

A series of states succeeded one another on the plains of Mesopotamia over several millennia. By the beginning of the Christian Era, the great kings Gilgamesh, Sargon, Hammurabi, Nebuchadnezzar, and many others had ruled and died. Empires had formed and collapsed. Alexander the Great passed through in 330 BC, and a few centuries later the Roman Empire incorporated large parts of the region.

Other early states in Eurasia are found in the Nile Valley in Egypt, in the Indus Valley in Pakistan, and in China. Egypt and the Indus civilization were possibly influenced by events in Mesopotamia, but developments in China were independent of western Asia and northeastern Africa. The state emerged in Egypt around 2500 BC with a dynasty of rulers that lasted for 2000 years. The evidence from *Lower Nubia* (Chapter 4) on population change comes largely from this dynastic period in Egypt. Large-scale political centralization was much more pronounced in Egypt than in Mesopotamia. In Egypt, the pharaoh was divine ruler and supreme leader. The pyramids of Egypt were tombs for these rulers, containing wealth and grandeur unsurpassed in the ancient Near East (Fig. A.7). The structures themselves reflect the power of the kings and the authority of the

Fig. A.7 The Sphinx and a pyramid in Egypt.

state—able to design and construct such imposing monuments. Another impressive structure is the temple of *Abu Simbel* (Chapter 17), one of the hallmarks of ancient Egypt.

The Harappan state arose in the Indus Valley in present-day Pakistan and India just a few centuries after the Egyptians. The two best-known centers were the cities of *Harappa* (Chapter 4) and *Mohenjo-Daro* (Chapter 11) at opposite ends of the valley. Although these South Asian sites have not yielded rich tombs, like those in Egypt and Mesopotamia, they are known for their highly developed craft industries. Indus centers were not as large as those in Mesopotamia, but they were more systematically planned, with extensive residential quarters, centralized drainage networks for individual houses, and city walls with controlled entrance gates.

Pristine states developed in North China around 2000 BC. Again, the emergence of cities and larger, territorial polities mark this new phenomenon. Massive walls and platforms of packed earth form the monumental architecture of this region. An-yang, the last capital of the Shang dynasty, is one of the best-known early Chinese cities. These Chinese cities were among the largest in the world with populations in the hundreds of thousands. One of the more remarkable features of these early Chinese states were the tombs of the rulers. During the reign of the Qin dynasty, for example, a magnificent tomb was built near the capital of *Xianyang* (Chapter 5) shortly before 200 BC. According to Chinese history, construction of the tomb required 700,000 laborers who worked for 36 years. Part of the tomb contents included a huge army of life-size terracotta (brown-orange earthenware) foot soldiers and cavalrymen. This massive project and construction documents the powerful military, strict class society, and wealth that existed in ancient China.

In Europe, the Bronze Age witnessed major changes, initially and most spectacularly in the southeastern part of the continent. The Aegean area was the center of this development, first on the island of Crete and shortly thereafter on the Greek mainland. The Minoan civilization on Crete emerged after 2000 BC and is well known from a series of palaces across the island. The Minoans controlled the eastern Mediterranean and dominated trade with the rest of Europe. As a result, Crete and the Aegean became a magnet for the raw materials of Europe. Metal ores of gold, copper, silver, and tin, amber, furs, and many other materials were funneled along major trade routes, rivers, and passes to the Aegean. There, craft specialists produced the wealth of finished products, including jewelry, metal weapons, cloth, wine and oil, that was traded for additional wealth and power. The site of *Akrotiri* (Chapter 13) on the island of Thera is a remarkable testament to these early civilizations and the extent of their trade. The Mycenaeans of mainland Greece took over Crete and the rest of the Aegean after 1400 BC, but the general pattern of trade with the rest of the continent continued. The Mycenaean period, which ended in 1100 BC, was the time of Homer's heroes and the Trojan War, as Greek warriors sailed to the west coast of Turkey and besieged the ancient city of *Troy* (Chapter 9).

The nodes of the major trade routes on the European continent were greatly influenced by the wealth and exchange that was taking place, and powerful societies grew up at these junctions. Wessex in England, Bohemia in the Czech Republic, and *Denmark* in Scandinavia witnessed rich Bronze Age societies (Chapter 16). The Bronze Age of northern Europe dates from the period around 2000 BC and provides a striking example of the distribution and significance of burial mounds, or barrows. Some of the more spectacular evidence from the later Stone Age and Bronze Age in northern Europe is seen in the rock art that adorns a number of areas in northern Scandinavia. The rock carvings at *Nämforsen*, Sweden, are discussed in Chapter 16.

The introduction of iron in Europe intensified trends initiated during the late Neolithic and Bronze Age and launched the start of the Iron Age there. The classic civilizations of Greece and Rome arose in the last millennium before Christ during the early Iron Age in Europe. In Greece, the Golden Age of Pericles, Athens, Sparta, and the foundations of democracy dominated much of the Mediterranean during its height from 600 to 336 BC. The *Parthenon* (Chapter 17) in Athens was completed during this period in 432 BC.

In much of the rest of Europe, the elite gained power and wealth and were buried in elaborate tombs. The *Lindow Man* (Chapter 7), in marked contrast, was executed and buried in a bog. Warfare and conflict were rampant as major fortified towns sprang up at the center of Iron Age societies. The great hall at *Gammel Lejre* (Chapter 6) was constructed during the Iron Age around AD 850. The societies of much of Central and Western Europe during this time have been lumped under the rubric of Celts. These groups dominated Western Europe until the rise of the Roman Empire.

Rome and the Romans conquered large parts of North Africa, Europe, and the Near East in the period between 285 BC and the birth of Christ, with an iron will and a powerful military. The empire stretched from the east to the northwest, from Damascus to Hadrian's Wall in the north of England. The Roman town of *Pompeii* (Chapter 8) was buried under the eruption of Mount Vesuvius near Naples, Italy, in AD 79. Pompeii is an example of early efforts at site protection. Exploration of the site began in 1748, largely as a search for objects of art, but by 1860 substantial efforts were being made to preserve the buildings and decorations. Excavations continue today and almost two-thirds of the town has been uncovered. The remaining sections will be left for posterity.

In Africa, following the spread of some agricultural species and the indigenous domestication of others in the sub-Saharan region, farming expanded in various ways to the south. By 1000 BC, agriculture was well established in West Africa and by 200 BC prosperous villages were growing, involved in the trade of iron, grinding stone, and eventually gold. Jenné-jeno emerged as a major center in this area, and by AD 700 it covered 33 ha (80 acres) inside massive mud fortification walls. A series of kingdoms rose and fell in this region over the last 2000 years, fueled by control of trade in gold, ivory, salt, and other valued commodities.

Elsewhere in East and South Africa, hunter-gatherer groups were being displaced by the expansion of iron-using cattle herders, probably belonging to the Bantu language family. Herding groups arrived in East Africa by 2000 BC and continued expansion to the south. Farming groups also were expanding and occupying primarily the wetter areas of the East African lake district and the Zambezi and the Limpopo rivers in South Africa by AD 400.

Trade in gold and ivory pushed societal changes in this region, as powerful trading towns, polities, and complex states arose, controlling the movement of goods between coastal demand and inland supply. During the last thousand years of African prehistory, complex states emerged in the central and southern regions. The best known of these states was centered at the site of Great Zimbabwe, in the country of Zimbabwe, on a tributary of the Zambezi River. Great Zimbabwe covered some 40 ha (100 acres) at its zenith around AD 1350, with a population estimated at 18,000.

THE AMERICAS

This section considers the first Americans who peopled the New World more than 10,000 years ago and their descendants. We follow the development of Native American cultures in North, South, and Middle America from the early hunter-gatherers to the origin and spread of agriculture, and the rise of major civilizations. The region of Mexico, Guatemala, Belize, and parts of Honduras and El Salvador where high civilizations arose is sometimes called Mesoamerica The timeline and map of sites for the New World is seen in Fig. A8.

Early Americans

Homo sapiens came to the New World for the first time sometime before 13,000 years ago. The passage to the Americas was across the "Bering Land Bridge," a dry-land connection between Siberia and Alaska provided by dramatically lower sea levels during the cold periods of the Pleistocene. Groups of hunters quickly expanded across both North and South America and may have been involved in the extinction of a number of animal species (see Chapter 12). The earliest known remains from this period come from the site of Monte Verde in southern Chile, dating to 13,000 years ago.

Archaeological remains in North America dating to around 10,000 years ago are generally known as Paleoindian. Sites from this period, like *Folsom* (Chapter 5) in New Mexico, are recognized by a specific type of stone spear tip, known as a fluted point (Fig. A.9). Paleoindian spear points document the presence of early Americans in North America between 11,000 and 9,000 years ago.

The period following the Paleoindian is known as the Archaic across the Americas and is characterized by hunter-gatherers involved in a wide range of subsistence activities, often in rich environments, and living in more permanent settlements. The Archaic in the eastern United States is also a fascinating period with large permanent sites in some areas and long-distance trade. The *Koster* (Chapter 6) and *Black Earth* (Chapter 4) sites in Illinois document this time and place. *Windover* (Chapter 5) in Florida is another important Archaic site from North America. In other areas, such as the basin and range topography of the intermontane western United States, a variety of hunting and gathering groups coped very successfully with the exigencies of their environment. Investigations in the *Reese River Valley* (Chapter 6) and *Carson Sink* (Chapter 10) in Nevada document such adaptations. Another find from this period was a skeleton found in 1996 along the banks of the Columbia River in Washington state at the town of *Kennewick*, dated to approximately 7000 BC. The ownership and disposition of this skeleton has been the subject of controversy between archaeologists and Native American groups in the area ever since, discussed in Chapter 17. The Emeryville Shellmound in California (Chapter 16) also documents a forager way of life in this area from approximately 600 BC to AD 1300.

Farming Villages

During the Archaic, plants became much more important in the human diet. A number of prehistoric groups began to utilize and eventually manipulate certain plant species more intensively in their environment. There are at least three primary centers of domestication in the New World—in Mexico, western South America, and eastern North America.

In Mexico, gourds and squash were domesticated during the eighth millennium BC; maize (corn) and possibly beans were cultivated by 5000 years ago. These crops provided the essential nutrients and calories for a healthy diet. Domesticated animals were never very important in this area, although turkeys, dogs, and the stingless honeybee were kept. The evidence in Mexico is very intriguing since domestication of a few plants happens very early while maize is domesticated somewhat later. Sedentary village farming does not appear for several thousand years after that date, around 2000 BC.

Sites in the highlands of Peru in South America contain evidence for the early domestication of gourds, tomatoes, beans, and potatoes by 3000 BC. Some of these plants may have reached the mountains from an original habitat in the lowland jungles, but little is known about the prehistory of the Amazon Basin and other tropical areas of South America. Potatoes certainly were an indigenous crop in the highlands; hundreds of varieties of wild and domesticated potatoes grow

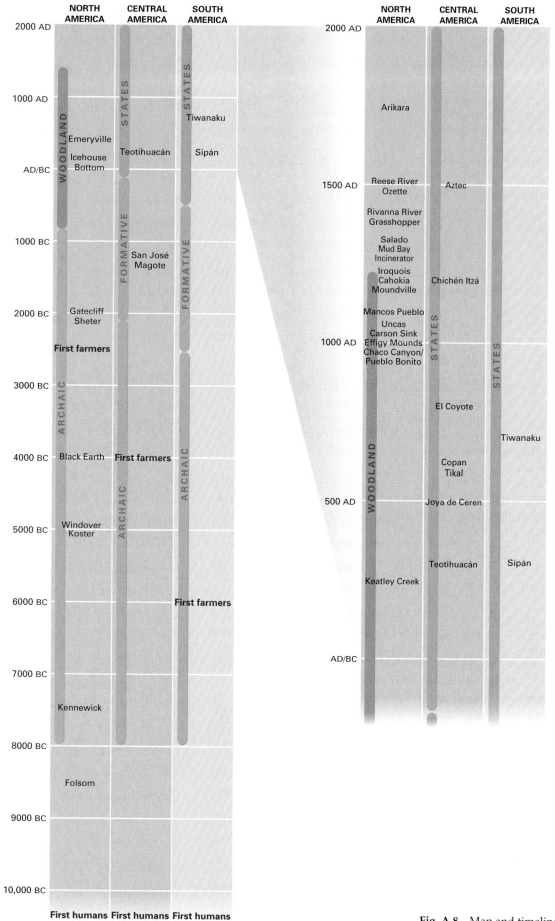

Fig. A.8 Map and timeline for the Americas.

GREENLAND

NORTH

AMERICA

Keatley Creek

PACIFIC OCEAN

ATLANTIC OCEAN

Teotihuacán
Aztec
San José Mogote
Chichén Itzá
Tikal
Copan
El Coyote
Joya de Ceren

Equator

SOUTH

AMERICA

Sipán

Tiwanaku

CONTINENTAL UNITED STATES

Ozette
Mud Bay
Kennewick
Little Bighorn
Iroquois
Arikara
Effigy Mounds
Carson Sink
Koster
Incinerator
Reese River
Cahokia
Emeryville
Gatecliff
Shelter
Mancos Pueblo
Folsom
Black Earth
Grasshopper
Pueblo
Uncas
Icehouse Bottom
Chaco Canyon/
Pueblo Bonito
Salado
Moundville
Windover

0   500 Mi
0   500   1000 Km

Fig. A.9 A fluted point from Wisconsin.

in this area today. Corn was introduced to South America from its source area in Mexico. In addition to plants, several animals were also domesticated. The guinea pig was used for food, while the llama was domesticated and used to transport goods around the mountains of South America. The alpaca, a camelid like the llama, may have been domesticated for both meat and wool.

North America (the United States and Canada) was a diverse area archaeologically in terms of subsistence and social complexity with a wide range of societies present in different parts of the continent. In the U.S. Southwest and Southeast, there were rather large and complex groups based on horticulture and later maize agriculture, involved in long-distance trade and building monumental structures. Domesticates arrived here from Mexico before 1000 BC. Large villages and even towns were not uncommon in these areas, as reported by the first Spanish explorers. Sites like **Pueblo Bonito** (Chapter 8) in **Chaco Canyon** (Chapter 6) are examples from the Pueblo cultures that developed in the American Southwest in the period after AD 1. **Mancos Pueblo** (Chapter 14) is discussed in the context of human cannibalism. The ceramics of the **Salado** culture are another focus in Chapter 11. The **Grasshopper Pueblo** site in east-central Arizona is the subject of the project for Chapter 6.

The **Uncas site** (Chapter 5) in Oklahoma is typical of the Plains adaptations in the Central United States around AD 1000. In eastern North America, several local plants such as sunflower, marsh elder, and lamb's quarter were domesticated by 1000 BC, toward the end of the Archaic period and prior to the introduction of corn from Mexico. Clearly this area participated in the global trend toward agriculture in the Holocene, and it is now considered one of the six known centers for the origins of agriculture. This native agriculture contributed to the growth of larger societies as a number of intriguing cultures appeared in the eastern United States. The term *Woodland* is generally used for the time period of these groups. The site of **Icehouse Bottom** (Chapter 11) in Tennessee dates from the Middle Woodland, ca. AD 150, and contains the earliest evidence for corn in the eastern United States along with a number of mounds and imported ceramics. The **Effigy Mounds** (Chapter 5) of Wisconsin and adjacent states are one of the remarkable manifestations of the period around AD 1000.

During the Late Woodland period, after AD 1000, the Mississippian culture dominated the midwestern United States with a major center at **Cahokia** (Chapter 16) near East St. Louis, Illinois. Cahokia, with its enormous earthen mounds and residential areas, was the largest settlement in North America at its zenith around AD 1200. Big, powerful centers continued to flourish in the southeastern United States until the European conquest, including the major center of Moundville (Chapter 14). The burial mound that Thomas Jefferson excavated along the **Rivanna River** (Chapter 3) probably belonged to this time.

In the northeastern United States, the arrival of maize agriculture also gave rise to larger societies. One of the best-known examples is the **Iroquois**, who controlled the region of what is today New York state and adjacent parts of Canada. The ceramics from this area are the subject of a study reported in Chapter 11.

Hunter-gatherers inhabited the western United States and Canada until European arrival, but a number of these groups, particularly along the Pacific coast, were large and sedentary. The best known in this area were the Northwest Coast groups, who built enormous longhouses and canoes of cedar wood, controlled the rights to fishing grounds, traded huge quantities of wealth at potlatch feasts, and made war on one another almost continuously. The site of **Keatley Creek** in interior British Columbia provides a glimpse of these western hunter-gatherers in the discussion in Chapter 9.

States and Empires

In Mesoamerica, the beginnings of sedentary village life mark the start of the Formative, or Preclassic, period around 1800 BC. Society changed very rapidly from that point as long-distance exchange, status differentiation, and monumental construction appeared on the Gulf Coast of Mexico where the *Olmec* culture emerged. The large farming village of *San José Magote* (Chapter 4) in Mexico dates from the time of the Olmec culture. The Olmec were succeeded around the time of the birth of Christ with the beginnings of Classic period civilizations both in highland Mexico and in the Maya region of Guatemala, Honduras, and the Yucatán of Mexico.

Major urban centers were established in the highlands of Mesoamerica. The city of *Teotihuacán* (Chapter 5) dominated much of Mesoamerica for the first 600 years after Christ. This planned metropolis was home to perhaps 120,000 people and extended its control and/or influence over both the highlands and parts of the Maya region as well. Many impressive centers, including Tikal, Palenque, and *Copan* (Chapter 15), were built in the Maya lowlands during the Classic era. While the Classic *Maya* (Chapter 14) developed Mesoamerica's most sophisticated writing system, none of their centers reached the size of Teotihuacán. The site of *El Coyote* is a smaller Maya center in Honduras that serves as an example for soil analysis described in Chapter 15. *Joya de Ceren*, in El Salvador, was a Maya farming village buried in a volcanic eruption. The later Maya site of *Chichén Itzá* (Chapter 3) was a capital of the northern Yucatán peninsula in Mexico.

Major changes took place in Mesoamerica between AD 700 and 1200 that involved the decline and depopulation of many centers and the rise of new political powers. Places like Tula, on Mesoamerica's northern frontier, and Chichén Itzá, in the northern Yucatán, rose to power for several centuries. The Postclassic Maya period was concentrated in the northern Yucatán. The *Aztec* (Chapter 16) are perhaps the best-known society from this time in the highlands, with an empire centered at Tenochtitlán, the largest city in the history of prehispanic Mesoamerica. Although its powerful rulers received tributary from as far away as highland Guatemala, they were defeated by the Spanish conquistador Hernando Cortés in AD 1521. Cortés and his men tore down the massive temple pyramids, destroyed books and other sacred relics of the Aztec, introduced a variety of European diseases, and founded modern Mexico City on the foundations of the Aztec capital. Mesoamerican civilizations flourished until the Spanish conquest without beasts of burden, wheeled transportation, or metal tools. The region was characterized by powerful states, major urban centers, and spectacular craftwork and architecture.

The prehistory of western South America is, in a general way, similar to that of Mesoamerica. In both areas, the earliest experiments with food production preceded the transition to sedentary village life. In South America, the centers of power and influence shifted back and forth between the coastal desert along the Pacific Ocean and the highlands of the adjacent Andes. The first villages date to 3500 BC and are found along the Pacific coast of Peru. The beginnings of monumental architecture and status differentiation are also found in this coastal region ca. 2000 BC The first indications of elite leadership and interregional influence, observed from the Pacific to the Amazon Basin, appear between 900 and 200 BC, and became known as the Chavín style.

In South America, the last centuries BC were marked by the rise of major centers that became states administering regional populations. The Moche culture, on the north coast of Peru, constructed some of the largest pyramids in the New World (along with Cahokia and several in the highlands of Mexico). The power of rulers and the pronounced status differences that marked this society are illustrated in the spectacular royal tombs unearthed at *Sipán*, described in Chapter 2. *Tiwanaku* (Chapter 6), a giant economic and religious center near the southern end of Lake Titicaca in the high Andes of Bolivia, began to incorporate larger areas outside its local region. Intensive agriculture along the lakeshore helped to feed the large population at the site. The scene shifted then again to the north coast where the Chimu kingdom was in power after AD 1000.

The Chimu were conquered by the expanding Inka civilization between AD 1462 and 1470. The Inka empire was centered on the city of Cuzco, the Inka capital in the highlands of Peru. At the time of the Spanish conquest of Peru, the Inka empire was one of the largest in the world, covering almost one million km² (an area the size of the states of Washington, Oregon, Idaho, and Montana combined). The empire's reach extended from Colombia in the north across the Andean highlands of Argentina, Bolivia, Peru, and Ecuador to Chile in the south.

THE PACIFIC

The Pacific Ocean covers one-third of the surface of the planet, some 181,300,000 km² (70,000,000 mi²), and contains half of the liquid water on earth. It is an enormous region, dotted with a few groups of tiny islands that have always been separated by thousands of kilometers. Try to imagine how and why these islands were first discovered and settled. Australia, Tasmania, New Guinea, and a few islands north of New Guinea were colonized some 30,000–40,000 years ago, but the open seas of much of the rest of the Pacific remained a formidable obstacle to human expansion until 3000 years or so ago.

The colonization of the Pacific islands is documented by the arrival of distinctively decorated Lapita pottery, brought and made by the first settlers. The pottery is named after a site where it was found in New Caledonia, but its origins are ultimately in Southeast Asia. The Lapita peoples were skilled seafarers who, beginning around 1500 BC, spread eastward through the islands of Melanesia and into the remote archipelagos of the central and eastern Pacific. The *Cook Islands* (Fig. A.10) are of interest because of the early arrival of sweet potato, discussed in Chapter 13. The burial ground of Roy Mata, dating to around 1350 AD, on the island of *Retoka* in Melanesia is discussed in Chapter 14.

These sailors and farmers reached Tonga and Samoa by roughly 1000 BC, the Marquesas by AD 300, and Hawaii by AD 600. Easter Island, one of the more remote places on earth, lies 1000 km (621 mi) from any other island and more than 2000 km (1200 mi) from the coast of Chile. Easter Island was colonized around AD 400 by the people who eventually raised hundreds of colossal stone heads on the island. New Zealand seems to have been bypassed in the expansion and was not colonized until AD 1000. The crossing of this great ocean and the settling of the many islands by sailors and farmers is a remarkable story, one that repeatedly raises the questions of how and why. Many explanations have been offered including new crops, new kinds of canoes, new navigation skills, wanderlust, and others, but the question remains unresolved.

HISTORICAL ARCHAEOLOGY

The archaeology of history is another important and expanding arena of study. Interest in the medieval period in Europe, in the industrial revolution, in battlefields, and in Colonial America, for example, has spawned new areas of research, more positions in departments and museums, and a better understanding of our more recent past. Historical archaeology is treated separately here to emphasize the relationship between written document (history) and archaeology.

Historical archaeology in the United States has actually been around for some time, in large part because of the interest in the Colonial period and the lack of substantive documents about the early history of the United States. Colonial Williamsburg in Virginia has been a center of archaeological and historical research since 1926 when a local minister convinced the wealthy magnate John D. Rockefeller to preserve and restore the city's many historical buildings. Subsequently, historical archaeology has expanded in this area to *Jamestown* (Chapter 8) and many other sites from the Colonial and Revolutionary War periods (Fig. A.10).

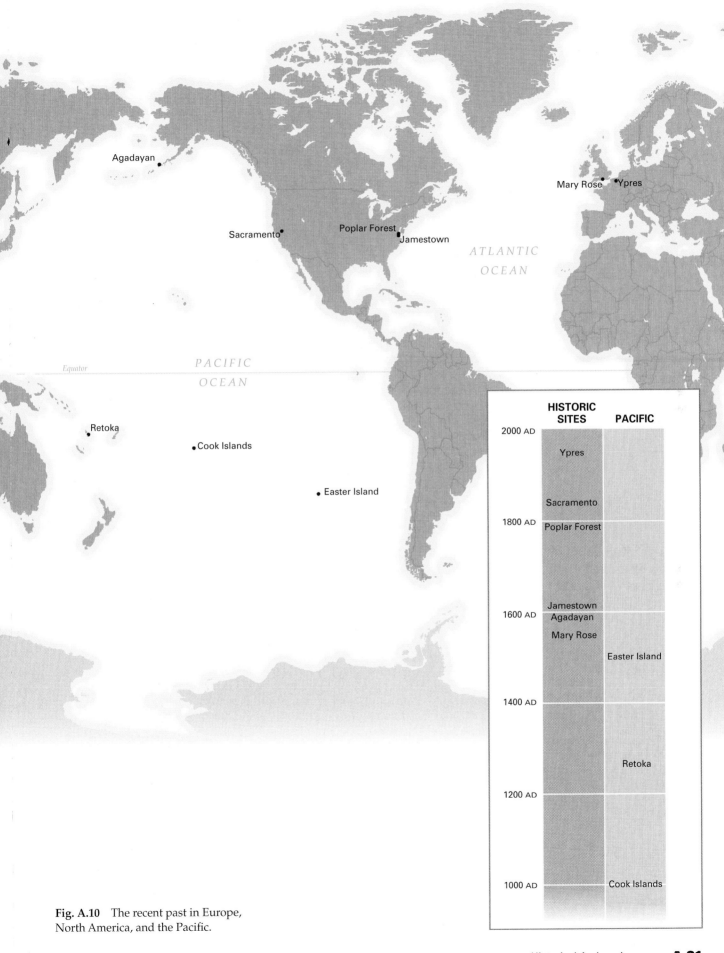

Fig. A.10 The recent past in Europe,
North America, and the Pacific.

Medieval archaeology has grown dramatically in Europe in the last 25 years, as the combination of urban renewal and new antiquity laws has produced many new discoveries. There are academic programs solely concerned with this period from ca. AD 500 to 1450, beginning in the late Iron Age when Christianity had conquered most of Europe, and epidemic disease and an exploitative feudal system left much of the continent in a ruinous state. It was a strange time in many ways when religion and rulers kept the populace in poverty. The religious atmosphere can be seen in the relic industry that arose in the thirteenth and fourteenth centuries when religious icons and sacred objects were sanctified, bought, or forged in large numbers. The **Shroud of Turin** is one example discussed in Chapter 8.

There were points of light in the Dark Ages, such as the exploration and settlement of the Vikings of Northern Europe. The period between AD 800 and 1050 was a time of this Viking expansion across the North Sea, the conquest and settlement of parts of England, Ireland, and France, and the discovery and colonization of Iceland, Greenland, and North America. It's a remarkable story. Part of this story is told in Chapter 5 in the section on the town of **York** in England, which the Vikings founded. The settlements on Greenland and in North America were also established by Vikings during a period of warmer climate and had to be abandoned when colder conditions returned. The story of the Vikings on *Greenland* is told in Chapter 14.

Historical shipwrecks are another important area of archaeological and public interest. The *Titanic* is probably the best-known historic shipwreck to be located in recent years, but other searches have been going on for decades. The Wasa in Sweden and more recently the **Mary Rose** (Chapter 14) in England are examples of ships that were the pride of their nations. The Wasa sank on launching in Stockholm's harbor in 1628 and was raised in 1961. The Mary Rose (Chapter 14), flagship of Henry VIII, sank accidentally during battle in 1545 in the waters off Portsmouth England and was discovered and eventually raised in 1982. Both ships sit today in spectacular museums and serve as major tourist attractions.

Studies at early American settlements such as Jamestown document historical archaeology in North America. The archaeozoological investigation of the meal remains of the gold miners of nineteenth-century Sacramento, California, provides another example of historical archaeology in action. The historical archaeology of the twentieth century focused on battlefields and industrial development. The Little Big Horn in Montana (Chapter 17) and the World War I site of *Ypres* (Chapter 17) in Belgium are examples of such studies.

CONCLUSIONS

Our human past is a long and extraordinary story, beginning more than 6 million years ago. Graphic depiction in any form only began with the art and decoration of the Upper Paleolithic, and written records were not invented until 5500 years ago. The only source of information that we have for the bulk of our vast past comes from archaeology. That's one of the reasons why what archaeologists do is so important.

Archaeology tells us about the first steps we humans took as bipedal relatives of the apes and about the long and complex path to our genus *Homo*. The first tools appear as broken stones as human technology begins to form the world around us. Big steps on the trail to the present included the move out of Africa and into Eurasia. At the same time, technology advanced very slowly and led to the invention of the handaxe. The control of fire would have been a major accomplishment, opening many new opportunities in cold, harsh climates. In those frigid parts, notably in Europe, evolution took a side trail as Neanderthals came on the scene, replaced in time by the arrival, again from Africa, of anatomically modern humans, bringing new technology and ideas.

The Upper Paleolithic was the culmination of many long trends—in biology and culture, in language and communication, in ritual and ideology, in social organization, in art and design, and in settlement and technology—that began several million years earlier. New continents were explored, and Australia, North America, and South America were colonized. From almost any perspective, the Upper Paleolithic represents a time of dramatic transition in human behavior, almost certainly associated with changes in the organization of the brain or in the use of language, or both. Essentially modern behavior appeared with this transformation, and the rapid change from ancestor to human, from archaic to modern, from the past to the present had begun.

Another major transition, this time marked by the domestication of plants and animals, started societies on the road to what we think of today as civilization. Permanent farming villages, larger populations, religion, monumental architecture, craft specialization, and social inequality had their beginnings at this time. The surpluses produced by agriculture fostered new social arrangements and underwrote a larger scale of construction, technology, and concept. Almost everything we humans did became new.

Farming spread like a virus, quickly moving across continents, replacing hunter-gatherer populations to the climatic limits of cultivation (with the exception of Australia). Farming villages eventually spread across much of the Americas as well, slightly later than in the Old World, and spawned more complex societies. Architecture became more common on archaeological sites, particularly large-scale construction in the form of public works and dramatic civic centers. Pyramids were erected in various places around the globe as powerful and predatory state-level societies moved to the fore. Those states continue today to parry and feint, to expand and conquer. Larger and larger political entities territorialized the continents.

This appendix is about what archaeologists know. Archaeology can show us how we came to our present point in time, the paths that our ancestors followed, the events that happened, and the processes that operated along the way. There is a great deal left to learn; the past remains a mysterious place. New methods and new ideas must be developed to better understand the record of the past that we have. This book is about some of those methods and ideas that archaeologists use to explore the past—how we know what we know.

REFERENCES

Fagan, B. 2000. *Ancient North America: The Archaeology of a Continent.* 3d ed. London: Thames & Hudson.

Gates, Charles. 2003. *Ancient Cities.* London: Routledge.

Klein, R. G. 1999. *The Human Career: Human Biological and Cultural Origins.* 2d ed. Chicago: University of Chicago Press.

Peregrine, Peter N., and Melvin Ember, eds. 2003. *Encyclopedia of Prehistory.* New York: Springer.

Price, T. D., and G. Feinman. 2005. *Images of the Past.* 4th ed. New York: McGraw-Hill. *A heavily illustrated textbook on world prehistory.*

Smith, B. D. 1998. *The Emergence of Agriculture.* 2d ed. New York: Scientific American Library. *A well-illustrated and up-to-date summary of agricultural beginnings worldwide.*

Tattersall, Ian, and J. H. Schwartz. 2000. *Extinct Humans.* Boulder: Westview Press. *This book argues that there have been many species of humans in the past and portrays their evolution.*

Common Measurement Conversions and Equivalents

LENGTH OR HEIGHT

1 centimeter (cm) = 0.394 inch (in)
1 inch = 2.54 centimeters
1 meter (m) = 3.281 feet (ft)
1 foot = 0.305 meter
1 meter = 1.0936 yards (yd)
1 yard = 0.9144 meter
1 kilometer (km) = 0.6214 mile (mi)
1 mile = 1.6094 kilometers

APPROXIMATE EQUIVALENTS	Feet	Meters
Average person	5.5	1.7
Height of basketball basket	10	3.0
High-diving platform	32.8	10
Bowling alley	60	18
Ten-story building	100	30
Arc de Triomphe	164	50
High ski jump	196.8	60
Football field	300	91
Washington Monument	555	169
Golf course	20,000	6098

AREA

1 square centimeter (sq cm) = 0.155 square inch (sq in)
1 square inch = 6.452 square centimeters
1 square meter (sq m) = 10.764 square feet (sq ft)
1 square foot = 0.0929 square meter
1 square meter = 1.196 square yards (sq yd)
1 square yard = 0.8361 square meter
1 square kilometer (sq km) = 0.386 square mile (sq mi)
1 square mile = 2.59 square kilometers
1 hectare (ha) = 10,000 square meters
1 hectare = 2.47 acres
1 acre = 0.405 hectare

VOLUME

1 cubic centimeter (cc) = 0.061 cubic inch (cu in)
1 cubic inch = 16.39 cubic centimeters
1 cubic meter (cu m) = 35.314 cubic feet (cu ft)
1 cubic foot = 0.0283 cubic meter
1 cubic meter = 1.308 cubic yards (cu yd)

APPROXIMATE EQUIVALENTS	Cubic Meters
Refrigerator	2
Home bathroom	10
UPS delivery truck	25
School bus	50
Large room	100
Medium-size house	1000
Small church	10,000
Modern oil tanker	100,000

DENSITY

25 people/sq km	=	0.2 person/soccer field	=	65 people/sq mi
500 people/sq km	=	4 people/soccer field	=	1300 people/sq mi
5000 people/sq km	=	40 people/soccer field	=	13,000 people/sq mi

APPROXIMATE EQUIVALENTS	Length	Width	Square Feet	Square Meters	Acres	Hectares
Average bedroom	12 ft	10 ft	120	11	0.0027	0.0011
Soccer goal	24 ft	8 ft	192	18	0.0045	0.0018
Doubles tennis court	36 ft	78 ft	2808	261	0.0645	0.0261
Basketball court	84 ft	45.75 ft	3843	357	0.0882	0.0357
Average house lot	80 ft	80 ft	6400	595	0.1469	0.0595
Baseball infield	90 ft	90 ft	8100	753	0.1859	0.0753
Olympic pool	50 m	21 m	11,298	1050	0.2594	0.1050
Football field	300 ft	60 ft	18,000	1673	0.4132	0.1673
Hockey rink	200 ft	100 ft	20,000	1859	0.4591	0.1859
Soccer field	100 m	80 m	86,080	8000	1.9760	0.8000
Union Square, New York City	650 ft	650 ft	422,500	39,250	9.6948	3.9250
Average city block	700 ft	700 ft	490,000	45,539	11.2481	4.5539

	Miles	Miles	Square Miles	Acres	Hectares
Churchill Downs (horse racetrack)	1.25	oval	0.018522	11.849	4.797
Indianapolis racetrack	2.5	oval	0.4112	263.057	106.501
Central Park, New York City	2.5	0.5	1.25	799.663	323.750
Manhattan Island	12.5	2.5	22	14,074.060	5698.000

Glossary

absolute dating   Method of dating that can provide an age in *calendar* years.

accelerator mass spectrometer (AMS)   A huge scientific instrument used for sorting and counting *isotopes*. AMS dating allows much smaller samples to be used in *archaeology*.

achieved status   Earned position of prestige in society determined by skills, abilities, and effort.

acropolis   Refers to the citadel or upper part of ancient cities in the classical world or Maya region.

activity area   Location of specific tasks or behaviors within a site.

additive techniques   A way of making things like ceramics or building a house that involves incremental steps and the addition of material to the object or structure. A bigger object is made from smaller pieces. Compare *subtractive techniques.*

adobe   A brick made of earth and straw and dried by the sun.

alidade   An optical surveying instrument used for making contour maps.

amateur archaeologist   In contrast to professional archaeologists, who are educated in the discipline, amateur or vocational archaeologists collect artifacts, study *archaeology,* and participate in professionally run excavations. Amateur archaeologists are an important part of the field and have made substantial contributions to our knowledge of the past.

amino acid   Simple organic compounds containing carbon, hydrogen, oxygen, nitrogen, and in certain cases sulfur. Twenty amino acids are the building blocks of proteins.

ancient DNA (aDNA)   Genetic material preserved in archaeological or *paleontological* remains.

annealing   A process of repeated heating and cooling to make metal tougher and less brittle.

anthropogenic   Created or produced by human activity, e.g., anthropogenic soils are a result of human activity.

anthropological archaeology   Archaeological investigations that seek to answer the larger, fundamental questions about humans and human behavior taught in departments of anthropology.

appendicular skeleton   The limbs (the clavicles, scapulae, bones of the pelvis, and the upper and lower limbs, including the hands and feet).

appliqué   Decorative technique for pottery involving the addition of *clay* pieces to the original *clay* vessel.

arboreal pollen (AP)   Pollen from trees.

archaeobotany (a.k.a. *paleobotany, paleoethnobotany*)   The study of archaeological plant remains.

archaeological chemistry   A part of archaeometry, the investigation of inorganic and organic composition, *elements* and *isotopes, molecules* and compounds in archaeological materials.

archaeological context   The buried or surface context in which archaeological remains are found; what survives to the present.

archaeological culture   A group of related materials from a region that indicate a common or shared way of doing things.

archaeological record   The body of information about the past that has survived to the present.

archaeological science   A generic term that includes noninstrumental areas such as faunal analysis, *paleoethnobotany,* and *human osteology.*

archaeology   The study of our human past, combining the themes of time and change, using the material remains that have survived.

archaeomagnetism   A dating technique based on the migration of the earth's north pole, known for the last 1000 years.

archaeometry   The measurement of the chemical or physical properties of an artifact in order to solve problems of chemical composition, *technology, chronology,* etc. Sometimes described as "instrumental" archaeology.

archaeozoology   The study of animal remains in *archaeology.*

articular   The portion of the bone that touches another bone, usually a surface at the end or edge of a bone.

artifacts   The objects and materials that people have made and used.

ascribed status   Inherited position of prestige in society determined by birth.

assemblage   A related set of different things.

association   A statistical term referring to related groups, or subsets, within a sample that have similar values. The members of the group are said to be associated.

atomic number   The number of protons in the nucleus of an atom.

attributes   Detailed characteristics of archaeological materials and information.

auger   (a.k.a. corer, borer) A tool for drilling holes, used in *archaeology* for coring into soil and taking samples.

aurochs   Wild cattle.

axial skeleton   The trunk and head (all the bones of the head and neck, the vertebrae, ribs and sternum).

band   Small-scale societies of *hunter-gatherers* where relationships are generally egalitarian and decision making is consensual.

bar graph   Visual display of *data;* basically a tally sheet with bars instead of tally marks, used to display nominal or ordinal scale data.

barrow   Earthen burial *mound.*

base   The lower part of a *ceramic* vessel.

bifacial   A term describing a flaked stone *tool* in which both faces or sides are retouched to make a thinner *tool.* See also *unifacial.*

bioarchaeology   The study of human remains from archaeological contexts.

bioerosion   Changes in the exterior surface on bone that indicate conditions of deposition.

biological anthropology   The study of the biological nature of our nearest relatives and ourselves.

bioturbation   Disturbance of the *archaeological record* from plant and animal activities such as root growth or animal digging.

bipedal   The human method of locomotion, walking on two legs; one of the first human characteristics to distinguish the early *hominins*, as opposed to quadrupedalism, walking on four legs.

blade A special kind of elongated *flake* with two parallel sides and a length at least twice the width of the piece. The regular manufacture of blades characterized the Upper Paleolithic, with an efficient way of producing mass quantities of cutting edges.

body sherd Fragment of broken *pottery* that does not include the rim of the vessel.

bronze A mixture of tin (or arsenic) and copper that produced a harder metal. Produced in both the Old and New Worlds.

brushing Decorative technique for pottery involving roughening of the surface.

bulb of percussion A partial cone of fracture that is seen on the inner surface of *flakes* as a slightly rounded protrusion or bulb.

bulbar surface (a.k.a. ventral) The inner, fresh surface of a *flake*.

bundle burial A disarticulated group of bones buried in a group, probably tied in a bundle or wrapped in a skin or cloth.

burial population The set of human remains found interred in a *site* or cemetery.

burin A distinctively edged stone *tool* combining a 90° edge and an oblique angled working edge.

burnishing Decorative technique for *pottery* involving smoothing or polishing of the surface.

calendar A system for organizing time into repeatable and predictable units.

calibration Correction of *radiocarbon* dates for the difference between *calendar* years and *radiocarbon* years.

camp Short-term, temporary settlement, usually associated with *hunter-gatherers* or nomads.

cassava Tropical root crop with starchy roots (a.k.a. manioc), source of tapioca.

cementum annuli Annual deposits of cementum around the base of teeth.

cenotaph An empty grave, without a body.

ceramic Fired *clay*.

ceramic petrography Microscopic technique for study of the mineral composition of *pottery*.

cervids Members of the deer family.

chaîne opératoire (French: *sequence of production*) The different stages of production from the acquisition of raw material to the final abandonment of the desired and/or used objects.

chenopod A variety of weedy herbs belonging to the goosefoot family, which includes spinach, beets, and pigweed.

chert A *cryptocrystalline* quartz with large crystal size and impurities that give it color and cloudiness.

chiefdom A large, kinship-based political unit of several communities where status is hereditary and assigned by birth order (*rank*).

chi-square (χ^2) A statistical test of association for nominal scale information.

chronology A framework of time to show the order of events, a dated sequence of events in the past.

city Urban agglomeration with population of 10,000 or more, internal differentiation, and distinct civic or ceremonial areas within its boundaries.

class Distinctions between groups of people that define levels, or strata, in society.

classical archaeology A branch of *archaeology* primarily concerned with the Mediterranean civilizations of Greece and Rome.

classification The process of putting objects into groups on the basis of shared characteristics.

clay A very fine-grained sediment, deposited in water and usually found in former lake or stream deposits; raw material for making *pottery*.

coefficient of stylistic variability A statistical measure of the strength of association among stylistic attributes.

coil technique *Pottery* vessel made by ropes of *clay* used to build up the walls of the vessel.

collagen The *protein* that makes up the organic portion of bone.

collar A vessel rim with added *clay* material.

commensals *Species* in a symbiotic relationship in which one *species* is benefited while the other is unaffected.

complexity Organization of society involving more units in society and more integration between those units.

component An *assemblage* from a single layer, *living floor*, or *occupation horizon*; a set of materials in contemporary use by the same group of people.

composition The mineral and organic contents in a petrographic thin section.

compounds Combinations of elements in either organic or inorganic molecules in nature.

conchoidal fracture Shell-like shape of the interior surface of a *flake*; the breakage pattern seen in flaking stone *tools*.

conservation Preservation and restoration of archaeological materials in the laboratory and museum.

context Place and association among the archaeological materials and the situation in which they occur.

contour map A schematic map of topography, the three-dimensional surface of the earth or other features. Contours are conventionally shown as a series of curved, concentric lines reflecting elevation or relief of a surface.

coprolites Preserved ancient feces.

cord-marked Decorative technique for *pottery* involving impressions of cord-wrapping in the *clay*.

cord-marking A distinctive decoration on *pottery* produced by pressing a cord-wrapped stick into the soft *clay* of a pot before firing.

core The stone from which other pieces or *flakes* are removed. Core *tools* are shaped by the removal of *flakes*.

correlation A measure of association between two sets of numbers.

cortex A heavily weathered rind on the outside of *flint* or *chert nodules*.

The presence of this cortex is the criterion for a *cortical flake*.

cortical bone   Hard, dense bone tissue commonly found in limbs and supporting structure of the skeleton.

cortical flake   A *flake* with some of the outer surface (*cortex*) of the stone *nodule* present.

cosmology   Explanations of the origins of the universe, of life, and of society.

country   A sovereign *region*, marked by boundaries, and defended by military power, usually associated with state-level societies.

cremation   A funereal practice involving immolation of the corpse. Cremation burials usually consist of ash and a few fragments of bone and teeth, and are often found in urns and small pits. Also, the incinerated remains of a human body. Contrast with *inhumation*.

cribra orbitalia   Pitting and thickening of the eye sockets in the skull caused by anemia or parasitic infections.

cryptocrystalline   Stone with microscopic crystals, formed from *silica* under pressure in marine deposits, such as quartz, *chert, flint*.

crystalline   Materials with atoms arranged in a regular geometric pattern, used in *X-ray diffraction* analysis.

cultural (social) anthropology   The study of living peoples with a focus on the shared aspects of the human experience.

cultural resource management (CRM)   Historical preservation in the United States; involves *survey* and *excavation* to determine that historical and cultural resources are not being destroyed by development and construction.

cultural transformation   Modification of the *archaeological record* through human activity.

culture   A means of human adaptation based on intelligence, experience, learning, and the use of *tools*; the general set of behaviors and knowledge that humans use to survive and adapt.

culture change   In *archaeology*, innovations or modification in *technology* or *material culture*.

curated tools   Special-purpose implements that require specific raw materials and substantial time and labor in manufacture. Curated tools can often be repaired or recycled and are normally discarded only when exhausted. Contrast with *expedient tools*.

cursus monument   Paired linear earthworks that mark an avenue or long, rectangular area in Neolithic Europe.

cut   Geomorphological terms for erosion of sediments, also human digging.

cutmarks   Scratches and cuts on bone indicating the use of stone *tools* for butchering.

data   Information; the observations and measurements of archaeological materials.

datum   A point with known locational coordinates and elevation; a fixed point for *surveying*.

débitage   (French) A term referring to all the pieces of *shatter* and *flakes* produced and not used when stone *tools* are made; also called *waste*.

deciduous teeth   The first set of "baby" teeth that are lost when the permanent teeth come in.

deconstruction   A form of literary analysis used to show the differences between the structure of a text and basic Western concepts about the meaning of reality.

demography   Study of human populations with a focus on size, age, and sex distribution, birth and death rates, and migration. Prehistoric demography is also known as paleodemography.

dendrochronology   The study of the annual growth rings of trees as a dating technique to build *chronologies*.

descriptive statistics   Numbers that are used to condense information in order to summarize and compare different sets of data.

diachronic   Dealing with change over time, comparing two or more time periods.

diagenesis   Physical and chemical changes in bone after burial.

diatom   Silicate shells of microscopic algae.

diffraction   Principle of X-rays being scattered when striking a crystal, used in X-ray diffraction analyses.

diffusion   The spread of new ideas or materials from one group to another.

discriminant analysis   Statistical technique for classifying a set of observations into predefined classes based on new measurement.

division of labor   Organization of tasks involving different groups doing different activities for the sake of efficiency.

DNA   The blueprints for life; hereditary material; a long molecular chain of molecules called chromosomes found both in the nucleus of the cell and in cell structures known as mitochrondria.

dorsal surface   The outer surface of a *flake*.

drawing grid   (a.k.a. planning frame) Normally a 1 m^2 (10 ft^2) frame of wood or aluminum fitted with a grid of string or wire at 20 cm (ca. 8 in) intervals. It is used for drawing detailed plans of vertical sections or horizontal floors in archaeological *excavations*.

dual-residence   A subsistence and settlement pattern observed among some groups of *hunter-gatherers* who live in two places at different seasons during the course of a year.

ecofacts   Unmodified, natural items found in archaeological contexts, often plant or animal material.

ecological constraint   Limitations on human activity imposed by the *environment*. For example, arid conditions are an ecological constraint on agriculture.

economy   The means and methods that society uses to obtain food, water, and resources for maintenance and growth.

effigy   An object or construction in the shape of a plant, animal, or human figure.

electron spin resonance (ESR)   A dating method based on trapped electrons in tooth enamel, assuming the accumulation rate is constant.

elements   Building blocks of matter, different atoms by weight.

empire   Large sovereign space, expanded by military conquest, and encompassing several countries and/or territories, associated with state-level societies.

enamel hypoplasia   Irregular lines in tooth enamel resulting from childhood stress or malnutrition.

environment   The natural and social milieu in which human societies operate.

enzyme   A protein that catalyzes a chemical reaction.

epiphysis   Joint ends of bones where growth occurs.

equifinality   A situation in which different initial conditions can lead to a similar end, making archaeological interpretation difficult.

ethnoarchaeology   Archaeological study of living societies for information to help better understand the past.

ethnographic   *Ethnography* is the study and description of human societies. Ethnographers are anthropologists who study societies in a variety of places around the world.

ethnographic analogy   Comparison between *ethnography* and *archaeology* to explain similar things.

ethnography   The detailed investigation of a group of people, traditionally non-Western, through participant observation and descriptions of practices, activities, behaviors, and beliefs.

ethnohistory   Branch of ethnography that combines sources from history, *archaeology,* and oral traditions in the search for answers about past peoples.

excavation   The exposure, recording, and recovery of buried materials from the past.

exchange   Transfer of material or information among individuals or groups.

exotic   Foreign, unusual; in *archaeology* refers to artifacts and other materials from nonlocal sources.

expedient tools   Implements that are quickly made, used, and discarded. The *technology* is fairly simple, production fairly rapid, use more general purpose, and discard immediate. Contrast with *curated tools.*

experimental archaeology   Modern experiments to reproduce *artifacts, architecture,* and/or techniques from the past.

extractive sites   Nonresidential localities where some members of the society obtain food or other resources.

fabric   The geometric relationship of the constituents in a petrographic thin section.

fatty acid   Organic compound in animal and vegetable fats and oils, made up of saturated or unsaturated fats.

fauna   Generic term for the archaeological remains of animals; the general class of animals.

faunal remains   The animal ecofacts found in *archaeological contexts,* including bone, teeth, antler, ivory, shell, scales, and the like.

features   The permanent facilities and structures that people construct in or on the earth.

Fertile Crescent   The arc-shaped zone of wetter uplands in Southwest Asia that stretches from the Mediterranean coast through the mountains of southeastern Turkey, to the mountains of southwestern Iran. The ancestral homeland of many *species* that were domesticated.

field notes   The records of a field project of *survey* or *excavation* with description of activities, finds, records of samples, drawings, photographs, and the like. An important document of the research project.

fieldwork   An important part of archaeological research involves *survey* for and *excavation* of archaeological materials, practices normally done outdoors (in the field) and collectively known as fieldwork.

fill   Geomorphological terms for deposition of *sediments,* also human filling.

flake   A type of stone *artifact* produced by removing a piece from a *core* by chipping or *knapping.* Flakes are made into a variety of different kinds of *tools* or used for their sharp edges (without further *retouching*).

flint   A hard, siliceous stone that breaks in predictable ways to produce sharp *flakes;* common raw material for stone *tools* in *prehistory.*

flintknapping   Chipping or flaking stone to make *tools* and other *artifacts.*

flora   Generic term for the archaeological remains of plants; the general class of plants.

floral   Plants, botanical materials, in contrast to *fauna,* or animals.

flot   The lighter, carbonized plant remains that "float" in the *flotation* methods of recovering plant remains.

flotation   An archaeological technique for recovering charred plant remains using water and density differences between heavy and light materials in sediments. Dry sediments are stirred into water and the lighter plant remains float to the top.

fluorine absorption   An archaeometric test for *relative dating* based on the assumption that fluorine accumulates at a constant rate in buried bone.

foragers   Nonfarmers; groups who subsist by hunting, collecting, fishing, and the like without domesticated plants or animals; see also *hunter-gatherers.*

forensic reconstruction   *Restoration* of the facial tissues on human skulls, both past and present.

foreshaft   Part of an arrow, designed to detach with the point after impacting the animal in order to preserve the longer shaft of the arrow, which falls away.

fossile directeur   (French: *indicator fossil*) A single fossil *species* as a marker of a time horizon.

fractionate   Process through which the ratio of *isotopes* in a material can be changed by heat, *photosynthesis, enzymes,* or other natural mechanisms.

fracture mechanics   The physics of how materials break.

fully modern humans (FMH)   A synonymous term for *Homo sapiens sapiens,* first appearing more than 100,000 years ago in Africa.

fume hood   A ventilation system for removal of toxic gas in a chemistry lab.

function   The use of an *artifact*; the action or activity for which it was made.

gas chromatography-mass spectrometry (GC-MS)   Archaeometric technique for organic materials; samples in gas state separate in a column and exit sequentially to a detector that produces a spectrum of the weight and amount of the molecules.

Geiger counter   A device for measuring radioactive emissions.

genus   A taxonomic group containing one or more related *species* (plural: genera).

geoarchaeology   Archaeological research concerned with geology and the earth sciences.

Geographic Information Systems (GIS)   A computer program(s) for the storage, display, and analysis of geographic and spatial data. The basic concept involves the use of overlaid maps of an area in combination with locational information and spatial analytical capabilities.

geomorphology   The branch of geology concerned with the study of the shape of the land, and involves *classification*, description, origin, and change of land forms.

glaze   A metallic or glass mixture used to change the surface of the *pottery* vessel for decorative purposes.

Global Positioning System (GPS)   A locational and navigational system for determining precise three-dimensional coordinates (longitude, latitude, and elevation) of any place on the earth's surface. Satellites broadcast locational information used by GPS equipment to determine the exact position of a place. Used instead of traditional, manual land *survey* methods.

glume   The husk that covers and protects cereal grains.

gorget   Jewelry worn on the chest.

grave goods   Food and/or other goods, often valuable, sometimes buried with deceased individuals.

gravity model   A concept from geography where interaction among settlements is based on size, similar to interaction among planets based on gravity. Bigger communities have more interaction and influence on smaller communities.

Ground Penetrating Radar (GPR) (a.k.a. georadar) An instrument that sends radar waves through the ground to reveal buried features.

grouping   The process of sorting things into piles, or groups, of similar items without predetermined categories.

guide   A listing of the different types, or *species*, that are present, and the distinguishing characteristics of each.

habitus   Unthinking dispositions and basic knowledge that constitute a practical cultural competence.

half-life   Conventional rate for radio-activity based on the time period for the decay of half the unstable *isotopes* in a known quantity of material.

hamlet   A small village with just a handful of houses and a small number of inhabitants.

hammer and anvil   A *hard hammer* percussion technique which involves striking the core (hammer) itself against a large rock in the ground (anvil) to produce a *flake*.

hammerstone   A stone used to knock *flakes* from *cores*; part of the toolkit of a *flintknapper*.

handaxe   The characteristic artifact of the Paleolithic: a large, teardrop-shaped stone *tool* bifacially flaked to a point at one end and a broader base at the other, for general-purpose use.

hand-thrown   *Pottery* made by hand.

hard hammer   A percussion technique for making stone *tools* by striking one stone, or *core*, with another stone, or hammer. See also *soft hammer* technique.

Harris lines   Interruption of growth evidenced in a skeleton by darker bands in the ends of long bones.

Harris matrix   A method for depicting intricate archaeological *stratigraphy* in a schematic way.

Hertzian Cone   Name for the bulb of force produced in fracture of *cryptocrystalline* materials.

hieroglyph   Originally, the pictographic script of ancient Egypt; any depictive, art-related system of writing, such as that of *Mesoamerica*; may also refer to an individual symbol.

histogram   A graph of the number of measurements in interval form.

historical archaeology   Refers primarily to the *archaeology* of the civilizations of the recent industrial era, since 1700 or so.

home range   The geographic area an animal uses for feeding and other activities; in *archaeology* the term generally refers to the area used by mobile *hunter-gatherers*.

hominin   Early human ancestor, fossil form (replaces the term *hominid*).

horizon   Layer or *assemblage* associated with geological strata or archaeological contents, e.g., usage includes a soil horizon, a cultural horizon; the geographic extent of similar artifacts and design in space.

human osteology   The study of human skeletal remains for information on past biology and behavior.

human taphonomy   Study of the placement and decomposition of the corpse in the grave.

hunter-gatherers   People who obtain their food from wild plants and animals, not domesticated *species*.

hydrocarbon   One of many *organic compounds* that contain only carbon and hydrogen.

hydrophilic   Chemical compounds with an affinity for water which are used to remove water from *artifacts* during *conservation*.

hydroxyapatite   The mineral component of bone.

iconography   The pictorial representations of beliefs, ideas, symbols, and concepts.

ideology   The explanation of human, natural, and supernatural relationships through belief, *ritual*, and ceremony.

impressing   Decorative technique for *pottery* involving impressions or incisions made with various small *tools*.

in situ (Latin)   An object in its original position of discard or deposition, in place, *primary context.*

incising   Decorative technique for *pottery* involving cutting or carving lines and other designs in the surface of the *clay.*

inductively coupled plasma–mass spectrometry (ICP-MS)   *Archaeometry* technique, in which samples introduced to a plasma source are ionized and elemental mass and concentration are measured.

industry   One object or *artifact* type that appears in a number of *assemblages.*

inferential statistics   Numbers that are used for making decisions about *data* and describing relationships among variables.

ingot   A casting of pure metal intended for transport and reuse, usually oblong or disk-shaped.

inhumation   Burial of all or part of the corpse; contrast with *cremation.*

inorganic compounds   Molecules that do contain carbon.

instrumental surveying   Making maps and plans of places and areas of archaeological interest using *survey* instruments such as a *total station* or global positioning satellite systems.

interface   The term used in *Harris matrix* for surfaces at a *site* that were places of activity before they were buried—for example, the surface of a pit.

invention   The creation or development of new ideas or techniques for solving problems.

ion   Electrically charged atoms that have lost or gained electrons.

isotopes   Slightly different atoms of the same element with the same *atomic number,* but a different numbers of *neutrons.*

key   Condensed guides, listing the characteristics of important types.

kiln   Fire for making *pottery,* can be open or closed, updraft or downdraft.

kinship   Relationships between individual members in society based on family ties.

knapping   (a.k.a. *flaking*) Intentionally removing a series of flakes, working stone.

kouros   Ancient stone statue of a nude Greek youth.

kurgans   Burial *mounds* in the steppe region of eastern Europe.

lake dwelling   Archaeological remains of settlements once thought to have stood over the water on raised pilings, but now known to have been situated along former shorelines, now submerged.

landscape   A humanly modified or perceived area.

leguminous plant (legume)   One of thousands of *species* with seed pods that split along both sides when ripe; more common legumes include beans, lentils, peanuts, peas, and soybeans; plants that absorb nitrogen from the atmosphere rather than from soil.

levee   A raised bank created by repeated flooding.

lineage   Genealogies, lines of descent that are used to extend relationships and determine membership in a group; the relationship between individual members in society on the basis of their family ties.

linguistics   The study of human languages.

lintel   A horizontal beam of wood or stone that supports the wall above a doorway or window.

lipids   A generic category of greasy compounds including fats, oils, waxes, sterols, and triglycerides, that are constituents of living tissues.

lithic assemblage   The complete set of stone *artifacts* found at an archaeological *site.*

lithics   A generic term used for stone *artifacts* in *archaeology* and more specifically for flaked stone *artifacts.*

living floor   The actual places where people lived and carried out their activities.

living horizon   (*occupation horizon, living floor*) The actual surface of occupation at an archaeological *site,* sometimes preserved under unusual conditions of deposition.

lost wax casting   A technique for creating detailed metal castings using wax as the mold. The molten metal replaces the wax and replicates the mold.

macroscopic   Visible to the naked eye.

magnetic polarity   A dating technique based on shifts in the location of the earth's magnetic pole.

magnetometer   (a.k.a. gradiometer) Measures the earth's magnetic field at an archaeological *site* to locate buried walls and pits.

mass spectrometer   Any analytical instrument that records components of a spectrum by weight.

material culture   Tangible, surviving evidence of human activities.

mean   The average for ratio scale data calculated by dividing the sum by the number of numbers.

median   The exact middle number of the nominal or ordinal values.

Mesoamerica   Anthropological term for the area of Mexico, Guatemala, Belize, and parts of Honduras and El Salvador where several early civilizations, including the Aztec and Maya, emerged.

metal detectors   Instruments that emit an electromagnetic field that is disrupted by the presence of metal objects in the ground, used for finding buried metal objects.

microburin   (1) A technique for making segments of *blades* into small geometric pieces (*microlith*); (2) waste products of the microburin process are also called microburins.

microlith   Small *blades* and geometric forms of stone *tools,* usually associated with the Mesolithic period in the Old World.

micromorphology   The study of *anthropogenic sediments* at a *microscopic* level.

microscopic   Visible only with magnification.

microwear analysis   Microscopic studies of damage and polish on the edges of stone *artifacts* to reveal the materials that were worked.

midden   Any substantial accumulation of garbage or waste at a locus of human activity; archaeological deposits of trash and/or shells that accumulate in heaps and mounds. A shell midden is a specific type of midden composed largely of mollusk shells.

Middle Range Theory   Used to describe a cultural system outside of a specific cultural context.

migration   Movement of new people into an area.

mitochondrial DNA (mtDNA)   Modern genetic material taken from the mitochondria, inherited only through the maternal line.

MNI   The minimum number of individuals, which is based on counts of the number of distinctive body parts from a particular *species*.

mode   The most common category in nominal or ordinal data or the highest peak in ratio scale data.

moieties   Organizational division of some societies into two large, kin-related groups; moieties are composed of clans.

molded   *Pottery* produced by pressing *clay* into prepared molds.

molecular archaeology   Sometimes used to refer to the organic component of archaeological chemistry and particularly to the investigation of ancient *DNA* in plant and animal remains, including humans. Sometimes called biomolecular archaeology.

molecule   A combination of atoms held together by chemical bonds.

mortuary analysis   Study of graves and their contents to learn about past societies and individuals.

mounds (a.k.a. *barrows*, tumuli)   A built pile or heap of earth or stones, resembling a very small hill, usually a burial monument.

multicomponent   A mixture of different episodes or periods of activity.

myoglobin   A *protein* found in human tissue; its presence in human feces is used as evidence for cannibalism.

Native American Graves Protection and Repatriation Act (NAGPRA)   Federal legislation intended to protect and return certain archaeological human remains and culturally significant artifacts to Native Americans.

natural transformation   Modification of the archaeological record by geological, hydrological, or chemical activity.

Neanderthal   An earlier human relative that lived largely in Europe from approximately 250,000 to 35,000 years ago when it became extinct. *Homo neanderthalensis.*

neck   The upper zone on a *pottery* vessel between the *shoulder* and the rim.

neutron   Particle in the core of an atom with no electrical charge; part of the nucleus of an atom.

neutron activation analysis (NAA)   *Archaeometry* technique using *neutron* bombardment to release detectable element-specific gamma rays in samples.

NISP   The number of identified specimens, the number of bones from a *species.*

nodule   Unworked pieces of stone, raw material for making stone *tools.*

nominal scale of measurement   Basic information recorded as unordered observations, often descriptive.

nonarboreal pollen (NAP)   Pollen from plants other than trees.

nonsite (off-site)   The areas between archaeological *sites* where there are occasional traces of human activity in the form of isolated *artifacts, features,* or other evidence.

normal curve   The standard, or normal, shape of measured values plotted in a frequency diagram.

nucleic acid   Compounds found in all living cells and viruses, composed of purines, pyrimidines, carbohydrates, and phosphoric acid.

nucleotides   Basic building blocks of DNA, each made up of one of four base units (adenine, cytosine, guanine, or thymine) that together make up the long molecules of chromosomes.

observation   Term used for each value recorded in a data set.

obsidian   A glassy rock produced from sand in volcanic conditions, used for making stone *tools* in the past.

obsidian hydration dating   A dating technique which relies on the accumulation of a hydration (weathering) layer on the fresh surface of *obsidian* objects.

occipital flattening   A flattening of the back of the head caused by hard crib boards in infancy. Noted among the Moche and many other Native American groups in the New World.

occupation horizon   The layer or strata that accumulates during an episode of human habitation and activity.

ochre   A red iron mineral sometimes found in prehistoric graves.

open-air sites   On land and uncovered, in contrast to *sites* in caves or *rockshelters.*

optimal foraging theory   Evolutionary ecology perspective based on efficient *foraging* strategies.

ordinal scale of measurement   Ranked information with an ordered relationship between numbers.

organic compounds   The molecules of living organisms with the element carbon as a base.

organization   Structure and interaction in human society, including relationships among individuals, groups, and other societies.

orifice   The opening or mouth of a *ceramic* vessel.

osteodontokeratic   ("bone-tooth-horn") A term coined to describe what might have been the earliest *tools;* lack of modification makes them impossible to identify.

oxbow lake   A stranded river meander left as a lake in a floodplain.

paddle-and-anvil technique   Use of two *tools* to press and shape the walls of a *ceramic* vessel.

paleobotany   Study of fossil plants.

paleoethnobotany   The study of plant use by both living and prehistoric peoples.

paleontology   Study of fossil animals.

paleopathology   The study of medical disorders and injury in human skeletal remains.

palynology   The study of pollen from plants for information on *species,* environment, and climate.

parenchymous tissues Parenchyma is plant storage tissue, commonly found in roots, tubers, rhizomes, and corms.

parry fracture A distinctive break in the forearm resulting from a blow to an arm raised in protection.

paste Mix of *clay* and other materials used to make *pottery*.

patination A weathering process that gradually changes the surface appearance of *flint* from shiny to dull, and often from one color to another over time; the new surface is described as a patina.

pectoral Wide, biblike necklaces or plates worn over the chest area; part of costume or armor.

pedologist Soil scientist.

percussion flaking A technique for producing stone *artifacts* by striking or *knapping crystalline* stone with a *hard* or *soft hammer.* See also *pressure flaking.*

petroglyphs *Rock art* made by removing the outer surface of a rock by carving or hammering.

petrographic microscope A specialized version of a binocular microscope designed for the study of thin sections of rock or *pottery.*

phase A particular period in time and space where an *assemblage* occurs.

photosynthesis Process in plants for manufacture of carbohydrates and oxygen from carbon dioxide and water in the presence of chlorophyll with sunlight as the energy source.

phytoliths Genus-specific silicate bodies inside plants.

pictographs *Rock art* made by the application of pigment to rock surfaces.

pithouse A dwelling constructed over a hole in the ground; semisubterranean structure; structure built on a semisubterranean foundation.

plan view A bird's-eye or top-down view of a *site* or *region.* A kind of map of the features and characteristics of a place. A standard representation of archaeological *sites* and areas.

plasma The gaseous state of hot ionized material consisting of *ions* and electrons used as a source for ions in spectrometry.

playa A dry lake bed, common *geomorphological* feature in the western United States.

plow zone The upper part of soil layers that has been disturbed by plowing.

point bar A low ridge of sand and gravel that forms underwater along the inner bank of a meandering stream.

pollen Covering of the gametes of flowering plants released in sexual reproduction.

polychrome Several colors; polychrome *pottery* is painted with at least two colors.

polymerase chain reaction (PCR) Technique in genetic studies to increase quantities of *DNA* sample by rapid cloning.

population (1) All of the people living at a place or in a *region.* An archaeological population generally refers to the people related through membership in the same group. (2) All of the items or units of interest in statistical sampling.

population density The number of people per unit of area, e.g., square kilometer.

positivism A philosophical view that the application of science and the evaluation of empirical evidence allow one to be objective.

posthole The hole or depression left when a post is removed from the ground, an indication of construction posts.

pottery *Ceramic* container or vessel.

preform (a.k.a. blank) A basic piece or blank form used to make a specific kind of finished product. Term is used in *lithic* studies to describe early stages in manufacture of certain kinds of *tools* like *projectile points.*

prehistory The time in the past before written history, often synonymous with *archaeology.*

pressure flaking A technique for producing stone *artifacts* by removing *flakes* from a stone *core* by pressing with a pointed implement. See also *percussion flaking.*

primary context An object in its original position of discard or deposition; in place (Latin: in situ).

primary inhumation Burial of the complete corpse after death.

profile A cross-section of archaeological or geological deposits showing the *stratigraphy,* sequence of layers. Also, the cross-section of the walls of a *ceramic* vessel, a measure of shape.

projectile point Generic name for the range of shapes and materials used to make a sharp end on weapons such as spears, darts, javelins, arrows, and the like (synonym: arrowhead, spearhead).

protein Complex organic macromolecule composed of more chains of *amino acids* containing carbon, hydrogen, oxygen, and nitrogen; fundamental components of all living cells and many substances such as enzymes, hormones, and antibodies.

proton Particle in the core of an atom with a positive electrical charge.

provenience The place of discovery or origin. Where an item is from (a.k.a. provenance in *classical archaeology*).

provenience postulate States that if differences within a source of material are less than differences with other sources, then it is possible to distinguish individual sources, or *provenience.*

pseudoscience False or misleading claims about the nature of the world or the past, masquerading as science.

pubic symphysis The "face" of the pelvis where the two halves join; important area for age determination in the skeleton.

punch A piece of antler, bone, or wood used as a pointed object between the hammer and the *core* to assist the removal of the *flake;* a kind of chisel for *flintknapping.*

punctate Decorative technique for *pottery* involving impressions of circular depressions in surface of *clay.*

punctuated equilibrium Abrupt and sudden changes in the pace of evolution.

rachis The stem that connects the grain seed to the main plant stalk in cereals.

radioactivity The process of decay of unstable *isotopes* over time through the spontaneous emission of radiation from the nucleus of an atom.

radiocarbon A radioactive *isotope* of carbon (^{14}C, carbon-14); an important dating technique in *archaeology.*

radiopotassium, or potassium-argon, dating Dating technique for old samples that is based on *half-life* for decay of potassium into argon in new rock.

raised fields A productive agricultural field system in wetlands using canals for water and built-up islands between canals for farmland.

range A measure of the spread of values using the minimum and maximum.

rank Inherited positions in societies based on birth order and ancestry.

ratio scale of measurement Measurements with a true zero point made using an instrument.

reciprocity The *exchange* of items of roughly equal value.

reconnaissance The search for *artifacts* and *sites* by *survey* or field walking.

redistribution The movement of goods to a central place from which they are rationed or portioned out to members of society.

reference collections Collections of modern plants, animal bones, human skeletal material, and other items to be used in the process of identification of archaeological remains. Prehistoric items are compared to modern to find the closest match.

refitting A technique for reassembling the scattered pieces of stone, *pottery,* or bone at an archaeological *site* to study patterns of manufacture and disposal.

regions Large geographic areas, containing a number of archaeological *sites,* that have been physically or conceptually modified.

relative dating Method of dating that determines whether an object or layer is older or younger than another.

religion Formalized *ritual,* a belief system that promotes *cosmology,* *ideology,* morals, and values in human society.

remote sensing A variety of techniques used for obtaining information about surface or buried objects. Above-ground techniques normally involve aircraft or satellites using photography, radar, and other methods to locate and map *features* on or near the surface. Below-ground techniques use radar, resistivity, magnetic properties, or chemistry to search for buried features.

research design The overall strategy of intended methods, research area, and planned analysis for answering a question or questions about the past.

residential sites Places of habitation where people live and carry out the everyday activities that sustain life.

resist A decorative technique for *pottery* involving materials which disappear on firing and leave a negative color on the surface of the vessel.

resistivity meter Used to measure electrical conductivity in soils that may be due to the presence of buried disturbances such as fireplaces, burials, or other structures.

restoration Altering the material and/or structure of an artifact or structure to return it to a more original condition.

retouch The shaping or sharpening of stone *artifacts* through *percussion* or *pressure flaking;* a technique of *flintknapping.*

rim sherd Fragment of broken *pottery* that includes part of the rim of the vessel.

ritual Symbolic, prescribed, and structured behaviors that are often repetitive in nature and related to belief systems.

rock art Decoration of rock surface by painting, pecking, or engraving.

rockshelter A shallow cave or overhang, defined by having a width greater than its depth.

root crop Plants that reproduce asexually from shoots or cuttings.

sample A portion of a whole (n); to take a part of a deposit, site, feature, or artifact for analysis (v). The term *sampling* describes the process of taking a sample. This can be a one-time event, a series of actions, or a statistical process. Statistical sampling is a specific method for taking samples that allows probability estimates to be made about the *population* that is being sampled. Archaeologists almost always take samples, but only rarely is this done in a statistical fashion.

saqia An oxen-powered water wheel used for irrigation in ancient Egypt.

scale (1) Different levels of discovery, analysis, and interpretation in *archaeology,* or (2) the size of a map relative to the area it portrays.

scale A ratio representing the size of an illustration, map, or reproduction in a publication.

scale of measurement Measurements can be made using nominal, ordinal, or ratio scales of numbers.

scanning electron microscope (SEM) An electronic (not optical) instrument for very high magnification of microscopic structures. The SEM uses electrons instead of light to form an image.

scatterplot A single graph combining two sets of numbers simultaneously.

screening Sifting or sieving of *sediments* through fine screens to separate them from *artifacts* and *ecofacts.*

seasonal round (a.k.a., annual cycle) The pattern of subsistence and settlement found among *hunter-gatherers* who change residence regularly during the course of a year.

seasonality The time of year a *site* was occupied, part of an annual cycle, usually related to *hunter-gatherer* settlement patterns.

secondary inhumation Reburial or burial of partial or skeletal human remains often missing some parts.

secondary products Both food and nonfood materials and energy that come from domestic animals in addition to meat.

section (a.k.a. *profile*) The walls of trenches and squares in *excavations* that show a cross section of the deposits and reveal the sequence and methods of formation.

sedentary Permanent or year-round settlement.

sediment Any particulate matter (*clay, sand, silt, mud, leaves, shell,* and other materials) that can be transported by water. Opposite of rock.

seed crop Plants that reproduce sexually by making and dispersing seeds.

selectionist School of archaeological theory that believes culture should be explained by natural selection and other Darwinian processes.

seriation An archaeological method for ordering.

sexual dimorphism Size difference between the males and females of the same *species.*

shaduf A manual water hoist used for irrigation in ancient Egypt.

shaman Specialist in ritual and healing; seer of the future in *hunter-gatherer* and *subsistence* farming societies.

shattering Seed dispersal mechanism.

shell midden A specialized kind of extractive site, a mound made up of large dumps of shell from mussels, oysters, or other *species.*

sherds Broken pieces of *pottery.*

shoulder The transition zone where the body ends and the neck begins on a *ceramic* vessel.

silica The mineral component of sand.

single component The remains of a single episode of human activities.

site formation The processes involved in the creation of archaeological *sites.*

sites Accumulations of artifacts and features, representing the places where people lived or carried out certain activities.

slab technique Pottery vessel made by rolling a single sheet of *clay* into a cylinder and attaching a base.

slip A coating of the surface of a *ceramic* vessel for decorative or functional reasons.

slopewash Gradual movement of sediments from higher to lower ground as a natural process of erosion and deposition.

sodalities Groups or clubs within society whose members come from different *lineages* and share common interests or goals.

soft hammer A flintknapping technique that involves the use of a hammer of bone, antler, or wood, rather than stone. See also *hard hammer.*

soil Surface sediments weathered *in situ.*

species A taxonomic group whose members can interbreed.

spondylus *Species* of large marine mollusk with a prized shell.

spore Microscopic gamete of non-flowering plant.

stadia rod Essentially, very long ruler that is held vertically and read by an optical surveying instrument to determine distance above the ground.

standard deviation (s.d.) The square root of the variance, a single measure of spread.

starch Microscopic grains of a complex carbohydrate found in certain *species* of plants.

state A large-scale, autonomous, and territorial political unit and class society, having a centralized government with the power to collect taxes, draft men for work or war, and decree and enforce laws.

stela A stone monument, carved and/or painted with designs and/or inscriptions, common in the Maya region (plural: stelae).

sterile Containing no archaeological materials.

sterol Unsaturated solid alcohol, such as cholesterol and ergosterol, present in the fatty tissues of plants and animals.

stratigraphy A sequence of layers in the ground.

striking platform The flat surface of a *core* where a blow is struck to remove *flake,* visible at the top of the *flake.*

study area A generic term for the *region* of focus of a research project.

style A distinctive way of being or doing.

subsistence The activities and materials that people use to obtain food.

subtractive techniques A way of making things like stone *tools* or wood carvings that involves the continuous removal of material from a larger original piece. Compare *additive techniques.*

superposition Principle that governs the interpretation of *stratigraphy*—in a sequence the oldest layers are on the bottom and the youngest layers are on top.

surface sites Visible on the surface of the ground.

survey (1) A systematic *reconnaissance* of the landscape for *artifacts* and *sites* on the ground through aerial photography, field walking, soil analysis, or geophysical prospecting; (2) mapping of *sites* and areas using surveying instruments such as a *total station* or *GPS.*

symbol Depiction or design which expresses a larger concept, often ideological.

synchronic Dealing with a moment in time, a single time period.

Synthetic Aperture Radar (SAR) An instrument that beams energy waves to the ground surface and records the reflected energy.

systemic context The actual use of *artifacts* and *features* in the past or present.

systems theory A method to explain the interaction of different variables within an organism or organization.

taphonomy The study of what happens to an organism between its death and the time it is found as a fossil or archaeological remain, including decomposition, postmortem transport, burial, and the biological, physical, and chemical changes.

taro Tropical root crop with slightly toxic potatolike tuber.

technology The material, equipment, techniques, and knowledge that allow humans to convert natural resources into *tools,* food, clothing, shelter, and other products they need or want.

tectonic Geological forces that move and deform the earth's crust.

tell An accumulated mound of occupation debris; man-made, settlement mounds of earth and trash that accumulate from the decomposition of mud brick, common in Southwest Asia and Southeast Europe.

temper A nonplastic substance intentionally added to *clay* in order to reduce breakage caused by shrinkage and firing.

teosinte Wild Mexican grass, probable ancestor of corn.

territory A recognized and defended area utilized by a group or society, often associated with agricultural societies.

texture The size and sorting of sediments, for example, in a petrographic thin section.

theory A generally accepted explanation of observed events or relationships.

Thermal Infrared Multispectral Scanner (TIMS) A satellite instrument that records multiple wavelengths of light reflected from the earth's surface.

thermoluminescence (TL) dating Technique for *absolute dating* based on the principle of the rate of accumulation of TL after heating, used with burned *flint* and *clay*.

tool Any equipment, weapon, object intentionally modified by humans to change the *environment* around them.

total station A modern *surveying* instrument using an infrared laser and computer to calculate distance and three-dimensional angles to determine the precise location of a target in terms of grid coordinates and elevation. Replaces levels, *alidades*, transits, and theodolites.

town Larger than a village with internal differentiation in size and location of structures and usually containing one or more public buildings.

trabecular bone Spongy bone tissue found in the interior of bone.

trade Economic transactions between individuals or groups involving bartering, buying, or selling.

tradition The continuity of similar *artifacts* and design through time.

tribe Small-scale societies of farmers where relationships are generally egalitarian and decision making is consensual.

trophic level Position in the food chain, e.g., herbivore, carnivore, bottom-feeder.

type list The set of types of *artifacts* for a specific area.

typology A formal system of classification for assigning time and space meaning to archaeological materials.

unifacial A term describing a flaked stone *tool* in which only one face or side is *retouched* to make a sharp edge. See also *bifacial*.

uniformitarianism Geological principle that the processes of erosion and deposition observed in action today also operated in the past.

uranium series dating An isotopic dating method based on radioactive decay of uranium.

variance A single measure of spread or range in ratio data.

varves Annual layers of deposits in cold-water lakes.

village Small residential unit of permanent houses with a population of less than a few hundred.

waste A term referring to all the pieces of *shatter* and *flakes* produced and not used when stone *tools* are made; also called *débitage*.

waster *Pottery* that broke or warped in the process of firing.

wattle-and-daub A construction technique that involves standing posts and interwoven horizontal branches (wattle) that are covered in mud (daub) to make a wall.

weathering Chemical and biological processes that break down and change the surface of the earth, altering its color, texture, or composition.

wet lab A chemistry facility with lab tables, equipment, and running water.

wheel-thrown Pottery produced on a wheel with distinctive manufacturing characteristics.

wiggle matching A technique for finding precise dates using a series of *radiocarbon* dates and the irregularities in the calibration curve.

X-ray diffraction (XRD) Archaeometric method for measuring mineral and elemental composition of most solids using distinctive patterns of X-ray scattering.

ziggurat A large, solid, mud-brick stepped tower. Stairways lead to a small temple on top.

Bibliography

Adams, Jenny L. 2002. *Ground Stone Analysis: A Technological Approach.* Salt Lake City: University of Utah Press.

Adams, W., and E. Adams. 1991. *Archaeology Typology and Practical Reality.* New York: Cambridge University Press.

Adington, Lucile R. 1986. *Lithic Illustration: Drawing Flaked Stone Artifacts for Publication.* Chicago: University of Chicago Press.

Ahler, S. A. 1979. Functional analysis of nonobsidian chipped stone artifacts: Terms, variables, and quantification. In *Lithic Use-Wear Analysis,* edited by B. Hayden, 301–328. New York: Academic Press.

———. 1989. Mass analysis of flaking debris: Studying the forest rather than the tree. In *Alternative Approaches to Lithic Analysis,* edited by D. O. Henry and G. H. Odell, 85–118. Washington, D.C.: American Anthropological Association.

Aitkin, Martin J. 1985. *Thermoluminescence Dating.* London: Academic Press.

———. 1990. *Science-Based Dating in Archaeology.* New York: Longman.

Aksu, A. E., R. N. Hiscott, P. J. Mudie, A. Rochon, M. A. Kaminski, T. Abrajano, and D. Yaşar. 2002. Persistent Holocene outflow from the Black Sea to the Eastern Mediterranean contradicts Noah's Flood hypothesis. *GSAToday* 12(5):4–9.

Alcock, Susan E., Carla M. Sinopoli, Terence N. D'Altroy, and Kathleen D. Morrison, eds. 2001. *Empires: Perspectives from Archaeology and History.* Cambridge: Cambridge University Press.

Alcock, Susan E., and Robin G. Osborne. n.d. *Classical Archaeology.* Oxford: Blackwell.

Aldenderfer, M. 1998. Quantitative methods in archaeology: A review of recent trends and developments. *Journal of Archaeological Research* 6(2):91–120.

Alexander, Brian. 1990. Archaeology and looting make a volatile mix. *Science* 250:1074–1075.

Allison, Penelope, ed. 1999. *The Archaeology of Household Activities.* New York: Routledge.

Alva, Walter. 1988. Discovering the New World's richest unlooted tomb. *National Geographic* 174(4):510–549.

———. 1990. New tomb of royal splendor. *National Geographic* 177(6):2–15.

———. 2001. The royal tombs of Sipán: Art and power in Moche society. In *Moche: Art and Archaeology in Ancient Peru,* edited by Joanne Pillsbury, 222–245. Washington, D.C.: National Gallery of Art.

Alva, Walter, and Christopher B. Donnan. 1993. *Royal Tombs of Sipán.* Los Angeles: UCLA Fowler Museum of Cultural History.

Ambrose, S. H., and Katzenberg, M. A., eds. 2001. *Biogeochemical Approaches to Paleodietary Analysis.* New York: Springer.

Andersen, S. H. 1987. Tybrind Vig: A submerged Ertebølle settlement in Denmark. In *European Wetlands in Prehistory,* edited by J. M. Coles and A. J. Lawson, 253–280. Oxford: Clarendon Press.

Andersen, S. H., and C. Malmros. 1984. "Madskorpe" på Ertebøllekar fra Tybrind Vig. Aarbøger Nord. Oldk. Hist. 1983: 78–95.

Anderson, A. 1984. *Interpreting Pottery.* London: Batsford.

Anderson, David G., and Michael K. Faught. 2000. Palaeoindian artefact distributions: Evidence and implications. *Antiquity* 74: 507–513.

Anderson, P. C. 1980. A testimony of prehistoric tasks: Diagnostic residues on stone tool working edges. *World Archaeology* 12(2):181–194.

Andrefsky, W. 1994. Raw-material availability and the organization of technology. *American Antiquity* 59:21–34.

———. 1998. *Lithics: Macroscopic Approaches to Analysis.* Cambridge: Cambridge University Press.

———, ed. 2001. *Lithic Debitage: Context, Form, Meaning.* Salt Lake City: University of Utah Press.

Arden, H. 1989. Who owns our past? *National Geographic* 175(3):376–392.

Arneborg, J., Jan Heinemeier, Niels Lynnerup, Henrik L. Nielsen, Niels Rud, Árny E. Sveinbjörnsdóttir. 1999. Change of diet of the Greenland Vikings determined from stable carbon isotope analysis and ^{14}C dating of their bones. *Radiocarbon* 41(2):157–168.

Arnold, Bettina. 1990. The past as propaganda: Totalitarian archaeology in Nazi Germany. *Antiquity* 64(244): 464–478.

Arnold, D. 1985. *Ceramic Theory and Cultural Process.* Cambridge: Cambridge University Press.

Ascher, R. 1968. Time's arrow and the archaeology of a contemporary community. In *Settlement Archaeology,* edited by K. C. Chang, 43–52. Palo Alto: National Press.

Ascher, Robert. 1961. Analogy in archaeological interpretation. *Southwestern Journal of Anthropology* 17:317–325.

Asouti, E., 2003. Wood charcoal from Santorini (Thera): New evidence for climate, vegetation and timber imports in the Aegean Bronze Age. *Antiquity* 77:471–484.

Aufderheide, A. C. 2003. *The Scientific Study of Mummies.* Cambridge: Cambridge University Press.

Babits, L. E., and H. van Tilburg. 1998. *Maritime Archaeology: A Reader of Substantive and Theoretical Contributions.* New York: Plenum.

Bahn, Paul G. 1998. *The Cambridge Illustrated History of Prehistoric Art.* Cambridge: Cambridge University Press.

———, ed. 1996. *The Story of Archaeology: The 100 Great Discoveries.* London: Weidenfeld & Nicolson.

———, ed. 1996. *The Cambridge Illustrated History of Archaeology.* Cambridge: Cambridge University Press.

———, ed. 2003. *Written in Bones: How Human Remains Unlock the Secrets of the Dead.* Buffalo: Firefly Books.

Baillie, M. G. L. 1995. *A Slice through Time: Dendrochronology and Precision Dating.* London: Batsford.

———. 2001. Tree ring records and environmental catastrophes. *Inter-*

disciplinary Science Reviews 26(2): 87–89.

Bak, P. 1996. *How Nature Works.* New York: Springer.

Bamforth, D. B. 1986. Technological efficiency and tool curation. *American Antiquity* 51:38–50.

———. 1988. Investigating microwear polishes with blind tests: The institute results in context. *Journal of Archaeological Science* 15:11–23.

———. 1991. Technological organization and hunter-gatherer land use: A California example. *American Antiquity* 56:216–235.

———. 2002. Evidence and metaphor in evolutionary archaeology. *American Antiquity* 67(3):435–452.

Bamforth, D. B., and M. S. Becker. 2000. Core/biface ratios, mobility, refitting, and artifact use-lives: A Paleoindian example. *Plains Anthropologist* 45:273–290.

Banning, E. B. 2000. *The Archaeologist's Laboratory: The Analysis of Archaeological Data.* New York: Kluwer.

Bannister, B. 1970. Dendrochronology. In *Science in Archaeology,* edited by D. Brothwell and E. Higgs, 191–205. New York: Praeger.

Barber, Russell J. 1994. Exercise 15: Mean ceramic dating. In *Doing Historical Archaeology: Exercises Using Documentary, Oral, and Material Evidence.* Englewood Cliffs, N.J.: Prentice Hall.

Bareis, Charles J., and James W. Porter, eds. 1984. *American Bottom Archaeology: A Summary of the FAI–270 Project Contribution to the Culture History of the Mississippi River Valley.* Urbana: University of Illinois Press.

Barnett, William, and John Hoopes, eds. 1995. *The Emergence of Pottery: Technology and Innovation in Prehistoric Societies.* Washington, D.C.: Smithsonian Institution Press.

Barrett, John C. 2001. Agency, the duality of structure, and the problem of the archaeological record. In *Archaeological Theory Today,* edited by Ian Hodder, 141–164. Cambridge: Polity Press.

Barton, C. M. 1997. Stone tools, style, and social identity: An evolutionary perspective on the archaeological record. *Rediscovering Darwin: Evolutionary Theory in Archaeological Explanation.* C. M. Barton and G. A. Clark. Washington, D.C., American Anthropological Association. 7: 141–156.

Barton, C. M., and G. A. Clark, eds. 1997. *Rediscovering Darwin: Evolutionary Theory and Archaeological Explanation.* Arlington, Va.: American Anthropological Association.

Bar-Yosef, O., B. Vandermeersch, B. Arensburg, A. Belfer-Cohen, P. Goldberg, H. Laville, L. Meignen, Y. Rak, J. D. Speth, E. Tchernov, A. M. Tillier, and S. Weiner, 1992. The excavations in Kebara Cave, Mt. Carmel. *Current Anthropology* 33:497–550.

Basalla, George. 1988. *The Evolution of Technology.* Cambridge: Cambridge University Press.

Bass, W. M. 1987. *Human Osteology: A Laboratory and Field Manual of the Human Skeleton.* 3d ed. Columbia, Mo.: Missouri Archaeological Society.

Bawden, G. 1982. Community organization reflected by the household: A study in Pre-Columbian dynamics. *Journal of Field Archaeology* 9:165–181.

Baxter, Michael. 2003. *Statistics in Archaeology.* London: Arnold.

Beaudry, Mary, ed. 1988. *Documentary Archaeology in the New World.* Cambridge: Cambridge University Press.

Beaudry, Mary, and Anne Elizabeth Yentsch, eds. 1992. *The Art and Mystery of Historical Archaeology: Essays in Honor of James Deetz.* Boca Raton, Fla: CRC Press.

Beck, Lane Anderson, ed. 1995. *Regional Approaches to Mortuary Analysis.* New York: Plenum.

Bell, J. A. 1994. *Reconstructing Prehistory: Scientific Method in Archaeology.* Philadelphia: Temple University Press.

Bentley, R. Alexander, and Herbert D. G. Maschner, eds. 2003. *Complex Systems and Archaeology.* Salt Lake City: University of Utah Press.

Bethell, P. H., R. P. Evershed and L. J. Goad. 1994. The investigation of lipids in organic residues by gas chromotography/mass spectrometry: Application to palaeodietary studies. In *Prehistoric Human Bone: Archaeology at the Molecular Level,* edited by Joseph B. Lambert and Gisela Grupe. Berlin: Springer.

Bettinger, R. L. 1991. *Hunter-Gatherers: Archaeological and Evolutionary Theory.* New York: Plenum.

Bettinger, R. L., R. Boyd, and P. J. Richerson. 1996. Style, function, and cultural evolutionary processes. In *Darwinian Archaeologies,* edited by H. Maschner, 133–164. New York: Plenum.

Binford, Lewis R. 1962. Archaeology as anthropology. *American Antiquity* 28:217–225.

———. 1978. *Nunamiut Ethnoarchaeology.* Academic Press, Orlando.

———. 1979. Organization and formation processes: Looking at curated technologies. *Journal of Anthropological Research* 35:172–197.

———. 1981. *Bones: Ancient Men and Modern Myths.* New York: Academic Press.

———. 1989. Science to seance, or processual to "post-processual" archaeology. In *Debating Archaeology,* by L. R. Binford, 27–40. New York: Academic Press.

———. 1989. Styles of style. *Journal of Anthropological Archaeology* 8:51–67.

Bintliff, John. 1991. The contribution of an annaliste/structural history approach to archaeology. In *The Annales School and Archaeology,* edited by J. Bintliff, 1–33. Leicester: Leicester University Press.

Birkeland, P. W. 1984. *Soils and Geomorphology.* New York: Oxford University Press.

Birmingham, Robert A., and Leslie E. Eisenberg. 2000. *Indian Mounds of Wisconsin.* Madison: University of Wisconsin Press.

Bishop, R. L., Robert L. Rands, and George R. Holley. 1982. Ceramic compositional analysis in archaeological perspective. In *Advances in Archaeological Method and Theory,* vol. 5, edited by M. B. Schiffer, 275–330. New York: Academic Press.

Blackman, M. James. 1984. Provenance studies of Middle Eastern obsidian from sites in highland Iran. In *Archaeological Chemistry III*, edited by Joseph Lambert, 19–50, ACS Advances in Chemistry Series No. 205. Washington, D.C.: American Chemical Society.

Blanton, R. E., S. A. Kowalewski, G. M. Feinman, and L. M. Finsten. 1993. *Ancient Mesoamerica: A Comparison of Change in Three Regions.* 2d ed. Cambridge: Cambridge University Press.

Bleed, P. 1986. The optimal design of hunting weapons: Maintainability or reliability? *American Antiquity* 51.

———. 2001. Trees of chains, links or branches: Conceptual alternative for consideration of stone tool production and other sequential activities. *Journal of Archaeological Method and Theory* 8(1):101–127.

Blitz, J. H. 1993. Big pots for big shots: Feasting and storage vessels in a Mississippian community. *American Antiquity* 58:80–96.

Blot, Jean-Yves. 1996. *Underwater Archaeology: Exploring the World Beneath the Sea.* Translated by Alexandra Campbell. Abrams, 1996.

Boddington, A. 1987. From bones to population: The problem of numbers. In *Death, Decay, and Reconstruction*, edited by A. Boddington, A. N. Garland, and R. C. Janaway, 180–197. Manchester: Manchester University Press.

Bonde, N., and A. E. Christensen. 1993. Dendrochronological dating of the Viking Age ship burials at Oseberg, Gokstad and Tune, Norway. *Antiquity* 67: 575–583.

Bonnichsen, Robson, and Marcella Sorg, eds. 1989. *Bone Modification.* Center for the Study of Early Man. Orono: University of Maine.

Boone, James L., and Eric Alden Smith. 1998. Is it evolution yet? A critique of evolutionary archaeology. *Current Anthropology* 39:141–174.

Bordes, F. 1969. Reflections on typology and techniques in the Paleolithic. *Arctic Anthropology* 6(1):1–29.

Bourdieu, P. 1977. *Outline of a Theory of Practice.* Cambridge: Cambridge University Press.

Bowman, S. 1990. *Radiocarbon Dating.* Berkeley: University of California Press.

———, ed. 1991. *Science and the Past.* London: British Museum Press for the Trustees of the British Museum.

Bradley, B. A. 1975. Lithic reduction sequences: A glossary and discussion. In *Lithic Technology: Making and Using Stone Tools,* edited by E. Swanson, 5–13. The Hague: Mouton.

Braun, David P. 1983. Pots as tools. In *Archaeological Hammers and Theories,* edited by J. A. Moore and A. S. Keene, 107–134. New York: Academic Press.

Braun, David P., and Stephen Plog. 1982. Evolution of "tribal" social networks: Theory and prehistoric North American evidence. *American Antiquity* 47:504–525.

Brodie, Neil, Jennifer Doole, and Colin Renfrew, eds. 2001. *Trade in Illicit Antiquities: The Destruction of the World's Archaeological Heritage.* Cambridge: McDonald Institute.

Brodie, N., and K. W. Tubb, eds. 2002. *Illicit Antiquities: The Theft of Culture and the Extinction of Archaeology.* London: Routledge.

Broida, M. A. 1984. An estimate of the percentage of maize in the diets of two Kentucky Fort Ancient villages. In *Late Prehistoric Research in Kentucky,* edited by D. L. Pollack, C. B. Hockensmith, and T. N. Sanders, 68–82. Frankfort: Kentucky Heritage Council.

Brothwell, D. R. 1981. *Digging Up Bones.* Ithaca: Cornell University Press.

Brothwell, D., and P. 1997. *Food in Antiquity. A Survey of the Diet of Early Peoples.* Baltimore: Johns Hopkins University Press.

Brothwell, D. R., and A. M. Pollard, eds. 2001. *Handbook of Archaeological Sciences.* Chichester: Wiley.

Brothwell, Don. 1987. *The Bog Man and the Archaeology of People.* Cambridge Mass.: Harvard University Press.

Broughton, J. M. 2002. Prey spatial structure and behavior affect archaeological tests of optimal foraging models: Examples from the Emery-

ville Shellmound vertebrate fauna. *World Archaeology* 34:60–83.

Broughton, Jack, and James F. O'Connell. 1999. On evolutionary ecology, selectionist archaeology, and behavioral archaeology. *American Antiquity* 64:153–164.

Browman, David L., and Stephen Williams, eds. 2002. *New Perspectives on the Origins of Americanist Archaeology.* Tuscaloosa: University of Alabama Press.

Brown, A. G. 1997. *Alluvial Geoarchaeology.* Cambridge: Cambridge University Press.

Brück, Johanna. 1999. Ritual and rationality: Some problems of interpretation in European archaeology. *European Journal of Archaeology* 2:313–344.

Bruhns, K. O. 1994. *Ancient South America.* New York: Cambridge University Press.

Brumfiel, E. 1991. Weaving and cooking: Women's production in Aztec Mexico. In *Engendering Archaeology: Women and Prehistory,* edited by Joan Gero and Margaret Conkey, eds., 224–251. Oxford: Blackwell.

———. 1992. Breaking and entering the ecosystem: Gender, class, and faction steal the show. *American Anthropologist* 94:551–567.

———. 1996. Figurines and the Aztec state: Testing the effectiveness of ideological domination. In *Gender in Archaeology: Research in Gender and Practice,* edited by R. P. Wright, 143–166. Philadelphia: University of Pennsylvania Press.

———. 2001. Asking about Aztec gender: The historical and archaeological evidence. In *Gender in Pre-Hispanic America,* edited by Cecelia F. Klein. Washington, D.C.: Dumbarton Oaks.

Bryant, Vaughn M., Jr., and Richard G. Holloway. 1983. The role of palynology in archaeology. *Advances in Archaeological Method and Theory* 6:191–224.

Buikstra, J. E. 1997. Paleodemography: Context and promise. In *Integrating Archaeological Demography: Multidisci-*

plinary Approaches to Prehistoric Population, edited by Richard R. Paine, 367–380. Carbondale, Ill.: Center for Archaeological Investigations.

Buikstra, J. E., and L. W. Konigsberg. 1985. Paleodemography: Critiques and controversies. *American Anthropologist* 87:316–333.

Buikstra, J. E., and D. H. Ubelaker, eds. 1994. Standards for data collection from human skeletal remains. Arkansas Archeological Survey Research Series No. 44. Fayetteville, Ark.: Arkansas Archeological Survey.

Burenhult, G., ed. 1994. *Old World Civilizations: The Rise of Cities and States.* San Francisco: HarperSanFrancisco.

Cahen, Daniel. 1989. Refitting stone artifacts: Why bother? In *The Human Uses of Flint and Chert,* edited by G. de G. Sieveking and M. H. Newcomer, 1–10. Cambridge: Cambridge University Press.

Cahen, D., and L. H. Keeley. 1980. Not less than two, not more than three. *World Archaeology* 12:166–180.

Campbell, B. G., and J. D. Loy. 2000. *Humankind Emerging.* 8th ed. Boston: Longman.

Cannon-Brookes, P. 1994. Antiquities in the market-place: Placing a price on documentation. *Antiquity* 68:349–350.

Caple, Chris. 2000. *Conservation Skills: Judgement, Method and Decision Making.* London: Routledge.

Carman, J. 2002. *Archaeology and Heritage: An Introduction.* London: Continuum.

Carniero, Robert. 1970. A theory of the origin of the state. *Science* 169:733–738.

Carr, Christopher, and J. C. Komorowski. 1995. Identifying the mineralogy of rock temper in ceramics using X-radiography. *American Antiquity* 60(4):723–749.

Carr, Christopher, and J. Neitzel. 1995. *Style, Society, and Person.* New York: Plenum.

Carter, Richard J. 1998. Reassessment of seasonality at the early Mesolithic site of Star Carr, Yorkshire based on radiographs of mandibular tooth development in red deer. *Journal of Archaeological Science* 25: 851–856.

Chamberlain, A.T., and M. Parker Pearson. 2001. *Earthly Remains: The History and Science of Preserved Human Remains.* London: British Museum Press.

Chang, K. C. 1967. Major aspects of the interrelationship of archaeology and ethnology. *Current Anthropology* 8:227–234.

Chapman, Jefferson.1973. *The Icehouse Bottom Site, 40MR23.* Department of Anthropology Report of Investigations, no. 13. Knoxville, Tenn.: University of Tennessee, Knoxville.

Chapman, Robert. 2003. *Archaeologies of Complexity.* London: Routledge.

Chatters, J. C. 1987. Hunter-gatherer adaptations and assemblage structure. *Journal of Anthropological Archaeology* 6(4):336–375.

Childe, V. Gordon. 1929. *The Danube in Prehistory.* Oxford: Clarendon Press.

Christaller, Walter. *1933. Die Zentralen Orte in Süddeutschland.* Jena: Gustav Fischer. Translated by Charlisle W. Baskin, as *Central Places in Southern Germany.* Prentice Hall, 1966.

Clark, Geoffrey A. 1993. Paradigms in science and archaeology. *Journal of Archaeological Research* 1:203–234.

Clark, J. G. D. 1954. *Excavations at Star Carr.* Cambridge: Cambridge University Press.

Clarke, D. L. 1968. *Analytical Archaeology.* London: Methuen.

Clarke, David. 1973. The loss of innocence. *American Antiquity* 47:6–18.

Classen, C. 1994. *Women in Archaeology.* Philadelphia: University of Pennsylvania Press.

Clutton-Brock, J. 1999. *A Natural History of Domesticated Animals.* Cambridge: Cambridge University Press.

Coles, B., and John Coles. 1989. *People of the Wetlands: Bogs, Bodies, and Lake-Dwellers.* New York: Thames & Hudson.

Coles, J. 1990. *Images of the Past. A Guide to the Rock Carvings and Other Ancient Monuments of Northern Bohuslän.* Tanum: Hällristningsmuseet Vitlycke.

Coles, J. M. 1979. *Archaeology by Experiment.* London: Hutchinson University Library.

Collins, Michael B. 1993. Comprehensive lithic studies: Context, technology, style, attrition, breakage, use-wear and organic residues. *Lithic Technology* 18:87–94.

Collis, John. 2001. *Digging up the Past: An Introduction to Archaeological Excavation.* Stroud: Sutton Publishing.

Condamin, J., F. Formenti, M. O. Metais, M. Michel, and P. Blond. 1976. The application of gas chromatography to the tracing of oil in ancient amphorae. *Archaeometry* 8:195–201.

Conkey, M., and C. Hastorf, eds. 1990. *The Uses of Style in Archaeology.* New Directions in Archaeology. Cambridge: Cambridge University Press.

Conkey, M., and J. Spector. 1984. Archaeology and the study of gender. *Advances in Archaeological Method and Theory* 7:1–38.

Conkey, Margaret W., and Joan M. Gero. 1997. Programme to practice: Gender and feminism in archaeology. *Annual Review of Anthropology* 26:411–437.

Cook, S. F. 1972. *Prehistoric Demography.* McCaleb Modules in Anthropology 16. Reading, Mass.: Addison-Wesley.

Cooper, Emmanuel. 2000. *Ten Thousand Years of Pottery.* Philadelphia: University of Pennsylvania Press.

Cooper, M. A., A. Firth, J. Carman, and D. Wheatley, eds. 1995. *Managing Archaeology.* London: Routledge.

Courty, M. A., Paul Goldberg, and Richard Macphail. 1989. *Soils and Micromorphology in Archaeology.* Cambridge: Cambridge University Press.

Crabtree, Don E. 1972. *An Introduction to Flintworking.* Pocatello, Idaho: Idaho State University Museum.

Craddock, P. T. 1995. *Early Metal Mining and Production.* Edinburgh: Edinburgh University Press.

Croes, D. R. 2003. Northwest Coast wet-site artifacts: A key to understanding resource procurement, storage, management, and exchange. In *Emerging from the Mist: Studies in Northwest Coast Culture History,* edited by R. G. Matson,

G. Coupland, and Q. Mackie, 51–75. Vancouver, B.C.: UBC Press.

Cronyn, J. M. 1990. *The Elements of Archaeological Conservation.* London: Routledge.

Crown, P. 1999. Socialization in American Southwest pottery decoration. In *Pottery and People: A Dynamic Interaction,* edited by J. M. Skibo and G. M. Feinman, 25–43. Salt Lake City: University of Utah Press.

Crumley, Carole. 1995. Heterarchy and the analysis of complex societies. In *Heterarchy and the Analysis of Complex Societies,* edited by R. Ehrenreich, C. Crumley, and J. Levy, 1–6. Archaeological Papers of the American Anthropological Association, no. 6. Arlington, Va.: American Anthropological Association.

Cziesla, E., and R. Kuper. 1989. Sitra—das Orakel der Steine: Momentaufnahmen aus der Steinzeit in den Siwa-Oasen. *Archäologie in Deutschland* 2 (Apr-Jun):11–16.

d'Errico, F., C. Henshilwood, and P. Nilssen. 2001. An engraved bone fragment from ca. 70,000-year-old Middle Stone Age levels at Blombos Cave, South Africa: Implications for the origin of symbolism and language. *Antiquity* 75:309–318.

Dalan, R. A., and B. W. Bevan. 2002. Geophysical indicators of culturally emplaced soils and sediments. *Geoarchaeology* 17(8):779–810.

Dales, G. F., and J. M. Kenoyer. 1986. *Excavations at Mohenjo Daro, Pakistan: The Pottery.* Philadelphia: University Museum Press.

D'Altroy, Terence N., and Christine Ann Hastorf. 2001. *Empire and Domestic Economy.* New York: Kluwer Academic/Plenum.

Damon, P. E., D. J. Donahue, B. H. Gore, A. L. Hatheway, A. J. T. Jull, T. W. Linick, P. J. Sercel, L. J. Toolin, C. R. Bronk, E. T. Hall, R. E. M. Hedges, R. Housley, I. A. Law, C. Perry, G. Bonani, S. Trumbore, W. Woelfli, J. C. Ambers, S. G. E. Bowman, M. N. Leese, and M. S. Tite. 1989. Radiocarbon dating of the Shroud of Turin. *Nature* 337:611–615.

Danforth, M. E. 1994. Stature change in the prehistoric Maya of the Southern Lowlands. *Latin American Antiquity* 5:206–211.

Daniel, G., and C. Chippendale, eds. 1989. *The Pastmasters: Eleven Modern Pioneers of Archaeology.* New York: Thames and Hudson.

Daniel, G., and C. Renfrew. 1988. *The Idea of Prehistory.* Edinburgh: University of Edinburgh Press.

Daniels, V. 1996. Selection of a conservation process for Lindow Man. In *Human Mummies: A Global Survey of Their Status and the Techniques of Conservation,* edited by K. Spindler, H. Wilfing, E. Rastbichler-Zissernig, D. zur Nedden, and H. Nothdurfter, 173–181. Vienna: Springer.

Dansgaard, W., S. J. Johnsen, N. Reeh, N. Gundestrup, H. B. Clauser, and C. U. Hammer. 1975. Climatic changes, Norsemen, and modern man. *Nature* 255:24–28.

Dark, K. R. 1995. *Theoretical Archaeology.* Ithaca: Cornell University Press.

David, Nicholas, and Carol Kramer. 2001. *Ethnoarchaeology in Action.* New York: Cambridge University Press.

Davis, Simon. 1995. *The Archaeology of Animals.* New Haven: Yale University Press.

Day, S. P., and P. A. Mellars. 1994. Absolute dating of Mesolithic human activity at Star Carr, Yorkshire: New palaeoecological studies and identification of the 9600 BP radiocarbon 'plateau'. *Proceedings of the Prehistoric Society* 60:417–423.

De Atley, S. P., and R. L. Bishop. 1991. Toward an integrated interface for archaeology and archaeometry. In *The Ceramic Legacy of Anna O. Shepard,* edited by R. L. Bishop and F. W. Lange, 358–380. Niwot: University Press of Colorado.

de Roever, J. P. 2004. *Swifterbant-Aardewerk. Een analyse van de neolithische nederzettingen bij Swifterbant, 5e millennium voor Christus.* Groningen: Groningen Archaeological Studies 2.

Deagan, Kathleen, and Darcie MacMahon. 1995. *Fort Mose: Colonial America's Black Fortress of Freedom.*

Gainesville: University Press of Florida.

DeBoer, W. 1991. The decorative burden: Design, medium, and change. In *Ceramic Ethnoarchaeology,* edited by W. A. Longacre. Tucson: University of Arizona Press.

Deetz, James. 1965. *The Dynamics of Stylistic Change in Arikara Ceramics.* Illinois Studies in Anthropology No. 4. Urbana: University of Illinois Press.

———. 1967. *Invitation to Archaeology.* Garden City, N.Y.: Natural History Press.

Diaz-Andreu, M., and M. L. Sorenson, eds. 1998. *Excavating Women: A History of Women in European Archaeology.* London: Routledge.

Dimbleby, G. W. 1978. *Plants and Archaeology.* London: Paladin.

———. 1985. *The Palynology of Archaeological Sites.* Orlando: Academic Press.

Dincauze, D. F. 2000. *Environmental Archaeology.* Cambridge: Cambridge University Press.

———. 2002. *Environmental Archaeology, Principles and Practice.* Cambridge: Cambridge University Press.

Dixon, J. E., J. R. Cann, and Colin Renfrew. 1968. Obsidian and the origins of trade. *Scientific American* 218(3):38–46.

Dobres, M. A., and J. E. Robb, eds. 2000. *Agency in Archaeology.* London: Routledge.

Donnan, Christopher B. 1978. *Moche Art of Peru.* Los Angeles: UCLA Fowler Museum of Culture History.

———. Archaeology and looting: Preserving the record. *Science* 251:498.

———. 1995. Moche funerary practices. In *Tombs for the Living: Andean Mortuary Practices,* edited by T. Dillehay, 111–160. Washington, D.C.: Dumbarton Oaks.

Doran, Glen H., ed. 2002. *Windover: Multidisciplinary Investigations of an Early Archaic Florida Cemetery.* Gainesville: University Presses of Florida.

Doran, Glen H., David N. Dickel, William E. Ballinger, Jr., O. Frank

Agee, Philip J. Laipis, and William W. Hauswirth. 1986. Anatomical, cellular and molecular analysis of 8,000-yr-old human brain tissue from the Windover archaeological site. *Nature* 323(6091):803–806.

Dornan, Jennifer. 2002. Agency and archaeology: Past, present and future directions. *Journal of Archaeological Method and Theory* 9:303–329.

Downum, C. E. 1993. Southwestern archaeology: Past, present, and future. *Expedition: Magazine of Archaeology and Anthropology* 35(1):4–13.

Downum, C. E., and G. B. Brown. 1998. The reliability of surface artifact assemblages as predictors of subsurface remains: A case study from southern Arizona. In *Surface Archaeology*, edited by A. P. Sullivan, 111–123. Albuquerque: University of New Mexico Press.

Drake, R. E., and G. H. Curtis. 1979. Radioisotope dating of the Laetoli beds, the Hadar formation, and the Koobi Fora-Shungura formations. *American Journal of Physical Anthropology* 50:433–434.

Drennan, Robert D. 1996. *Statistics for Archaeologists.* New York: Plenum.

Duday, H., P. Courtaud, E. Crubezy, P. Sellier, and A. M. Tillier. 1990. L'anthropologie de "terrain": Reconnaissance et interpretation des gestes funeraires. *Bulletins et Memoires de la Société d'Anthropologie de Paris* 2(3–4):26–49.

Dugmore, Andrew J., Anthony J. Newton, Gurún Larsen, and Gordon T. Cook. 2000. Tephrochronology, environmental change and the Norse settlement of Iceland. *Environmental Archaeology* 5:21–34.

Dunnell, R. C. 1971. *Systematics in Prehistory.* New York: Free Press.

———. 1978. Style and function: A fundamental dichotomy. *American Antiquity* 43:192–202.

———. 1989. Aspects of the application of evolutionary theory in archaeology. In *Archaeological Thought in America*, edited by C. C. Lamberg-Karlovsky, 35–49. Cambridge: Cambridge University Press.

Earle, Tim. 1997. *How Chiefs Come to Power: The Political Economy in Prehistory.* Palo Alto: Stanford University Press.

Earle, T. K., and J. E. Ericson, eds. 1977. *Exchange Systems in Prehistory.* New York: Academic Press.

Earle, Tim, and A. Johnson. 2000. *The Evolution of Human Societies: From Forager Group to Agrarian State.* 2d ed. Palo Alto: Stanford University Press.

Earle, Timothy K., and Robert W. Preucel. 1987. Processual archaeology and the radical critique. *Current Anthropology* 28:501–538.

Ehmann, W. D., and D. E. Vance. 1991. *Radiochemistry and Nuclear Methods of Analysis.* New York: Wiley.

Eighmy, J. L., and R. S. Sternberg, eds. 1990. *Archaeomagnetic Dating.* Tucson: University of Arizona Press.

Engelstad, E. 1991. Images of power and contradiction: Feminist theory and post-processual archaeology. *Antiquity* 65:502–514.

England, P. A., and L. Van Zelst, eds. 1985. *Application of Science in Examination of Works of Art: Proceedings of the Seminar, September 7–9, 1983.* Boston: Research Laboratory, Museum of Fine Arts.

Erickson, Clark. 2003. Agricultural landscapes as world heritage: Raised field agriculture in Bolivia and Peru. In *Managing Change: Sustainable Approaches to the Conservation of the Built Environment*, edited by J. M. Teutonico and F. Matero, 181–204. Los Angeles: Getty Conservation Institute.

Evans, J., and T. O'Connor. 2001. *Environmental Archaeology, Principles and Method.* Stroud: Sutton.

Evans, Susan Toby. 2004. *Ancient Mexico and Central America: Archaeology and Culture History.* New York: Thames & Hudson.

Faegri, Knut, Johs. Iversen, Peter Emil Kaland, and Knut Krzywinski. 2000. *Textbook of Pollen Analysis.* 4th ed. 1950. Reprint, Caldwell, N.J.: Blackburn.

Fagan, B. M. 1994. *Quest for the Past: Great Discoveries in Archaeology.* Prospect Heights, Ill.: Waveland Press.

———. 2000 *Ancient North America: The Archaeology of a Continent.* 3rd ed. London:. Thames & Hudson.

———. 2003. *Archaeologists: Explorers of the Human Past.* Oxford University Press.

———. 1998, ed. *Eyewitness to Discovery: First-Person Accounts of More Than Fifty of the World's Greatest Archaeological Discoveries.* Oxford: Oxford University Press.

Falchetti, Ana María. 2003. The seed of life: The symbolic power of gold-copper alloys and metallurgical transformations. In *Gold and Power in Ancient Costa Rica, Panama, and Colombia*, edited by J. Quilter and J. W. Hoopes, 345–381. Washington, D.C.: Dumbarton Oaks Research Library and Collections.

Feder, K. 2005. *Frauds, Myths, and Mysteries: Science and Pseudoscience in Archaeology.* 5th ed. New York: McGraw-Hill.

Feinman, G., Steadman Upham, and Kent Lightfoot. 1981. The production step measure: An ordinal index of labor input in ceramic manufacture. *American Antiquity* 46:871–884.

Feinman, G. M., and J. Marcus, eds. 1998. *Archaic States.* Santa Fe: School of American Research Press.

Feinman, G. M., and T. D. Price. 2001. *Archaeology at the Millennium.* New York: Kluwer.

Ferguson, Leland. 1992. *Uncommon Ground: Archaeology and Early African America, 1650–1800.* Washington, D.C.: Smithsonian Institution Press.

Fergusson, T. J. 1996. Native Americans and the practice of archaeology. *Annual Review of Anthropology* 25:63–79.

Ferring, C. R. 2001. Geoarchaeology in alluvial landscapes. In *Earth Sciences and Archaeology*, edited by P. Goldberg, V. T. Holliday, and C. R. Ferring, 77–106. New York: Kluwer Academic/Plenum.

Fischer, J. L. 1961. Art styles as cultural cognitive maps. *American Anthropologist* 63:79–93.

Fisher, C., and T. Thurston, eds. 1999. Dynamic landscapes as socio-political process: The topography of anthropogenic environments in global perspective. *Antiquity* 73: 630ff.

Flannery, K. 1967. Culture history vs. culture process: A debate in American archaeology. *Scientific American* 217:119–122.

———. 1968. Archaeological systems theory and early Mesoamerica. In *Anthropological Archaeology in the Americas*, edited by B. J. Meggers, 67–87. Washington, D.C.: Anthropological Society of Washington.

———. 1972. The cultural evolution of civilization. *Annual Review of Ecology and Systematics* 3:399–426.

———. 1973. Archaeology with a capital "S." In *Research and Theory in Current Archaeology*, edited by C. Redman, 47–53. New York: Wiley.

———, 1982. Golden Marshalltown: A parable for the archeology of the 1980's. *American Anthropologist:* 84 (2):265–278.

———, ed. 1976. *The Early Mesoamerican Village.* New York: Academic Press.

Flannery, Kent, and Joyce Marcus. 1976. Formative Oaxaca and the Zapotec cosmos. *American Scientist* 64:374–387.

———. 1993. Cognitive archaeology. *Cambridge Journal of Archaeology* 3:260–270.

Fleming, S. J. 1979. *Thermoluminescence Techniques in Archaeology.* Oxford: Clarendon.

Ford, James A. 1952. *Measurements of Some Prehistoric Design Developments in the Southeastern States.* Anthropological Papers 44(3):313–384. New York: American Museum of Natural History.

———. 1954. The type concept revisited. *American Anthropologist* 56:42–53.

Foster, Rhonda, and Dale R. Croes. 2001. Archaeology/Anthropology— Native American coordination, an example of sharing the research. Paper presented at the American Anthropological Association, Washington, D.C.

———. 2004. Joint Tribal/College Wet Site Investigations—A Critical Need for Native American Expertise. *Journal of Wetland Archaeology* 4:127–139.

Fowler, Brenda. 2000. *Iceman: Uncovering the Life and Times of a Prehistoric Man Found in an Alpine Glacier.* New York: Random House.

Fowler, C. 2004. *The Archaeology of Personhood.* London: Routledge.

Fowler, Melvin L. 1978. Cahokia and the American Bottom: Settlement archaeology. In *Mississippian Settlement Patterns*, edited by B. Smith, 455–478.

Fox, Richard Allan. 1997. *Archaeology, History, and Custer's Last Battle: The Little Big Horn Reexamined.* Norman: University of Oklahoma Press.

France, D. L. 2001. *Lab Manual and Workbook for Physical Anthropology.* Belmont, Calif.: Wadsworth.

French, Charles. 2003. *Geoarchaeology in Action: Studies in Soil Micromorphology and Landscape Evolution.* London: Routledge.

Fricke, Henry C., James R. O'Neil, and Niels Lynnerup. 1995. Oxygen isotope composition of human tooth enamel from medieval Greenland: Linking climate and society. *Geology* 23:869–872.

Gaffney, V., and J. Gater. 2003. *Revealing the Buried Past: Geophysics for Archaeologists.* Stroud: Tempus.

Garanger, J. 1972. *Archéologie des Nouvelles-Hébrides, contribution à la connaissances des îles du centre.* Paris: Office de la Recherche Scientifique et Technique Outre-Mer.

Gardner, Andrew. 2004. *Agency Uncovered: Archaeological Perspectives on Social Agency, Power, and Being Human.* London: UCL Press

Garland, N., and R. Janaway. 1989. The taphonomy of inhumation burials. In *Burial Archaeology: Current Research, Methods and Developments*, edited by C. A. Roberts, F. Lee, and J. Bintliff, 14–38. London: University of London.

Gates, Charles. 2003. *Ancient Cities.* London: Routledge.

Gero, Joan. 1985. Socio-politics of archaeology and the woman-at-home ideology. *American Antiquity* 50:342–350.

Gero, Joan, and Margaret Conkey, eds. 1991. *Engendering Archaeology: Women and Prehistory.* Oxford: Basil Blackwell.

Gibbon, G. 1989. *Explanation in Archaeology.* Oxford: Basil Blackwell.

Gibson, Alex M., ed. 2003. *Prehistoric Pottery: People, Pattern and Purpose.* Oxford: Archaeopress.

Gibson, Alex M., and Ann Woods. 1997. *Prehistoric Pottery for the Archaeologist.* 2d ed. London: Leicester University Press.

Giddens, A. 1979. *Central Problems in Social Theory: Action, Structure, and Contradiction in Social Analysis.* Berkeley: University of California Press.

Gilbert, R. I., and J. H. Mielke, eds. 1985. *The Analysis of Prehistoric Diets.* Orlando: Academic Press.

Given, Michael. 2004. *Archaeology of the Colonized.* London: Routledge.

Glascock, M. D., and H. Neff. 2003. Neutron activation analysis and provenance research in archaeology. *Measurement Science and Technology* 14:1516–1526.

Glob, P. V. 1969. *The Bog People: Iron-Age Man Preserved.* Ithaca: Cornell University Press.

Goldberg, Paul. 2000. Micromorphological aspects of site formation at Keatley Creek. In *The Ancient Past of Keatley Creek*, vol. 1, edited by Brian Hayden, 79–95. Burnaby, B.C.: Archaeology Press.

Goldberg, Paul, M. A. Courty, R. I. Macphail. 1989. *Soils and Micromorphology in Archaeology.* Cambridge: Cambridge University Press.

Goldberg, Paul, V. T. Holliday, and C. Reid Ferring, eds. 2001. *Earth Sciences and Archaeology.* New York: Kluwer/Plenum.

Goldberg, Paul, M. Petraglia, and D. T. Nash, eds. 1993. *Formation Processes in Context.* Madison: Prehistory Press.

Goldstein, L., and Keith Kintigh. 1990. Ethics and the reburial controversy. *American Antiquity* 55:585–591.

Görür, N., M. N. Çağatay, Ö. Emre, B. Alpar, M. Sakınç, Y. İslamoğlu, O. Algan, T. Erkal, M. Keçer, R. Akkök, and G. Karlık, 2001. Is the abrupt drowning of the Black Sea shelf at 7150 yr BP a myth? *Marine Geology* 176:65–73.

Gosselain, O. P. 1992. Technology and style: Potters and pottery among Bafia of Cameroon. *Man* 27(3):559–586.

Gould, R. 1980. *Living Archaeology.* Cambridge: Cambridge University Press.

Grace, R. 1989. *Interpreting the Function of Stone Tools: The Quantification and Computerisation of Microwear Analysis.* Oxford: B.A.R.

———. 1990. The limitations and applications of functional analysis. In *The Interpretative Possibilities of Microwear Studies,* edited by B. Gräslund, H. Knutsson, K. Knutsson, and J. Taffinder. *Aun* 14:9–14.

Grant, A. 2004. The analysis of urban animal bones assemblages: A handbook for archaeologists. *International Journal of Osteoarchaeology* 14:481–482.

Grauer, Anne L., ed. 1995. *Bodies of Evidence: Reconstructing History through Skeletal Analysis.* New York: Wiley.

Grayson, Donald K. 1984. *Quantitative Zooarchaeology: Topics in the Analysis of Archaeological Faunas.* Orlando: Academic Press.

Green, E. L., ed. 1984. *Ethics and Values in Archaeology.* New York: Free Press.

Greene, D. L., D. P. Van Gerven, and G. J. Armelagos. 1986. Life and death in ancient populations: Bones of contention in paleodemography. *Human Evolution* 1:193–207.

Greene, Kevin. 2002. *Archaeology: An Introduction.* 4th ed. London: Routledge.

Greenfield, Jeanette. 1996. *The Return of Cultural Treasures.* New York: Cambridge University Press.

Grupe, G., and J. Peters. 2003. *Deciphering Ancient Bones.* Rahden, Germany: Marie Leidorf.

Haglund, William D., and Marcella H. Sorg, eds. 1997. *Forensic Taphonomy: The Postmortem Fate of Human Remains.* Boca Raton, Fla.: CRC Press.

Hall, Martin, and Stephen Silliman. 2006. *Historical Archaeology.* Oxford: Blackwell Publishing.

Hanson, Julie. 1994. Beyond the site: Palaeoethnobotany in regional perspective. In *Beyond the Site in the Aegean Area,* edited by N. Kardulias, 173–190. Lanham, Md.: University Press of America.

Hardesty, Donald L., and Barbara J. Little. 2000. *Assessing Site Significance: A Guide for Archaeologists and Historians.* Walnut Creek, Calif.: Alta Mira.

Hardin, Margaret Friedrich. 1970. Design structure and social interaction: Archeological implications of an ethnographic analysis. *American Antiquity* 35.

———. 1977. Individual style in San Jose pottery painting: The role of deliberate choice. In *The Individual in Prehistory,* edited by J. Hill and J. Gunn, 109–136. New York: Academic Press.

———. 2000. The social and historical context of short-term stylistic replacement: A Zuni case study. *Journal of Archaeological Method and Theory* 8(3).

Harlan, J. R. 1967. A wild wheat harvest in Turkey. *Archaeology* 20:197–201.

Harrington, J. C. 1954. Dating stem fragments of seventeenth and eighteenth century clay tobacco pipes. *Quarterly Bulletin: Archaeological Society of Virginia* 9(1).

Harris, E. C. 1989. *Principles of Archaeological Stratigraphy.* 2d ed. London: Academic Press.

Harris, E. C., M. R. Brown, and G. J. Brown, eds. 1993. *Practices of Archaeological Stratigraphy.* London: Academic Press.

Hassan, F. 1981. *Demographic Archaeology.* London: Academic Press.

Hastorf, Christine. 1998. The cultural life of early domestic plant use. *Antiquity* 72:773–782.

———. 1999. Recent research and innovations in paleoethnobotany. *Journal of Archaeological Research* 7:55–103.

Hastorf, C. A., and V. S. Popper, eds. 1988. *Current Paleoethnobotany, Analytical Methods and Cultural Interpretations of Plant Remains.* Chicago: University of Chicago Press.

Hather, Jonathan G. 1991. The identification of charred archaeological remains of vegetative parenchymous tissue. *Journal of Archaeological Science* 18:661–675.

———. 1993. *An Archaeobotanical Guide to Root and Tuber Identification.* Oxford: Oxbow Books.

Hather, Jonathan G., and Patrick V. Kirch. 1991. Prehistoric sweet potato (*Ipomoea batatas*) from Mangaia Island, Central Polynesia. *Antiquity* 65:887–893.

Haviland, W. A. 1967. Stature at Tikal, Guatemala: Implications for ancient demography and social organization. *American Antiquity* 32:316–325.

Hawkes, C. F. C. 1954. Archaeological theory and method: Some suggestions from the Old World. *American Anthropologist* 56:155–168.

Hayden, B. 1984. Are emic types relevant to archaeology? *Ethnohistory* 29(4).

———. 1997. *The Pithouses of Keatley Creek.* New York: Harcourt, Brace.

———. 1998. Practical and prestige technologies: The evolution of material systems. *Journal of Archaeological Method and Theory* 5:1–55.

———, ed. 2000. *The Ancient Past of Keatley Creek.* Burnaby, B.C.: Archaeology Press.

Heath, Barbara. 1999. Buttons, beads and buckles: Self-definition within the bonds of slavery. In *Historical Archaeology, Identity Formation and the Interpretation of Ethnicity,* edited by Maria Franklin and Garrett R. Fesler, 47–68. Colonial Williamsburg Research Publications, Dietz Press, Richmond.

———. 1999. *Hidden Lives: The Archaeology of Slave Life at Thomas Jefferson's Poplar Forest.* Charlottesville: University of Virginia Press.

Hegmon, M. 1992. Archaeological research on style. *Annual Review of Anthropology* 21:517–536

———. 1998. Technology, style and social practices: Archaeological approaches. In *The Archaeology of Social Boundaries,* edited by M. T. Stark, 264–279. Washington, D.C.: Smithsonian Institution Press.

Heizer, R. F., and L. K. Napton. 1969. Biological and cultural evidence from prehistoric human coprolites. *Science* 165(893):563–568.

Henderson, J. 1987. Factors determining the state of preservation of human remains. In *Death, Decay and Reconstruction: Approaches to archaeology and forensic science,* edited by A. Boddington, N. A. Garland, and R. C. Janaway, 43–54. Manchester: Manchester University Press.

———. 2000. *The Science and Archaeology of Materials: An Investigation of Inorganic Materials.* London: Routledge.

Henshilwood, C. S., F. d'Errico, R. Yates, Z. Jacobs, C. Tribolo, G. A. T. Duller, N. Mercier, J. C. Sealy, H. Valladas, I. Watts, and A. Wintle. 2002. Emergence of modern human behaviour: Middle Stone Age engravings from South Africa. *Science* 295:1278–1280.

Hermann, B., and S. Hummel, eds. 1994. *Ancient DNA: Recovery and Analysis of Genetic Material from Paleontological, Archaeological, Museum, Medical, and Forensic Specimens.* New York: Springer.

Heron, C., E. P. Evershed, L. J. Goad, and V. Denham. 1990. New approaches to the analysis of organic residues from archaeological ceramics. In *Archaeological Sciences 1989,* edited by P. Budd, B. Chapman, C. Jackson, R. Janaway, and B. Ottaway, 332–339. Oxbow Monograph. Oxford: Oxbow.

Hesse, Brian, and Paula Wapnish. 1985. *Animal Bone Archeology: From Objectives to Analysis.* Washington, D.C.: Taraxacum.

Hill, James, and Robert K. Evans. 1972. A model of classification and typology. In *Models in Archaeology,* edited by David L. Clarke, 231–273. London: Methuen.

Hill, K., H. Kaplan, K. Hawkes, and A. Hurtado. 1987. Foraging decisions among Ache hunter-gatherers: New data and implications for optimal foraging models. *Ethology and Sociobiology* 8:1–36.

Hillam, J. 1995. Theoretical and applied dendrochronology: How to make a date with a tree. In *The Archaeologist and the Laboratory,* edited by P. Phillips, 17–23. London: Council of British Archaeology.

Hillman, G. C. 1981. Reconstructing crop husbandry practices from charred remains of crops. In *Farming Practices in British Prehistory,* edited by R. Mercer, 123–162. Edinburgh: Edinburgh University Press.

Hoadley, R. Bruce. 1990. *Identifying Wood: Accurate Results with Simple Tools.* Newtown, Conn.: Taunton Press.

Hodder, I. 1982. *The Present Past: An Introduction to Anthropology for Archaeologists.* New York: Pica Press.

———. 1985. Postprocessual archaeology. *Advances in Archaeological Method and Theory* 8:1–26.

———. 1992. *Theory and Practice in Archaeology.* London: Routledge.

———. 1995. *Theory and Practice in Archaeology.* London: Routledge.

———, ed. 2001. *Archaeological Theory Today.* Cambridge: Polity Press.

Hodder, I., M. Shanks, A. Alexandri, V. Buchli, J. Carman, J. Last, and G. Lucas, eds. 1995. *Interpreting Archaeology: Finding Meaning in the Past.* London: Routledge.

Hoffman, Brian. 2001. The organization of complexity: A study of late prehistoric village organization in the Eastern Aleutian region. Ph.D. diss., University of Wisconsin-Madison.

Hofman, J. L., and J. Enloe, eds. 1992. *Piecing Together the Past; Applications of Refitting Studies in Archaeology.* Oxford: British Archaeological Reports.

Holliday, V. T. 2004. *Soils in Archaeological Research.* New York: Oxford University Press.

Horne, Lee. 1998. Ur and its treasures: The Royal Tombs. *Expedition Magazine* 40, no. 2.

Hosler, D., J. A. Sabloff, and D. Runge. 1977. Simulation model development: A case study of the Classic Maya collapse. In *Social Processes in Maya Prehistory,* edited by N. Hammond, 552–590. London: Academic Press.

Hughes, M. K., and H. F. Diaz. 1994. Was there a "Medieval Warm Period" and if so, when and where? *Climatic Change* 26:109–142.

Hummel, Susanne. 2003. *Ancient DNA Typing: Methods, Strategies, and Applications.* New York: Springer.

Hummert, J. R., and D. P. Van Gerven. 1985. Observations on the formation and persistence of radiopaque transverse lines. *American Journal of Physical Anthropology* 66:297–306.

Huntley, B., and J. B. Birks. 1983. *An Atlas of Past and Present Pollen Maps for Europe 0–13,000 Years Ago.* Cambridge: Cambridge University Press.

Hurt, Teresa D., and Gordon F. M. Rakita, eds. 2001. *Style and Function: Conceptual Issues in Evolutionary Archaeology.* Westport, Conn.: Bergin & Garvey.

Huss-Ashmore, R., A. Goodman, and G. T. Armelagos. 1982. Nutritional inference from paleopathology. In *Advances in Archaeological Method and Theory,* edited by M. Schiffer, 5:395–474. New York: Academic Press.

Hutchinson, Dale L., and Clark Spencer Larsen. 1990. Stress and lifeway change on the Georgia Coast: The evidence from enamel hypoplasias. In *The Archaeology of Mission Santa Catalina de Guale: 2. Biocultural Interpretations of a Population in Transition,* edited by Clark Spencer Larsen, 50–65, Anthropological Papers of the American Museum of Natural History, vol. 68.

Insoll, T. 2004. *Archaeology, Ritual, Religion.* London: Routledge.

Isçan, M. Y. 1989. *Age Markers in the Human Skeleton*. Springfield, Ill.: Charles C. Thomas.

Isçan, M. Y., and K. A. R. Kennedy, eds. 1989. *Reconstruction of Life from the Skeleton*. New York: Liss.

James, P., and N. Thorpe. 1994. *Ancient Inventions*. New York: Ballantine Books.

Jane, F. W. 1970. *The Structure of Wood*. 2d ed. London: Adam & Charles Black.

Jeffries, Richard W. 1987. *The Archaeology of Carrier Mills: 10,000 Years in the Saline Valley of Illinois*. Carbondale: Southern Illinois University Press.

Jeffries, Richard W., and Brian M. Butler, eds. 1982. *The Carrier Mills Archaeological Project: Human Adaptation in the Saline Valley, Illinois*. Research paper, no. 33, Center for Archaeological Investigations. Carbondale, Ill.: Southern Illinois University.

Johansen, K. L., S. T. Laursen, and M. K. Holst. 2004. Spatial patterns of social organization in the Early Bronze Age of South Scandinavia. *Journal of Anthropological Archaeology* 23:33–55.

Johnson, G. A. 1973. *Local Exchange and Early State Development in Southwestern Iran*. Ann Arbor: University of Michigan Museum of Anthropology papers, no 51.

———. 1977. Aspects of regional analysis in archaeology. *Annual Review of Anthropology* 6:479–508.

Johnson, Matthew. 1999. *Archaeological Theory: An Introduction*. Oxford: Blackwell.

Johnston, Francis E., and Louise O. Zimmer. 1989. Assessment of growth and age in the immature skeleton. In *Reconstruction of Life from the Skeleton*, edited by Mehmet Yaşar Işcan and Kenneth A. R. Kennedy, 11–21. New York: Wiley-Liss.

Jones, Andrew. 2002. *Archaeological Theory and Scientific Practice*. Cambridge: Cambridge University Press.

Jones, G. 1986. *The Norse Atlantic Saga*. 2d ed. Oxford: Oxford University Press.

Jones, Martin. 2003. *The Molecule Hunt: Archaeology and the Search for Ancient DNA*. New York: Arcade Publishing.

Jones, S. 1997. *The Archaeology of Ethnicity: Constructing Identities in the Past*. London: Routledge.

Joyce, Rosemary. 2001. *Gender and Power in Prehispanic Mesoamerica*. Austin: University of Texas Press.

Juel Jensen, H. 1988. Functional analysis of prehistoric flint tools by high-power microscopy: A review of West European research. *Journal of World Prehistory* 2:53–88.

Kardulias, P. Nick, and Richard W. Yerkes. 2003. *Written in Stone: The Multiple Dimensions of Lithic Analysis*. Lanham, MD: Rowman & Littlefield.

Karsten, P., and B. Knarrström. 2003. *The Tågerup Excavations*. Lund: Riksantikvarieämbetet.

Katzenberg, M. A., and R. G. Harrison. 1997. What's in a bone? Recent advances in archaeological bone chemistry. *Journal of Archaeological Research* 5:265–293.

Keeley, L. H. 1977. The function of Palaeolithic flint tools. *Scientific American* 237:108–126.

———. 1980. *Experimental Determination of Stone Tool Use: A Microwear Analysis*. Chicago: University of Chicago Press.

———. 1982. Hafting and retooling: Effects on the archaeological record. *American Antiquity* 47:798–809.

Kelly, R. L. 1988. The three sides of a biface. *American Antiquity* 53:717–734.

Kelly, Robert L. 1992. Mobility/sedentism: Concepts, archaeological measures, and effects. *Annual Review of Anthropology* 21:43–66.

———. 1995. *The Foraging Spectrum*. Washington, D.C.: Smithsonian Institution Press.

Kelly, R. L., and M. Prasciunas. 2004. Did the ancestors of Native Americans cause animal extinctions in Late Pleistocene North America? In *Reconsidering the Ecological Indian*, edited by M. E. Harkin and D. R. Lewis. Lincoln: University of Nebraska Press.

Kennett, D. J. 1996. Seasonality studies. In *The Oxford Companion to Archaeology*, edited by Brian Fagan, 631–632. New York: Oxford University Press.

Kenyon, Ian T., and P. A. Lennox. 1996. Missing the Point: A consideration of small sites archaeology. Proceedings of the 1996 OAS Symposium, Kingston, Ontario, Canada.

King, T. F. 1998. *Cultural Resource Laws and Practice: An Introductory Guide*. Walnut Creek, Calif.: AltaMira.

———. 2000. *Federal Planning and Historical Places: The Section 106 Process*. Walnut Creek, Calif.: AltaMira.

———. 2002. *Thinking about Cultural Resource Management: Essays from the Edge*. Lanham, Md.: Rowman & Littlefield.

Kirkpatrick, Sidney D. 1992. *Lords of Sipán: A True Story of Pre-Inca Tombs, Archaeology, and Crime*. New York: William Morrow and Company.

Klein, Richard G., and Kathryn Cruz-Uribe. 1984. *The Analysis of Animal Bones from Archaeological Sites*. Prehistoric Archaeology and Ecology series. Chicago: University of Chicago Press.

Klein, R. G. 1999. *The Human Career: Human Biological and Cultural Origins*. 2d ed. Chicago: University of Chicago Press.

Knapp, B. 1996. Archaeology without gravity: Postmodernism and the past. *Journal of Archaeological Method and Theory* 3:127–158.

Koetje, Todd. 1999. Unit issues in archaeology: Measuring time, space, and material. *American Antiquity* 64:373–375.

Kohl, Philip L. 1985. Symbolic cognitive archaeology: A new loss of innocence. *Dialectical Anthropology* 9:105–117.

———. 1993. Limits to a post-processual archaeology (or, the dangers of a new scholasticism). In *Archaeological Theory: Who Sets the Agenda?*, edited by N. Yoffee and A. Sherratt, 13–19. Cambridge: Cambridge University Press.

Kohl, P. L., and C. Fawcett, eds. 1995. *Nationalism, Politics, and the Practice of Archaeology.* Cambridge: Cambridge University Press.

Kohler, Timothy A., and George J. Gummerman, eds. 2000. *Dynamics in Human and Primate Societies: Agent-Based Modeling of Social and Spatial Processes.* Oxford: Oxford University Press.

Kolata, Alan. 1993. *The Tiwanaku: Portrait of an Andean Civilization.* Cambridge: Blackwell.

Konigsberg, L. W., and S. R. Frankenberg. 1992. Estimation of age structure in anthropological demography. *American Journal of Physical Anthropology* 89:235–256.

———. 1994. Paleodemography: "Not Quite Dead." *Evolutionary Anthropology* 3:92–105.

Kooyman, B. P. 2000. *Understanding Stone Tools and Archaeological Sites.* Albuquerque: University of New Mexico Press.

Kosso, Peter. 2001. *Knowing the Past: Philosophical Issues of History and Archaeology.* Amherst, N.Y.: Humanity Press.

Kraft, John C., Ilhan Kayan, and Oguz Erol. 1980. Geomorphic reconstructions in the environs of ancient Troy. *Science* 209:776–782.

Kraft, John C., George (Rip) Rapp, Ilhan Kayan, and John V. Luce. 2003. Harbor areas at ancient Troy: Sedimentology and geomorphology complement Homer's *Illiad. Geology* 31:163–166.

Krieger, A. D. 1944. The typological concept. *American Antiquity* 9:271–288.

Krogman, Wilton Marion, and Mehemet Yaşar Işcan. 1986. *The Human Skeleton in Forensic Medicine.* Springfield, Ill.: Charles C. Thomas.

Kruger, P. 1971. *Principles of Activation Analysis.* New York: Wiley-Interscience.

Kuijt, I. 2001. Reconsidering the "cause" of cultural collapse in the Lillooet area of British Columbia, Canada: A geoarchaeological perspective. *American Antiquity* 66:692–703.

Kus, S. 1997. Archaeologist as anthropologist: Much ado about something

after all? *Journal of Archaeological Method and Theory* 4:199–213.

Lamberg-Karlovsky, C. C., ed. 1989. *Archaeological Thought in America.* Cambridge: Cambridge University Press.

Lambert, J. 1997. *Traces of the Past: Unraveling the Secrets of Archaeology through Chemistry.* New York: Addison Wesley Longman.

Larsen, C. S. 1987. Bioarchaeological interpretations of subsistence economy and behavior from human skeletal remains. In *Advances in Archaeological Method and Theory,* vol. 10, edited by Michael B. Schiffer, 339–445. San Diego: Academic Press.

———. 1997. *Bioarchaeology: Interpreting Behavior from the Human Skeleton.* Cambridge: Cambridge University Press.

———. 2000. *Skeletons in Our Closet: Revealing Our Past through Bioarchaeology.* Princeton: Princeton University Press.

Larson, Daniel. 1995. Population growth, agricultural intensification, and culture change among the virgin branch Anasazi. *Journal of Field Archaeology* 22:1–22.

Leach, E. K. 1992. On the definition of geoarchaeology. *Geoarchaeology* 7:405–417.

LeBlanc, S. 1971. An addition to Naroll's suggested floor area and settlement population relationship. *American Antiquity* 36:210–211.

Lechtman, Heather, A. Erly, and E. J. Barry, Jr. 1982. New perspectives on Moche metallurgy: Techniques of gilding copper at Loma Negra, Northern Peru. *American Antiquity* 47:3–30.

Legge, A. J., and Rowley-Conwy, P. A. 1988. *Star Carr Revisited.* London: Centre for Extra Mural Studies.

Lennox, P. A. 1986. The Innes site: A plow disturbed Archaic component, Brant County, Ontario. *Midcontinental Journal of Archaeology* 11(2):221–268.

Leone, Mark. 1982. Some opinions about recovering mind. *American Antiquity* 47:742–760.

———. 1986. Symbolic, structural, and critical archaeology. In *American Archaeology Past and Future,* edited by D. J. Meltzer, D. D. Fowler, and J. A. Sabloff. Washington, D.C.: Smithsonian Institution.

Leone, Mark, Parker Potter, and Paul Shackel. 1987. Toward a critical archaeology. *Current Anthropology* 28:283–302.

Lewin, R. 1998. *Principles of Human Evolution.* Malden, Mass.: Blackwell.

Lewis, B. 1986. The analysis of contingency tables in archaeology. *Archaeological Method and Theory* 9:277–310. New York: Academic Press.

Lewis, R. Barry, and Charles Stout, eds. 1998. *Mississippian Towns and Sacred Spaces: Searching for an Architectural Grammar.* Tuscaloosa: University of Alabama Press.

Lewis-Williams, J. D. 1983. *The Rock Art of Southern Africa.* Cambridge: Cambridge University Press.

———. 2002. *The Mind in the Cave: Consciousness and the Origins of Art.* New York: Thames & Hudson.

Lieberman, D. E. 1993. Life history variables preserved in dental cementum microstructure. *Science* 261:1162–1164.

———. 1993. The rise and fall of seasonal mobility among hunter-gatherers: The case for the southern Levant. *Current Anthropology* 34:599–632.

Lightfoot, R. R. 1994. Household organization. In *The Duckfoot Site Volume 2: Archaeology of the House and Household,* 145–171. Occasional Papers, no. 4. Cortez, Colo.: Crow Canyon Archaeological Center.

Lindsay, Alexander J., and Calvin H. Jennings, eds. 1968. *Salado Red Ware Conference: Ninth Southwestern Ceramic Seminar.* Flagstaff: Museum of Northern Arizona.

Little, Barbara J. 2002. *Public Benefits of Archaeology.* Gainesville: University Press of Florida.

Lock, Gary. 2003. *Using Computers in Archaeology: Towards Virtual Pasts.* London: Routledge.

Lomborg, Ebbe, 1973. The flint daggers of Denmark. *Norwegian Archaeological Review* 8/2. Oslo.

Longacre, W. A. 1985. Pottery use-life among the Kalinga, Northern Luzon, the Philippines. In *Decoding Prehistoric Ceramics*, edited by B. A. Nelson, 334–346. Carbondale: Southern Illinois University Press

Longacre, W. A., Kenneth L. Kvamme, and Masashi Kobayashi. Southwestern pottery standardization: An ethnoarchaeological view from the Philippines. *The Kiva* 53:101–112.

Lowe, John. 1985. *The Dynamics of Collapse: A Systems Simulation of the Classic Maya.* Albuquerque: University of New Mexico Press.

Loy, T. H. 1994. Methods in the analysis of starch residues on prehistoric stone tools. In *Tropical Archaeobotany*, edited by Jon G. Hather, 86–114. London: Routledge.

Lucas, Gavin. 2005. *The Archaeology of Time.* London: Routledge.

Lucy, D., A. M. Pollard, and C. A. Roberts. 1995. A comparison of three dental techniques for estimating age of death in humans. *Journal of Archaeological Science* 22:417–428.

Lyman, R. Lee. 1994. *Vertebrate Taphonomy.* Cambridge Manuals in Archaeology. Cambridge: Cambridge University Press.

Lynott, M. J., and A. Wylie. 1995. *Ethics in American Archaeology: Challenges for the 1990s.* Washington, D.C.: Society for American Archaeology.

Macauley, Rose. 1953. *The Pleasure of Ruins.* London: Weidenfeld and Nicolson.

MacGregor, A. 1985. *Bone, Antler, Ivory, and Horn Technology.* London: Croom Helm.

Manzanilla, Linda. 1996. Corporate groups and domestic activities at Teotihuacan. *Latin American Antiquity* 7:228–246.

Manzanilla, Linda, and Luis Barba. 1990. The study of activities in classic households: Two case studies from Coba and Teotihuacan. *Ancient Mesoamerica* 1:41–49.

Marcus, Joyce, and Kent V. Flannery. 2004. The coevolution of ritual and society: New ^{14}C dates from ancient Mexico. *Proceedings of the National Academy of Sciences* 101:18257–18261.

Maruyama, Magoroh. 1963. The second cybernetics: Deviation-amplifying, mutual causal processes. *American Scientist* 51:164–179.

Maschner, H. D. G., ed. 1996. *Darwinian Archaeologies.* New York: Plenum.

Masson, Marilyn A., and David Freidel, eds. 2002. *Ancient Maya Political Economies.* Walnut Creek, Calif.: AltaMira.

Matson, F. R., ed. 1965. *Ceramics and Man.* Chicago: Aldine.

Matthews, W., C. A. I. French, T. Lawrence, D. F. Cutler, and M. K. Jones. 1997. Microstratigraphic traces of site formation processes and human activities. *World Archaeology* 29:281–308.

Mays, Simon. 1998. *The Archaeology of Human Bones.* London: Routledge.

McBryde, I., ed. 1985. *Who Owns the Past?* Papers from the Annual Symposium of the Australian Academy of the Humanities. Melbourne and New York: Oxford University Press.

McCoy, F., and G. Heiken, eds., 2000. *Volcanic Hazards and Disasters in Human Antiquity.* Special Paper 345. Boulder, Colo.: Geological Society of America.

McDougall, I. 1995. Potassium-argon dating in the Pleistocene. In *Dating Methods for Quaternary Deposits*, edited by N. W. Rutter and N. R. Catto, 1–14. Ottawa: Geological Association of Canada.

McEvedy, C., and R. Jones. 1978. *Atlas of world population history.* Harmondsworth: Penguin.

McGovern, P. 1995. Science in archaeology: A review. *American Journal of Archaeology* 99:79–142.

McGovern, Thomas H., and Sophia Perdikaris. 2000. The Vikings' silent saga: What went wrong with the Scandinavian westward expansion? *Natural History Magazine* October: 51–59.

McGuire, R. H. 1992. *A Marxist Archaeology.* San Diego: Academic Press.

McIntosh, Jane. *The Practical Archaeologist: How We Know What We Know about the Past.* 2d ed. 1999. New York: Facts on File.

Mckillop, Heather. 2004. *The Ancient Maya.* Santa Barbara: ABC-Clio Publisher.

McPherron, Shannon, and Harold L. Dibble. 2002. *Using Computers in Archaeology: A Practical Guide.* New York: McGraw-Hill.

Mellars, P., and P. Dark, eds., 1998. *Star Carr in Context.* Cambridge: Macdonald Institute for Archaeological Research.

Meltzer, D. J., D. D. Fowler, and J. A. Sabloff, eds. 1986. *American Archaeology: Past and Future.* Washington, D.C.: Smithsonian Institution Press.

Menotti, Francesco, ed. 2004. *Living on the Lake in Prehistoric Europe.* London: Routledge.

Merriman, N., ed. 2003. *Public Archaeology.* New York: Routledge.

Meskell, Lynn. 1998. An archaeology of social relations in an Egyptian village. *Journal of Archaeological Method and Theory* 5:209–243.

———. 1999. *Archaeologies of Social Life: Age, Sex, Class, Etcetera in Ancient Egypt.* Oxford: Blackwell.

Meskell, Lynn, and Peter Pels. 2004. *Ethical Locations: Anthropological Moralities on the Boundaries of the Public and the Professional.* Oxford: Berg.

Messenger, P. M., ed. 1999. *The Ethics of Collecting Cultural Property: Whose Culture? Whose Property?* 2d ed. Albuquerque: University of New Mexico Press.

Meunier, Jean D., and Fabrice Colin, eds. 2001. *Phytoliths: Applications in Earth Sciences and Human History.* Lisse (Netherlands): A. A. Balkema Publishers.

Michels, Joseph W., and Ignatius S. T. Tsong. 1980. Obsidian hydration dating: A coming of age. In *Advances in Archaeological Method and Theory*, vol. 3, edited by M. B. Schiffer, 405–444. New York: Academic Press.

Mills, B. J. 1989. Integrating functional analyses of vessels and sherds through models of ceramic assemblage formation. *World Archaeology* 21:133–147.

Milner, G. R., 2004. *The Moundbuilders: Ancient Peoples of Eastern North America.* London: Thames & Hudson.

Milner, G. R., J. W. Wood, and J. L. Boldsen. 2000. Paleodemography. In *Biological Anthropology of the Human Skeleton,* edited by S. R. Saunders and M. A. Katzenberg, 467–497. New York: Wiley-Liss.

Mithen, Steven J. 1996. *The Prehistory of the Mind: The Cognitive Origins of Art, Religion, and Science.* Cambridge: Cambridge University Press.

Molleson, T. 1994. The eloquent bones of Abu Hureyra. *Scientific American* 271(2):70–75.

Monks, G. G. 1981. Seasonality studies. *Advances in Archaeological Method and Theory* 4:177–240.

Moore, A. M. T., G. C. Hillman, and A. J. Legge. 2000. *Village on the Euphrates.* London and New York: Oxford University Press.

Moore, P. D., J. Webb, and M. C. Collinson. 1991. *Pollen Analysis.* Oxford: Blackwell.

Morrow, T. A. 1996. Lithic refitting and archaeological site formation processes. In *Stone Tools,* edited by G. H. Odell, 345–373.

Moseley, M. E. 1992. *The Incas and Their Ancestors: The Archaeology of Peru.* New York: Thames & Hudson.

Murowchick, R. E., ed. 1994. *China: Ancient Culture, Modern Land.* Cradles of Civilization series. Norman: University of Oklahoma Press.

Nagaoka, Lisa. 2002. The effects of resource depression on foraging efficiency, diet breadth, and patch use in southern New Zealand. *Journal of Anthropological Archaeology* 21:419–442.

Napton, L. K. 1970. *Archaeological Investigations at Lovelock Cave, Nevada.* Unpublished Ph.D. diss. University of California-Berkeley.

Naroll, R. 1962. Floor area and settlement population. *American Antiquity* 27:587–589.

Nash, D.T., and M. Petraglia, eds. 1987. *Natural Formation Processes and the Archaeological Record.* Oxford: British Archaeological Reports 352.

Nash, Stephen Edward, ed. 2000. *It's About Time: A History of Archaeological Dating in North America.* Salt Lake City: University of Utah Press.

Neiman, Fraser D. 1995. Stylistic variation in evolutionary perspective: Inferences from decorative diversity and interassemblage distance in Illinois Woodland ceramic assemblages. *American Antiquity* 60:1–37.

Nelson, Ben, ed. 1985. Decoding prehistoric ceramics. Carbondale: Southern Illinois University Press.

Neumann, Thomas N., and Robert M. Sanford. 2001. *Cultural Resources Archaeology.* London: Rowman & Littlefield.

———. 2001. *Practicing Archaeology.* Walnut Creek, Calif.: AltaMira.

Newcomer, M. H., R. Grace, and R. Unger-Hamilton. 1986. Investigating microwear polishes with blind tests. *Journal of Archaeological Science* 13:203–217.

Newsom, L.A. 2002. Windover paleoethnobotany. In *Multidisciplinary Investigations of an Archaic Cemetery: Windover, Florida,* edited by G. Doran. Gainesville: University Presses of Florida.

O'Brien, M. J., ed. 1996. *Evolutionary Archaeology: Theory and Application.* Salt Lake City: University of Utah Press.

O'Brien, Michael J., and R. Lee Lyman. 1999. *Seriation, Stratigraphy, and Index Fossils: The Backbone of Archaeological Dating.* New York: Kluwer Academic/Plenum.

O'Connor, Terry. 2000. *The Archaeology of Animal Bones.* College Station: Texas A&M University Press.

Oddy, Andrew, ed. 1992. *The Art of the Conservator.* Washington, D.C.: Smithsonian Institution Press.

Odell, George H. 2004. *Lithic Analysis.* New York: Kluwer.

Olin, J. S., and A. D. Franklin, eds. 1982. *Archaeological Ceramics.* Washington, D.C.: Smithsonian Institution Press.

Olson, S. 2002. *Mapping Human History: Discovering the Past through Our Genes.* Boston: Houghton Mifflin.

Orser, C. E., and B. Fagan. 1995. *Historical Archaeology.* New York: Harper-Collins.

Ortiz Díaz, Edith. 2003. Activity areas and domestic cult contexts in Oztoyahualco, Teotihuacan. *Internet Journal for Teotihuacan Archaeology and Iconography.* Notes I–4.

Ortner, Donald J., and Walter G. Putschar. 1985. *Identification of Pathological Conditions in Human Skeletal Remains.* Washington, D.C.: Smithsonian Institution Press.

Orton, C., P. Tyers, and A. Vince. 1993. *Pottery in Archaeology.* Cambridge: Cambridge University Press.

O'Shea, John M. 1984. *Mortuary Variability: An Archaeological Investigation.* Orlando: Academic Press.

Pääbo, S. 1993. Ancient DNA: Genetic information that had seemed lost forever turns out to linger in the remains of long-dead plants and animals. *Scientific American* 1993:87–92.

Paine, R. R., ed. 1997. *Integrating Archaeological Demography: Multidisciplinary Approaches to Prehistoric Population.* Occasional Paper, no. 24. Carbondale, Ill.: Center for Archaeological Investigations, Southern Illinois University.

Parkes, P. A. 1986. *Current Scientific Techniques in Archaeology.* New York: St. Martin's Press.

Parry, W. J., and R. L. Kelly. 1987. Expedient core technology and sedentism. In *The Organization of Core Technology,* edited by J. K. Johnson and C. A. Marrow, 285–304. Boulder, Colo.: Westview Press.

Pate, F. D. 1994. Bone chemistry and paleodiet. *Journal of Archaeological Method and Theory* 1:161–209.

Patterson, Thomas C. 1995. *Toward a Social History of Archaeology in the United States.* Fort Worth: Harcourt Brace.

Pauketat, Tim. 2001. Practice and history in archaeology: An emerging paradigm. *Anthropological Theory* 1:73–98.

Pearsall, Deborah M. 2000. *Paleoethno-botany. A Handbook of Procedures.* 2d ed. San Diego: Academic Press.

Pearsall, Deborah M., and Dolores R. Piperno, eds. 1993. *Current Research in Phytolith Analysis: Applications in Archaeology and Paleoecology.* Philadelphia: University of Pennsylvania Museum.

Peebles, Christopher, and Susan Kus. 1977. Some archaeological correlates of ranked societies. *American Antiquity* 42:421–448.

Peglar, S. M., and H. J. B. Birks. 1993. The mid-Holocene *Ulmus* fall at Diss Mere, south-east England: Disease and human impact? *Vegetation History and Archaeobotany* 2:61–68.

Pelegrin, Jacques. 1990. Prehistoric lithic technology: Some aspects of research. *Cambridge Archaeological Review* 9:116–125.

Peregrine, Peter N. 2001. *Archaeological Research: A Brief Introduction.* Upper Saddle River, NJ: Prentice Hall.

Peregrine, Peter N., and Melvin Ember, eds. 2003. *Encyclopedia of Prehistory.* New York: Springer.

Petersen, W. 1975. A demographer's view of prehistoric demography. *Current Anthropology* 16:227–245.

Petrequin, Pierre, and Rose-Marie Arbogast. 1998. Demographic growth, environmental changes, and technical adaptations: Responses of an agricultural community from the 32nd to the 30th centuries BC. *World Archaeology* 30:181–192.

Piperno, Dolores R. 1988. *Phytolith Analysis: An Archaeological and Geological Perspective.* San Diego: Academic Press.

———. 2006. Phytoliths: A Comprehensive Guide for Archaeologists and Paleocologists. Lanham, Md.: AltaMira Press.

Pitman, Walter C., and William B. F. Ryan. 1998. *Noah's Flood: The New Scientific Discoveries about the Event That Changed History.* New York: Simon & Schuster.

Plog, Stephen. 1980. *Stylistic Variation in Prehistoric Ceramics.* Cambridge: Cambridge University Press.

———. 1985. Estimating vessel orifice diameters: Measurement methods and measurement error. In *Decoding Prehistoric Ceramics,* edited by B. A. Nelson, 243–253. Carbondale: Southern Illinois University Press.

Poirier, David A., and Nicholas F. Bellantoni, eds. 1997. *In Remembrance: Archaeology and Death.* Westport, Conn.: Bergin and Garvey.

Pollard, M., and C. Heron. 1996. *Archaeological Chemistry.* Cambridge: Royal Society of Chemistry.

Pollock, Susan. 1999. *Ancient Mesopotamia: The Eden That Never Was.* Cambridge: Cambridge University Press.

Powell, S., C. Garza, and A. Hendricks. 1993. Ethics and ownership of the past: The reburial and repatriation controversy. *Journal of Archaeological Method and Theory* 5:1–42.

Praetzellis, Adrian. 2000. *Death by Theory: A Tale of Mystery and Archaeological Theory.* Lanham, Md.: Rowman & Littlefield.

Prag, John, and Richard Neave. 1999. *Making Faces.* London: British Museum Press.

Prentiss, William C., Michael Lenert, Thomas A. Foor, Nathan B. Goodale, and Trinity Schlegel. 2003. Calibrated radiocarbon dating at Keatley Creek: The chronology of occupation at a complex hunter-gatherer village. *American Antiquity* 68:719–736.

Preucel, R. 1991. *Processual and Postprocessual Archaeologies: Multiple Ways of Knowing the Past.* Carbondale: Southern Illinois University Press.

———. 1995. The postprocessual condition. *Journal of Archaeological Research* 3:147–175.

Preucel, Robert, and Ian Hodder, eds. 1996. *Contemporary Archaeology in Theory.* London: Blackwell.

Price, T. D., and G. Feinman. 2005. *Images of the Past.* 4th ed. New York: McGraw-Hill.

Price, T. D., and A. B. Gebauer. 1995. *Last Hunters, First Farmers: New Perspectives on the Transition to Agriculture.* Santa Fe: School of American Research Press.

———. 2005. *Smakkerup Huse: A Coastal Late Mesolithic Site in Denmark.* Aarhus: Aarhus University Press.

Quine, T. A. 1995. Soil analysis and archaeological site formation processes. In *Archaeological Soils and Sediments: Analysis, Interpretation and Management,* edited by A. J. Barham and R. I. Macphail, 77–98. London: Institute of Archaeology.

Raab, M. L., and A. C. Goodyear. 1984. Middle-range theory in archaeology: A critical review of origins and applications. *American Antiquity* 49:255–268.

Rackham, James. 1994. *Animal Bones.* London: British Museum Press.

Rafferty, Sean M., and Rob Mann, eds. 2004. *Smoking and Culture: The Archaeology of Tobacco Pipes in Eastern North America.* Knoxville: University of Tennessee Press.

Ramenofsky, Anne F. 1998. Evolutionary theory and the Native American record of artifact replacement. In *Studies in Culture Contact: Interaction, Culture Change, and Archaeology,* edited by J. Cusick, 77–101. Carbondale: Southern Illinois University Press.

Rapp, G., and C. L. Hill. 1998. *Geoarchaeology.* New Haven: Yale University Press.

Rappaport, R. A. 1971. Ritual, sanctity, and cybernetics. *American Anthropologist* 73:59–76.

———. 1971. The sacred in human evolution. *Annual Review of Ecology and Systematics* 2:23–44.

Reents-Budet, D., J. Ball, R. Bishop, V. Fields, and B. MacLeod. 1994. *Painting the Maya Universe: Royal Ceramics of the Classic Period.* Durham: Duke University Press in association with Duke University Museum of Art.

Reichert, E. T. 1913. *The Differentiation and Specificity of Starches in Relation to Genera, Species, Etc.* Washington, D.C.: Carnegie Institution of Washington.

Reina, Rubin E., and Robert M. Hill, II. 1978. *The Traditional Pottery of Guatemala.* Austin: University of Texas Press.

Reitz, E. J., L. A. Newsom, and S. J. Scudder, eds. 1996. *Case Studies in Environmental Archaeology.* New York: Plenum.

Reitz, Elizabeth J., and Elizabeth S. Wing. 1999. *Zooarchaeology.* Cambridge Manuals in Archaeology. Cambridge: Cambridge University Press.

Renfrew, Colin. 1993. Cognitive archaeology: Some thoughts on the archaeology of thought. *Cambridge Journal of Archaeology* 3:248–250.

———. 1993. Collectors are the real looters. *Archaeology* 46(3):16–17.

———. 2000. *Loot, Legitimacy and Ownership: The Ethical Crisis in Archaeology.* London: Duckworth Publishing.

Renfrew, Colin, and Paul Bahn, eds. 2005. *Archaeology: The Key Concepts.* London: Routledge.

Renfrew, Colin, and John Dixon. 1976. Obsidian in Western Asia: A review. In *Problems in Economic and Social Archaeology,* edited by G. de G. Sieveking, I. H. Longworth, and K. E. Wilson, 137–150. London: Duckworth.

Renfrew, Colin, and E. B. W. Zubrow, eds. 1994. *The Ancient Mind.* Cambridge: Cambridge University Press.

Reyman, J. E., ed. 1992. *Rediscovering Our Past: Essays on the History of American Archaeology.* Brookfield, Vt.: Avebury.

Rice, P. 1990. Functions and uses of archaeological ceramics. In *The Changing Roles of Ceramics and Society: 26,000 B.P. to the Present,* edited by W. D. Kingery, 1–10, Ceramics and Civilization, vol. 5. 5 vols. Westerville, Ohio: American Ceramic Society.

———. 1991. Specialization, standardization, and diversity: A retrospective. In *The Ceramic Legacy of Anna O. Shepard,* edited by R. L. Bishop. and F. W. Lange, 257–279. Boulder: University of Colorado Press.

———. 1991. Women and prehistoric pottery production. In *The Archaeology of Gender: Proceedings of the 22nd Annual Chacmool Conference,* edited by D. Walde and N. D. Willows, 436–443. Calgary: Archaeological Association of the University of Calgary.

Rice, Prudence. 1984. *Pots and Potters: Current Approaches in Ceramic Archaeology.* Monograph 24. Los Angeles: Institute of Archaeology, U.C.L.A.

———. 1987. *Pottery Analysis: A Sourcebook.* Chicago: University of Chicago Press.

Rocek, Thomas, and Ofer Bar-Yosef, eds. 1998. *Seasonality and Sedentism: Archaeological Perspectives from Old and New World Perspectives.* Cambridge, Mass.: Peabody Museum of Archaeology and Ethnology.

Rodgers, Bradley A. 2004. *The Archaeologist's Manual for Conservation: A Guide to Non-Toxic, Minimal Intervention Artifact Stabilization.* New York: Kluwer Academic/Plenum.

Rosenfeld, A. 1965. *The Inorganic Raw Materials of Antiquity.* New York: Praeger.

Roskams, Steve. 2001. *Excavation.* Cambridge Manuals in Archaeology. Cambridge: Cambridge University Press.

Rowe, Chandler. 1956. *The Effigy Mound Culture of Wisconsin.* Westport, Conn.: Greenwood Press.

Rowley-Conwy, P. A., ed. 2000. *Animal Bones, Human Societies.* Oxford: Oxbow Books.

Rye, O. S. 1981. *Pottery Technology, Principles and Reconstruction.* Washington, D.C.: Taraxacum.

Sagan, Carl. 1995. The fine art of baloney detection. In *The Demon-Haunted World.* New York: Random House.

Sandford, M. K., ed. 1993. *Investigations of Ancient Human Tissue: Chemical Analyses in Anthropology.* Amsterdam: Gordon and Breach.

Saul, F. P. 1972. *The Human Skeletal Remains of Altar de Sacrificios.* Papers of the Peabody Museum of Archaeology and Ethnology, vol. 63, no. 2. Cambridge, Mass.: Harvard University.

Saunders, Nicholas, ed. 2005. *Matters of Conflict: Material Culture, Memory and the First World War.* London: Routledge.

Saunders, Shelley Rae. 1989. Nonmetric skeletal variation. In *Reconstruction of Life from the Skeleton,* edited by Mehmet Yaşar Işcan and Kenneth A. R. Kennedy, 95–108. New York: Liss.

Saunders, Shelley R., and D. Ann Herring, eds. 1995. *Grave Reflections: Portraying the Past through Cemetery Studies.* Toronto: Canadian Scholars' Press.

Saunders, Shelley R., and M. Anne Katzenberg. 1992. *Skeletal Biology of Past Peoples: Research Methods.* New York: Wiley-Liss.

Saxe, A. A. 1971. Social dimensions of mortuary practices in Mesolithic populations from Wade Halfa, Sudan. In *Approaches to the Social Dimensions of Mortuary Practices,* edited by J. A. Brown, no. 25:39–56. Memoirs of the Society for American Archaeology. Washington, D.C.: Society for American Archaeology.

Schick, Kathy, and Nick Toth. 1993. *Making Silent Stones Speak.* New York: Simon & Schuster.

Schiffer, M. B. 1976. *Behavioral Archeology.* New York: Academic Press.

———. 1987. *Formation Processes of the Archaeological Record.* Albuquerque: University of New Mexico Press.

———. 1988. The structure of archaeological theory. *American Antiquity* 53:461–485.

———, ed. 2001. *Anthropological Perspectives on Technology.* New World Studies, vol. 5. Dragoon, Ariz.: Amerind Foundation.

Schiffer, M. B., James M. Skibo, Tamara C. Boelke, Mark A. Neupert, and Meredith Aronson. 1994. New perspectives on experimental archaeology: Surface treatments and thermal response of the clay cooking pot. *American Antiquity* 59(2):197–217.

Schmid, Elisabeth. 1972. *Atlas of Animal Bones.* Amsterdam: Elsevier.

Schoeninger, Margaret P., and M. J. DeNiro. 1984. Nitrogen and carbon isotopic composition of bone collagen from marine and terrestrial animals. *Geochimica et Cosmochimica Acta* 48:625–639.

Schoeninger, Margaret P., and Katherine Moore. 1992. Bone stable isotope studies in archaeology. *Journal of World Prehistory* 6:247–296.

Schulz, Peter D., and Sherri Gust. 1983. Faunal remains and social status in 19th century Sacramento. *Historical Archaeology* 17:44–53.

Schwarcz, Henry P., and Margaret P. Schoeninger. 1991. Stable isotope analyses in human nutritional ecology. *Yearbook of Physical Anthropology* 34:283–321.

Sciulli, P. W., K. N. Schneider, and M. C. Mahaney. 1990. Stature estimation in prehistoric Native Americans of Ohio. *American Journal of Physical Anthropology* 83:275–280.

Sease, Catherine. 1994. *A Conservation Manual for the Field Archaeologist.* 3d ed. Los Angeles: Los Angeles Institute of Archaeology.

———. 2002. The conservation of archaeological materials. In *Archaeology: Original Readings in Method and Practice,* edited by P. N. Peregrine, C. R. Ember, and M. Ember, 36–47. Upper Saddle River, N.J.: Prentice Hall.

Seeman, M. F. 1996. The Hopewell core and its many margins: Deconstructing upland and hinterland relations. In *A View from the Core: A Synthesis of Ohio Hopewell Archaeology,* edited by P. Pacheco, 304–315. Columbus: Ohio Archaeological Council.

Sellars, Wilfrid. 1962. Philosophy and the scientific image of man. In *Frontiers of Science and Philosophy,* edited by Robert Colodny, 5–78. Pittsburgh: University of Pittsburgh Press.

Semenov, S. A. 1964. *Prehistoric Technology.* London: Adams and Dart.

Shanks, M., and C. Tilley. 1987. *Re-Constructing Archaeology.* Cambridge: Cambridge University Press.

Shapiro, G. 1984. Ceramic vessels, site permanence, and group size: A Mississippi example. *American Antiquity* 49:696–712.

Sharer, R. J. 1994. *The ancient Maya.* 5th ed. Palo Alto: Stanford University Press.

Shea, J. J. 2003. Neandertals, competition, and the origin of modern human behavior in the Levant. *Evolutionary Anthropology* 12:173–187.

Sheets, Payson. 2005. *The Ceren Site: Prehistoric Village Buried by Volcanic Ash in Central America.* 2d ed. Belmont, Calif.: Wadsworth.

Shennan, S. 2003. *Genes, Memes, and Human History: Darwinian Archaeology and Cultural Evolution.* London: Thames & Hudson.

Shennan, Stephen J. 1988. *Quantifying Archaeology.* Edinburgh: Edinburgh University Press.

Shepard, A. O. 1956. *Ceramics for the Archaeologist.* Washington, D.C.: Carnegie Institution of Washington.

———. 1964. Temper identification: Technological sherd-splitting or unanswered challenge. *American Antiquity* 29(4):518–520.

———. 1982. *Ceramics for the Archaeologist.* Washington, D.C.: Carnegie Institution of Washington.

Shermer, Michael. 1997. *Why People Believe Weird Things: Pseudoscience, Superstition, and Other Confusions of Our Time.* New York: W.H. Freeman and Company.

Shopland, Norena. 2006. *A Finds Manual: Excavating, Processing and Storing.* Stroud UK: Tempus Publishing.

Shott, M. J. 1996. Innovation and selection in prehistory: A case study from the American Bottom. In *Stone Tools: Theoretical Insights into Human Prehistory,* edited by G. H. Odell, 279–309. New York: Springer.

———. 1998. Status and role of formation theory in contemporary archaeological practice. *Journal of Archaeological Research* 6:299–329.

Simon, Arleyn W., James H. Burton, and David R. Abbott. 1998. Intraregional connections in the development and distribution of Salado polychromes in Central Arizona. *Journal of Anthropological Research* 54:521–550.

Singleton, Theresa A., ed. 1985. *The Archaeology of Slavery and Plantation Life.* Orlando: Academic Press.

Sinopoli, Carla M. 1991. *Approaches to Archaeological Ceramics.* New York: Plenum.

Skibo, J. 1992. *Pottery Function: A Use-Alteration Perspective.* New York: Plenum.

Skibo, J., and G. Feinman, eds. 1999. *Pottery and People: A Dynamic Interaction.* Salt Lake City: University of Utah Press.

Skibo, James M., and Michael B. Schiffer. 1995. The clay cooking pot: An exploration of women's technology. In *Expanding Archaeology, edited by* J. M. Skibo, W. H. Walker, and A. E. Nielsen, 80–91. Salt Lake City: University of Utah Press.

Smith, Adam T. 2003. *The Political Landscape: Constellations of Authority in Early Complex Polities.* Berkeley: University of California Press.

Smith, Bruce D. 1998. *The Emergence of Agriculture.* 2d ed. New York: Scientific American Library.

Smith, David Glenn, Ripan S. Malhi, Jason Eshleman, Joseph G. Lorenz, and Frederika A. Kaestle. 1999. Distribution of mtDNA haplogroup X among Native Americans. *American Journal of Physical Anthropology* 110:271–284.

Smith, Eric A., and Bruce Winterhalder, eds. *Evolutionary Ecology and Human Behavior.* New York: Aldine.

Smith, Monica. 1999. The role of ordinary goods in premodern exchange. *Journal of Archaeological Method and Theory* 6:109–136.

Snow, D. R. 1994. *The Iroquois.* Oxford: Basil Blackwell.

Sørensen, Marie Louise Stig. 2000. *Gender Archaeology.* Cambridge (UK): Polity Press.

Sorg, M. H., and W. D. Haglund, eds. 2001. *Advances in Forensic Taphonomy.* Boca Raton: CRC Press.

South, Stanley. 1977. *Method and Theory in Historical Archaeology.* New York: Academic Press.

Spaulding, Albert C. 1953. Statistical techniques for the discovery of artifact types. *American Antiquity* 18:305–313.

————. 1954. Reply to Ford. *American Anthropologist* 56:112–114.

Spencer, C. S. 1997. Evolutionary approaches in archaeology. *Journal of Archaeological Research* 5:209–264.

Spielmann, K. A., ed. 1998. *Migration and Reorganization: The Pueblo IV Period in the American Southwest.* Anthropological Research Papers, 51. Tempe: Arizona State University.

Spindler, Konrad. 1995. *Der Mann im Eis: Neue Funde und Ergebnisse.* Wien: Springer.

Spindler, K., et al., eds. 1996. *Human Mummies: A Global Survey of Their Status and the Techniques of Conservation.* Vienna: Springer.

St. Hoyme, Lucile E., and Mehmet Yaşar Işcan. 1989. Determination of sex and race: Accuracy and assumptions. In *Reconstruction of Life from the Skeleton*, edited by Mehmet Yaşar Işcan and Kenneth A. R. Kennedy, 53–93. New York: Wiley-Liss.

Stanish, Charles. 1989. Household Archaeology. *American Anthropologist* 91:7–24.

Stead, I. M., J. B. Bourke, and Don Brothwell. 1986. *Lindow Man: The Body in the Bog.* Ithaca: Cornell University Press.

Stein, J. K. 1987. Deposits for archaeologists. *Advances in Archaeological Method and Theory*, 11:337–395.

————. 1990. Archaeological stratigraphy. In *Archaeological Geology of North America*, edited by N. P. Lasca and J. Donahue, 513–523, Centennial Special Volume 4. Boulder, Colo.: Geological Society of America.

————. 2001. A review of site formation processes and their relevance to geoarchaeology. In *Earth Sciences and Archaeology*, edited by P. Goldberg, V. T. Holliday, and C. R. Ferring, 37–51. New York: Kluwer Academic/Plenum.

Stein, J. K., and W. R. Farrand, eds. 1985. *Archaeological Sediments in Context.* Orono: Center for the Study of Early Man, University of Maine.

Steponaitis, Vincas P. 1981. Settlement hierarchies and political complexity in nonmarket societies: The formative period of the Valley of Mexico. *American Anthropologist* 83:320–363.

Steward, J. H. 1954. Types of type. *American Anthropologist* 56:54–57.

Stiebing, W. H. 1994. *Uncovering the Past: A History of Archaeological Thought.* New York: Oxford University Press.

Stirland, Ann. 1999. *Human Bones in Archaeology.* Buckinghamshire (UK): Shire Publications.

Stirling, A. J. 2000. *Raising the Dead: The Skeleton Crew of King Henry VIII's Great Ship, the Mary Rose.* Chichester: Wiley.

Stokes, Marvin A., and Terah L. Smiley. 1996. *An Introduction to Tree-Ring Dating.* Tucson: University of Arizona Press.

Stoltman, James B. 1991. Ceramic petrography as a technique for documenting cultural interaction: An example from the Upper Mississippi Valley. *American Antiquity* 56:103–121.

Stone, Elizabeth C., and Paul Zimansky. 2004. *The Anatomy of a Mesopotamian City: Survey and Soundings at Mashkan-Shapir.* Winona Lake, Ind.: Eisenbrauns.

Stothers, David M., and Richard A. Yarnell. 1977. An agricultural revolution in the Lower Great Lakes. In *Geobotany*, edited by R. D. Romans, 209–232. New York: Plenum.

Strecker, Matthias, and Paul Bahn, eds. 1999. *Dating and the Earliest Known Rock Art.* Oxford: Oxbow Books.

Stuart, George E., and Francis P. McManamon. 1996. *Archaeology and You.* Washington, D.C.: Society for American Archaeology.

Sullivan, Allan P. 1978. Inference and evidence in archaeology: A discussion of the conceptual problems. *Advances in Archaeological Method and Theory* 1:183–222.

Sutton, Mark Q., and Brooke S. Arkush. 2002. *Archaeological Laboratory Methods: An Introduction.* 3d ed. Dubuque: Kendall/Hunt.

Tait, H., ed. 2004. *Five Thousand Years of Glass.* Rev. ed. Philadelphia: University of Pennsylvania Press.

Tattersall, Ian, and J. H. Schwartz. 2000. *Extinct Humans.* Boulder, Colo.: Westview Press.

Taylor, R. E., and M. J. Aitken. 1997. *Chronometric Dating in Archaeology.* New York: Plenum.

Taylor, W. W. 1948. *A Study of Archaeology.* Originally published as Memoir 69, Memoirs of the American Anthropological Association.

Thomas, David H. 1986. *Refiguring Anthropology: First Principles of Probability and Statistics.* 2d ed. Prospect Heights, Ill: Waveland Press.

————. 2000. *Skull Wars: Kennewick Man, Archaeology, and the Battle for Native American Identity.* New York: Basic Books.

Tilley, Chris. 1991. *Material Culture and Text: The Art of Ambiguity.* London: Routledge.

————. 1994. *A Phenomenology of Landscape: Places, Paths, and Monuments.* Oxford: Berg.

Tite, M. S. 1972. *Methods of Physical Examination in Archaeology.* London: Seminar Press.

————. 1999. Pottery production, distribution, and consumption—The contribution of the physical sciences. *Journal of Archaeological Method and Theory* 6:181–233.

Todd, Lawrence C. 1991. Seasonality studies and Paleoindian subsistence strategies. In *Human Predators and Prey Mortality*, edited by M. Stiner, 217–238. Boulder, Colo.: Westview Press.

Torrence, R., and J. P, Grattan, eds. 2002. *Natural Disasters and Cultural Change.* London: Routledge.

Townsend, Richard F. 2004. *Hero, Hawk, and Open Hand: American Indian Art of the Ancient Midwest and South.* New Haven: Yale University Press.

Trigger, Bruce G. 1965. *History and Settlement in Lower Nubia.* Yale University Publications in Anthropology, no. 61. New Haven: Yale.

———. 1968. The determinants of settlement patterns. In *Settlement Archaeology,* edited by K. C. Chang, 53–78. Palo Alto: National Press.

———. 1989. Archaeology's relations with the physical and biological sciences. In *Archaeometry Proceedings of the 25th International Symposium,* 1–9. Toronto: Elsevier.

———. 1990. *A History of Archaeological Thought.* Cambridge: Cambridge University Press.

———. 1991. Distinguished lecture in archaeology: Constraint and freedom—A new synthesis for archaeological explanation. *American Anthropologist* 93:551–569.

———. 2003. *Understanding Early Civilizations: A Comparative Study.* Cambridge: Cambridge University Press.

Tubb, K. W., ed. 1995. *Antiquities Trade or Betrayed: Legal, Ethical, and Conservation Issues.* London: Archetype.

Tufte, Edward. 2001. *The Visual Display of Quantitative Information.* 2d ed. Cheshire, Conn.: Graphics Press.

Turner, Christy G., and Jacqueline A. Turner. 1999. *Man Corn: Cannibalism and Violence in the Prehistoric American Southwest.* Salt Lake City: University of Utah Press.

Turner, R. C., and R. G. Scaife. 1995. *Bog Bodies: New Discoveries and New Perspectives.* London: British Museum Press.

Tuross, N., I. Barnes, and R. Potts. 1996. Protein identification of blood residues on experimental tools. *Journal of Archaeological Science* 23:289–296.

Tykot, Robert H. 1996. Obsidian procurement and distribution in the central and western Mediterranean. *Journal of Mediterranean Archaeology* 9(1):39–82.

Tyler, Norman. 1999. *Historic Preservation: An Introduction to Its History, Principles, and Practice.* New York: W.H. Norton.

Ubelaker, D. H. 1978. *Human Skeletal Remains.* Chicago: Aldine.

Valladas, H., J. L. Reyss, J. L. Joron, G. Valladas, O. Bar-Yosef, and B. Vandermeersch. 1988. Thermolumines-

cence dating of Mousterian Proto-Cro-Magnon remains from Israel and the origin of modern man. *Nature* 331:614–616.

Van Biema, David. 1998. Science and the Shroud. *Time,* April 20.

Van der Leeuw, S. E., and A. C. Pritchard, eds. 1984. *The Many Dimensions of Pottery.* Amsterdam: Universiteit van Amsterdam.

Van Noten, F., D. Cahen, and L. Keeley. 1980. A Paleolithic campsite in Belgium. *Scientific American* 242(4):48–55.

Van Noten, F. L., ed. 1978. Les Chasseurs de Meer. Diss. Archaeologicae Gandenses 18. Brugge: De Tempel.

Vehik, Susan, 1982. Archaeological excavations at the early plains village Uncas site (34Ka–172). *Oklahoma Anthropological Society Bulletin* 31:1–70.

Verano, John. 1997. Human skeletal remains from Tomb I, Sipán (Lambayeque river valley, Peru), and their social implications. *Antiquity* 71: 670–682.

Vidale, M., J. M. Kenoyer, and K. K. Bhan. 1991. Ethnoarchaeological excavations of the bead making workshops of Khambhat: A view from beneath the floors. In *South Asian Archaeology,* edited by A. J. Gail and G. J. Mevissen, 273–288. Stuttgart: G.J.R. Verlag.

Villa, P. 1982. Conjoinable pieces and site formation processes. *American Antiquity* 47:276–290.

Vitelli, Karen, ed. 1996. *Archaeological Ethics.* Walnut Creek, Calif.: Rowman & Littlefield.

W. B. Emery. 1962. A funerary repast in an Egyptian tomb of the Archaic Period. *Scholae Adriani de Buck Memoriae Dicatae* 1. Leiden: Nederlands Instituut voor het Nabije Oosten.

Wagner, Gail E. 1996. Feast or famine? Seasonal diet at a Fort Ancient community. In *Case Studies in Environmental Archaeology,* edited by E. J. Reitz, L. A. Newsom, and S. J. Scudder, 255–271. New York: Plenum.

Wagner, Gunther, Ernst Pernicka, and Hans-Peter Uerpmann, eds. 2003.

Troia and the Troad. New York: Springer.

Wahl, J., and H. G. König. 1987. *Anthropologisch-traumatologische Untersuchung der menschlichen Skelettreste aus dem bandkeramischen Massengrab bei Talheim, Kreis Hilbronn.* Fundberichte aus Baden-Wurttenberg 12:65–194.

Waldorf, D. C. 2001. *The Art of Flintknapping.* Washburn, Mo.: Mound Builder Books.

Waldron, T. 2001. *Shadows in the Soil: Human Bones and Archaeology.* Stroud: Tempus.

Waldrop, Mitchell M. 1992. *Complexity: The Emerging Science at the Edge of Order and Chaos.* New York: Simon & Schuster.

Walker, P. L., J. R. Johnson, and P. M. Lambert. 1988. Age and sex biases in the preservation of human skeletal remains. *American Journal of Physical Anthropology* 76:183–188.

Walter, R. C. 1997. Potassium-argon/argon-argon dating methods. In *Chronometric Dating in Archaeology,* edited by R. E. Taylor and M. J. Aitken, 97–126. New York: Plenum.

Waters, Michael R. 1992. *Principles of Geoarchaeology: A North American Perspective.* Tucson: University of Arizona Press.

Waters, Michael R., and David D. Kuehn. 1996. The geoarchaeology of place: The effect of geological processes on the preservation and interpretation of the archaeological record. *American Antiquity* 61:483–497.

Watson, Jacqui. 2004. The freeze-drying of wet and waterlogged materials from archaeological excavations. *Physics Education* 39:171–176.

Watson, Patty Jo. 1995. Archaeology, anthropology and the culture concept. *American Anthropologist* 97:683–694.

Watson, Patty Jo, and Mary C. Kennedy. 1991. The development of horticulture in the eastern Woodlands in North America: Women's role. In *Engendering Archaeology: Women and Prehistory,* edited by Joan M. Gero and M. W. Conkey, 255–277. Oxford: Basil Blackwell.

Watson, P. J., Steven LeBlanc, and Charles Redman. 1984. *Archaeological Explanation: The Scientific Method in Archaeology.* New York: Columbia University Press.

Watson, Richard A. 1992. The place of archaeology in science. In *Meta-archaeology: Reflections by Archaeologists and Philosophers,* edited by L. Embree, 255–267. Dordrecht: Kluwer.

Webster, David. 2002. *The Fall of the Ancient Maya: Solving the Mystery of the Maya Collapse.* London: Thames & Hudson.

Weigand, P. C., G. Harbottle, and E. V. Sayre. 1977. Turquoise sources and source analysis in Mesoamerica and the Southwestern U.S.A. In *Exchange Systems in Prehistory,* edited by T. K. Earle and J. E. Ericson. New York: Academic Press.

Weiss, Harvey. 2005. *Collapse: How Sudden Climate Change Destroyed Civilization and Shaped History.* London: Routledge.

Weiss, K. M. 1973. *Demographic Models for Anthropology.* Memoirs of the Society for American Archaeology, no. 27. Washington, D.C.: Society for American Archaeology.

Whallon, Robert. 1968. Investigations of Late Prehistoric Social Organization in New York State. In *New Perspectives in Archaeology,* edited by L. R. Binford and S. R. Binford, 223–244. Chicago: Aldine.

Whallon, R., and J. A. Brown, eds. 1982. *Essays on Archaeological Typology.* Evanston, Ill.: Center for American Archeology Press.

White, Tim D. 1992. *Prehistoric Cannibalism at Mancos 5MTUMR-2346.* Princeton: Princeton University Press.

White, Tim D., and Pieter A. Folkens. 2000. *Human Osteology.* 2d ed. Orlando: Academic Press.

Whitley, David S., ed. 1998. *Reader in Archaeological Theory: Post-Processual and Cognitive Approaches.* London: Routledge.

Whittaker, J. C. 1994. *Flintknapping: Making and Understanding Stone Tools.* Austin: University of Texas Press.

Whittaker, J., D. Caulkins, and K. Kamp. 1998. Evaluating consistency in typology and classification. *Journal of Archaeological Method and Theory* 5(2):129–164.

Wiessner, P. 1983. Style and social information in Kalahari San projectile points. *American Antiquity* 48:253–276.

———. 1984. Reconsidering the behavioral basis for style: A case study among the Kalahari San. *Journal of Anthropological Archaeology* 3:190–234.

———. 1988. Style and changing relations between the individual and society. In *The Meaning of Things: Material Culture and Symbolic Expression,* edited by Ian Hodder. London: Allen and Unwin.

Wilk, R. R. 1991. The household in anthropology: Problem or Panacea? *Reviews in Anthropology* 20:1–12.

Wilkinson, Caroline. 2004. *Forensic Facial Reconstruction.* Cambridge: Cambridge University Press.

Wilkinson, K. N., and C. J. Stevens, 2003. *Environmental Archaeology: Approaches, Techniques and Applications.* Stroud: Tempus.

Willey, G. R., and J. A. Sabloff. 1993. *A History of American Archaeology.* 3d ed. New York: W.H. Freeman and Company.

Williams-Thorpe, Olwen. 1995. Obsidian in the Mediterranean and Near East: A provenancing success story. *Archaeometry* 37:217–248.

Wilson, A. L. 1978. Elemental Analysis of Pottery in the Study of its Provenance: A Review. *Journal of Archaeological Science* 5:219–236.

Winstone, H. V. F. 1990. *Woolley of Ur: The Life of Sir Leonard Woolley.* London: Secker & Warburg.

Winterhalder, Bruce, and Eric A. Smith. 1992. Evolutionary ecology and the social sciences. In *Evolutionary Ecology and Human Behavior,* edited by E. Smith and B. Winterhalder, 3–24. Hawthorne, N.Y.: Aldine de Gruyter.

———, eds. 1981. *Hunter-Gatherer Foraging Strategies: Ethnographic and Archaeological Analyses.* Chicago: University of Chicago Press.

Wintle, A. G. 1996. Archaeologically relevant dating techniques for the next century. *Journal of Archaeological Science* 23:123–138.

Wisseman, S. U., and W. S. Williams, eds. 1994. *Ancient Technologies and Archaeological Materials.* Amsterdam: Gordon and Breach.

Wobst, H. M. 1977. Stylistic behavior and information exchange. In *For the Director: Research Essays in Honor of James B. Griffin,* edited by C. E. Cleland, 317–342. Museum of Anthropology Paper 61. Ann Arbor: University of Michigan.

Wobst, Martin. 1978. The archaeo-ethnology of hunter-gatherers or the tyranny of the ethnographic record in archaeology. *American Antiquity* 43:303–309.

Wood, Bernard F. 2002. Hominid revelations from Chad. *Nature* 418:133–135.

Woolley, C. Leonard. 1982. *Ur "of the Chaldees": A Revised and Updated Edition of Sir Leonard Woolley's Excavations at Ur,* by P. R. S. Moorey. Ithaca: Cornell University Press.

Wright, Gary A. 1969. *Obsidian Analysis and Prehistoric Near Eastern Trade: 7500–3500 B.C.* University of Michigan Museum of Anthropology Anthropological Papers 37.

Wright, Henry T. 1986. The evolution of civilizations. In *American Archaeology Past and Future,* edited by D. J. Meltzer, D. Fowler, and J. Sabloff. Washington, D.C.: Smithsonian Institution Press.

Wright, H. T., and G. A. Johnson. 1975. Population, exchange, and early state formation in southwestern Iran. *American Anthropologist* 77:267–289.

Wright, Patti J. 2005. Flotation samples and some paleoethnobotanical implications. *Journal of Archaeological Science* 32:19–26.

Wylie, A. 1985. The reaction against analogy. *Advances in Archaeological Method and Theory* 8:63–111.

Yanko-Hombach, Valentina. 2003. "Noah's Flood" and the Late Quaternary history of the Black Sea and its adjacent basins: A critical overview of the flood hypotheses. GSA Annual Meeting, November 2–5, 2003, Seattle.

Yarmin, Rebecca, and Karen Bescherer Metheny, eds. 1996. *Landscape Archaeology: Reading and Interpreting the American Historical Landscape.* Knoxville: University of Tennessee Press.

Yates, R., J. Parkington, and T. Manhire. 1990. *Pictures from the Past: A History of the Interpretation of Rock Paintings and Engravings of Southern Africa.* Pietermaritzburg (South Africa): Centaur Publications.

Yellin, Joseph, Thomas E. Levy, and Yorke M. Rowan. 1996. New evidence on prehistoric trade routes: The obsidian evidence from Gilat, Israel. *Journal of Field Archaeology* 23:361–368.

Yoffee, N., and G. L. Cowgill, eds. 1988. *The Collapse of Ancient States and Civilizations.* Tucson: University of Arizona Press.

Yoffee, N., and A. Sherratt. 1993. *Archaeological Theory: Who Sets the Agenda?* Cambridge: Cambridge University Press.

Zeder, Melinda. 1997. *The American Archaeologist: A Profile.* Walnut Creek, Calif.: AltaMira.

Zimmerman, Larry J., Karen D. Vitelli, and Julie Hollowell-Zimmer. 2003. *Ethical Issues in Archaeology.* Walnut Creek, Calif.: AltaMira.

Zimmerman, L. J., and William Green. 2003. *The Archaeologist's Toolkit.* Walnut Creek, Calif.: AltaMira.

Zohary, D., and M. Hopf. 2000. *Domestication of Plants in the Old World.* 3d ed. Oxford: Oxford University Press.

Zubrow, Ezra. 1976. *Demographic Anthropology: Quantitative Approaches.* Albuquerque: University of New Mexico Press.

Zurer, P. S. 1983. Archaeological chemistry: Physical science helps to unravel human history. *Chemical and Engineering News* 61:26–44.

Credits

Janes / printed with permission. From Robert A. Birmingham and Leslie E. Eisenberg, *Indian Mounds of Wisconsin.* Madison, WI: University of Wisconsin Press, 2000; 5.14, © Amelia R. Janes / printed with permission. From Robert A. Birmingham and Leslie E. Eisenberg, *Indian Mounds of Wisconsin.* Madison, WI: University of Wisconsin Press, 2000; 5.15, © Gilles Tosello; 5.16, © AP/Wide World Photos; 5.17, adapted from T. Douglas Price and Gary M. Feinman, *Images of the Past,* 4th edition, p. 166. Copyright © 2005 by The McGraw-Hill Companies, Inc. Reprinted with permission; 5.18, Reproduced from *Past Worlds: The Times Atlas of Archaeology* by kind permission of Times Books, Ltd., London; 5.19, from Linda Manzanilla, "Corporate Groups and Domestic Activities at Teotihuacan." Reproduced with permission of the Society for American Archaeology from *Latin American Antiquity,* Vol. 7, No. 3 (1996), pp. 228–46, Figure 7 (modified); 5.20, illustration by Fernando Botas from Linda Manzanilla, ed., *Anatomía de un conjunto residencial teotihuacano en Oztoyahualco.* UNAM, Mexico: Instituto de Investigaciones Antropológicas, © 1993 UNAM and Linda Manzanilla. Reprinted by permission of Linda Manzanilla; 5.21, © Werner Foreman/Art Resource, NY; 5.22, from Archeological Management and Research Center, Department of Anthropology, University of Oklahoma. Reprinted by permission of the Department of Anthropology, University of Oklahoma; 5.23, from Brian W. Hoffman, *The Organization of Complexity: A Study of Late Prehistoric Village Organization in the Eastern Aleutian Region.* Thesis (Ph.D.), University of Wisconsin, Madison, 2002, Figure 4.3. By permission of Brian W. Hoffman. Based on a field sketch by Steve Klingler, U.S. Fish and Wildlife Service, 1985; 5.24, © National Maritime Museum, London; 5.25, adapted from Anders Fischer, "People and the Sea—Settlement and Fishing along the Mesolithic Coasts." In Lisbeth Pedersen, Anders Fischer, and Bent Aaby, *The Danish Storaebaelt since the Ice Age: Man, Sea and Forest.* Copenhagen: Storaebaelt Fixed Link, 1997. By permission of Anders Fischer; 5.26, from *The Illustrated History of Mankind, Volume 2: People of the Stone Age.* Weldon Owen, 1993, p. 62. Illustration by Mike Gorman. © Weldon Owen Pty Ltd.; 5.27, redrawn from K. C. Chang, *Settlement Patterns in Archaeology.* Reading: MA: Addison-Wesley, 1972; 5.28, © Gilles Tosello; Table 5.2, from Mark Q. Sutton, Robert M. Yohe, *Archaeology: The Science of the Human Past.* Published by Allyn & Bacon, Boston, MA. Copyright © 2003 by Pearson Education. Adapted by permission of the publisher; 5.29, from Mark Q. Sutton, Robert M. Yohe, *Archaeology: The Science of the Human Past.* Published by Allyn & Bacon, Boston, MA. Copyright © 2003 by Pearson Education. Adapted by permission of the publisher; 5.30, from Robert J. Sharer and Wendy Ashmore, *Archaeology: Discovering Our Past,* 3rd edition, p. 129. Copyright © 2003 by The McGraw-Hill Companies, Inc. Reprinted with permission; 5.31, adapted from Glynn LL. Isaac, "The Archaeology of Human Origins: Studies of the Lower Pleistocene in East Africa 1971–1981." In *Advances in World Archaeology,* Vol. 3, ed. Fred Wendorf and Angela Close. Academic Press, 1984, p. 35, Figure 1.9; 5.32, from Göran Burenhult, *Arkeologi i Norden.* Stockholm, 1999. Drawings by Sven Österholm. Reprinted by permission of Sven Österholm and Göran Burenhult; 5.33, from Clifford J. Jolly and Randall White, *Physical Anthropology and Archaeology,* 5th edition, p. 298. Copyright © 1995 by The McGraw-Hill Companies, Inc. Reprinted with permission; Table 5.3, from Sutton & Yohe, *Archaeology: The Science of the Human Past.* Published by Allyn & Bacon, Boston, MA. Copyright © 2003 by Pearson Education. Reprinted by permission of the publisher; 5.34, 5.35, Courtesy Glen Doran; 5.36, from Glen H. Doran, ed., *Windover: Multidisciplinary Investigations of an Early Archaic Florida Cemetery.* Gainesville, FL: 2002. Reprinted with permission of the University Press of Florida; 5.37, Forschungsinstitut für Alpine Vorzeit 5.38, from *Invitation to Archaeology* by James Deetz, copyright © 1967 by James Deetz. Used by permission of Doubleday, a division of Random House, Inc. **Chapter 6** CO-6, ©

Center for American Archaeology, Kampsville; 6.1, T.D. Price; 6.2, David Hurst Thomas, American Museum of Natural History; 6.3, from David Hurst Thomas, "An Empirical Test for Steward's Model of Great Basin Settlement Patterns." Reproduced by permission of the Society for American Archaeology from *American Antiquity,* Volume 38, No. 2 (April 1973), pp. 155–76, Figure 6 (modified); 6.4, T.D. Price; 6.5, Courtesy Clive Waddington; 6.6, T.D. Price; 6.7, © York Archaeological Trust; 6.8, © Jonathan Blair/Corbis; 6.9, © Tom Christensen/Roskilde Museum; 6.10, illustration by Tom Christensen, by permission of The Roskilde Museum; 6.11, Courtesy Sönke Harty; 6.12, © Lynn Roebuck; 6.13, © Arne Hodalic/Corbis; 6.14, 6.15, from T. Douglas Price and Anne Birgitte Gebauer, *Adventures in Fugawiland,* 3rd edition, pp. 12–13. Copyright © 2002 by The McGraw-Hill Companies, Inc. Reprinted with permission; 6.16, Courtesy Mickey Kienity; 6.18, © John W. Rick; 6.21, reproduced by permission of Ordnance Survey on behalf of HMSO. © Crown copyright 2006. All rights reserved. Ordnance Survey License number 100045274; and by permission of HP Visual and Spatial Technology Centre, University of Birmingham, U.K.; 6.22, T.D. Price; 6.23, Peregrine, Peter N.; Ember, Carol R.; and Ember, Melvin, *Archaeology: Original Readings in Method and Practice,* 1st edition, © 2002. Adapted by permission of Pearson Education, Inc., Upper Saddle River, NJ; 6.24, Courtesy NASA; 6.25, from T. Douglas Price and Gary M. Feinman, *Images of the Past,* 4th edition, p. 300. Copyright © 2005 by The McGraw-Hill Companies, Inc. Reprinted with permission; 6.26a, Courtesy Lawrence Conyers; 6.26b, part b adapted from Lawrence B. Conyers, Eileen G. Ernenwein, and Leigh-Ann Bedal, "Ground-Penetrating Radar (GPR) Mapping as a Method for Planning Excavation Strategies, Petra, Jordan," *e-tiquity,* 2002, Number 1. http://e-tiquity.saa.org/~etiquity/1. By permission of Lawrence B. Conyers; 6.27, Courtesy Paul Green; 6.28, 6.29, 6.30, 6.31 from T. Douglas Price and Anne Birgitte Gebauer, *Adventures in Fugawiland,* 3rd edition, pp. 95–97. Copyright © 2002 by The McGraw-Hill Companies, Inc. Reprinted with permission. **Part 3** Mark Downey/Getty Images **Chapter 7** CO-7, © H. Robertson/Iziko Museums of Cape Town; 7.1, from Pauline Wiessner, "Style and Social Information in Kalahari San Projectile Points." Reproduced by permission of the Society for American Archaeology from *American Antiquity,* Vol. 49, No. 2 (1983), pp. 253–76; 7.2, Courtesy Mickey Kienity; 7.3, Courtesy Robert Sharer; 7.4, © York Archaeological Trust; 7.5, © The British Museum, London; 7.6, Courtesy Bo Knarrström; 7.7, adapted from James A. Ford, "On the Concept of Types: The Type Concept Revisited," *American Anthropologist,* Vol. 56, No. 1 (February 1954), p. 46; 7.8, reprinted by permission of the illustrator, G. L. "Buck" Damone III/Damone Illustration. www.midrivers.com/~gdamone; 7.9, from *Analytical Archaeology* by David L. Clarke, 2nd edition revised by Bob Chapman, p. 176. Copyright © 1968, 1978 Estate of David L. Clarke. Reprinted with permission of Columbia University Press; 7.10, a portion of this figure is from Robert Whallon, Jr., "Investigations of Late Prehistoric Social Organization in New York State." In *New Perspectives in Archeology,* ed. Sally R. Binford and Lewis R. Binford. Chicago: Aldine Publishing Company, 1968, pp. 223–44. By permission of Robert Whallon, Jr.; 7.13, from Eric Sloane, *A Museum of Early American Tools.* New York: Funk & Wagnalls, 1964, p. 13. Reprint, Dover Publications, 2002. Reprinted by permission of The Estate of Eric Sloane, N.A. (1905–1985) & Michael Wigley Galleries, Santa Fe, NM; 7.14, Courtesy K.L. Feder; 7.15, adapted from *Invitation to Archaeology* by James Deetz, copyright © 1967 by James Deetz. Used by permission of Doubleday, a division of Random House, Inc.; 7.16, from Robert J. Sharer and Wendy Ashmore, *Archaeology: Discovering Our Past,* 3rd edition, p. 315. Copyright © 2003 by The McGraw-Hill Companies, Inc. Reprinted with permission; 7.18, From James A. Ford, "Measurements of Some Prehistoric Design Developments in the Southeastern

States." Anthropological Papers 44(3): 313–84. American Museum of Natural History. 1952; 7.19, from David G. Anderson and Michael K. Faught, "The Distribution of Fluted Paleoindian Projectile Points: Update 1998," *Archaeology of Eastern North America,* Vol. 26, pp. 163–87, Figure 1. © Copyright 1998 Eastern States Archaeological Federation. Reprinted with permission; 7.29, from *Past Worlds: The Times Atlas of Archaeology,* p. 39. Reprinted by permission of HarperCollins Publishers Ltd. Copyright © 1988 Times Books Limited; 7.33, from *Grasshopper Pueblo: A Story of Archaeology and Ancient Life* by Jefferson Reid and Stephanie Whittlesey, © 1999 The Arizona Board of Regents. Reprinted by permission of the University of Arizona Press; 7.34, Courtesy J. Jefferson Reid **Chapter 8** CO-8, © Richard T. Nowitz/Corbis; 8.1, from Niels Bonde and Arne Emil Christensen, "Dendrochronological Dating of the Viking Age Ship Burials at Oseberg, Gokstad and Tune, Norway, *Antiquity,* Vol. 67, No. 256, September 1, 1993, pp. 575–83. Reprinted by permission of the publisher; 8.2, from J. C. Harrington, "Dating Stem Fragments of Seventeenth and Eighteenth Century Clay Tobacco Pipes," *Quarterly Bulletin: Archaeological Society of Virginia,* vol. 9, no. 1 (1954). Reprinted by permission of the Archaeological Society of Virginia; 8.3, courtesy of the National Park Service, Colonial National Historical Park. http://nps.gov/gis/mapbook/archeology/colo_pipes.html; 8.4, by Annick Boothe. From *Archaeology: Theories, Methods and Practice* by Colin Renfrew and Paul Bahn, 4th ed., published by Thames & Hudson Inc., New York; 8.6, adapted from Penelope A. Parkes, *Current Scientific Techniques in Archaeology,* Fig. 4.2. St. Martin's Press, New York. © 1986 P. A. Parkes. Reproduced with permission of Palgrave Macmillan; 8.7, Courtesy Henri D. Grissino-Mayer, Department of Geography, University of Tennessee.; 8.8, from *Archaeology,* 2nd edition by Thomas. © 1989. Reprinted with permission of Wadsworth, a division of Thomson Learning: www.thomsonrights.com. Fax 800 730-2215; 8.9, Courtesy Paul Logsdon; 8.10, Courtesy Musee Dauphinois. Grenoble, France; 8.11, from Pierre Pétrequin et al., "Demographic Growth, Environmental Changes and Technical Adaptations: Responses of an Agricultural Community from the 32nd to the 30th Centuries BC," *World Archaeology,* Vol. 30, No. 2 (October 1998), p. 188. Reprinted by permission of the author and Taylor & Francis Ltd. http://www.tandf.co.uk/journals; 8.12, Photo by Time Life Pictures/Time Magazine, Copyright Time Inc./Time Life Pictures/Getty Images; 8.13, from T. Douglas Price and Gary M. Feinman, *Images of the Past,* 4th edition, p. 143. Copyright © 2005 by The McGraw-Hill Companies, Inc. Reprinted with permission; 8.15, Courtesy Jan Heinemeier; 8.16, from Bruce D. Smith, *The Emergence of Agriculture.* New York: Scientific American Library, 1995, p. 38. Reprinted by permission of the author; 8.17, © Corbis/Sygma; 8.18, sata from Damon, P. E. et al., "Radiocarbon Dating of the Shroud of Turin," *Nature,* 337 (1989), pp. 611–15; 8.19, from E. B. Banning, *The Archaeologist's Laboratory: The Analysis of Archaeological Data,* p. 269. © 2000 Kluwer Academic / Plenum Publishers. With kind permission from Springer Science and Business Media; 8.20, adapted from Davis, O. K., Dai, K., Dean, J. S., Parks, J., and Kalin, R. M. 1996. Radiocarbon dating of buried trees, and climatic change in west-central Oklahoma. *Radiocarbon* 37 (2): 611–14. Used with permission of the publisher and Owen K. Davis; 8.21, 8.22, © John Reader/ Photo Researchers, Inc.; 8.23, Courtesy Martin Trtilek, Photon Systems Instruments Ltd. **Chapter 9** CO-9, © NGS Image Collection; 9.1, by ML Design. From *Archaeology: Theories, Methods and Practice* by Colin Renfrew and Paul Bahn, 4th ed., published by Thames & Hudson Inc., New York; 9.2 top, modified from H.-E. Reineck and I. B. Singh, *Depositional Sedimentary Environments,* p. 230. © by Springer-Verlag Berlin and Heidelberg 1973. With kind permission from Springer Science and Business Media. 9.2 bottom, modified from Karl W. Butzer, *Geomorphology from the*

Earth. New York: Harper & Row, 1976. By permission of the author; 9.3, United States Department of Agriculture, Natural Resources Conservation Service. http://www.soils.usda.gov/education/resources/k_12/lessons/profile/; 9.4, reprinted with permission from *Science,* Vol. 209, 15 August 1980; John C. Kraft, Ilhan Kayan, and O_uz Erol, "Geomorphic Reconstructions in the Environs of Ancient Troy," pp. 776–82, Fig. 6. Copyright 1980 AAAS; 9.5, *Archaeology,* 2004 by Trevor Barnes. © Kingfisher 2004. Reproduced by permission of Kingfisher Publications Plc. All rights reserved.; 9.6, Courtesy Torben Malm9.7, Courtesy David Hurst Thomas. American Museum of Natural History; 9.8, Courtesy GretagMacbeth; 9.10, p. 256 Courtesy of Sönke Hartz; 9.11, from *Archaeology,* 1st edition by Rathje. © 1982. Reprinted with permission of Wadsworth, a division of Thomson Learning: www.thomsonrights.com. Fax 800 730-2215; 9.13, courtesy of Edward Harris, adapted from *Principles of Archaeological Stratigraphy,* 1989, Fig. 12, p. 39; 9.14, Courtesy Anne Argast, Indiana University-Purdue University, Fort Wayne; 9.15, 9.17, Courtesy Brian Hayden; 9.18, from Brian Hayden, *The Pithouses of Keatley Creek: Complex Hunter-Gatherers of the Northwest Plateau.* Fort Worth, TX: Harcourt Brace College Publishers, 1997, Figure 3.8, p. 38. Reprinted by permission of the author; 9.19, Courtesy Paul Goldberg; 9.20, from Diana Alexander, "Excavations in Housepit 9." In *The Ancient Past of Keatley Creek.* Volume III: Excavations and Artifacts, ed. Brian Hayden (2003). Courtesy of Archaeology Press, Simon Fraser University; 9.21, courtesy of William Middleton; 9.22, Courtesy Dr. Payson Sheets **Chapter 10** CO-10, © The National Museum of Denmark; 10.1, Courtesy Bo Knarrström; 10.2, from William Watson, *Flint Implements: An Account of Stone Age Techniques and Cultures,* 3rd edition, p. 27, Fig. 1. © 1968, The Trustees of the British Museum. Reprinted by permission; 10.4, from Nicholas Toth, "The First Technology," *Scientific American,* April 1987. By permission of the illustrator, Edward L. Hanson; 10.5, from François Bordes, *The Old Stone Age,* translated from the French by J. E. Anderson, p. 25. Copyright © 1968 by The McGraw-Hill Companies, Inc. Reprinted with permission; 10.6, © The National Museum of Denmark; 10.7, 10.8 from T. Douglas Price and Gary M. Feinman, *Images of the Past,* 4th edition, p. 123 & 125. Copyright © 2005 by The McGraw-Hill Companies, Inc. Reprinted with permission; 10.9, from a translation of an unpublished paper by Jacques Tixier; 10.10, Photo courtesy of 3D Visualization Program, Geo-Marine, Inc.; 10.12, Photo courtesy F. Clark Howell; 10.14, from Roger Grace, "The 'chaîne opératoire' approach to lithic analysis," Figure 18. http://www.hf.uio.no/iakk/roger/lithic/opchainpaper.html. Reprinted by permission of Roger Grace; 10.15, from William Andrefsky, Jr., *Lithics: Macroscopic Approaches to Analysis,* p. 204. © Cambridge University Press 1998. Reprinted with the permission of Cambridge University Press; 10.16, from Robert L. Kelly, "The Three Sides of a Biface." Reproduced by permission of the Society for American Archaeology from *American Antiquity,* Vol. 53, No. 4 (1988), pp. 717–34, Figure 2 (modified); 10.17, courtesy of Erwin Cziesla; 10.18, from Erwin Cziesla, "Investigations into the archaeology of the Sitra-Hatiyet, northwestern Egypt." In L. Krzyaniak, M. Kobusiewicz, and J. Alexander (Eds.), *Proceedings of the 3rd International Symposium: Environmental Change and Human Culture in the Nile Basin and Northern Africa until the Second Millennium BC.* Pozna_ Archaeological Museum, Vol. 4 (1993), pp. 185–97. Reprinted by permission of Erwin Cziesla; 10.19, from Paola Villa, "Coinjoinable Pieces and Site Formation Processes." Reproduced by permission of the Society for American Archaeology from *American Antiquity,* Vol. 47, No. 2 (1982), pp. 276–90, Figure 1; 10.20, reprinted with the permission of Simon & Schuster Adult Publishing Group from *Making Silent Stones Speak* by Kathy D. Schick and Nicholas Toth. Copyright © 1993 by Kathy D. Schick and Nicholas Toth; 10.21, Courtesy Monika

Derndarsky; 10.22, © Professor Leroi-Gourhan. From *The Old Stone Age*, p. 236. Weidenfeld & Nicholson Ltd.; 10.23, from F. Van Noten, D. Cahen, and L. Keeley, "A Paleolithic Campsite in Belgium," *Scientific American*, Vol. 242, No. 4 (1980), pp. 48–55. Reprinted by permission of the illustrator, Andrew M. Tomko III; 10.24, from D. Cahen, L. H. Keeley, and F. L. Van Noten, "Stone Tools, Tool Kits and Human Behavior in Prehistory," *Current Anthropology*, Vol. 20, No. 4 (1979), pp. 661–83, Figure 9. Copyright © 1979 by The Wenner-Gren Foundation for Anthropological Research. Reprinted by permission of The University of Chicago Press; 10.25, from F. Van Noten, D. Cahen, and L. Keeley, "A Paleolithic Campsite in Belgium," *Scientific American*, Vol. 242, No. 4 (1980), pp. 48–55. Reprinted by permission of the illustrator, Andrew M. Tomko III; 10.26, © National Museum of Ethnology, Holland (4436-86A); 10.27, from A. Leroi-Gourhan, *Prehistoric Man*, translated by Wade Baskin. Philosophical Library, New York, 1957. Reprinted by permission of the publisher **Chapter 11** CO-11 © Justin Kerr/Kerr Associates; 11.1, © Sakamoto Photo Research Laboratory/Corbis; 11.2, from T. Douglas Price and Anne Birgitte Gebauer, *Adventures in Fugawiland*, 3rd edition, p. 80. Copyright © 2002 by The McGraw-Hill Companies, Inc. Reprinted with permission; 11.3, from John P. Staeck, *Back to the Earth: An Introduction to Archaeology*, 1st edition. Mountain View, CA: Mayfield, 2002, p. 195. Reprinted by permission of the author; 11.4, from John P. Staeck, *Back to the Earth: An Introduction to Archaeology*, 1st edition. Mountain View, CA: Mayfield, 2002, p. 195. Reprinted by permission of the author; 11.5, from C. Garth Sampson, *Stylistic Boundaries among Mobile Hunter-Foragers*. Washington, DC: Smithsonian Institution Press, 1988, p. 55. Reprinted by permission of the author; 11.6, from T. Douglas Price and Gary M. Feinman, *Images of the Past*, 4th edition, p. 234. Copyright © 2005 by The McGraw-Hill Companies, Inc. Reprinted with permission; 11.7, from T. Douglas Price and Gary M. Feinman, *Images of the Past*, 4th edition, p. 234. Copyright © 2005 by The McGraw-Hill Companies, Inc. Reprinted with permission; 11.8, © Hulton-Deutsch Collection/Corbis; 11.9, from Fagan, Brian M., *Archaeology: A Brief Introduction*, 9th edition, © 2006. Adapted by permission of Pearson Education, Inc., Upper Saddle River, NJ; 11.10, from Clive Orton, *Mathematics in Archaeology*, p. 34, Fig. 2.8. © Clive Orton 1980. Reprinted with the permission of Cambridge University Press; 11.12, © Jim Sugar/Corbis; 11.13, © Roger Wood/Corbis; 11.14, from Søren H. Andersen and C. Malmros. 1984. "Madskorpe" på Ertebøllekar fra Tybrind Vig. *Aarbøger for Nordisk Oldkyndighed og Historie* 1983, pp. 78–95, Fig. 6. Courtesy of J. Kirkeby/S. H. Andersen; 11.15, Courtesy S.H. Andersen; 11.16, from John P. Staeck, *Back to the Earth: An Introduction to Archaeology*, 1st edition. Mountain View, CA: Mayfield, 2002, p. 28. Reprinted by permission of the author; 11.17, adapted from Ruben E. Reina and Robert M. Hill II, *The Traditional Pottery of Guatemala*. Austin: University of Texas Press, 1978. By permission of Ruben E. Reina; 11.18, reprinted from Margaret Ann Hardin, "Individual Style in San José Pottery Painting: The Role of Deliberate Choice," in *The Individual in Prehistory*, ed. James N. Hill and Joel Gunn. New York: Academic Press, 1977, p. 121, with permission from Elsevier; 11.19, p. 315 Courtesy of Robert Whallon; 11.20, after Whallon, 1968; 11.21, from T. Douglas Price and Gary M. Feinman, *Images of the Past*, 4th edition, p. 274. Copyright © 2005 by The McGraw-Hill Companies, Inc. Reprinted with permission; 11.22, Courtesy James Stoltman; 11.23, Beloit College, Logan Museum of Anthropology (16359); 11.25, adapted from an illustration by Linda Price Thomson, from David E. Doyel, "The Prehistoric Hohokam of the Arizona Desert," *American Scientist*, Vol. 67, No. 5 (September–October 1979), pp. 544–54, Figure 10. Used by permission of the publisher; 11.26, after figure 102 from G. F. Dales and J. M. Kenoyer, *Excavations at Mohenjo Daro, Pakistan: The Pottery*. Philadelphia, PA: University of Pennsyl-

vania Museum of Archaeology and Anthropology, 1986. By permission of the publisher and J. M. Kenoyer; Table 11.1, data from Stanley A. South, *Method and Theory in Historical Archaeology*. New York: Academic Press, 1977, pp. 210–12 **Chapter 12** CO-12, Aaris-Sorensen and Brinch Petersen, STRIAE, 24: 111–17. Photo by Geert Brovad; 12.1, © Kim Aaris-Sorensen; 12.2, © Statens Historiska Museum. Photo: Soren Hallgren; 12.3, from David H. Jurney and Susan L. Andrews, *Archaeological Investigations at 41DL279: Site of the John F. Kennedy Exhibit, Dallas County Administration Building, Dallas, Texas*. Erie, PA: Mercyhurst College, 1995, Figure E.1. Reprinted by permission of James M. Adovasio, Principal Investigator; 12.4, from Fagan, Brian M., *In the Beginning: An Introduction to Archaeology*, 10th Edition, © 2001. Adapted by permission of Pearson Education, Inc., Upper Saddle River, NJ; 12.5, Courtesy Colonial Williamsburg Foundation; 12.6, T.D. Price; 12.7, from T. Douglas Price and Gary M. Feinman, *Images of the Past*, 4th edition, p. 154. Copyright © 2005 by The McGraw-Hill Companies, Inc. Reprinted with permission; 12.8, from Colin Renfrew and Paul Bahn, *Archaeology: Theories, Methods, and Practice*, 4th ed. London and New York: Thames & Hudson, 2004. Reprinted by permission of the publisher; 12.9, © Texas Parks and Wildlife Department; 12.10, Courtesy Chris O'Brien; 12.11, from Clifford J. Jolly and Randall White, *Physical Anthropology and Archaeology*, 5th edition. Copyright © 1995 by The McGraw-Hill Companies, Inc. Reprinted with permission; 12.13, From J.G.D. Clark, 1954. Star Carr. New York: Cambridge University Press; 12.14, from Grahame Clark, *Excavations at Star Carr*. Cambridge University Press, 1954, Fig. 31, p. 94. Reprinted with the permission of Cambridge University Press; 12.15, from A. J. Legge and P. A. Rowley-Conwy, *Star Carr Revisited*. Centre for Extra Mural Studies, Birkbeck College, University of London, 1988. Reprinted by permission of Anthony J. Legge; 12.16, after Jean Perrot, Centre de Recherche Francais de Jerusalem; 12.17, Courtesy Daniel Lieberman, Harvard University; 12.18, from Sutton & Yohe, *Archaeology: The Science of the Human Past*. Published by Allyn & Bacon, Boston, MA. Copyright © 2003 by Pearson Education. Reprinted by permission of the publisher; 12.19, Courtesy Kathy Schick and Nicholas Toth, Co-Directors, Stone Age Institute, www.stoneageinstitute.org; 12.20, Courtesy Richard Potts; 12.21, "Figure 12.14 (a)" from Robert Boyd and Joan B. Silk, *How Humans Evolved*, 3rd edition, by Robert Boyd and Joan B. Silk. Copyright © 2003, 2000, 1997 by W. W. Norton & Company, Inc. Used by permission of W. W. Norton & Company, Inc.; 12.22, p. 345 From *Archaeology*, 2nd edition by Thomas. © 2001. Reprinted with permission of Wadsworth, a division of Thomson Learning: www.thomsonrights.com. Fax 800 730-2215; 12.23, Courtesy Søren Andersen; 12.24, Courtesy Nicky Milner, University of York; 12.25, T.D. Price **Chapter 13** CO-13, © David Cavagnaro/Peter Arnold, Inc.; 13.1, from Kenneth L. Feder and Michael Alan Park, *Human Antiquity: An Introduction to Physical Anthropology and Archaeology*, 4th edition, p. 475. Copyright © 2001 by The McGraw-Hill Companies, Inc. Reprinted with permission; 13.2, Courtesy Institute of Archaeology, University College, London; 13.3, Photo by Grant D. Hall, courtesy of the Archaeology Laboratory, Department of Sociology, Anthropology & Social Work, Texas Tech University; 13.4, Courtesy Charles M. Niquette, Cultural Resource Analysts, Inc.; 13.5, Courtesy Peter Woodman; 13.6, Braidwood and Howe, *Prehistoric Investigations in Iraqi Kurdistan*, University of Chicago Press, 1960. Plate 27b. Courtesy Oriental Institute Publications; 13.7, courtesy The Dayton Society of Natural History; 13.8, © Jill Malusky/SunWatch Indian Village; Table 13.1, from Gail E. Wagner, "Feast or Famine? Seasonal Diet at a Fort Ancient Community." In *Case Studies in Environmental Archaeology*, ed. E. J. Reitz, L. A. Newsom, and S. J. Scudder, pp. 255–71. © 1996 Plenum Press, New York. With kind permission from Springer Science and Business Media; 13.9, adapted from Gail

E. Wagner, "Feast or Famine? Seasonal Diet at a Fort Ancient Community," in *Case Studies in Environmental Archaeology*, ed. E. J. Reitz, L. A. Newsom, and S. J. Scudder, pp. 255–71. © 1996 Plenum Press, New York. With kind permission from Springer Science and Business Media; 13.10, © Chip Clark; 13.11, courtesy Institute of Archaeology, University College London; 13.12, from T. Douglas Price and Gary M. Feinman, *Images of the Past*, 4th edition, p. 220. Copyright © 2005 by The McGraw-Hill Companies, Inc. Reprinted with permission; 13.13, Courtesy Jack Harlan; 13.14, "Figures 14.1 and 14.4," from *Village on the Euphrates: From Foraging to Farming at Abu Hureyra* by A. M. T. Moore and G. C. Hillman and A. J. Legge, copyright © 1999 by Oxford University Press, Inc. Used by permission of Oxford University Press, Inc.; 13.15, Courtesy Kathleen Pigg; 13.16, © Lawrence Migdale/Photo Researchers, Inc.; 13.18, © Kristi J. Black/Corbis; 13.19, Courtesy E. Asouti; 13.20, Courtesy Arlene M. Rosen; 13.21, © Eric V. Grave / Photo Researchers, Inc.; 13.22, Courtesy Don Ugent; 13.23, © Dennis Kunkel/Phototake. All rights reserved; 13.24, Irish Peatland Conservation Council. www.ipcc.ie. Reprinted with permission **Chapter 14** CO-14, Unit of Art in Medicine, University of Manchester; 14.1, Courtesy Dr. Caroline Wilkinson; 14.2, Courtesy Dr. Joachim Wahl; 14.3, © Michael A. Hampshire/NGS Image Collection; 14.4, © Jonathan Blair/Corbis; 14.5, from James L. Theler and Robert F. Boszhardt, *Twelve Millennia: Archaeology of the Upper Mississippi River Valley*. Iowa City: University of Iowa Press, 2003, Figure 1.5. Reprinted by permission of the illustrator, Laura Jankowski; 14.7, from T. Douglas Price and Gary M. Feinman, *Images of the Past*, 4th edition, p. 185. Copyright © 2005 by The McGraw-Hill Companies, Inc. Reprinted with permission; 14.8, © Bettmann/Corbis; 14.9, adapted from Philip L. Stein and Bruce R. Rowe, *Physical Anthropology*, 8th edition, p. 467. Copyright © 2003 by The McGraw-Hill Companies, Inc. Used with permission; 14.12, from Nikola Koepke and Joerg Baten, "The Biological Standard of Living in Europe during the Last Two Millennia," *European Review of Economic History*, vol. 9, no. 1 (April 2005), pp. 61–95, Figure 4. © 2005 Cambridge University Press. Reprinted with the permission of Cambridge University Press; 14.13, from J. Wahl and H. G. König, "Anthropologisch-traumatologische Untersuchung der menschlichen Skelettreste aus dem bandkeramischen Massengrab bei Talheim, Kreis Heilbronn." *Fundberichte aus Baden-Württemberg 12*, 1987, pp. 65–193, Figure 6. Reprinted by permission of Joachim Wahl; 14.15, Courtesy C.S. Larsen, Ohio State University; 14.17, © Pepys Library, Magdalene College, Cambridge; 14.18, from Kenneth L. Feder and Michael Alan Park, *Human Antiquity: An Introduction to Physical Anthropology and Archaeology*, 4th edition, p. 71. Copyright © 2001 by The McGraw-Hill Companies, Inc. Reprinted with permission; 14.19, Illustration © Gilles Tosello/Musee de Prehistorie d'Ile-de-France, Nemours; 14.20, adapted from Igor Ovchinnikov and William Goodwin, "The Isolation and Identification of Neanderthal Mitochondrial DNA," *Profiles in DNA*, January 2001, p. 9. By permission of William Goodwin; 14.21, Courtesy of the Museum of Archaeology in Varna, Bulgaria; 14.22, © CNRS UMR 7041; 14.23, from A. Sherratt, "Resources, Technology and Trade: An Essay in Early European Metallurgy." In *Problems in Economic and Social Archaeology*, ed. G. de G. Sieveking et al. London: Duckworth, 1976, pp. 557–82, Fig. 8. Reprinted by permission of Gerald Duckworth & Co. Ltd.; 14.24, from *Past Worlds: The Times Atlas of Archaeology*, pp. 48–49. Reprinted by permission of HarperCollins Publishers Ltd. Copyright © 1988 Times Books Limited; 14.25, reprinted by permission of the illustrator, Steven Patricia. © Steven Patricia. From *Hero, Hawk, and Open Hand: American Indian Art of the Ancient Midwest and South*, Richard F. Townsend, General Editor. Art Institute of Chicago, 2004, p. 168 **Chapter 15** CO-15, © Nimatallah/Art Resource, NY; 15.1, from Michael D. Glascock, "An Overview of Neutron Activation Analysis," Figure 1. http://www.missouri.edu/~glascock/naa_over.htm. By permission of Michael D. Glascock; 15.3, T.D. Price; 15.4, Courtesy Bruker AXS; 15.5, adapted with permission from Bruker AXS Inc., Madison, Wisconsin; 15.7, from C. Bernes, *Persistent Organic Pollutants—A Swedish View of an International Problem*. Swedish Environmental Protection Agency, Stockholm, 1998. Reprinted with permission; 15.8, Courtesy Jason Knudsen; 15.9, T.D. Price; 15.10, redrawn and modified from J. E. Dixon, J. R. Cann, and Colin Renfrew, "Obsidian and the Origins of Trade," *Scientific American*, Vol. 218, No. 3 (March 1968), pp. 38–46; 15.11, adapted from Colin Renfrew and John Dixon, "Obsidian in Western Asia: A Review." In *Problems in Economic and Social Archaeology*, ed. G. de G. Sieveking et al. London: Duckworth, 1976, pp. 137–50. Reprinted by permission of Gerald Duckworth & Co. Ltd.; 15.13, from E. C. Wells, "Investigating Activity Patterns in Prehispanic Plazas: Weak Acid-Extraction ICP-AES Analysis of Anthrosols at Classic Period El Coyote, Northwestern Honduras," *Archaeometry*, Vol. 46, No. 1 (2004), pp. 67–84, Figure 2. Reprinted by permission of Blackwell Publishing; 15.14, from T. Douglas Price and Gary M. Feinman, *Images of the Past*, 4th edition, p. 170. Copyright © 2005 by The McGraw-Hill Companies, Inc. Reprinted with permission; 15.15, some of the data are from Tauber, H., "13C Evidence for Dietary Habits of Prehistoric Man in Denmark," *Nature*, Vol. 292 (July 23, 1981), pp. 332–33; 15.16, from Margaret J. Schoeninger and Katherine Moore, "Bone Stable Isotope Studies in Archaeology," *Journal of World Prehistory*, Vol. 6 (1992), pp. 247–96, Fig. 1. With kind permission from Springer Science and Business Media; 15.17, reprinted from Margaret J. Schoeninger and M. J. DeNiro, "Nitrogen and Carbon Isotopic Composition of Bone Collagen from Marine and Terrestrial Animals," *Geochimica et Cosmochimica Acta*, Vol. 48 (1984), pp. 625–39, Figure 1, with permission from Elsevier; 15.18, from Thomas H. McGovern and Sophia Perdikaris, "The Vikings' Silent Saga: What Went Wrong with the Scandinavian Westward Expansion?" *Natural History Magazine*, October 2000, p. 54. Reprinted by permission of the illustrator, Marcia Bakry; 15.19, data from Arneborg, J., Jan Heinemeier, Niels Lynnerup, Henrik L. Nielsen, Niels Raud, Árny E. Sveinbjörnsdóttir. 1999. Change of diet of the Greenland Vikings determined from stable carbon isotope analysis and 14C dating of their bones. *Radiocarbon* 41: 157–68; and Dansgaard, W., et al. 1975. Climate changes, Norsemen, and modern man. *Nature* 255: 24–28; 15.20, Courtesy Jason Krantz; 15.21, © Christopher A. Klein/NGS Image Collection; 15.22, Used by permission of the Early Copan Acropolis Program, University of Pennsylvania Museum of Archaeology & Anthropology **Part 4** Adalberto Rios Szalay/Sexto Sol/Getty Images **Chapter 16** CO-16, reprinted by permission of the Institute of Archaeology, University College London, from V. Gordon Childe, *The Danube in Prehistory*. Oxford: Clarendon Press, 1929; 16.1, Lewis R. Binford/*In Pursuit of the Past*/© 2002/The Regents of the University of California; 16.2, From *Analytical Archaeology* by David Clarke. © 1981 Columbia University Press. Reprinted with permission of the publisher.; 16.3, from Robert L. Kelly, *The Foraging Spectrum: Diversity in Hunter-Gatherer Lifeways*. Washington, DC: Smithsonian Institution Press, 1995, Figure 6–7, p. 255. Reprinted by permission of the illustrator, Daniel G. Delaney; 16.4, Four bronze age barrows along the coast of Denmark. From *Danish Prehistoric Monuments*, by P.V. Glob, 1971, page 27, figure 4. Reprinted with permission of Glydendal, Copenhagen.; 16.5, reprinted from K. L. Johansen, S. T. Laursen, and M. K. Holst, "Spatial Patterns of Social Organization in the Early Bronze Age of South Scandinavia," *Journal of Anthropological Archaeology*, Vol. 23 (2004), pp. 33–55, with permission from Elsevier; 16.6, © The National Museum of Denmark; 16.7, from T. Douglas Price and Gary M. Feinman, *Images of the Past*, 4th edition, p. 318. Copyright © 2005 by The McGraw-Hill Companies, Inc. Reprinted with permission; 16.8, figure 2 from Raymond Sidrys and Rainer Berger, "Lowland Maya Radiocarbon Dates and the Classic Maya Collapse," *Nature,* Vol. 277 (1979), pp. 269–74. Copyright 1979 by Nature Publishing Group. Reproduced with permission of Nature Publishing Group via Copyright Clearance Center; 16.9, from John Lowe, *The Dynamics of Collapse: A Systems Simulation of the Classic Maya.* Albuquerque, NM: University of New Mexico Press, 1985. Reprinted by permission of the publisher; 16.10, from David Webster, *The Fall of the Ancient Maya.* London: Thames & Hudson, 2002, pp. 328–29. Reprinted by permission of the author; 16.11, from Jeremy A. Sabloff, *The New Archaeology and the Ancient Maya.* New York: Scientific American Library/W. H. Freeman, 1994, p. 121. Reprinted by permission of the author; 16.12, Courtesy Ian Hodder, Stanford University; 16.13, Book cover courtesy Polity Press. Image courtesy Galleria Emi Fontana, Milano.; 16.14, From *Death by Theory* by Adrian Praetzellis. 2000. Walnut Creek: Altamira Press, p. 139; 16.15, Photo by Johan Olofsson, Environmental Archaeology Lab. Umeå University, Sweden; 16.16, © Per Byrgren; 16.17, from Christopher Tilley, *Material Culture and Text: The Art of Ambiguity.* London: Routledge, 1991, Figure 12. Reprinted by permission of the author; Table 16.2, from Christopher Tilley, *Material Culture and Text: The Art of Ambiguity.* London: Routledge, 1991. Reprinted by permission of the author; 16.18, from Christopher Tilley, *Material Culture and Text: The Art of Ambiguity.* London: Routledge, 1991. Reprinted by permission of the author; 16.19, from Christopher Tilley, *Material Culture and Text: The Art of Ambiguity.* London: Routledge, 1991, Figure 7.3. Reprinted by permission of the author; 16.20, Used by permission of Springer Verlag; 16.21, data from David P. Braun, "Pots as Tools." In *Archaeological Hammers and Theories,* ed. J. A. Moore and A. S. Keene. New York: Academic Press, 1983, pp. 107–34. Reprinted by permission of David P. Braun; 16.22, Courtesy of the Phoebe Hearst Msueum of Anthropology and the Regents of the University of California (15-7792); 16.23, adapted from J. M. Broughton, "Prey Spatial Structure and Behavior Affect Archaeological Tests of Optimal Foraging Models: Examples from the Emeryville Shellmound Vertebrate Fauna," *World Archaeology,* Vol. 34, No. 1 (1 June 2002), pp. 60–83; 16.24, Blackwell Publishers; 16.25, Photo by Jason Jones. Courtesy Liz Brumfiel; 16.26, © The Bodleian Library, University of Oxford, MS. Arch. Seld.A.1; 16.27, from Melinda A. Zeder, *The American Archaeologist: A Profile.* Copyright © 1997 by Society for American Archaeology. Reprinted with permission of AltaMira Press, a division of Rowman & Littlefield Publishers, Inc.; 16.28, data from Melinda A. Zeder, *The American Archaeologist: A Profile.* AltaMira Press, 1997; 16.29, adapted from Kurt A. Richardson, "'Methodological Implications of Complex Systems Approaches to Sociality': Some Further Remarks," *Journal of Artificial Societies and Social Simulation,* Vol. 5, No. 2 (2002), Figure 1. By permission of the publisher **Chapter 17** CO-17, Courtesy Dr. Dale Croes; pp. 478–79, from Rhonda Foster and Dale R. Croes, "Archaeology/Anthropology—Native American Coordination: An Example of Sharing the Research." Paper presented at the American Anthropological Association Symposium entitled Current Issues in Anthropology: Five Fields Update, Washington, DC, November 29, 2001. Reprinted by permission of the authors; 17.1, 17.2, Courtesy Clark Erickson; 17.3, © Reuters/Corbis; Table 17.1, UNESCO World Heritage Centre; 17.4, ©Georg Gerster/Photo Researchers, Inc.; 17.5, Courtesy Cheryl Ann Munson (Indiana University) and David Pollack (Kentucky Heritage Council); 17.6, © Reuters/Corbis; 17.7, from Elizabeth Gilgan, "Looting and the Market for Maya Objects: A Belizean Perspective." In *Trade in Illicit Antiquities: The Destruction of the World's Archaeological Heritage,* ed. Neil Brodie, Jennifer Doole, and Colin Renfrew. Cambridge, UK: McDonald Institute for Archaeological Research, 2001, pp. 73–88. Reprinted by permission of The McDonald Institute for Archaeological Research; 17.8, © AP/Wide World Photos; p. 489, definition of "Ethics" from *Webster 1913 Dictionary.* Patrick J. Cassidy, 1913. *Answers.com* 13 . 2006. http://www.answers.com/topic/ethics-legal-term; 17.9, 17.10, Courtesy Aurel Sercu; 17.10, Courtesy JW Ball; Table 17.4, from http://www.saa.org/aboutSAA/committees/curriculum/principles.html. Reproduced by permission of the Society for American Archaeology; pp. 495–97, Joe Ball, "The Other Side of the Story." Reprinted by permission of the author; 17.11, Poster courtesy of the State Historic Preservation Office, Arizona State Parks, Phoenix, Arizona **Appendix** A-3, from B. Wood, "Paleoanthropology," *Nature,* Vol. 418 (11 July 2002), p. 134. Copyright 2002 by Nature Publishing Group. Reproduced with permission of Nature Publishing Group via Copyright Clearance Center; Fig. A-4, from Barry Cunliffe, *Oxford Illustrated Prehistory of Europe.* Oxford: Oxford University Press, 1994. Reprinted by permission of Paul A. Mellars; A-5, Photo by Jean Vertut, Issey-les-Molineaux, France; A-7, © Royalty-Free/Corbis; A-9, © Tom Pleger ; A6, from Kenneth L. Feder and Michael Alan Park, *Human Antiquity: An Introduction to Physical Anthropology and Archaeology,* 4th edition, p. 437. Copyright © 2001 by The McGraw-Hill Companies, Inc. Reprinted with permission; p. 526 from T. Douglas Price and Gary M. Feinman, *Images of the Past,* 4th edition. Copyright © 2005 by The McGraw-Hill Companies, Inc. Reprinted with permission.

Index

by geographic distribution, 196, *196*
importance of, 184–185, *185*, 187
of Iroquois pottery, 190, *190*
of Northwestern Plains projectile points, *188*
raw materials and, 189–191, *190*
of San arrows, 179–180, *180*
seriation, 193–195, *193, 194, 195*
splitters and lumpers, 185
typologies, 186–187, *188*
See also data
class societies, 85
clay
definition of, 300
in pottery, 301–302
in soil texture, 255, *255*
See also ceramic
clay smoking pipes, 217–218, *218*
cleaning artifacts, 181–182, *181*
climate
extinction and, 330
Little Ice Age, 435, *435*
Medieval Warm Period, 434–435, *434, 435*
relevance of, 482
society and, 72
tree ring data on, *242*
cloth. *See* textiles
clustered patterns, 209, *209*
CMRAE (Center for Materials Research in Archaeology and Ethnology), 41
coefficient of stylistic variability, 313, *313*
cognitive archaeology, 474–475
coil technique, 302, *302*
coins, 13–14
collagen, bone, 430
collars, pot, 306–307
commensals, 337
commercialization of artifacts, *489*, 492, 493
complexity, 86–87, *87*
complexity theory, 473
components, 111–112, *112, 138*
composition
ceramic, 316–318, *317, 318*
sediment, 256
compounds, 418–419
conchoidal fractures, 275
Conkey, Meg, 471, *471*
conservation of materials, 182–183, *183*
context, 105–106, *105*, 130
contingency tables, 203–205, *204*
contour maps, 155–158, *156, 157, 158*
Conyers, Lawrence, *165*
Cook Islands, 524
Copan site (Honduras), 436–438, *436, 437*
copper, 42, 77, 137
Coppergate Site (England), 100, *100*
coprolites, 207, *208*, 373, 385–386
cord-marking, 83, 304
cores, 274
corn. *See* maize
correlations, 208–209, *209*

Cortés, Hernando, 522
cortex, of stone tools, 279–280
cortical bone, 383, *383*
cortical flakes, 280
cosmology, 88, 89
Cosquer cave (France), 153
country, definition of, 73
creationism, 16, 216
Cree Indians, snowmobiles and, 468
cremation, 109, 149, 381
cribra orbitalia, 392, *393*
critical theory, 460
CRM. *See* cultural resource management
Crumley, Carole, 167
cryptocrystalline materials, 274–275, *275*
crystalline materials, 422–423
cultural (social) anthropology, 8
cultural (evolutionary) archaeology, 467–468, *467*, 471, 475, 476
cultural landscapes, 116
cultural resource management (CRM)
academic archaeology and, 9
careers in, 20, *20*, 24–25, *24*
definition of, 480
in FAI–270 project, 58–62, *59, 60, 61, 62, 63*
overlooking regulations during business operations, 497–498
Squaxin Island Tribe and, *478*, 479–481
cultural transformation, 130, *132*
culture
adaptation and, 15, 70–71
components of, 71–72, *71*
definition of, 70, 450
demography and, 72–75, *74, 75*
economy in, 81–83, *81, 82*
environment and, 72, *73*
ideology and, 87–91, *88, 89, 91*
as means for human adaptation, 15, 70–71
organization of, 84–87, *85, 86, 87*
technology and, 80–81, *80, 81*
culture change, definition of, 433
culture history, 51, 56, 475, *476*
culture process, 56–57
curated tools, 283
cursus monuments, *160*
Curtis, Garniss, 234
Custer Battlefield National Monument, 217
Custer's Last Stand, 8–9, 217
cut, 256, *256*
cutmarks, 339–341, *340, 341*
cylindrical vases, *298, 299, 303*
Cziesla, Erwin, 286

Daniel, Glyn, 64
Dart, Raymond, 342
Darwin, Charles, 15, 49, 217
data, 196–209
basic statistics, 198–205, *201, 202, 203, 204*
numbers, 197–198, *198*
qualitative *vs.* quantitative, 198

visual display of, 205–209, *205, 206, 207, 208, 209*
See also classification
dating methods, 215–243
accelerator mass spectrometer dating, 228–230, *229*
applications of, 225, 227, 230–232, *231*
archaeomagnetic, *221, 222, 222, 223*
association, 216–217
calendars, 219–220, *220*
calibration of, 232–233, *232, 233*
chronologies, 215, 217
dendrochronology, 215, *216*, 223–225, *224*, 240–242
example project on, 239–242, *239, 240, 241, 242*
fluorine absorption, 419
overview of methods, 221–222, *221, 222*
radiopotassium dating, *221, 222, 222*, 234–236, *234, 235*
relative *vs.* absolute, 216, 237
for rock art, 115
sample size required, *229*
seriation, 193–195, *193, 194, 195*
stratigraphy, 216–217
thermoluminescence dating, 115, *221, 222*, 236–237, *237*
datum, 155–156
Dawson, Charles, 10–11, *11*
death
age at, 388–389, *388, 389*
cause of, 391–392, *392, 393*
death's head motif, 193, *193*
débitage, 277, *285*
decapitators, 38
deciduous teeth, 388
deconstruction, 460
Deetz, James, 193, 312, 314
demography
analysis at Black Earth site, 77–79, *78, 79, 80*
culture and, 72–75, *74, 75*
definition of, 72
at Windover Pond (Florida), 136, *136*
See also age distribution
dendrochronology
application example, 240–242, *241, 242*
in Oseberg ship burial, 215, *216*
overview of method, 223–225, *224*
Denmark
barrows, Bronze Age, 454–456, *454, 455, 456*
hunter-gatherer camp on seacoast, *127*
Lejre site, *68, 69*, 151–152, *152*
Mesolithic sites, 119–121, *120, 149*, 151
Smakkerup Huse site, 333, *333*, 513
Tybrind Vig site, 310, *310*
density units, 528
Description de l'Egypt, 48, *48*
descriptive statistics, 199, *199*
diachronic explanations, 453
diagenesis, 339, 438

extinction, 329–330, *329, 330*

extractive sites, 112, 114

fabric of sediments, 256

Fagan, Brian, 55

FAI–270 project (Illinois), 58–62, *59, 60, 61, 62, 63*

The Fall of the Ancient Maya (Webster), 458–459, *459*

fatty acids, 438–439

fauna, 108. *See also* animals

faunal remains, 326–327, *327*. *See also* animal remains; archaeozoology

features, 108–109

feminist archaeology, 471–473, *471, 472*

Fertile Crescent, 360, *361*

field crews, 166–168

field notes, 146

field recording, 381–382, *382*

field schools, 169

fieldwork, 141–175

   contour maps, 155–158, *156, 157, 158*

   definition of, 142

   equipment for, 169, *169*

   field notes, 146

   field recording, 381–382, *382*

   geographic information systems, 158–160, *160*

   horizontal excavations, 148–150, *149*

   maps and grids, 154–160, *155, 156, 157, 158*

   opportunities in, 168–169, 495

   personnel in, 164–169

   remote sensing, 161–164, *162, 163*

   screening and flotation, 150–151, *150, 354*

   selecting sites for excavation, 146–147

   soil sampling, 150, 160–161, *161*

   surveys, 143–146, *143, 145*

   test pits, 147–148, *147*

   total stations, 158, *158*

   vertical excavations, 148

fill, 256, *256*

Fiorelli, Giuseppe, 49

fishing, 83

flakes

   cortical, 280

   fracture mechanics and, 274–276, *275, 276*

   from percussion flaking, 276, *277*

Flannery, Kent, 57, 90

flexed burials, 382, *383*

Flinders Petrie, William Matthew, 50, *50*, 194, *194*

flint, 274, *275*

flintknapping, 276–277, *277*

flora, 108

floral remains, 352. *See also* plant remains

flot, 353, *354*

flotation, 151, 353, *353, 354*

fluorine absorption test, 419

FMH (fully modern humans), 506. *See also Homo sapiens sapiens*

Folsom Paleoindian points, 105, *105*, 518

footprints, 235–236, *235*

foragers, 81. *See also* hunter-gatherers

Ford, James, 187, 195, *195*

forensic reconstruction, *378, 379, 380, 383*

foreshafts, 179

formal analogy, 92

Fort Ancient culture, 355–358, *355, 356, 357, 358*

fossile directeur, 187

fractionate, 429

fracture mechanics, 274–276, *275, 276*

France

   Cosquer cave, 153

   lake dwellings, 226–227, *226, 227*

   Pincevent site, *290*

   Pont du Gard, 7

   St. Acheul site, 280–281

   Terra Amata site, 287, *287*

frequency seriation, 194

"Frequently Asked Questions about Careers in Archaeology" (Carlson), 19

fully modern humans (FMH), 506. *See also Homo sapiens sapiens*

fume hoods, 424

function, 191–193, *193*

functional views, 451

Gammel Lejre (Denmark), 151–152, *152*, 517

Garanger, José, 403–405

Garaycochea, Ignacio, 483

Garrod, Dorothy, 52, *52*

gas chromatography-mass spectrometry (GC-MS), 423, *423*

Gatecliff Shelter (Nevada), 253, *254*

gazelles, 336, 362–363

GCI (Getty Conservation Institute), 236

Geiger counters, 228

gender archaeology, 471–473, *471, 472*

gender differences. *See* sex distinctions

genealogy, DNA evidence of, 398

genus, definition of, 326

geoarchaeology, 245–271

   Black Sea Flood Hypothesis, *244*, 245–246

   catastrophes, 264, *265*

   definition of, 246

   geomorphology, 246–249, *247, 248, 249*

   micromorphology, 256–265 (*See also* micromorphology)

   stratigraphy, 252–256, *252, 253, 254, 255, 256*

geographic information systems (GIS), 158–160, *160*

geological time, 506–507, *507*

geomorphology

   Homer's Troy and, 250–251, *250, 251*

   processes in, 246–249, *247, 248, 249*

georadar (ground penetrating radar), 164–165, *165*

Gero, Joan, *471*

Getty Conservation Institute (GCI), 236

Getty *kouros, 416,* 417–418

giant sloths, 329

Giddens, Anthony, 474

gilding technique, 42

GIS (geographic information systems), 158

glazes, 305

global positioning satellites (GPS), 158, *159*

glumes, 359–360, *359*

gold

   in Bronze Age barrows, 455, *455*

   in Moche culture, 42, 43

   in Varna site (Bulgaria), *401*

Goldberg, Paul, 261

Gold Rush menus, 340–341, *341*

gorgets, 406

Gould, Stephen Jay, 15–16

GPR (ground penetrating radar), 164–165, *165*

GPS (global positioning satellites), 158, *159*

Grace, Roger, 283

gradiometers, 164

graphs

   bar, 205–207, *205*

   box and whisker plots, 207, *207*

   histograms, 201–202, *201, 202, 203*, 205–207, *206*

   pie charts, 207, *208*

   scatterplots, 208–209, *208, 209*

   stem and leaf plots, 205, *205*

Grasshopper Pueblo (Arizona), 211–212, *211, 212*

grave goods

   at Black Earth site (Illinois), 77, *78*

   information from, 400

   at Moundville site (Alabama), 405–407, *405, 406*

   at Nitra cemetery (Slovakia), 402–403, *402, 403*

   at Roy Mata burial ground (Retoka), 403–405, *404*

   at Tomb of the Lord of Sipán (Peru), 35–36, *36*

gravestones, style of, 193, *193*

gravity model, 128–129

Great Basin (North America), 144

Great Hall at Lejre (Denmark), 151–152, *152*

Great Zimbabwe, 518

Green, Paul R., 167

Greenland

   Eskimo diet in, 431, *431*

   Viking explorations of, 434–435, *434, 435*

Gregorian calendar, 219

grids, 155, *155*

grid points, 157, *158*

Griffin, James, 62

ground penetrating radar (GPR), 164–165, *165*

ground stone artifacts, 292

grouping, 185–186

guides, in classification, 186–187

Gust, Sherri, 341

habitation zones, 144–145, *145*
habitus, 474
half-life, 228, *228, 229*
Hallström, Gustaf, 462–464, *464*
hamlets, 112
hammer and anvil method, 276
hammer and sickle symbol, 192, *192*
hammers, 80–81, *80*, 276, *278, 281*
hammerstones, 276
handaxes, 280–281, *281*
handedness, 292
hand-thrown ceramics, 303
Harappan culture (Indus Valley), 96–97, *96, 97,* 516
hard hammers, 276, *281*
Hardin, Margaret, 312
Harris, Edward, 258
Harris lines, 392
Harris Matrix, 258–259, *259*
Haviland, William, 391
Hawkes, Christopher, 450
Hayden, Brian, 257
hermeneutic interpretation, 461, 464, 466
Hertzian cones, 275, *275*
Hesse, Brian, 332
hierarchical societies, 85–88, *86, 87*
hieroglyphic writing, Mayan, 52, 299
Hill, James, 477
Hillman, Gordon, 361
Hisarlik site (Turkey), 250–251, *250, 251*
histograms
    of bone chemistry data, 441, *442*
    construction of, 205–207, *206*
    normal curve and, 201–202, *201, 202, 203*
historical archaeology, 8, 524–526, *525*
history of archaeology, 47–64
    before 1900, 48–51, *48, 49, 50*
    from 1900–1950, 51–55, *52, 53, 54, 55*
    from 1950–2000, 55–62, *57, 58, 60, 61, 62, 63*
    academic degrees and positions in, 49, 52
Hodder, Ian
    Archaeological Theory Today, 461, *461*
    on ethnographic analogy, 92
    Reading the Past, 57, *58*
Hoffman, Brian, 124
Hohokam pottery, 317, *317*
Holocene period
    Abu Hureyra site (Syria), 362–364, *362, 363*
    dates of, 506, *507*
Homeland Security, cultural resources and, 498
home range, 73
Homer's Troy, 250–251, *250, 251*
hominins, 104, *104*
Homo erectus, 507, 509–511
Homo habilis, 509
Homo neanderthalensis. See Neanderthals
Homo sapiens
    compared with neanderthals, 398–399, *398, 399*

emergence of, 511
    in New World, 518
Homo sapiens sapiens
    emergence of, *507,* 511
    mitochondrial DNA and, 398–399
Hopewell period, 314–316, *315, 316*
horizons, site, 112, 248
horizons, soil, 248–249, *249*
horizontal excavations, 148–150, *149*
horses, in North America, 467–468
Hosler, Dorothy, 459–460
houses and households
    floor chemistry studies, 262–263, 265, *265*
    lake dwellings, 226–227, *226, 227*
    longhouses, 92, *92,* 264
    Mayan, 264–265, *265*
    pithouses, 83, 225, *225,* 258–264, *261–263*
    Unalaska, *125*
    wattle-and-daub buildings, 353, *353*
    within-site spatial analysis of, 122–125, *123, 124, 125*
Huaca de la Luna (Peru), 31
Huaca del Sol (Peru), 31
Huaca Rajada (Peru), 32, *33*
human osteology, 379. *See also* bioarchaeology
human prehistory, 505–527
    in Africa, 507–509, *508, 509*
    creative explosion in Upper Paleolithic, 511–513, *512, 513*
    early Americans, 518–520, *520*
    geological time and, 506–507, *507*
    major human fossil forms, *510*
    New World farming villages, 520–521
    New World states and empires, 521–522
    Old World states and empires, 515–518, *516*
    origins of agriculture, 513–515, *514,* 520–521
    out of Africa, 509–510
    timelines for, *508*
human remains
    ethical issues, 408, 490, *490*
    Kennewick Man, 490–491, *491*
    Mary Rose Trust Code of Practice, 397
    of Native Americans, 498–499
    paleopathology, 390–396, *392, 393, 394*
    See also bioarchaeology
human sacrifice, 39, 42
human skeleton, 380, *381,* 383–384, *384*
human taphonomy, 400–401
hunter-gatherers
    in the Americas, 518, 520, 521
    camps of, 118, 120–121
    definition of, 81
    in most of human history, 17–18
    optimal foraging theory, 469–471, *470*
    population density among, 74
    at Reese River Valley site (Nevada), 144–145, *144, 145*
    regional spatial analysis of, 126–129, *127, 128*
    rock art of, 465–466, *465, 466*

seasonality and, 333–335, *333, 335*
    stone tools of, 284–285, *284, 285*
    at Windover Pond (Florida), 135–136, *135, 136*
hunting overkill, extinction from, 330
hydrocarbon residues, 438
hydrophilic lubricants, 184
hydroxyapatite, 419

Ice Age. *See* Pleistocene
Icehouse Bottom (Tennessee), 314–316, *315, 316,* 521
Iceman (Europe), 136–137, *136, 137,* 139, 515
iconography, 88, 89
ICP-AES (inductively coupled plasma-atomic emission spectrometry), 424
ICP-MS (inductively coupled plasma-mass spectrometry), 421, *421*
ideology, culture and, 72, 87–91, *88, 89, 91*
Iliad (Homer), 250–251, *250, 251*
impressing pottery, 304, *304*
Incidents of Travel (Stephens and Catherwood), 47, 49
Incinerator site (Ohio), 355–359, *355, 356, 357, 358*
incised decorations, 304, *304*
indirect punch technique, *277*
inductively coupled plasma-atomic emission spectrometry (ICP-AES), 424
inductively coupled plasma-mass spectrometry (ICP-MS), 421, *421*
industry, definition of, 111
infant mortality, 79, *79, 80*
inferential statistics, 199, 202
ingots, 36
inhumation, 109, 149, 381
injuries, 390
Inka culture, 43, 45, 52, *52,* 522
inorganic compounds, 419
In Pursuit of the Past (Binford), 452
in situ, 106
Institute of Archaeology (Beijing), 8
Institute of Archaeology (London), 8
instrumental surveying, 143, 154–155
instrumentation, 420–424
    gas chromatography-mass spectrometry, 423, *423*
    inductively coupled plasma-atomic emission spectrometry, 424
    inductively coupled plasma-mass spectrometry, 421, *421*
    neutron activation analysis, 420, *420*
    X-ray diffraction, 422–423, *422, 423*
intellectual property, *492, 493*
intelligent design, 16
interfaces, in profiles, 258
"interpretative archaeologies," 461
Inuit culture, 92–93, *93*
invention, definition of, 81
ions, 418

Quarter Site, Poplar Forest (Virginia), 3–5, *4*
quartiles, 207, *207*

rachis, 359–360, *359*
radar instruments, 162, 164–165, *165*
radioactivity, 227–228
radiocarbon dating, 227–233
  accelerator mass spectrometer dating,
    228–230, *229*
  calibration of, 232–233, *232, 233*
  discovery of, 227, *227*
  example calculations, 239–242, *239, 240, 241,*
    242
  limit of, 228, *229*
  range of measurements, *221, 222, 222*
  of rock art, 115
  sites used in, 225, *227,* 230–232, *231*
radiopotassium dating, *221, 222, 222,* 234–236,
  234, 235
raised beds, at Tiwanaku, 482–484, *483*
Ramenofsky, Ann, 467–468
random sampling, 144
range, 200
rank, in society, 85
Rappaport, Roy, 90
ratio scale data, 198, *198,* 205–206
raw materials, 189–191, *190*
Reading the Past (Hodder), 57, *58*
reciprocity, 82. *See also* trade
reconnaisance, 143
reconstructions, *378,* 379, *380,* 383
recordkeeping, in the field, 146, 381–382, *382*
redistribution, 82
Reese River Valley (Nevada), 144–145, *144, 145*
reference collections, of botanic materials, 354
refitting, 279, 283–287, *285, 286, 287, 291*
regional spatial analysis, 126–129, *127, 128*
regions, 101, 116
relational analogy, 92
relationship structures, 84–85, *85*
relative dating methods, 216–218, 237, 419
relativism, 461
religion
  aspects of ideology, 88–89, *88*
  components of, 90–91
  Native American, 499
remote sensing, 161–164, *162, 163*
research design, 70
residential sites, 112, *113. See also* houses and
  households
resistivity meters, 164
resists, in pottery, 305
responsibilities, 479–502
  ethical principles, 492–493, *492*
  human remains, 490–491, *491*
  ownership of archaeological resources,
    488–490, *488, 489, 490*
  protection of archaeological resources,
    484–487, *484, 486, 487,* 492
  public access to information, 500

publication of results, 500
relevancy of archaeology, 481–482
responsible archaeologists, 500
teaching archaeology, 495–499, *496, 498*
See also cultural resource management;
  ethical issues
restoration of artifacts, 182–183, *183*
Retoka site (Melanesia), 403–405, *404*
retouching, 278–279, *278*
Reuvens, C. J. C., 48
Rich Neck Slave Quarter site (Virginia), *328*
rim sherds, 306, *307*
ritual, 88–90, *91*
Rivanna River burial mound (Virginia), 51, 521
roads, in Chaco Canyon (New Mexico),
  162–163, *163*
rock art
  Lascaux cave, *513*
  Nämforsen site (Sweden), 462–466, *463, 464,*
    465, 466
  South African, 114–115, *114, 115*
  Upper Paleolithic, 512–513, *513*
rockshelters, 112
Roman calendar, 219
Romulus and Remus, 88
root crops, 358
Royal Tombs of Sipán Museum, Lambayeque,
  Peru, 43, *43*
Roy Mata burial ground (Retoka), 403–405,
  404, 524
Runge, Dale, 459
Ryan, William, 245–246
rye, 362

Sabloff, Jeremy, 459
sacrifice, 39, 42, 90
Sahelanthropus tchadensis, 507
Salado polychromes, 317–318, *317, 318*
sale of artifacts, *489,* 492, 493
samples, 144
San culture, arrows from, *178,* 179–180, *180,*
  199
San Jose Mogoté (Mexico), 90, *91, 312,* 521
saqia, 75, *75*
SAR (Synthetic Aperture Radar), 162
satellite photography, 161–163, *162, 163*
scaffold burials, 382, *383*
scale, 102–105, *103,* 157
scale of time, 102, 104–105, *104*
scales of measurement, 197–198, *198*
scanning electron microscope (SEM), 358,
  364–365, *364, 365, 367*
scapulamancy, 90
scatterplots, 208–209, *208, 209,* 443
scavengers, humans as, 340
scepters, 38, 42
Schiffer, Michael, *Behavioral Archaeology,* 130
Schliemann, Heinrich, 50, 250
schools of thought, 450–473
  agency-based, 474

Bronze Age barrows and, 454–456, *454, 455,*
  456
cognitive archaeology, 474–475
complexity theory, 473
evolutionary ecology, 467, 468–471, *470*
gender archaeology, 471–473, *471, 472*
Maya civilization collapse and, 456–460, *457,*
  458, 459
Nämforsen rock art and, 462–466, *463, 464,*
  465, 466
popularity of, 475–476, *476*
post-processual overview, 460–462, *461, 462,*
  475, *476*
practice-based, 474
processual overview, 451–453, *454, 475, 476*
selectionist archaeology, 467–468
self-organizing systems, 473–474
Schulz, Peter, 341
scientific method, 6, 13–15, *14*
scientific publication, 500
scrapers, 282, *282,* 287
screening, 150–151, *150*
sculpture
  from Harappan culture, *96*
  from Jericho, 99
  from Olmec culture, *89*
  from Teotihuacán, *122*
Scythian tombs, 239–242, *239, 240, 241, 242*
seasonality
  Abu Hureyra site (Syria), 363, *363*
  animal remains and, 333–337, *333, 334, 335,*
    343, *344,* 355
  example determination of, 345–348, *345, 346,*
    347, 348
  floral remains and, *357,* 358, *358*
  in the Preneolithic, 336–337, *337*
  Star Carr site (England), 334–335, *334, 335*
seasonal rounds, 144
secondary inhumations, 149, 382
secondary products, 342
sections, 148
sedentary settlements, 336–337, *337*
sediments
  anthropogenic, 256, 427–429, *428*
  categories and size criteria, 254–255, *255*
  composition of, 256
  definition of, 247–248, *248*
  Munsell soil color chart, 253, *254*
  plow zone, 256
  texture of, 255, *255*
  See also soil
seed crops, 358
selectionist archaeology, 467–468
self-organizing systems, 473–474
Sellars, Wilfred, 450
SEM (scanning electron microscope), 358,
  364–365, *364, 365, 367*
Semenov, Sergei, 287
September 11, 2001 terrorist attacks, 482
seriation, 193–195, *193, 194, 195*

settlement patterns, 145
settlements, 119, *119*, *120*
sex distinctions
    of adult humans, 387–390, *387*, *390*
    of children, 402
    in faunal remains, 330–331
    in life span, 79, *79*
sexual dimorphism, 331
shaduf, 75, *75*
shamans, 87, 412
Shanks, Michael, 461
Sharer, Robert, 437
shattering, 359
shell middens, 114, 253, 343, 469–471, *470*
shells and shellfish, 343, *344*
sherds, 300, 306
Shipman, Pat, 340
shipwrecks
    Mary Rose, 394–397, *394*, *395*, 526
    Titanic, 524
    Wasa, 524, 526
Shoshonean culture, 144–145, *144*, *145*
shoulders, pot, 306
shovel testing, 147–148
Shroud of Turin, 230–232, *231*
silica, in obsidian, 425
silver, in Moche culture, 42, 43
Simon, Arelyn, 318
single component layers and sites, 111
Sipán site (Peru)
    artwork from, *28*, 29
    looting of, 32–34, *33*, 44–45, 493
Siq, 165
Sistine Chapel, Vatican (Michelangelo), *88*
site discovery, 142–153
    archaeological surveys, 143–146, *143*, *145*
    excavation, 146–151, *147*, *149*, *150* (See also
        excavations)
    at Great Hall at Lejre (Denmark), 151–152,
        152
    preliminary research, 142–143
    project on, 171–174, *171*, *172*, *173*, *174*
    in underwater archaeology, 153, *153*
site grids, 155, *155*
sites
    definition of, 101
    excavation of (See excavations)
    grids on, 155, *155*
    looting of, 32–34, *33*, 44–45, 493
    preservation of, 132–135, *133*, *134*
    protection of, 123
    site analysis, 126, *127*
    site formation, 129–132, *129*, *130*, *131*, *132*,
        133
    types of, 112–114, *113*
    See also under names of individual sites; site
        discovery
Sitra site (Egypt), *285*, 286, *286*
skeletal bones, *328*, 383–384, *384*
skulls, sex differences in, *388*, 389

slab technique, 302, *303*
Slack Farm site (Kentucky), *487*
slavery, at Poplar Forest site, 3–5, *4*
slips, 305
slopewash, 130
Smakkerup Huse site (Denmark), 333, *333*, 513
Smith, Eric Alden, 467
Society for American Archaeology (SAA)
    Ethical Principles, 492–493, *492*
    "Frequently Asked Questions about Careers
        in Archaeology" (Carlson), 19
    on teaching archaeology, 495, *496*
sodalities, 85
soft hammers, 276, *278*, 281
soil
    chemistry studies, 262–263, 265, *265*, 429
    horizon formation, 248–249, *249*
    Munsell color chart, 253, *254*
    sampling of, 150, 160–161, *161*
    texture categories, 255, *255*
Solutrean period, 512, *512*
sorghum, 4
South, Stanley, 321–322
South African rock art, 114–115, *114*, *115*
South America
    agriculture in, 520–521
    earliest humans in, 518
    Huaca de la Luna (Peru), 31
    Huaca del Sol (Peru), 31
    Huaca Rajada (Peru), 32, *33*
    Inka culture, 43, 45, 52, *52*, 522
    Macchu Picchu (Peru), 52, *52*
    states and empires in, 522
    Tiwanaku culture, 482–484, *482*, *483*, 522
    Tomb of the Lord of Sipán (Peru), 34–40,
        34–40
    See also Moche culture
South Asia
    Harappan culture (Indus Valley), 96–97, *96*,
        97, 516
    Mohenjo Daro site (Pakistan), 316–318, *319*
Spadework (Woolley), 55
spatial archaeology, 118–129
    activity areas and features, 118–121, *119*, *120*
    gravity model in, 128–129
    houses and households, 122–125, *123*, *124*,
        125
    regional spatial analysis, 126–129, *127*, *128*
    site analysis, 126, *127*
    spatial units in, *119*
spatial patterning, 126
Spaulding, Al, 187
species
    commensals, 337
    definition of, 326
    extinction of, 329–330, *329*, *330*
    species lists, 328
Spector, Janet, 471
splitters, 185
spondylus, 402

spores, 368–369
squash, 358, *358*
Squaxin Island Tribe (Washington), 479–481
St. Acheul site (France), 280–281
stadia rods, 156
standard deviation (s.d.), 200, *201*, 202
5β stanol, 439
Star Carr site (England), 334–335, *334*, *335*,
    513
starch, identification of, 369–370, *370*
state archaeologists, 24–25, *24*
states, 86–87, *87*
statistics, 198–205
    chi-square and contingency tables, 203–205,
        204
    correlations, 208–209, *209*
    descriptive *vs.* inferential, 199, *199*
    mean, 199, 202
    median, 199–200
    mode, 200
    normal curve, 201–202, *202*, *203*
    range, 200
    standard deviation, 200, *201*, 202, *202*
    variance, 200
stature, estimates of, 389–391, *390*, *391*
status, 86, 400
stelae, definition of, 116, 437
stem and leaf plots, 205, *205*
Stephens, John Lloyd, 47, 49, 50
"sterile," *256*
sterols, 438–439
Steward, Julian, 144–145
stirrup-spout portrait vessels, 32, *32*
Stoltman, James, 315–316
Stonehenge site (England), 159, *160*
stone points. *See* projectile points
stone tools, 273–297
    bamboo substituting for, 191
    chaîne opératoire method, 279, 282–283,
        283
    cutting edges over time, *294*
    expedient *vs.* curated, 283
    flakes, 274–276, *275*, *276*, *277*, 280
    fracture mechanics, 274–276, *275*, *276*
    ground stone artifacts, 292
    hammers, 80–81, *80*, 276, *278*, 281
    handaxes, 280–281, *281*
    human behavior and, 273–274
    hunter-gatherers in western Nevada and,
        284–285, *284*, *285*
    making, 276–279, *277*, *278*, *279*
    at the Meer site (Belgium), 289–292, *289*, *290*,
        291
    microwear analysis, 279, 286–289, *288*
    New World *vs.* Old World, 281–282, *282*
    possible functions for, *288*, 289
    refitting, 279, 283–287, *285*, *286*, *287*
    stone for, 274
    typology of, 279, 280–282, *281*, *282*
    See also projectile points